CLASSICAL MYTH

THIRD EDITION

BARRY B. POWELL

UNIVERSITY OF WISCONSIN-MADISON

with new translations of ancient
texts by Herbert M. Howe

Prentice
Hall

Upper Saddle River, NJ 07458

Library of Congress Cataloging-in-Publication Data
Powell, Barry B.
    Classical myth/Barry B. Powell.–3rd ed.
        p. cm.
    Includes bibliographical references and index.
    ISBN 0-13-088442-1
    1. Mythology, Clasical.   I. Title.

BL722 .P68 2000
292.1'3–dc21   99-087714

President: J. Philip Miller
Editor-in-chief: Leah Jewell
Acquisitions Editor: J. Philip Miller
VP, Director of Production and Manufacturing: Barbara Kittle
Managing Editor: Mary Rottino
Production Editor: Randy Pettit
Prepress and Manufacturing Manager: Nick Sklitsis
Prepress and Manufacturing Buyer: Mary Ann Gloriarde
Marketing Director: Gina Sluss
Marketing Manager: Rachel Falk
Cover Design: Jayne Conte
Cover Art: "VAS Schoen 80", Staatliche Antikensammlungen and Glyptothek München, Photograph by Kopperman.
Photo Researcher: Pat Powell

For permission to use copyrighted material, grateful
acknowledgment is made to the copyright holders listed
throughout the text, which is considered an extension
of this copyright page.

This book was set in 10/12 Baskerville by The Composing Room of Michigan, Inc.
and printed and bound by R.R. Donnelley & Sons Company.
The cover was printed by Phoenix Color Corp.

©2001 by Prentice-Hall Inc.
A Pearson Education Company
Upper Saddle River, New Jersey 07458

Printed in the United States of America
10 9 8 7 6 5 4 3 2

0-13-088442-1

Prentice-Hall International (UK) Limited, *London*
Prentice-Hall of Australia Pty. Limited, *Sydney*
Prentice-Hall Hispanoamerica, S.A., *Mexico*
Prentice-Hall of India Private Limited, *New Delhi*
Prentice-Hall of Japan, Inc., *Tokyo*
Editora Prentice-Hall do Brasil, Ltda., *Rio de Janeiro*

Herbert M. Howe

Quomodo Romani scriptores, quomodo Grai
naturam rerum arcanis operire solerent
fabellis per te didici, longosque per annos
tu mihi tam iucundus eras, o amice, magister
quam fuit herbiferis in Pelei uallibus olim
aequoreae Thetidis nato Philyreius heros.

CONTENTS

PART II
Divine Myths

PART III
Legends

12. Introduction to Heroic Myth   313

13. Perseus and Myths of the Argive Plain   322

19. The Trojan War: The House of Atreus; The Anger of Achilles   509

PREFACE

What does our great historical hunger signify, our clutching about us of
countless cultures, our consuming desire for knowledge, if not the loss of
myth, of a mythic home, the mythic womb?

FRIEDRICH NIETZSCHE, *The Birth of Tragedy*, 1872

The category "classical myth" exists more in the minds of contemporary teachers than it did in the ancient world itself, but it has nonetheless come to serve a useful pedagogical purpose. For some time now, courses bearing this or a similar title
have been a vehicle for introducing college students to the cultures of the ancient
Greeks and Romans, hence to the roots of Western civilization. Studying the myths
of the ancients primarily through the literary works in which they have been preserved, students are exposed to important classical authors, as well as to stories and
figures which have sustained interest and kindled imaginations throughout the history of Western culture.

The present text began as a modern introduction to classical myth, a comprehensive and flexible resource for college-level courses that would reflect the best recent scholarship in the field. The fact that the first and second editions were used in
many such courses throughout North America, by instructors with different academic backgrounds teaching in a wide variety of educational settings, has been a
gratifying confirmation of my sense that a book of this type was needed. In this third
edition, I have made improvements to the book based on suggestions from instructors who have used the first two editions in their classes, as well as on my own experiences in teaching with it. But the central goals of the book remain unchanged. I

have again included a large number of translations from ancient literary sources, organized around mythical figures or themes. I have again provided substantial background information and interpretive commentary to accompany these selections. And again, in both the translations and the background material, I have sought to take account of the needs of today's students as well as of the many new perspectives on the ancient world opened up in recent years by scholars working in various areas of classical studies.

The first two editions were unique among texts in classical myth in the extent to which they emphasized the context in which the ancient stories were told. In this emphasis I believe I was reflecting the direction of much contemporary scholarship, and in the third edition I have once again sought to place the myths in their anthropological, historical, religious, sociological, and economic contexts. Where possible I have extended and improved the coverage of these topics. In this edition I have grouped the male and female gods in separate chapters, whereas earlier they were organized according to family relation. In this way it is possible more easily to explore issues of gender and sexual identity that have preoccupied commentators in recent years. In a new chapter, "An Introduction to Heroic Myth" (Chapter 12), I use the Mesopotamian story of Gilgamesh as a model for understanding the complex myths of heroes in Greece, whereas the earlier editions did not single out the topic of the "hero." The other chapters have been compressed and revised, and new comments on context have been added to the discussion of specific myths in various chapters.

The first and second editions were also unique in the emphasis they placed on the historical development of classical myth. Only when we see how myth changes over time, yet somehow remains the same, can we grasp its essence. For this reason I included in the first editions an extensive discussion of the Mesopotamian antecedents of classical myth, but in this edition I discuss such myths at the same time as their later expressions in classical civilization, so that their relation can be better understood.

In the third edition, as in the first two, I have included as many passages from ancient literary works as space permits. Many of these are from well-known sources, but I have not hesitated to present lesser-known passages rarely seen in books of this type, when that seemed appropriate. Whenever possible I have used Greek sources rather than Latin ones, but I have nonetheless included selections from Ovid's highly influential Latin retelling of the Greek myths when the myth is found in no other ancient literary source. The complete text of the *Metamorphoses* will form a natural, though not necessary, adjunct to this text, as will complete translations of Greek tragedies, or modern works which reflect ancient patterns of myth or similar concerns.

Most translations of these selections, which were prepared specifically for inclusion in this volume, are largely unchanged in this edition. Translations of most Greek, Latin, Hebrew, and Italian sources were prepared by Herbert M. Howe; I did some of these, however, and am also responsible for translations of the Akkadian, Egyptian, and modern Greek passages. In our translations we have sought a modern idiom, unrhymed, with a regular beat in the poetic lines; poetry, then as now, has its own rules of expression, and the translator can only try to recreate in modern tongue thoughts and manners distant from our own. Those who wish to examine the original Greek and Latin sources should consult the exhaustive references given in Pierre Grimal, *The Dictionary of Classical Mythology* (Oxford, 1986) and in Keith Aldrich's translation and commentary on Apollodorus, *The Library of Greek Mythology* (Lawrence, Kansas, 1975).

I believe that ancient works of art can play a valuable role in helping students visualize mythical figures and events as the ancients themselves did, and therefore I have included many additional illustrations from classical sources: some one hundred ninety-seven reproductions of vase paintings, sculptural works, architectural monuments, and other works of art from the ancient and modern worlds.

Like the first two editions, the third stresses the importance of interpretation in the study of myth, though without relying exclusively on any one interpretive perspective. No single approach to interpretation can ever be adequate to the enormous range and complexity of classical myth. The subject of interpretation is briefly introduced in Chapter 1, and throughout the text I offer interpretive comments on individual myths as they are examined—comments that I know will be used as a basis as much for objection as for agreement. The subject of interpretation is dealt with most extensively, however, in Chapter 23, "Theories of Myth Interpretation." I am fully aware that some instructors will prefer to deal with theories of interpretation early on in the course, and even though this chapter is placed at the end of the book, it can be introduced at any point, without loss of coherence.

The third edition remains committed to the principle that when we study classical myth, we also study the roots of Western culture. Like the first two editions, therefore, it includes in most chapters one or more "Perspective" boxes that examine the uses of classical myth in the medieval, Renaissance, or modern periods. Many of the Perspectives incorporate excerpts from or reproductions of the literary and artistic works discussed. My intent is to help students see how stories and figures from classical myth were appropriated and interpreted at later stages of history, often for purposes very different from those of the ancient world itself.

The study of classical myth inevitably presents students with hundreds of new and unfamiliar names. To assist students with the pronunciation of these, I have provided an English pronunciation guide the first time each difficult name appears in the text. (The pronunciation guides are repeated in the index.) I have also used **bold** letters to highlight the names that are of greatest importance, those which one really ought to know to claim competence in the topic. These names are repeated in a list of important terms at the end of each chapter, with page numbers of where the term first appears. I leave names of lesser importance in ordinary type, though in many cases I give pronunciations for these as well. Finally, in the index I have included a capsule identification for important names.

This edition is accompanied by a Companion Website™ located at

http://www.prenhall.com/powell

which provides up-to-date links, organized by chapters in the text, to a vast array of resources relevant to the study of classical myth, including electronic texts, fine art images, and background information on Greek culture and society. It also offers a comprehensive interactive study guide, complete with self-scoring quizzes and other resources designed to assist students in mastering the course material.

ACKNOWLEDGMENTS

This book grew out of a course in classical myth offered for many decades without interruption at the University of Wisconsin-Madison. The course was created in the 1930s by Walter "Ray" Agard, whom the famous educator Alexander Meiklejohn brought to Madison from Amherst in 1927 to teach in the Meiklejohn Experimental College. Herbert M. Howe taught the course from 1957 to 1975. Since that time I have taught the course regularly. I am grateful to my predecessors for the insights I gained from them about how to present this material to undergraduate students.

J. Philip Miller of Prentice Hall has worked with me on the organization of this book from its inception. Many others have helped as well, and they continue to offer advice. Paul Plass, emeritus professor at the University of Wisconsin-Madison, who for long taught a course on the history of the interpretation of Greek myth, wrote the first draft of Chapter 22, for which I am very grateful. John Lenz, of Drew University, saved me from embarrassing errors. I also gratefully thank the following people for the comments on the manuscript: Borimir Jordan, University of California, Santa Barbara; Patricia A. Marquardt, Marquette University; F. Carter Philips, Vanderbilt University; Edward A. Shaw, University of Central Florida; John Foley, University of Missouri; Kirk Freudenburg, Ohio State University; Eva Stehle, University of Maryland; Holly An' Oyster, State University of New York-Buffalo; Kristin Thompson, Madison, Wisconsin; Eugene Miller, Madison, Wisconsin; Michael L. Robertson, Johnson County Community College; E. N. Genovese, San Diego State University; David Mulroy, University of Wisconsin-Milwaukee; David Leitao, San Francisco State University. John Adams, California State University, Northridge; David Engel, Penn State University; Laura McClure, University of Wisconsin-Madison; Lisa Maurizio, University of Massachusetts, Amherst; Joseph F. O'Connor, Georgetown University; Gregory A. Staley, University of Maryland; Robert F. Sutton, Jr., Indiana University-Purdue University, Indianapolis. I want to thank Dale Grote especially, for his superb labors on the website, which has enhanced the value of the text. Last and far from least, I wish to thank my wife Patricia for her indefatigable labor in tracking down the photos printed here, and for reading this book in manuscript again and again.

In the preparation of my own English versions of Mesopotamian and Egyptian literary texts I owe a general indebtedness to the following translations: James B. Pritchard, editor, *Ancient Near Eastern Texts Relating to the Old Testament* (Princeton, N.J., 1969); A. Heidel, *The Gilgamesh Epic and Old Testament Parallels* (Chicago, 1949); Thorkild Jacobsen, *The Treasures of Darkness* (New Haven, Conn., 1976); Samuel Noah Kramer, *Sumerian Mythology* (New York, 1961) and *The Sumerians: Their History, Culture, and Character* (Chicago, 1963); Stephanie Dalley, *Myths from Mesopotamia* (Oxford, 1989). I thank Frederick W. Schwink for his translation of the Hittite "Kingship in Heaven." I thank J. C. McKeown for the verse epigraph.

I also thank Random House for permission to quote "Musée des Beaux Arts" from *The Collected Poems of W. H. Auden* (1945); Simon & Schuster, to quote "Leda and the Swan" from W. B. Yeats's *Collected Poems* (1951); and New Directions Publishing Corporation to quote "Adonis" from *Collected Poems 1912–1944* by H. D.

We wish also to thank the museums, libraries, galleries, and other collections

that have kindly allowed reproduction of items in their collections and have provided the necessary photographs. Photographs from these and other sources are
gratefully acknowledged in the text.

I welcome comments on this edition from instructors and students who have
used it, as these will help me plan improvements for future editions of the book. I
can be contacted at the address listed below.

—*B.B.P.*

Madison, 2000

Barry B. Powell
Halls-Bascom Professor of Classics
University of Wisconsin-Madison
email: bbpowell@facstaff.wisc.edu

CHAPTER 1

THE NATURE OF MYTH

The longer I occupy myself with questions of ancient mythology, the more diffident I become of success in dealing with them, and I am apt to think that we who spend our years in searching for solutions of these insoluble problems are like Sisyphus perpetually rolling his stone uphill only to see it revolve again into the valley.

Sir James G. Frazer (1854–1941),
author of *The Golden Bough*

T HE Western Roman Empire ended more than fifteen hundred years ago, but the stories of classical gods and goddesses, of Greek and Roman warriors and leaders, live on in their old vigor. Zeus, Venus, Helen, Odysseus, Achilles, Aeneas— these familiar names stood in the background as later Western art and literature advanced, and they stand there still today. They were bequeathed to us in the writings of the Greeks and Romans, but their names and stories are much older than the written word. They go back to an earlier era, before the introduction of writing, an era when classical myth first took a shape we can recognize.

Later chapters examine specific myths that have come down to us from the Greeks and Romans, but in this chapter we limit ourselves to some preliminary matters essential to a clear understanding of classical myth. We discuss the definition of myth and the three main types of myth: divine myth, legend, and folktale. We also look briefly at some aspects of the study of myth.

WHAT IS A MYTH?

Human beings have told stories from time immemorial, for stories are a natural product of spoken language, an outgrowth of the imaginative power that most clearly separates us from other animals. The story is a universal ingredient of human culture, bringing relief from the tedium of everyday labor and reminding listeners of their own values, beliefs, and history.

This book is concerned with a certain type of story known as myth. The term *myth* is hard to define, in part because of the enormous variety of stories gathered from many cultures by ethnographers, anthropologists, and literary historians. Originally, the Greek word *mythos* simply meant "authoritative speech," "story," or "plot," but later writers used the term *myth* in more restricted ways. Some recent authorities, exasperated by the complexity of the phenomenon, deny that the term *myth* expresses a coherent concept. A definition widely agreed on is that myth is a traditional story. We can accept this definition, but we must consider carefully what it means.

To say that a myth is a story is to say, first of all, that it has a plot, a narrative structure consisting of a beginning, middle, and end. In the beginning of a typical story, we are introduced to characters whom we find in a certain situation, usually one involving conflict with other characters, with misfortune, or within themselves. In the middle, the situation grows more complex and tension develops. In the end, the tension is somehow resolved. Today we might find an example of this basic structure in the plot that is repeated in so many novels and feature films: Boy meets girl (the beginning), boy loses girl (the middle), boy finds girl (the end). Plot is an essential feature of myth. Without a beginning, middle, and end, there can be no story and hence no myth. In casual speech we sometimes say that the Greek god Zeus, for example, is a myth. However, strictly speaking, Zeus is not a myth, but a character in myth, in the plotted stories that tell of his exploits. Belief in the existence of a particular god, the observance of a ritual in a god's honor, and religious symbols are not myths.

Like all other stories, myths have characters as well as plots.[1] In myths, the characters may be gods, goddesses, or other supernatural beings, but they may also be human beings or even animals who speak and act in the manner of human beings. Another element of myth is setting. The setting is the time and place in which the action of the story unfolds. Myths are never set in the present or the recent past; the action always takes place in the distant past, or in a shadowy time altogether outside human chronology. The setting of myths may or may not be in identifiable places. In some Greek myths, the setting is an actual city, such as Athens or Thebes, or some other location familiar to the audience. In others, the setting is an obscure place: the underworld, which no one ever visited, or Mount Olympus, which really exists but in myth is the home of the gods, or Crete of a very long time ago. Myth transcends our everyday notions of time and space.

Thus, like all other stories, myths have plot, characters, and setting. However, a myth is not just any story, but a certain kind of story, which we describe as traditional.

---

[1] *Character* comes from a Greek word meaning "a certain mental imprint." Hamlet cannot make up his mind, Macbeth is ambitious, King Lear is blind to the character of others; character is the sum of the choices one makes.

Our word *traditional* comes from Latin *trado,* "hand over," and a traditional story is one that has been "handed over" orally from one storyteller to another without the intervention of writing. In societies that do not use writing, stories must be handed on by word of mouth, so traditional tales are the vehicle for transmitting one generation's thought to another. In this way traditional tales maintain contact with the past and pass inherited wisdom on to the future. They explain a society to itself, promulgating its concerns and values. They describe patterns of behavior that serve as models for members of a society, especially in times of crisis. For example, in Homer's *Iliad* (written down in the eighth century B.C.), Achilles tries to persuade King Priam of Troy to eat at a time when Priam is heartbroken for his son Hector, whom Achilles himself has killed. Achilles tells the story of Niobê, a Theban princess: Although Artemis and Apollo had killed her seven sons and seven daughters, still she ate, and so should Priam. Four hundred years later, when the philosopher Socrates was on trial for his life, he defended his insistence on telling the truth in spite of threats against him by recalling the example of Achilles, who was ashamed to live as a coward and chose to die bravely before the walls of Troy.

Because they are traditional, myths are also anonymous. In contrast to such modern forms of storytelling as Leo Tolstoy's *War and Peace,* Toni Morrison's *Beloved,* or George Lucas' film *Star Wars,* myths never have identifiable authors; literary works based on myth may indeed have authors, but not the myths themselves. The Greek dramatist Sophocles wrote a play about Oedipus the king, but the *myth* of Oedipus existed long before, and no one can say who created it.

This anonymity helps us to understand why the Greeks, following the lead of the philosopher Plato, eventually came to contrast *mythos,* "story" or "myth," with *logos,* "account." The teller of a *logos* takes responsibility for the truth of what is said; a *logos* is a reasoned explanation of something that emphasizes a continuing causal sequence, as in the proofs of plane geometry. We still use the suffix *-logy* to indicate a reasoned inquiry into a topic, as anthropo*logy,* "study of human beings," bio*logy,* "study of life forms," or even mytho*logy,* "study of myth" (although *mythology* often is used casually as a synonym for *myth*). By contrast, the teller of a *mythos* does not claim personal responsibility for what is said. After all, the teller did not invent the story, but only passed it on.

During oral transmission, a traditional tale is subject to constant change. Different narrators of a story have different motives and emphasize or embroider on different aspects. The story of Niobê could easily illustrate the dangers of self-assertion (Niobê bragged that she had more children than the mother of Apollo and Artemis), but Achilles uses the story to prove that grief can be lessened by food. Homer describes Achilles' anguished choice between a short, glorious life and a long, inglorious one but never presents the choice as between courage and cowardice. In the written works in which Greek myths have been preserved, we often find strikingly different versions of the same myth. The poets Homer and Sophocles both report that Oedipus, king of Thebes, killed his father and married his mother, but in Homer's account Oedipus continues to rule after the truth comes out, whereas in Sophocles' play he pokes pins in his eyes and leaves the city, a wretched wanderer. Neither is the "true" version of which the other is a variant, although we might argue that a version originating before writing is more traditional; the myth of Oedipus is the complex of all the variants, however many there may be. A retelling of every variant of every Greek myth would require a book of enormous length; here we concentrate on the best-known variants, often those of some great literary work. Sophocles' version of the myth of Oedipus is far better known than is Homer's passing reference. Virtually every group of humankind has its store of traditional narrative, but in this book we limit ourselves to the myths of Greece and Rome, only occasionally referring to earlier and parallel traditions, especially those from the ancient Near East.

TYPES OF MYTH

Modern scholars often distinguish between several types of myth based on the nature of the principal characters and the function the story fulfilled for listener and teller. **Divine myths** (sometimes called true myths or myths proper) are stories in which supernatural beings are the main actors; such stories generally explain why the world, or some aspect of it, is the way it is. **Legends** (or sagas) are stories of the great deeds of human heroes or heroines;[2] legends narrate the events of the human past. **Folktales** are stories whose actors are ordinary people or animals; folktales entertain the audience and teach or justify customary patterns of behavior.

The more we learn about myth, the more we discover how difficult it can be to separate one type from another. For example, stories that appear to be legends sometimes turn out to incorporate elements of folktales or to explain the nature of things, as do divine myths. Such distinctions are nonetheless valuable because they allow us to isolate and study various aspects of myth. Let us look more closely at each type.

Divine Myth

The supernatural beings who are the principal characters in divine myth are depicted as superior to humans in power and splendor. Sometimes they can take on human or animal shape at will. They control awesome forces of nature: thunder, storm, rain, fire, earthquake, or fecundity. When these beings appear in their own form, they are often enormous and of stunning beauty or ugliness. Conflicts between them can take place on an immense scale and involve whole continents, high mountains, and vast seas.

Sometimes the supernatural characters in divine myth are little more than personified abstractions without clearly defined personalities. In Greek myth, for example, Nikê (**nī**-kē), "Victory," is just the abstract concept (see Fig. 1.1). In other cases, the supernatural beings are gods, goddesses, or demons with well-developed and distinctive personalities of their own. Zeus, the sky god in Greek myth, is much

[2]From Latin *legenda*, "things that should be read," that is, originally, morally uplifting stories of Christian saints.

FIG. 1.1. Stars descend before Sun. The stars, represented as boys, leap into the sea before the approach of Helius in his horse-drawn chariot (the nimbus around his head is one origin of the medieval halo around the heads of saints), on an Attic wine-bowl, c. 435 B.C. As the goddess Nikê personifies an event, the Stars, or Helius, personify natural forces.

(British Museum, London, E 466)

more than a personification of the sky; he is depicted as a powerful father, an often unfaithful husband, and the upholder of justice in human communities.

The events of divine myth usually take place in a world before or outside the present order where time and often space have different meanings from those familiar to human beings. For example, one Greek myth explained how Zeus came to rule the world: He fought against the Titans, an earlier race of gods,[3] defeated them in a terrible battle, and established his empire on the ruin of theirs. It would be pointless to ask when these events occurred, even within the context of the story, because they are set in a time before human chronology has meaning. Moreover, many divine myths of the Greeks are set in a place far removed from the familiar world of human beings—on Mount Olympus, far away and unapproachable.

Understandably, many of the gods about whom traditional tales were told were both actors in the stories and cult objects. Zeus is a character in Greek myth, but he was also a god for whom the Greeks built temples, carried out sacrifices, and celebrated festivals. Because of this double function of the gods, divine myth is easily confused with religion, but the two must be clearly distinguished. Myths are traditional stories; religion is belief and the course of action that follows from belief. *Belief* is best defined as "what you accept (with or without proof) as a basis for action." For example, the Greeks believed that Zeus caused the rain to fall; therefore, they sacrificed animals in times of drought to persuade him to bring rain. Myths often justify

---

[3]The word *God* (capital *G*) should be limited to a single all-powerful being in any religion—Jewish, Christian, Muslim, or other. A small *g* shows that you are talking about one of many immortal powers. A demigod is the offspring of a god and a human who sometimes becomes a god at death. *Deity* covers all these concepts.

a religious practice or a form of religious behavior, but we can retell a myth, even a myth about divine beings, without engaging in religious behavior. The relationship between myth and religion is complicated, and we will have more to say about it later, but we must remember that myth is a traditional story, whereas religion is a set of beliefs that motivates a course of action.

Divine myths served a function in ancient cultures analogous to that of theoretical science in our own: They explained why the world is the way it is. Many of these myths tell of the origin and destruction of grand things: the universe, the gods, and ourselves; the relations of gods with one another and with human beings; and the divine origin of such human economic and social institutions as the growing of crops, the cycle of the seasons, the making of wine, and prophecy and oracles. Many divine myths deal with limited matters, such as the origin of local customs and practices.

In more technical language, we can describe such explanatory myths as etiological, from the Greek word *aition,* "cause." A creation myth is an example of an etiological tale because it explains the causes that brought the world into existence. An etiological myth explained the origin of Mount Etna, a dangerous volcano in Sicily: Beneath it Zeus imprisoned the fire-breathing monster Typhoeus, who continued to spew forth smoke and lava. Another example is the myth of Persephonê, daughter of the wheat goddess Demeter. Persephonê must spend four months of the year in the underworld, and Demeter refuses to let anything grow during those months—the hot, barren summer. The change of seasons is "explained," according to many, by the myth. Another etiological myth made clear why Demeter was worshiped in one part of Greece in the form of a mare. According to the story, Demeter changed herself into a mare in an unsuccessful attempt to escape the amorous attentions of Poseidon, god of the sea. Of course, an etiological tale such as this does not explain the real cause of a practice. In reality, Demeter probably was represented as a mare because at some stage in the evolution of her cult horses had a special importance. The etiological tale expresses a conjecture about the cause of something that existed long before the explanation.

Both divine myth and modern science offer explanations of why the world is the way it is, but they do so in very different ways. Scientific explanations are based on impersonal general laws and statistical probabilities discovered, or at least verified, by repeatable quantitative experiments, whereas mythic explanations, expressed in traditional tales, assume that supernatural beings control the world through the exercise of personal will. The ascription of human qualities, especially unpredictability, to the forces that stand behind the world is characteristic of the world-view we find in myth. Thunder is an expression of Zeus's anger, not the necessary result of impersonal physical forces. Greek myth could thus blame sudden and puzzling deaths on the will of the gods, as in the story of how, out of spite, the gods Artemis and Apollo struck down the fourteen children of Niobê. Modern scientists may be puzzled by death from cancer, but they do not blame such death on a divine and irrational agent. The modern world was born from the struggle of scientific thought against traditional explanations for why and how things happen in the world.

In Part II of this text we examine more closely the divine myths of the ancient Greeks.

Legend

If divine myth in oral cultures is analogous to science in modern, literate Western society, legend is analogous to history. Both legend and modern historical writing attempt to answer the question, "What happened in the human past?" Because the human past explains and justifies the human present, the telling of legends was an important activity in the cultural life of many ancient peoples, and never more so than among the ancient Greeks. In legends, the central characters are human beings, not gods and goddesses. Although supernatural beings often play a part, their roles are subordinate to those of the human characters. In the legend of Orestes, the god Apollo orders Orestes to kill his mother, but the emphasis of the story is on Orestes' carrying out the order and facing the terrible consequences.

The principal actors of legend are heroes and heroines. Drawn from the ranks of the nobility, they are kings and queens, princes and princesses, and other members of an aristocratic elite. They have extraordinary physical and personal qualities and are stronger, more beautiful, or more courageous than ordinary people. Most Greeks had no doubt that such legendary figures really lived, and members of important families regarded themselves as descended from them. Whereas divine myth is set in a different or previous world order, legendary events belong to our own, although they took place in the distant past, at the very beginning of human time when mighty heroes and heroines lived on earth, great cities were founded, difficult quests undertaken, fearful monsters slain, and momentous wars waged.

Most ancient Greeks, then, had no doubt that such events as the Trojan War really did occur, and they pointed out the tombs of legendary heroes and the actual sites of heroes' exploits. But the Greeks had no way to compare their traditions with historical reality. Today, armed with the insights of archaeology and techniques of historical investigation, modern scholars recognize that the oral transmitters of traditional tales had little respect for historical truth. Greek myth tells us more about the circumstances and concerns of its transmitters than it does about life in the distant past.

Still, legends can contain an element of truth. Modern scholars have long thought that Greek legend does reflect, however dimly, major events and power relations of a historical period now known to us through archaeological remains. Many or most of the figures in Greek legend probably did live at some time, most likely in the Mycenaean civilization of the Late Bronze Age (c. 1600–1200 B.C.; see Chronological Chart). Their very names provide one bit of evidence. For example, the name of Menelaüs, the legendary husband of Helen of Troy, means something like "upholder of the people." This distinctive name is appropriate to the aristocracy that certainly existed during this period, and similar names appear in written documents of the time (the Linear B tablets, the writings of the Mycenaeans, discussed in Chapter 2).

Further evidence is provided by archaeology. Excavation has shown that many of the places associated with important legendary events were great centers of civilization during the Bronze Age. Troy, for example, was a city of considerable importance until it was destroyed about 1250 B.C. Although we have no proof that it was destroyed by Greek warriors, as Greek legends assert, there remains a tantalizing correspondence between the legend and the archaeological evidence (Fig. 1.2).

FIG. 1.2. The walls of Troy. The earliest settlement at Troy can be dated to about 3000 B.C., but the walls shown here belong to the sixth level of occupation, about 1400 B.C. Constructed of neatly cut blocks of limestone that slope inward, the wall had at least four gateways, two of them protected by towers. Inside the walls, the ground slopes upward in concentric terraces. The palace would have been on the summit, but no trace remains because much later the hill was leveled to construct a temple to Athena. Troy VI was destroyed by an earthquake about 1300 B.C. The same inhabitants rebuilt, on a more modest scale, Troy VIIa. This city was destroyed by enemy action about 1250 B.C., perhaps in the very war remembered in Greek tradition. After a brief further occupation, the site was deserted for four hundred years, then resettled about 700 B.C.   (Author's photo)

Like divine myths, some legends also served a specific etiological function. Thus, one Greek story explained why, at the spring wine festival, Athenians brought their own cups, although at other festivals they drank from a communal bowl. According to the legend, the Mycenaean prince Orestes, who had killed his own mother to avenge her murder of his father, came to Athens at the time of the festival. The king of Athens did not want to send Orestes away impolitely, but neither did he want the Athenian people to be polluted by sharing a bowl with a man who had murdered his mother, so the king had every man drink from his own cup. In fact, the use of separate cups probably arose from a fear of contagion from ghosts, thought to be abroad at this season. The practice had nothing to do with a visit from Orestes, and the story was invented well after the custom was established.

We examine the legends of the ancient Greeks and Romans in detail in Part III of this text, with further remarks on general patterns in heroic myth (Chapter 12).

Folktale

Folktale is more difficult to define than is divine myth or legend because of the variety of traditional stories grouped together under this heading. Some scholars describe as a folktale any traditional story that is not a divine myth or legend. This category would encompass such familiar fairytales as "Cinderella" and "Snow White," which are among the many German stories written down from oral sources in the early nineteenth century by the brothers Jacob and Wilhelm Grimm. Likewise, the beast fables attributed to the Greek writer Aesop (sixth century B.C.), such as "The Tortoise and the Hare," could also be considered folktales, as could a story such as "Sinbad the Sailor" from the *Arabian Nights* and most oral tales recorded in North America and Africa during the last two hundred years.

Within this diversity we can still discern common traits. As in legend, the central characters in folktales are human beings, even though gods and spirits appear and play important roles. But in folktales the main characters usually are ordinary men, women, and children rather than kings and queens and others of exalted personal qualities or social status, hence the term *folktale*, a story about common people. Even in fables, a kind of folktale in which the characters are animals, the animals speak and act as though they were ordinary humans.

Unlike legends, folktales do not pretend to tell us what happened in the human past. No one believes that Snow White, Cinderella, Hansel and Gretel, or the American Indian trickster Crow really existed, as the Greeks believed that Achilles, Helen, and Orestes did. Often the main characters in folktales have low social status, at least at the beginning of the story, and are persecuted or victimized in some way by other characters. The folktale hero may be an outcast whose intelligence and virtue are not recognized by those in power. The hero often is the youngest child, the third of three brothers or sisters, abused by siblings or by a wicked stepmother. Very often the end of the story brings a reversal of fortunes, the happy ending for which folktales are well known. Initially taken to be stupid or ineffectual, the folktale hero triumphs over all obstacles and receives an appropriate reward.

Whereas divine myths explain why the world is the way it is and legends tell what happened in the human past, the primary function of folktales is to entertain, although they may also play an important role in teaching and justifying customary patterns of behavior. Folktales draw on such universal human experiences as the child's place in the hierarchy of the family and appeal to such universal human instincts as the belief that good is rewarded and evil punished eventually. In modern literate culture, the novel and the feature film have functions analogous to that of the folktale in oral society.

Although few pure folktales have come down to us from the Greeks and Romans, this type of traditional tale is of central importance to the study of Greek myth. To understand why, we must take note of a distinctive aspect of the folktale: the regular appearance of identifiable folktale types, even in stories from cultures widely separated in space or time. Folktale types are made up of smaller elements called motifs that can be recombined in endless variety. We might think of folktale motifs as the cells that make up the body of a tale. Common examples are the dragon that guards a spring or a magic object that protects against attack. Modern scholars have exhaustively described and organized the bewildering variety of folktale motifs, which number in the thousands.

Scholars recognize more than seven hundred folktale types in traditions around the globe. Sometimes a folktale type is named after a famous example. The Cinderella type, for example, is any story in which an abused younger sister, assisted by a spirit, appears in fancy dress at a ball, disappears from the prince's admiring glance, then is recognized and marries the prince. A general type often found in Greek myth is the quest. Compelled to seek some special object, the folktale hero journeys to a strange, terrifying, or wonderful land. There he must face a powerful antagonist: a dragon, monster, ogre, or thoroughly wicked man. To overcome his antagonist, the hero needs the assistance of animals, ghosts, divine beings, or magical weapons or devices. The hero is often a clever trickster, whereas his adversary is brutish, stupid, and cruel. The adversary succeeds in imprisoning, enchanting, or even killing the hero, but at last, often through a trick, the hero escapes, overcomes the enemy, and dispatches him in some cruel or gruesome way. Taking the object he sought, the hero returns to his native land, where his reward is the hand of a princess in marriage, or a part of the kingdom, or a great treasure.

Many of these motifs appear in the Greek story of Perseus (see Chapter 13), who was sent on a dangerous journey by an evil king who wanted to marry Perseus' mother. Assisted by nymphs, the goddess Athena, and an array of magical objects, Perseus went to the ends of the earth and slew the deadly Gorgon. On his return journey, carrying the Gorgon's death-dealing head in a pouch, he killed a sea monster that threatened a young woman chained to a rock. He took the woman back to Greece, married her, and killed the wicked king. This story illustrates the way Greek myth can use folktale motifs to elaborate on what would otherwise be considered a legend. About Perseus, for example, we are also told that he was born in the town of Argos and brought up by a poor fisherman on the island of Seriphus, that he accidentally killed his grandfather Acrisius in the town of Larissa, and that he moved to Tiryns and founded Mycenae, where his children later ruled. These are details appropriate to a widespread legend. The myth of Perseus, then, is neither pure legend nor pure folktale, but rather a mixture of the two.

In general, we may describe much of Greek myth as legend strongly colored by folktale. The main characters in these stories often have names appropriate to men and women who might really have lived, members of a social elite whose stories are attached to prominent Greek towns. Yet their adventures are of a sort we expect to find in folktale. The distinctions we have drawn between types of myth are of great value in organizing our thinking about myth, but we should remember that our distinctions are the results of intellectual analysis; they would not have been recognized by the Greeks themselves.

THE STUDY OF MYTH

The word *mythology* should mean "the study of myth" (by analogy with *biology, anthropology,* and the like). The word can mean that, but in common usage *mythology* typically refers more loosely to the myths themselves, or to a particular group of myths, not to the study of myth. Such statements as "I like mythology" are therefore taken to mean "I like myths as such," and the myths of Greece and Rome are often called classical mythology. The present book studies one particular group of myths, those of ancient Greece and Rome. To be clear, we avoid the ambiguous term *mythology* altogether, using instead *myth* or *myths*, on one hand, and *the study of myth* on the other.

The study of myth is multifaceted. There are many different ways in which modern scholars approach the study of myth, but they can be grouped into four general categories:

The recording and compiling of a given culture's myths
The analysis of the role specific myths play or played within the culture
The study of how one culture's myths are related to those of other cultures
Assessment of the lasting human significance of specific myths or groups of myths

Let us first discuss the recording and compiling of a given culture's myths. The spread of alphabetic literacy in the modern world has greatly reduced the degree to which myths serve as a guide to everyday life, but many cultures still maintain a vital oral tradition. One task undertaken by anthropologists and others who study such cultures is to record, in writing or by other means, the oral tales that are still passed on from generation to generation.

For such ancient cultures as those of Greece and Rome, whose myths are no longer part of a living tradition, direct recording of oral tales is no longer possible. If we are to study the myths of these cultures, they must have been recorded already. Typically the ancient myths were recorded not by scholars studying the myths for their own sakes, but by members of the culture who had other goals. In addition, oral tales exist in many different variants; the variant that was recorded on one occasion could be very different from that recorded on another. As a result, the records that have come down to us are contradictory, confusing, and incomplete. Careful study and considerable experience are needed to move from existing records to a coherent picture of any one myth.

The principal source for the study of ancient myths is works of literature. A literary work can take the form of a narrative and thus have the same structure as an oral tale (beginning, middle, end; plot, character, setting). That is because literary works, encoded in writing, take their concepts of structure directly from oral tales. Therefore, the study of myth has much in common with the study of literature. However, the structural similarities between the original oral tale and the written work of literature in which it is recorded can be deceptive. The literary work typically is the creation of a single person whose name we often know, whereas myths are anonymous. While creating his or her own version of a given myth, the author of the literary work introduces variations not present in the different oral retellings of the tale. Moreover, the author may not have taken the myth directly from the oral tradition at all, but may have worked from versions recorded in previous literary works. We know of many such instances in classical culture, so that often we are not sure whether we are dealing with myths or with something else.

Another valuable source of information about the myths of ancient peoples is the archaeological record. Painting, sculpture, and other nonliterary artifacts can provide valuable clues about variants not contained in the literary record and about who told particular myths, where, and when. A picture is not by itself a story; at most a picture can represent a character or scene from myth. Still, much can be learned about a culture's mythic traditions by correlating artistic depictions with tales known from other sources. It is often difficult to identify positively a mythical scene or character depicted on such artifacts, but in some cases figures are identified by labels or attributes that make correlations possible. In other cases, inference and educated guesses are the best we can do. A major problem in the study of mythical representations in ancient art is determining whether such images were inspired by written or unwritten sources. In any event, we have a great number of such artifacts from ancient Greece and Rome, and much has been learned about classical myth through study of them. For that reason, this book contains abundant illustrations from Greek pottery and other artifacts.

A second way in which scholars approach the study of myth is to examine the functions of specific myths in the context of a given society. In a society with a living oral tradition, myths must always be told by someone to someone and on some occasion. Both the tellers of tales and their audience must have a certain identity and status within the culture. They are male or female, wealthy or poor, powerful or not. To understand the myth fully, we need to know how it functioned for the people who took part in its retelling. We have already mentioned that myths can be etiological, offering an explanation for beliefs or practices that already exist. But a myth can function in other ways as well. Did it enhance the prestige of those who told the tale or heard it told? Did it justify the existing distribution of power and wealth or perhaps express a protest? Just what was so interesting to the people who listened to this tale?

A third way in which scholars study myth is to trace relationships between the myths of one culture and those of others. We have already mentioned that many folktale motifs are found in the same or similar form in many different cultures around the world. We can also look at the way specific myths have migrated from one culture to another but were transformed to suit the adopting culture's needs and traditions. The migration of myths from the ancient Near East to Greece is an event of extraordinary importance in the history of culture, and we spend some time on this problem.

Finally, some scholars involved in the study of myth are concerned above all with the assessment of myths. What is the deeper human significance of these old tales? Why have they fascinated so many for so long, in many cases even after the culture that produced them ceased to exist? Is there some sense in which truth resides in these fantastic tales?

Questions of the deeper meaning and truth of myth have played an important role dating back to antiquity. Some have sought to find a deep philosophical or psychological truth in myth by moving beyond the obvious surface meaning to a deeper, less apparent meaning. But to say that this or that is the genuine meaning of a myth is always a matter for dispute. Although some interpretations can be more successful than others, it is never possible to offer conclusive proof. Still, good interpretations require sensitivity and insight, knowledge of the society that produced the myth, and knowledge of one's own mind, which likes to see what it wants, unaware of its own prejudgments. Truly, in studying the history of the interpretation of myth we study more how peoples' prejudgments have changed than we study myth itself. For some scholars, nonetheless, the assessment of a myth's meaning is the most important aspect of their study, and in this book we offer many interpretations. When not compelling, we hope that our interpretations at least provide a basis for disagreement. Chapter 23 is devoted solely to an examination of the interpretation of myth and the many different theoretical frameworks.

KEY TERMS

divine myth, 4
legend, 4
folktale, 4

FURTHER READING

Carpenter, Thomas H., *Art and Myth in Ancient Greece* (London, 1991). The representation of Greek myths in Greek art, arranged by subject, with many illustrations.

Detienne, Marcel, *The Creation of Mythology*, trans. M. Cook (Chicago, 1986). Doubts that the category "myth" is valid.

Grimm's Fairy Tales. Collection of eighteenth-century German folktales by the brothers Grimm; established, more than any other book, what we think of as a folktale. There are many editions.

Havelock, E. A., *Preface to Plato* (Cambridge, Mass., 1963; reprinted 1982). Classic study of the relationship between the oral culture of prealphabetic Greece and its literate culture.

Lexicon iconographicum mythologiae classicae (LIMC) (Zurich, 1981–1999). Massive multivolume compilation of every representation of every myth, with scholarly commentary, in many languages (but mostly English). The single leading resource for the study of myth and art in the ancient world.

Lloyd, G.E.R., *Magic, Reason and Experience. Studies in the Origin and Development of Greek Science* (Cambridge, Mass., 1979). Describes the shift in thought from mythic to scientific.

Propp, V., *Morphology of the Folktale*, 2nd ed. (Austin, Tex., 1968; Russian original, 1928). English translation of the great Russian folklorist's seminal study of narrative pattern in folktale.

Shapiro, H. A., *Myth into Art. Poet and Painter in Classical Greece* (New York, 1994). A study of Greek iconography, focusing on the depiction of myth on Greek painted pottery.

Thompson, Stith, *The Folktale* (New York, 1946; reprinted Berkeley, 1977). Still the standard survey of the nature and forms of the folktale, by the most distinguished modern scholar of the folktale.

——— *Motif-index of Folk-literature*, 6 vols. (Bloomington, Ind., 1993). The basic reference work for folktale motifs throughout the world.

Veyne, Paul. *Did the Greeks Believe in Their Myths?* (Chicago, 1988). Influential, sometimes abstruse meditation on the nature of belief and the meaning of truth.

For bibliographic items dealing explicitly with the interpretation of myth, see the list at the end of Chapter 23.

CHAPTER 2

THE CULTURAL CONTEXT
OF CLASSICAL MYTH

Is there anyone to whom you entrust a greater number of serious matters than your wife? And is there anyone with whom you have fewer conversations?

SOCRATES TO CRITOBULOS,
in Xenophon's *Oikonomikos* 3.11–13

MYTHS REFLECT the society that produces them. They cannot be separated from the physical, social, and spiritual worlds in which a people lives or from a people's history. In this chapter we consider the background of the Greeks (and, briefly, the Romans), the nature of the land they lived in, their origins and history, how they lived as groups and individuals, and something about their values—what they hoped to achieve in life and how they hoped to do it. Later, when we turn to Roman myth (Chapter 22), we discuss their world in greater detail, which was rather different from that of the Greeks.

GREEK GEOGRAPHY

Greece was a poor country, barren and dry, in ancient times as today. Unlike the rich river valleys of Egypt and Mesopotamia, the rugged Balkan peninsula, the southeasternmost extension of Europe, does not seem to be a likely setting for the ancient civilization it produced (see Map I, inside front cover). Its rivers are too small to be

MAP II. Southern and Cultural Greece

SOUTHERN AND CENTRAL GREECE

navigable, and they dry up in the blazing heat of the mostly rainless summers. The Greek landscape is dominated by high mountains, which occupy about three quarters of the land. A towering range, the Pindus, runs down the center of the peninsula, then continues into the sea, where its peaks appear as dry, rocky islands. Pindus is intersected by other ranges, which cut across the peninsula. Between these ranges lie a series of small, isolated plains, the only places in Greece suitable for agriculture. Here, on these plains nestled between the mountains and the sea, Greek civilization developed.

To the northeast on the Balkan peninsula are the plains of Thessaly and Macedonia (see Map V, inside back cover). To their south lies the plain of **Boeotia** (bē-ō-sha, "cow-land"), whose principal settlement in ancient times was the city of Thebes, and the plain of **Attica,** whose capital was Athens. Farther south, on the smaller peninsula known as the Peloponnesus (pel-o-pon-**nē**-sus; see Map II, Southern and Central Greece), are other cultivable plains: Argolis, whose principal settlements were, in the Bronze Age, Tiryns and Mycenae (mī-**sē**-nē) and later, in the Classical Period, Argos and Corinth; Laconia, with the town of Sparta, also called Lacedaemon (las-e-**dē**-mon); Messenia (mes-**sē**-ni-a), whose most important settlement was Pylos; and Elis, site of the Olympic Games. All of these places are important in Greek myth.

On these small plains the ancient Greeks grew wheat and barley, planted early in winter, when the rainy season began, and harvested in May. The olive, whose small, compact gray leaves resist the ferocious summer sun, grew abundantly in the lowlands and provided a delightful light oil for cooking, cleansing and anointing the body, and burning in lamps. Wine grapes grew on vines planted on the slopes that surrounded the plains. Goats, sheep, and pigs were kept for wool, milk, cheese, leather, and meat, but cattle were few because of the lack of forage. Horses were also scarce, and therefore highly valued; they were a source of great prestige, the pride of the ruling class.

As cultivable land was limited in Greece, so were other resources. There was some gold in Thrace (far in the north), but none in Greece proper. There were a few deposits of silver (one of them, at Laurium in Attica, contributed to Athenian economic and military power). Most iron was imported, although important iron deposits in Laconia contributed to Spartan military supremacy. Greece imported copper from Cyprus. The source of tin, alloyed with copper to produce bronze, remains unknown.

The Greeks did have access to excellent deposits of limestone and clay. The best limestone was found on the island of **Euboea** (ū-bē-a), just east of the mainland, on several smaller islands, and in Thessaly. Under high pressure, limestone crystallizes into marble, a lovely, workable stone used by the Greeks for sculpture and for the finest temples, such as the Parthenon in Athens, which celebrated the goddess Athena.

Important deposits of marble were found on Mount Pentelicus near Athens (Fig. 2.1) and on the islands of Naxos and Paros. The finest clay, especially that found near Athens and Corinth, provided material for pottery, which the Greeks produced in great abundance and variety. Once fired, ceramic material is breakable, but its fragments are virtually indestructible. Exquisitely decorated Greek pots, which imi-

FIG. 2.1. Athens, from the west. To the left, the Parthenon, "temple to the virgin," stands on the summit of the Acropolis, a high limestone outcropping; the small temple to Nikê, Victory, and the elaborate entranceway is just visible before it at the very edge of the photograph. Below the Parthenon lies the valley of the agora, where Socrates taught and Athenian business was conducted. The rise in the foreground leads to the steps of the *pnyx,* a hillside (off the photo to the right) where the *demos* of Athens met to decide issues of peace and war. In the center distance is Mount Pentelicon, where the marble for constructing the Parthenon was quarried. This photo was taken in the 1940s, before urban sprawl engulfed modern Athens. (University of Wisconsin Photo Archive, Madison)

tated precious exemplars in silver and gold that now are lost, often expressly for use in burials, have been found all over the Mediterranean world and especially in Italy. The pictures painted on these pots provide us with vivid illustrations of Greek myths (many of which are illustrated in this book) and wonderfully illuminate many details of Greek social life.

But perhaps the greatest Greek natural resource was the sea. The **Aegean** (ē-jē-an) **Sea,** between the Balkan peninsula and Asia Minor, played a central role in the life of the ancient Greeks. Most of them lived near the sea and took from it the fish that was one of the staples of their diet, although Homeric heroes preferred to eat only flesh. The sea was also an avenue of communication with the world beyond the mountains that enclosed them.

Because of the islands scattered across the Aegean, a seafarer is almost never out of sight of land, and the Greeks learned early to travel long distances in small open boats. Several large islands dominate the others. Crete, the southernmost Aegean island, had an especially important role in the early history of Greece, but Euboea, Rhodes, Chios, and Lesbos also stand out. There are two principal groups of islands: the **Cyclades** (**sik**-la-dēz, "circle islands"), placed in a rough circle around the tiny central island of Delos, sacred to Apollo and Artemis; and the Sporades, "scattered islands," which extend along the coast of **Ionia,** the western coast of Asia Minor.[1]

The paucity of cultivable land and natural resources led the Greeks to trade with other nations. A mastery of the sea allowed them to transport goods to and from foreign lands. They exported wine, olive oil, and pottery and brought back the metals and other goods they needed, especially grain and prestige items of exquisite quality. Later, they established colonies across the sea, on the coasts of Asia Minor to the east and in Italy to the west.

The geography of the Balkan peninsula influenced both the history and the myths of the Greeks. The extremely mountainous terrain discouraged communication by land and favored political independence; through most of ancient Greek history, the various cities remained autonomous political entities. Many Greek legends told of the great deeds of these cities' founders and early rulers. Myths also reflect the fact that the Greeks were the greatest seafaring people of the ancient world (together with the Semitic Phoenicians), as exemplified by the story of Odysseus, whose perilous sea journey home from the Trojan War lasted ten years.

GREEK HISTORY

Greece was occupied even in the Paleolithic ("Old Stone") Age, before 7000 B.C., but almost nothing is known of these early inhabitants. From the Neolithic ("New Stone") Age, 6000–3000 B.C., survive foundation stones of houses, pottery, stone tools, and graves. These peoples lived in settled communities and practiced a rudimentary agriculture. Our evidence becomes richer with the advent of the Bronze Age around 3000 B.C., after which we divide the archaeological and historical record into the following periods:

Early/Middle Bronze Age	3000–1600 B.C.
Mycenaean Age (Late Bronze Age)	1600–1200 B.C.
Dark Age	1200–800 B.C.
Archaic Period	800–480 B.C.

[1]Curiously, the Ionian Sea and the Ionian Islands are to the west of Greece, far removed from Ionia itself.

Classical Period	480–323 B.C.
Hellenistic Period	323–31 B.C.

The dates for these periods are to some extent arbitrary and conventional, but this scheme provides a useful framework for discussion.

The Early/Middle Bronze Age (3000–1600 B.C.): The Origin of the Greeks

We do not regard the inhabitants of the mainland during the Early Bronze Age as Greeks because their cultural traditions were very different from those of the people who eventually became known by that name. We know nothing of their race or the language they spoke. They seem to have been modest farmers who worshiped goddesses of fertility to increase the yield of their crops, a religion still vital among later Greeks and reflected prominently in some Greek myths.

We are far better informed about the inhabitants of the island of Crete, called Minoans after Minos, the legendary Cretan king, although again we know nothing of their ethnic affinities or language. From c. 2200 B.C. into the Mycenaean Age, c. 1450 B.C., they built elaborate and wealthy palaces. The bull was important in their religious ritual, as was the double ax, or *labrys* (hence "labyrinth"), presumably the special tool by which bulls were sacrificed. They also worshiped a goddess of fertility. The Minoan palaces were not encircled by defensive walls, a fact that lends support to the remark by the Greek historian Thucydides (c. 460–c. 401 B.C.) that the mythical "kingdom of Minos" dominated the seas.

The people later called the Greeks belonged to a cultural and linguistic group known as the **Indo-Europeans,** whose original homeland apparently was in central Asia, perhaps east of the Caspian Sea. Beginning in the fourth millennium B.C., the Indo-Europeans seem to have migrated in all directions into Europe and Asia, bringing with them their linguistic and cultural traditions. The exact date of their arrival in Greece cannot be established definitively, but the destruction of existing settlements around 2100 B.C. at the transition from Early to Middle Bronze Age suggests the arrival of a new people. From about the same time we find the first evidence in Greece of the domestic horse, an animal elsewhere associated with the Indo-Europeans.

Much of what we know about the Indo-Europeans today is inferred by scholars from a reconstruction of the language they spoke, called proto-Indo-European. Although we have no written record or other direct evidence of this long-extinct hypothetical language, some of its vocabulary, and even some of its grammatical structure, can be inferred from the many ancient and modern languages descended from it.[2]

---

[2]Every language spoken today in Europe (except Basque, Finnish, Hungarian, and Estonian) belongs to this family. Today more than 1.6 billion people, on every continent, speak or at least understand Indo-European languages. Europe's colonial expansion into the Americas, Africa, Asia, and Australia carried English, Spanish, Portuguese, Russian, and French into new lands, where today they continue to absorb and replace native languages. The spread of the Indo-European language family, now assisted further by the Internet, is one of the most remarkable events in the history of the human race.

According to the elusive evidence, Indo-European society may have been divided into three groups whose membership was determined by birth: kings and priests, warriors, and food producers. They had a highly developed family life, and they were devoted to war. Some think that some basic patterns in Greek myth go back to the Indo-Europeans.

The Greek language of later eras probably was not the tongue of the early Indo-European immigrants but developed over the centuries after their arrival. The basic vocabulary of Greek is derived from the hypothetical proto–Indo-European parent language, but many words—particularly those for places, plants, and animals—seem to have been taken from the language of the earlier inhabitants, just as in America the names *Manhattan, Chicago,* and *Wisconsin* were taken from languages of pre-European inhabitants. There were also many Semitic words in Greek, reflecting the Greeks' enormous debt to earlier Semitic culture.

The Mycenaean Age (1600–1200 B.C.)

We have little archaeological evidence from the Early and Middle Bronze Age in Greece, but spectacular ruins and written documents survive from the Late Bronze or **Mycenaean Age,** named for the enormous stone citadel of Mycenae in the Peloponnesus (compare Fig. 13.1). The site was taken over by Greek-speaking Indo-Europeans about 1650 B.C.; immensely wealthy tombs from about 1600 B.C. prove its richness and importance and provide a convenient date for the beginning of the Mycenaean Age.

In the Mycenaean Age the Greeks were ruled by powerful kings. The kings and their retainers constituted a military and aristocratic elite; they were lovers of war who used bronze weapons, rode to battle in horse-drawn chariots, and concentrated great wealth. Independent kings built impressive strongholds from which they supervised highly controlled and centralized, although local, economies. Their greatest centers of power, in addition to Mycenae, were Thebes and Orchomenus in Boeotia, Athens in Attica, Pylos in Messenia, and Sparta in Laconia. All these centers (except Orchomenus) figure prominently in Greek myth, and we encounter them repeatedly in the following chapters. Unlike the Minoan settlements, Mycenaean palaces were strongly fortified. The Mycenaean Greeks may have called themselves **Achaeans** (a-kē-anz), a word Homer uses to describe the men who attacked Troy.

About 1450 B.C. the Minoan civilization was destroyed and the palaces burned, perhaps by Mycenaeans from the mainland, when Mycenaeans occupied and rebuilt the principal palace at Cnossus. The palace was destroyed again in 1400 B.C. by an unknown agency, never to be rebuilt. In the ruins we have found documents written in Greek in a nonalphabetic script called **Linear B.** Minoan art and religion made a deep impression on the Mycenaean Greeks and, through them, on subsequent European culture.

English architect Michael Ventris deciphered Linear B, the form of writing used by the Mycenaeans, in 1952, one of the great intellectual accomplishments of the twentieth century. Ventris proved that the writing consisted of about eighty nonalphabetic signs, each of which stood for a syllable. In addition to the tablets found at

Cnossus in Crete, documents in Linear B have turned up at Pylos, Mycenae, and Thebes on the mainland, proving the cultural uniformity of the Mycenaeans. Linear B, preserved on clay tablets, may have originated as a modification of the earlier, undeciphered Linear A writing, which may have preserved the Minoan language, presumably unrelated to Greek. Linear B was used only for keeping economic accounts. Although these records give us a great deal of information, Linear B was not used for recording literature.

The coincidence between centers of power in Mycenaean times and important locations in cycles of Greek legend—the Mycenae of Agamemnon, the Tiryns of Heracles, and the Thebes of Oedipus—indicates that many Greek legends probably originated during the Mycenaean period. In the absence of some form of writing suitable for recording them, however, these tales could only be transmitted orally from one generation to the next. Sometimes non-Greek cities, Cnossus in Crete and Troy in Asia Minor, were provided with cycles of legend, but always as seen through Greek eyes. Of native traditions from such cities, we have no direct information.

The Dark Age (1200–800 B.C.)

When Troy was destroyed by human hands about 1250 B.C., the people then occupying the site were raising horses and using pottery similar to that found in Greece; the Trojans of this period may have been Greeks. Most scholars associate the destruction of 1250 B.C. with the legend of the Trojan War (although there is plenty of room for disagreement). Soon after 1200 B.C., fire also destroyed most of the Mycenaean palaces on the mainland. Linear B writing disappeared forever. Greece sank into a **Dark Age** that lasted some four hundred years.

Later Greeks attributed this destruction to an invasion by Greek-speaking peoples from northwest Greece, whom they called the **Dorians,** equated with the Sons of Heracles in Greek legend, about whom important stories were told. Although modern scholars cannot confirm the Dorian invasion, it seems a plausible explanation of the archaeological evidence. The Dorians, whether or not descendants of Heracles, apparently overthrew the Mycenaeans who earlier dominated Greece, except for remote and mountainous central Arcadia in the Peloponnesus. They then pushed across the Aegean to Crete and other nearby islands and to the southern strip of Asia Minor.

Of the mainland settlements, Athens alone withstood the invaders. Many Greeks from other regions migrated eastward and resettled the Aegean islands. Refugees from the Peloponnesus, passing through Athens and now called Ionians, took possession of the central islands of the Aegean and founded colonies in the central sector of the western coast of Asia Minor. This central region, henceforth known as **Ionia,** had its greatest center at Miletus (see Maps I and V, inside front and back covers). Other refugees, the Aeolians, crossed from Thessaly to the island of Lesbos and to the northern portion of the coast of Asia Minor, henceforth called Aeolis. The famous poet Sappho, whose poems are nearly the only documents to survive in the odd Aeolic dialect, lived on Lesbos. By 900 B.C., the map of Greece had been completely redrawn.

Very few archaeological remains survive from the Dark Age, a time of profound social disorganization, depopulation, and impoverishment. Petty kings with only local authority replaced the great monarchs of the Mycenaean Age. To judge from later traditions, Greek society was organized around the family and village. Many settlements were split by tribal and family feuds and, in the Dorian areas, by a great gulf between masters and subjects. What civilization remained seems to have centered on the long island of Euboea, just east of the mainland, where recent excavations have revealed rich burials, one a spectacular grave containing a warrior and his wife, with many rare and valuable objects, some of gold. We are now learning that Euboean settlements were the only Greek towns to carry on direct trade with the Near East throughout the Dark Age. These relations were to play a central role in the subsequent revival of Greek culture: The alphabet first appears on Euboea, where the poems of Homer and Hesiod may have been written down.

The Archaic Period (800~480 B.C.)

About 800 B.C., someone familiar with Phoenician writing, probably a Euboean, invented the Greek alphabet by requiring that a rough indication of the vowel accompany each consonantal sign (Fig. 2.2). Phoenician writing had only signs for consonants and could not be pronounced except by a native. The Greek alphabet was the first writing that encoded an approximation of the actual sound of the human voice, hence potentially a writing applicable to any human language. It is one of the most important inventions in the history of culture, the basis for all Western civilization and, except for minor changes, the same system of writing that appears on this page.

Within a generation, the revolutionary alphabetic technology had spread throughout the Greek people. At the same time, under Euboean leadership, the Greeks sent out colonies to the west, to southern Italy and Sicily, where they built cities and prospered greatly. The period of political and cultural revival that began with the invention of the alphabet marks the beginning of a new era in Greek history, the **Archaic Period** (800–480 B.C.).

The Archaic Period witnessed the emergence of the Greek *polis,* the politically independent city-state. Unlike the villagers of earlier eras, who defined their position by family relations, the members of a *polis* owed their allegiance to a social group defined by geography. In the *polis* appeared for the first time the explicit concept of citizenship ("city-membership"), so important to the modern state. Only men were citizens and could participate in political affairs; women lived in a separate world. Within the *polis,* the Greek citizen was in relentless competition with his neighbor. Greek cultural values depended on the spirit of male competition (unlike in Egypt, for example, where cooperation was the highest social value), and these values permeate the stories they told.

Another important development during the Archaic Period was the rebirth of commerce, which ebbed throughout the Dark Age. The Greeks' dependence on the sea for commerce, transportation, and food was essential to the formation of their character and had a direct influence on their social structure. Greece was never so-

FIG. 2.2. Greek papyrus. A typical letter (you can see the signature at the bottom), from the second century A.D. All ancient Greek literature was recorded on papyrus, made of thin strips of the papyrus plant laid in two cross-grained layers. When complete, the papyrus was rolled (hence our word *volume;* Latin *volumen,* "a thing rolled"), making it difficult to look anything up. Tens of thousands of papyri have survived in the dry sands of Egypt, including most of what we possess of Sappho and other early poets.   (From "The Wisconsin Papyri," no. 76, University of Wisconsin Photo Archive, Madison)

cially stratified in the elaborate fashion of the heavily populated and extravagantly wealthy river monarchies that grew up along the Nile and in Mesopotamia, between the Tigris and Euphrates rivers, and the Greeks' dependence on the sea further reduced class distinctions. The sea is an equalizer: The sudden dangerous storms of the Aegean threatened captain and crew alike, so claims to good birth and upbringing had no survival value. Seafaring encouraged extreme individualism and offered rich rewards to the skilled adventurer willing to take risks. Seafaring was practiced almost entirely by free citizens, and in the *Odyssey* the Greeks invented the world's first tale of danger and wonder on the high sea.

In the sixth century B.C. commerce received an enormous stimulus from the introduction of coinage, universally accepted weights of portable, indestructible metal certified by civic authority. Before this time, money as we think of it did not exist. Coined money made possible capitalism and the enrichment of the new social classes by commerce. The traditional aristocracy looked down on and bitterly opposed these upstarts, skillful only at accumulating wealth, and called them *kakoi,* the "bad men," while calling themselves *aristoi,* the "best men" (hence our "aristocrat"). Despite the scorn of the *aristoi,* economic and political power fell more and more into the hands of the *kakoi.*

Between 650 and 500 B.C., many Greek city-states were ruled by strong men known as *tyrants,* who represented the interests of the commercial class against the traditional aristocracy. The word *tyrant* comes from a non-Greek language of Asia Minor and originally meant something like "ruler," but by the sixth century B.C. it referred to a leader who had taken power by "unconstitutional" (that is, nontraditional) means. In the eyes of their aristocratic opponents, the tyrants were arbitrary despots, but tyrants often did much to enhance the wealth and power of the cities they ruled. Rarely did a tyrant give up power voluntarily. In cultural matters, however, the aristocracy clung to power. As the most literate citizens, its members were creators or sponsors of most Greek literature, art, and philosophy. They gave to *tyrant* the pejorative meaning it still has today. When speaking of Greek culture, we refer, with few exceptions, to the literary monuments produced by and for the *aristoi,* the free male citizens descended from old families. About the *kakoi,* the poor, slaves, women, and other noncitizens, most of whom were illiterate, we have little direct information.

The Classical Period (480–323 B.C.)

During the latter part of the Archaic Period, Greece was threatened by a powerful rival from the East. The Persians, an Indo-European people living on the Iranian plateau east of Mesopotamia (modern Iraq), had developed into a dynamic warrior state under the leadership of Cyrus the Great (600?–529 B.C.). Conquering and absorbing first the Semitic states of Mesopotamia, then Egypt, and finally advancing into Anatolia (modern Turkey) and southern Russia, Persia became the greatest empire the world had seen. Soon Persia absorbed the Greek colonies on the eastern coast of Asia Minor.

In 508 B.C., in Athens, a remarkable development took place: the emergence of the world's first democracy ("rule by the people"; *dêmos* = "people"), an outgrowth of the centuries-long dispute between *kakoi* and *aristoi.* Under the leadership of Clisthenes (**klīs**-the-nēz), the social and political basis of the *polis* was completely reorganized so as to place decision-making power in the hands of all adult male citizens, who may have numbered about 25,000. Citizens lived both in the countryside and in the city. Henceforth, authority in government came not from wealth and prominence of family, but from one's ability to persuade the large, unruly assembly of citizens.

From this unique political climate emerged many of the forms of civilization familiar to us today: written law, the rules of reason, the need for evidence, history, popular entertainment, science, and philosophy. In Athens, ancient myths were recast as a new form of entertainment and instruction in the annual presentations of Athenian tragedy. Democracy made the ordinary citizen feel he had responsibility for his own destiny. The Persian army discovered to their sorrow the explosive power of this new form of government when they invaded mainland Greece in 490 B.C. In a tremendous battle near the village of Marathon, about twenty-five miles from

FIG. 2.3. A Greek hoplite (heavy-armed soldier) drives his spear into a Persian, Attic vase, c. 460 B.C. Note the Greek's bronze helmet, linen cuirass (body protector), and bronze shield held by an arm strap and hand grip. In real life the hoplite also covered his feet and calves with bronze. The Persian, wearing long pants, a shirt, and a leather cap with tassels, is armored only with a linen cuirass and carries a sword, bow, and arrow. Later, Amazons were portrayed in the same garb and identified with the Persian enemy. The Athenian's love of freedom, as well as his superior armor, contributed to his military victory over the Persians in 490 and 480 B.C.   (The Metropolitan Museum of Art, New York, Rogers Fund, 06.1021.117)

Athens, Athenian citizen soldiers smashed the professional Persian army and drove the invaders into the sea. "This proved," wrote the historian Herodotus, "if there were need of proof, how noble a thing is freedom" (*Histories* 5.78). An even greater Persian campaign launched ten years later, in 480 B.C., also met with disaster, first in a naval battle off the island of Salamis near Athens and then on land near Plataea, in Boeotia (Fig. 2.3). This second stunning victory over the Persians, under Athenian leadership at sea and Spartan on land, fired the Greeks, and especially the Athenians, with an unprecedented self-confidence and eagerness to try out new forms of thought, social organization, and artistic expression. These amazing victories inspired the first study of history (Herodotus coined the word, which means "inquiry," in his great book) and mark the beginning of the brief **Classical Period.** In the popular Marathon race the Athenian victory of 490 B.C. is still celebrated around the world.[3]

During the Classical Period, the Golden Age of Greece, lived many of the most influential thinkers, artists, and politicians: historians Herodotus and Thucydides; tragedians Aeschylus, Sophocles, and Euripides; comic dramatist Aristophanes; statesman Pericles; philosophers Socrates, Plato, and Aristotle; Ictinus, architect of the Parthenon; sculptor Phidias; and orator Demosthenes, to name only the most prominent. All these men were residents of Athens, a testimony to the city's cultural supremacy, fostered by its radical democracy. From other cities during the Classical Period came the poet Pindar; Democritus, who fashioned the atomic theory of matter; and Hippocrates, "the father of medicine."

During the Classical Period the *polis* reached its greatest effectiveness but also showed its worst faults. Some of the tragedies of this era illuminate the violent tensions many citizens no doubt felt between ancient loyalty to the family and current loyalty to the political state. Still, the *polis* triumphed as the ideal of social life. In the fourth century B.C., Aristotle described the *polis* as the perfect and natural fruit of a long social evolution. According to him, "man is by nature a political animal," that is, a being who reaches full potential only by living in a *polis.*

Although the proud and politically independent city-states struggled constantly and murderously against one another, the Greeks nonetheless maintained the sense of being a single people. They spoke a common language and used a common technology of writing and called themselves Hellenes (**hel**-ēnz), implying a common descent from the legendary Hellen (**hel**-len).[4] They worshiped the same pantheon of gods and participated in panhellenic religious and athletic festivals, especially at Olympia. Such regional events as the annual Panathenaic ("All-Athenian") festival in Athens gave the Greeks a sense of ethnic community. But political unity was beyond the reach of the freedom-loving Greeks. In the crisis of the Persian wars they combined briefly against the barbarian invader. Once the Persian threat receded, however, they settled into two loosely organized rival leagues, one led by Sparta, a military state ruled by an old-fashioned aristocracy, the other by democratic Athens (Fig. 2.4). From 431 to 404 B.C., these leagues fought each other in a ruinous conflict known as the **Peloponnesian War.** Greece never recovered.

The Classical Period saw the development of Greek philosophy and history as powerful intellectual rivals to traditional myth. Such physicians as Hippocrates and such philosophers as Protagoras and later Plato and Aristotle challenged mythic accounts of the origin and nature of the universe, and the historian Thucydides rejected the conviction, heretofore universal, that gods determine the outcome of human events. The stories of gods and heroes were the common birthright of all Greece and were celebrated in painting, sculpture, song, and drama, but they were given new meanings in the intellectual ferment of this extraordinary age.

---

[3]After the defeat of the Persians, a runner ran the twenty-five miles to Athens, announced the victory, and dropped dead. In the Olympic Games at Athens in 1896, the Marathon race was instituted to commemorate this event. In 1908 the distance was standardized at 26 miles, 385 yards.

[4]Not to be confused with Helen of Troy. See the myth of Deucalion (Chapter 5). The term *Graioi*, "Greeks," comes from the Romans, who took it from a northwestern Greek tribe living in Epirus, the backward territory across the Ionian Sea, which separates Italy from Greece.

FIG. 2.4. The modern village of Sparta in the plain beneath towering Mount Taygetus. Little remains of the ancient city, proving the wisdom of the Greek historian Thucydides, who remarked in his history of the Peloponnesian War, "If the Spartans should abandon their city, and leave behind their temples and the foundations of their permanent structures, no doubt after a considerable time had elapsed posterity would be very skeptical indeed about their power . . . since they do not live in a real city and do not have any rich or beautiful shrines and public buildings, but dwell in scattered villages in the ancient Greek style. . . . On the other hand, if the same thing happened to Athens, the visible evidence would lead people to estimate the city's power at twice its true value."   (University of Wisconsin Photo Archive, Madison)

The Hellenistic Period (323~31 B.C.)

The social and political system based on the *polis* was crippled in 338 B.C. when Philip II of Macedon, a region to the north of Greece (see Map V, inside back cover), over-ran the Greek city-states and imposed his will on them. The Macedonian state was a monarchy and altogether unlike the Greek *polis;* although Philip admired Greek intellectual culture and Greek economic enterprise, he had no patience with the endless squabbles conducted in the name of "freedom." When he was killed in 336 B.C. in a palace intrigue, his twenty-year-old son Alexander inherited the throne. Moved by legends of the Trojan War and seeing himself as a latter-day Achilles, Alexander attacked the enormous Persian Empire, ostensibly to avenge the Persian invasions 150 years earlier. In a series of brilliant battles, he destroyed the Persian empire and occupied its vast territories. His conquests took him even beyond Persian domains into India. From 323 B.C., when Alexander died of a fever (or was poisoned by rivals) at age thirty-two, we date what is known as the **Hellenistic Period** of Greek history.[5]

After his death Alexander's empire quickly broke up into separate and hostile kingdoms, but Greek culture became world culture. Everywhere throughout the ancient East—in Syria, Mesopotamia, Palestine, and Egypt—cities were established on the Greek model, decorated in the Greek style, ruled by Greeks and speakers of Greek. The cultural capital shifted from Athens to Alexandria, a city Alexander himself had founded in the western delta of Egypt.

In 146 B.C., the Greek mainland was conquered by Rome, and other centers of Hellenistic culture met a similar fate in the years that followed. The end of the period can be dated to 31 B.C., when Alexandria fell into Roman hands after the suicide of Cleopatra VII, the last ruling descendant of the generals of Alexander.

GREEK SOCIETY

Greek myths reflect the society in which they were transmitted, and to understand them we need to understand something about the social life of ancient Greece. Unfortunately, our knowledge of Greek society is rather limited. About conditions in the Bronze and Iron ages we have archaeological evidence but no written information except the accounting documents of Linear B. For the Archaic Period, we have the long poems of Homer and Hesiod, who lived in the eighth century B.C., but almost nothing after them. We know more about Greek society in the Classical Period, largely because of the tragedies and other literary works that have survived from this era. But even here our knowledge is incomplete. Almost all the literary sources are of Athenian origin, and almost all were composed by aristocratic men. Most so-called descriptions of Greek social life are really descriptions of Athenian social life of the fifth and fourth centuries B.C., although Athens was in many ways a unique community in ancient Greece. In this section we nonetheless attempt to describe the general aspects of Greek society reflected in myth, especially the aspects that seem to us most foreign and distant.

Men

Much of Greek social life revolved around the free men who were dominant in both the private and the public spheres. In Classical Athens, there were about 25,000 such

---

[5] *Hellenic* refers to anything Greek (from the legendary Hellen, founder of the Greek race); *Hellenistic* refers to the historical period that began with the death of Alexander the Great.

FIG. 2.5. An older bearded man and a younger beardless man dance the *komos,* "revel" (whence the word *comedy*), c. 490 B.C., on the inside of a wine cup (*kylix*). The pedagogue's instruction in alphabetic literacy and in playing the lyre led to close friendships and intimate relations, suggested by the bearded man's posture and gesture with his staff. (Toledo Museum of Art, 64.126)

men, out of a total population of around 200,000. They held final authority over their wives and the other members of their households. They alone were obligated to fight in wars, and they alone were eligible to become citizens of the *polis.* They were prepared for these roles by an education that began in early childhood and taught them not only to read and write, but also to be athletic, in rigorous control of their appetites, and fearless in battle and the hunt. They grew up in a small, tightly knit, relentlessly competitive community where everyone knew everyone's worth and there was no forgiveness for failure. An individual man was celebrated for victories over his enemies in war and politics and for his wit and ability to entertain at the all-male *symposium,* "drinking party," the Greek man's principal form of social life and principal setting for the telling of Greek myths.

In the Classical Period, when a boy was born, his father was at least thirty years old. Between six and thirteen he received instruction from a *pedagogue* ("trainer of boys"), who taught him how to read, write, and memorize the poetry of Homer and other poets from written texts, which he could recite before his male friends (Fig. 2.5). The boy still lived in the women's quarters of the house, but every day he exercised naked with his friends to harden his body against the day when, in defense of the *polis,* he would take up armor and stand against the enemy.

Isolated from the other sex, men in their twenties gathered at the exercise ground to admire the prepubescent boys and to court them through gifts and poetry, a practice called **pederasty,** "love for boys." Greek pederasty has no good modern counterparts, and no other facet of ancient Greek social life seems more odd, a measure of our enormous distance from the Greeks of the Classical Period. Teenage boys also attended the symposium as cupbearers, where such courtship could continue. If the boy accepted a suitor's attentions (he need not), he would submit to kissing and fondling and, eventually, to copulation from the front between the boy's thighs, or even anal penetration (Fig. 2.6). The boy was expected to derive little or no physical pleasure from his lover's attentions, in keeping with Greek moral education in self-control: In the many surviving pederastic illustrations on pots, the boy,

FIG. 2.6. Pederastic scene on an Attic two-handled drinking cup from the sixth century B.C. The mature man fondles the genitals of the boy, who reaches up affectionately to touch the man on the chin. The grape vines on either side refer to the wine drunk from the cup. Such erotic scenes, homosexual and heterosexual, are common on Greek pottery used in the symposium. No other art tradition, except that of Japan, rivals the Greek in the explicit portrayal of lovemaking. (Museum of Fine Arts, Boston, 08.292)

always beardless, is never shown with an erection, whereas the man, always bearded, often has one. We learn of few instances of homosexual activity between adults, a practice held up to savage ridicule by the Greek comic poet Aristophanes (c. 450–338 B.C.). Pederasty was an aspect of Greek preparation for manhood and war and was thought to enhance the refined moral qualities of loyalty, respect, affection, and courage.

At age eighteen, when half the boys had lost their fathers in war, a male in Athens became a *citizen,* a "member of the city," able to vote in elections and speak in public. Between eighteen and twenty he was called an *ephebe* (**e**-fēb), "one who has come of age," and in an initiatory rite of passage he spent time outside the city practicing military procedure and honing his hunting skills. In one ephebic festival dedicated to the hero Theseus, men dressed as women, a common practice in many tribal cultures to mark the transition from youth to full manhood. Apparently the purpose of the ritual was to identify with the female sex that had heretofore controlled the young boys, then by disrobing to break away from women's ways forever. At this same time the boy prepared to leave the women's part of the house.

When in his early twenties the young man sought out prepubescent boys for friendship and sexual pleasure, his marriage was still ten years away, and even when he married pederastic attachments might continue. No longer a cupbearer at the symposium, but an equal participant in it, the young citizen reclined to eat and drink on one of the fourteen or sixteen couches placed around the walls of the *andreion,* the "man's room," which had a separate entrance from that into the rest of the house. Here he competed in wit and poetry with his friends, many of whom he had grown up with.

The symposium is the setting for Plato's famous dialogue *The Symposium*, where drunken companions attempt to define the nature of sexual love. The topic is suitable because in addition to the handsome boys who served wine, female courtesans called *hetairai,* "female companions," offered every kind of sexual service for pay. *Hetairai* also sang and danced and are often represented on Greek pottery, which was designed to be used at the symposium. They seem often to have been foreign women or slaves and with few exceptions had no standing in respectable society (Fig. 2.7).

War was a looming concern for every Greek male, who could expect at some time to face the enemy in hand-to-hand combat and throughout his life prepared for that moment. Half would die by the sword. In the Bronze and Dark ages warfare seems to have been conducted between unorganized gangs from which some hero might emerge, an Achilles eager for glory and reputation, to challenge the best fighter from the other side; so do men fight in Homer's *Iliad*. In the Classical Period, by contrast, a citizen fought for the glory of his *polis*. War was conducted on open plains between opposing lines, many ranks deep, of heavily armed men called **hoplites** (see Fig. 2.3; *hoplon* = "shield," "armor"). Each man had to pay for his own equipment. The principal weapon was the thrusting spear, but a fighter also carried

FIG. 2.7. The symposium ("drinking party"). On a fifth-century B.C. Attic vase a nude *hetaira* entertains the male diners by playing on the double flute. On the far right a diner plays the game of *kottabos;* the idea is to twirl the large, flat drinking cup called a *kylix* (see Fig. 2.5) on the forefinger, then fling the dregs of the wine across the room to knock down a small statuette, usually of a satyr, perched atop a stand. The diner to his left reaches out to the *hetaira,* while on the far left two elderly men are deep in their cups; one holds two *kylikes.* Note the lyre on the wall, used to accompany the poetry sung at the symposium.   (Master and Fellows of Corpus Christi College, Cambridge, England)

a one-edged sword for slashing in close encounter. Advancing in tight ranks, one line attempted to break the other and win the battle. Afterwards, a truce was called, the dead buried, and a *trophy* set up by the winning side (*tropaion* = "place of turning"). In Homer the heroes go into battle in chariots, then jump down and fight on foot. Cavalry—warriors mounted on individual horses—was not important in Greek warfare until the Hellenistic Period, and even then the lack of saddle and stirrup (introduced to Europe from China in the Middle Ages) and the small size of the horses limited the cavalry's effectiveness.

Social institutions encouraged the cultivation and refinement of the warrior's spirit. In the *gymnasium* (from Greek *gymnos*, "naked"), the Greek male practiced nonlethal forms of war. Our tradition of athletics (from Greek *athlos*, "contest") began in Greece (Fig. 2.8). As sport to the Greek was practice for war, war was a kind of sport, and strict rules governed the behavior of the citizen armies. Competitive rules similar to those regulating Greek warfare extended off the battlefield into every realm of social life. In the Archaic and Classical periods, a man divided his social relations into clear camps of friends and enemies; a man was measured by the richness of gifts to his friends and the thorough punishment he gave to his enemies. In Athenian tragedy, poets recast ancient myths to reflect contemporary concerns as they competed vigorously for first prize under the critical gaze of their fellow citi-

FIG. 2.8. A foot race on an Athenian amphora (two-handled jar), c. 460 B.C., offered as a prize for victory in the athletic games held every four years during the Panathenaic festival. Homer calls Achilles "swift-footed," as a successful warrior had to be.   (The Metropolitan Museum of Art, New York, Rogers Fund, 14.130.12)

zens. In Athenian law courts, one sought not justice, but victory. The notion of "natural rights" to life or property or happiness, so prominent in our own thinking, simply did not exist.

Women

Although our lack of sources hinders the study of all aspects of ancient Greek society, we find it particularly difficult to form an accurate picture of the lives of women. Almost all the literary sources were composed by male authors, who often present a biased, unsympathetic, and contradictory picture of women. On one hand, these sources suggest, the ideal Greek woman was tall, beautiful, submissive, fertile, chaste, and silent, virtually invisible to those outside the home. As the statesman Pericles told the widows of soldiers killed in battle, "Your reputation is great when you do not prove inferior to your own nature and when there is the least possible talk about you among men, whether, in praise or in blame" (Thucydides 1.45.2). But the sources also imply that real women were likely to behave in ways that contrasted sharply with this ideal. Fired by an insatiable sexual appetite, the women depicted in literature often are ready to lie and scheme to achieve their aims. It is difficult to distill the truth about women's lives from the sources that are available to us, but we can make at least some observations with a reasonable level of confidence.

A little girl learned the values of modesty, obedience, and restraint in the care of a nurse as she grew up in the *gynaikeion*, "women's quarters," located in the back of the house or on an upper floor. In the *gynaikeion* she also learned the female arts of spinning wool and making cloth, a woman's principal occupation throughout life, except for childbearing and care of the dead (Fig. 2.9). Only rarely did women learn to read and write. In the inner rooms of the *gynaikeion* women met with other women friends and entertained one another with gossip and music. Although women may have told stories, myths, to one another and to their children, we have no direct evidence that they did; as far as we know, Greek myth, like Greek literary education, was an invention of men, a fact of paramount importance in our attempts to understand it.

A Greek proverb noted that a woman knew two great moments in her life: her marriage and her death. Unlike other ancient peoples (except possibly the Etruscans), the Greeks were monogamous; that is, offspring from one wife at a time were the man's legitimate heirs. The origins of Greek monogamy are unknown, but no other social practice affected more deeply the way Greek men and women behaved toward one another. Marriage was not based on mutual affection, but arranged between families on political and economic grounds. Even the Athenian *polis*, despite the institutions of democracy, was governed by its leading families. The family provided the woman with a dowry, which allowed the bride's family to retain some control even after marriage: In case of divorce the husband was compelled to return the dowry intact. The bride may never have set eyes on her husband until the wedding day. The groom was a mature adult, usually in his thirties, with wide experience of life and war; the bride was a girl in her teens, around fourteen years old, who offered her dolls in a temple as her last act before marriage. The husband had wide sexual

FIG. 2.9. Greek village women, from about 1920, spinning wool. The women represent all age groups: a middle-aged woman on the left with her young daughter, also spinning, then a teenage girl, then two old women flanking a prepubescent girl. Another girl stands behind at a higher level. The women hold distaffs under their right arms that support masses of wool. With their right hands, they detach the wool while the left hand guides the thread to a spindle that spins like a top, dropping gradually to the ground as the thread lengthens, when the spinner must stop and wind the thread around the spindle's shaft. Ancient spinning was done in precisely this fashion. Seven tenths of the time needed to produce woven cloth is taken up by spinning, woman's archetypal activity until modern times. The women are dressed in dark colors and cover their heads. Their activity and dress are remarkably similar to those of women in ancient Greece. (University of Wisconsin Photo Archive, Madison)

experience, sometimes orgiastic, with women and other men; the bride was a ***parthenos***, "virgin" (Fig. 2.10). No respectable man would knowingly marry a woman who had prior sexual experience, and a father could sell into slavery a daughter guilty of it, even if she were the victim of rape. For these reasons Greek girls were married off as soon as possible after first menstruation.

The period between first menstruation and marriage was one of great danger to the girl, her family, and society itself. As *parthenos,* the girl was thought to be wild and dangerous, like the goddess Artemis, to whom the *parthenos* was often compared and whose cult young girls served. Most heroines of Greek myth are *parthenoi,* in a momentary position of freedom to do immense harm or bring great advantage to her people. Fortunately, in marriage a woman could gain *sophrosynê,* "self-control." Tamed by the authority of her husband, in willing submission to the weighty demands of pleasing her husband sexually and bearing him children, a woman could overcome her natural weakness and live a modest and silent life away from the scrutiny of others.

The wedding, high point of a girl's life, ordinarily was held at night, when the new bride moved out of her mother's *gynaikeion* into that of her mother-in-law, where she first experienced intercourse, bore children, and lived until she died, often in childbirth at a young age. The myth of the abduction of Persephonê (Chapter 9) must reflect the young Greek girl's psychological experience on the wedding night. Terrified when snatched up by Lord Death as she played with her virgin friends, she soon accepted her changed condition in life.

FIG. 2.10. Statue of a *korê*, "maiden." Such statues stood on the Acropolis, where they were dedicated by wealthy citizens in honor of their daughters, presumably so that by magical sympathy the young women could stand in Athena's protection. The *korê*'s hair is made into elaborate tresses and falls over a linen dress called a *peplos*. The statues, made of limestone, were brightly colored. Her "archaic smile" is characteristic of Greek statues from the late sixth century B.C. The statues have survived because when the Athenians cleaned up the Acropolis after the Persian sack of 480 B.C., they threw the broken statuary into a pit, whence it has been recovered in modern times. (Acropolis Museum, Athens; author's photo)

The groom traveled to the bride's house in a cart, where he took her wrist in a special gesture implying a staged abduction (Fig. 2.11); at this moment she left behind the authority of her father and entered within the authority of her husband and her husband's mother. To the accompaniment of music, dance, song, and crackling torches the cart made its way to the house of the groom. In the morning, the girl's friends visited her in the bridal chamber and brought gifts (Fig. 2.12).

As a virgin, or *parthenos*, the Greek girl was called *korê* (an alternate name for Persephonê). After marriage and intercourse she was a *nymphê*, "bride" (hence our word *nymph*). Not until she bore her first child did she become a *gynê*, "woman" (as in *gynecology*), when she assumed full authority over the *oikos*, "family,"[6] which included not only the female and young unmarried male members of the household, but also the slaves and domestic animals, the house itself, and its inner storeroom filled with storage vessels; in myth, women are closely associated with vessels, as they are with textiles. By her late teens a Greek woman was a mother and by age thirty a grandmother. By age forty-five she was a great-grandmother, if she lived that long.

A Greek wife did not even eat with her husband, but monogamy placed enor-

---

[6]From which comes our word *economy*, "the management of the family," and *ecology*, "study of the habitat." The Latin *familia* had approximately the same meaning.

FIG. 2.11. A Greek wedding, on an Attic wedding vase (*loutrophoros*), which held the water by which the bride purified herself, c. 540 B.C. The bridegroom moves to the right, having clasped the bride by the hand; the Greek wedding was a mock abduction. He gazes at the bride, whose face has just been revealed. Over his head is written the Greek word for "handsome." The bride inclines her head slightly, in the expected attitude of modesty and shame. Cloth covers her head (compare Fig. 2.9), and she wears a bridal crown. Two cupids, called *erotes* (singular, *eros*), flutter about her head, symbolizing sexual desire. Women attendants stand on either side. The column on the right edge of the photo represents the bridal chamber, where the groom is leading the bride. (Boston Museum of Fine Arts, 03.802)

mous power in her hands (about which we hear endless complaints in Greek myth). Monogamy also isolated her in a way unknown within the polygamous societies of the rest of the ancient world, where women of the harem had constant companionship. Increased prosperity heightened still more the isolation of Athenian women of the Classical Period, for whom abundant slaves performed such menial but social work as gathering water and nursing children. Ordinarily a respectable women went outdoors only during certain religious festivals, when she averted her eyes from the gaze of men and covered her head.

Several festivals were restricted to women alone, and close study of their symbols and rituals shows how in these festivals the fertility of the earth, and by extension the well-being of the community, were connected closely to the woman's ability to bring forth from her body new life. Childbirth was a moment of personal crisis, because many women died from it, but also of enormous pollution, called **miasma**, "stench," because of the blood and other fluids that attend childbirth. No man would come close to a woman in labor. Women's ability to purify the chamber and the child af-

FIG. 2.12. The day after the wedding, in the women's quarters, from a fifth-century B.C. Attic *epinêtron,* an odd ceramic object with roughed upper surface to serve as a knee-cover for wool-working. On the right, the bride rests against a couch; behind her, the double doors of the bridal chamber stand open. The pillar before her indicates that this is an interior view. Outside, friends of the bride bring gifts. One woman talks to a dove, the bird of Aphrodite. At the left, a woman arranges myrtle in a *loutrophoros* (see Fig. 2.11). From the wall hang a mirror, symbol of the bride, and a wreath. All the figures are named; the bride is called Alcestis, after the legendary wife who died so that her husband could live (Chapter 14), and the other women also have mythical names.   (National Archaeological Museum, Athens, 5127, Deutsch Archaologisches Institut, Athens)

ter birth extended to their care of the dead. Only women could touch a dead body to clean it for burial. After burial they tended the family graves, pouring offerings and tying ribbons around gravestones. Myths are filled with events surrounding birth and death and the special power of women to withstand and control the two crises through which every human being must pass.

Our evidence about family size from the Classical Period is poor, but in the Hellenistic Period an average Greek family consisted of three children, preferably two boys and one girl: one boy to die in the endless wars, another to carry on the family line, and one girl to assist in the formation of interfamilial alliances. Girls were disadvantageous because they required a dowry and did not carry on the family name. Additional children were often exposed, abandoned in the wilds. Most died, but some were found and raised as slaves or prostitutes. There are famous foundlings in Greek myth, including Oedipus of Thebes.

Athenian women probably fared somewhat better in the Archaic Period, when great families were in power, than in the Classical Period under the democracy, when citizenship became all-important. To be a citizen meant not to be a woman or a slave.

In affirmation of the solidarity of the group, Athenian men met together every year in a gigantic civic symposium, the festival of Dionysus, god of wine, where they witnessed the tragedies and light-hearted satyr plays, for which the chorus dressed as sexually excited men.[7] Although powerful women often appear in Greek plays, their fascination emerges directly from the shocking reversal of ordinary roles. In Aeschylus' tragedy *Agamemnon,* Clytemnestra ruled the city of Mycenae while her husband, Agamemnon, fought at Troy, then murdered him in a bathtub. In Aristophanes' comedy *Lysistrata,* the women of the Greek cities banded together, went on a sex strike, and took over Athens. To the male audience, this amusing reversal seemed as absurd as if the birds in the sky conquered the world, as they actually do in another of Aristophanes' plays.

Although social tensions between Greek men and women were high and never resolved, the sexes were capable of genuine affection toward each other. Helen's infidelity, so the story went, caused the Trojan War, but Odysseus' longing for home and family led him to abandon an offer of immortal life with a nymph far more beautiful than his wife. Among the most touching works of Greek art are the sculptured gravestones showing the deceased in loving company with husbands, wives, or children. In rare cases, women even participated in public life: Aspasia, the non-Athenian mistress of Pericles from the city of Miletus, was highly cultivated, knew Socrates and other powerful people, and was said to have advised Pericles on his foreign policy.

Slavery

Without slaves, ancient civilizations could not have existed. Tribal societies kill captives taken in war, or sometimes adopt the women and children, but the ancient Mediterranean civilizations of Greece and Rome were sufficiently wealthy to support vast numbers of slaves, on whom their economies depended. Slaves made up one fourth or one third of the workforce in classical Athens, and even men of modest means owned them. They made possible the leisure essential to Athenian democracy, allowing the citizens to argue in the law courts, debate public policy in the assembly, fight their enemies on land and sea, and practice the arts of rhetoric, philosophy, history, and science. The slaves in Greece were mostly captured in Thrace or further north in the Danube region, or they came from Asia Minor, sold into Greece by slave traders.

Slaves were chattel property and had no enforceable rights. They could be killed or sexually used with impunity: In one of his adventures, Heracles is sold as a slave to a foreign queen to serve as her sexual playmate. Slaves had no legal families of their own. They served in the household, but male slaves also performed work outside it, doing the same tasks as free men, with whom they often worked side by side on farms and in factories. Most unfortunate were those who worked, in atrocious conditions, in the Athenian silver mines at Laurium, as many as 40,000 at one time.

[7]Although no clear evidence shows whether women were present at tragedies, their presence would nullify the all-male esprit that the citizen festival was intended to affirm and violate the conventional sense of feminine modesty.

Slaves could receive salaries and often saved up enough money to purchase their freedom. In Roman civilization, freedmen—those born as slaves who had purchased their freedom—formed a powerful social caste and were highly influential in the governance of the Roman empire.

Religion

Christians, Jews, and Muslims believe that there is one God who made the world. He stands outside it, yet dwells in the human heart. His nature is love, and he works for good in the world. His plan for humans is revealed through sacred writings, which specialists (priests, rabbis, and mullahs) interpret to the masses within buildings set aside for this purpose (churches, synagogues, and mosques). Christian clerics usually are paid and devote their lives to interpreting God's will. God demands of his followers love, faith, and adherence to a strict code of moral behavior, including sexual behavior. Christians who follow his commandments can expect to be rewarded in another world after death. These religions once had, and to some extent still have, important social and political missions.

The Greeks, by contrast, had many gods, who did not make the world, but dwelled within it. Zeus was their leader, but Void (Chaos), Earth (Gaea), Night (Nyx), and other gods existed before him and his brothers and sisters; they continued to exist even after Zeus, by force, achieved ascendancy. No Greek god was all-powerful, but each controlled a certain sphere of interest, which sometimes overlapped with that of other gods. The Greek gods had personalities like those of humans and struggled with one another for position and power. They did not love humans (although some had favorites) and did not ask to be loved by them. They did not impose codes of behavior. They expected to be given respect and honor but could act contrary to human needs and desires. They did not reveal their will in writing; their priests, having no writings to interpret, were required only to perform appropriate rituals. Because there were male and female gods, there were male and female priests to perform such rituals.

The appropriate ritual was always a form of sacrifice: the killing of an animal or many animals or the offering of foodstuffs. Although human sacrifice is often mentioned in Greek myths, it appears to have been highly uncommon during the historical period, and archaeology has produced only one clear example from the Bronze Age (from Crete). The underlying logic of sacrifice was always the same: In order to gain the god's good will, destroy what you value most. Sacrifice was performed outside the god's house on an altar, usually to the east of the temple; the temple was not itself a place of worship. There was no official priestly organization with social or political missions. Priests and priestesses came from local families or were sometimes chosen by lot. When one wanted to know the god's will, one went to a seer or to an oracle. Religious activity—appropriate sacrifice—could help in this life, but had no effect on one's lot in the next world (the mysteries at Eleusis were a notable exception; see Chapter 9). Notions of guilt or sin, which arise from disobeying God's rules of universal application, were unknown; there were no such rules to obey.

The Greek gods were capricious and terrifying, not to be taken lightly. Yet the Athenian comedians made fun of them, and Greek intellectuals criticized them for the immoral behavior reported in Greek myth. A small minority even questioned the existence of the gods and sought other than divine causes behind the phenomena of the world. The thinking of these radical intellectuals led to the proposition that gods do not fashion human misery or happiness, success in war or love, or anything else. Humans make their own world, a fundamental principle of what we think of as Western civilization.

Beliefs and Customs

Underlying many Greek myths is a way of thinking about the world that most people today would reject, at least in principle. For us to comprehend these myths, we must make an effort to understand their world-view, one shared by many preliterate societies throughout the world.

One aspect of this view is a belief in magic. We have already mentioned, in our discussion of divine myth, the ascription of human qualities to natural forces. Although modern science rejects this notion, it was present in virtually all ancient societies and still has wide appeal; even today we speak of Mother Nature and Father Time. Modern science rejects the theory that we can manipulate the outside world by means of rituals and spells, but ancient peoples (and some modern ones) were certain that magic was effective. Myths talk endlessly about magical objects: amulets, a necklace that bears a curse, or such fanciful objects as a hat that makes the wearer invisible, sandals that enable one to fly, or a fruit that gives everlasting life.

Today we consider words to be unconnected to the objects or ideas that they represent (so that the same thought can be expressed in many languages), but magical theory assumes that words embody creative and effective power. If one commands emphatically that this or that take place, it will take place. Curses on the lips of the dying are extremely dangerous. The word or the name is the thing itself, its essence or soul.[8]

Closely related to the belief in magic is the conviction that the world is inhabited by spirits, the ghosts of the dead (see Chapter 11). From the fear of ghosts comes the belief in blood guilt, which the Greeks called *miasma*, "pollution," the same word used to describe the pollution of childbirth. *Miasma* was thought to afflict a murderer because he was pursued by the spirit that lived in the blood he spilled. For this reason murderers were very dangerous company: Their misfortune, destined to come, will afflict those around them. Fortunately, spirits and ghosts could be coerced by means of ritual or spells or persuaded by sacrifice or prayer.

Another common feature of the world-view underlying myth is the **taboo,** a strict prohibition against some form of behavior. Many folktales turn on the plot of the violated prohibition and describe the terrible consequences that follow when one acts contrary to an authoritative command. An example appears in the folktale "Bluebeard." Bluebeard tells his new wife never to open a certain door, but she does so

---

[8]Hence the biblical commandment, "You shall not take the name of the Lord in vain."

and discovers the corpses of Bluebeard's many earlier wives. Sometimes the violated prohibition has deep moral connotations, as in the biblical story of Adam and Eve. God commands, "You may freely eat of every tree of the garden, but of the tree of the knowledge of good and evil you must not eat." The penalty for violating this prohibition is that man must toil for his food, woman must suffer in childbirth, and both must die at last.

We divide the human world sharply from the natural, but to the ancient Greeks such distinctions were not necessary. Animals may have human qualities, including the power of speech. For example, in Homer's *Iliad* the horses of Achilles speak to him at a critical moment, warning him of impending death. A human may be born not of woman, but of something in the natural world: The handsome Adonis was born from a tree. Animals may raise humans, as in the story of the twins Romulus and Remus, the eventual founders of Rome; abandoned as infants, they were suckled by a wolf. Transformation of humans into animal or natural forms (rocks, trees, mountains, or stars) is common. A famous story was told about Narcissus (nar-**sis**-sus), a youth of tremendous good looks. His parents wanted to know whether their son would have a long life. "Very long," a prophet replied, "if he does not look at his own face." When Narcissus was grown, he saw his face reflected in a spring. Reaching for the beautiful figure, he fell in and drowned (hence our term *narcissism*, meaning "self love"). His body was changed into the flower that still bears his name.

Similarly, the supernatural world mixes easily with the human. A human being may be born of a god or spirit: Achilles' mother was Thetis, a sea nymph. Male gods commonly have intercourse with mortal women, who bear them mortal but superior human children; far less often, goddesses have intercourse with mortal men. The line between human and divine is not firmly drawn. Although Heracles was born a mortal, he became a god at death. Dionysus and Zeus were both gods, but both had tombs where their spirits were honored as those of dead mortals.

We think of the world as a complex machine, governed by natural law, through which we wander, dodging misfortune and doing the best we can. God may have made the world, but appears not to intervene directly in it (although in Christian doctrine God sent his son). However, the theory of natural law is a Greek invention of the fifth century B.C.; it did not exist when Greek myth was forming and probably was never accepted by most Greeks. According to traditional Greek views, there are no chance events; every event in the world is connected with every other, if only we see how. At remote Dodona (do-**dō**-na) in northwestern Greece, servants of Zeus and his consort Dionê could interpret the rustling of the wind in an oak to answer questions written on lead tablets; some of these have survived. Especially important among the Etruscans and later the Romans was information drawn from examining the entrails of sacrificed animals and observing the flight of birds (called *augury*, hence our word *inauguration*). Professional prophets and seers play an important role in Greek myth.

Dreams were another way to discover hints of the future, for in sleep the spirit is loosely attached to the body and is in communication with the realms of Apollo, lord of prophecy. When Hecabê, queen of Troy, was pregnant, she dreamed that she gave birth to a bundle of sticks, from which emerged fiery serpents who set fire to Troy. A Trojan seer explained that the child would bring destruction to the city. He ordered the baby exposed on the mountain. Rescued by a shepherd, the child grew up to be Paris, who caused the war that destroyed Troy.

Greek myths often refer to social mores that, although common among preliterate societies, differ sharply from those of Greek society itself, at least in the historical period. Cannibalism, human sacrifice, cattle rustling, wife-theft, and blood vendetta as the ordinary response to homicide all figure prominently in Greek myth. For example, Thyestes, a prince of Mycenae, ate his own sons cooked in a stew; his nephew Agamemnon killed his own daughter, Iphigenia, to appease the goddess Artemis; one of Heracles' labors was to rustle the cattle of the monstrous Geryon; the Trojan War began when Paris abducted Helen, wife of Menelaüs; and Orestes, son of Agamemnon, killed his mother to avenge her murder of his father. Such practices were not characteristic of Greek society in the Archaic Period and after. Cannibalism had long since disappeared in Greece, if it ever existed, and blood vendetta and human sacrifice were quickly disappearing. Of course, a gory description of an outmoded or outrageous social practice is a good way for a storyteller to attract attention from a restless audience, as makers of modern horror films well understand.

GREECE AND ROME

Classical myth comprises not just the stories of the Greeks, but also Roman versions of those stories and some stories native to Rome. The Romans remade Greek culture in their own image, and they, not the Greeks, passed the classical tradition to modern Europe.

When Alexander "conquered the world" in 336–323 B.C., he did not conquer Italy or any other region west of the Adriatic Sea (Map IV, Chapter 22). The western lands were still remote, although Greek cities had flourished in Italy and Sicily since the eighth century B.C. But even in Alexander's day a small tribe of Indo-European speakers south of the Tiber river, living in and near the city of Rome and possessing a superior political and military organization, had begun a course of relentless expansion without parallel in human history. Controlling perhaps a few hundred square miles in the sixth century B.C., by the time of Christ the Romans governed virtually the entire Mediterranean world and large territories to the north and east of the Mediterranean. Greece itself became a Roman province in 146 B.C., as did Asia Minor in 133 B.C. and Syria in 63 B.C., but the **Roman Period** in ancient history, as distinguished from the Hellenistic Period, may conveniently be dated from 31 B.C., when Egypt, the Hellenistic cultural center, fell into Roman hands. The western Roman Empire crumbled in the fifth century A.D., but its Greek-speaking eastern part lasted until A.D. 1453, preserving virtually all the records we have of ancient Greece.

As Rome was in early times surrounded by hostile peoples speaking different languages, so it was isolated by geography. Greece is made up of innumerable islands, large and small, and, on the mainland, coastal pockets suited to seaborne commerce and international exchange with the East and its extraordinary cultures. Italy, by contrast, is a long boot-shaped peninsula, split down the middle by the rugged Apennine range that cuts off Italy from the East (see Map IV, Chapter 22). Seas to the east and west of Italy are noted for their sudden storms, and the whole peninsula had few good harbors, only one on the coast facing Greece. To cross the peninsula from east to west, one had to cross high bandit-ridden mountains, and traffic from north to south by land was slow and dangerous until the construction of the famous Roman military roads; the first, the Appian Way, was not built until 312 B.C. We need not be surprised, then, that Italy remained so long on the periphery of ancient Mediterranean culture.

Italy was a melting pot of diverse peoples who spoke many languages. The Romans spoke Latin, an Indo-European language, but there were many other Indo-European Italic dialects whose speakers could scarcely understand each other. North of Rome lived the powerful and influential Etruscans, who, like the Greeks, resided in independent city-states.[9] Their origin is unknown, but some think they emigrated from Asia Minor sometime in the twelfth century B.C. The culturally powerful Etruscans spoke a non–Indo-European tongue of unknown affiliation but took over the Greek alphabet from Greeks living near the Bay of Naples within decades of the alphabet's invention around 800 B.C. The Etruscans gave this writing to the Romans and the Romans gave it to us. With the alphabet came the riches of Greek culture, and above all Greek myth.

The Etruscans ruled the city of Rome during the sixth century B.C., bequeathing a rich legacy to Roman society, government, and religion; the very name *Roma* may be Etruscan. The Roman gladiatorial games developed from Etruscan funeral games in which prisoners were killed in honor of the dead as a form of human sacrifice. The unique genius of the Roman people was to absorb cultural achievements from foreign peoples and yet remain Roman; in the fourth century A.D. they even took over the Christian church, of Jewish origin. While other peoples made things of beauty, the Roman destiny was to rule, as the Romans often explained to themselves.

In early times Rome was an oligarchy, ruled by a council of aristocrats, the Senate ("body of old men"); this period is called the *Republic* (from the Latin *res publica*, "public business"). The Republic broke down after a hundred years of civil war between competing factions within the oligarchy, and Augustus Caesar, the grand-nephew of Julius Caesar, defeated his rivals and took power about the time of Christ. Augustus, pretending that the Republic still existed, modestly called himself *princeps*, "first citizen" (the source of our *prince*) and *imperator*, "commander" (or "emperor"). Henceforth Rome was in reality a monarchy, ruled by one man.

Although the Romans had their own religious heritage, they had few traditional stories, as far as we know. They happily adopted Greek legends, which they learned mostly from Greek poets of the Hellenistic Period. No legend was more important than the story of Aeneas, a Trojan hero in Homer's *Iliad*. By accepting Aeneas as their actual progenitor, the founder of their race, the Romans aggressively laid claim to the rich and prestigious cultural tradition of Greece. Still, as we will see in Chapter 22, myth functioned rather differently among the Romans than among the Greeks.

[9]The modern name of Tuscany is derived from the ancient name Etruria.

KEY TERMS

Boeotia, 17	Ionia, 23
Attica, 17	Archaic Period, 23
Euboea, 17	*polis*, 23
Aegean Sea, 19	Classical Period, 27
Cyclades, 19	Peloponnesian War, 27
Ionia, 19	Hellenistic Period, 29
Indo-Europeans, 20	pederasty, 31
Mycenaean Age, 21	hoplites, 32
Achaeans, 21	*parthenos*, 36
Linear B, 22	*miasma*, 39
Dark Age, 22	taboo, 42
Dorians, 22	Roman Period, 44

FURTHER READING

GENERAL

Beard, Mary, *Classics: A Very Short Introduction* (Oxford, U.K., 1996). Classics today, in 100 pages, organized around the temple of Apollo at Bassae.

Cartledge, Paul, *The Greeks* (Oxford, U.K., 1993). Fine essays on history and myth, men and women, citizens and aliens.

Finley, M. I., *The Ancient Greeks* (New York, 1987). An overview by a leading historian.

The World of Athens: An Introduction to Classical Athenian Culture (Cambridge, U.K., 1984). Jointly composed by the Association of Classical Teachers to accompany a textbook in ancient Greek, this comprehensive guide contains chapters on geography, society, politics, war, and much more.

ARCHAEOLOGY AND HISTORY

Boedeker, Deborah, and Kurt Raaflaub, eds., *Democracy, Empire and the Arts in Fifth-century Athens* (Cambridge, Mass., 1998). Excellent collection of essays by established scholars.

Bury, J. B., and R. Meiggs, *A History of Greece to the Death of Alexander the Great,* 4th ed. (New York, 1975). Since 1909 the standard one-volume history, with emphasis on military and political events.

The Cambridge Ancient History, 2nd and 3rd eds. Massive survey in twelve volumes (varying dates) by leading scholars on every aspect of Greek and Roman history.

Chadwick, John, *The Mycenaean World* (Cambridge, U.K., 1976). Overview with excellent illustrations. Chadwick collaborated with Michael Ventris in deciphering Linear B.

Drews, Robert, *The Coming of the Greeks* (Princeton, N.J., 1988). Discusses the arrival of the Indo-Europeans in the Aegean and the Near East.

Murray, Oswyn, *Early Greece* (Stanford, Calif., 1983). Reflections of Homer's own time in the *Iliad* and *Odyssey.*

Snodgrass, A. M., *Archaic Greece: The Age of Experiment* (Berkeley, Calif., 1980). Superior analysis of the formative period of Greek classical civilization.

Ober, Josiah, *Mass and Elite in Democratic Athens: Rhetoric, Ideology, and the Power of the People* (Princeton, N.J., 1991). Modern survey of politics in Athens' golden age.

Vermeule, Emily, *Greece in the Bronze Age* (Chicago, 1972). Scholarly review, with rich bibliography.

RELIGION

Burkert, Walter, *Greek Religion,* trans. John Raffan (Cambridge, Mass., 1985). A standard scientific description of Greek religion.

Mikalson, Jon D., *Athenian Popular Religion* (Chapel Hill, N.C., 1983).

———, *Honor Thy Gods: Popular Religion in Greek Tragedy* (Chapel Hill, N.C., 1991). Both books provide an understanding of how common people, as opposed to poets and intellectuals, perceived their religion.

Nilsson, Martin, *Greek Folk Religion* (Philadelphia, 1972). Religion of the common people.

———, *A History of Greek Religion,* 3rd ed. (New York, 1980). An English-language compressed version of his authoritative (and enormous) study in German; Nilsson was one of the great scholars of Greek religion.

Pollard, J.R.T., "Greek Religion," in *The New Encyclopaedia Britannica, Macropaedia,* 15th ed., vol. 8, pp. 406–11 (1974–1984 printings only). Superb summary, with bibliography.

Vernant, Jean-Pierre, "Greek Religion," in Mircea Eleade, ed., *The Encyclopedia of Religion* (New York, 1987), vol. 6, pp. 99–118.

SOCIETY

Blundell, Sue, *Women in Classical Athens* (London, 1998). A concise summary of what is known about women and their status in Athens in the fifth and fourth centuries B.C.

Davidson, James, *Courtesans and Fishcakes* (New York, 1998). A new appraisal of the Greek pleasures of eating, drinking, and sex.

Dover, K. J., *Greek Homosexuality* (Cambridge, Mass., 1978). Scientific treatment of a difficult topic.

Fantham, E., H. P. Foley, N. B. Kampen, and S. B. Pomeroy, *Women in the Classical World* (Oxford, U.K., 1994). Superb review of artistic and literary evidence, clear and jargon-free.

Hawley, Richard, and Barbara Levick, eds., *Women in Antiquity: New Assessments* (New York, 1995). Wide-ranging topics, both Greek and Roman, in essays by different scholars.

Lefkowitz, Mary R., *Women in Greek Myth* (Baltimore, 1990). The types of women in Greek tragedy and their relationship to real Greek women, by a leading scholar; good on the Amazons.

Peradotto, J., and J. P. Sullivan, eds., *Women in the Ancient World* (Albany, N.Y., 1987). Essays from a feminist perspective.

Pomeroy, Sarah, *Goddesses, Whores, Wives and Slaves* (New York, 1975). A pioneering survey of the roles assigned to women in ancient Greece.

Rowlandson, Jane, ed., *Women and Society in Greek and Roman Egypt: A Sourcebook* (Cambridge, U.K., 1998). Excellent collection of original sources for the lives of women in Greco-Roman Egypt.

Sergent, Bernard, *Homosexuality in Greek Myth,* with a preface by G. Dumézil (Boston, 1986). Explores the social practice as reflected in traditional story.

Vernant, Jean-Pierre, *Myth and Society in Ancient Greece* (New York, 1988). Opposing older notions, this leading French scholar exposes the realities of ancient slavery, blood sacrifice, ritualized warfare, ceremonial hunting, and ecstasy. Includes chapters on war, marriage, and the city-state.

WRITING

Chadwick, John, *The Decipherment of Linear B,* 2nd ed. (Cambridge, U.K., 1990). Fascinating account of the unraveling of the mysteries of this syllabic script.

Powell, Barry B., *Homer and the Origin of the Greek Alphabet* (Cambridge, U.K., 1991). Gathers the complex evidence supporting the thesis that a Euboean invented the Greek alphabet c. 800 B.C. to record the poems of Homer.

CHAPTER 3

THE DEVELOPMENT
OF CLASSICAL MYTH

Men imagine not only the forms of the gods but their ways of life to be
like our own.

ARISTOTLE, Politics 1252b

MYTH BEGINS in the primordial past; it is possible (although it cannot be proved)
that features of myth found in the classical period first appeared 10,000 or
even 100,000 years ago, long before the Greeks and Romans existed. In thinking
about the beginnings of classical myth, we can try to peer beyond our earliest written
records to reconstruct myths, or religious beliefs, that may have been current in prehistoric times. Comparative material, archaeological and linguistic, may offer some opportunity to do this, as does the study of just how myth was transmitted before writing.
In this chapter we review the earliest information we can infer about the history of
myth, then review how myth developed through the historical periods in the pre-Hellenic cultures of the ancient Near East and in Greece and Rome themselves. Surprisingly, the Greeks seem to have owed little to the indigenous cultures of the southern
Balkans and a great deal to Mesopotamian culture; more and more, scholars view
Greek culture as an offshoot of the Mesopotamian rather than as an independent development, very much as Roman culture was an offshoot of the Greek.

THE BEGINNINGS OF GREEK MYTH

Conspicuous in the museums of southeast Europe and the Near East are figurines
that have exaggerated sexual organs and plump buttocks and breasts. Such objects

FIG. 3.1. Goddess giving birth from Çatal Hüyük, c. 6500–5700 B.C. (The Museum of Anatolian Civilizations, Ankara)

are the oldest freestanding sculptures in the world. Male figurines, often with an erect penis, are also found, but in far fewer numbers. Some have tried to connect such figures with goddesses and gods of fertility known from the historical period and prominent in myth.

Figure 3.1 shows one of the best known of these small statues, several inches high and made c. 6500–5700 B.C. in Çatal Hüyük (**cha**-tal **hoo**-yuk), in south central Turkey, the oldest known agricultural community in the world. While seated in a throne, a woman is giving birth. Leopards, on which she rests her hands, crouch on either side. Another type of European female figurine comes from the Aegean islands of the Cyclades (Fig. 3.2), carved in local marble during the third millennium B.C. Sharp angles intersect pleasingly with plane surfaces, nose and breasts are reduced to protrusions, and genitals are large and clearly marked. Although most such figures are small, this one is life-sized. Rediscovered in modern times, the Cycladic idols had a strong influence on European sculptors of the early twentieth century. We have neither names to apply to these figurines, made before the invention of writing, nor information about their purpose. Because most are found in graves, of both men and women, we can guess that they had a magical power to produce new life, which somehow enhanced the ghost's well-being. Because fertility is a permanent concern among human societies, we may also assume that gods of fertility were important in this period too. Figure 3.3, from a Greek vase of the sixth century B.C., was made six thousand years after the figurine from Çatal Hüyük but is similarly

FIG. 3.2. Cycladic mother figurine, c. 3000 B.C.   (The N. P. Goulandris Foundation, Museum of Cycladic Art, Athens; Author's photo)

placed between two wild animals. She holds a spotted leopard in her right hand and a stag in her left. The Greeks called this figure of Artemis ***Potnia Therôn,*** "lady of the beasts," whose role in Greek religion was to promote the abundance of game. In this case, the historic cult of the goddess Artemis, who protected wild game, appears to be many thousands of years old; perhaps elements of her myths also reach back into the very distant past. Unfortunately, we can never be sure which details in the stories preserved to us are old and which are recent. The relationship between the archaeological and written record is always difficult, but never more so than when dealing with prehistoric myth and religion.

Another way of trying to reconstruct prehistoric myths is by comparing the myths of different Indo-European peoples. The Indo-Europeans must have had their myths and their religion, which they brought with them as they spread from their homeland into and across Europe, and perhaps through comparative means we can learn something about them. From their linguistic roots, we know that the names of the Greek god Zeus and the Roman god Jupiter are descended from the same Indo-European word, and most would agree that the Indo-Europeans did worship a sky god. Unfortunately, we cannot go much further than that. Gods change their nature; we cannot be sure what role that god may have played in Indo-European society. Because several figures in the myths of Indo-European peoples have a name that seems to mean "twin," and because in classical myth we find stories about twins, some scholars speculate that Indo-European myth included such a story. They even speculate about an early cultural dualism between the left (dangerous, evil) and the right (lucky, good) and about a primordial war between two of the social orders, the priests and warriors, against the third social order, the food producers (the myth of the Tro-

FIG. 3.3. Artemis Potnia Therôn, c. 570 B.C. (Museo Archeologico Nazionale, Florence)

jan War could be a classical descendant). However, so much is left to hypothesis in these reconstructions, and so contradictory is the evidence or explicable in other ways, that few scholars have accepted such explanations with confidence. It is striking how few traces of Indo-European culture we find among the Greeks (for more on Indo-European myth, see Chapter 23).

Of great interest to students of the origins of classical myth are names found on Linear B tablets of numerous gods, named as the recipients of offerings, who are familiar from later Greek literature: Zeus and Hera, Poseidon, Athena, Artemis, Hermes, Enyalius (an alternate name for Ares), Paean (an alternate name for Apollo), and Eileithyia (the birth goddess) are all found. Dionysus, a deity long thought to have entered Greek religion after the Bronze Age, is also mentioned (or it is a man named after him). *Potnia,* "Lady," as in *Potnia Therôn* or as a common classical epithet of Athena, seems to be a separate deity, perhaps the name of a Mycenaean mother goddess. Deities completely unknown in classical times also appear. We may be sure, therefore, that some of the classical Greek gods did exist in the Mycenaean Age, but as far as we know only as objects of religious cult. We have no stories or hints of stories preserved in the Linear B records. Although interesting frescoes representing a sea battle have been found recently on the island of Thera in the Cyclades, perhaps a Minoan outpost, we cannot identify one single Minoan or Mycenaean myth.

Perhaps the best approach to understanding the beginnings of Greek myth is found not in the substance of the myths themselves but in the means by which myths must have been transmitted before writing. On the basis of comparative evidence gathered in modern times, we now think that in prehistoric Greece and on through the Archaic Period illiterate singers called in Greek *aoidoi* (a-**oi**-doi, related to our "ode") entertained in aristocratic courts and perhaps elsewhere. We usually translate *aoidos* (the singular form) as "bard" or "oral poet." Early in life an *aoidos* learned through association with a master, through unconscious absorption, a special language of poetic composition. As ordinary language is shaped by unconscious grammatical patterns, this one was shaped by an unconscious rhythm, which we analyze in written versions as a poetic line called dactylic hexameter.[1] The special language contained many preset rhythmical phrases, such as "swift-footed Achilles," which helped the *aoidoi* to compose a poem even as they sang it to the accompaniment of a lyre.

Homer was such a poet, and Hesiod was another (eighth and seventh centuries B.C.). Homer himself gives us an account of the blind *aoidos* Demodocus (de-**mo**-di-kus) in Book 8 of the *Odyssey*. At an assembly in the morning, the king tells a messenger, "Summon the glorious *aoidos* / Demodocus, on whom a god immortal has poured great skill at reciting. / His song will surely delight us, whatever subjects he fancies." In the course of the festivities, Demodocus sings and plays several times: "They stretched out their hands for the dinner which lay on the table before them; / then, when they all were content and their hunger and thirst were both satisfied," the Muse reminds the *aoidos* of a song of the quarrel between Odysseus and Achilles, which he sings. After an interval, Demodocus is called on to accompany a group of expert young dancers; he is a skilled musician, as well as a singer of songs. He now sings the racy story of the trapping of adulterous Ares and Aphrodite in bed (see Chapter 8). After another interval, Demodocus is brought back in and congratulated. Odysseus gives him a token of honor and requests a new song. Demodocus again invokes the Muse and sings of the Trojan Horse. Many think that Demodocus is a self-portrait of Homer himself, and most of what we know about the social context of Homer's own singing comes from these descriptions.

Although making use of traditional stories and motifs, *aoidoi* must always have spoken to contemporary concerns and, of course, had no concept of history. The *aoidoi* were the myth-makers of early Greece. Real warriors are interested in hearing about real wars, especially if they themselves fought in them or if their fathers or grandfathers did. For this reason it is likely that the great cycles of myth surrounding the Trojan War and the war against Thebes do go back to campaigns waged in the Bronze Age, rumors of which were passed on by generations of oral poets.

THE INFLUENCE OF NEAR EASTERN MYTH

Whereas such myths as those of the Trojan War appear to be Greek in origin and to go back to the Bronze Age or earlier, other very important stories had their beginnings not in Greece, but in the non–Indo-European Near East. Ancient **Mesopotamia,** the "land between the rivers," which occupies the region of the Tigris and Euphrates rivers in what is today Iraq (see Map V, inside back cover), was a particularly important source. The Greek myth of the origin of the present world order

[1]Six feet per line, each foot (except the last) being a dactyl (¯˘˘, e.g., "hamburger") or spondee (--, e.g., "hormone"). An example in English would be "Dōwn ĭn ă | dēēp dārk | hōle săt ăn | ōld cōw | mūnchĭng ă | bēānstălk."

in a battle of the gods, for example, was certainly of Mesopotamian origin. Such stories may have come to Greece in the Bronze Age, but far more likely were imported from Eastern ports in the late Dark Age at the same time that the Greeks invented the alphabet on the basis of the earlier Phoenician writing (c. 800 B.C.), or they may have been learned from Semitic peoples living in Greece at this time.

Until about three hundred years ago, Western Europe knew very little about the ancient Near East, and most of what was known came from the Old Testament, preserved in its original Hebrew and Aramaic (closely related to Hebrew) and in translations into Greek (c. 300 B.C.) and Latin (c. A.D. 400). There are also many references, usually inaccurate, to the Near East in Greek and Latin authors and in the fathers of the Christian church. Reliance on the literal accuracy of the first five books of the Bible, the Pentateuch (**pen**-ta-took), led to a telescoped notion of the length of history: In 1654 Archbishop James Ussher of Armagh, Ireland dated the creation of the world at 4004 B.C. Ideas of historical change assumed either decay from a golden age or a cyclical process of development followed by recession.

But in the seventeenth century European travelers began to enter the lands of the ancient Near East and bring back firsthand reports. Pietro della Valle, an Italian nobleman, journeyed to Constantinople, Egypt, Palestine, and Syria, and in Persepolis, the ancient capital of Persia (559–332 B.C.), copied from the palace doors several inscriptions written in three different forms of an unknown script. In 1700 an Oxford scholar, although unable to read the script, gave the name *cuneiform* ("wedge-shaped") to the writing.

From this time onward a stream of archaeological material from the Near East poured into western European museums, including many inscribed clay tablets, and the languages of the region were deciphered gradually. In 1872 British scholar George Smith reported that he had deciphered a fragment of a tablet with a description of a universal flood that had destroyed all humankind. The next year, in Iraq, Smith found the text of the Babylonian story of creation, the *Enuma Elish*. The much later composer of Genesis, the biblical book of creation, evidently borrowed such stories, so that Genesis could no longer be regarded as an original and divine revelation. Not surprisingly, these and similar discoveries forced a reconsideration of the meaning of myth.

The Near Eastern background for prominent Greek myths is so important that we must now say something about these stories that leaped cultural and linguistic barriers to influence the Greeks and, through them, the entire Western world.

Sumerian Myth

Not until World War II did reliable information about Sumerian myth come to light. Few stories have come down to us complete, and those must be inferred from cryptic texts inscribed on badly broken clay tablets in a difficult script that records a dead language poorly understood. We must depend heavily on reconstructions by a few scholars, whose translations are not so much a literal rendering of the meaning of the original text as conjectures about possible meanings. The **Sumerians,** of unknown racial stock, spoke a language unrelated to any other that we know. They lived close to the Persian Gulf in the treeless and stoneless mudlands near the estuary of the Tigris and Euphrates rivers (see Map III). Their culture appeared rather suddenly, about 4000 B.C. According to their own traditions, they came from somewhere outside Mesopotamia, perhaps from Iran (Persia) or India. Supported by irrigation agriculture, which they invented, the Sumerians created the first full-fledged city-states by 3000 B.C., with as many as forty or fifty thousand inhabitants each.

Each Sumerian city had its own protective deity with which its fortunes were closely bound, and one city's triumph over another represented a victory of the local deity. The deity lived in a temple in the city's center, often at the top of a tall, terraced pyramid of successively receding stories known as a *ziggurat*. Times of prosperity brought slaves, gold, animals, exotic clothes, and spices, but some great cities, such as Ur, sank into desolation and disappeared.

Irrigation agriculture greatly increased the food supply, but it demanded social cooperation. The ruling elite's most powerful tool was cuneiform writing (c. 3400 B.C.), the first known true writing. Despite its immense complexity, cuneiform was the most widely used system of writing in the ancient world before the Greek alphabet and recorded many languages, some unrelated, during its three-thousand-year history. The earliest myths on earth are recorded in cuneiform writing.

As in all polytheisms, there were dozens, even hundreds, of gods and goddesses in the Sumerian pantheon, but some stand out above the others. **An,** "Sky," was god of the infinite expanse of the dome above us, across which the sun travels and from which the rain falls. He was originally the supreme authority, the source of order in the worlds of gods above and humans below. *Anitu,* "Anu-ship," the institution of human kingship that made Mesopotamian civilization possible, came down from the sky. An began as an important figure in myths of creation, then shrank to a remote being with little influence on human affairs, very much like Uranus, "Sky," in Greek myth.

Often said to be An's daughter, **Inanna** (in-**an**-na), "queen of heaven," was goddess of sexual love and, curiously, of war. Her lust was insatiable, all-consuming, and dangerous. One Sumerian text notes that even 120 lovers could not satisfy her. Inanna is like Aphrodite in Greek myth, and somehow their names seem to be related.

As An embodied divine authority, **Enlil** (en-lēl), "lord of the storm," embodied force, power, the unruly violence of the thunderstorm. But he was also a king, An's agent on earth, and was personally involved in earthly events. He possessed the Tablets of Destiny by which the fates of gods and humans were decreed (a reflection of the power of cuneiform writing within Sumerian society). He could be beneficial, the bringer of fertilizing rain, or destructive, the drier-up of the flood waters, the bringer of locusts and the wild, destructive hordes of hillmen eager to prey on the lowland cities. Enlil's position was similar to that of Zeus in Greek myth.

Enki, "lord of earth," was so named because he ruled the sweet ground water found beneath the soil (Fig. 3.4). He was the active fertilizing principle. As water wends its devious path beneath and around obstacles, Enki was the clever, crafty god, the trickster of Sumerian myth. He was also the god of wisdom and magic who instructed humankind in all the arts and crafts. Enki has much in common with Hermes but also shares features with Hephaestus, Prometheus, Poseidon, and Dionysus.

MAP III The Ancient Near East

FIG. 3.4. Akkadian seal-impression, c. 2360–2180 B.C., showing in the center Shamash, the sun god, rising from the eastern horizon, rays springing from his shoulder. He holds a saw in his hand, evidently so he can cut through the mountains (or symbolic of his role as judge). To the left of Shamash stands Ishtar (= Sumerian Inanna) beside a somewhat bedraggled tree and, perhaps, the hero Gilgamesh with his bow. To the right of Shamash is a bird (perhaps Anzu, which according to one story stole the Tablets of Destiny) and Ea (= Sumerian Enki), his watery nature indicated by fish-filled streams that pour from his shoulders. To the right of Ea is the two-faced messenger god, Isimud.   (British Museum, London, 2180)

The Great Mother goddess of the Sumerians had many names, and sometimes was just Ki (kē), "Earth"). She was always Mother Earth, the rich silt built up from the river floods, who united with Enki to produce the first vegetation. In some ways she is similar to the Greek Demeter. **Ereshkigal** (er-esh-**kē**-gal), "queen of the great below," the Sumerian goddess of death, is an aspect of Ki, the dark soil into which the bodies of the dead were laid. She is like Persephonê in Greek myth.

Mesopotamian myths are vague about the physical appearance of the gods. Many "mythical" representations survive, but they rarely give a clear idea about who or what is being shown (Fig. 3.5). However, all the Sumerian gods are anthropomorphic, "human-shaped" in both appearance and behavior. Their society resembles that of humans, with an assembly of elders presided over by an executive leader, a king. They are related to one another in a large family (just how is not always clear). In Sumerian literary accounts, the gods are devoted or capricious, like humans, and are susceptible to human passions, including ambition, anger, and lust. They gossip, scheme, backbite, give speeches, win victories, lament defeats, and constantly struggle among themselves, as did the cities they protected.

The Sumerian gods figured in an important cycle of legends about the hero Gilgamesh (see Chapter 12). However, most Sumerian myths are divine myths, stories of the doings of superhuman beings. Their themes range from the creation of the

FIG. 3.5. Mesopotamian terracotta relief from Khafaje, c. 1700 B.C., showing a god cutting a one-eyed female demon down the middle. Rays come from her head, and her hands are tied behind her back. As so often in Mesopotamian art, which rarely illustrates known myths, we cannot be sure of the identity of either god or monster. (Iraq Museum, Bagdad; Oriental Institute of the University of Chicago)

universe and underworld to the creation of humankind and the universal flood. Somehow all these story patterns traveled from Iraq to the Mediterranean, where they formed part of our own cultural heritage.

Semitic Myth

By 2000 B.C. Sumer had fallen under the control of **Semites,** seminomadic peoples who inhabited the steppe at the fringes of the Arabian desert and pushed constantly against the river cultures of Mesopotamia. The Semites were not a united people or race; the term is a modern one, taken from the Hebrew Bible (Genesis 10.21–31), where Shem (hence "Semite"), the son of Noah, is called the father of Ashur (hence the "Assyrians," another Semitic people), Aram (the Semitic "Aramaeans"), and Eber (the Semitic "Hebrews"). *Semitic* designates both a linguistic group and its associated cultural patterns.

The Semitic **Akkadians,** led by the great Sargon (c. 2340 B.C.) and named after their capital, Akkad, took over the southern Sumerian cities and adopted Sumerian culture. Identifying the Sumerian gods with their own deities (see Chart 3.1), the Akkadians appropriated Sumerian myths, refashioned them, and preserved them in

Sumerian Name	Akkadian/Babylonian Name
An	Anu
Inanna	Ishtar
Enlil	Enlil, Marduk
Enki	Ea
Ninhursag, Ki	—
Ereshkigal	—
Utu	Shamash

CHART 3.1. Near Eastern Gods and Goddesses

cuneiform script on clay tablets. The Sumerian language itself disappeared as a living, spoken language by 2000 B.C. and henceforth was used only by scholars and priests, like Latin in recent times, often to record myths.

Later, in the geographically ill-defined Mesopotamian river basin, a reorganization of power led to the ascendancy of the Semitic Babylonians, whose capital was the famous city of Babylon. Under their leader Hammurabi (1750 B.C.), whose collection of legal decisions has survived on a column with 3,600 lines of cuneiform writing, the Babylonians fashioned a temporary political unity from the scattered city-states of southern Sumer. After Hammurabi's death, the empire succumbed to attacks from the nomadic and seminomadic mountain dwellers to the east. The biblical story of the Tower of Babel (**bā**-bel, *babel* = "gate of God") may have been inspired by the great *ziggurat* in Babylon, built by Hammurabi. From Babylon comes one of our most important pre-Greek myths, the epic poem of creation, called *Enuma Elish,* from its first two words meaning "When on high." Most Mesopotamian cuneiform documents were written by scribes to educate other scribes, but the *Enuma Elish* appears to have been read aloud at the annual New Year's festival. It is a real cult hymn. The poem recounts a divine myth, the making of the world and its present arrangement, and we study it when discussing the Greek account of creation.

The **Hebrews,** by far the best known of the Semitic peoples, traced their ancestry back to Abraham (c. 2000? B.C.), who came from "Ur of the Chaldees" in southern Mesopotamia (that is, from Sumer; the biblical reference to the Chaldeans is an anachronism). According to the tradition, Abraham migrated to Canaan (present-day Israel and Jordan) after God promised that he would become the father of a mighty nation destined to possess this land. Abraham's descendants drifted into Egypt, where they became slaves to Pharaoh, apparently remaining there for several centuries. This tradition remains today a basis for Jewish self-explanation.

The great teacher Moses (c. 1200? B.C.), evidently inheriting teachings of the Egyptian monotheistic pharaoh Akhenaten (fourteenth century B.C.), later led the Hebrews out of Egypt and, in the Sinai peninsula, gave them the Ten Commandments, the ethical foundation of Judaism. The first of God's commandments to the Hebrews was "You shall have no other gods before me." Moses insisted that his people put aside the polytheistic practices characteristic of Egypt and Mesopotamia and devote themselves exclusively to the powerful God called Yahweh (he had other names), who had delivered them from Egyptian bondage. Moses' monotheistic vision prevailed, but many of the stories the Hebrews told about their ancestors and their God—for example, the story of creation and the story of the universal flood—were adapted from Mesopotamian myth.

Under Moses' successors, the Hebrews invaded Canaan and waged a successful war against the Philistines, who were probably Mycenaean Greeks from Crete, for control of the land. The acme of Hebrew political power came about 1000 B.C. under Solomon, who built the first temple at Jerusalem. In 586 B.C. the Chaldeans, a Babylonian dynasty led by the famous Nebuchadnezzar, captured Jerusalem. He destroyed Solomon's temple and deported the Hebrew leaders to Babylon, where they and their descendants remained for almost fifty years. The Babylonian Captivity was a time of deep soul-searching for the Hebrews. Asking why God had abandoned them, the Hebrews took stock of their ancient myths, many preserved in written texts dating back to 800 B.C. or earlier. They combined these texts with accounts of their recent history and admonishments by "prophets" written down at different dates to form the books which later, around 90 A.D., became the Hebrew Bible (or Old Testament, as it is known to Christians).

The writing system used by the Hebrews often is called the Phoenician alphabet, but is really a highly condensed syllabary of twenty-two signs, each of which stood for a single syllable in which only the consonant was specified. Phoenician writing was a great advance over the clumsy cuneiform and was widely used to record many Semitic languages after about 1000 B.C. In the great empire of the Semitic Assyrians (ninth to seventh centuries B.C.) on the Tigris river, records were kept in duplicate: one in cuneiform on tablets in the Akkadian language and another in the Phoenician system on papyrus in a Semitic language called Aramaic. Because the vowels were not specified, Phoenician writing was difficult to read, a fact that has given great prestige to the *rabbi* (Hebrew for "my teacher"), who can read and interpret the ancient texts. The Phoenician system of syllabic writing was of great importance in the history of writing. Modern Arabic script, used all over the world, is a slightly modified form of it, and the revolutionary Greek alphabet, which specified two kinds of signs, one consonantal and the other vocalic, was adapted from it.

Other Sources

Some related myths, but with their own innovative features, come from the non-Semitic **Hittites,** one of the most powerful and important peoples of the Late Bronze Age, who controlled central Anatolia (Asia Minor) from about 1600 to 1200 B.C. Their myths were preserved on clay tablets in cuneiform writing (and in their own special hieroglyphic writing) from the thirteenth century B.C., found in the archives at their capital city of Hattussas in modern north-central Turkey. Although the Hittites were Indo-European speakers—the earliest attested—they inherited cultural traditions first formulated among the Sumerians and later refined by the Sumerians' Semitic successors.

Non-Semitic ancient Egypt had few myths.[2] Literary texts from Egypt are mostly

---

[2]The Egyptian language belongs to the Hamitic family (after Ham, son of Noah), now usually called the Afro-Asiatic family; similar in structure to Semitic languages, ancient Egyptian shares almost no common vocabulary with Semitic languages.

collections of wise sayings, reports of a man's important achievements, hymns that praise gods (without telling stories), and sophisticated and amusing tales for scribal instruction and entertainment. The most important myth by far in ancient Egypt told of the murder of the god Osiris and his resurrection, but nowhere do the Egyptians themselves tell the complete story; we must depend on an account in Greek.

We examine specific ancient Near Eastern myths in subsequent chapters as we investigate the Greek myths that depend on them.

GREEK MYTH IN THE ARCHAIC PERIOD

Although many Greek myths may have taken shape during the Mycenaean and Dark ages of Greek history and even earlier, it was not until the Archaic Period that myths were committed to writing. Consequently, we derive most of our knowledge of Greek myth from writings of this and later periods. Additional information from the Archaic and Classical periods also comes to us from the 50,000 pictured Greek vase paintings that survive, and occasionally from sculpture. Scholars estimate surviving pictured vases to represent about 1% of the original production, giving us some idea of the explosion of images that flooded ancient Greece and Italy in this period, for which there is no parallel in the ancient world. Many images on Greek pots represented myths, often inspired by literary accounts, and some are reproduced in this book.

Earlier we discussed myths as being traditional oral tales that eventually were taken down in alphabetic writing. The earliest Greek literature is the poems of **Homer,** the *Iliad* and the *Odyssey*. We know nothing for certain about Homer's life. Later tradition has him born somewhere in Asia Minor, perhaps in the city of Smyrna or on the island of Chios, but his poems show wide knowledge of the Aegean and Greece. He must have lived just at the moment that the alphabet was introduced into Greece, for (with one exception) Homer knows nothing about writing or the revolutionary effects it had on social behavior. The absence of descriptions of writing in Homer is one of the principal reasons for placing him in the eighth century B.C., when the alphabet was new and unfamiliar.[3] It would have been impossible to record Homer in the earlier Linear B or Phoenician syllabic scripts because the complex rhythms of his poetic line depended on the alternations of long and short vowels, which these scripts were incapable of notating. The extraordinary Greek alphabet made possible the writing down of Homer's poems, and, according to one theory, a poetry-loving Greek invented the alphabet for just this purpose.

The *Iliad*, a long poem (about 16,000 lines), is set in a period of several weeks during the ninth year of the Trojan War. Its principal theme is the wrath of Achilles, his anger over being mistreated by the leader of the expedition, Agamemnon. Within this frame Homer includes a wealth of subordinate myths. The *Odyssey*, about 12,000 lines, narrates the return of Odysseus to his home after an absence of twenty years.

---

[3]The many problems surrounding the genesis of the Homeric poems, still hotly debated, are called the Homeric Question.

The *Iliad* and the *Odyssey* define what we mean by **epic** (*epos* = "song"): a long narrative poem celebrating the deeds of heroes. To judge from Homer's own descriptions in the *Odyssey* of the *aoidoi,* his audiences were all or mostly male (in the *Odyssey,* the only woman mentioned at a poetic performance is a queen). Under what conditions he may have sung songs as long as the *Iliad* or *Odyssey* remains unclear. These poems probably were never presented in the form in which we know them. The poems we have are the result of artificial conditions created by the writing down of the poems, when the poet was no longer forced to sing rapidly and had no audience to entertain and so could greatly expand his narrative.

Views differ widely about the reality of the world Homer portrays. The famous archaeologist Heinrich Schliemann, who in 1876 claimed to have found the ruins of Troy in northwestern Turkey, thought they were literal descriptions of the Bronze Age, and we have given reasons for thinking that the stories of the Trojan War may go back to this period. In other respects, however, Homer knows little or nothing about the Bronze Age. For example, in Homer the dead are cremated on a large pyre, then their ashes gathered and buried in an urn. But the Mycenaean Greeks interred the bodies of the dead in graves lined with stone slabs or, if royalty, in enormous underground beehive-shaped tombs. Homeric society consists of petty chieftains, each ruling a small territory; in the Bronze Age great centers of power kept careful watch over a controlled economy by means of a professional bureaucracy. Although Homer mentions a certain kind of helmet made of boars' tusks and several other objects familiar only in the Bronze Age, such objects may have been preserved as heirlooms long after the destruction of Mycenae. Others think that the conditions Homer describes are those of the Dark Age, or that Homer's world is an imaginary mixture of details from different periods, although the *Odyssey*'s description of dangerous seafaring in the far west depends on real Greek exploration there beginning about 800 B.C. On balance, it seems most plausible that Homer incorporated various features from earlier periods preserved through the oral tradition but that his poems, and especially the social and religious values that move the actors, reflect Homer's own age, the eighth century B.C.

The influence of Homer's poems on Greek and later culture is inestimable. Less influential but perhaps more important to the study of myth is his near contemporary **Hesiod** (700? B.C.). Unlike the anonymous Homer, who conceals his personality behind his poems, Hesiod tells us a little about himself in his two surviving poems, the *Theogony* and *Works and Days.* His father had lived in Asia Minor, then moved to mainland Greece to a small forlorn village at the foot of Mount Helicon near Thebes, where Hesiod lived. Like Homer, he became an *aoidos.* While he was tending his flocks on Helicon, the Muses, inspirers of poetry, came to him in a vision and gave him the power of song.[4] Hesiod's remarkable description of the Muses and his meeting contains many names, which we will examine later in this book, but is worth quoting here in full because it identifies him as the first European author (Homer never identifies himself), gives the first definition of a *poet* (= "maker"), and explains why a poet can speak with authority about past, present, and future: because he is inspired by the Muses with a mission divinely ordained.

---

[4]Thus Helicon is synonymous with poetic inspiration in the Western literary tradition.

Let us begin our song with the Muses of Helicon,
who dwell upon the great and rugged mount of Helicon
and dance with gentle feet around the indigo spring
and around the altar of Cronus' mighty son.
5   When they have washed their tender bodies
in Permessus, or in the Horse's Spring, or holy Olmeius,
they make lovely, longing dances on the top of Helicon
and move with thumping feet. From there they rise, go forth by night,
veiled in dark mist to utter their song in darling voice,
10   singing of Zeus who holds the aegis [a magic shield] and mistress Hera
of Argos, who walks on golden sandals,
and of the blue-eyed Athena, daughter of Zeus the aegis-holder,
and of Phoebus Apollo, and Artemis who thrills to the arrow,
and Poseidon, who holds the earth and shakes it,
15   and honorable Themis [Law] and glancing-eyed Aphrodite
and Hebê [Youth] with crown of gold and beautiful Dionê,
Leto, Iapetus, and Cronus of crafty counsels,
Êos [Dawn] and great Helius [Sun] and bright Selenê [Moon],
Earth too, and great Oceanus and dark Night
20   and the sacred race of all the other ones who never die.
One day they taught Hesiod glorious song [aoidê, hence aoidos]
while he was shepherding his lambs under holy Helicon.

Now Hesiod offers the first statement in the history of European literary criticism,
one that has obsessed commentators ever since: How much truth do myths contain?

Here is the first word [muthos, hence "myth"] the goddesses said to me—
the Muses of Olympus, daughters [korai, i.e., virgins] of Zeus who holds the
    aegis:
25   "You stupid rustic shepherds, bellies and nothing more,
we are the ones who can tell you lies that look like truth.
We can also, if we please, proclaim what indeed is true."
    So spoke the trustworthy daughters of mighty Zeus,
and gave me a leafy branch of laurel to pluck for a staff.
30   Then into me they breathed the inspired art of the poet,
to sing of things of the past and those that are yet to be.
They told me to sing of the blessed immortal race of the gods,
always beginning and ending my song with the Muses themselves.

HESIOD, *Theogony* (1–33)

In another poem, *Works and Days,* Hesiod also tells us that he was a singer at funeral games in honor of a dead prince on the nearby island of Euboea, a detail that
may explain how his poems came to be written down: The Euboeans were the earliest possessors of the Greek alphabet.

The *Theogony,* a description of the creation of the present world order, owes a
great deal to Mesopotamian myths. It tells how Zeus overcame an earlier generation
of gods and monsters in battle and established his own power. The *Theogony* is one
of the most important mythical texts to survive from antiquity, and we devote the
next chapter to it. *Works and Days* describes a bitter dispute between Hesiod and his

brother over the disposition of their father's property, a theme that allows Hesiod to range widely over issues of right and wrong, which he illustrates by telling such myths as the story of Pandora. We call this kind of literature "wisdom literature," a well-established genre in the Near East and another sign of Hesiod's closeness to Eastern sources.

We know that many other epic poems, now lost, were written down during the Archaic Period, and that they contained many myths; commentaries surviving from a later date summarize their contents. These post-Homeric epics are called the Cyclic Poems because they were constructed in a circle (*kuklos* = "circle") around the *Iliad* and the *Odyssey,* telling parts of the Trojan War story not covered in Homer. The Cyclic Poems had an enormous influence on Greek art and on the Athenian tragedians of the fifth century B.C.

Another important source from the Archaic Period is a collection of poems known as the **Homeric Hymns.** Like the poems of Homer and Hesiod, they were composed orally and, in antiquity, were believed to be by Homer himself. In fact they are from a later date, mostly from the seventh and sixth centuries B.C. Four are several hundred lines long: those to Demeter, Apollo, Hermes, and Aphrodite. A hymn is a metrical address invoking a god or goddess by listing cultic names and telling an important story about the deity. The Homeric Hymns are a literary elaboration of this old tradition and very unlike Near Eastern hymns in their focus on mythic narrative. Whereas epic seems to have been performed before elite male audiences, hymns were performed in public places, at festivals that may have included women and a broader range of social classes. Yet, like epic, they were composed in performance by specially trained *aoidoi.*

In Homer's poems, action is always described in the third person. From the sixth century B.C. comes a small body of personal lyric poems (including the fragments of Sappho's work), on a wide variety of topics, but celebrating notably the individual's pain in love and the uncertainty of war. Many of these poems touch on mythical themes. Unlike the Homeric, Hesiodic, and Cyclic poems, however, this poetry was not composed in performance and recorded by dictation, but was composed directly in writing, meant to be memorized by others and represented orally. This shift in the way literature was created was to have epoch-making consequences.

GREEK MYTH IN THE CLASSICAL PERIOD

We must remember that there never was an agreed-upon version of any Greek myth because there was no text (like the Bible) with sacred authority and no organization (like the Christian church) to establish an official version. As the Muses in Hesiod explained, they were capable of disseminating lies as easily as the truth: The gods were not a source of truth. For this reason the Greeks invented ethics, a way to tell right from wrong without divine authority, and secular law, which together make up **humanism.** The poets gave form to Greek myths, but no one poet, not even Homer, could claim to promulgate an official version.

Those adept at the memorization of written epic and at the effective public delivery of such memorized texts were called *rhapsodes,*[5] who performed while leaning

FIG. 3.6. An *aoidos* sings to a lyre on an Attic cup, c. 515 B.C. He wears his hair in a turban and has a cloak thrown over one shoulder. Meaningless letters spill from his mouth to represent his song, by now equated with alphabetic writing. (Elvehjem Museum, University of Wisconsin, Madison, 1979.122)

on a staff. They were not themselves poets. Oral poets, *aoidoi,* were like jazz musicians who do not use a written score and never play a given tune the same way twice (Fig. 3.6); *rhapsodes* were like classical musicians who recreate from a written score someone else's invention. *Rhapsodes* may be as old as the alphabet itself, which made them possible, and they were still a conspicuous feature of Greek life in the fourth century B.C., when Plato complained about them. Certainly rhapsodic performance of epic song rapidly popularized Greek myths, previously confined to the immediate small aristocratic audiences of *aoidoi,* who could never have been many in number. One often hears, or assumes, that myths were also told by mothers to their children or in other family contexts, but the evidence for this is slight; such stories seem to have been of the bogey-man variety and were certainly not what we think of as Greek myth.

The *aoidoi* continued to exist in Greece through the Archaic Period and continued to perform and to dictate their songs, or perhaps in some cases to write them down themselves, but by the early fifth century B.C., when composition in writing had become the rule, the *aoidoi* had disappeared. In addition to lyric poetry, the new technique of composition in writing made possible choral song, memorized for public presentation by a group of twelve or more boy or girl dancers (Greek *choros* = "dance"). Often the chorus would speak for itself in the first person, a fact that has created great confusion because until recently readers equated the "I" of such poetry with the personality of the poet. Greatest of the choral poets was **Pindar** (518–438 B.C.). Much of his poetry is lost, but a large body of victory odes to athletes survives. These odes ordinarily contain a myth that in some way reflects on the glory of the athlete being praised. Some of our earliest versions of Greek myths are found in Pindar and in surviving poems by his contemporary Bacchylides (ba-**kil**-i-dēz) from the island of Ceos, who also wrote choral poetry.

---

[5]The source of our word *rhapsody. Rhapsode* seems to derive from the Greek work *rhabdos,* "staff." Although the Muses gave a *rhabdos* to Hesiod, he seems to have been an *aoidos,* an oral poet.

FIG. 3.7. Representation of a fourth-century theatrical presentation from a south Italian fragment of a wine-mixing bowl, c. 350 B.C. Perhaps the play illustrated is the lost *Stheneboea* of Euripides. Stheneboea (a masked man) peeks from the half-open central door of the scene building (*skēnē*) to overhear Bellerophon, whom she has falsely accused of rape, as he meets her husband Proetus on the far right (see Chapter 15). At the top of the scene building is Bellerophon mounted on the winged horse Pegasus, in the center, while Proetus (?) pursues with a sword on the right and Bellerophon flees on the left. (Würzburg, Martin-von-Wagner-Museum, H 4696-4701)

By far our most important source from the Classical Period is the tragic plays, performed in Athens during the fifth century B.C. The origin of *tragedy* is obscure.[6] The word *tragoidia* seems to mean "goat song." Because the goat was an animal associated with Dionysus, at whose spring festival in Athens tragedies were staged, perhaps the name is taken from the song sung during the sacrifice of a goat in the god's honor. Composed in writing, the script of a tragic play was like a modern screenplay, meant not to be read but to serve as a prompt book for a live performance. Although afterward the texts could be studied by students and quoted by intellectuals, all of Greek literature was meant to be heard, not read silently as we are reading this book and the literary selections within it.

The actors were always male (as the audience probably was) and never more than three in number. They wore masks with stereotypical features to distinguish their roles (for example, old man, young girl, or king). They could communicate emotion only through the use of words and gestures, not by facial expression (Fig. 3.7).

Tragedy was a form of popular entertainment, directed to the complex concerns of the Athenian citizen, including his taste for patriotic propaganda, horror, violence, and conflict between the sexes, themes that still command an attentive audience. Dionysus, the divine patron of tragedy, was a god of the *demos*, the "people" (i.e., the men). Pisistratus, an Athenian tyrant of the sixth century B.C., encouraged production of the plays, no doubt to favor the emerging mercantile class who had placed him in power.

Aristotle, the first literary critic, attempted to explain the function of the violent

[6]For further discussion of the origin of tragedy, see Chapter 10.

plots of many tragedies by suggesting that, in beholding the dramatization of the destruction of a noble man or woman, the audience was cleansed "through pity and fear" (*Poetics* 6.2): pity for the protagonist (= "first actor") and fear that the same fate might become one's own. Tragedy allowed the audience to experience intense, sometimes disturbing emotions that could not be experienced in real life without terrible cost. Tragedy painlessly expanded one's experience as a human being. No more effective answer has ever been offered to the censors who, throughout human history, have policed public entertainment to make it conform to preconceived notions of what is proper.

Aristotle also discussed the structure of Greek tragedy, noting how the protagonist is greater than we, rises to high fortune, then in a "turning around" (*peripeteia*) comes to a "down-turning" (*katastrophê,* our word *catastrophe*) as the result of a "missing of the mark" or "mistake." The Greek word *hamartia,* "mistake," was early mistranslated as "flaw," leading to a misunderstanding of Greek tragedy that is still encountered today. Other explanations of the protagonist's misfortune attribute it to *hubris,* often translated as "pride," but really *hubris* means "violence" and only by extension the thoughtless behavior that encourages violence. Surely *hubris,* "violence," is punished in Greek myth—Clytemnestra killed her husband Agamemnon because he had killed their daughter, and the gods hated him because he had burned the temples of Troy—but neither "tragic flaw" nor "pride" is a useful category for understanding Greek myth.

Aeschylus (525–456 B.C.) is the earliest tragedian whose works survive. We have seven plays of the more than eighty he wrote. Aeschylus loved long and elaborate descriptions, especially of foreign lands, and high-flown metaphorical language. He used myth to explore such grand moral issues as the conflict between individual will and divine destiny, and his characters tend to be types or to embody some principle. Aeschylus lived when Athens basked in its greatest glory, and in his epitaph, which he himself composed, he mentioned only that he fought at Marathon. Aeschylus' play, the *Persians,* about events of his own time, is the only surviving tragedy that does not have a mythical theme.

The career of **Sophocles** (496–406 B.C.) exactly coincides with the political and cultural dominance of Athens. Born six years before the battle of Marathon, he died two years before Athens' humiliation by Sparta at the end of the Peloponnesian War. Of the 123 plays he wrote, 7 survive. The vivid characters of his tightly plotted dramas typically are locked in bitter conflict. Sophocles likes to show the dignity of human beings in conflict with superior, often divine forces, a noble person caught in overwhelming crisis. His heroes are lonely and unbending. They learn too late how they should act. He is deeply influenced by folklore, especially by the theme of fulfillment of an oracle: In all his plays a prophecy or oracle predicts an unexpected outcome.

From **Euripides** (485–406 B.C.) more plays survive than from Aeschylus and Sophocles combined, nineteen from the more than ninety he wrote. Euripides was a poet of great range who subjected the traditional myths to rigorous scrutiny and sometimes severe criticism. His characters are often deflated heroes, mere mortals caught up in some all-too-human squabble. His characters often veer off into abnormal mental states. Aristotle remarked that Sophocles showed men as they ought to be, but Euripides showed them as they really are. He reflects contemporary Athenian rhetoric; most of his plays center on a long debate. He has been called an irrationalist because he likes to celebrate the power of emotion over reason.

In Aeschylus, the inherited curse and divine will motivate the action; in Sophocles, fate stands behind events; in Euripides, passionate, often erotic, and especially female emotion drives the action. He is the most modern of the tragedians. His plays were often revived in antiquity and are commonly performed today.[7] Euripides loved sensational bloody scenes and was not above happy endings.

The myths in tragedy are a web of interlocking family histories. Of the thousand tragedies performed between the end of the sixth century B.C. and the end of the fifth, not a single one was concerned exclusively with the doings of gods and goddesses, as far as we know. Tragedy shows little interest in the large mythic cycle Hesiod describes, of creation, the battles of Titans and Olympians, and the births and loves of the gods (the *Prometheus* of Aeschylus stands almost alone). Although gods and goddesses appear on stage and have important roles, the focus is always on the men and women of the Greek legendary past and often on the passions and horrors of family life. No possibility is omitted: Sons kill their mothers, wives kill their husbands, sons kill their fathers, mothers kill their children, a father kills his daughter or son or all his children, a daughter kills her father, brothers kill each other, sons kill their stepmothers, mothers expose their infants to die, men and women kill themselves. Every chord is struck on the theme of sexual trespass: A son sleeps with his mother, a father rapes his daughter, adultery is rampant, lustful women seduce honorable men (never the reverse), husbands desert their wives and mistresses. Complementing such extreme dishonesty are family relations characterized by intense love and devotion: between brother and sister, brother and brother, father and son, husband and wife, father and daughter.

In their loves and hates, the characters in Attic drama can be extreme cases, and in no sense do such tales reflect ordinary life. Yet the audience must have experienced corresponding emotions, although more muted, in their own lives, even as we experience the same emotions today. At precisely the same time as the tragedies were being performed, with their gory scenes and exaggerated emotions, Greek philosophy and Greek science were coming into being. Some intellectuals, such as Anaxagoras, already subjected myth to a rigorous criticism, denying its validity as a means to achieve understanding (for the rise of rationalism and the critique of myth, see Chapter 23).

GREEK MYTH IN THE HELLENISTIC PERIOD

The conquests of Alexander the Great spread Greek culture throughout the eastern Mediterranean and deep into Asia. In 331 B.C. he founded Alexandria in the western delta in Egypt; ironically, for the next 300 years the center of Greek culture was to lie outside Greece. At Alexandria was established the first real library, the *Mou-*

---

[7]During the Vietnam War, the *Trojan Women*, an antiwar play, ran for more than ten years in New York.

seion, "Hall of the Muses," where the classics of Greek literature were gathered together and edited in standard editions. For the first time scholars appeared in the modern sense; they established critical principles to determine the original form of texts corrupted through repeated copying. All Greek texts that survive today passed through the hands of the Alexandrians, who pursued many other branches of learning, especially mathematics, astronomy, and medicine.

While *aoidoi* composed their poems in performance, and rhapsodes and tragic actors memorized their parts from a written prompt to display in public, literature in the Hellenistic Period seems to have been read aloud from the actual scroll, probably to a small audience of friends. (The practice of silent reading so familiar to us did not appear until the fourth century A.D.) The psychological effect of this shift was enormous. Literature was now written to be read, not performed, and as a result it became more self-conscious and learned; it was sometimes extremely abstract and difficult.

The Alexandrian librarian scholars, keenly interested in myth, produced highly complex poems on mythical topics.[8] Such learned, allusive poetry is called Alexandrian. The great scholar Callimachus (c. 305–240 B.C.), author of the first scientific history of literature, wrote mythical poetry of this kind. Although most of his work is lost, Callimachus profoundly influenced the Roman poets, and through them all subsequent Western literature. Another example is his learned pupil Apollonius of Rhodes (third century B.C.), who wrote an epic poem on Jason in the style of Homer, the *Argonautica,* our most important treatment of this myth.

The Hellenistic Greeks were also keenly interested in the essential truth of myth; influenced by the philosophical school of Stoicism founded by Zeno of Citium (a town in Cyprus), they refined the allegorical method of interpreting the ancient stories (see Chapter 23). As early as the fifth century B.C., Greek scholars called mythographers began to gather into collections traditional stories about the doings of gods and heroes. In the Hellenistic Period these efforts increased. The most important survivor is the ***Library of Apollodorus*** (C. A.D. 120), which is not a work of art but a straightforward account of mythical events from the creation of the world to the death of Odysseus. It is one of our best sources of information about many Greek myths, especially those told in the lost Cyclic Poems. Another handbook, a geographical survey of Greece by Pausanias (C. A.D. 150), also preserves much mythical material otherwise unknown.[9]

THE ROMAN APPROPRIATION OF GREEK MYTH

Careful students of Greek culture from an early date, the Romans eventually took over the whole body of Greek myths, with minor modifications, substituting similar Roman divinities for the Greek gods and goddesses (see chart, The Greek and Ro-

---

[8]One such poem, the *Alexandra* (the Trojan princess Cassandra) by Lycophron, contains about 3,000 words, of which 518 are found nowhere else.
[9]One of the founders of modern anthropology, classical scholar Sir James Frazer (1854–1941), author of *The Golden Bough* (see Chapter 23), derived many of his theories about the nature of myth from his study of Pausanias, on whom he wrote a famous commentary.

man Pantheon, at back of book). Catullus (84–54 B.C.), a contemporary of Julius Caesar, is best known for his love poems but also wrote on mythical themes. **Vergil** (70–19 B.C.), the greatest Romen poet, told the story of Aeneas in his epic the *Aeneid*. This poem has one of our fullest descriptions of the underworld and our most vivid account of the sack of Troy. The poem also preserves the legends of Dido, queen of Carthage, and of Hercules' battle against the monster Cacus.

The poetry of the Roman **Ovid** (c. 43 B.C.–A.D. 17), a generation younger than Vergil, is our most important source from the period of the early Roman Empire. Ovid was a man-about-town in Rome, of good birth, famed for his clever and witty verse. He moved in the highest society. Implicated in a sexual scandal that touched the emperor Augustus' own house, he was exiled in A.D. 8 to the town of Tomis on the Black Sea—remote, lonely, and cold—and there he died.

Ovid left behind a large body of poetry, but none more influential than the *Metamorphoses* (met-a-mor-**fō**-sēz), by far the most substantial and influential repertory of Greek myth. This highly original work is a handbook in its own right, a compendium of more than two hundred stories ingeniously united by the theme of the transformation of shape. The poem is itself ever-changing, beginning with the transformation of chaos into cosmos and ending with the transformation of Julius Caesar, Augustus' great-uncle, into a star. But in Ovid's literate and urbane retelling, the old Greek tales have lost the religious overtones of the Greek versions; almost every story he tells is a love story, appealing to the refined, good-humored taste of the powerful but often idle Roman elite. Clever, engaging, irreverent, sometimes salacious, his *Metamorphoses,* more than any other single work, defines what the world thinks of as classical myth. Ovid wrote much love poetry besides the *Metamorphoses* that also alludes to myth. For centuries, from the Roman Period through the Middle Ages and the Renaissance, Ovid was the most important source of classical myth for artists, writers, and others. Every museum has pictures inspired by his accounts.

The Roman historian Livy (59 B.C.–A.D. 17), Ovid's contemporary, wrote an enormous work describing the history of Rome from the beginning down to his own time, about a fourth of which survives. The early books of Livy give legendary accounts that belong more to the study of myth than to history, and we examine them in Chapter 22. Seneca, tutor to the emperor Nero (A.D. 54–68) and defender of Nero's crimes before the Roman senate, wrote voluminously, including several tragedies on mythical subjects. Characterized by extreme violence and savage emotion—hence we speak of Senecan tragedy—these plays made a deep impression on the literature of the Renaissance and on Shakespeare above all.

As long as myths were transmitted orally, they were subject to endless change and local variation; written versions also introduced change to fit the concerns and conditions of the day. Eventually, however, and certainly by the Hellenistic Period, standard versions began to emerge of certain myths because of their treatment by such poets as Homer or Sophocles. A difficulty we face in studying Greek myth is to separate the myth from the work of literature in which it is embodied. A focus on the myths alone would give us a bare-bones list of all the extant variations of, say, the story of Oedipus. A literary analysis, on the other hand, might concentrate on how Sophocles portrays character in his play *Oedipus the King*. Although this book is primarily about myth, which exists independently of any specific version, we touch on literary features of works that have made some myths better known than others. After all, we care about Achilles not because he fought at Troy but because Homer described his personal torment in a way that speaks to us all as human beings.

This book has more in common with the method and intellectual interests of the Hellenistic mythographers than it does with the literary sources for myth, especially of the Greek Archaic and Classical periods. When we piece together, for example, the "myth of Dionysus" from different sources widely separated in time, interest, point of view, and even language (see Chapter 10), we present a special version of the myth that was never part of the direct experience of anyone in the ancient world. But such has always been the fate of myth: to be recast and reformed according to the ideas of the day. The mystery is why such stories continue to be so interesting.

KEY TERMS

FURTHER READING

Baldry, H. C., *The Greek Tragic Theatre* (New York, 1973). What the Athenian stage looked like, how the actors performed, the Athenian tragic contests, and other topics.

Bell, Robert E., *Women of Classical Mythology, A Biographical Dictionary* (Oxford, U.K., 1993). Short articles on women, arranged alphabetically.

Bonnefoy, Yves, compiler, *Mythologies,* 2 vols. (Chicago, 1991). An English translation of the French encyclopedia *Dictionnaire des mythologies et des religions des sociétés traditionnelles et du monde antique*. Essays by French scholars on myths from around the world, with an extensive section on Greek myth (in Vol. 1).

Brooks, Otis, *Ovid as an Epic Poet,* 2nd ed. (Cambridge, U.K., 1970). One of the best general studies of the poet, with emphasis on the *Metamorphoses.*

Burkert, Walter, *The Orientalizing Revolution: Near Eastern Influence on Greek Culture in the Early Archaic Age* (Cambridge, Mass., 1992). Demonstrates the direct influence of Eastern myth on Greece.

Easterling, P. E., ed., *The Cambridge Companion to Greek Tragedy* (Cambridge, U.K., 1997). Various essays focused on performance and reception, especially to productions of tragedy on stage and in film since the Renaissance.

Forbes-Irving, P.M.C., *Metamorphosis in Greek Myths* (Oxford, U.K., 1992). Thorough review of this feature, based on early religious belief, in Greek myth.

Frankfort, H., and others, *The Intellectual Adventure of Ancient Man* (Chicago, 1946). Exciting and penetrating account of myth and culture in Egypt, Mesopotamia, and Palestine in the Bronze Age. See also *Before Philosophy* (New York, 1949), a shortened edition of the same book.

Friedman, Richard Elliott, *Who Wrote the Bible?* (New York, 1989). Lucid summary of two hundred years of biblical scholarship, explaining how our present text came into being.

Galinsky, G. Karl, *Ovid's Metamorphoses, An Introduction to the Basic Aspects* (Oxford, U.K., 1975). The best general book on Ovid's poem, with excellent analysis of the differences between Greek and Roman myth.

Gantz, Timothy, *Early Greek Myth, A Guide to Literary and Artistic Sources* (Baltimore, 1993). A modernization and rewriting in English of the nineteenth-century German *Griechische Mythologie* by Carl Robert and Ludwig Preller, this invaluable handbook lucidly traces in detail the historical development of each myth, giving original ancient sources for each variant and including references to many ancient artistic representations.

Gelb, I. J., *A Study of Writing* (Chicago, 1963). Pioneering work on the nature and history of writing.

Gimbutas, Marija, *The Goddesses and Gods of Old Europe 7000–3500 B.C.: Myths, Legends, and Cult Images* (Berkeley, Calif., 1982). This prehistorian argues that ancient Greek mythical images of goddesses go back to the Neolithic Period.

Graf, Fritz, *Greek Mythology, An Introduction* (Baltimore, 1993). Readable and learned overview.

Huxley, G. L., *Greek Epic Poetry* (Cambridge, Mass., 1969). Reconstructs the contents of lost epic poems.

Jacobsen, Thorkild, *The Treasures of Darkness: A History of Mesopotamian Religion* (New Haven, Conn., and London, 1976). A survey of Mesopotamian, Sumerian, and Semitic myth, organized chronologically, with sophisticated analyses of individual myths.

Lesky, Albin, *Greek Tragedy* (London, 1976). Astute literary analyses of the surviving plays.

Lewis, David M., and Arthur Pickard-Cambridge, *The Dramatic Festivals of Athens*, 2nd ed., ed. John Gould (Oxford, U.K., 1989). The standard scholarly study of the festivals at which tragedy was performed, tragic costume, how the prize was awarded, makeup of the audience, and training of actors.

Lord, Albert, *The Singer of Tales* (New York, 1965; reprinted 1976). The theory that Homer was an oral poet who composed without the aid of writing, by a student of Milman Parry. One of the most influential works of literary criticism of the twentieth century.

McCall, Henrietta, *Mesopotamian Myths* (Austin, Tex., 1990). The best short introduction to the topic.

Parry, M., *The Making of Homeric Verse*, ed. A. Parry (Oxford, U.K., 1971). The introduction is the best presentation of Parry's views.

The Perseus Project, at http://www.perseus.tufts.edu/ ed. G. Crane, et al. Has thousands of links to texts, works of art, maps, lexica, and other aids to understanding myth and the classical world.

Pritchard, James B., ed., *Ancient Near Eastern Texts: Relating to the Old Testament*, 3rd ed. (Princeton, N.J., 1996). The standard collection of translations by many experts, with commentary, of original texts written in the many languages and scripts from the ancient Near East; a book of incomparable scholarly value.

Rose, H. J., *A Handbook of Greek Mythology: Including Its Extension to Rome*, 6th ed. (New York,

1959). The standard English-language handbook of Greek myth for many years, it is still a good reference book, although old-fashioned in style and interpretation.

Simpson, Michael, *Gods and Heroes of the Greeks: The "Library" of Apollodorus* (Amherst, Mass., 1976). A translation of an ancient Greek handbook of mythology. The notes and introduction are valuable compendia of scholarship.

Taplin, Oliver, *Greek Fire* (New York, 1990). Based on a BBC series available on videotape from the University of Illinois Press.

Tripp, Edward, *The Meridian Handbook of Classical Mythology* (New York, 1974). Excellent desktop reference work to Greek myths if you just want to know the stories. Useful references to primary sources.

Wilkinson, L. P., *Ovid Recalled* (Cambridge, U.K., 1990). Excellent survey of this important poet (a shorter paperback version published as *Ovid Surveyed*).

Winkler, John J., and Froma I. Zeitlin, eds., *Nothing to Do with Dionysus?* (Princeton, N.J., 1992). Essays by scholars on Athenian drama in its social context.

CHAPTER 4

MYTHS OF CREATION
THE RISE OF ZEUS

Sing all this to me, Muses, you who dwell on Olympus:
from the beginning tell me, which of the gods first came to be.

HESIOD, *Theogony* 114–115

IN CONTRAST TO THE FAMILIAR STORY told in the biblical book of Genesis (see Perspective 4.2), where God stands outside his creation and exists before it, the most authoritative Greek account, by Hesiod, tells of the origin of the universe through succeeding generations of gods. **Cosmogony,** a story that explains the origin of the world, is for Hesiod the same as **theogony,** a story that explains the origin of the gods and their rise to power. Hesiod's thousand-line poem, the *Theogony,* composed in the eighth century B.C., is in external form an elaborate hymn to Zeus, the Greek version of the Indo-European sky god, and we have already examined Hesiod's invocation to the Muses, who grant him the power to sing this song. To explain Zeus's supremacy Hesiod must go back to the beginning of all things, to the generations of **Chaos** (kā-os), "Chasm," **Gaea** (jē-a), "Earth," and **Uranus** (ūr-a-nus), "Sky."

THE CHILDREN OF CHAOS

Hesiod begins his account thus (see Chart 4.1):

[116]   Chaos was first to appear, then Gaea, earth, the broad-bosomed,
          unshakable base of things, then Tartarus, windswept and dark,

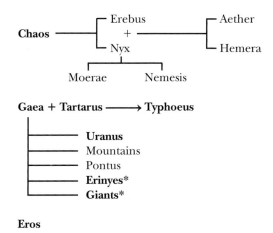

CHART 4.1. The First Generation of Gods

120   deep in the caverns of broad-wayed earth. And Eros, the fairest
       of all the immortals, arose, who frees us all from our sorrows,
       but ruins our hearts' good sense, breaking the wisest intentions
       of gods and mortals alike. From Chaos came Erebus, darkness,
       and Nyx, night, mother of Aether, radiance, and Hemera, day;
       these Nyx conceived by uniting with Erebus, gloomy and somber.

HESIOD, *Theogony* (116–125)[1]

Hesiod's cosmogony is hard to understand; it abounds in contradictions and its meaning is still hotly debated. Myths come from a time when the laws of physics, chemistry, and mathematics were unknown, when even probability was uncertain; when time, space, and causality were almost impossible to formulate. We must remember, too, that language grows: Coining new words for new concepts is a slow process, especially when the art of permanent recording is new. Certainly first came Chaos, a being of some kind that was not always there; where it comes from Hesiod does not say, and we are not sure what Hesiod meant by it. Chaos is related etymologically to our words *gap* and *yawn;* we might translate it as "Chasm," and some understand it as the opening from which the other primordial beings arose. Implicit in the word is the separation of two things to make a gap in the middle. After Chaos came Gaea, Mother Earth, the personification of the earth beneath us, the solid, sure foundation of the world. Tartarus is some place below Earth and often confused in Greek myth with the abode of Hades, but Hesiod personifies Tartarus as one of the primordial elements by which Gaea later has offspring. Hesiod is struggling to de-

---

[1]For convenience, line numbers are given to the left of the translations of poetic texts; the first line numbered in brackets corresponds with the line having the same number in the standard Greek text; subsequent numbers correspond to the lines in the translation. The extent of the whole passage in the original Greek is given in parentheses at the end of the translated text.

lineate space in mythical terms, working toward the scheme Olympus/topmost, Gaea/middle, and Tartarus/bottommost.[2] After Chaos there appeared **Eros,** "Sexual Love" or "Attraction," the first motion, which brings sexual beings together to produce still more offspring. Eros is a being as well as a force that drives Hesiod's complex genealogies. Hesiod does not seem to think that Gaea or Eros sprang from Chaos or from each other, but that the three formed aspects of the primeval stuff from which the world emerged: a gaping (Chaos), the foundation of all that is (Gaea), and the principle of sexual attraction, which ensures future generation and change (Eros).

Erebus (**er**-e-bus), "Darkness," and Nyx (nux), "Night," which sprang from Chaos, are really qualities of Chaos.[3] Hesiod later tells how from Nyx sprang the personifications of the dark necessities: the **Moerae** (**mē**-rē), "Fates," who apportion birth, the length of life, and the time of death, and Nemesis (**nem**-e-sis), "Retribution," who brings pain and just punishment for the wicked. Then Erebus and Nyx came together sexually to produce their opposites, Aether (**ē**-ther), "Radiance," and Hemera (**hē**-mer-a), "Day."[4] Darkness (Erebus) implies light (Aether), and night (Nyx) implies day (Hemera). Such personified forces of nature play little part in subsequent myth.

According to the short *Homeric Hymn to Gaea,* the Mother of All Things, Gaea is simply the source of life and all that is good in life:

> I lift a song to the mother of all things, firm-rooted Gaea,
> mother and nurse of whatever is born into life on the earth.
> Beasts of the shining land, fishes that swim in the waters,
> flying birds of the air—all feed at your bountiful breast.
> 5 From you, O mistress of life, all fruit and increase arises;
> mortals too must concur if you give them life or deny it.
> Happy the man you honor, on whom your benevolence settles.
> All his labors are fruitful: his field is heavy with corn,
> fat cattle graze on his pasture, good grain runs over his bins.
> 10 Equity governs the law such men dispense in their village;
> fair women dwell in the town, attended by riches and plenty.
> Children laugh and sing as the earth gives ever-new bounties.
> Chattering girls run braiding new blossoms into their tresses;
> laughing, they dance in the soft and flowery grass of the meadows
> 15 in steps to delight even you, O reverend, bountiful lady.
> Hail then, mother of gods, bride of the star-studded heaven;
> grant me, as pay for my song, a life of happy contentment,
> that I once more may compose another song of your praises.

Homeric Hymn to Gaea

---

[2]*Olympus* appears to be a pre-Greek word meaning simply "mountain." There were at least ten Mount Olympuses in Greek geography, but *the* Mount Olympus, poetic site of Zeus's throne, is between Thessaly and Macedonia. Olympia, site of the Olympic games, is in the northwest Peloponnesus, on a flat plain beside a stream.

[3]Cf. the biblical account: "The earth was without form and void, and darkness was upon the face of the deep" (Genesis 1.2).

[4]Cf. the biblical account: "And there was evening and there was morning, the first day" (Genesis 1.5).

The Children of Gaea: The Titans and Their Cousins

From Earth, the foundation of all that is, sprang a whole host of beings, bewildering in their complexity and the obscurity of their origins and nature. Most important were the **Titans** (tī-tans), but the monstrous **Cyclopes** (sī-klō-pēz) and the even stranger **Hecatonchires** (he-ka-ton-**kī**-rēz) had important roles to play in the world's early days.

The Titans

According to Hesiod, Gaea first bore, asexually, Uranus ("Sky"), the Mountains on her upper side that rise into the sky, and her watery doublet, Pontus ("Sea"). In sexual union with her son Uranus/Sky, Gaea/Earth produced the six male and six female Titans, a word of unknown meaning (Chart 4.2). **Cronus** (**krō**-nus), who will be Uranus' rival for power, is named as the last born. The Titans rarely are represented in art and do not often play a role in later stories or in religious cult. However, their unions were to produce a whole cycle of divinities:

[126]   The first of the children of Gaea, equal in size to herself,
hiding her body completely, was Uranus, star-studded heaven.
The blessed gods needed solider ground to support their feet;
she bore long ranges of Mountains, pleasant haunts of immortals.
130   Pontus she bore, the unharvested sea with its raging swell,
without the pleasure of love. Thereafter Gaea was bedded
with Uranus, lord of heaven, and bore deep-swirling Oceanus,
Coeus, Crius, Hyperion, Iapetus, Theia and Rhea, Themis,
Mnemosynê, gold Phoebê, and fair-featured Tethys.
135   Last of all she gave birth to Cronus, that scheming intriguer,
cleverest child of her brood, who hated his lecherous father.

HESIOD, *Theogony* (126–138)

Uranus evidently was the same size as Gaea and covered her completely, as if locked in perpetual sexual embrace (Fig. 4.1). The birth of Pontus, "Sea," reminds

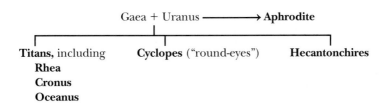

CHART 4.2. The Offspring of Gaea and Uranus

FIG. 4.1. Sky and Earth, from the Egyptian Papyrus of Tameniu, c. 1000 B.C. The notion that Sky and Earth are beings once united in sexual embrace, who were separated at the moment of creation, was widespread in the ancient world, as in this representation, which shows Sky as a woman (= Nut, pronounced "noot") and Earth (= Geb) as a sexually excited man, longing to be reunited with his mate. Most ancient peoples thought of the earth as female, the sky as male, but the Egyptians, as the Greek historian Herodotus remarked, "did everything backwards." To the right, the air god, who separates Sky from Earth, shows adoration to his parents. (British Museum, London)

us of the watery nature of the primordial element in the Mesopotamian myths, which we examine later in this chapter. Although the oppositions of Up/Down, Sky/Earth have now appeared, the separation of the primal opposites is yet to be fixed and made permanent.

Two notable Titans are the watery male **Oceanus** (ō-sē-a-nus) and female Tethys (tē-this). According to a passing reference in Homer, Oceanus and Tethys themselves gave birth to all the gods. Oceanus is a river that encircles the world, where the dome of the sky touches the flat surface of the earth. All the waters that emerge from wells, springs, fountains, and rivers are also fed by the flow of Oceanus. The pair united to give birth to the six thousand Oceanids (ō-sē-a-nids), spirits of the sea, rivers, and springs.

Coeus, Crius, and Theia, "Divine," are scarcely more than names. Phoebê, "Brilliant," must have something to do with the light of the sky, as Themis, "Law," refers to the earth, that which is fixed and settled, like the oracles delivered in her name: The oracular shrine of Delphi belonged to Themis before Apollo took it over. Themis will bear children to Zeus, as will Mnemosynê (nē-**mos**-i-nē), "Memory." The name of Iapetus may be related to that of the biblical Japheth, the son of Noah and, in the biblical account, the ancestor of the Europeans. Cronus and **Rhea** (rē-a), doublets for Uranus and Gaea, are parents of the twelve Olympians, including Zeus, the king of the gods and the principal object of praise in Hesiod's poem.

Cyclopes, Hecatonchires

In addition to the Titans, Gaea bore, after union with Uranus, three Cyclopes, "Round-eyes," and the mighty Hecatonchires, the "Hundred-handers":

[139]   Then Gaea gave birth to Cyclopes, strong and abrupt of emotion,
140   Brontes, Steropes, Arges, stubborn, determined of spirit,
     forgers of thunder for Zeus and makers of bolts of his lightning.
     For the most part, they resembled in features the other immortals,
     but each had only one eye, in the middle part of his forehead.
     Violence, power, and shrewdness attended each of their actions.
145   Still other children were born to Uranus, bedded with Gaea:
     three huge powerful beings, whose names can scarcely be spoken,
     Cottus, Briareus, Gyes, offspring of terrible power.
     A hundred terrible arms hung down from their muscular shoulders,
     and fifty heads surmounted their mighty necks and their limbs.
150   Invincible terrible power glared out from each of the monsters.
     Of all the children descended from Uranus, husband of Gaea,
     these their father most hated, from the very day of their birth.

HESIOD, Theogony (139–155)

Unlike the simple shepherd Cyclops Polyphemus, son of Poseidon, who imprisoned Odysseus in his cave (see Chapter 21), Hesiod's Cyclopes combined the wisdom of the metallurgist with great strength. They are the clever smiths of the gods. Taking raw iron from the depths of earth, their mother, they made the irresistible weapon of victory: lightning. Their names Brontes, "Thunderer," Steropes, "Flasher," and Arges, "Brightener," reflect the noise and brilliance of their marvelous weapon.

Finally, Uranus and Gaea bore the three Hecatonchires, each of whom had a hundred arms that shot from his shoulders, as well as fifty heads. Named Cottus (meaning unknown), Briareus (bri-ā-rūs), "Strength," and Gyes (jī-ēz), meaning unknown, perhaps "Primeval," they are beings of invincible strength who can easily crush any opponent in their mighty hands.

Hyperion's Children: Sun, Moon, Dawn

The Titan Hyperion (perhaps "he who goes above") is a sun god. He is father to the better-known **Helius,** also a sun god; Selenê (se-lē-nē), the moon; and **Eos** (ē-os), the dawn. The *Homeric Hymn to Helius* portrays the journey of Helius across the sky in his chariot, an image familiar in the history of art:

Calliopê,° daughter of Zeus, a hymn to the Sun in its glory!
whom soft-eyed Euryphaëssa° bore to a child of the Earth
and the starry Sky above. For Hyperion wedded his sister,

---

1. *Calliopê.* "Fair-voiced," one of the Muses.   2. *Euryphaëssa:* "Wide-shining," probably another name for the Titaness Theia, whom Hesiod names as the wife of Hyperion.

the farfamed Euryphaëssa, who bore him beautiful children:
5   rosy-armed Eos, the dawn; Selenê, the flowing-haired moon;
       and Helius, the sun never weary, handsome as any immortal.°
       Driving his horses, casting his light on gods and on humans,
       he darts a keen-eyed gaze from under the gold of his helmet.
       His gleaming rays flash out; by ruddy forehead and temples
10   is framed the light of his face. The mantle around his body
       rustles and shines afar in the wake of his galloping stallions.
       For a moment he halts the rush of his hurrying golden car,
       then expertly lashes his team through Sky and on to the Ocean.
       Hail, Lord Helius; grant me a life of comfort and pleasure.
15   From you I advance to applauding a mortal race of mankind,
       the demigods, whose actions the gods° have displayed to us humans.

Homeric Hymn to Helius

6. *immortal*: Of course he was an immortal, a good example of a conventional epithet, common in oral poetry. Sometimes the phrase may be inappropriate, as here.   16. *the gods*: Presumably the Muses. The hymn seems to have served as a prelude to a story about some hero.

A story made famous by Ovid is told about **Phaëthon** (**fā**-e-thon), a son of Helius and Clymenê, an Oceanid. It is a good example how, in the hands of the urbane Roman Ovid, descriptions of the world's early days became a prettified fantasy embodying the teasing morals, "Don't be too curious about your origins, and don't get too big for your breeches!" Although Phaëthon's mother was married to the king of Ethiopia, she assured her son that his father was none other than the sun. Overhearing a companion doubt his parentage, Phaëthon begged his mother for confirmation. She urged him to journey to the house of Helius himself, where the boy wondered at the sun god's shining palace and its brilliant columns. Helius set aside the crown of rays coming from his head so that he might embrace his son. To prove that he was truly Phaëthon's father, Helius gave him one wish: anything he desired. To Helius' horror, Phaëthon asked that he be allowed to drive the chariot of the sun across the sky.

Helius warned Phaëthon, but he could not go back on his promise. At first Phaëthon drove carefully along the paths of the sky, but soon the four horses sensed the unsure hand on the reins and leaped from their accustomed path in the heaven. Frightened by the animals of the zodiac blazing above him, Phaëthon lost control of the car, and the horses dashed down close to earth, nearly setting the world ablaze. Libya, still a desert today, was scorched and seared and the skin of the Ethiopians burned black. Then the horses soared high toward the stars. To save the world, Zeus blasted the boy from the car. He fell into the river Eridanus (= the Po, in northern Italy). His sisters, the Heliades ("Daughters of Helius"), buried him and wept so hard over his death that they turned to poplar trees and their tears to golden amber.

Only one story was told of Selenê, the moon, a favorite with love poets ancient and modern. Having fallen in love with the handsome shepherd Endymion (see Fig. 1.1), Selenê seduced him while he slept in his cave, and eventually bore him fifty daughters. At Selenê's request, Zeus placed Endymion in an eternal sleep, that he might never grow old.

Eos, the dawn, was even more lascivious than Selenê and had many affairs. Above all she loved **Tithonus** (ti-**thō**-nus), a Trojan prince. Tithonus received a similar boon, but with less serene outcome. The story is told as an aside in the *Homeric Hymn to Aphrodite:*[5]

[218]   So too golden-throned Eos abducted the noble Tithonus,
       another man of your race,° and one who resembled the gods.
220   She went to beg for a favor from Cronus' dark-clouded son,
       that Tithonus should be an immortal, living on forever and ever.
          Zeus nodded assent to her prayer. But Eos, poor foolish lady,
       neglected to ask that her lover might never be subject to aging.
       As long as the springtime of life continued, a happy Tithonus
225   rejoiced with his Eos the golden-throned, the early-born goddess.
       But when gray hair appeared on Tithonus' cheeks and his temples,
       more and more Lady Eos avoided their once happy bed.
       She attended him still in her house, rendering all her affection,
       giving him food and ambrosia and clothing his chilly old body.
230   But finally gloomy old age laid its ponderous burden upon him;
       no more could he lift his bones to totter, decrepit and feeble.
       At last the goddess agreed on this as the plan she must follow:
       she closed him up in his room, and locked up the glorious portal.
       Inside, his piping old voice droned endlessly. Gone is the vigor
235   he used to enjoy, and the use of limbs once handsome and supple.

                    Homeric Hymn to Aphrodite (218–238)

219. *your race:* The Trojans.

Later versions report that Tithonus was turned into a cicada, chirping uselessly in the wind.

CRONUS AGAINST URANUS

Although Uranus and Gaea bore many children, at first none could come forth into the light, for Uranus/Sky hated his own offspring:

[156]   As soon as each child was conceived, Uranus kept it well hidden,
       refusing it access to light, deep in the womb of the earth,
       and gloated over his action, while Gaea groaned in her travail.
       But she planned a treacherous scheme: first inventing gray steel°
160   (till that day unknown), she fashioned a terrible sickle.
       She told her children the plan, hoping to stiffen their courage,
       though sorely disturbed herself. "O children, you whom I bore
       to a wicked and terrible father, if you will only support me,
       we can avenge the shame and disgrace he has loaded upon you.

159. *steel:* The sickle is actually said to be adamantine, "invincible," a mythical hard substance often translated "steel," which it probably was not. The word is the source of *diamond.*

[5]The rest of the hymn appears in Chapter 8.

165   For he it was who was first to devise such hideous actions."
       At that fear silenced them all. Nobody dared give an answer,
       till the wily Cronus bravely replied to the lady his mother:
       "Mother, I am quite ready to carry through with this matter,
       for I scorn our accursed father, who plotted such terrible things."
170   So he spoke, and the heart of Gaea leaped up in delight.
       She hid him, couched in an ambush, and into his hands she delivered
       the sickle, toothed like a saw. Her plot worked out as she planned it:
       when Uranus came to her presence, bringing with him the darkness,
       and, panting with lust, embraced the mighty body of Gaea,
175   from ambush Cronus' left hand seized the genital parts of his father;
       he reached out his right with the sickle, saw-toothed, deadly, and sharp.
       Like a reaper, he sliced away the genitals of his own father,
       flinging them over his shoulder, to roll wherever chance bade them.
       But they did not fly from his hand down to the earth, ineffective,
180   for Gaea absorbed the gory drops that rained down upon her,
       and after a year had passed she bore the frightful Erinyes,
       the Giants, gleaming in armor, holding long spears in their hands,
       and the Melian Nymphs, whom mortals reverence all the world over.

                                   HESIOD, *Theogony* (156–187)

Although Hesiod speaks of Uranus "bringing with him the darkness and panting with lust," the meaning of the story depends on an image of Uranus/Sky and
Gaea/Earth as locked in perpetual intercourse. Uranus/Sky lay constantly across
Gaea/Earth, fecundating her but never allowing his children to emerge from the
mother's body. There is no space where the activity of the world can take place. By
slicing away his genitals, Cronus broke away Sky, allowing him to rise to the place
where he belonged. A provisional separation of the two primal elements is now made
permanent; the world has reached its proper configuration, Sky above and Earth beneath, with Tartarus attached somewhere below. All round flows Oceanus, the primordial water. All of this has emerged from Chaos.

But the permanent separation of the first elements is bought at the high cost of
deceit and violence of son against father: Uranus/Sky mightily cursed his treacherous son Cronus. Fecundated by the drops of blood that fell from the ghastly wound
of Uranus/Sky, Earth gave birth to the **Erinyes** (e-**rin**-i-ēz), the Furies, ferocious female spirits who haunt anyone who sheds kindred blood, driving them into madness. The Erinyes are especially malignant because kindred blood is, in a sense, one's
own. From other drops of the bloody gore sprang up the **Giants,** "Earthborn Ones,"
beings of enormous strength and unbridled violence, who one day will bring their
power against Zeus and his Olympian brothers and sisters.

The Birth of Aphrodite, Monsters, and Sea Deities

Hesiod goes on to describe the birth of Aphrodite:

[188]   As for the genitals, slashed away by the sickle of steel,
        their impetus carried them out from shore to the tide of the sea.

190 For years the waters swilled them about, as white foam kept oozing
     from out the immortal flesh. Within it there grew up a maiden
     who drifted first to holy Cythera,° then on to Cyprus.
     There she emerged from the sea as a modest and beautiful goddess,
     around whose slim-ankled feet arose all the flowers of springtime.
195 Gods and mortals alike call her Aphrodite, the *Foamborn*,
     or else Cytherea, to honor the island where first she was seen.
     Eros walked by her side, and fair Desire came after,
     as she joined the race of the gods. These are the honors she holds:
     giggling whispers of girls, the smiling deceptions they practice,
200 as well as the honeyed delights and all the allurements of passion.

HESIOD, Theogony (188–206)

192. *Cythera:* An island off the southeastern coast of the Peloponnesus.

The blood fell on the earth, but the genitals themselves fell into the sea. The sea foam, mixed with semen, sloshed around them until from the "foam" (= Greek *aphros*) appeared a being of dreadful power, Aphrodite, goddess of sexual love (Fig. 4.2; compare Fig. P 8.1a). Born from the bloody genitals of a cosmic deity, Aphrodite represents the universal force of irresistible sexual desire, a fruit of mutilation and violence. The destructive power of sexual attraction is a central theme in Greek myth. The Titans, the Cyclopes, and the Hecatonchires were born of Gaea's union with her son Uranus, but she also had sexual relations with Pontus, another of her

FIG. 4.2. Aphrodite (Venus) rising from the sea, from the so-called Ludovisi Throne, c. 465 B.C. The relief, which was found in Rome during the Renaissance, seems once to have decorated an altar in a Greek city in southern Italy. The goddess wears a simple chiton (a type of dress). Two of the Horae, "Seasons" standing on a pebbled shore, help to lift her from a deep pool between two rocks. (Museo Nazionale delle Terme, Rome; author's photo)

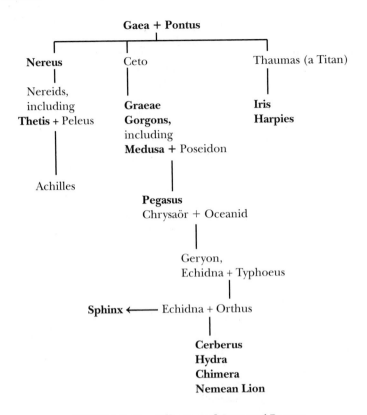

Gaea + Pontus

Nereus   Ceto   Thaumas (a Titan)

Nereids,
including   **Graeae**   **Iris**
Thetis + Peleus   **Gorgons,**   **Harpies**
                     including
                     Medusa + Poseidon

Achilles

                     Pegasus
                     Chrysaör + Oceanid

                     Geryon,
                     Echidna + Typhoeus

Sphinx ←——— Echidna + Orthus

                     Cerberus
                     Hydra
                     Chimera
                     Nemean Lion

CHART 4.3. The Offspring of Gaea and Pontus

sons. From this union came a host of other offspring (Chart 4.3), most of whom have little importance in later myth or make only a brief appearance in heroic legend. Some are notable for their monstrous shape or, like the sea that begot them, are changeable in appearance. Etymologically, *monster* means "that at which you point in surprise," and in Greek art the monstrous descendants of Sea and Earth were most often represented as mixtures of animal and human parts. This tradition derives from Mesopotamian and Egyptian art, but the Greeks changed the meanings of the fabulous creatures whose forms they copied. For example, the Egyptians represented the souls of the dead as human-headed birds; being ghosts, they could fly where they wanted and enjoy the pleasant gardens before their tombs and the offerings placed there by pious relatives. In Greek art, human-headed birds were the Harpies, "Snatchers," grandchildren of Gaea and Pontus, hostile spirits of storm who appeared from nowhere to carry away the living.[6] Another example is the **Sphinx,** also a descendant of Gaea and Pontus. The Egyptians symbolized the divine power of Pharaoh as a human-headed lion, and in this form Pharaoh watched over Egypt in death as in life. The Greeks changed the Sphinx's sex from male to female, added

[6]The Sirens, who lured sailors to their deaths, were shown in the same way, but the Sirens were not descended from Gaea and Pontus. Compare Fig. 21.3.

wings, and explained the name as meaning "Strangler," a deadly spirit of plague who besieged the city of Thebes (see Fig. 17.4).

The Greeks also invented their own ways to portray monsters in their art, although they preserved the Near Eastern practice of combining parts from different creatures or simply reduplicating normal parts. The Gorgons had a woman's body to which wings were attached, snakes instead of hair, and boar's tusks for teeth (see Fig. 13.7a). Geryon (**jer**-i-on), an enemy of Heracles, had three bodies jointed at the waist; his dog Orthus had two heads. **Cerberus** was a fifty-headed (or three-headed) hound who guarded the gates of Hades' realm (Fig. 4.3). The water serpent Hydra, "Watery," sometimes had seven heads. Echidna was an ordinary woman from the buttocks up, but a serpent below, "a glimmering flesh-eater in the inky caverns of hallowed earth," as Hesiod puts it. Most bizarre was **Chimera** (ki-**mē**-ra), "She-goat," a lion with a snake's tail and a goat's head growing from its back (Fig. 4.4).

The shapes of the descendants of Gaea and Pontus could also be drawn from nature, although they possessed extraordinary powers. Ceto (**sē**-to), "Sea Monster," was a whale or enormous fish. The Graeae (**grē**-ē), "Gray Ones," were "fair-cheeked hags,

FIG. 4.3. Heracles and Cerberus. The tyrant Eurystheus compelled Heracles to perform twelve tasks, the last to capture Cerberus and drag him to the upper world. Here Heracles shows the beast to Eurystheus, who raises his hands in terror and stands in a bronze pot for protection. Heracles has the dog on a leash; he raises his club in his other hand. Snakes spring from Cerberus' forelegs and head. This pot was found in Cerveteri in Italy (ancient Etruscan Caere) and was either made there by a Greek immigrant c. 530 B.C. or imported from a Greek city in Asia Minor. (Musée du Louvre, Paris; Hirmer Fotoarchiv, Munich)

FIG. 4.4. The Chimera, an Etruscan bronze from the fifth century B.C., with a lion's body, the head of a goat protruding from its back, and a serpent's tail. According to a variant on the folktale called "Potiphar's Wife," the hero Bellerophon killed the Chimera (see Chapter 15).   (Museo Archeologico Nazionale, Florence; University of Wisconsin, Madison Photo Archive)

gray from birth," as Hesiod describes them. The Nemean lion looked like a lion but could not be killed by ordinary means (see Fig. 14.2). Nereus (**nē**-rūs) was the wise Old Man of the Sea, a prophetic deity, as are many sea gods. Ordinarily he had a human shape, but he could also change his shape at will into fire, a leopard, a serpent, or a tree. He sired the fifty-two Nereids (**nē**-rē-idz),[7] a group of sea spirits hard to distinguish from their cousins the Oceanids but far fewer in number. The Nereids live at the bottom of the sea seated on golden thrones and embody the lovely, gentle aspect of the sea. The best known Nereid was Thetis (**thē**-tis), mother of Achilles. Like her father, Thetis could change her shape at will (see Fig. 19.2).

ZEUS AGAINST CRONUS: THE BATTLE WITH THE TITANS

Hesiod tells how Uranus tyrannized Gaea with his sexual demands, smothering her and keeping her and all else down. With the overthrow of Uranus, Cronus became the first king of the world. he ruled over a complex realm filled with many new beings. He had to be underhanded, violent, and suspicious to maintain his power. Told by his parents that he would fall victim to one of his children, Cronus feared his chil-

---

[7]The suffix --*id* = "daughter" or "descendant."

dren and swallowed them as fast as they issued forth from his wife and sister, Rhea. These children were Hestia, Demeter, Hera, Hades, Poseidon, and Zeus, six gods who as the Olympians would one day divide the power of the world (see Chart 6.1):

[453] Rhea, submitting to Cronus, bore to him wonderful children:
       Hestia, gold-sandaled Hera, Demeter, and Hades the mighty,
455   implacable, him whose dwelling is under the earth in the darkness;
       Poseidon, thundering shaker of earth, and Zeus the wiliest schemer,
       father of gods and men, whose thunder shatters the cosmos.
       Each of them Cronus devoured as they came from the holy womb
       to the knees of Rhea. All this, lest she bear him a lordly successor,
460   to hold high honor and rule in heaven among the immortals.
       For his fate, as starry Uranus told him, and Gaea, his mother,
       was one day to fall from his throne, displaced by one of his children,
       in spite of the power he held, through the plottings of great Zeus.
       He therefore kept vigilant watch, and lay in wait to devour
465   each of his children at birth. Rhea mourned, but she never forgot.

HESIOD, *Theogony* (453–467)

Rhea went to her parents, Gaea and Uranus, for advice. They instructed her to journey to Crete and there to bear her youngest child, Zeus. This she did, then hid him in a mountain cave, where he was brought up by nymphs on milk from the goat Amalthea (am-al-**thē**-a) and honey from Melissa, the bee. His infant cries were drowned by the clashing cymbals of the Corybantes (kor-i-**ban**-tēz), perhaps "Whirlers," also called Curetes (kur-**ē**-tēz), "Young Men," or warriors. When Cronus asked for the latest child, she gave him a stone wrapped in swaddling clothes. Stupid Cronus gulped it down. In this way Zeus was saved and grew into manhood.

Hesiod is strangely silent about what happened next, noting only that Zeus eventually forced Cronus to vomit up the children, Zeus's brothers and sisters. Later sources say that the Oceanid Metis, "Cleverness," gave Cronus an emetic potion and that Cronus vomited out the children in reverse order. The stone came out too and was later displayed for all to see in Apollo's shrine at Delphi. Conical and decorated with carving, this stone was called the *omphalos*, "navel." Oil was poured on it every day, and unspun wool decked it during festivals.

Now Zeus became king of the gods, and he and his brothers and sisters took up abode on Mount Olympus. But the Titans resented their rule. They banded together and attacked the Olympians in the stupendous **Titanomachy** (tī-tan-**a**-ma-kē), "battle of the Titans" (*machê* in Greek means "battle"). Only the Titan Themis and her son **Prometheus** (prō-**mē**-thūs) dared side with Zeus in the conflict:

[629] For a long time the Titans and the other gods sprung of Cronus
630   savagely battled each other. The lordly Titans came charging
       down from the heights of Othrys;° the gods, bestowers of blessings,
       whom fair-haired Rhea had borne, bedding in union with Cronus,

631. *Othrys:* A mountain south of the plain of Thessaly.

Goya's *Saturn Devouring His Children*

Francisco de Goya (1746–1828), a Spanish artist of eccentric vision, stood apart from his contemporaries in his perception of demonic forces and the terrors of the human experience. Late in life, suffering from deafness, witness to many horrors, he retired to his house and covered the walls with nightmarish devil-worshipers, subhuman monsters, and other haunting images, including a representation of Saturn devouring his children (Fig. P 4.1).

Saturn ("the Sower"), an Italian spirit of the harvest, is the Latin equivalent of Cronus, whom Greek intellectuals had equated with Chronos ("Time"). In this way, the myth of Cronus eating his children could be explained as an allegory for "time devours all things" (see Chapter 23; the scythe of our Father Time would be the sickle whereby Cronus = Chronos severed his father's genitals). Hesiod tells us that Cronus swallowed his children whole, as if in one gulp, but Goya heightens the hor-

FIG. P 4.1. Francisco Goya (1746–1828), *Saturn Devouring His Children* (detail), 1819–1823, oil on plaster transferred to canvas. (Museo del Prado, Madrid; University of Wisconsin Photo Archive, Madison)

ror of the scene through an exaggerated fantasy of Saturn as a ghastly cannibal giant, chomping up one child—male or female, we cannot tell—bit by bit. Even so does ravenous, unforgiving Time destroy all in its bloody, grinding jaws; even so do the demonic forces in human nature, reflecting nature itself, destroy all that is childlike and innocent.

> counterattacked from Olympus.° For ten full years did they battle;
> no rest, no truce in the strife; no victory crowning their efforts.

HESIOD, Theogony (629–638)

633. *Olympus:* North of the Thessalian plain.

Zeus learned from Gaea that he could win the battle only with the help of the three Hecatonchires, the Hundredhanders. He released them and the Cyclopes from Tartarus, where Uranus, fearing their power, had imprisoned them. Weakened from long confinement, the Hacatonchires partook of a mythical drink called *nectar* (perhaps meaning "that which overcomes death") and an equally mythical food known as *ambrosia* ("undying") and soon regained strength. In gratitude, the Cyclopes, wonderful smiths, made for Zeus the thunderbolt, his special weapon:

[666]   On that very day the immortals began their terrible contest,
      male and female, the Titans and those descended from Cronus,
      and those whom Zeus had freed from Erebus,° deep in the darkness,
      back to the light of day. A hundred hands, strong and brawny,
670   grew from the shoulders of each, with fifty heads in the middle.
      Forward they marched to war with the Titans, giving no quarter,
      each one brandishing broken-off fragments of cliff as his missiles.
      Against them advanced the Titans, each one urging his fellows,
      each side eagerly vaunting the strength and skill of its ranks.
675   The mighty sea howled around, and the earth resounded beneath them;
      broad heaven trembled above, and the roots of Olympus were shaken
      by the clash of immortals, resounding louder than echoing thunder,
      as far as windy Tartarus—rushing of feet as they hurried,
      screaming darts in their flight, shouted cries as they rallied.
680   All this rang to the stars as the two sides clashed with each other.
         Now Zeus no longer held back his might. From now on his spirit
      seethed in his rage as he showed the full extent of his power.
      Down from the heaven he rushed, from the highest peak of Olympus,
      hurling in endless showers the flashing bolts of his lightning.
685   Forth from his mighty hand flashed glare commingled with thunder,
      ceasing for never a moment. Earth, giver of life, could but cower,
      tormented and scorched by her burns; great forests choked in the fire,
      as the water of earth boiled off, and the surging tides of the ocean,
      even the harvestless sea. The fiery blast soared on upward
690   to the quiet expanse of the heaven,° and down to the arrogant Titans,
      shriveling sight from their eyes.

HESIOD, Theogony (666–698)

668. *Erebus:* Used here for Tartarus.

The tide of battle turned. Helped by the Hecatonchires, Zeus cast the Titans into darkest Tartarus:

[713]   Leading the bitter struggle were Cottus, Briareus, Gyes,
    lusting for battle, each hurling a good three-hundred terrible boulders
715   in fire so rapid the stones quite overshadowed the Titans.
    Some they hurled to their ruin, down under the wide-wayed earth
    as far underground as earth itself is lower than heaven,
    where they bound them in biting chains, curbing their arrogant spirit.
        Drop an anvil from heaven; it falls nine days and nine nights,
720   reaching the earth on the tenth. Just so a great brazen anvil,
    if dropped from the earth, for an equal time would go hurtling downward,
    and would land at last on the tenth day, deep in Tartarus' depths.
        Round Tartarus runs a wall of brass, at whose narrowest portion
    threefold night gushes out. Below are the roots of the earth,
725   and those of unharvested sea. Within it the Titans are buried,
    by design of Zeus who assembles the clouds. No way of escape
    lies open, for mighty Poseidon set gates of bronze, and around them
    the wall hems them in on both sides. There Cottus, Briareus, Gyes,
    mighty of heart, all dwell,° strong henchmen of Zeus of the aegis.

HESIOD, *Theogony* (713–735)

729. *all dwell:* As jailers.

Atlas, either a Titan (a son of Uranus) or a giant (son of Iapetus and an Oceanid), was condemned by Zeus to live at the edge of the world, where he held up the heavens (see Fig. 5.1), ensuring the continued separation of Sky and Earth. Later, Atlas was equated with a mountain range in Morocco near the Atlantic Ocean (whence comes its name) and gave his name to the fanciful continent Atlantis, said by Plato to lie in the far west beyond the Pillars of Heracles, the hills of Gibraltar and of Ceuta in Morocco.

ZEUS'S BATTLE WITH TYPHOEUS

But Zeus's struggles were not ended. Gaea, who had advised Zeus to summon the Hecatonchires in his struggle against her own children the Titans, for some reason now resented Zeus's victory; she became his greatest enemy. Coupling with her own offspring Tartarus, she gave birth to the monstrous **Typhoeus** (tī-fē-ūs), also called Typhon (tī-phon):

[820]   When Zeus had driven the Titans out of the sky into exile,
    mighty Gaea gave birth to the last of her children, Typhoeus,
    born of Tartarus' lust and the wiles of gold-haired Aphrodite.
    Typhoeus had muscular arms, fit for laborious action,
    and the tireless feet of a god of might. Surmounting his shoulders
825   sprouted the hundred heads of a terrible serpentine dragon,
    flicking their dark livid tongues. The eyes of each sinister forehead

spat out a jet of flame from under its shadowing eyebrows,
and each indescribable mouth had a voice of ineffable volume,
uttering words only gods can know: now the arrogant cry of a bull,
830   a lordly bellow of strength, now the terrible roar of a lion,
shameless and angry. Again, the eager bark of the mastiff,
or the hunter's echoing whistle that makes the mountains resound.
      No defense could be found, from the day of birth of the monster,
and Typhoeus would soon have been despot alike of gods and of humans,
835   had not the wit of the father of mortal men and immortals
seen through the threat, and sounded his irresistible thunder.
All earth quaked at the sound, and the wide-flung arches of heaven,
the springs of Ocean, the seas, and the gloomy depths of the earth.
Under the thundering tread of its monarch marching to battle,
840   huge Olympus was shaken, and all earth trembled and whimpered.
The purple face of the sea was seared by the flames of both rulers,
by Zeus's thunder and lightning, by fire that flashed from Typhoeus:
the lightning bolts of the one, the scorching winds of the other.
All earth boiled, and all heaven; the sea surged over its headlands,
845   its crashing waves driven up and around by the blast of the powers.
      Uncontrollable shaking seized all the earth and the heavens;
and even Hades, the lord of the lifeless shades, shook in terror,
and the Titans, buried in Tartarus, huddled together with Cronus.
Now Zeus kindled his rage and eagerly snatched up his missiles,
850   thunder and lightning and fire from heaven, crashing and blazing.
He bounded forward, and shot from the lofty top of Olympus;
the fiery blast ignited the marvelous heads of the monster.
Typhoeus, scourged and shattered by Zeus's terrible weapons,
hamstrung, sank to his knees, as the mighty earth groaned in despair.
855   From the fall of the stricken ruler, blasted by heavenly lightning,
flames leaped out like those in the woods of rugged Mount Etna,
when it too is struck. For miles the whole great earth was enkindled
by the blast of heavenly wind. It melted like wax in a ladle
worked by a brawny-armed smith, or iron, toughest of metals,
860   smelted in mountain forests and worked in the heat of a forge.
Just so the earth was melted in the white-hot gleam of the fire.

HESIOD, Theogony (820–867)

Apollodorus, author of the oldest surviving "handbook of Greek myth" (second century A.D.), adds interesting details to this account of Hesiod. Typhoeus, he says, was born in Cilicia (the southern coast of modern Turkey) and was so huge that he towered above the mountains and his head struck the stars. One hand reached the western horizon, the other the eastern. From the waist down he was a tangle of hissing vipers; he had majestic wings, and shaggy hair covered his body (Fig. 4.5). Typhoeus hurled fiery rocks at heaven, then charged, hooting and spewing fire from his mouths. The Olympian gods fled to Egypt and disguised themselves as various animals; that is why Egyptian gods have animal shapes. Zeus charged, pitching thunderbolts and brandishing a sickle (perhaps the one with which Cronus had castrated Uranus). Hotly pursued, Typhoeus fled to Mount Casius in north Syria. Zeus threw down his sickle and grappled with the monster hand to hand, but Typhoeus caught

FIG. 4.5. The Typhonomachy, from a vase found in Etruria but probably painted by a Euboean Greek living in Italy, c. 525 B.C. Zeus is shown brandishing his thunderbolt in his right hand while he takes aim with his left. Typhoeus is winged with snaky limbs beneath the waist, with a full beard, gnarled nose, and pointy ears. (Staatliche Antikensammlungen und Glyptothek, Munich)˙

Zeus in his coils, seized the sickle, and sliced out the sinews of Zeus's hands and feet, which he stored in a jar. He carried the god, limp as a rag doll, to a cave in Cilicia, threw him in a corner, hid the sinews under a bearskin, and placed a dragon to guard the cave.

Fortunately, Zeus's son Hermes and a goat-shaped woodland spirit named Aegipan ("Goatpan") slipped past Typhoeus, took the sinews from the jar, and restored them to Zeus, who mounted a glorious chariot drawn by winged horses. He pursued Typhoeus across the earth, flinging thunderbolts. In Thrace the monster took his stand, ripped out whole mountains, and threw them. Zeus caught and threw them back, badly wounding Typhoeus, whose blood covered an entire mountain, henceforth known as Mount Haemus ("Bloody").

Zeus finally ran Typhoeus down in the far west and buried him beneath Mount Etna in eastern Sicily. When today the mountain smokes, it is from the fusillade of lightning that Zeus poured upon him, or it may be the fire of Typhoeus himself, escaping from the earth.

ZEUS'S BATTLE WITH THE GIANTS

Although he had won wars against the Titans and Typhoeus, Zeus was still not secure. The logic of the **succession myth** seemed to demand that he too be overthrown.

Cronus was more clever than Uranus, and Zeus more clever than Cronus. Who would be more clever than Zeus? No one, once Zeus married cleverness herself, the Oceanid **Metis** (mē-tis), "Cleverness." Metis, who had given the emetic to Cronus, was the first of Zeus's seven consorts (see Chart 6.2). She was already pregnant with Athena when Zeus learned from Uranus and Gaea that his wife's next child, after Athena, would be the one to depose him. Uranus had attempted to preserve his power by keeping his offspring down in the body of the mother, Cronus swallowed his children, and Zeus discovered the craftiest trick of all: He swallowed the mother herself before the child was born. Thus did Metis, "Cleverness," become part of his own being, inaccessible except through Zeus himself.

Later, suffering a severe headache, Zeus cried out for assistance. Either Prometheus or Hephaestus struck his head with an ax. Out sprang Athena, fully formed, fully armed, screaming the war cry (Fig. 4.6). Thus Athena was the child of Zeus alone, his agent and supporter, female in sex but virgin in body and masculine in thought and behavior. The child who would have overthrown him was never born. Zeus defied the prophecy by defying the biological logic according to which only the female gives birth.

Hesiod does not tell it, but very popular in classical art was the story of another enemy who rose against him. The Giants, conceived from the blood of Uranus' sev-

FIG. 4.6. The birth of Athena from the head of Zeus on an Attic cup, c. 560 B.C. Hephaestus, who has just struck open Zeus's head with his ax, turns to run, startled at the result. Athena springs forth, armed with shield and spear, while an indifferent Zeus holds a thunderbolt aloft in his right hand. (British Museum, London; PS 147431)

FIG. 4.7. Battle of the gods and giants, from the Great Altar at Pergamum in Asia Minor, east face, third–second centuries B.C. A giant with snaky tails has seized a god around the waist and bites him on the biceps, while the head of one tail bites the (missing) head, perhaps Ares because of the shield in the lower right corner. In the upper right Heracles, recognizable from the paw of his lionskin cloak, prepares to swing his club. The contorted features and writhing, violent postures are typical of Hellenistic art (compare Fig. 20.4). (Staatliche Museen, Berlin; University of Wisconsin, Madison Photo Archive)

ered genitals and urged on by Gaea, attacked the Olympians in the **Gigantomachy** (jī-gan-**ta**-ma-kē), "Battle of the Giants," hurling rocks and burning trees into the sky. Literary accounts and artistic representations pair individual gods with individual giants. The Giants were shown as enormous and bearded, often with snaky legs and long, disheveled hair (Fig. 4.7). The mortal Heracles, son of Zeus, joined the Olympians in the war, for an oracle declared that the gods could not win without a mortal's assistance. The chronology of the world's childhood is vague, yet Heracles' presence indicates that the Gigantomachy was considerably later than the primordial events of the Titanomachy and the Typhonomachy.

The Giants at last were overcome. Now the three male gods, Zeus, Hades, and Poseidon, cast lots to divide the world between them. Zeus took heaven, Poseidon the gray sea, and Hades the dark mist at the world's end. But the earth and the heights of Olympus were common to all.

PROMINENT THEMES IN THE GREEK CREATION STORY

The Greek story of the creation of the world and of the gods, especially as told by Hesiod, is an example of what we have called divine myth; its subject is the actions of gods and the description of grand events and their consequences. Yet the narrative patterns underlying the story owe much to folktale. Here gods act as ogres (Uranus, Cronus) and tricksters (Cronus, Zeus); goddesses behave as sexual victims (Gaea, Rhea), as dangerous enemies (Gaea), and as beneficent protectors (Gaea, Rhea). Typhoeus is a dragon; Zeus is his killer. Vicious family conflict drives the action: Wife plots against husband (Gaea versus Uranus), son against father (Cronus versus Uranus, Zeus versus Cronus), and father against children (Uranus versus the Titans, Cronus versus the Olympians). Ancient traditional material has been remodeled to make an exciting tale that answers the question, "How did Zeus come to rule the world?"

The universe portrayed by Hesiod is not a static creation, spoken into existence by God once and for all. It comes from successive growth and change, from progressive proliferation and differentiation away from original unity. First was Chaos/Chasm, after which emerged Night and Darkness, primal entities that generate their opposites, Day and Radiance. Then came Gaea/Earth, the first really animate being, female in nature, who nonetheless gave birth asexually to Pontus/Sea and Uranus/Sky. Eros/Love propelled the expanding creation. Later Gaea/Earth had intercourse with her own children, and henceforth, with few exceptions, reproduction is by sexual means.

The Greek cosmogony/theogony is a tale of the gradual ascent to power of male over female. In the beginning was female Gaea/Earth, mother of all; in the end is the male Zeus, ruler of the universe. At the beginning of the evolutionary development, Gaea produced children asexually; at the end, Zeus does the same when Athena springs from his head. For the Greeks it seemed natural to suppose that an orderly universe, like an orderly household or city, would be one that was ruled by a clever and powerful male; after all, this was the social ideal. But the power of Gaea/Earth can never be removed completely: She is the ultimate base on which stands the world.

Gaea, although wife and mother to Uranus/Sky, conspired with her son, clever Cronus, to mutilate Uranus and ruin his power. Uranus was an ogre; he opposed life and the future and cared only for his own lust. Like a hero in folktale, wily Cronus sprang from an ambush to destroy the dragon who sexually threatened the woman. Cronus castrated his father with a steel sickle, a special weapon of the sort folktale heroes need to overcome their enemies. As in so many folktales, the story is set within the contradictions of the human family: A father begets a son in the hope that one day the son may replace him, not destroy him!

Uranus was a bad father and deserved his fate, but Cronus was hardly better. Uranus kept his children in Gaea's womb; the cannibal Cronus swallowed them into his own stomach (the Greek word *nêdus* means both "womb" and "stomach"). Uranus and Gaea then worked together, advising Rhea how to outwit her husband. The once clever Cronus himself became a stupid ogre who mistook a stone for his own child. Rhea, a doublet of Gaea, carried her child to a cave, earth's womb, on the island of Crete, where a new champion, the clever Zeus, grew to manhood.

In the detail of Zeus's rearing on Crete, folktale is influenced by historical religion. On Crete flourished an ancient cult of a young male god, perhaps the consort of a mother-goddess worshiped deep in Cretan caves. When the invading Indo-Europeans encountered the male god of the indigenous inhabitants of Crete, they seem to have identified him with their own male god, Zeus, although as a dying god of nature (see Chapter 7) the Cretan god was utterly unlike the Indo-European god of storm. The Greeks sometimes called him the Cretan Zeus to distinguish him from the Olympian; islanders could point out the tomb of Cretan Zeus. According to Cretan tradition, Rhea handed over the infant Zeus to the Curetes, who did a war dance, loudly banging spears against their bronze shields to hide the infant's cries from Cronus. In historical times, the Curetes on Crete were in fact orgiastic worshipers of a mother-goddess.

The Titans, whatever their actual origins, came in general to represent the untamed forces of nature. Their offspring were the seas, rivers, and heavenly bodies. Clever Zeus, the fully anthropomorphized god of historical Greece, could not defeat them unassisted, by raw force alone. Forging a new system of power, he acted as statesman, righting the wrongs of the past and releasing the Cyclopes and the Hecatonchires from Tartarus, where Cronus had imprisoned them. The Cyclopes became Zeus's armorers, who made the thunderbolt. The Hecatonchires served as his mercenary soldiers, and only with their assistance was he able to cast the Titans into darkness and overwhelm Typhoeus.

The ambivalence of the female is prominent in the Greek story. Gaea at first favors progressive change, then, resentful of the Titans' overthrow, opposes it. She bears Typhoeus, enemy of the new world order. Later, Gaea/Earth also incites the Giants to revolt. Although born of Uranus' blood, the Giants are her children and represent her interests, in this case malevolent.

In Apollodorus' version of the Typhoeus story, Zeus's special weapon, following the folktale pattern, is the same steel sickle with which Cronus castrated Uranus. Like many folktale heroes, in this version Zeus is temporarily overcome. Paralyzed, without sinews, he lies in the darkness of the womblike, tomblike cave. Thanks to Hermes, the messenger god who connects this world with the next, and Aegipan, god of natural vitality, Zeus returns to life. He cannot quite kill Typhoeus, any more than he can overcome Gaea/Earth herself, so he imprisons him beneath Mount Etna, whence emanates irresistible volcanic fire. In Hesiod's version, Typhoeus is still present in our world in the violent winds that rock the sea.[8] As his reward for overcoming the dragon, Zeus becomes king, takes a wife, and bears many children.

In the cycle of Greek creation myths, the motifs of separation, succession, and dragon combat are ingeniously melded to tell the story of the fashioning of the ordered and diverse world from the disordered and homogeneous one that preceded it.

EASTERN CREATION STORIES

Scholars once thought that the story of Zeus's war against the Titans must reflect a historical conflict between the Greek Indo-European invaders with their new gods

---

[8]Our word *typhoon*, really from the Chinese term *tai fung*, "violent wind," derives its form by analogy with Typhon (= Typhoeus). *Typhus* and *typhoid fever* also come from the Greek monster, for both arouse a wild delirium in the patient.

(especially Zeus) on one side against the indigenous peoples with their (mostly female) deities on the other. However, the recovery of ancient Near Eastern myths leaves no doubt that the story of war in heaven and other features of the Greek account are taken from earlier Eastern cultures; the story's origin is not historical (at least not in Greece). We are not sure how Eastern stories crossed barriers of language and culture to enter Greece, but they did.

The Babylonian *Enuma Elish*

The best example of Mesopotamian creation myth is the Babylonian poem *Enuma Elish,* "When on High," recited on the fourth day of the New Year's festival in Babylon in honor of the god of the city, Marduk. The text reached its present form before 1100 B.C., although it preserves far older material. Telling of the first days of the creation, the story had the magical power to renew the world at the critical joining of one year with the next. There is little drama or suspense; it is our best example from Mesopotamia of a myth we know to have been told during a religious ritual.

The poem opens with the gods of the primordial waters, male Apsu, fresh water, and female **Tiamat** (tē-a-mat), salt water, mingled together in an indeterminate mass:

> When on high heaven was not yet named,
> nor was the hard ground below called by name—
> there was nothing but primordial Apsu, the begetter,
> and Mother Tiamat, she who gave birth to everything.
> The waters of Tiamat and Apsu were mingled together as a single body.
> No one had woven a reed hut. There was no marsh land.
> It was a time before the gods had come into being,
> or were called by name, or their destinies determined—
> this was when the gods took form within them.°
> Lahmu and Lahamu° were brought forth, called by their names
> Before they had grown.
> Anshar and Kishar° took form, greater than the others.
> They made the days long, added on years.°
> Anu was their heir, rival to his own fathers.

. . . within them: That is, the waters of Apsu and Tiamat. To name is to create, for the essence of a creature resides in the word that designates it.   *Lahmu and Lahamu:* Perhaps "Mr. and Mrs. Mud," the primordial slime.   *Anshar and Kishar:* Probably Heaven and Earth, Up and Down, to judge from the roots *An* ("sky") and *Ki* ("earth")   *. . . added on years:* Time passed.

With Lahmu and Lahamu, "mud," the creation began even as Gaea, "Earth," appeared out of Chaos. From Apsu and Tiamat came four generations of gods, **Anu** (Sky, = Sumerian An) and **Ea** (ē-a) (= Sumerian Enki) among them. Eros, who is attraction or the notion of first motion, accompanied Gaea as she emerged from Chaos, and in *Enuma Elish* the new gods came together to dance. Their activity and noise disturbed Apsu's rest, and with his officer Mummu, Apsu went to Tiamat to complain:

I cannot stand their ways!
The day brings no respite, and the night no rest.
I will ruin their ways and drive them away!
Then may peace come again, and sleep!

Although the loving mother Tiamat vigorously opposed Apsu's wish to destroy their troublesome offspring, Mummu urged it, and his advice so pleased Apsu that Apsu's face grew radiant and he kissed his officer.

When the younger gods heard of the plan to destroy them, they fell into a panic. Only Ea, "who knows everything, the skillful, the wise," kept his head. He cast a spell over Apsu and Mummu, sending them into a deep sleep. He killed Apsu, strung a rope through Mummu's nose, and imprisoned him. On top of the dead Apsu, Ea built his house, into which he moved with his wife. She soon gave birth to the real hero of the poem, **Marduk,** god of Babylon, in every way an extraordinary being:

He sucked from the teats of goddesses.
His nurse filled him with glory.
His body was charming, sparkling his eyes.
He was born fully developed, mighty from the start.
When his father Ea looked upon him,
he rejoiced and beamed; his heart was gladdened.
He made him perfect, a god twice over.
Exalted above them all, he was superlative in every way.
His limbs were well made, impossible to describe,
beyond comprehension, hard to perceive.
Four were his eyes, four were his ears.
When he opened his mouth, fire shot forth.
His four ears were huge,
his four eyes saw all that was.
His limbs were immense, he was enormously handsome.

His grandfather Anu was so proud that he fashioned four winds for Marduk's plaything. The winds blew constantly to and fro, once more stirring the waters of Tiamat, and again the older gods complained. Tiamat, who earlier defended the younger gods, was now (like erratic Gaea in the Greek story) determined to destroy them, and she begot an army of monsters to help her:

She set up the snake with horns, the dragon, the lahmu-hero,°
the lion demon, rabid dog, and scorpion-man,
savage ûmu-devils,° fishman, bullman.

lahmu-hero: It is not clear what is meant.   *ûmu:* A word of unknown meaning.

To lead the horde, she chose a new husband, Kingu, "her only lover." She placed him on a throne and armed him with the mysterious Tablet of Destiny, which gave power over the universe.

When Ea heard of the fresh preparations, he lost his nerve and ran to the god Anshar. In consternation Anshar bit his lip and slapped his thigh and demanded that Ea war against Tiamat. At this point the tablet is broken, but apparently Ea was unsuccessful, for when the text resumes, it is Anu who attacks Tiamat. But she put her hand against him, and Anu ran away in terror. At the moment of crisis, the gods lost all hope and sank into despair, as they do in many Mesopotamian myths.

Then Anshar remembered Marduk, whose moment had come. He kissed Marduk on the lips, and Marduk agreed to fight Tiamat and her army of monsters, but only on condition that he be given absolute power as reward:

> "My word alone shall establish fate, not yours!
> What I fashion shall last forever!
> What my lips decree, shall never be changed, never altered!"

Hastily, the gods agreed.

> They gave him a scepter, a throne, a royal robe.
> They gave him relentless weapons to overwhelm the foe:
> "Go slice the throat of Tiamat!
> Let the winds bring her blood, tidings of joy!"

Taking bow and arrows, a mace and net, with lightning flashing before him, with seven winds at his back, Marduk mounted his chariot—the image of a thunderstorm. The chariot's team were named Killer, Ruthless, Racer, and Flyer, and their teeth dripped poison. Radiant with power, he roared down the road toward Tiamat, but when he saw her, he (like Ea and Anu before him) lost his nerve and had to endure the taunts of Tiamat. But he soon regained his courage and rebuked her, so that she was seized by uncontrollable rage, let out a roar, and attacked:

> Tiamat and Marduk, the wisest god, locked together.
> They tangled in the hand-to-hand, clasped in battle.
> Marduk spread out his net to catch her.
> The storm that followed behind him, he splashed in her face.
> When Tiamat opened wide her mouth to swallow him,
> he drove down the storm so she could not close her lips.
> The savage winds swelled her belly,
> her body puffed up and her mouth opened wide.
> He fired his arrow, it burst her belly,
> carved through her guts and split the heart,
> wrecked and extinguished her life.
> He threw down the corpse and trod upon it.

The army of monsters tried to flee, but Marduk caught them in his net, fixed them with nose-ropes, and bound their arms. He imprisoned Kingu and took control of the Tablet of Destiny. Then (Fig. 4.8)

> Marduk trod on Tiamat's legs.
> With his mighty mace he smashed her skull.
> When he had sliced open the arteries of her blood,
> the North Wind bore it to places unknown.
> When the gods saw what had happened, they were joyous, radiant.
> They brought gifts of homage to Marduk.
> But the lord paused to look at her corpse,
> so that he might divide the monster and fashion clever things.

FIG. 4.8. Bronze statuette of a four-faced god who steps on a ram, from Ischali, c. 1800 B.C. The god wears a long, flounced dress and carries in his right hand a sickle-ax. The god's identity is unknown, but some think he may be Marduk with the ram Tiamat, embodiment of chaos.
(Oriental Institute of the University of Chicago; A7119)

He split her like a clamshell into two parts.
Half he raised up high, calling it sky.
He lowered the bar and set up watchmen.
He commanded them never to let her waters escape.

On top of the corpse Marduk built a large temple and cult centers for Anu, Enlil, and Ea. He made the constellations, set up the calendar, put the north star in its place, and brought forth the sun and moon. From Tiamat's spittle he made the surging clouds, the wind, the rain; from her poison, the billowing fog. He heaped a mountain over her head and pierced her eyes, from which flow the rivers Tigris and Euphrates. Other mountains he heaped over her breasts, then bent her tail into the sky to make the Milky Way. With her crotch he held up the sky.

Marduk returned him in triumph, delivered the Tablet of Destiny to Anu, and presented his captives before the gods. He washed off the gore of battle, dressed in royal attire, and sat on a high throne to receive homage from the gods. He proclaimed that he would build a great temple, a luxurious dwelling for himself and for all the gods, when they came to visit. He announced another plan:

"I will mash blood together and bones
and make a primeval man: Man shall be his name.
His purpose will be to serve the gods,
that they might be at ease!"

He brought the rebel Kingu before the assembly:

> They tied him up and dragged him in before Ea.
> They carried out the execution, severed his arteries.
> From his blood they made man.
> Ea made labor to be man's lot, but the gods he set free.

Marduk then divided the gods into those who live in the sky and those beneath the earth. The grateful gods eagerly began to build the palace of which Marduk had spoken, and after two years they completed the great ziggurat (an artificial mountain) of Babylon. A banquet was held and Marduk proclaimed lord of the universe. The story ends with a long list of the fifty names of Marduk (more than one fourth of the total poem), with detailed explanations of each name. In this way was the world made, and the same order of kingship was established among the gods as in Babylon itself.

In *Enuma Elish* and other Mesopotamian myths, the original creative element is watery, feminine, and ambivalent, both life giving and life destroying. Above the earth the waters may descend as life-giving rain, but below the earth they bound the land of the dead. The same ambivalence as that of the original, primeval element of the universe is displayed by female deities, who both nurture and destroy (see the story of Inanna and Dumuzi in Chapter 9). The dangerous, chaotic waters may be represented by a monster or dragon who is overcome by a hero who fashions the cosmos. There is a complex association between water, chaos, monsters, and death. Dragon combat and cosmogony can be one and the same. The hero establishes the world order and his own permanent reign over the corpse of the monster.

Mesopotamian divine myths, like Hesiod's story, envision the formation and organization of the world and of human society as process and change. The world has not always been the way it is now; its initial unity in the primeval waters has moved to diversity. Creation arises not from nothing but, as in Hesiod, from a primordial chaos by means of sexual reproduction and a series of successively more powerful generations. A younger generation opposes, overcomes, and controls or destroys an older, until the present world order comes into being.

The Hittite *Kingship in Heaven* and the *Song of Ullikummi*

Other Eastern myths important to the later classical tradition come from the mighty Indo-European **Hittites,** who ruled the central Anatolian plain in the Late Bronze Age. Their powerful capital was near modern Ankara, and their art and culture were strong well into the eighth century B.C. in what is today southeastern Turkey and northern Syria. Only small portions of a poem called *Kingship in Heaven* survive, but the myth has clear relevance to the Greek cosmogony:

> In earlier years, Alalush was king in heaven.
> Alalush sits there on his throne.
> And strong Anush [= Anu], first of the gods, is his servant.
> He bows to him at his feet.

5   He always gives him great cups
       to drink into his hand.
           For nine years of rule, Alalush was king in heaven.
       After nine years, Anush made war against Alalush.
       He defeated Alalush
10   who fled under the dark earth,
       but Anush sat on the throne.
       Anush is there on his throne
       and strong Kumarbi always gives him food to eat
       and he always bows at his feet
15   and always gives him great cups into his hand.
           For nine years Anush ruled as king in heaven.
       In the ninth year, Anush made war with Kumarbi.
       The eyes of Kumarbi he could not defeat.
       He slipped from Kumarbi's hand and fled.
20   Anush the eagle flew in the sky
       and Kumarbi closed in behind him,
       grabbed his feet
       and pulled him down from the sky.
           He [Kumarbi] bit off his genitals.
25   His sperm went into Kumarbi's stomach.
       He swallowed Anush's sperm
       and was happy and he laughed.
           And Anush turned back to him
       and began to speak to Kumarbi:
30   "You are really pleased about your stomach.
       It swallowed my sperm.
       You should not rejoice!
       I have placed a burden in your middle.
       First, I have made you pregnant with the storm god;
35   second, with the river Aranzakh°
       third, with the heavy Tasmishu.°
       And I placed the burden, the terrible gods into your middle!
       You will perish, hitting your head on the mountain Tashshu!"
       When Anush finished speaking, he disappeared.
40   Then Kumarbi went high into the heavens.
       He spit from his mouth.
       The stricken king spit from his mouth upwards.
       That which had been ingested, Kumarbi spit out.

35. *Aranzakh:* The Tigris.   36. *Tasmishu:* An attendant of the storm god.

There the tablet breaks off. When it resumes, we learn that Anush argued with the storm god, who was still within the body of Kumarbi, over how the storm god should escape from Kumarbi's body. Kumarbi felt dizzy and asked Aya (= Ea) for something to eat. He ate something that hurt his mouth. At last the storm god, warned not to come forth through various openings, especially not through Kumarbi's anus, came out of the "good place," apparently Kumarbi's penis. The rest is lost, but somehow the storm god escaped from Kumarbi's body, overthrew him, and became king of heaven.

Another Hittite tale, the *Song of Ullikummi,* tells us more about the celestial kingship and Kumarbi's struggle for ascendancy. Kumarbi planned destruction for the storm god Teshub, who seems to be Kumarbi's own son. Kumarbi "took wisdom unto his mind," rose from his chair, took a staff, put sandals on his feet, and set out to a place called Cool Pond. There Kumarbi had intercourse with a huge rock, "five times he possessed it, and again ten times he possessed it."

The rock became pregnant and gave birth to a stone child. The child was placed on Kumarbi's knees and Kumarbi named him Ullikummi (= "Destroyer of Kummiya," the city of Teshub). Kumarbi then delivered the child to Ubelluri, a giant who, like the Greek Atlas, carried heaven and earth. Ubelluri placed the child on his shoulder. Soon Ullikummi, who grew an acre each month, was so big that the sea came only to his waist and his head reached the sky. Teshub learned of the monster and, to get a better look, ascended Mount Casius in northwestern Syria. Realizing the danger, he marshaled his forces and attacked. Teshub was temporarily defeated, but Aya obtained the very tool by which heaven and earth had first been separated and with it cut away Ullikummi from Ubelluri, reducing Ullikummi's power. Teshub took heart and mounted his chariot, prepared to fight again. Here the tablet breaks off, but certainly Teshub, highest god of the Hittite pantheon, did overcome the dragon Ullikummi to become king of heaven.

Observations: The Succession Myth in Hesiod and the Near East

In *Enuma Elish,* first came a theogony, the generation of Apsu and Tiamat and their descendants. These new gods bring a principle of movement into the world (their dance), which contrasts sharply with the older forces of chaos, which stand for inactivity and inertia (symbolized by their desire to sleep). The primordial gods' resistance to change leads to a battle in which newer gods overthrow the older. This succession motif, as we have seen, is important in Greek myth as well.

In the first round of the battle of the gods, the wise and clever Ea overcomes wicked Apsu by a spell; his magical power resides in the spoken word. Ea's wisdom and cleverness are contrasted with Apsu's brutish lust to destroy, a common folktale motif; the dragon-slayer is clever and tricky, his opponent dull and stupid. Tiamat, like Gaea, manages to be both beneficent and malevolent. She first opposes her husband's destructive designs, but when Apsu is killed she herself becomes the destructive monster. Later, in a repetition of the succession motif, Tiamat is destroyed by her grandson Marduk, who becomes ruler of the world.

The Hittite *Kingship in Heaven* is similarly based on the succession motif: First Alalush was king, then Anush, then Kumarbi. The *Song of Ullikummi* carries the conflict one generation further: Now Kumarbi must be overthrown. To defend his power, Kumarbi, like Tiamat, begets a terrible monster with which the storm god Teshub must contend for supremacy.

In both *Enuma Elish* and Hesiod's *Theogony* the first generation of gods is made up of primal pairs: Apsu, the male sweet waters, and Tiamat, the female salt waters, and Uranus and Gaea. The fathers Apsu and Uranus hate the first children, who are begotten within the mother. In an initial round of conflict the clever sons Ea and

The Biblical Creation Story

For many Westerners, the best-known story of creation is that reported in the biblical book of Genesis (1.1–2.4a). The story is so familiar that many people find it hard to hear the words in their original meanings. But a close examination of the Hebrew text's opening lines reveals some striking parallels with the creation myths of ancient Mesopotamia:

> In the beginning, when God created the heaven and the earth, the earth was a formless and unbounded mass, with darkness covering its fluid chaos, and with a wind° from God sweeping over it. God said, "Let there be light!" and there was light.° God saw the goodness of the light and separated it from the darkness; the light he called° "day" and the darkness "night." Thus evening and morning came into being, a complete day. Then God said, "Let there be a partition° in the middle of the watery chaos, spreading out to separate the waters." So it came about, and the partition divided the waters below it from those above; God called the partition "sky." The evening came and the morning, making up the second day.

GENESIS 1.1–8.

wind: The word in Hebrew is *ruach,* which, like Greek *pneuma* and Latin *spiritus,* may mean air in motion, breath, psychological power.   *light*: Light is what makes it possible for one to distinguish things.   *called:* The Hebrew word for name is broader than the English; it connotes "essence," "identity," "power." Later in Genesis (1.19–20), God gives Adam the task of naming the animals: "and whatever he should call them was to be its name."   *partition:* Literally, "something solid." Except in religious usage, the English "firmament" is nearly obsolete.

The Hebrew text of Genesis, which did not reach its final form until perhaps 400 B.C., is an edited account based on several earlier sources, some of which used different names for God. From these different sources Hebrew scholars have created a text suitable to the doctrinal needs of a monotheistic religion. The Hebrew account differs from the Mesopotamian in its notion of a single transcendent God, with no rivals, who stands before and beyond the creation, but is similar to the Mesopotamian myth in its picture of a universe beginning in a watery mass that is split into an above and a below, Heaven and Earth. In the Mesopotamian and Hittite accounts, the great elements of nature are deified, whereas in the Hebrew account the powers that made the world are stripped of personal names and attributes. So An/Anu/Anush becomes simply "sky"; Enlil/Marduk/Teshub, god of storm, becomes the "wind" that moves across the water; Ki is the dry land; and Enki/Ea is the waters from which the dry land is separated, the earthly waters as opposed to those that existed before the creation. For centuries Christian theologians have debated whether creation took place *ex nihilo,* "out of nothing," or out of something formless (not unlike the modern notion of matter in a state of entropy), but the Hebrew text, like its Mesopotamian forebears, clearly envisions creation as a process of separation.

In *Enuma Elish* the primordial waters are personified as the great dragon Tiamat, whom the creator of the cosmos must overcome. Although not a part of the biblical creation story, this myth is dimly reflected in other biblical passages: "In that day the Lord with his hard and great and strong sword will punish Leviathan [= "twister," "coiler"] the fleeing serpent, Leviathan the twisting serpent, and he will slay the dragon that is in the sea" (Isaiah 27.1). Ullikummi, too, stands in the sea, whom Teshub attacks with a special cutting tool—the very one by which Heaven was first separated from Earth.

Cronus overthrow their fathers. In a second round of conflict, gods of the third generation—Marduk and the storm god Zeus—revolt against an earlier divine generation. Terrible monsters are overcome: Tiamat and her army in *Enuma Elish,* and the Titans, Typhoeus, and the Giants, all children of Gaea, in the Greek story. The storm god is then made king. Mesopotamian and Greek myths alike report a cosmic history that begins with mighty powers of nature and ends in the organization of the universe as a monarchic, patriarchal state. Both mythical traditions make use of the motifs of succession and dragon combat.

Similarities between the Hittite and Greek myths are equally striking (Chart 4.4). According to *Kingship in Heaven,* first a primordial god (Alalush) was ruler, then the sky god (Anush) ruled, then another god (Kumarbi), and then, probably, the storm god (Teshub). The same sequence of generations appears in Hesiod: First came Chaos (= Alalush?), then Uranus/Sky (= Anush), then Cronus (= Kumarbi), then the storm god Zeus (= Teshub). Both Anu and Uranus were castrated by their sons, and gods were born from the severed organs. As long as heaven and earth are locked in sexual embrace, forming a solid whole, there is no space within which the created world can appear. Castration was a real practice imposed on enemies taken in war, but in the logic of the myth castration is separation, and separation is creation. Both Kumarbi and Cronus have children within themselves. The children of each, Teshub and Zeus, both storm gods, overcome their fathers to win victory in heaven.

According to the Hittite *Song of Ullikummi,* the Hittite storm god Teshub must defend his reign against a dragon of chaos, Ullikummi, just as Zeus takes on the formidable Typhoeus. The Hittite Aya/Ea uses the weapon by which heaven and earth were separated to cut the enormous Ullikummi, born from a rock, away from Ubel-

Hittite *Kingship in Heaven*	Hesiod's *Theogony*
Alalush	Chaos
↓	↓
Anush (= Sumerian Anu, "Sky"); castrated by his son	Uranus ("Sky"); castrated by his son
↓	↓
Kumarbi	Cronus
↓	↓
Teshub (storm god)	Zeus (storm god)

CHART 4.4. Hittite and Greek Theogonies Compared

luri, the giant who holds up the world; Zeus too uses a special weapon against Ty-phoeus, the same sickle by which Cronus castrated Uranus. Teshub takes his stand on Mount Casius in Syria to view Ullikummi, the same mountain on which the Ty-phonomachy takes place.

There are differences in detail and profound differences in tone between the Eastern and the Greek stories: The writing systems of the Mesopotamians and Hit-tites, unlike the Greek alphabet, were unable to record the suppleness and color of spoken language. Nonetheless, there are enough similarities to remove all doubt that transmission somehow took place. The Greek cosmogonic traditions are old and have been passed across linguistic, cultural, and racial lines. Greek cosmogonic myth partly reflects the Greeks' own attitudes, but its basic structure, and many of its cultural assumptions, come from non-Greek peoples. In trying to understand Greek myth, we are also trying to understand our much older precursors.

KEY TERMS

cosmogony, 72	Rhea, 76	Prometheus, 85
theogony, 72	Helius, 77	Atlas, 88
Chaos, 72	Eos, 77	Typhoeus, 88
Gaea, 72	Phaëthon, 78	succession myth, 90
Uranus, 72	Tithonus, 79	Metis, 91
Eros, 74	Erinyes, 80	Gigantomachy, 92
Moerae, 74	Giants, 80	Tiamat, 95
Titans, 75	Sphinx, 82	Anu, 95
Cyclopes, 75	Cerberus, 83	Ea, 95
Hecatonchires, 75	Chimera, 83	Marduk, 96
Cronus, 75	Titanomachy, 85	Hittites, 99
Oceanus, 76		

FURTHER READING

Athanassakis, Apostolos, *Hesiod: Theogony, Works and Days* (Baltimore, 1983). Good translation with valuable notes.

Black, Jeremy, and Anthony Green, *Gods, Demons and Symbols of Ancient Mesopotamia* (Austin, Tex., 1992). Excellent compact reference to images and names.

Brown, Norman O., *Theogony. Hesiod* (New York, 1953). A lucid prose translation prefaced by one of the best essays on the *Theogony* in English.

Caldwell, Richard S., *Hesiod's Theogony*, translated, with introduction, commentary, and interpretive essay (Cambridge, Mass., 1987). Readable, literate translation with comprehensive commentary and general interpretation (but along Freudian lines).

Hoffner, Harry A., and Gary M. Beckman, eds., *Hittite Myths* (New York, 1998). Up-to-date treatment.

Kramer, S. N., ed., *Mythologies of the Ancient World* (New York, 1961). Contains a valuable essay on Hittite mythology by Hans G. Göterbock, as well as other useful essays on Egyptian,

Mesopotamian, Canaanite, Greek, Indian, Persian, Chinese, Japanese, and Mexican myth.

Lamberton, Robert, *Hesiod* (New Haven, Conn., 1988). A compact survey of the poet, his times, and his work.

Macqueen, J. G., *The Hittites and Their Contemporaries in Asia Minor,* revised edition (London, 1986). Best general survey.

Penglase, C., *Greek Myths and Mesopotamia* (New York, 1994). Parallels and influence in the Homeric Hymns and Hesiod.

West, M. L., *Theogony* (Oxford, U.K., 1966) and *Works and Days* (Oxford, U.K., 1978). These scholarly editions of the Greek text contain invaluable introductory essays and commentary on all aspects of the poems and their mythical background.

CHAPTER 5

MYTHS OF CREATION
THE ORIGINS OF MORTALS

What does ravaging time not ruin?
The age of our fathers, worse than the one before,
brought forth ourselves, worse men than our fathers,
who will beget offspring more vicious still.

HORACE, *Odes* III 6.45−48

WHERE DO HUMAN BEINGS COME FROM? What sets them apart from other creatures? Why is it their fate to labor, suffer, and die? The myths of the ancient Greeks and Romans offered answers to these questions. Certain elements of the stories they told about human origins and the human condition are strikingly similar to corresponding stories from ancient Mesopotamia and the Bible. As we will see, many Greek myths were shaped in important ways by contact with the ancient Near East, just as the myths of creation examined in Chapter 4 were. Still, the tales presented by Hesiod, Aeschylus, and Ovid reflect the distinctive characteristics of the Greek (and Roman) experience of human life.

PROMETHEUS, MAKER OF MORTALS

The Greek tradition shows curiously little interest in the ultimate origins of mortals. Hesiod offers no explanation at all, although he does discuss other matters pertaining to the early life of human beings, as we will see later in this chapter. Scattered references in later authors often are contradictory. Sometimes Zeus himself is identified as the creator of mortals, sometimes various gods working together. But most often the maker of human beings is said to be **Prometheus** (prō-**mē**-thŭs), the Titan who took Zeus's side in the battle against his brother and sister Titans.

Like Cronus, and like Zeus himself, Prometheus was known especially for being clever, the inventor of many things, including the race of mortals. He was said to have fashioned human beings from mud and water or from mud combined with wind. The Roman poet Ovid gives the fullest surviving version of the story. After describing the emergence of the world from Chaos, Ovid tells us that Prometheus made the human race by mixing primeval earth and water. Because the earth contained divine seed, the human was a superior being:

[76]   An animal blessed with a higher soul was still needed,
        one abler to reason more deeply, one able to govern the others.
        So man was born. Perhaps the maker of all things° produced him
        of heavenly seed, in hopes of creating a yet better world.
80   Or perhaps the newborn world, freshly set off from the ether,
        still retained a few seeds of the heaven from which it had come.
        The son of Iapetus° fashioned earth and water commingled
        into the image of gods, who are rulers of all things created.
        The other beasts, four-footed, gaze at the earth, looking downward;
85   but man was given a posture which forces his eyes to the heavens,
        walking erect and lifting his sight to the stars in their courses.

                                        OVID, *Metamorphoses* (1.76–86)

78. *maker of all things:* Jupiter.   82. *son of Iapetus:* Prometheus.

We have already seen (Chapter 4) how in the *Enuma Elish* human beings were made from the blood of Kingu as servants to the gods, which is why humans are so disposed to wickedness and why they must work constantly. A related Eastern story also told how humans were made from mud or clay. Hence our bodies turn to dust when we die, a version that entered the biblical narrative of how "the Lord God formed man of dust from the ground and breathed into his nostrils the breath of life; and man became a living being" (Genesis 2.4). But the story is far older than the Bible.

The Sumerian Creation of Man from Mud

A Sumerian poem too fragmentary to quote presents our earliest known example of this myth, from the third millennium B.C. The gods did not have enough to eat, especially after the creation of the female deities, who consumed more than their share. The gods complained bitterly. **Enki,** the clever god, might have helped, but he was sound asleep in the *apsu* (here = "the abyss"). At length the goddess Nammu, who like Tiamat represents the primeval sea, aroused him. Enki instructed **Ki,** "Earth,"[1] and together they fashioned servants of clay to provide for the gods' needs—the prototypes of ordinary humans.

[1]She is called Ninmah, "exalted lady," in the text.

To celebrate the happy event, a great feast was held. Enki and Ki became uproariously drunk and competed in a contest of creation. Ki pinched off clay from the edge of the abyss and fashioned six more humans, but they were freaks, each with some defect: a woman who could not bear children and a being without sexual organs (a eunuch). Enki was challenged to declare their "fates," that is, to find a place for them in the social order, which he did in every case.

Enki now proposed that they switch roles, that he do the creating and let mother Ki define the "fates." We cannot read his first effort, for the text is damaged, but Enki's second creation was a creature called "my day is far off," a very old man. Enki's freak was so wretched that it could not talk, eat, stand, or sit. Ki tried to speak to him, but he could not speak; she offered him bread, but he could not take it. She upbraided Enki, but he only laughed and reminded her how he was able to cope with *her* freaks. The exasperated Ki cursed Enki, and there the text breaks off.

The story explains the origin of ordinary human beings; a creature so made and destined to serve as slave of the gods can never hope for happiness. It also explains the origin of defective humans, some of whom could be accommodated in Sumerian society (Ki's freaks) and others who had no place in it (Enki's freak). Such deformed humans were not part of the original plan but were created as the aftermath of a drunken party and an irresponsible wager between two gods.

The story seems to distinguish between the superior creative power of Ki, whose creatures, although freaks, had some place in the world order, and the inferior power of Enki, whose creatures were without hope. The story may embody an element of the male's fear and envy of the female's evidently superior ability to create life. Although Ki is the maker of defective humans, her creatures receive their "fates"; they have a function in the social order, whereas Enki's creature is so deformed that it is not even human.

PROMETHEUS, PROTECTOR OF MORTALS

Prometheus had much in common with his Eastern predecessor Enki, and in the classical tradition he was the creator of mortals. He was also their protector, an important figure to modern European culture. His lineage was as lofty as that of Zeus, for his father Iapetus was a Titan, brother of Cronus. Prometheus' essential quality is encoded in his name, which means "forethinker," like a character from folklore. His name has the same linguistic root as *Metis,* "Cleverness," Zeus's first consort, and points to his inventive intelligence. Prometheus is the folktale trickster who delights in outwitting those who appear more powerful. In a contrast typical of folklore, "Forethinker" has a brother "Afterthinker": Epimetheus, or "Dummy."

In Chapter 4, we looked at Hesiod's story of Zeus's rise to power. Through violence and deceit, Zeus overcame the older generation of gods and became the ruler of the universe. He remained on guard, however, against anyone who might usurp his power, and he was particularly jealous and fearful of Prometheus, as we see in the following tale told by Hesiod about an incident at Meconê (me-**kō**-nē, another name for Sicyon in the northern Peloponnesus). We can see why Zeus was so nervous about this mortal-loving, dangerous being:

[535] For once, when gods and mortals were gathered to feast at Meconê,
Prometheus, trying to hoodwink great Zeus's wits and attention,
had cheerfully butchered and served up the succulent flesh of an ox.
To the others, gods and men, he handed the meat in due portions,
and sweetbreads, dripping with suet, wrapped in the outermost layer
540 of the ox's stomach, a haggis. But the white bones he slyly concealed
in shining fat, and to Zeus he presented the neatly wrapped bundle.
Pausing a moment, the father of mortals and gods asked politely,
  "Son of Iapetus, you are surely the cleverest man now alive,
but haven't you split the portions as unequally as can be?"
545 So spoke the inscrutable Zeus; to him Prometheus answered,
assuming a treacherous smile, "O Zeus, the noblest and greatest
of all the eternal gods, pick whichever your heart may desire."
This was only deceit. But Zeus, unchanging of purpose,
saw through the trick at once, and planned in his vengeful spirit
550 a terrible future for mortal men, one they could never evade.
He took the white suet in his hands, but within him his heart raged with anger,
as he saw that the tempting outside held the ox's white bones beneath.
And ever since then, men of every race on the face of the earth
burn the white bones on the altar in sacrifice to the immortals.

HESIOD, Theogony (535–557)

The pile of glistening fat was more appetizing than the repulsive stomach, and Zeus accepted the fat and the bones hidden beneath. For this reason, at a sacrifice the Greeks ate the meat but burned the bones to the gods: It is an etiological myth to explain a detail of Greek sacrifice. Hesiod excuses Zeus's stupidity by explaining that he had really seen through the trick and made the wrong choice to justify the pain he was planning to inflict on humans. In an earlier version, however, we cannot doubt that Zeus was the stupid ogre, as gullible as his father, Cronus, who could not distinguish a stone wrapped in swaddling clothes from a live baby.

Zeus was so angered by what happened at Meconê that, to punish Prometheus' favorites, he removed fire from the trees where it had lurked before, available to mortals when lightning struck or when branches, rubbing against one another, burst into flame. Mortals who had learned to sustain themselves by eating cooked meat now must starve. But Prometheus pitied his beloved mortals and stole fire from heaven by hiding it in a fennel stalk, a thick plant stem with a soft inflammable pith and a hard fire-resistant coat, used in early times to transport live coals. Ever since, human beings have enjoyed the permanent possession of fire, although only constant labor at gathering fuel could maintain it. After the incident at Meconê, human life was one of unremitting labor.

Zeus now turned on the Titan himself, who twice had deceived him, who even threatened his rule. Zeus ordered Strength (*Kratos*) and Violence (*Bia*), children of the underworld river Styx, to bind Prometheus to a pillar in the Caucasus Mountains (Fig. 5.1):

[521] He bound Prometheus the schemer in inescapable fetters,
a torment to bear, and through them he drove a mighty stone pylon,
and sent a long-winged eagle to gnaw his incorruptible liver.

FIG. 5.1. The punishment of the Titans Atlas and Prometheus on a Spartan cup from the sixth century B.C. On the left, Atlas holds up the sky on his shoulders; the snake probably represents the great serpent Ladon, thought to protect the tree of life that grew in the magical Garden of the Hesperides, at the end of the world. Prometheus, in a position like that in which real prisoners were bound, hangs from a pillar while an eagle tears his liver.   (Vatican Museum, Rome; XXXIV-36-15)

By day the bird fed upon it, but each night as much as was replenished
525   as was lost on the day before.

HESIOD, *Theogony* (521–525)

This method of punishment actually existed: Vicious criminals were taken to the boundaries of a territory, stripped naked, nailed to a post, and allowed to die miserably when eaters of carrion consumed their flesh (Jesus, too, was crucified "outside the city"). Prometheus, being immortal, can never die; his liver grows back each day, an image of everlasting intolerable torment. He did it for us. In Aeschylus' play *Prometheus Bound*, the Titan, hanging in his unbreakable bonds, describes the many benefits he conferred on mortals, for which he now suffered:

[442]   Now listen while I tell of mortals' pain,
          how primitive they were till I fired their wits.

445

450

455

460

> I tell you, not from disgust at men, but showing
> how much they owe me. Before then, they had eyes
> that blankly gazed, ears hearing empty sound.
> Shapes in a dream, they blundered through long years;
> they built no house of brick to catch the sun,
> or even of wood, but antlike dwelt in ditches,
> crowding in lightless crannies, with no sign
> to show when winter would come or flowery spring,
> or summer with its crops. Their work was mindless
> till I explained the courses of the stars.
> I taught them mathematics, wisdom's lore,
> and words in letters, of all things remembrancer,
> mother and servant of arts. I was the first
> to harness beasts with saddle, yoke, and chain,
> thus making them inherit mortals' sweat.
> I set the horse, exulting in his reins,
> to draw the car, image of wealthy pride.
> Who before me, pray, made canvas wings
> for sea-battered ships? I was the one
> who found all this for men—but for myself,
> no way to freedom from these pressing toils.

AESCHYLUS, *Prometheus Bound* (442–471)

Ancient myth usually depicts early human beings as having lived in a paradise, now lost, a biblical Eden. The Greeks (and Mesopotamians) also told stories of a better time in the remote past, as we shall see, but as Aeschylus tells it, early humans were rude, witless, savage, and lacking self-consciousness. Prometheus taught them brickmaking, woodworking, the calendar, numbers, writing, animal husbandry, and seafaring. Prometheus boasts of his other contributions:

[476]

480

485

490

> Now hear the rest, and, hearing, wonder more
> at the devices that I planned for men.
> Until my time, whenever men fell ill
> there was no help in diet, potion, ointment,
> or draft; men simply shriveled up and died
> for lack of drugs. I showed them gentle compounds,
> remedies saving men from all disease.
> I ferreted out dark ways of prophecy,
> and was the first to teach the lore of dreams,
> what men would face when they awoke from sleep.
> I taught them to divine from random sounds,
> chance meetings in the road, the swoop of birds;
> some signs are good by nature, some are not;
> I showed men which is which. The ways they live,
> their loves and hates, with whom they flock—these too.
> I showed the art of entrails: were they smooth?
> what color should they have to please the god?
> The liver too: its lobes of checkered beauty.
> By burning joints and haunch, well wrapped in fat,

495   and showing them the unknown signs in flame,
      I set them on the way to prophetic art.
      So much for that. Who before me dared claim
      to show men metals hidden deep in the earth—
      copper and iron, silver, even gold?
500   No one. So, to put it in a word,
      all human arts came from Prometheus.

AESCHYLUS, Prometheus Bound (476–506)

The highest human skills, then, are the gifts of Prometheus: medicine, metal-lurgy, and prophecy from dreams, the shape of intestines, and astronomical phe-nomena. Prometheus is the great culture-bearer. He made human life what it is. (We will see in Chapter 7 that Apollo presides over medicine and prophecy, which Prometheus invented.)

At last, the hero Heracles killed the devouring eagle and freed the Titan. Zeus did not object, for Prometheus had by then done Zeus a great favor. When an ora-cle declared that a child greater than its father would be born to a certain woman, only Prometheus knew that the oracle referred to the Nereid Thetis, whom Zeus ad-mired. While bound in chains, Prometheus the forethinker revealed the truth, and Zeus compelled Thetis to marry a mortal. This was Peleus, father of Achilles, a son greater indeed than his father.

PANDORA

Zeus punished Prometheus for stealing fire, but he also punished man by imposing what Hesiod regarded as the greatest affliction: woman. Hesiod tells the story in both the *Theogony* and the *Works and Days*. Here is the version from *Works and Days:*

[42]   The gods control our livelihood, holding it back from us mortals.
      You ought to be able to earn enough by a single day's labor
      as now you could in a year—and that in a leisurely fashion.
45   At the end of that day you could hang your rudder to dry in the smoke;
      the ox's toil would be finished, and that of long-suffering mules.
      But Zeus in his irritation holds back that sort of existence,
      because Prometheus fooled him, devising a treacherous scheme.
      Ever since then Zeus has plotted terrible pain for us mortals.
50   Zeus had deprived us of fire. But the noble son of Iapetus,
      to counter the schemes of Zeus, then stole it back for mankind.
      Stealthily hidden, it smoldered away in a dry stalk of fennel.
      The raging Compeller of Clouds upbraided defiant Prometheus:
      "Son of Iapetus, you surely are the slyest schemer of all.
55   You really delighted in swindling me by stealing the fire,
      but soon you will find it a curse to yourself and to men yet to be.
      I shall give them a present to compensate for the fire;
      may they all be merry at heart, forever embracing this horror!"
      With a nasty smile, the father of men and gods
60   told famous Hephaestus to hurry, to knead the water and clay,

Prometheus and the Romantics

In the eighteenth century the established political order of Europe seemed entirely corrupt, and the figure of Prometheus inspired many romantic rebels, especially during and after the French Revolution. The Romantic movement in literature, which these rebels generated, usually is dated from the publication of the *Lyrical Ballads* (1798) of Coleridge and Wordsworth, two of the intellectual heirs of the American and French revolutions. Inspired by their call for a new world order, Englishman Percy Bysshe Shelley (1792–1822), a well-to-do but wild-eyed political and moral radical, wrote a verse drama, *Prometheus Unbound* (1820), a sort of sequel to the *Prometheus Bound* of Aeschylus. Shelley's Titan is a heroic rebel for the sake of humankind; his opponent, Jupiter, is all cruelty and evil. Prometheus is finally relieved from his torments, Jupiter is driven from the throne, and a new era of love begins. The play ends as follows:

> To suffer woes which Hope thinks infinite;
> To forgive wrongs darker than death or night;
>   To defy power which seems omnipotent;
> To love and bear; to hope till Hope creates
> From its own wreck the thing it contemplates;
>   Neither to change, nor falter, nor repent—
> This, like thy glory, Titan, is to be
> Good, great, and joyous, beautiful and free;
> This is alone Life, Joy, Empire, and Victory.

At about the same time Shelley wrote *Prometheus Unbound,* his wife, Mary Wollstonecraft Shelley (daughter of the early feminist author of *The Vindication of the Rights of Women,* 1792) wrote *Frankenstein, or, The Modern Prometheus.* The young student Frankenstein, amoral and irresponsible, creates from bits taken from dissecting rooms and cemeteries a humanlike creature, a *tabula rasa* ("clean palette") ready to accept whatever he is taught by his environment (hence the novel's title, because Frankenstein, like Prometheus, makes a man). First the nameless monster learns love and morality from a family he secretly observes; then he learns to be angry and cruel when, after seeking his maker, he is denied respect and love. He kills Frankenstein's brother and his bride, and finally Frankenstein himself, then disappears.

Other Romantics worked in the same vein, such as Lord Byron (1788–1824), who died of fever while fighting to free Greece from the Turks. Byron's life was a titillating series of scandals. His verse was enormously and deservedly popular, and his death gave the proof that he meant what he had said in a short poem, *Prometheus* (1816):

Thy godlike crime was to be kind,
   to render with thy precepts less
   the sum of human wretchedness,
and strengthen Man with his own mind.
   But, baffled as thou wert from high,
   still, in thy patient energy,
in the endurance and repulse
   of thine impenetrable spirit
which Earth and Heaven could not convulse,
   a mighty lesson we inherit.

The spirit of the Romantic poets is still very much alive in the icons of popular culture. Like Byron and Shelley, rock musicians Janis Joplin, Jim Morrison, Jimi Hendrix, and Kurt Cobain led unconventional lives, inspired millions, and died young. Like their many musical heirs, these modern romantics rebelled against the constraints of convention, finding life's meaning in feeling, not reason.

to add human speech and strength, to give it a goddess's form
and the lovely face of a maiden. Next he ordered Athena
to teach her womanly skill, to weave on a well-built loom.
Aphrodite the golden he told to crown her head with desire,
65   but with heartbreak as well, and all the aching sorrow of love.
Last of all he had Hermes the herald, the killer of Argus,
to give her thievish morals, and to add the soul of a bitch.
Thus he decreed. The immortals obeyed Lord Zeus, son of Cronus.
The famous lame craftsman° molded a lump of clay to an image,
70   the form of a modest girl, as the son of Cronus designed it;
the gray-eyed goddess Athena saw to her clothing and hair.
The Graces and Lady Persuasion decked her with golden jewelry,
to accent the bloom of her flesh, and the fair-haired seasons together
crowned her with flowers of spring.
75   Then the killer of Argus, the guide, the herald of gods,
filled her with lies, with swindles, all sorts of thievish behavior,
and named the woman Pandora,° since all who dwell on Olympus
gave her their gifts—a curse to men who must live by bread.
When the father at last had completed this inescapable trap,
80   he sent the famous killer of Argus, swift messenger of the gods,
to bring her to Epimetheus. But he in his folly ignored
Prometheus' warning, to accept no gift from Zeus of Olympus,
but to send it right back, lest it bring eternal trouble to men.
Epimetheus gladly received her, remembering too late the injunction.
85   Till then the human race had lived on the face of the earth
far from all ills, without torment, pain, or dreadful disease,
that bring men down to their graves. But now the hands of the woman
lifted the jar's° heavy lid and allowed them all to escape,

69. *craftsman:* Hephaestus.   77. *Pandora:* "All-gifted."   88. *jar's:* Hesiod does not tell where she got the jar, but introduces it suddenly into the narrative. Presumably it contained the gifts of the gods mentioned in lines 78–79. Medieval tradition falsely reported it to be a box, hence our expression "to open Pandora's box" for "to let loose a host of troubles."

planning the bitterest sorrows for men. Hope only remained
90 in a prison she could not escape, under the lip of the jar.
She could not fly out, for the woman replaced the great heavy lid.
But the other numberless miseries were spread over all humankind.
The earth is crowded with anguish, equally so the sea;
some pestilence strikes men by day; some comes on as it will
95 in night's quiet dark, its voice being silenced by Zeus's command.

HESIOD, *Works and Days* (42–104)

The folktale of **Pandora,** like the biblical story of Adam and Eve, is etiological to explain the origin of woman, marriage, and suffering in the world: They are all mixed together. Prometheus offered Zeus something that looked good on the outside, covered in glistening fat; within was only bones. Zeus now offered a similar deception to man: It looked good on the outside, but within was filled with "lies, with swindles, all sorts of thievish behavior." Fortunately, we still have Hope (this seems to be his meaning, but how this can be, when Hope was left inside the jar, Hesiod does not explain).

In Aeschylus, Prometheus presents an evolutionary vision of primitive human conditions, which Prometheus himself alleviated by introducing the arts of civilized life. In Hesiod's woman-hating story, life once was good—he is not bothered by the problem of reproduction in a unisexual world—before Pandora opened the jar. Now life is labor, misery, and disease, with death at the end. Oddly, Hesiod does not tell us that Pandora was forbidden to open the jar, perhaps because that was obvious. However, Epimetheus was explicitly told not to accept gifts from the gods, yet he disobeyed (Fig. 5.2). As in the biblical folktale, which also depends on a violated prohibition ("Don't eat from the Tree of the Knowledge of Good and Evil"), the woman is responsible for suffering in the world.

Pandora's descendants, the "race" (*genos*) of women, are a species apart who contribute nothing to the production of food, but like a bottomless pit consume vast quantities of it:

[591] From her descends the ruinous race and tribe of women,
who live as a curse and cause of sorrow to mortal men.
No partners in grim poverty, but only useless excesses.
As bees in their dome-shaped hive faithfully tend to the drones,
595 who take no part in hard work while the workers toil through the day;
till sunset they keep on loading their honey in the white comb,
while the drones sit lazily peering out from the arching hive,
sweeping the fruit of this labor into their own slow bellies°—
just so Zeus, who thunders on high, saw to it that women,
600 curse of us mortal men, should invent work utterly useless.

HESIOD, *Theogony* (591–602)

598. *bellies:* Hesiod did not know that drone bees are males, workers sterile females.

As Prometheus had covered the good part of the sacrifice with the stomach, so is Pandora nothing but a stomach, a consumer of food and wealth. The male is the food producer, the female the unproductive consumer, reminiscent in the

FIG. 5.2. Epimetheus seduced by Pandora on an Attic vase, c. 450 B.C. Zeus, on the far left, leans on his staff of office, while at his command Hermes conveys Pandora to Epimetheus; the two gods, party to a deception, exchange conspiratorial glances. Pandora's negative qualities in fact were the gift of Hermes, god of deception. Hermes holds a flower, sign that a gift is about to be exchanged. Epimetheus, oblivious to the danger, reaches out to Pandora as she rises from the earth, wearing the adornments that Hesiod describes: a lovely garment, veil, and crown. Their eyes lock together, the gaze of sexual attraction symbolized by the Eros above Pandora, who mocks the modesty expected of the bride by throwing wide her arms. The hammer in the hand of Epimetheus usually is associated with Hephaestus and is a puzzle: Perhaps the scene illustrates a lost play by Sophocles (c. 460 B.C.) called *Pandora,* or *The Hammerers.*   (Ashmolean Museum, Oxford; G.275/V.575)

mortal realm of the Sumerian story given earlier, which explains how excessive consumption by the female gods required the creation of a race of slaves: humans. Hesiod does not mention and has no respect for woman's tireless labor in the production of cloth and in the maintenance of the household. Still, there is no hope of altogether abandoning women, Pandora's descendants:

[603]   Whoever keeps clear of marriage and the trouble fomented by women,
          and is quite content to stay single, must expect a gloomy old age,

605   with no one at hand to attend him. He may have plenty of money,
       but when he dies his relations, often far distant, divide it.°
       Even if someone is married to a wise and compatible woman,
       all through his life he will find that trouble is mixed with his joy.

                                HESIOD, *Theogony* (603–610)

606. *divide it:* In Hesiod's time the inheritance of a man's property seems generally to have been
limited to his family, first to his son and then to his brothers and more distant relations.

Modern readers are struck by the virulence of Hesiod's attack on women (there
are other examples in early Greek literature), presented as an unavoidable evil and
a punishment for bad relations with the gods. Even the Bible, whose story of Eve's
betrayal bears a similar message, accords to woman a partnership in the propagation
of the species, a role that Hesiod barely mentions. The roots of misogyny are varied
and not easily understood, especially in an age when women's rights are a prominent political issue. In early times women were kept separate from men from a magical fear of woman's menses, considered an extremely dangerous and polluting substance, requiring the menstruating woman's rigorous separation from contact with
males.[2] Among the Greeks, however, misogyny seems to be based not so much on
primitive magical terror, or economic resentment as in Hesiod's surly complaint, as
on a male resentment of the institution of monogamy itself. Greek myth is obsessed
with hostile relations between the sexes, especially between married couples. In considering the meaning of such passages we need to remember that, with minor exceptions, ancient literature was composed by men for men in an environment ruled
by men (as was the Bible).

Hesiod explains Pandora's name as reflecting the fact that every god and goddess endowed her with a charm, "All-gifted," but the name probably means "All-
giver," another name for the mother-goddess, like Gaea, the giver of all things, here
transformed into a young girl with "thievish morals" and "the soul of a bitch." She
is irresistible to the male gaze from without, but within, like Gaea, she is mud,
clay. Poor dumb Epimetheus, violating a prohibition, was duped by her beauty,
Aphrodite's gift. In Pandora is mirrored in miniature the grand mythical ambiguity
of Gaea/Rhea. Pretty outside in fine attire and jewels of gold, within she is Earth,
within which the male must plant his seed if he hopes to sire an heir and, in this small
way, defy mortality.

Observations: Women as Containers

It is no coincidence that Pandora is associated in myth with a jar. In Greek myth, as
in Greek art and religious rituals, and even in the Greek language, we often encounter
the image of woman as a box or container whose contents can either help or harm,

[2]Compare the biblical "When a woman has a discharge of blood . . . this uncleanness of her monthly
period shall last for seven days. . . . Anyone who touches her will be unclean until evening. Any bed
she lies on in this state will be unclean," and so on (Leviticus 15.19–20).

give life or take it away. In Greek society women carried water to the house, a daily task, and jars with big bellies, called *hydriae,* "water jars," often have pictures on them revealing scenes from women's daily lives. Next to one of the most famous statues of antiquity, the naked Aphrodite of Praxiteles (fourth century B.C.), stood such a jar, explicitly compared with the body of the goddess of sexual desire (Fig. 5.3).

The word *amnion* is used both for the membrane that surrounds the fetus (hence our "amniotic fluid") and for a jar that holds the blood of sacrifice. In Greek religious ritual, women and girls often carry baskets, including the basket that contains

FIG. 5.3. The Capitoline Aphrodite, a Roman copy that goes back to a celebrated statue by Praxiteles, fourth century B.C., made as the cult statue of Aphrodite for her temple at Cnidos in southwest Asia Minor. The earliest Greek sculpture, from the eighth century B.C., represented males naked, but women were almost always represented clothed. About the original statue (known only from Roman copies) Aphrodite was said to have asked, "When did Praxiteles see me nude?" The soft, languorous, sensuous style of Praxiteles, with the S-curve of the body, continued to have influence for hundreds of years. The nudity of the goddess is explained by her having just arisen from a bath, taken in antiquity by pouring water over the body from a jug, here shown at her side, partially draped. The gesture of the left hand, covering the pelvis, is taken from ancient Eastern sculpture.   (Museo Capitolino, Rome; author's photo)

the sacrificial knife hidden in a heap of wheat. The wheat is life, the knife is death, which through the shedding of blood guarantees new life. The basket and its contents, like the woman, are a mystery: When the young virgin *Arrephoroi*, "Basket-carriers," in the myths of Athens (see Chapter 15) peer into a basket supposedly containing the young Athenian prince Erichthonius, they are driven mad and leap to their deaths from the Acropolis. Painted Greek pots again and again show women receiving vessels, boxes, baskets, and jars, always from other women, never from men. At her wedding, especially, a Greek woman is surrounded by boxes (even as today some prepare a hope chest for marriage). To the graves women carry a special flat basket containing magical objects for the dead. On the Parthenon reliefs, Demeter and Persephonê, who guarantee fertility, are seated on baskets. In a curious ritual widespread in the ancient world, dedicated to the hero Adonis, who died young, women planted seeds in broken jars, then allowed the hot sun to destroy the young plants. Perhaps the ritual's meaning was to drive away danger to the human young by providing a substitute for hostile spirits, a ransom; so will the woman's jar, her womb, be unbroken and her seed will live. The Greeks called a pregnant woman a closed jar; the Danaïds, who refused proper marriage and pregnancy when they killed their husbands on their wedding night (see Chapter 13), were condemned to try forever to pour water into broken jugs. The jugs are symbols for their own bodies.

Earth is the great container of seed (and of the dead), and a phrase in the Greek wedding ceremony urged the husband to "plow his wife for the begetting of new children"; she too is the earth, holding concealment, treasure, and mystery, all mixed up with sex. The male enters into the dark recesses of the virgin's body, a treasure, and spills his milky fluid to mix with the woman's clay, a new treasure, the future's hope; to marry without virginity would be to buy an empty jar, unthinkable in ancient Greek society.

The Greeks stored grain and oil and treasure in just such jars as Pandora received from the gods. In the myth of Perseus, the virgin Danaë is buried in an underground chamber to ensure her virginity, for treasures abide underground. But Zeus fell into the chamber as a different treasure, a rain of gold, and impregnated her.

As female brought male into the world, so does woman, who is earth that holds dead bodies, foresee his death. Thetis tells Achilles how he will die, and in Greek society the dangerous practice of burial was given entirely to women. As only women dared touch the bodies of the dead to clean them and rub them with scented oils, so only women touched the bloody, soiled newborn to clean it and make it shine.

As earth and jars contain, so do they consume; Hesiod is depressed by the economic hardship imposed by female mouths. In myth, as in the story of Pereus, babies are placed into jars or chests, from which they emerge born again, but into jars also go the bones of the dead. A euphemism for exposing one's newborn to die was "putting it in a pot."

In the myth of Pandora and the jar is the emblem of woman herself, the first woman. From her came all evils, out of the womb, the tomb, into the world. Hope, still within the jar, is like the child in the womb: unfulfilled, a possibility for good or ill. From the womb come children who in Greek myth will kill or curse their parents or go to bed with them or make them proud; still, Hope remains in the jar, and there is no other way.

THE FIVE RACES

In the *Works and Days* Hesiod relates another story, which must have a separate origin, describing the decline of humankind from a blessed past to a wretched present, the myth of the Five Races (= *genera*, the same word Hesiod uses to describe the "race," *genos*, of women):

[106]   If you wish, I will use my skill to sketch you another story
      of how both men and immortals arose at the start of things.
      I promise you all my skill, so plant this account in your memory.
        The first race of men the gods who life on Olympus created,
110   in the days when Cronus was ruler in heaven, was fashioned of gold.
      They lived like gods, with hearts all unacquainted with trouble,
      removed far away from labor and sorrow. Old age and depression
      had not yet appeared, but vigorous of hand and foot, ever youthful,
      they passed their days in feasting, unaging, youthful of body,
115   and when they died at last, they vanished away like a dream.
      All good things were theirs: the land yielded grain in abundance,
      in harvests demanding no toil. They lived, contented and quiet,
      surrounded by blessings, with each man looking after his duties.
        But at last Earth covered this race, and now, by Zeus's design,
120   they walk the earth, kindly spirits, guards and defenders of men.
      Hidden in cloud, they wander everywhere over the earth,
      defenders of justice and firmness, givers of wealth and of plenty,
      wielding the royal powers, their privilege and their reward.
        The gods who live on Olympus made a second, inferior race,
125   of silver, unlike the golden in form, and duller in reason.
      At the side of its lady mother, nursing and playing at home,
      a child spent a hundred years, no better, indeed, than a baby.
      When finally he grew up and reached the measure of manhood,
      he lived for a few years more, in trouble through his own folly.
130   Men could not hold back their hands from violence aimed at each other,
      and refused to honor the gods with sacrifice at the high altars,
      an old universal tradition. So Zeus, the son of great Cronus,
      angrily buried them out of his sight for their stiff-necked refusal
      to honor the blessed gods, the dwellers on lofty Olympus.
135   But even though earth has hidden this race deep under the ground,
      mortals still call them blessed, though subterranean, spirits—
      second in rank, no doubt, but yet entitled to honor.
        Zeus the Father then made yet another, a third race of mortals,
      this one fashioned of bronze, a terrible race and warlike,
140   sprung from ash-trees, concerned with the bloody labor of Ares.
      They ate no bread from the earth, for their spirits were bent upon plunder.
      No one dared to approach them, so mighty and strong were the hands
      that grew from invincible arms beneath their muscular shoulders.
      This race's weapons were bronze, and bronze as well were its houses;
145   all its works were of bronze, for it had not discovered black iron.
      They fell by each other's hands, and nameless they all descended
      to the mildewy house of cold Hades, in spite of their terrible power;
      when black Death seized them, they fled from the glorious light of the sun.

Now when the grave had covered this generation as well,
150   Zeus, son of Cronus, created a fourth on the life-giving earth,
braver and juster by far, the godlike race of the heroes.
Indeed, they are called half-gods, this race preceding our era,
over the whole wide earth. Dread warfare and terrible slaughter
carried some of them off at Thebes, in the land of old Cadmus,°
155   fighting each other for plunder, to loot King Oedipus'° cattle.
Warfare took others in ships over the sea's surging billows,
to fight for the sake of Helen, the woman with beautiful hair.
For most of them, death was the end which hid them away from our vision,
but on some, father Zeus, son of Cronus, bestowed a new way of living,
160   far from the haunts of men, at the very end of the world.

There they remain, untroubled at heart and free from disturbance,
in the far-away Isles of the Blessed, by the swirling waters of Ocean,
prosperous heroes, to whom three harvests a year are accorded.
Cronus rules as their king, for the father of men and immortals
165   set him free from his chains and granted him power and honor.
But after them, broad-fronted Zeus made no such glorious race
to dwell on the face of the earth, the fertile mother of all.

O, that I did not live with men of the fifth generation!
that I had perished before it, or else had been born hereafter.
170   For now as things are, our fellow-humans are people of iron.
Will the day never come for ceasing unending labor and warfare,
or a night to stop the destruction? Or will the immortals forever
keep piling fresh bitter causes of quarrels and hatred upon us?
Yet for a while some good will still be mixed with the evil,
175   till Zeus destroys this race like the others, when finally comes the time
when children are born with the cynical grizzled hair of old age;
when father shares no more with his son or son with his father;
when guest and host are at odds, oldest friend with his comrade;
when your brother no more is your truest friend, as he used to be.
180   When people abuse their parents as these grow older and weaker;
sarcastic and proud, they will mock the certain revenge of the gods,
refusing any return for the cost and pain of their rearing.
Trusting in force, they will raid and plunder each other's dominions.
The faithful will win no regard, nor even the just or the honest;
185   only the cynical doer of evil will win the world's admiration,
he who thinks his might makes right, whose heart is empty of scruple.
Knaves will cheat honest men, backing their falsehoods with oaths.
Mischievous envy, sour in face and tongue, will lay ambush,
entrapping all who are poor, entrapping all who are honest.
190   When all this comes to pass, Shame and Indignation,
shrouding their honest faces from human sight with white veils,
will abandon mortals and hurry far from the wide-wayed earth,
fleeing back to Olympus and its gods, leaving only the prospect
to mortals of sorrow and pain, with no defenses against them.

HESIOD, *Works and Days* (106–201)

154. *Cadmus:* Founder of the city of Thebes.   155. *Oedipus:* A legendary king of Thebes.

All later mention of a golden age depends ultimately on this passage in Hesiod and his description of the Golden Race, who lived in the days of Cronus. They were happy and blessed[3] and at death became spirits on the earth, watching over and protecting mortals. The next race, of silver, was far worse than the first. A child would stay young for a hundred years, then grow up suddenly, age and die. The Silver Race committed crimes against one another and did not respect the gods. Still, when they died, they became spirits who live under the ground. The third race, made of bronze, was worse than the silver. Born from ash trees, from which the shafts of spears were made, they were terrible, strong, and violent. Their weapons and houses were of bronze; they did not understand ironworking. Unlike the preceding two races, at death they descended into the realm of Hades, where they dwell in darkness. The fourth race, that of heroes, was in some ways better than the bronze. This race fought at seven-gated Thebes and on the windy plain of Troy to take back lovely Helen. Some heroes never died at all but were transported to the Isles of the Blessed at the end of the world. They live there still, never knowing sorrow. The fifth race, of iron, is Hesiod's own.

Hesiod has inherited from the East a classification of the phases of human existence into gold, silver, bronze, and iron, a picture of ever-worsening conditions;[4] a similar myth built around a metallic metaphor was told in ancient Persia, where many think the myth originated. Under the influence of the Greek oral tradition, which told of wars against Thebes and Troy, Hesiod has inserted the race of heroes between the race of bronze and his own iron world of crime and sorrow.

Hesiod's poems reflect the disturbances of a time of radical economic change in Greece. Land was moving from group to private ownership. The poor, forced to mortgage and finally lose their plots, sank into slavery or were forced to emigrate to the cities or to colonies in Sicily, Italy, and elsewhere. Trade in oil and wine was growing, coinage was beginning, and traditional social hierarchies were shaken. Cities of artisans and sailors were increasing in size, and political and legal systems did not keep pace.

Later commentators interpreted Hesiod's account as a chronological one and attempted, with little success, to slot in such unrelated mythical events as the universal flood and the career of Prometheus. A basic contradiction always remained: that the Golden Race lived under Cronus, who according to the more widespread account was tyrannous and evil. In this detail we can see how myth works and how Hesiod came to his description: Cronus was an early king, the Golden Race was the first, so Cronus ruled in the era of the Golden Race.

Hesiod's description of his own era reflects the same pessimism that characterized Mesopotamian myth, although his wish "that I had perished before it, or else had been born hereafter" suggests that conditions may improve in the future and

[3]As in the times before Zeus sent down Pandora, but Hesiod does not explicitly associate the myth of Pandora with the myth of the Five Races.
[4]Compare the great idol in Nebuchadnezzar's dream in the biblical Book of Daniel (2.31–33): "You looked, O king, and there before you stood a large statue—an enormous, dazzling statue, awesome in appearance. The head of the statue was made of pure gold, its chest and arms of silver, its belly and thighs of bronze, its legs of iron, its feet partly of iron and partly of baked clay," hence our expression "feet of clay." The idol refers to a sequence of kingdoms.

perhaps even return to those of the Golden Race. Hesiod does not so much picture a world in constant decline (although his mythical models certainly did) as he contrasts the Silver, Bronze, Heroic, and Iron races with that of Gold, when humans lived in Paradise. The races that followed were all degenerate, although in different ways. Vergil, a Roman poet influenced by Hesiod, writing around the time of Christ after a hundred years of bitter and brutal civil war, reinterpreted Hesiod's myth as a historical chronology and declared that a golden age (not a Golden Race) had returned to earth under the enlightened rule of the emperor Augustus (see Chapter 22). Many believed him.

THE UNIVERSAL FLOOD

In the biblical flood story, "the Lord [Yahweh] saw that the wickedness of man was great in the earth, and that every imagination of the thoughts of his heart was only evil continually. And the Lord was sorry that he had made man on the earth, and it grieved him to his heart. So the Lord said, 'I will blot out man, whom I have created from the face of the ground, man and beast and creeping things and birds of the air, for I am sorry that I have made them.'" Only Noah, because of his goodness, was saved from the flood that God sent. When the waters receded, Noah sent out a dove, which first returned because it found no place to rest. He released it again; this time it came back with an olive twig. He let it go a third time, but by now it had no need of the ark and disappeared for good (Genesis 6–8). The waters receded, and Noah built an altar and sacrificed to God.

This story is far older than the Bible, although the biblical account has made it perhaps the most widely known story on Earth. Let us first consider the origin of the flood story in Mesopotamia, then the classical version, which Greece's dry and riverless terrain proves to be a foreign importation.

Ziusudra, Atrahasis, and Noah

Earlier (Chapter 3) we described how in 1872 a young Assyriologist, George Smith, shocked the world when he revealed his discovery of a prebiblical account of the deluge. Smith read this account on a cuneiform tablet from the library of the Assyrian king Assurbanipal; the library was destroyed in 612 B.C. Scholars have since discovered several other Mesopotamian prebiblical descriptions of the flood, including one from Sumer dating to the third millennium B.C. It is badly preserved, but it is the oldest existing account.

The Sumerian story begins with the creation of humans, the animals, and the foundation of five important cities. The next part of the tablet is broken; when it resumes, the gods have decreed the destruction of humankind by means of a universal flood. Some gods were opposed to their plan, and Enki intervened to save **Ziusudra** (zē-u-**sū**-dra), "long life," a pious man. Enki advised Ziusudra to build a large boat:

All the winds, amazingly strong and powerful, attacked,
and the deluge rampaged over the earth.

For seven days and nights,
the deluge rampaged in the land.
The huge boat was slung about on the vast waters.
Then Utu° came forth, he who sheds light on heaven and earth.
Ziusudra drew open a window of the huge boat,
Ziusudra, the king, threw himself down on the ground before Utu.
He killed an ox, slaughtered a sheep.

Utu: The sun god.

Most of the rest of the tablet is lost. We learn only that Ziusudra was made to be like a god and transported to Dilmun, a mysterious land in the East where there is no pain or suffering, the Sumerian paradise.

The later myth of **Atrahasis** (a-tra-**hā**-sis), c. 1700 B.C., preserved in the Semitic Akkadian language, adds many other details to the story. The hero there is called Atrahasis ("exceeding wise," another name for Ziusudra). Soon after creation, before humans were made, the gods had to toil constantly, digging out the Tigris and Euphrates river channels. After 3,600 years, weary of their labors, they revolted, burned their tools, and surrounded the house of the storm god Enlil.

Terrified, Enlil tried to mediate the dispute, then burst into tears. He offered to resign as king of the gods. Ea (= Sumerian Enki) proposed a compromise: The gods should create humans from mud. The womb goddess Beletili, "Mistress of the Gods," did just this, pinching off some clay from the edge of the abyss. She made seven males and seven females, the ancestors of the human race—another version of the myth of humans made from mud to serve the needs of the gods.

The solution worked too well. After 1,200 years, the world was so filled with the shouting masses of humankind that Enlil (like Apsu in the *Enuma Elish*) could not get any sleep. To reduce the population, Enlil, with the other gods' approval, sent first a plague, then a drought, then a famine, but each time the population rebounded. Enlil devised the final solution: a great flood to exterminate humankind. Although bound by oath not to reveal Enlil's plan, Ea warned Atrahasis, whom he favored for his goodness, to build a huge boat and lock inside it all kinds of animals and his family:

The great flood roared like a bull,
the winds howled like the screaming of a wild ass,
darkness was all, the sun blotted out.

The gods were horrified at the violence of the flood. Everyone but Atrahasis and his family perished (the folktale motif of "all but one"), so that no offerings came to sustain the gods, and they began to starve. The storm raged for seven days and nights before the rain stopped and the ship ran aground. Atrahasis prepared a sacrifice, around which the hungry gods gathered like flies to a carcass of meat—all except Enlil, furious that a mortal had escaped. But he too was appeased when the gods devised various means to control the population: Some women would henceforth be barren, some would remain chaste for ritual reasons, and a demon would appear to kill some babies at birth. These new measures would prevent the world from again being overrun by humans.

Archaeological evidence proves that devastating floods sometimes took place in Mesopotamia when the rampaging Euphrates burst its banks and spilled across the flatland to the lower Tigris channel. The story may go back to an actual flood, although no cultural break ever involved all Mesopotamia. Still, many variants of the story circulated in that region and spread to Palestine, Anatolia, and Greece. Although the basic themes are constant, details reflect different environments and national interests. The Mesopotamian story of Ziusudra/Atrahasis, in which divine powers send destruction to correct overpopulation, reflects human insecurity before the capricious powers of the gods; it also explains the origin of barren women and stillbirths.

The Hebrew account, on the other hand, presents God as destroying humans because of their wickedness, their moral failure. Omnipotent though he is, after the flood God voluntarily limits his power by striking a covenant with Noah, and Noahs' descendants: He will never again destroy the human race, but he demands that certain laws be observed. If one man kills another or an animal whose flesh he then eats with the blood, he must forfeit his own life (Genesis 9.4.1–17). The biblical story also is etiological, explaining the origin of Hebrew customs concerning homicide and abstinence from blood. The story of Noah attempts to explain the origin of the special relationship between God and the Hebrews.

The myth of the flood must also be understood in the context of Mesopotamian cosmogonic myth. The universal flood is a return to the watery conditions before the creation, when Tiamat, the salt water, was mixed with Apsu, the sweet, reminiscent of the biblical description of when "darkness was upon the face of the deep," perhaps reflected in the biblical description of the flood: "All the fountains of the great deep burst forth, and the windows of the heavens were opened" (Genesis 7.11). The Hebrew word *tehom,* translated "fluid chaos" in the first chapter of Genesis, probably is related etymologically to the Akkadian name *Tiamat.*

Lycaon, Deucalion, and Pyrrha

In the classical tradition the earliest direct accounts of the flood are from the Roman Period, in Ovid and Apollodorus, but certainly based on much earlier Greek examples. Hearing that all men were vicious and corrupt, Zeus descended among them disguised as an ordinary man. Human wickedness was exemplified by **Lycaon** (li-**kā**-on), king of Arcadia, who practiced human sacrifice and cannibalism. In Ovid's telling of the story, Zeus is reporting to the other gods what happened:

[211]   "Stories had come to my ears of the wicked ways of mankind;
          hoping to find them false, I came down from the top of Olympus,
          and, god though I am, I examined the earth in the guise of a human.
          Merely to list the crimes I discovered all over the world
215   would be a tedious task, and the rumors fell short of the truth.
          Crossing the Maenala region, alive with the lairs of wild creatures,
          and the pinewoods of cold Lycaeus, along the hills of Cyllenê,°

217. *Cyllenê:* Maenala, Lycaneus, and Cyllenê are all mountains in Arcadia. the first was named after Maenalus, a son of Lycaon; on the peaks of Lycaeus, human sacrifice was offered to Zeus, reportedly down to classical times; on Cyllenê, in northeast Arcadia, was born the god Hermes

as darkness drew on to night, I came to a grim-fronted palace,
the home of the tyrant king of Arcadia. I gave him a signal
220   to show that a god was present, and his people started to worship.
At first Lycaon just laughed at the pious prayers they murmured,
then boasted, "I soon shall discover if this is a god or a mortal,
by a sure and certain test; no shadow of doubt will remain."
This was his test: at night, when I was buried in slumber,
225   he planned to put me to death, in a way no man could expect.
That was Lycaon's idea of a rigorous test of the truth.
But even this was too little: he cut the throat of a hostage
(one of a group of Molossians°), cut up his half-dead remains,
stewed some parts in hot water, while broiling some on the fire,
230   and set the meal on the table. . . . With a crash of my vengeful lightning,
I split the house on the heads of its lord and his lickspittle gods,
who ran off in fright to the fields, to win some refuge in silence.
Safe, as he thought, he attempted to speak, but an animal's howling
was all that came out. His face was wet with the froth of his madness,
235   and his grisly craving for murder was turned against cattle and sheep.
His royal robe turned shaggy, his arms were an animal's forepaws;
though now a wolf, he retains some trace of his human appearance.
His hair is still gray, his face displays its bloodthirsty features,
his eyes still gleam with the flashing of the same cruel animal glare.
240   This one household has fallen, as many households deserve,
for as far as the wide earth stretches, the savage Furies hold sway.
You would think all men had conspired; the sooner, then, let them pay
the penalty that they deserve! This is great Jupiter's° sentence."
    Some of the listening gods approved great Jupiter's decision,
245   and poured their oil on his fire; some gave assent by their silence,
Yet all were saddened to think of the unforeseen liquidation
of all the race of mankind; what will the world be like,
they asked, without population? who will sacrifice at our altars?
does Jupiter plan to abandon the earth to savage wild beasts?
250   Foreseeing new problems arising, they raised such questions as these.
The king of the heavens calmed them and told them they need not worry:
he promised to raise a new race, unlike the one that they knew,
born in a wonderful way. He was about to rain thunderbolts over the nations,
when a worrying thought gave him pause: would the sacred ether on high
255   be ignited by this conflagration? Would the axis of Earth take fire?
His mind recalled the warning of Fate: "The day is approaching,
when the fabric of earth and sea and the lofty palace of heaven
will pass away in fire,° and the world's great mass will be shaken."
He hastily stored away the thunderbolts, forged by Cyclopes,
260   and conceived a different design, of opening dark heavy rain clouds,
In every quarter of heaven, and drowning mankind in the waters.

           OVID, *Metamorphoses* (1.211–261)

---

228. *Molossians:* A people who lived in Epirus, in northwestern Greece   243. *Jupiter's:* Ovid, of course , uses Roman equivalents for the Greek gods (see Chart at the back of this book).
258. *pass away in fire:* A reference to Stoic cosmology, which predicted just such an end to the world.

Ovid goes on to describe the destruction of humanity. Only Prometheus' son **Deucalion** (dū-kā-li-on) and his wife, **Pyrrha** (**pir**-ra), a daughter of Pandora and Epimetheus, survived:

[313]   Phocis,° a fruitful land (as long as dry land existed)
         divides the land of Boeotia from that surrounding Mount Oeta.°
315   But in the time of our story it was only an arm of the ocean,
         a wide-spreading waste of waters, after the deluge of rain.
         The rugged mountain Parnassus° stretches twin peaks to the heavens,
         with tops rising over the clouds, where Deucalion, the only survivor,
         (the sea had covered all others) was carried with Pyrrha, his wife,
320   saved as they clung to a raft which drifted onto the mountain.
         Together the pair paid homage to the local gods and the nymphs,
         and to Themis, Destiny's mouthpiece, who then was the oracle's ruler.
             No better man ever existed, nor one more devoted to justice
         than he; no woman showed greater respect for the gods than did Pyrrha.
325   When Jupiter saw that the world was awash with slow-moving water,
         that of all its thousands of men one only remained alive,
         that one woman only was left of all its thousands of women,
         both of them guiltless of crime, for pious souls were they both,
         he scattered the clouds and dispersed the rain with a northwest wind,
330   and made the land show its face to the sky and the sky to the earth.
         The wrath of the sea was calmed by Neptune, ruler of ocean,
         who, laying his trident aside, summoned the sea-green Triton,°
         who rose from the deep, displaying his barnacle-crusted shoulders.
         Neptune gave him an order to sound trumpet calls on his conch shell
335   to recall, as if by a signal, the rivers and waves to their places.
         He took up his hollow trumpet, a twisted shell whose mouth
         comes spiraling off to one side. This horn of Triton, when sounded
         even far out in the sea, fills the coastlines in either direction.
         So now, as the sea god raised it to his mouth and his dripping beard,
340   the waters, both fresh and salt, all heard it sound the retreat,
         which forced the listening currents at once to obey its command.
         Down sank the rivers, making mountains seem to be rising;
         the sea was bounded by shores, the rivers contained by their channels,
         the ground emerged once more as the waters ebbed. Landmarks appeared,
345   and woods, though naked of foliage, once more raised branches on high,
         their tattered leaves still fluttering, brown and slimy with mud.
         The circle of lands was completed. Deucalion viewed the bleak desert,
         a desolate land, one plunged in silence, profound and unbroken.
         Tears welled up in his eyes as he opened his heart to his Pyrrha:
350   "My sister, my wife, the only woman alive on the earth,
         joined as cousin and kin, as bride, and as partner in danger,

---

313. *Phocis:* The territory around Delphi.   314. *Mount Oeta:* In southern Thessaly. Where Mount Oeta touches the sea is Thermopylae, the "Hot Gates." There the Spartan king Leonidas and his 300 companions fought to the death against the Persian invaders in 480 B.C.   317. *Parnassus:* Dephi, Apollo's oracle in classical times, is built on the south slope of this precipitous mountain, the Mount Ararat (where Noah's ark alighted, variously identified) of Greek myth.   332. *Triton:* A god of the sea, son of Poseidon.

we are the whole population of the world, from the rise of the sun
to where it sets in the west. The ocean has swallowed all else.
And how can we be assured that our own lives will safely continue,
355   under these threatening clouds, which arouse such fear in my heart?
What hope, poor thing, would you have, if fate had left you alone;
how could you master your terror? who would comfort you in distress?
If you too had drowned in the sea, I would follow, dearest of women,
and—truly I swear it—I too would have perished, drowned in the sea.
360   How I wish I had mastered the arts possessed by my father Prometheus
by which to repeople the earth, mixing life-giving spirit and clay!
The mortal race of humanity now is reduced to us two,
to serve as the pattern of men, for so the gods have decided."
    Both of them wept at his words, but asked help of the gods above.
365   Hand in hand they hurried away to the stream of Cephisus,°
which, murky still with silt, was at least contained in its channel.
They solemnly purified their clothing and heads with its water,
then turned their steps to the shrine of Themis,° reverend goddess,
whose roof was stained with moss, whose altars stood without fire.
370   Reaching the temple steps, they prostrated themselves on the earth,
and, trembling, each pressed a pious kiss on the cold lifeless stones.
    "O goddess," they murmured, "if ever divinity softens at prayers,
won by the faith of their givers, if angry gods can be swayed,
tell us, O goddess, we pray, how to ward off our race's destruction,
375   and grant your unfailing help to a world engulfed in disaster."
The goddess, stirred by their plea, returned this cryptic reply:
"Veil your heads when you leave; undo the knots of your clothing;°
then toss the bones of your mighty mother over your shoulders."
For a while they stared in surprise. Pyrrha first broke the silence,
380   by refusing the goddess's orders, and begging in tremulous accents
for pardon; she trembled to think of insulting the ghost of her mother
by tossing her bones about. But as they repeated the riddle
concealed in the cryptic words of the oracle's strange revelation,
Prometheus' son's quiet words calmed Epimetheus' daughter:
385   "Either my wits have gone wrong," said he, "or the oracle's message
is urging us on to no sin. The earth is our mighty mother,
rocks, no doubt, are her bones; it is they we are bidden to throw."
    The daughter of Titans respected her husband's plausible guess,
but neither trusted the outcome, both doubted the oracle's word.
390   Still, how could it hurt them to try? Down they went from the temple,
veiled their heads, unfastened the knotted belts of their tunics,
and threw the stones, as ordered, behind them into their footprints.
Who would believe what happened, had not tradition assured us?
The stones began to give up their rigid inflexible structure,
395   and presently started to soften, and, softened, acquired new form.
Soon, as they reached full size, and their gentler nature developed,
the human form could be seen in a doubtful, tentative fashion

---

365. *Cephisus:* A river northeast of Delphi.   368. *Themis:* At Delphi, where the Titaness gave oracles before Apollo took over the shrine.   377. *knots of your clothing:* The knot would magically tie up the mysterious power Deucalion is about to exercise.

as we see it in statues the sculptor has just begun to rough out
from a block of unfashioned stone, not ready yet for display.

400   The earthly part of their matter became their muscles and sinews;
the solider part, which cannot be bent, turned into their bones;
the part of marble called "veins" still keeps that name in our bodies.
And soon by the will of the gods the stones from the hand of the man
acquired the features of men, those thrown by the woman were women.

405   This, then, is the reason our race is tough and enduring in hardship,
why each of us shows his proof of the source from which we descended.
The earth on its own gave birth to the rest of the animal kingdom,
each animal after its kind. As the waters warmed in the sunshine,
and the spongy ooze of the marshes swelled with the growing warmth,

410   the fertile seeds of things grew fat in the quickening mud;
as a fetus does in the womb, they grew and acquired new features.

OVID, Metamorphoses (1.313–421)

Most important of the children of Deucalion and Pyrrha was their son **Hellen,** who gave his name to the whole Greek race, the Hellenes. Hellen had three sons, Dorus, Aeolus, and Xuthus. Dorus and Aeolus were the founders of the Dorians and the Aeolians, peoples who spoke two of the principal Greek dialects. Xuthus, the brother of Dorus and Aeolus, was father to Ion, from which descended the Ionians, the third principal group of Greeks, which included the Athenians. These figures are **eponymous ancestors** of the Greeks as a whole (= Hellenes) and of the three principal ethnic divisions among the Greeks (= Dorians, Ionians, Aeolians). *Eponymous* means "giving one's name to something," a place, people, city, or institution, and an *eponym* is the person whose name is so given. There are many eponyms in mythology, but most are really named after the fact.

PROMINENT THEMES IN CLASSICAL STORIES OF HUMAN ORIGINS

The Greeks and Romans did not have a book of Genesis to decree what one should believe about the origin of humans and their early life in the long-ago faraway times when mortals lived close to gods. Hesiod's account was by far the most popular, but other traditions abounded. Although different in detail, most reports agreed that humans came from the earth, a theme that first appeared in Mesopotamian myth. Of course, the notion that Earth is a mother is logical and may appear independently in any culture.

Humans may simply emerge from the earth, growing like plants from seeds or semen placed within it. Deucalion threw stones over his shoulder like a man sowing a furrow, and up sprang men;[5] the Giants, too, were born when the semen-blood from Uranus' severed genitals fell to the earth. In a variation on this theme, Hesiod's Bronze Race sprang from ash trees.

A second way for mortals to issue from the earth is at the hands of an artisan god. So Hephaestus made Pandora from clay.[6] A tradition later than Hesiod says that

[5]In Greek versions, there is a play on words between the Greek *laos,* "people," and *laas,* "stone."
[6]Although in Figure 5.2 she is portrayed emerging from the ground (= clay).

Plato's Aristophanes on Love and Human Origins

An important utility of myth, especially after the invention of writing, is to offer a body of common knowledge for allusion to those who know the stories—the opportunity to make in-jokes and impress friends. Plato, enjoyed today as much for his literary artistry as for his deep questions about knowledge, opposed the old myths because they did not teach correct values. However, he was not above making up his own stories, "myths" in a broader sense, to answer some old questions. A memorable tale about the nature of Eros/Love and the origin of humans is told in his dialogue the *Symposium* ("drinking party," about 360 B.C.), a brilliant picture of the all-male social environment in which Greek myth flourished. Socrates is there, as are other prominent Athenians, but this story is told by Aristophanes (c. 450–388 B.C.), the greatest comic poet of the ancient world (eleven of his forty-four plays survive). Plato appropriately makes his story an entertaining one:

> "All right then," said Aristophanes, "I'm going to talk about Eros in a different way. It seems to me that nobody has the slightest idea about his power; if they did, they would give him the biggest altars and temples and feasts—not like now, when they do nothing of the sort, as they damn well ought to. Does any god do more for people than Eros? He's the god who cares most for us; he's the one who most looks after us; he's the best doctor there is, especially if you've caught something whose cure is the best luck a man can have. Well then, I'm going to try to show you what his power really is, so you will be able to teach other people.
>
> "First of all, you have to understand human nature and its troubles. Originally, we were not the same as now. There were three sexes—not just two, men and women, but also a third, a combination of both. . . . This group is gone, and only its name survives, but there were once man–woman beings, who under this name shared the appearance of both men and women. They themselves are extinct, and by now the name is only a slander. Secondly, all humans were round in shape, with backs and bellies making a circle. They had four hands and the same number of feet. One head had two faces looking opposite ways, perched on a single round neck, the same shape behind as before. They had two pairs of ears and two sets of sex organs—and that's enough for you to guess what the rest of their bodies looked like! They could walk standing up, as people still do, or, if they wanted to run really fast, they could flip up onto their hands like gymnasts and move in a series of hand-springs, swinging all eight limbs around at a great rate.
>
> "Well, then, there were three sexes, all like this. . . . The strength and speed of these people was terrific, and their ambitions likewise; indeed, they even attacked the gods. So, when Homer talks about the giants Ephialtes and Otus, he really means these men I have described, and how they tried to mount to heaven so that they could assault the immortals.
>
> "At that Zeus and the other gods debated what they should do, but could

not make up their minds. They felt they could not just kill them, like the Giants, destroyed utterly by thunder—then they would lose the honors and observances they had from men. On the other hand, they could not endure this horrid rioting. Zeus, putting all his wits together, spoke at last and said: 'Well, I think I can arrange it so, without ceasing to exist, men will give up their iniquity through a lessening of their strength. I propose to slice every one of them in two, so that while making them weaker we will find them more useful, because there will be many more of them. And they shall walk erect on two legs. If they continue to be turbulent and do not shut up, I will do it again,' said he, 'slice everyone in two, and then they must go on one leg, hip-hopping.'

"So saying, he sliced each human being in half, just as they slice apples to make a dry preserve, or eggs with hairs and at the splitting of each he ordered Apollo to turn its face and half-neck to the cut side, to subdue them by the sight of the knife's work; then the god was to heal them up. So Apollo turned their faces around and pulled their skin together from the edges over what is now called the belly, just like purses which you draw close with a string. The little opening he tied up in the middle of the belly, making what we call the navel. He smoothed away the puckers and molded the breast with an instrument such as shoemakers use to smooth the wrinkles of leather on the shoe-mold, although he left a few around the belly and navel to remind us of our early fall. Now when our first form was cut in two, each half, longing for its other half, would come to it again, and they would fling their arms around each other and in mutual embrace long to be grafted together, until they began to perish of hunger and indolence, because they refused to do anything apart. And whenever on the death of one half the other was left alone, that half went searching and embracing to see if it might find that half of the whole woman which now we call a woman, or maybe the half of the whole man. In this fix they were perishing, when Zeus in his pity provided a new plan. He moved their private parts to the front—for until then they had these, like everything else, on the outside, and did their begetting and giving birth not on each other but on the earth, like the crickets. These parts he shifted to the front, to be used for propagating on each other—in the female member by means of the male, so that a man should happen on a woman and embrace her, there might be conception and continuation of their kind. And if male met with male, they might be satisfied through their union and find relief, and thus turn their hands to their labors and their interest to ordinary life. So ancient is mutual attraction ingrained in humankind, recalling how once we were, and attempting to combine two in one and heal the human sore."

PLATO, Symposium (189c–190e)

Aristophanes' playful explanation of sexual attraction—between men and women, men and men, and women and women—is not a real myth because it is not a traditional tale. It is fiction, a fresh creation sprung from the brain of Plato in the spirit of the real Aristophanes' genius for wit and exaggeration. The story would have been unknown to anyone outside Plato's circle, yet ingeniously explains a common feeling in sexual union, that two are made one, by appealing to traditional mythical categories: the power of Eros and the triumph of Zeus over disorder.

Prometheus mixed clay with wind to make the first humans, as in the biblical story the creator made Adam by breathing on the dust of the earth.

The image of humans growing from the earth is derived from agriculture; the tradition of the artisan god derives from potterymaking. The first image is more common. Many city-states had local traditions that told how the inhabitants, the first anywhere, had come from the earth. These humans were ordinarily male, no doubt because the principal role of such stories was to glorify the local male nobility who claimed descent from the "first inhabitants" (as today people in the United States claim prestige from ancestors who sailed on the Mayflower); males are the myth-telling animals in the ancient world, and they did not accept the notion that females belonged to the same species.

A recurrent theme in these stories is that the human world did not arise all at once; there were delays and new beginnings. First came males, then females. First the gods made the Golden Race, then the Silver, Bronze, Heroic, and Iron. Zeus once destroyed all humanity in a flood. Only Deucalion and Pyrrha survived, who sowed the earth with stone seeds to provide a fresh start.

The essential quality of humans is to be mortal, destined to die. This quality separates us forever from the company of the gods. Because gods too emerged from Gaea/Earth, they and mortals share a common origin, and once upon a time men had dined on ambrosia and nectar in association with the gods. They were free from work and women and did not suffer from disease, poverty, or even death: The Golden Race did not so much die as become disembodied spirits. But some fault broke the intimacy between gods and humans. Now we live apart from the gods, eat cooked meat, labor for our keep, marry to reproduce, and die.

Hesiod's account of the incident at Meconê explains how this separation came about. Prometheus, by a trick, tried to give humans an advantage when the terms of sacrificial ritual were established. Zeus was angered, and humans attempted through sacrifice, the act that first offended Zeus, to restore good relations. Sacrifice was the central act of Greek religion and life and defined the human place in things: Animals, which eat their food raw, are sacrificed; humans, who eat their food cooked, sacrifice animals in honor of the gods, then eat the cooked flesh; gods, who eat neither raw food nor cooked, but dine on ambrosia and nectar, receive the smoke of the sacrifice performed in their honor.

The separation between human and divine became irrevocable when Zeus punished mortals for Prometheus' second offense, the stealing of fire. He sent "a curse for men": woman. She is beautiful, evil, costly, and insincere, a thorough calamity. Hesiod's word for "humans" before Pandora is *anthropoi*,[7] "human beings," not *andres*,[8] "males." After she appears, he distinguishes between *andres*, "males," and *gynaikes*, "females," both of whom are *anthropoi*. The story is a fantasy of male dominance, a world without women.

How is woman to be integrated within humanity, *anthropoi*, when she is something completely other from the males? In the Hebrew account, Eve is taken from

---

[7]Hence *anthropology*, "study of humans."
[8]Hence *androgen*, the male hormone.

Adam's body.[9] Pandora, by contrast, has a completely separate origin from the male. She is an artifact made by Hephaestus, not so much human as an imitation. Hesiod shows some confusion about Pandora's descendants, at one place saying that all women descend from her, but otherwise implying that from her womb all future humanity, male and female, will come forth, so that Pandora/All-giver discharges for humanity the same function as Gaea/Earth did in the times of the world's formation. The social institution of the male's union with the female in human marriage grows directly from the final separation between humans and gods.

There were many local traditions about the first men and women, and Deucalion and Pyrrha were ancestors of all the Greeks, but no classical myth tells the story of the origin of the human species as a whole. In thinking of themselves as alone being descended from the first humans, the Greeks followed a common tradition: Most ancient peoples did not include within humanity those who lived beyond their own racial and linguistic boundaries. In this sense, the biblical story of Adam, which explains the origin of the whole human race, is unique; division into races does not come until after Noah's flood.

KEY TERMS

Prometheus, 107

Enki, 107

Ki, 107

Pandora, 115

Ziusudra, 123

Atrahasis, 124

Lycaon, 125

Deucalion, 127

Pyrrha, 127

Hellen, 129

eponymous ancestors, 129

FURTHER READING

Detienne, Marcel, and Jean-Pierre Vernant, *Cunning Intelligence in Greek Culture and Society,* trans. Janet Lloyd (Chicago, 1991). Traces the role of *mêtis,* "cunning," throughout Greek life and thought, including its role in the stories of Zeus's rise to kingship and his contest with Prometheus.

Dundes, Alan, ed., *The Flood Myth* (Berkeley, Calif., 1988). A collection of essays offering a history of the discovery of a prebiblical story of the universal flood and a wide variety of interpretations.

Panofsky, Dora, and Erwin Panofsky, *Pandora's Box: The Changing Aspects of a Mythical Symbol* (New York, 1962; reprinted Princeton, 1991). The influence of this powerful myth from Hesiod to modern times.

Reeder, Ellen D., ed., *Pandora: Women in Classical Greece* (Princeton, N.J., 1995). Lavishly illustrated, with illuminating, sometimes penetrating essays.

Vernant, Jean-Pierre, *Myth and Society in Ancient Greece,* trans. Janet Lloyd (New York, 1980). Contains an important essay on the myth of Prometheus.

---

[9]After the woman has sinned by eating the forbidden fruit, she is given a name: Eve, the mother of all the living (her name is derived from a Hebrew root meaning "to live").

CHAPTER 6

MYTHS OF THE OLYMPIANS
ZEUS AND HERA

Homer and Hesiod have attributed to the gods all things that bring rebuke and blame among men—stealing, adultery, deceit.

XENOPHANES OF COLOPHON, fragment 11 (Diels–Kranz)

W E HAVE SEEN that two contradictory traditions attached to the reign of Cronus: that he was a cannibal tyrant who devoured his children and that he presided over the world when the Golden Race lived, when want and disease and hardship were unknown. In any event, his rule belonged to an era before his sons and daughters by Rhea came to power. These six sons and daughters were Zeus, Hera, Poseidon, Demeter, Hestia, and Hades. According to Hesiod, Aphrodite was born of the foam that gathered around the severed genitals of Uranus. She is a primordial goddess, older than the children of Cronus. According to other accounts, however, she is a daughter of Zeus.

Except for Hades, ruler of the underworld, all these deities were said to live on Mount Olympus, the tallest mountain in Greece, on the northern border of Thessaly. Together with six of Zeus's and Hera's children, they were known collectively as the Olympians (see Chart 6.1). By the sixth century B.C., a body of twelve Olympian gods and goddesses had been recognized; an altar to "The Twelve" was built in Athens, from which all distances in Attica were measured. The list did not remain fixed, however. Eventually, at least according to some sources, the colorless Hestia was replaced by Zeus's divine son Dionysus (discussed in Chapter 10).

Taken together, the twelve Olympians made up the divine family—brilliant, headstrong, quarreling, conspiring, feasting, loving and hating, immortal and im-

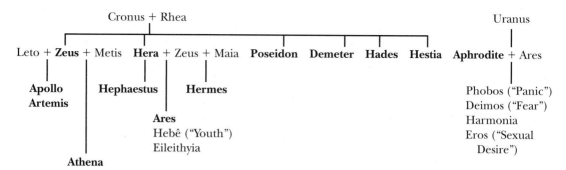

CHART 6.1. The Twelve Olympians

moral. Zeus stands at their head, "father" of gods and men. Although he makes every final decision, he can be won over by flattery, charm, bribery, and deception. Hera, his sister and wife, presides over the family, while his brother Poseidon rules the sea, his sister Hestia watches the fire, and his sister Demeter brings fertility to the earth. Hades rules the underworld. Hephaestus inspires the craftsmen, workers in metal, who made classical civilization possible. Ares is war. Athena, who knew no mother, presides over women's skills and practical knowledge of all kinds, including the art of war.

The children, too, have their spheres of influence. Apollo, god of prophecy and healing, often called Phoebus (**fē**-bus), perhaps meaning "Shiner," is one of the most important Greek gods; he is also by far the most complex and difficult to understand. In many stories he is inseparable from Artemis (the Roman Diana), goddess of wild animals and the hunt. In other myths, Artemis acts independently and achieves an identity of her own. Finally, the trickster Hermes, god of open spaces, traveled from high to low and from near to far, even from this world to the next. As a traveler, dependent on his wits, he was master of deception, lies, and (therefore) commerce.

The Olympian gods were a projection onto cosmic canvas of the concerns and activities of the Greeks themselves, and the organization of the Greek family and the tensions between the sexes are reflected in the family of the gods. The mighty Zeus rules his palace with an iron hand, but Hera, jealous and complaining, subverts his authority constantly. While Zeus pursues women and boys, his vengeful wife insults and annoys him and takes revenge against women who foolishly submit to his caress. Athena and Artemis were beings of great power, but they were celibate, without husband or child; in the human world, such power was broken through marriage. Demeter sponsored fertility but seemed to have no husband; the fecundity of the female was an unfathomed mystery. Aphrodite was violent, like the sexual urges of young men, although men liked to tell story after story of how frail woman surrendered to immoral urges.

Although in Homer and Hesiod the familial relationships are well established, all these gods and goddesses have separate origins. In this chapter we examine the greatest Olympians, Zeus and Hera. In the following two chapters, we examine first the male Olympians, then the females; of Demeter and Hades we have much more to say in later chapters.

FIG. 6.1. The temple of Olympian Zeus at Athens, with the ruins of the Parthenon in the background atop the Acropolis, c. 550 B.C.–130 A.D. The largest temple in Greece, it was begun under the Athenian tyrant Pisistratus in the sixth century B.C. but not completed until the Roman emperor Hadrian. Its magnificent Corinthian columns were made of Pentelic marble, like those of the Parthenon. This photo was taken in the 1920s.   (University of Wisconsin, Madison Photo Archive)

ZEUS, LORD OF THE SKY

The name **Zeus** is derived from an Indo-European root *di-* meaning "shine" or "sky." Other Indo-European peoples, as we mentioned in Chapter 3, have gods with the same derivation: The Germanic god Tiu's name also means "sky" (hence Tuesday, "the day of Tiu"), and that of the Indic god Dyaus Pitar means "Father Sky." Likewise the Roman god Jupiter, who was eventually identified with the Greek Zeus: His name also means "Father Sky." Presumably, all these gods, including Zeus, are derived from an earlier Indo-European deity associated with the luminous heaven.

In Greek myth and religion, Zeus was identified with the sky in general, but more particularly with the weather. It was he who gathered the clouds and caused the rain; Homer calls him the cloud-gatherer. His natural abode is on the tops of mountains, where the dark clouds gather before a storm; for this reason, no doubt, the Greek poets thought of his court as existing on Greece's highest mountain, Olympus, although Mount Ida near Troy was also his special abode (Fig. 6.1).

Zeus's outstanding attribute is his irresistible strength. In the *Iliad* he warns the other gods to remain aloof from the fighting at Troy. If they do not, they will

[17]   Learn how much stronger am I than all the rest of you gods,
          If you really want to know and to prove it to other immortals,
          let drop a golden cord from the heavens, and seize the end,
20   O all you gods and goddesses! Pull it with all your might.
          Try as you will to drag me from heaven down to the earth—
          you cannot move me a bit! I am Zeus, the highest and wisest.
          But suppose I really wanted to pull you up to the heavens:
          up you would come, and behind you would come both land and sea.
25   The cord I would fasten securely to the highest peak of Olympus,
          leaving its burden to hang, twisting there in the wind.
          That is how far I surpass in power both gods and mortals!

                                        HOMER, *Iliad* (8.17–27)

The **aegis**, "goat skin," was an emblem of Zeus's power, a magical object that inspired abject terror in all who beheld it. Perhaps derived from a goatskin shield used in primitive times, it symbolized the storm cloud of the weather god. In art it is shown as a shield with snake-headed tassels; Athena, to whom Zeus lent it, often wears it as a breastplate (see Fig. 8.5). The thunderbolt is Zeus's weapon; he used it to overcome the Titans, the Giants, and the monster Typhoeus. Where lightning struck, the Greeks would erect a shrine to Zeus *kataibatês*, "Zeus who descends." In art the lightning bolt is shown as a two-pointed object (see Figs. 4.5 and 4.6). The bull, because of its immense power and fecundity, was Zeus's special animal and was sacrificed to him ritually. The eagle, lord of the sky, was also associated with Zeus.

As ruler of the world, Zeus presided over law and justice. But at least in the early stages of Greek history, law and justice were not abstract ideals. They referred simply to what had always been done and was therefore right—in other words, to custom.[1] Zeus upheld the customary ways of Greek society. Those who acted illegally or unjustly—that is, against custom—also acted against Zeus.

Above all, Zeus protected the custom called **xenia** (ksen-ē-a), which we can roughly translate as "a formal institution of friendship" (*xenos* means "guest" or "stranger," as in English *xenophobia* = "fear of strangers"). *Xenia* enabled Greeks to travel safely to distant lands where other Greeks lived. A relationship was established when a wanderer was received into someone's household, entertained, and given a gift. Should the host one day visit the wanderer's home, he could expect to be received similarly. Obligations of reciprocal hospitality fell not only on the individuals involved originally, but also on their entire families and on their descendants. A host violated *xenia* if he killed or robbed his guest, as did a guest who stole from his host or seduced his host's wife. The legendary Trojan Paris seduced Helen, wife of his host, Menelaüs; this violation of *xenia* began the Trojan War and ensured Zeus's ap-

---

[1]The Greek word for justice was *dikê*, a word whose root means "to point out" (as in *digit* = "finger"). *Dikê* is a critical term in the history of Greek and Western thought. Plato's famous dialogue *The Republic* is an elaborate effort to define what is meant by *justice*.

proval of Troy's destruction, despite his love for the city. Similarly, Homer's *Odyssey* can be viewed as a study in appropriate and inappropriate expressions of *xenia*.

Figuratively, Zeus is father of gods and men, overseer of all that happens on earth and in heaven. In a more literal sense, he is father of numerous other gods and of many human heroes who are the legendary founders of historical Greek cities and peoples. As we might expect of a god who produced so many offspring, Zeus was celebrated for his numerous consorts or wives and his many dalliances with mortal women. Hellenistic commentators counted 115 of them. The origin of these tales, which distressed later moralizing commentators, is complex. As in Mesopotamian myth, sexual generation is a form of divine providence; it is the way the world and all things within it were made. The Eastern sexual metaphor, applied to the growth of crops, supported this thinking: The rain is semen and the receiving earth is woman's womb. In certain mystery cults (see Chapter 9), a leader looked to heaven and cried, "Send rain!" then, looking down at the earth, cried, "Conceive!" (in Greek, the words rhyme).

A humorous passage in the *Iliad* suggests the connection of Zeus's sexual exploits and the growth of plants. With the assistance of a magical embroidered belt lent her by the sex goddess Aphrodite, Zeus's wife, Hera, seduces him while he sits atop Mount Ida and watches the Trojan War (Fig. 6.2). Hera intends to distract Zeus so that she may assist the Greeks without his knowledge. The magical belt makes her so lovely that Zeus is overcome by desire, which he compares with desire earlier felt for other women:

[314] "Come with me, my Hera; we two will lie down in love.
315   Desire for goddess or mortal has never so flooded my heart
       or made it thump in my chest as now my passion for you.
       Not when I fell in love with Ixion's lovely bride,°
       mother by me of the wise Pirithoüs, wise as the gods;
       not in pursuit of Danaë, fair-ankled child of Acrisius,°
320   who bore me Perseus, my son, most honored of mortal men;
       not in abducting Europa,° daughter of glorious Phoenix,
       who bore me Minos the wise and the godlike Rhadamanthys;
       not in my loves for Semelê° or Alcmenê,° women of Thebes—
       the one bore Dionysus, the greatest joy of mankind,
325   the second gave birth to my son Heracles, mighty of spirit—
       not in my love for Demeter,° lady with soft fair braids,
       nor that for glorious Leto°—nor my love, my darling, for you!
       None ever shook my heart with the passion that now I feel."

HOMER, *Iliad* (14.314–328)

317. *bride:* Dia, who otherwise plays no part in myth.   319. *Acrisius:* Following an oracle, Acrisius imprisoned Danaë in an underground chamber, but Zeus came to her in the form of a shower of gold that fell through the grating.   321. *Europa:* When Zeus appeared to her in the form of a bull, she climbed on his back; he swam to Crete and there possessed her.   323. *Semelê:* She saw Zeus "as he appeared to Hera" and was burned to a crisp.   323. *Alcmenê:* Zeus came to her in the guise of her own husband.   326. *Demeter:* The goddess of the harvest.   327. *Leto:* Mother of Apollo and Artemis.

FIG. 6.2. The wedding of Zeus and Hera, a carving from a temple in Selinus on the southwest coast of Sicily, c. 550 B.C. Hera unveils herself, preparing for marriage with Zeus, while Zeus, holding her by the left arm, pulls her closer. Zeus's pose, seated on a throne, is typical of the Classical Period.   (Museo Archeologico Nazionale, Palermo; University of Wisconsin; Madison Photo Archive; author's photo)

The passage is a joke. Homer's male audience must have laughed at a husband seducing his own wife by listing all the women with whom he had betrayed her! Yet behind the humor stands the fructifying religious union of Father Sky with Mother Earth that is central to ancient myth and religion. The cloud-gatherer Zeus took his wife in his arms, assuring her that no one will see them:

[342]   "Hera, don't be afraid of a peeper, immortal or human;
         I'll bundle you up in a curtain of mist—opaque, yes, but golden,
         baffling even to Helius, keenest-eyed of immortals."
345   With that the son of great Cronus stretched out his arms like a bridegroom.

> Beneath from the radiant earth shot sweet young grasses of springtime,
> with lotuses, hyacinth, crocus, all flowers blushing and tender,
> all spring up to the light to curtain the amorous couple.
> So they embraced, reclined in a nimbus gleaming and golden,
> 350   their ardor cooled by glittering drops of the fresh-fallen dew.

HOMER, Iliad (14.342–351)

After intercourse, Zeus falls asleep, then wakes up later to discover that Hera has sneaked off to rouse the other gods against the Trojans. The male heavenly principle of fecundation becomes the enraged patriarch abused by a scheming wife:

> [13]   Zeus, with a savage glare, poured his reproach on Hera:
> "I should have known; it was your dirty trick
> 15   that put lord Hector° out of the way and made his army panic!
> Maybe you'll learn a lesson, if you yourself are the first,
> lashed by a bolt of lightning, to suffer the consequence.
> Don't you remember the time I strung you up by your wrists,
> tied your arms with golden cords, hung an anvil on each leg,
> 20   and left you dangling up there in the winds and the clouds?
> Of course, the gods were sorry, all over mighty Olympus,
> but dared not come to help: whoever I caught I flung
> headlong out of the door to land, more dead than alive,
> down on the earth. . . . So maybe you'll listen to me for once
> 25   and give up all your attempts to fool me, when once you have learned
> that all the alluring wiggling of your hips from side to side
> by which you used to get me into bed, away from the other gods,
> will never work again as a sexy hoax to deceive me."

HOMER, Iliad (15.13–33)

15. *Hector:* Leader of the Trojan forces.

Various explanations are given for the stories of Zeus's sexual unions with goddesses (Chart 6.2). Some are perhaps mythical reflections of a historical fact, the triumph of the invading Greeks' male sky god over the mother-goddess of indigenous peoples. Other unions have different meanings. Some are allegories illuminating the nature of Zeus and the universe.[2] Zeus's marriage with Metis, "Cleverness," whom he swallowed while she was pregnant with Athena, is an allegory: The rule of Zeus combines force with intelligence. His second consort was the Titaness Themis, "Things-established" (i.e., "the unchangeable laws of the universe"), who personifies the notion that the world is governed by rules. Zeus's union with her explains allegorically that under Zeus's reign the universe is governed by law, not force and whim. Their offspring are representations of visible order in the world. The (usually) three Horae (**hō**-rē), "Seasons," personify the regularly recurring divisions of the agricultural year but also embody good customs, orderly arrangement within human society, as suggested by their names: Eurynomê (ū-**ri**-no-mē), "Wide-spread Custom"; Dikê (**dē**-kē), "Justice"; and Eirenê (**ē**-rē-nē), "Peace."[3] They are usually three, rep-

[2]For the large topic of allegory in myth, see Chapter 23.
[3]Hence our name *Irene.*

The Loves of Zeus

The many dalliances of the king of the gods offered to European artists rich opportunities for the representation of erotic themes and female nudes; the great regard in which classical authors were then held, especially Ovid, offered a guard against reproach from the church and other authorities. Apollodorus also was studied assiduously and seems to have been the basis for Titian's (Italian, 1488/90–1576) *Danaë* (Fig. P 6.1a). In the twentieth century Titian is the most revered of the Old Masters, but he was also immensely successful in his lifetime, equally at home painting religious subjects, portraits, and scenes from myth, which he visualized as taking place in the natural world inhabited by humans like himself; he used live models.

According to Book 2 of Apollodorus' *The Library,* the daughter of Acrisius was imprisoned in a subterranean bronze chamber, but Titian shows her in a typical sev-

FIG. P 6.1a. *Danaë,* by Titian (Tiziano Vecelli) (Italian, 1488/90–1576), 1533–34, oil on canvas.   (Hermitage Museum, St. Petersburg; Art Resource, New York)

FIG. P 6.1b. *Leda and the Swan* by Antonio Allegri Correggio (Italian, 1489/94 – 1534), c. 1534, oil on canvas.   (Staatliche Museen, Berlin)

enteenth-century boudoir among sumptuous bed hangings. She is the reclining nude, a beloved subject in sophisticated Venetian court circles during the Renaissance, especially when sanctioned by a mythical setting. A hideous woman, not in Apollodorus' account, greedily attempts to snatch the golden coins that fall toward the virgin's legs, spread to receive them.

The well-known story of Leda and the swan does not appear in Homer or Hesiod but is found first in Euripides' play *Helen,* in the prologue. (Apollodorus also tells the story in *The Library,* Book 3.) The theme was a great favorite of Renaissance painters, who were just then recovering the antique past. Here (Fig. P 6.1b) Italian artist Antonio Allegri Correggio (1489/94 – 1534), who was influenced by Leonardo da Vinci and Michelangelo and sometimes admired as their equal, shows a narrative sequence in which Zeus as swan and Leda are represented three times: the arrival of the swan on the right as Leda, surprised and defensive, bathes in a pond; the moment of coition in the center, where she wears an expression of bemused pleasure; and the swan's departure watched by Leda and two female companions. The

FIG. P 6.1c. *Jupiter Abducting Ganymede,* by Charles-Joseph Natoire (French, 1700–1777), c. 1731, oil on canvas. (Musée des Beaux-Artes et d'Archeologie, Troyes; 835.11)

events are accompanied by three cupid musicians on the left, one playing the lyre, one blowing a horn, and one playing the pan-pipes. Correggio's softly modeled forms are illuminated by the light in the upper right. The somber colors of the trees and earth highlight the flesh of the women and the whiteness of the swan.

Based on the description in Book 10 of Ovid's *Metamorphoses, Jupiter Abducting Ganymede* (Fig. P 6.1c) by Charles-Joseph Natoire (French, 1700–1777) is portrayed with a mixture of passion and tenderness. Natoire had as patrons both the king and members of court, whose houses he decorated with mythical subjects, but he also accepted religious commissions and was director of the prestigious French Academy in Rome beginning in 1751. Here a dreamy Ganymede looks adoringly into the eagle's eye and with his left hand gently caresses the bird's head while his right hand clenches a red fabric that wraps around both boy and bird. The massive claw wrapped around the boy's right leg leaves no doubt about Jupiter's intentions. Natoire made the painting for a private country house in a room entirely decorated by the loves of Jupiter, including also Leda, Europa, and Danaë.

In Fig. P 6.1d, Jean-Baptiste-Marie Pierre (French, 1713–1789) represents *The Rape of Europa* (1750), where Jupiter appears as an eagle in the dark cloud to the right of Europa and as the bull she rides upon. Closely following Ovid's story, Pierre shows the bull's muscular neck, small polished horns decked with garlands, and his friendly expression. Pierre captures the moment in the abduction when Europa's mood changes from gaiety to fear, as described by Ovid, but her anxious glance to shore is understated: There is no real sense of danger, but more of wonderment.

Three cupids watch from the sky, carrying the flowers of love, while tritons (mermen) and sea nymphs swarm around her. One triton feeds the bull flowers as he rides on a sea-monster whose enormous fishy eye peers out of the waves.

FIG. P 6.1d. *The Rape of Europa,* by Jean-Baptiste-Marie Pierre (French, 1713–1789), 1750, oil on canvas.   (Dallas Museum of Art, Foundation for the Arts Collection, Mrs. John B. O'Hara Fund)

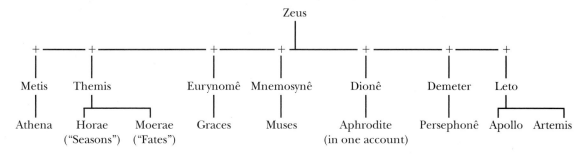

CHART 6.2. Zeus's Divine Consorts and Their Children

resented as women holding grass, grain, and fruit. Hesiod's *Theogony* tells us first that the **Moerae** (**mē**-rē), "Fates," were the children of Night, representing dark and implacable destiny, but later he says that they were children of Zeus and Themis, sisters of the Seasons: They establish the allotment that each mortal receives in life.[4] In Hellenistic times they are portrayed as three extremely old women, spinners of the threads of destiny: Clotho (**klō**-thō), "Spinner," who makes the thread; Lachesis (**lak**-e-sis), "Apportioner," who measures it; and Atropos (**a**-tro-pos), "she who cannot be turned aside," who cuts it off.

In Greek popular thought, one's fate, one's portion, can never be changed. Everyone is subject to unalterable fate, even mighty Zeus. In the *Iliad* Zeus wonders at one point whether he should act against fate and save his son Sarpedon from death, but Hera calls him up short:

[440]   "O mighty son of Cronus, what is this you suggest?
          Do you want to exempt a mortal, long since destined to die,
          from the gloomy decree of fate? Very well. Do as you please,
          but realize that not all the immortals will clap their hands.
          One thing I must point out for you to consider with care:
445   if you send Sarpedon back to his homeland, still alive,
          why should some other god not also want to deliver
          his own dear son from the deadly gamble of battle?
          Many of those who fight for the mighty city of Priam°
          are also sons of gods. Is exciting their rage what you want?"

                                             HOMER, *Iliad* (16.440–449)

448. *city of Priam:* Troy.

The passage implies that Zeus could act against fate, but that to do so would upset the scheme of things. In fact he never does; paradoxically, he is subject to the dictates of his own daughters, the Moerae. Although in the Classical Period and later Zeus was exalted as the origin and purpose of creation, Zeus's subordination to fate,

---

[4]The Romans called them *Parcae,* "Bringers Forth."

The Three Graces

In ancient representations the Graces are always shown as in this example (Fig. P 6.2a) from Pompeii from about 60 A.D., perhaps imitating a sculptural group. Stark naked, the central figure turns her back, while the outside figures face the viewer. Their hair is wreathed with crowns woven of leaves, and the outer figures hold a sprig. Shown like nymphs, virginal, small-breasted, and lovely, they stand in a country setting indicated by plants and rocks. Their eyes look demurely away, none seeing the other.

The iconography ("way of representing") of the Graces was rediscovered in the fifteenth century when a Hellenistic sculptural group was unearthed at Rome. The Renaissance artist Raphael made a painting of them (c. 1500 A.D.), and thereafter "The Three Graces" type became so popular that it was the way to indicate a brothel in Renaissance Italy.

FIG. P 6.2a. The three Graces, from a wall painting in Pompeii, c. 60 A.D.   (University of Wisconsin, Madison Photo Archive)

In this example by Flemish painter Peter Paul Rubens (1577–1640) (Fig. P 6.2b), painted 1,600 years later than that from Pompeii, the Graces adopt an ideal of feminine beauty unfashionable in our day. Rubens' figures seem to move and breathe. They adopt roughly the traditional posture, but the left-hand goddess turns inward as her gaze meets that of the middle figure, and the third Grace on the right gazes at both. In the painting from Pompeii the Graces touch one another, but in Rubens' version they seem actually to feel one another's flesh: The middle figure holds very tightly the other goddess' biceps, perhaps encouraging her to smile. Their faces are distinct, as is the color and arrangement of their hair: They are portraits of real women of Rubens' circle, a common practice in European art of the seventeenth century.

Unlike the formal setting of the painting from Pompeii, Rubens' scene has been cast in a partially realistic mode, with deer and trees and flowers in the background and the clothes the goddesses wore draped from the tree at the upper left. Evidently they have gone into the meadows, disrobed, and now prepare to dance. But symbols remain. The garland of roses over their heads stands for their loveliness, while the cherub holding a cornucopia in the upper right symbolizes their fecundity, their flushness and ripeness for burgeoning new life.

FIG. P 6.2b. Peter Paul Rubens (1577–1640), *The Three Graces,* c. 1620, oil on canvas.
(University of Wisconsin, Madison Photo Archive)

according to this conception, prevented the Greeks from evolving a true monotheism where a single god rules all things.

From Zeus's union with Eurynomê (not one of the Hours but an Oceanid with the same name) were born the **Graces** (Greek *Charites*, Latin *Gratiae*), usually considered three in number. The Graces personify the feminine qualities that make young women attractive to men, and they are often portrayed in the company of the goddess Aphrodite.

Zeus then united with Mnemosynê (nē-**mos**-i-nē), "Memory," to beget the Muses, who inspire poets and musicians.[5] The story is an allegory for the fact that such oral poets as Homer and Hesiod generated their poetry from an enormous stock of themes and story patterns held within their memory, passed on by tradition. Homer and Hesiod (as we have seen) begin their poems with a prayer to the Muses, setting a fashion in literature that remained vigorous until modern times.

Zeus's first four partners are allegorical figures. His fifth consort, by contrast, was Dionê, a Titaness or Oceanid, whose name is linguistically a feminine form of Zeus's own. Dionê may have been Zeus's earliest consort, before the Greeks migrated into the Balkan peninsula, where Hera replaced her. At the oracular shrine of Dodona in northwest Greece, Dionê was still with Zeus well into Christian times. In the alternative tradition that Aphrodite was Zeus's daughter (and not born from the sea), Dionê was her mother.

We will leave Zeus's many affairs with mortal women to our discussion of Greek legend. In addition to his relations with women, human and divine, Zeus was also a lover of boys, as were Greek aristocrats of the Classical Period. He fell in love with **Ganymede** (**gan**-i-mēd), most beautiful of mortals, a prince of the Trojan royal house. One day while Ganymede shepherded his flocks on Mount Ida, Zeus came upon him or sent an eagle to carry him to Olympus (Fig. 6.3). There Ganymede remained as cupbearer to the gods, serving the same function as did handsome boys in the Greek symposium.[6]

HERA, QUEEN OF HEAVEN

Zeus's proper wife is Hera (identified with Juno by the Romans). The meaning of her name, probably of pre-Hellenic origin, is unclear, although some explain it as meaning "ruler" or "lady," the feminine of *hero*. Hera was chiefly a goddess of marriage and of women's sexuality and fertility, but earlier she may have been a mother-goddess sponsoring the fertility of cattle and crops. The cow was her special animal; in Homer she is called "cow-eyed." Some of the earliest and most splendid temples

---

[5]The Muses were all concerned with communication: Clio, "Making Famous," ruled history; Euterpê, "Delighter," flute-playing; Thalia, "Flowering," comedy; Melpomenê, "Song and Dance," tragedy; Erato, "Lovable," love lyric; Terpsichorê, "Delighting in Dance," dance; Polyhymnia, "With Many Songs," pantomime; Urania, "Heavenly," astrology; and Calliopê, "Fair-voiced," epic poetry.
[6]In Rome Ganymede's name was corrupted to *catamitus*, the origin of our word *catamite*, a boy who submits to anal intercourse.

FIG. 6.3. Zeus and Ganymede on an Attic cup, c. 455 B.C. Zeus has dropped his thunderbolt and scepter, symbols of his power and his office, to seize the handsome boy. Although Zeus tries to catch the boy with his eye, Ganymede looks shyly to the ground (compare the similar posture of the symposiasts in Fig. 2.7). The rooster to the right is a common gift in pederastic relations.   (Museo Archeologico Nazionale, Ferrara; 9351)

in Greece were built to Hera: in Argos, on the island of Samos, and at Olympia, where her temple was older than Zeus's (Fig. 6.4). Hera's association with Argos is reflected in her eager sponsorship of the Greeks in the Trojan War, the subject of many myths told about her. Homer often calls the Greeks "Argives," that is, the men of Argos, near where stood the Heraeum, one of the oldest and holiest temples in Greece. Agamemnon, the leader of the Greek army, had his castle on the Argive plain, very near the Heraeum.

Adultery is the great threat to monogamous marriage and the orderly inheritance of property and rank, and perhaps for this reason Hera vindictively persecutes Zeus's many mistresses and illegitimate children, especially the hero Heracles. Despite Hera's role in protecting the family, she is never addressed in religious cult as "Mother" or represented with her children. Her own discordant marriage produced

FIG. 6.4. The temple of Hera at Olympia in the northwest corner of the great sanctuary to Zeus, c. 600 B.C. The original columns were wood, gradually replaced by local fieldstone and shell limestone as the timbers rotted. It is the earliest monumental temple in Greece, one hundred years older than the nearby great temple to Zeus, which held a famous statue by Phidias, one of the Seven Wonders of the Ancient World. Because of Hera's importance and precedence in Zeus's shrine, the sanctuary may have belonged to a mother-goddess in primordial times.
(University of Wisconsin, Madison Photo Archive)

but three children: Ares, whom Zeus called "most hated of gods"; the divine midwife **Eileithyia** (ē-lē-thī-ya), whose name may mean the "coming" (i.e., of the child) and who presided over the special function of childbirth (sometimes Hera herself was confused with Eileithyia); and Hebê (**hē-bē**), "Youth," a colorless abstraction. None of these figures played a central role in Greek myth.

Although later traditions make Hephaestus a child of Zeus and Hera, Hesiod reports that Hera conceived him asexually, jealous because Zeus had given birth to Athena without the intervention of woman. Perhaps his lack of a father explains why Hephaestus was born a cripple, a fact that caused Hera some consternation. According to one passage in the *Iliad* (presented later in this chapter), Hephaestus complains that Zeus threw him from heaven, but according to a second version in the *Iliad,* Hera herself cast him out, disgusted by his deformity. From incidental references we also learn that Hera joined with Poseidon and Athena in a palace conspiracy against Zeus. They actually succeeded in binding him, until Thetis summoned from Tartarus the Hundred-hander Briareus, who released Zeus from his bondage.

ZEUS AND HERA AT HOME ON OLYMPUS

Zeus, the king, had married Queen Hera in a formal ceremony on the islands of the Hesperides ("Nymphs of the West"), far away in the western ocean. As a wedding gift, Gaea/Earth gave her granddaughter Hera golden apples that grew on a magical tree (Fig. 6.5). Although married (and often henpecked), Zeus had a roving eye. As in any unhappy marriage, tension ran high. Homer indelibly influenced the Greek tradition with his portrayal of these squabbling, all-too-human gods near the opening of the *Iliad*. The Nereid Thetis has come to Zeus to beg a favor for her son Achilles, but a prying, jealous Hera overhears their conversation:

[536] When Hera saw him enter, she knew that he and Thetis,
the Nereid nymph, had been putting their heads together,
and she bitterly screamed at her husband Zeus, the son of Cronus.
"Who's this who's plotting with you to set the divine agenda?
540 You never miss a chance of waiting till I'm out of sight
to publish some scheme that you two have secretly plotted already,
and you haven't got the guts to tell me what you have in mind!"

HOMER, *Iliad* (1.536–543)

The father of gods furiously rebukes his wife:

[561] "Lady, you're always suspicious. You never miss a thing.
A lot of good it will do if you make me angrier still—
if you go on with your nagging, it will be a cold day for you!

FIG. 6.5. The three "Nymphs of the West," the tree of the Hesperides, guarded by the serpent Ladon, who winds around it, on an Attic water jug, c. 460 B.C. One of Heracles' labors was to steal the golden apples from this tree, which gave eternal life to whoever ate from them. Here he has taken three of the apples and flees to the left, while one nymph gestures toward him, another raises her arms in dismay, and the third tries to calm the angry serpent. (Krannert Art Museum, Champaign, Illinois; 70-8-4)

That's the way things are, because that's the way that I want them.
565 So sit down and shut up, and listen to what I am going to say:
Not all the gods on Olympus will give you a bit of assistance
if I get sore and lay my irresistible hand upon you!"
     At that the terrified Hera sat down and silently fumed,
and even in Zeus's house the heavenly gods were resentful.
570 But Hephaestus of skillful hands got up and spoke with a smile,
in favor of Hera, his mother, the goddess of milky-white shoulders:
     "Disgraceful indeed it will be, a state we cannot endure,
if you two start to squabble like this, and all because of a mortal,
wrangling among the gods! Our dinners will give us no pleasure,
575 if lesser matters distract from them our fullest attention.
I beg you, dearest mother, intelligent soul that you are,
to humor Zeus my father, lest he quarrel with you again,
ruining all the banquet and upsetting us all in addition.
For if the whim should seize the Olympian, hurler of thunder,
580 he could blast us out of our seats—he is mightier than we by far!
So please! try to soften him down with gentle affectionate words.
Then the Olympian again will show a benevolent face."
     So saying, he rose and put the two-handled cup
into his dear mother's hands, and continued his sound advice:
585 "Courage, dear mother; be cheerful, however gloomy you feel.
I don't want to stand by helpless, while I watch him beating you up.
For however great my anguish, I could not help you at all.
The Olympian—this I can assure you—is a hard man to oppose.
     "Do you remember the time, only a little while back,
590 when I was trying my best to stand up in your defense?
He grabbed me by one ankle and flung me out through the door.
For full twelve hours I fell. When the sun was about to set,
I hit the ground in Lemnos,° rather more dead than alive,
but the Sintians° promptly saved me by giving me first aid."
595   His rueful-comical tale restored her former good humor
to Hera the white-shouldered goddess. Smiling, she took the cup
from the hand of her son, who moved in a clockwise direction,
drew nectar out of the krater° and passed it on to the others.
And endless laughter arose among the immortal gods
600 as they watched Hephaestus puffing around the banqueting hall.
     So they feasted all day, until the coming of evening,
at the banquet where nothing was lacking, whatever the heart might desire—
not the sound of the lyre so skillfully plucked by Apollo,
to accompany the notes of the Muses' clear-ringing treble.
605 The gleaming disk of the sun descended at last in the west.
Returning to his own house, each Olympian lay down to slumber
in the home that the lame Hephaestus had cleverly built for each one.
To his own familiar bed, a comfort when weariness crushed him,
went lightning-throwing Zeus, to embrace the golden-throned Hera.

                              HOMER, *Iliad* (1.561–611)

593. *Lemnos:* A large island in the northern Aegean.   594. *Sintians:* The native inhabitants of Lemnos.   598. *krater:* A large bowl used to mix wine with water before serving.

In the *Iliad* Homer gives a picture of the gods' life, politically monarchical and socially monogamous, an image of Greek life in the preliterate ages, on which to some extent this picture must be based. Hephaestus, god of smiths, is the dutiful cup-bearing son, himself a past victim of Zeus's overwhelming power, and sad to see his parents quarrel. Apollo, who presides over music, plays the same role on Olympus that such bards as Homer played in human society: to entertain at the banquet. Here he accompanies the singing of the Muses, inspirers of oral song. Homer's monogamous and sometimes misogynistic male audience must have enjoyed his tales of a disagreeable wife threatened with violence to keep her in her place!

Observations: Greek Anthropomorphism

Influenced by the Mesopotamian tradition, the Greeks portrayed their gods as beings in the shape of men and women who act and think like human beings, honor kings, live in families, marry, procreate, have sexual liaisons, wrangle, intrigue, dine at banquets served by cupbearers, and are entertained by songs sung to the lyre. Such is Greek **anthropomorphism.** These gods have bodies and eat (although they do not excrete, which would be unseemly), and in their veins flows a divine fluid called *ichor* instead of blood. They can even be wounded, as Ares is in Homer's description of the meeting of the war god with the Greek hero Diomedes (assisted by Athena) on the Trojan plain:

[855]   Once more Diomedes, screaming, struck with his brazen spear.
Athena added her weight. The point took Ares right in the belly,
a little above his belt, and gave him a terrible wound,
and the flesh was ripped when Diomedes yanked it back.
Ares let out a bellow like nine or ten thousand soldiers
860   when battle lines clash in war. Greeks and Trojans alike
shook in terror to hear the screaming of pitiless Ares.

HOMER, *Iliad* (5.855–863)

Ares flees to heaven. Paieon (**pē**-e-on), a name associated with Apollo as healing god, cares for the wound:

[899]   With this Zeus ordered Paieon to heal the wounded Ares,
900   which he did by sprinkling pain-killing drugs on the wound.
He healed the god only because a god is not fated to die.
If you drop the acid juice of a fig into liquid white milk,
it promptly curdles to solid; just so the torn flesh of Ares
was healed by the drug. Then Hebê washed him and dressed him,
905   and once more he sat beside Zeus, proudly vaunting his glory.

HOMER, *Iliad* (5.899–906)

Anthropomorphism makes possible a large and diverse body of myths. Gods who are colorless abstractions, like the native Roman gods, or who take animal or other nonhuman form, like many of the gods of Egypt and India, make dull actors because it is hard to fit them into a plot—a story whose outcome is not predetermined. Homer's gods are like us, having the powers we do, although in greater abundance. But life itself, which "the dying ones"—humans—one day will lose, is possessed forever by "the deathless ones"—the gods. This makes the Greek gods, exempt from the serious business of dying, a fit subject for comedy, even burlesque. For death gives weight and meaning to human acts.

Freed from mortality, Homer's gods live amid perpetual good times. Their world is a light-hearted wish-fulfillment of the humans who described it. Yet when Homer's poems were composed, and for a thousand years thereafter, the Greeks built temples to these gods, made pious sacrifice to them, and were inspired by fear and awe in their presence. Thus we must distinguish between gods as actors in myth and gods as powers fit to receive sacrifice and to be adored in religious cult. Greek myths were in no sense "gospels," to be accepted by pious Greeks as trustworthy records of literal truth about divine beings.

In addition to the great gods who made the universe and who live on Olympus or beneath the earth, there were innumerable minor anthropomorphic deities in Greek myth, mostly personifications of natural powers. The broadest category is that of the **nymphs,** a word meaning "young women," thought of as lovely beings, often amorous, who inhabit wild places or who accompany the greater gods and goddesses.[7] Although divine, the nymphs were not necessarily immortal; they were something like the fairies of European folklore. Nymphs were usually closely bound to a particular place and were favorite subjects of love poetry throughout antiquity. Many of the stories in Ovid's *Metamorphoses* describe their doings. Nereids and Oceanids were nymphs of the sea; the Nereid Thetis and the Oceanid Dionê (probably not the consort of Zeus) had considerable importance. We will meet various other categories of nymphs and spirits in this book.

KEY TERMS

Zeus, 136	Moerae, 141	Eileithyia, 146
aegis, 137	Graces, 144	anthropomorphism, 149
xenia, 137	Ganymede, 144	nymphs, 150

FURTHER READING

Cook, A. B., *Zeus,* 3 parts (New York, 1964; orig. 1914–1940). An enormous work tracking the development of Zeus, according to the cultural theories of Sir James G. Frazer, author of *The Golden Bough* (see Chapter 23).

---

[7]As we saw in Chapter 2, a young virgin was called *korê,* "maid"; after marriage, she was *gynê,* "woman"; between the time of betrothal and the wedding, she was *nymphê.*

CHAPTER 7

MYTHS OF THE OLYMPIANS
THE MALE DEITIES

He whom the lord Apollo, who works from afar, makes a prophet,
    knows in advance what evil is lying in wait for a man.
The gods themselves give warning. But neither knowledge of omens
    nor sacrificial bribes can avert the sentence of Fate.
Other men are physicians, with the skills of drug-dealing Paeön,°
    but even they cannot promise certain success for their work;
too often horrible torment arises from trifling ailments,
    which no one could possibly cure by gentle conservative means.

SOLON, C. 594 B.C., fragment 1, 53–62 (Diehl)

Paeön: Apollo. In Homer Paeön was an independent god of medicine who healed Hades when Heracles shot him with an arrow. Later, *paeön* (**pē**-on) was an epithet applied to Apollo and Asclepius (Paeön is mentioned in the Linear B tablets).

As projections of human concerns, the male gods specialized in typically male activities. Zeus ruled the family and all humankind because men did just that in human society. The nether family was like a mirror-image of the upper, so Hades was King of Death (in ancient Mesopotamia Death was a woman, Ereshkigal in Sumerian myth). Knowledge was open only to men in ancient Greece, and Apollo guided them, although often through the mouth of a woman. Poseidon caused the devastating storms that afflicted Greek sailors, always male, but he was also the god of earthquake, which afflicted everyone. Only men were smiths and warriors, and Hephaestus and Ares represented their interests, just as Hermes helped the traveling merchant, an exclusively male occupation.

POSEIDON, LORD OF THE DEEP

Having won their victory over the Titans, the gods drew lots to apportion the world among them. Zeus won the heavens, Hades the underworld, and **Poseidon** (the Roman Neptune) the sea. The first part of the name *Poseidon* is Greek for "husband" or "lord" (*posis*), but the second part resists explanation. Some scholars take it to be the same as in *De*-meter, somehow meaning "wheat." Poseidon, then, would be the "wheat husband," the male consort of the earth mother and, like her, a god of fertility. This view finds some support in the myth that Poseidon pursued Demeter across the plains of Arcadia. To escape, she changed herself into a mare,[1] but Poseidon became a stallion and possessed her anyway. Their offspring was the famous horse Arion (a-**rī**-on), who saved the Argive hero Adrastus in the war of the Seven against Thebes.[2]

Some have theorized that Poseidon originally was an Indo-European god of freshwater streams who became identified with the sea after the Greek migration into the Balkans. His presence in Greece at an early date is evidenced by his name on Linear B tablets from Pylos in the southwestern Peloponnesus (c. 1200 B.C.).

By the time of Homer, Poseidon is preeminently Lord of the Deep, married to Amphitrite (am-fi-**trī**-tē), a Nereid. Their child Triton (**trī**-ton) was shown in art as a merman, half-human, half-fish; when Triton blew his conch shell, the seas were calmed. As often with minor deities, we sometimes hear of Tritons in the plural (compare Fig. P 6.1d).

Poseidon lived at the bottom of the sea and traveled across it in a chariot drawn by horses or sea monsters. Homer's description of him setting off to fight at Troy has colored for all time our conception of him:

[17]   Down from the mountain's rugged crags he thundered
with flying steps. High hills and trees shook at the tread
of his immortal feet as the lord Poseidon advanced.
20   Three mighty steps he took; the fourth one brought him home,
to Aegae,° where his home arose in the depths of the gulf,
gleaming and golden, a palace built to endure forever.
He harnessed his pair of brazen-hoofed wind-swift horses,
golden of mane, to his car. He buckled his golden armor
25   over his own strong limbs, took his strong and golden whip,
mounted his chariot's box, and scudded over the surge.
Beneath, great fish skipped up on every side from the deep,
and the laughing waves gave way, acknowledging their lord.
So the god and his team sped on, dry-axled, over the sea,
30   till the leaping horses reached the huddled Achaean vessels.
    A spacious cavern lies deep near the bottom of the strait
that runs between rocky Imbros and Tenedos, the island off Troy.

21. *Aegae:* A town in the northern Peloponnesus.

---

[1]The story is etiological, to explain a horse-headed statue of Demeter in the Peloponnesus, almost the only Greek example of a common Egyptian way of representing a deity.
[2]A distinguished journal of classical studies is called *Arion.*

Poseidon, shaker of earth, there halted his sweating team,
unhitched them from his car, and gave them ambrosial fodder.
35 Around their fetlocks he set unbreakable golden hobbles,
to keep them from wandering off before their lord returned.
Then he himself set off to the Achaean encampment.

HOMER, *Iliad* (13.17–38)

Poseidon's association with horses is richly attested, although no one has convincingly explained why; the association may go back to the horse-riding Indo-Europeans, who knew far more about horses than about water. Horses were drowned in sacrifice to him. He impregnated the Gorgon Medusa; from her neck, when Per-

FIG. 7.1. Poseidon or Zeus, c. 470–450 B.C. One of the most celebrated sculptures to survive from the ancient world, this over–life-sized bronze statue represents either Zeus or Poseidon majestically poised to strike with either thunderbolt or trident (the weapon has been lost). The statue was found in the sea north of the island of Euboea, evidently lost in a shipwreck. Few bronzes survive from the ancient world; most were later melted down to recover the valuable metal.
(National Archaeological Museum, Athens; University of Wisconsin, Madison Photo Archive)

seus beheaded her, sprang the warrior Chrysaör and the flying horse Pegasus (compare Chart 4.3), which Bellerophon mounted to slay the Chimera.

Poseidon has much in common with Zeus; he too admires women and from time to time imposes himself on them against their will. Both are represented in art as stern and lordly figures, not easily distinguished, except when Poseidon is shown carrying his characteristic trident (Fig. 7.1). That he may have originally been a male fertility god is suggested by his association with freshwater springs. Wherever he struck his trident, a spring burst forth. Competing with Athena for the allegiance of Athens, he demonstrated his power by striking the Acropolis. From the rock there sprang a well, although in this case one of sea water; it is not hard to see why the Athenians chose Athena as their patron, who gave them the domestic olive tree, basis of the Athenian economy. Poseidon, furious at the decision, flooded the Attic plain. In the Classical Period what was supposed to be Athena's original olive tree still grew beside the temple called the Erechtheum, and an opening was left in the roof and porch to show where Poseidon had struck the earth (see Fig. 15.1).

To Poseidon's lot fell one third of the world, but he lacked Zeus's good will toward humans. The Greeks did not like the sea: They knew too much about it. Poseidon was also the god of earthquake, a logical role for a power that dwells in the depths. Greece and the Aegean are geologically unstable and subject to frequent and violent earthquakes; this was Poseidon's doing. Homer calls him "shaker of earth." He is no friendly god, but master of the terrifying movement of the earth and the sea and the roaring thunder of horses' hooves beating over the plain.

HADES, KING OF THE DEAD

Together with Zeus and Poseidon, **Hades** (hā-dēz) shared the governance of the universe. His name means "the invisible," appropriate as the embodiment of the unseen dead, hidden beneath the ground but present on the earth as wandering and treacherous ghosts. Being dangerous to name, he was often called Pluto, the "enricher," from the agricultural riches that spring from the earth and from precious metals. The Cyclopes gave him a magical helmet that made him invisible; other deities, and even mortal heroes, occasionally borrowed it. His childless marriage to Persephonê, daughter of Demeter, is described in the *Homeric Hymn to Demeter*, translated in Chapter 9. He commanded legions of demons. A pitiless master, he never willingly allowed any who came to him to return to the land of the living. We examine the geography and inhabitants of his realm in Chapter 11.

APOLLO THE FAR-DARTER, GOD OF PROPHECY

The historical origin of Apollo is unknown, as is the meaning of his name. Many think his cult must have come from Asia Minor because he is called Lycian—that is, from Lycia—and because in Asia Minor there were many sites of his cult. However, *Lycian* could just as well mean "wolflike," perhaps because at an early stage he protected shepherds from wolves. Wherever Apollo's cult comes from, it has taken on

FIG. 7.2. Apollo and Dionysus at Delphi, Attic vase, fourth century B.C. The ecstatic aspect of Apollo's oracle brought it into natural alliance with the religion of Dionysus, who ruled Delphi during the three winter months while Apollo was away among the Hyperboreans. Even the grave of Dionysus could be seen in Apollo's precinct. Apollo, shown as a beardless youth with a crown of laurel, takes leave of Dionysus, bearded and wearing tragic garb and carrying the thyrsus. Beneath them is the Delphic omphalos or navel, and behind a palm tree. The other figures are maenads and satyrs. (Hermitage Museum, St. Petersburg)

associations with the far north: In winter, while Dionysus ruled at **Delphi,** Apollo dwelled among the Hyperboreans (hi-per-bor-ē-anz), "the men beyond the North Wind" (Fig. 7.2). By the time alphabetic literacy was established in Greece in the eighth century B.C., Apollo was already a great god.

With their mother, Leto, a Titan, Apollo and Artemis formed a sort of divine family, although in origin they had nothing to do with one another. Leto is evidently an ancient mother-goddess (always a convenient explanation) and was worshiped as such in Lycia and perhaps on Crete, but in Greek myth she is simply the mother of the divine twins, who are ever ready to defend her honor. In the Classical Period, Apollo is sometimes called a sun god—as Artemis was by then thought to represent the dark and the moon—but in origin he had no connection with the sun.[3] Although represented as an archer-god, he is not a god of hunters; his arrows are the shafts of disease, emerging from the spirit world, irresistible, unseen, striking down the luckless (Fig. 7.3). This association is made explicit in our oldest reference to him, at the beginning of the *Iliad* (c. 800 B.C.) where Apollo is the dangerous god of plague, called Lord of Mice, the plague-bringers.

The daughter of Chryses (**kri**-sēz), a Trojan priest of Apollo, has been captured by the Greeks and given as booty to King Agamemnon. Chryses comes to the Greek camp and begs for the return of his daughter, offering generous ransom. But Agamemnon, snarling and rude, refuses to give her up. Enraged, Chryses leaves the

[3]In the Hellenistic Period, when the Babylonian sky religion was imported into the Hellenic world, the names of the Olympians were assigned to the other planets, which still bear them today: Mercury (= Hermes), Venus (= Aphrodite), Mars (= Ares), and so forth.

FIG. 7.3. The temple to Apollo at Bassae, one of the best-preserved of all Greek temples, c. 450 B.C., in the wilderness of southwestern Arcadia, designed by Ictinus, architect of the Parthenon, and dedicated to Apollo in thanksgiving for release from a plague. Several years ago the temple was covered by an enormous, ugly canvas tent to protect it.   (University of Wisconsin, Madison Photo Archive)

Greek camp, walks along the much-resounding sea, and raises his arms in prayer to Apollo, his patron and protector:

[35]   "Hear me, O god of the silver bow, the guardian of Chrysê,
       the guardian of Cilla, who rules over Tenedos° with your power,
       Lord of the Mice! If ever I roofed your glorious temple
       or burnt fat flesh of bulls or of goats on your altar,
       grant that the Greeks may feel the piercing sting of your arrows,
40   and thus make reparation for their insults and all my tears."
           So he spoke, and Phoebus Apollo heard his prayer.
       Raging, down he came at a bound from the heights of Olympus,
       his bow on his shoulder, its quiver firmly boxed at both ends.
       The whining arrows sped out from the furious archer's shoulder;
45   black he stood as night, aiming now this way, now that.
       First he knelt at a distance, far from the ships, aimed, and shot.
       Terribly, shrilly, resounded the twang of his silver bow.
       First he aimed at the mules, then at the keen-scented hounds,
       then at the huddled men. The death fires burned day and night.

                               HOMER, *Iliad* (1.35–52)

36. *Chrysê . . . Tenedos:* Chrysê and Cilla seem to have been villages near Troy; Chryses takes his name from the first of them. Tenedos is the island just off the coast of Troy.

The Birth of Apollo on Delos

One of the longest of the Homeric Hymns is dedicated to Apollo. The first part, "To the Delian Apollo," describes how he was born, his parentage, and the greatness of his power; the second part, "To the Delphian Apollo," probably originally a separate and later composition, tells about the founding of Apollo's oracle at Delphi.

The Titaness Leto (daughter of Coeus and Phoebê) was a mistress of Zeus and, like so many others in a similar position, was persecuted by Hera. When pregnant Leto came to term, Hera maliciously decreed that no land that sees the light of day should receive her children. Bursting with pain, Leto wandered the earth seeking a place to give birth, but no land would accept her. At last, two tiny waterless islands in the center of the Cyclades agreed: **Delos** (dē-los), "clear, bright," and nearby Ortygia, "Quail Island." Delos and Ortygia were exempt from Hera's decree because they were floating islands, sometimes bobbing beneath the surface. Artemis was born on Ortygia and Apollo on Delos, although the Delian hymn mentions the birth of Artemis only in passing. Other versions of the story relate how Artemis was born first—and then with divine precocity assisted in the birth of her twin brother!

The hymn begins with a description of Apollo's honored place on Olympus:

[1]   Let me not forget to sing of Apollo who shoots from afar.
        In Zeus's house the immortals shake at Apollo's arrival,
        rising up from their seats as he tightens his wonderful bow.
        Leto alone keeps her place at the side of Zeus, lord of thunder;
5   it is she who looses his bowstring, she who closes his quiver.
        She lifts it off from his shoulders, to hang on a peg of gold
        driven into a pillar supporting the house of his father.
        She leads her son to his seat, as his father offers Apollo
        a golden goblet of nectar. The others, taking their places,
10   rejoice that Leto has borne her mighty son, archer Apollo.
        Hail to you, blessed Leto, the mother of glorious children,
        the lordly Apollo and Artemis, she who delights in her arrows.
        Her she bore on Ortygia, him on the rocky island of Delos,
        bracing her back against the towering rock of Mount Cynthus,°
15   close to the palm tree that flourishes green, on the bank of Inopus.°
            How can I challenge the songs already sung to your glory?
        Everywhere, Phoebus, the strains of music resound in your honor,
        on the mainland, teeming with cattle, on islands girt by the sea.
        All crags and beetling ridges of mountains gladden your spirit,
20   rivers that flow to the sea, headlands awash with salt water,
        and harbors locked from the sea.
            Shall I then sing the travail of Leto, the goddess who bore you,
        joy to mankind, who braced herself on the Cynthian mountain,
        on rocky Delos, the isle surrounded by sea? The dark surges

---

14. *Mount Cynthus:* Cynthus is the only peak (368 feet high) on this small island. From Cynthus comes our proper name *Cynthia,* "woman born by Mount Cynthus," that is, Artemis (= Diana).
15. *Inopus:* A tiny stream.

25   smashed in on either side, pressed by the whistling breezes.
        There you were born, there first you arose, the lord of mankind.

Homeric Hymn to Apollo (1–29)

The poem goes on to list thirty-two places Leto visits in her search for somewhere
to give birth; fearing Hera's anger, none would admit her. When at last she came to
poverty-stricken Delos, she proclaimed the advantages that would accrue to the place
willing to allow the birth of the great god:

[45]   To all these places in turn came Leto, her labor upon her,
        seeking a place of refuge for the birth of far-shooting Apollo.
        But all of them, even the richest, trembled with cowardly fear,
        and none dared welcome the god, till Leto happened on Delos.
        There to the island she spoke in anguished and bitter words:
50   "O Delos, I wish you were willing to offer a home for Apollo,
        my son, and in it be willing to build him a well-endowed temple!
        For otherwise no one would dream of coming to you for a visit.
        I cannot see your island as rich in sheep, wines, or cattle,
        and you surely will never have trees. But if you erected a temple
55   to Apollo, who works from afar, men would come from all over the world
        with sacrificial cattle. The savory smoke of their offerings
        would rise up on high forever, and you could provide for your rulers
        the product of other men's hands—a blessing, for under the land
        you have no wealth of your own."
60   So she spoke, and the island of Delos replied in delight to the goddess:
        "Leto, noble daughter of Coeus, I would be happy
        to win the glorious honor of bearing the far-shooting lord.
        I have a poor reputation, and doubtless you can improve it.
        But one thing, Leto, is scary. I must be frank, for they tell me
65   Apollo will be high and mighty, pushing himself to the fore,
        whenever immortals assemble, and among us mortals as well,
        here on the grain-giving earth. My personal feeling is this:
        from the very day he is born and looks to the light of the sun,
        he will scorn this poor little island, call it a desolate rockpile,
70   and stomp it into the sea. But the thing that really alarms me,
        like surf breaking over my head, is that some day, on a mere fancy,
        he will leave us to go somewhere else to build his wonderful temple,
        surrounded by bushes and parks. After that, the octopus doubtless,
        and the sleek black seal can use me—if ever they run out of rocks—
75   as a place for making their homes. So, goddess, if you dare promise,
        swear a great oath that here on Delos your son will first raise
        his glorious temple, an oracle shrine for the whole of mankind—
        then, once it is finished, he may build wherever he pleases."
        So Delos spoke, and Leto swore the great oath of the gods:
80   "Witness, O Earth, and you, the wide-spreading Heavens above,
        and you, slow waters of Styx, the greatest, most terrible oath
        that binds the blessed gods: here on this isle shall remain
        forever the fragrant temple and altar of Phoebus Apollo,
        and to you he will grant, O Delos, the highest honor of all."

Homeric Hymn to Apollo (45–88)

Even after nine days of labor Leto had not yet delivered. Although all the goddesses gathered to help (except, of course, Hera), Leto could not bring the god forth. Iris, "Rainbow," the messenger goddess, was sent to Hera to beg for her daughter Eileithyia, the divine midwife. Hera, although truculent, at last agreed, according to one account only after being bribed by a necklace of gold and amber 30 feet thick!

[116] At once delivery started, and Leto labored in childbirth,
      embracing the trunk of a palm, bracing her knees in the grass;
      The earth smiled in joy, and the goddesses shouted for pleasure
      as the god sprang into the light.

                        Homeric Hymn to Apollo (116–119)

As soon as Artemis and Apollo were born, the hitherto floating islands of Delos and Ortygia were anchored in their present places. The sacred palm that Leto grasped was a landmark outside the elaborate temple complex that sprang up on Delos during the Classical Period; true to Leto's prediction, Delos, whose area is only two square miles, became one of the richest and most celebrated religious shrines in all Greece (today the island is uninhabited). Another tradition reports that, only days after the twins' birth, Hera released the giant Tityus from the earth to rape Leto, but Apollo and Artemis cut him down in a shower of arrows, and Zeus condemned him to eternal punishment in Hades (see Fig. 11.2).

Apollo at Delphi

Apollo's role in prophecy was especially associated with the oracular shrine to him at Delphi, perched on a precipitous slope of Mount Parnassus near the Corinthian Gulf. The second part of the *Homeric Hymn to Apollo* begins with a pretty account of how Apollo, after being born, joined the gods on Olympus:

[186] He passes, swift as thought, soaring up from this world to Olympus,
      to the palace of Zeus, where he joins with a crowd of the other immortals.
      There the thoughts of the gods are turned to dancing and song.
      The clear-voiced Muses together add their refrain to the hymn.
190   They chant the right of the gods to an endless and blissful existence,
      and the misery of men, whose lives drag, helpless and blinded,
      who have no cure for death, no defense against helpless old age.
      The fair-haired Graces dance in a ring, and the light-hearted Horae,
      joining their hands in a chain, and with them Harmonia, Hebê,
195   and Aphrodite, daughter of Zeus. No dancer is ugly or dwarfish,
      least of all Artemis, wondrously beauteous, stately, and tall,
      she who delights in her arrows, brought up with her brother Apollo.
      Joining the dance is Hermes, the far-seeing slayer of Argus.
      Apollo plays on his lyre, to lead the dance and the singing,
200   while glory shines all about from his robe and his dancing feet.
      Leto of golden hair and Zeus, designer of counsel,
      rejoice as they watch their dear son playing amid the immortals.

                        Homeric Hymn to Apollo (186–206)

FIG. 7.4. The temple of Apollo at Delphi, on the precipitous slopes of Mount Parnassus, which rise behind it in the mist. These reconstructed columns stand near the entrance to the east; the adytum of the oracle was at the other end, to the left.
(V. Papaioannou; University of Wisconsin, Madison Photo Archive)

Apollo fulfills in the divine community the same function as the oral poet in the human, playing for choral dance and singing and entertaining at the banquet. As the oral poet was the bearer, through his song, of traditional male aristocratic Greek culture, Apollo the singer became the god of the Greek *aristoi*, a projection of their own self-image. Many stories were told about Apollo's skill with the lyre, in art his most common attribute. According to a story made famous by Ovid and beloved by European painters of the sixteenth to eighteenth centuries, the satyr Marsyas (**mar-si-as**), master of the double-flute, challenged Apollo to a musical contest, the winner being allowed to do as he liked; Apollo won easily and flayed Marsyas alive.

After being presented on Olympus, Apollo wandered over the earth, searching for a place to establish his oracle. He headed south and came eventually to a spring in Boeotia called Telphusa (tel-**fū**-sa), after a prophetic nymph who dwelled within it. Apollo tells the nymph that he wants to build his oracle here, but Telphusa, fearing competition, persuades Apollo to move on to the precipitous slopes of Parnassus (Fig. 7.4):

[282]   So forth you went, O archer, to Crisa,
　　　　a western foothill of snowy Parnassus, where crags of the mountain
　　　　hang over the place up above; beneath is a rough rocky cavern.
285　　　"This is the place where I plan to build my glorious temple,
　　　　an oracular shrine, to which mankind may forever
　　　　bring me unblemished offerings from rich Peloponnesus,

from Europe, and from the wave-washed islands around in the sea.
Whatever they ask, I will offer them all unfailing advice,
290 telling them what is to be, from within my opulent temple."
  With this Phoebus Apollo laid out all the foundations,
their breadth and their great length. The sons of Erginus,°
dear to the deathless gods, Trophonius and Agamedes,
laid on these the footings of stone. Countless tribes of men
295 above them built a temple of carefully polished ashlars,
the theme of song forever. Nearby was a sweet-flowing spring,°
where the lord, son of Zeus, loosed his bow and slew a dread female dragon:°
a great fat savage beast, who used to do dreadful things,
not only to thin-legged sheep, but to their owners as well,
300 crimson plague that she was. . . .
  If anyone stumbled upon her,
doomsday carried him off—till Apollo, who works from afar,
let fly a death-dealing arrow. Tortured by horrible pangs,
she lay there, twisting in pain and painfully gasping for breath.
305 Her racking screams reechoed as she squirmed about in the wood.
At last she gave up her life, coughing it out with her blood.
  Over her Phoebus Apollo proudly shouted his boast:
"Lie here now and rot unburied, here in the man-feeding ground!
No longer will you survive, you deadly plague to mankind.
310 They will eat the fruits of the earth, the supporter of many,
and hither they will bring me their offerings free of all blemish.
Typhoeus will be no help, nor evil-reputed Chimera,
against the pangs of your death; dark earth and shining Hyperion
will bring it about that you, at least, will the sooner decay."
315 So he boasted, and darkness covered the dragoness's eyes.
The holy power of the sun soon made her rot in corruption,
which is why, right down to this day, she bears the name of the Python,°
and men give Apollo the title "Pythian," since in the spot where she perished
the burning might of the sun rotted the monster away.

Homeric Hymn to Apollo (282–304, 356–374)

292. *Erginus:* An enemy of Heracles and king of Orchomenus in Boeotia; his sons, Agamedes and Trophonius, were famous builders.　296. *spring:* The Castalian Spring.　297. *dragon:* Python. 317. *Python:* Greek *pythō* means "to rot."

Apollo's destruction of the serpent Python is a Greek form of the ancient Eastern story of the dragon combat. The rest of the hymn reports Apollo's vengeance against Telphusa for sending him to a dragon-infested mountain: He buries her beneath a cliff and builds a small shrine for himself.

While wondering how to get priests for his temple, Apollo spies a Cretan ship at sea. Taking the form of a dolphin, he leaps on board, a terrifying portent. The sailors huddle together while Apollo guides the ship to Crisa, the coastal village near Delphi. There he reveals himself as a handsome man in his prime, with long locks drooping over his shoulders, and makes them priests of his temple. (Evidently the poet derives Delphi from Greek *delphis,* "dolphin," the form in which the god appeared to the sailors.) When the Cretans see Delphi perched on a precipitous

FIG. 7.5. Orestes purified by Apollo, South Italian vase, c. 400 B.C. On the left the ghost of Orestes' slain mother, Clytemnestra, awakens the Erinyes, personifications of ghost-miasma, and urges them to perse-cute the son who has murdered her, Orestes, who is seated before the Delphic omphalos (the egg-like ob-ject behind his left shoulder). He holds his sword drawn to ward off the Erinyes while Apollo, holding the sacred laurel in his left hand, Artemis at his side, drips the blood of a piglet over Orestes' head: by blood shall spilled blood be cleansed.   (Musée du Louvre, Paris; CP 790)

slope, with no place for crops or herds, they fall into despair. But Apollo comforts them: They will have plenty to eat from the rich offerings brought there. And so they did.

Other sources complete the tale. Having killed the dragon, Apollo had to be cleansed from miasma, "blood pollution." He therefore traveled to the Valley of Tempê in Thessaly at the foot of towering Mount Olympus; there he was ritually cleansed. Every eight years the Delphians celebrated the death of Python and the cleansing of Apollo. Because Apollo was himself cleansed of miasma, he could free others from it too, and many pilgrims journeyed to his temple at Delphi to submit to the appropriate ritual of purification (Fig. 7.5).

Observations: The Delphic Oracle

The second half of the *Homeric Hymn to Apollo* makes much of the god's eagerness to establish an oracular shrine so that he might enjoy its income and renown, but it tells us little about the history of the shrine and even less about the procedure followed there. Like the shrine at Delos, Delphi was a pan-Hellenic religious center to which all Greeks paid respect, regardless of their unending political differences. The ora-cle at Delphi functioned under Apollo for over a thousand years (c. 800 B.C.–A.D. 394); it was the most renowned oracle of the ancient world. The Greeks regarded Delphi as the center of the world, a location determined by Zeus when he sent out two eagles, one from each horizon, to see where they would cross. In the temple at Delphi stood a conical stone called the omphalos, marking the site as the world's navel (see Fig. 7.2).

According to legend, there was an earlier oracle at Delphi, which functioned un-der the goddess Gaea or Themis, and many scholars interpret the slaying of Python, the earth monster, to stand for Apollo's displacement of the earlier earth oracle. The notion of the world-navel, in addition to the fact that at Delphi oracular responses were always given by a woman, encourages the view that the shrine did once belong to an earth goddess, but archaeologists have found no evidence to confirm it.

The prophetess at Delphi was called the **Pythia** after the dragon Python. Originally she was a young virgin from the local village, but older women later served in this office. She seems to have had no special training. Most scholars understand her to have functioned as a medium, someone whose body served as an instrument for divine orders, but the precise nature of her inspiration remains a mystery. Ancient traditions report that she inhaled vapors from a chasm in order to achieve a state of ecstasy; however, no chasm has been found beneath the temple. Other accounts state that she chewed hallucinogenic laurel leaves, but the laurel, sacred to Apollo, has no hallucinogenic power. The Greeks were as puzzled as we by how the Pythia functioned.

When preparing to answer questions, the Pythia took her seat on a bronze tripod in the inner sanctum or adytum, the section "not to be entered," of Apollo's temple (Fig. 7.6). Questions were put by a male priest after the inquirer had made

FIG. 7.6. Aegeus before Themis in the shrine at Delphi, on an Attic drinking cup, c. 450 B.C. Aegeus, earthly father of Theseus, went to Delphi to learn whether he could beget a son. The Pythia (Themis) sits on the sacred tripod and gazes into a *phialê,* a kind of flat dish used to make drink offerings. In her other hand she holds a sprig of laurel. The column indicates that they are in the adytum of the temple at Delphi. The names of the figures are written above them.   (Staatliche Museen, Berlin; F2538)

appropriate sacrifice (the priests received the meat). The Pythia, possessed by the god, made replies, which the priests recast in a poetic form to give to the inquirer.

Although most questions were of a personal nature, questions of communal interest also were asked. In the days of western colonization, during the eighth century B.C. and later, Apollo was consulted about where to settle, what gods to worship, and what form of government to adopt, and Delphi became a center for the exchange of information about all of the Mediterranean world. The literary accounts of Delphic responses are famous for their dark ambiguity, however. Herodotus tells us about Croesus, king of Lydia, a rich and powerful ruler threatened by the Persians, who considered making a preemptive strike. Although not a Greek, he sent messengers with gifts to Delphi and asked what the outcome of the struggle would be. "If you make war on the Persians," he was informed, "you will destroy a mighty empire." Thus encouraged, he attacked, but was defeated and captured; the empire he destroyed was his own. In such literary accounts of oracular responses we must remember the prejudices and preferences of our written sources, whose principal purpose was to tell a good story.

In addition to its role in prophecy, the shrine at Delphi came to have a broadly ethical authority, encouraging the virtues of moderation and restraint and denying projects that were reckless or did not take sufficient account of the uncertainty of human fortune. Carved on the temple were the exhortations "Know yourself" and "Nothing too much," mottoes with similar meaning: You are only human, so don't try more than you are able (or you will pay the consequences). A recurring theme in Greek myth is the man or woman who loses sight of human limitations and acts arrogantly and with violence, as if immortal.

Apollo's Unhappy Loves

Apollo was father to many children and often was claimed as ancestor by families of prophets. However, many stories tell of his unsuccessful love affairs, which for some reason were numerous and beloved in late antiquity; Ovid makes much of them in his *Metamorphoses*.

Such stories sometimes refer to Apollo's power to make human beings prophets and the riddle and danger of this power. Priam, king of Troy, and his wife, Hecabê (**he**-ka-bē), had twins, Helenus (**hel**-e-nus) and **Cassandra** (kas-**san**-dra). Cassandra grew into a woman beautiful enough to rouse the lust of Apollo and shrewd enough to demand that he make her a prophet in return for her favors. Apollo agreed, but Cassandra nonetheless refused to sleep with him. Instead of taking back his gift, Apollo added a condition: Although Cassandra would always speak the truth, no one would believe her. Repeatedly she prophesied the ruin of Troy; no one listened. When Troy fell, Cassandra was carried off as booty by Agamemnon and butchered, along with her captor, by Agamemnon's wife, Clytemnestra (see Chapter 20). Today we call a Cassandra someone whose truthful words are ignored.

A similar story is told of his love for the first **Sibyl at Cumae,** to whom he gave as many years of life as the grains of sand she could scoop up in her hands. She accepted the gift, then refused to sleep with him. Apollo, though true to his word, failed to

Bernini's *Apollo and Daphnê*

Between about 1550 and 1700, the predominant style in European art and architecture was the baroque, typified by dramatic, bold, curving forms and elaborate ornamentation. Gianlorenzo Bernini (1598–1680) was the greatest sculptor–architect of the period. Later in his career he designed the Piazza in front of St. Peter's in Rome and, inside St. Peter's, the exuberant bronze canopy, supported by twisting columns, that protects the main altar under the soaring dome. In sculpture, the great innovation of the baroque was to create the illusion of a living scene, a moment captured yet recalling events before and after, an illusion in stone, as if the scene before us were actually taking place, as on a stage.

His renowned *Apollo and Daphnê* (Fig. P 7.1) is a youthful work, full of tension and excitement. The figures are life-size. Following Ovid's account closely, Bernini presents Daphnê just at the moment when the gods hear her pathetic pleas and change her into a laurel tree. She is nude, save for a strip of bark that strategically hides her genitals and buttocks. Behind her a youthful, beardless Apollo reaches around with his left hand to touch her bare abdomen, realizing at the moment of victory that he has lost his prey. The admixture of excitement, prettiness, sexual desire, and pathetic emotion perfectly mirrored the aesthetic taste of the aristocracy in seventeenth-century Europe, who loved Ovid and his stories for the Roman idle rich: They were the idle rich too. Bernini worked the marble marvelously to catch the texture of the flowing drapery, floating hair, the bark, leaves and branches, a dream of painting in exquisite marble.

FIG. P 7.1. Gianlorenzo Bernini (Italian, 1598–1680), *Apollo and Daphnê,* 1622–25, marble, life size. (Villa Borghese, Rome; Alinari/Art Resource, NY)

FIG. 7.7. Apollo pursues Daphnê (?), on an Attic water jug, c. 450 B.C. The god is identified by his laurel wreath and the laurel branch he carries. To the left, Hermes departs in a winged chariot. Such pursuit scenes are quite common on vases from the first half of the fifth century B.C., sometimes of gods and nymphs, sometimes of heroes or unidentified figures. They also appear on a special kind of vase intended for the bride's bath: The female figure, who may be Daphnê, seems to spread her arms in alarm, but may signify her willingness to be caught, as often on such vases, by turning back to Apollo and meeting his gaze. (British Museum, London; E 170)

grant a lasting youth to accompany her very long life. The Sibyl grew older and older until she shriveled up like a cicada.[4]

One of the best-known affairs is his love for **Daphnê** (**daf**-nē), a nymph, daughter of the river god Peneus in Thessaly. She rejected him, but he pursued her into the mountains (Fig. 7.7). To escape, she prayed to her father, who changed her into a laurel tree. The story is etiological to explain why the laurel is Apollo's sacred plant (Greek *daphnê* means "laurel").

Apollo, no less than Zeus, was subject to the attractions of young men. He loved Hyacinth (**hī**-a-sinth), a beautiful boy. One day they were practicing the discus (as good aristocrats do). A gust of wind caught the discus so that it swerved into Hyacinth's head and killed him. Apollo caused the hyacinth flower to grow from his blood. Ever after, the dead youth was honored each year at his tomb near Sparta. Hyacinth's name is certainly pre-Greek, perhaps originally a dying god of fertility (see Chapter 9).

---

[4]In the famous Roman novel *Satyricon* (first century A.D.), by Petronius, the "master of elegance" for the emperor Nero, an uncultured parvenu in southern Italy named Trimalchio boasts before his dinner guests that, "Once with my own eyes I saw the sibyl hanging in a bottle, and when those boys asked [he switches from Latin to Greek], 'What do you want?' she replied, 'I want to die.'" T. S. Eliot quotes these words (in Latin and Greek) as an epigraph to his celebrated poem *The Waste Land* (1922).

Apollo, god of prophecy, is also god of healing, and one of his tragic love affairs was connected with the origin of the Greek god of medicine, **Asclepius** (as-**klē**-pi-us), whom he conceived on a mortal woman, **Coronis** (ko-**rō**-nis). While pregnant with Asclepius, foolish Coronis slept with a mortal named Ischys, a thoughtless deed witnessed by a crow, who reported it to Apollo. Ovid tells the story:

[542]   Coronis, a girl of Larissa, was the loveliest woman of all
    who lived in Haemonia's land.° Even you, O Delphic Apollo,
    found she was just to your liking, as long as she either was true,
545   or at least was not caught at her tricks. But Phoebus' pet, a white raven,
    nosed out her games, and, brimming with incorruptible virtue,
    ran off to tattle the story . . . how he had noticed Coronis,
    snuggling down together with a good-looking boy from Haemonia.
    As the tale unfolded, the laurels° slipped from the brow of Apollo;
550   the color abandoned his features, the plectrum° fell from his hand.
    As his anger swelled and his heart was fueled with burning emotion,
    he reached for the bow, a weapon whose uses he knew so well;
    he pulled it back till the string came all the way to his shoulder;
    the arrow sped through the breast so often so close to his own.
555   With a groan the girl tore the dart away from her fair white flesh,
    which, as she watched, was crimsoned by blood that poured from her wound.
    Her dying words were these: "I deserve this punishment, Phoebus,
    but equally I deserve to have first given birth to our child.
    As it is, both he and I are destined to perish together."
560   At that she breathed her last, and her life ebbed out with her blood.
    As lover, Apollo repented—too late!—his terrible vengeance;
    he cursed his bow and his arrows, his hand that had brought them together.
    Stroking the lifeless corpse, with all the arts of the healer
    he attempted, too late and in vain, to annul grim Destiny's orders.
565   At last he knew he was helpless. He heard the sound of the servants
    building her funeral pyre to burn her remains in its flames.
    But Phoebus flatly refused to allow the child of his loins
    to crumble to ashes, cremated in the funeral pyre of its mother.
    Seizing the child from the womb, he bore it off to the cavern
570   where dwelt the double-formed Chiron, the Centaur. And as for the raven,
    who expected a great reward—after all, he had spoken the truth—
    Apollo erased him forever from the number of snowy-white birds.

OVID, *Metamorphoses* (2.542–547, 598–632)

543. *Haemonia's land:* Thessaly, in northeastern Greece.   549. *the laurels:* Sacred to Apollo. At the games given at Delphi the prize was a crown of laurel, which became the emblem of excellence in Apollo's arts; thus, the official royal poet of England is the poet laureate, and a Nobel prizewinner is a Nobel laureate.   550. *plectrum:* The pick for playing the lyre.

The wise and virtuous Centaur Chiron, the tutor of many heroes, understood well the art of medicine (although we are not told where he learned it) and taught the infant brought to him, Asclepius, all that he knew. Asclepius became a great doctor, even raising the dead. Athena had taken from the neck of the slain Gorgon Medusa two phials of blood: That from the left side of her neck cured all ailments, that from the right brought immediate death. The first phial she gave to Asclepius, who with it revived Hippolytus, son of Theseus, dragged to death over jagged rocks after Theseus cursed him (see Chapter 15).[5]

Asclepius generally is pictured with a serpent, often wound about a staff, no doubt because the snake has the ability to restore its health and vigor by shedding its skin;[6] serpents were kept in his shrines. The name of Hygieia (hī-jē-a), "health" personified, said to be his wife or daughter, gives rise to our word *hygiene*.

Observations: Apollo, God of Shamans

In most preliterate societies appears a figure, usually male, who specializes in understanding the secret meaning behind ordinary appearance. He is of the highest social standing and receives the respect of all. He can read the inner meaning behind such signs and omens as the flight of birds, the appearance of entrails in sacrificed animals, and lightning or other heavenly phenomena. He can summon the spirits of the dead, and dreams reveal to him what will come to pass. Through his superior knowledge he controls the invisible and dangerous forces that interfere constantly in the lives of human beings, including the most dangerous and puzzling of all, disease. This is the medicine man of popular lore, so called from the French *médecin*, "doctor." For the seer is also the healer.

One kind of medicine man, the shaman (Siberian for "he who knows"), can even leave his body behind in trance and travel through faraway realms to acquire knowledge of the future; he combats directly the hostile spirits that cause disease. He has friends in the spirit world, who may occupy his body and use his tongue to speak, although the voice is changed. Anthropological literature is filled with descriptions of such practices. In Greek religion, Apollo is the god of people who can do things like this (although Orpheus too, as we will see in Chapter 11, has many shamanistic qualities). Uniting inner and outer worlds, imparting knowledge, bringing healing, Apollo also embodies the aristocratic privilege accorded to the shaman of preliterate societies. Although the shaman ordinarily is male, he deemphasizes his masculinity and often wears a woman's clothes and behaves like a woman. In Greek religion and myth, Apollo inspired both men and women, but in different ways. Apollo inspired male seers, who through heightened awareness saw hidden meaning behind appearance and healed the sick. But he also took possession of female mediums, who gave themselves up—even against their will—to the god, lost consciousness of themselves, and communicated the god's knowledge of past, present, and future.

In his functions as god of prophecy and healing and of the musical and poetic

---

[5]Resurrected, Hippolytus became the minor Italian god Virbius, who protected a grove at a place named Aricia, near what was to be Rome. A priest ruled over the grove. If a runaway slave entered it and broke a branch, a golden bough, from a sacred oak, the priest was compelled to fight the man; if he was killed, the slave became the new priest. The priests of Virbius were always runaway slaves and always killed their predecessors. From this story Sir James Frazer took the theme and title of his influential book *The Golden Bough* (see Chapter 23).

[6]His staff, with mistakenly doubled snakes, was chosen by the American Medical Association for its emblem. In fact the staff with two serpents is the caduceus, Hermes' wand, by which he conducts the dead to Hades.

FIG. 7.8. Apollo, from the west pediment of the temple of Zeus at Olympia. The subject of the pediment was the Centaurs' rape of the Lapith women (from Thessaly). Apollo stands at the center of the melee, quietly reaching out his arm. Sculpted in the mid-fifth century B.C., the mythical theme was a transparent allegory for the Greek victory over the Persians, understood as the triumph of reason and order over barbarian chaos.   (Olympia Museum; Alison Frantz)

skills so valued by the Greek aristocracy, Apollo came to embody order against barbarism, reason against unreason, and what many have called "the Hellenic spirit." In the Classical Period Apollo represented the Greek aristocratic ideal of young, vigorous manhood. On the pediment of the temple to Zeus at Olympia, whose cult statue was one of the Seven Wonders of the Ancient World, Apollo stands calm and beardless, arm outstretched against the savage Centaurs trying to carry off Greek women (Fig. 7.8).

In the Persian Wars, by supporting nonresistance to the invaders through many oracles, the Delphic Oracle lost much of its old respect, but in matters affecting individuals it remained influential. A friend of Socrates asked, "Who is the wisest of men?" The oracle replied, "Socrates." This puzzled the philosopher, until he realized that other men thought that they knew a lot; Socrates alone realized his own ignorance.

About A.D. 100 Plutarch, himself a priest of Apollo, wrote a gloomy work on the growing decay of the oracles. They were finally closed down by the emperor Theodosius about A.D. 390. Long before this, we are told by the Christian historian Eusebius in a burst of wishful thinking that the emperor Augustus (27 B.C.–A.D. 14) went to Delphi to ask who would reign after him. The Pythia gave no answer, so Augustus asked why the prophetic shrine was silent. At last the god replied through the priestess:

A son of the Hebrews, a god and ruler over the blessed,
has bidden me leave this house and return to the realm of Hades.
Depart from this altar in silence, and never come back with your queries.

HEPHAESTUS, GOD OF SMITHS

Hephaestus (he-fēs-tus) (the Roman Vulcan) is non-Greek in origin and probably derives from the island of Lemnos in the Aegean Sea. We know that a non-Greek people, the Tyrsenoi, lived on Lemnos until the sixth century B.C., with Hephaestias as their capital. Presumably Hephaestus was in origin a god of this people. A sense of Hephaestus' connection with Lemnos is preserved in Greek myth: On this island he landed when Zeus threw him from heaven for taking his mother Hera's side in a dispute (see Chapter 6).

Lemnos was once the site of an active volcano, and perhaps it was for this reason that Greek myths also associated Hephaestus with volcanoes and with the Cyclopes, who worked at their forges deep within them. He is sometimes simply the personification of fire, as Zeus is of rain: not the fire of the hearth, who is Hestia, or the celestial fire of Zeus's thunderbolt, but the fire of the metalworker's forge. He is the god of smiths, the patron of those who worked with their hands to form metals into useful or beautiful objects. As such he was one of the chief promoters of civilization and city life; his temple (today the best-preserved in Greek lands) overlooked the Athenian agora, where manufactured goods were traded.

The ancient Greeks had ambiguous feelings toward such workers. On one hand, bronze- and ironworking were technologies of central importance. The warriors in Homer are "bronze-clad," and many of the stunning achievements of Greek art, especially realistic sculpture, depended on smelting intractable copper ores (bronze is an alloy of copper and tin) (Fig. 7.9). On the other hand, the filthy business of metalworking was repulsive to Greek aristocrats, who would not sully their hands with manual labor and who felt that the artisan class was beneath notice. Today we marvel at the elegance of Greek decorated pottery, of which fifty thousand examples survive (some illustrated in this book), but only once in all Greek literature, in a brief remark of the comic poet Aristophanes, does any mention of this craft appear: The potter, like the smith, had no social standing (although some were literate and signed their works). Greek *aristoi* also despised lameness and physical ugliness, and the fact that slow-moving cripples sometimes became smiths inspired further scorn toward such workers.

This ambiguous relationship was reflected in the Hephaestus of Greek myth. To

FIG. 7.9. A blacksmith's shop, from a drinking cup, c. 460 B.C. On the left a bronzeworker, wearing a cap often seen on Hephaestus, pokes at the coals in an upright furnace, while an apprentice, leaning on a hammer, looks on. To the right the bronzeworker assembles a hollow bronze statue (compare Fig. 7.1): its head, waiting to be attached, is on the ground beneath his feet. From the wall hang other parts for statues and bronzeworker's tools.   (Staatliche Museen, Berlin; F2294)

him was attributed the working of all elegant and ingenious objects, as well as weapons and other less glamorous things. He fashioned Pandora from clay and made the manacles that bound Prometheus to the Caucasus. He was important and given a place among the Olympians, but he remained a pretender, a slum-born upstart without proper parentage, an object of ridicule, almost a monster. His marriage to the sex-goddess Aphrodite was a laughable perversion: a union of beauty and the beast. No one need wonder why Aphrodite preferred the handsome, swashbuckling Ares as her lover.

According to the version in which Hera threw Hephaestus from heaven, Hephaestus fell not to Lemnos but into the sea, from which Thetis and her sister Nereids rescued him. They treated him kindly and kept him with them in a cavern for nine years. There he learned his metalworking skills. Enraged by Hera's ill treatment, he manufactured a marvelous golden throne to which was attached a golden mesh so fine as to be invisible, which he sent to his mother on her birthday. As soon as she sat in it, the net bound her tightly. Only Hephaestus could free her, but he refused to return to heaven. At last Dionysus gained his confidence, plied him with wine, and led him to Olympus, drunk. Hephaestus then let Hera go. The return of Hephaestus to Olympus was a common subject of Greek art and, in fact, is unattested in any literary account (Fig. 7.10).

FIG. 7.10. The return of Hephaestus to Olympus, on an Attic vase, c. 430 B.C. Hephaestus, drunk, crowned with ivy, is supported by a satyr, while Dionysus, to the far right, leads him to Olympus. Hephaestus carries the blacksmith's tools, a hammer in his left hand and tongs in his right. (Museum Antiker Kleinkunst, Munich)

ARES, INCARNATION OF BLOOD LUST

Ares, the other son of Zeus and Hera, is often simply an embodiment of war and battle. Ares (the Roman Mars) personifies blood lust, the successful warrior's exaggerated desire to kill his fellow man. Under Ares' influence, the warrior is merciless, fearless, and indifferent to pain in the frenzy of combat. Ares was little worshiped in Greek religion and has few myths; in art he is indistinguishable from any warrior. He was father to many, but had no regular wife, although he carried on an adulterous affair with Aphrodite long enough to father four children. Two of them, Phobos, "Panic," and Deimos, "Fear," allegorical figures, were fit offspring of the god of war.[7] Another was Harmonia, "Harmony," who married Cadmus of Thebes. The fourth, according to some sources, was Eros (Cupid), companion (or irresponsible child) of Aphrodite and personification of sexual attraction.

Ares' adultery with Aphrodite was by far the most famous myth about him (Fig. 7.11; compare Fig. P 8.1b). Because of its immoral content, this story, more than any other, inspired the Greeks of the Classical Period to question the veracity of their myths. But Homer tells the tale with humorous intent, placing it in the mouth of the oral poet Demodocus, who sings before a male, aristocratic audience with a taste for the salacious and irreverent:

[7]In modern times the two moons of the planet Mars are named after them.

FIG. 7.11. The adultery of Aphrodite and Ares on a fresco from Pompeii from the first century A.D. Ares (= Mars) reaches his hand inside Aphrodite's (= Venus') blouse while Eros (= Cupid), personification of erotic attraction, looks on. (Museo Archeologico Nazionale, Naples; Author's photo)

[266] Sounding his lyre, the singer began his beautiful song,
a tale of the dalliance of Ares and fair-crowned Aphrodite,
how they embraced in secret in the very house of Hephaestus.
Loading the goddess with gifts, Ares sullied the nuptial bed
270   of the lord Hephaestus, to whom Helius° carried the story,
that he himself had seen the couple embracing in passion.
Hephaestus listened in silence to the news that broke his heart,
then hurried into his workshop, contriving a fit retribution.
Firm on a solid base he set a ponderous anvil and forged
275   a chain that could not be broken, escaped, or even unfastened.
At last he finished his trap, and, seething in anger at Ares,
carried it up to the chamber housing the couch of love.
Around the bed-posts he draped his chain in voluptuous swirls,
coiled directly over the bed, looping down from the rafters.
280   Yet it was fine as a cobweb, not to be noticed by watchers,
even the blessed gods, such skill went into its making.
Finally, when his trap was arranged all over the bedstead,
he pretended important business in Lemnos, that well-managed city,
"dearest by far," said he, "of all the cities of men."
285   Now Ares, golden-reined, had kept his eye on Hephaestus.
Learning the god of craftsmen would be gone an indefinite period,

270. *Helius:* As the sun god, he sees all.

he wasted no time, but ran at once to the home of Hephaestus,
panting with lust to possess the beautiful-crowned Cytherea.
She had just said goodbye to her father, the mighty son of great Cronus,
290 and was sitting there by herself. Ares scratched at the door,
squeezed her hand, and murmured tender endearments of love:
    "Sweetheart, off we go, to snuggle down in the blankets.
Your husband? He's gone off; by now he must be in Lemnos,
amusing himself with Sintian women,° with voices like crows."
295   Aphrodite agreed: bed seemed to offer amusement;
up the pair went to slumber together. Down came the chain,
tightly embracing the two, as wily Hephaestus had planned it.
Neither could move an inch and neither could lift up a finger.
They knew at once they had no possible way of escaping.
300   The famous lame craftsman, meanwhile, had turned back to his house,
before he got to Lemnos, warned by Helius, his trusty informant;
savage with rage he approached, but checked himself in the doorway,
then yelled at the top of his voice to summon all the immortals:
    "Here, father Zeus and you other blessed immortal gods,
305 if you really want to guffaw at something shameful to see.
Aphrodite, daughter of Zeus, is always mocking my lameness,
billing and cooing with Ares, her muscular pretty-boy vandal.
So, I was born with a limp. Nobody can blame me for that;
charge the fault to my parents, who didn't have to beget me!
310 Just look here at the lovebirds, snuggled so sweetly together—
and in my bed, if you please. You wonder why I resent it?
Well, somehow I don't imagine they want to stay any longer;
however fond they may be, they'd rather have separate beds.
But this little gadget will chain them fast in loving embrace,
315 till Daddy repays every penny I gave for the lecherous slut.
Sure, his daughter is pretty, but empty of sense or of morals."
At this the gods rushed up and clustered around his door—
Poseidon, embracer of earth; Hermes the helper of mortals;
and the lord Apollo, who hurls his flying darts from afar.
320 (The feminine goddesses stayed at home for modesty's sake,
while the gods, the givers of blessings, gaped at the pair through the door.)
Unceasing bawdy laughter broke out from the blessed gods,
eyeing the clever device contrived by inventive Hephaestus.
Each slapped another's back as he flung him a salty jest:
325 "Crime never pays?" they asked. "The slow outrunning the swift?
why not, if limping Hephaestus can catch the swift-footed Ares,
nimblest of all the gods who hold domain on Olympus?"
"What if his legs are lame? his brain is certainly working."
    So they were joking together, and Apollo, son of Zeus,
330 questioned Lord Hermes thus: "O Hermes, giver of blessings,
even if you were shackled with inescapable fetters,
wouldn't you like to recline with Aphrodite the golden?"
Hermes the guide, the slayer of Argus, promptly retorted:
"O, what wouldn't I give for that, far-shooting Apollo!
335 I'd gladly be bound by thrice as many unbreakable chains,

294. *Sintian women:* Native inhabitants of Lemnos.

while all you gods looked on—yes, and the goddesses too—
as long as I might lie there with Aphrodite the golden!"
    At this reply the immortals burst into hootings of laughter:
but Poseidon, unamused, kept begging the famous inventor
340   to let poor Ares go. His words went straight to the point:
"Loose him. I promise to pay you whatever you may demand,
whatever is found satisfactory among the immortal gods."°
    The famous smith, who is crippled in both his legs, gave this answer:
"Poseidon, embracer of earth, please don't ask this of me.
345   Promises made by the worthless are so much worthless wind.
What can I claim from you before the immortals' assembly,
if once this Ares escapes, eluding me and my bonds?"°
    Poseidon, shaker of earth, unhappily gave this reply:
"Hephaestus, if Ares attempts to escape by jumping his bail,
350   I promise to make up his bond, repaying all that he owes."
    The crippled smith replied to Poseidon in these words:
"I cannot refuse your offer; to do so would be impolite."
So mighty Hephaestus unfastened the chain, and the lovers,
once set free from its links, slender but terribly strong,
355   jumped up in silence and parted, Ares to warlike Thrace,°
Aphrodite, lover of smiles, to her shrine in Cyprian Paphos,
with gardens around the temple and a fragrant altar within.
The Graces washed and anointed her flesh with ambrosial oil,
of the sort laid up for immortals, and clothed the goddess
360   in robes of the loveliest sort, a wonder to see.

HOMER, *Odyssey* (8.266–366)

342. *among the immortal gods:* According to Greek laws surviving from Athens and Crete, the adulterer, when caught in the act, could be detained until appropriate compensation was paid; in Athens, he could lawfully be killed on the spot. Poseidon is volunteering to put up bail for Ares. 347. *my bonds:* Hephaestus is at first reluctant to let Ares go, even on Poseidon's promise to guarantee Ares' payment of compensation. Ares will surely default, forcing Hephaestus to take action against Poseidon, which he does not want to do.   355. *Thrace:* Often said to be Ares' homeland.

HERMES, TRICKSTER GOD OF WAYFARERS

Except for Zeus, **Hermes** alone of the Olympians has a name of transparent meaning: "he of the stone heap" (Greek *herma* = "stone heap"). Most interpreters explain his origin from the common practice of marking trails through remote areas with a heap of stones. Each traveler throws a stone on the pile for good luck. Thus Hermes is the spirit that lives in the stone pile, the protector of travelers and of those who live on the limits of civilization. Like Artemis and the woodland spirit Pan, he was most at home in remote Arcadia, where he looked after shepherds and their flocks. Later, the stone pile was stylized into a small pillar with a human head and an erect phallus, used as a milestone or a marker of property boundaries (Fig. 7.12).[8]

[8]The use of the phallus apotropaically, "to turn away evil," is older than our species; among higher primates aggressive males show their erect penis to warn off intruders (even as we "flip the bird" to those who act abusively, to turn their aggression back on them).

FIG. 7.12. A herm from the island of Siphnos, c. 520 B.C. Such stone pillars with bearded head and erect phallus were used as boundary stones and as milestones and also placed before Athenian houses, to mark the boundary and ward off intruders. Just before the Athenians embarked on the disastrous expedition against Syracuse in 415 B.C., most of the herms in the city were mutilated in one night by vandals. Suspicion immediately fell on the most conservative faction, who were accused of conspiracy "to bring about a revolution and upset the democracy." The already divided command was so shaken by the charge that it was unable to act effectively, and the expedition was a catastrophic failure.   (National Archaeological Museum, Athens; 3728)

Hermes' role in protecting travelers leads to additional functions. He protects thieves, for thieves travel through the night, taking what they want through intelligence and stealth. He protects merchants, who must travel to bring their goods to market, and in the marketplace thieves sell what they have taken. (Our words *merchant* and *commerce* come from Latin *merx*, "merchandise," from which is derived *Mercury*, the Roman name for Hermes.) He is the herald of the gods and protects human heralds, elect men who travel from one hostile community to the other and who must not be harmed; as an emblem of their office they carry the god's wand, the caduceus, a staff intertwined with two snakes copulating (see Figs. 5.2, 11.1). Hermes also protects orators, for orators persuade just as heralds and diplomats do. Finally, Hermes plays a role in the most momentous form of travel, that from this world to the next: As *psychopompos*, "soul guide," he leads the dead into the House of Hades (see Figs. 11.1, 11.3).

One of Hermes' most famous deeds was the slaying of a hundred-eyed monster named Argus, whom Hera set up to watch over Io, a mistress of Zeus (see Fig. 13.2).

From this deed Hermes was ever after called Argeiphontes (ar-jē-**fon**-tēz), "slayer of Argus."

The most amusing of all surviving oral poems recorded by dictation (and one of the latest) is the *Hymn to Hermes,* probably from the sixth century B.C., which tells of the birth and extraordinary precocity of this trickster god. When only several hours old he invented the lyre, stole the cattle of his brother Apollo, then lied about it all to Apollo and Zeus. The poem is very funny in its celebration of rascality over pompous authority, but it may reflect deep social currents because it comes from a time when the social classes favored by Hermes, the merchants, were gaining in influence over the old aristocracy, whose god was Apollo:

[1]   Sing, Muse, a song to Hermes, the son of Maia° and Zeus,
       lord of Arcadian Cyllenê,° land of sheep beyond number,
       the helper, the herald of gods. Maia, a fair-braided nymph,
       bore him to Zeus, as fruit of her bashful joining in dalliance.
5   She had shunned the noisy gathering of all the rest of the blest ones
       to hide in a shady cavern, but Zeus, soon hunting her out,
       embraced the fair-haired goddess in the darkest hour of nighttime,
       when sweetest sleep would hold the eyes of the white-armed Hera,
       when he might elude both gods immortal and men who must perish.
10   So he attained his desire. Ten months° were marked in the heavens.
       The child sprang into the light, to bring about wonderful things.
       Maia's infant was clever—a swindler, a robber, a liar,
       rustler of cattle, fast talker, burglar and cracker of safes,
       who promptly practiced his tricks on even the wisest immortals.
15   Born at the break of day, by noon he was twanging the lyre
       (This on the fourth of the month° when lady Maia had born him);
       before the evening had come he had stolen Phoebus's cattle.
       Once he had sprung from the deathless thighs of the lady his mother,
       he wasted no time in the winnowing fan° that served as his cradle,
20   but jumped out and promptly departed to find the herds of Apollo.
       Just as he crossed the threshold of the cavern, high, overarching,
       he stumbled upon a tortoise, destined to make him a fortune,
       for Hermes was first to construct a musical sweet-singing lyre.°
       He met the beast in the courtyard, just in front of the doorway,
25   nibbling the soft sweet grass as it walked with its delicate feet.
       The helper, the son of Zeus, watched it, giggled, and addressed it:
       "Good morning to you, my omen of luck whom I must not disparage;
       How fair your face! how nimble your feet! what fun at a party!

1. *Maia:* A word meaning "venerable old woman" or "midwife." The daughter of Atlas and an Oceanid, she plays no part in myth except as the mother of Hermes.   2. *Cyllenê:* A mountain in the northeast corner of Arcadia in the Peloponnesus.   10. *ten months:* The ancients usually counted both ends in expressions of time; we would say nine months.   16. *fourth of the month:* Some days, like the fourth, were lucky, and both Aphrodite and Hermes were born on it; others were unlucky.   19. *fan:* The ancient Greeks used a kind of woven scoop to winnow the harvest (separate the grain from the hulls). The grain was first trampled by oxen, then tossed into the air, preferably in a breeze that would blow the chaff away. Hermes was put into a winnowing fan as a sort of bassinet (see Fig. 7.13).   23. *sweet-singing lyre:* Tortoise shells served as the sounding boxes for Greek lyres.

How happy I am to see you. Pray where did you get your fine costume?
30   that dappled shell that looks like a tortoise who lives in the hills?
Let me pick you up and take you inside, where I'm sure I can use you.
You'll be treated with all respect, since first you will benefit me.
You'd be safer inside the house, for the outdoors is always a danger.
While you live, you will be my defense against the perils of magic,
35   and, should you happen to die, you will warble the loveliest music."
So he addressed the tortoise, and, picking it up in his fingers,
he went back into the house, bearing his beautiful trophy.
With a gouge of sharp gray steel he scooped out the tortoise's entrails.
As fast as a passing thought traverses the breast of a thinker,
40   one whom repeated problems keep forcing to alter his plans;
as fast as the beams of vision flash from a viewer's eye,
so fast did glorious Hermes combine his thought with his action.
He carved a reed into slices of length which he carefully measured,
and fastened them tight in holes bored through the back of the shell.
45   Trusting his native wits, around them he mounted a drumhead.
Goat horns on either side were joined by a bridge up above,
whence seven harmonious strings of sheep gut stretched to the body.
When he had finished constructing his beautiful new invention,
he strummed each string with his hand, evoking melodious twanging.
50   Accompanied by the sound, the god improvised a sweet lyric,
just as young men at a feast compete with responding lampoons.
He sang the story of Zeus, son of Cronus, and fair-sandaled Maia,
their billing and cooing and whispered murmurs of love and affection,
and he sang of his own conception and birth, making much of his name.
55   He glorified the household, the splendid home of his mother:
the tripods and brazen cauldrons to be found all over the house.
But even while singing away, he was pondering various matters.
He bedded the hollow lyre in the holy winnowing fan,
for a whim had entered his mind that a juicy steak would be pleasant.
60   So he ran from the scented house to see what he might discover.
meanwhile plotting a scheme like those thieves make in the darkness.
    The sun, with chariot and horses, had set over dry land and sea,
when Hermes came to the shades of Pieria,° hill of the Muses,
where the herds of the blessed gods were safely shut in for the night,
65   well fed by a long day's grazing in meadows fragrant and blooming.
Of these the son of Maia, the far-sighted slayer of Argus,
picked out and drove away fifty mooing head from the cowpens.
By twisted byways he drove them, and wherever the roadway was sandy,
turned them about back to front, reversing the hoofprints' direction
70   by driving them backward, while he himself proceeded on forward.°
By the sandy shore of the sea he wove himself sandals of wicker,
wonderful, hard to believe! of tamarisk twiglets and myrtle.
A bundle of fresh green branches, verdant and heavy with foliage,
he had plucked in his preparations for the rugged Pierian journey.

---

63. *Pieria:* A mountain in Macedonia, just north of Olympus, sacred to the Muses.   70. . . . *proceeded on forward:* This method was used by Greek cattle rustlers down to the early twentieth century.

75   These light and flexible sandals, tied firmly under his insteps,
      saved him the labor of plodding the length of a long sandy road.
          An old man working a vineyard noticed the passing of Hermes
      as he went by Onchestus'° meadows, and then on down to the plain.
      Before he could ask a question, the son of Maia addressed him:
80   "Old man, bending your back as you dig away in the vineyard,
      you'll have a noble vintage, when all these vines bear their clusters.
      But listen, now, to my warning: if anyone asks you a question,
      tell him you've not seen a thing; just mutter, forgetting the truth:
      say you're deaf as a post, though your hearing is actually perfect.
85   Keep your mouth shut tight, if you know what's really your interest."
      That was enough; famous Hermes prodded the cattle together,
      past many a hill, by many a meadow or flowering plain.
      Most of the misty darkness of night, his accomplice, had vanished,
      and beauteous Selenê had started to travel her rounds yet again
90   (Selenê was daughter of Pallas,° the son of the lord Megamedes),
      when the mighty son of Zeus drove the broad-browed cows of Apollo
      to the river Alpheus,° whose current they freely shambled across,
      and freely at last they arrived at the cattle enclosure of Hermes,
      to drink from troughs full of water at the edge of a beautiful meadow.
95   When he had given their fill of grass to the bellowing cattle,
      and driven them all in a herd back to their pens for the night,
      champing, as on they plodded, at lotus or dew-dripping cypress,
      he gathered a load of dry wood and invented the kindling of fire.
      Choosing a slab of laurel, he smoothed it down with a drawknife,
100   over it twirled a drill, and blew on the smoldering tinder.
      Thus Hermes discovered the way to kindle a fire by friction.
      To the fire-pit dug in the earth he carried a burden of faggots,
      unsplit, but as dry as tinder, and piled them over the fire.
      The flame blazed high and scattered its beams out into the darkness.
105   While the potent tool of Hephaestus, far-famed god of the craftsman,
      was still blazing up, he dragged two bellowing crumple-horned cattle
      out of their pen to the fire, displaying his muscular power,
      by wrestling the panting beasts, belly up, to lie on the ground.
      He twisted and rolled them over, then cut their throats with a knife.
110   One task succeeded another: he sliced the rich fatty sirloins;
      he speared the cuts to be roasted on skewers whittled of wood;
      the rest he stuffed—yes, even the tenderloin, token of honor—
      and the blackish blood, deep down in the gut, inventing the blutwurst.
      All this he left by the fire, but the skins he dried on a layer
115   of rock, on which to this day those ancient hides have endured.°
          Then Hermes, merry of heart, slid the greasy fruit of his labor

---

78. *Onchestus:* A town of Boeotia, northwest of Thebes.   90. *Pallas:* Hesiod tells us that Selenê
(and Helius) were children of Hyperion and Theia; the Hymn apparently makes the Titan Pallas
(not Athena—several mythical figures had this name) her father. Megamedes is otherwise unknown.   92. *Alpheus:* The largest river of the Peloponnesus, flowing from Arcadia west past
Olympia and into the Ionian Sea. It was said to duck underground and emerge in the harbor of
Syracuse in Sicily.   115. . . . *endured:* Evidently rock formations, shown to pilgrims as the hides
that Hermes had spread out.

onto a smooth stone slab, and carved it into twelve portions.
These he assigned by lot, and topped each plate with a tidbit.°
Yet noble Hermes himself longed for the meat he had offered;
120 immortal though he might be, he drooled at the wonderful fragrance,
but still his heart refrained from stuffing his gullet with goodies.
The fat and the meat he brought to the cavern, high, overarching,
storing it well out of sight, a sign of his skill as a rustler.
Fetching more wood, in the blaze of the fire he burned heads and feet.
125 This housework finished, he tossed his sandals into the river
Alpheus, swirling and deep. He quenched the fire and leveled
the ashes, working all night by the light of a silvery moon.
At dawn he ran back once again to the shining crest of Cyllenê,
and met not a soul all the way, no human, no blessed immortal;
130 no dog dared bark at Hermes, son of Zeus and bringer of fortune.
Squirming his way through the keyhole, he stole back into the cavern,
entering the house like a mist that comes in the chill of the autumn,
hurrying in on tiptoe and making no sound on the pavement.
The famous Hermes hastily jumped right into his cradle,
135 and, as any baby would do, rucked the blanket up round his shoulder.
He lay there, his fingers twisting the clothes on his fat little legs,
and cuddled the lovely tortoise, hugged in the crook of his elbow.
God though he was, his mother gave him a vigorous scolding:
"You naughty shameless boy, where have you been, to get home
140 at such an hour of the night? Leto's son will certainly get you,
and take you away, tied so tightly that even you can't escape him.
Or else you'll turn into a bandit, prowling about in the mountains.
Whatever you stole, take it back! Your father created a nuisance
for mortals and gods alike, the night when you were begotten!"
145 With a crafty answer Hermes replied to the lady his mother:
"Madam, why do you scold me as if I were only a baby,
whose heart has never been touched by blame or words of reproval?
Do you think I will timidly whimper because my mother is angry?
No; I shall pick whatever career may offer most promise,
150 with an eye to both of our welfares. Why should we two be contented,
we who are both divine, whose place is among the immortals,
without the honors of prayer and sacrifice, here in this hovel?
If that is what you are suggesting, I know a far better future:
let us spend our days amusing ourselves among the immortals,
155 in a life of abundance and wealth, like lords of many an acre,
rather than twiddling our thumbs in this drafty echoing cavern.
And as for honor and rank, I too want the same as Apollo.
If my dear father won't grant it, I'll try—and I'm sure to succeed—
to earn the honor and riches that belong to the patron of thieves.
160 If the glorious son of Leto attempts to follow my traces,
I think he may run into something far bigger than he can expect.
I'll make my way to Delphi and tunnel into the temple,
where I'll find plenty of loot, like beautiful tripods and caldrons;

118. *tidbit:* One for each of the Olympian gods; this is the earliest known reference to the Twelve Gods.

I'll make off with all the gold and the iron I may require,
165   not to mention the fabrics. You'll see, my mother, you'll see!"
      The pair exchanged such words, as they sat and chatted together,
the son of Zeus of the aegis, and lady Maia, his mother,
till early-born dawn appeared, bringing her light to us mortals,
rising from ocean's deep tides. Then Apollo came to Onchestus,
170   the lovely grove that is sacred to the rumbling shaker of earth.°
By the road he found the old peasant feeding his ugly old beast,
his trusty transport in the vineyard. The son of Leto addressed him:
      "Ancient grubber of thorns in the vineyards of grassy Onchestus,
hither I come from Pieria, hunting about for my cattle,
175   heifers all from my herd, with crumpled horns on their foreheads.
My black-skinned bull was grazing alone, left there by the others,
except four fierce-eyed dogs, who followed like trusty retainers.
The dogs and the bull alone remained, to my utter amazement,
for all the cattle returned last night, when the sun had descended,
180   back from their pleasant pasture, from the fragrant flowery meadow.
So tell me, you ancient man, have you seen a rustler of cattle,
passing along this road and driving the cows on before him?"
      The old man answered the question with subtle words of evasion:
"My friend, it's not at all easy, reporting all that you've noticed.
185   Moreover, a great many travelers choose this road as their highway,
some with nefarious schemes, some on their lawful occasions.
How can I tell which is which? I was digging away at my vineyard,
all through the livelong day, right down to the hour of sunset.
But, sir, I may have seen—I really can't tell you for certain—
190   what looked like a little moppet tending his spreading-horned heifers.
He carried a great long stick and skipped from one side to the other,
as he drove them along from behind, but he himself facing backwards."
      The old man finished; Apollo listened and hurried his footsteps.
Consulting a long-winged bird, he knew that the thief was none other
195   than the newborn boy who was fathered by mighty Zeus, son of Cronus.
The lord Apollo, himself Zeus's son, sped quickly to Pylos,°
down by the sandy shore, to hunt for his shambling cattle,
wrapping his brawny shoulders in a misty cloud for concealment.
There he who shoots from afar saw the tracks of cattle and shouted:
200   "What in the name of Heaven is this that startles my eyes!
It looks to me like the track of a herd of longhorned cattle,
but why are they turned the wrong way, to the meadow of asphodel?
And these—they can't be the tracks of mortal man or of woman,
nor yet of gray wolves or bears, or even of ravenous lions.
205   I can scarcely believe it's the track of a shaggy-necked Centaur,
yet something nasty has traveled this pathway on hurrying feet:
one set of tracks is horrendous, the other is simply appalling!"
      So speaking, the lord Apollo, son of Zeus, continued his journey,
and presently came to Cyllenê, the mountain covered with forest,

---

170. *shaker of the earth:* Poseidon, lord of earthquakes.   196. *Pylos:* Apparently not the famous Pylos on the southwest coast of the Peloponnesus, but another one in Elis, about thirty-five miles north of the other.

FIG. 7.13. Hermes and the cattle of Apollo, Attic vase, c. 490 B.C. Hermes, back in Maia's cave, huddles down in his basket cradle after stealing Apollo's cattle. Wrapped in his swaddling clothes, he still wears his traveler's cap (*petasos*). Maia, to his left, reproves him for the theft, while the herd of cows stands in the background; one cow licks the cradle.   (Vatican Museum, Rome; XXXII-23-45)

210   to a shadowy cave in the rock, where dwelt the nymph, the immortal,
wherein she had given birth to the child of Zeus, son of Cronus.
A wonderful perfume distilled all over the mystical mountain,
where flocks of long-limbed sheep stood nibbling succulent pasture.
Apollo, who shoots from afar, rushed up, crossed over the threshold,
215   and entered in all his radiance into the gloom of the cave.
    The son of Zeus and Maia knew him at once for Apollo,
the god who shoots from afar, enraged at the loss of his cattle,
and snuggled down the deeper in his sweet-smelling swaddling bands (Fig.
    7.13].
As coals burning deep in a log are hidden by layers of ashes,
220   so Hermes huddled at sight of the god who works from afar,
contracting into small space his head and his hands and his feet.
He looked like a newborn baby, just washed and ready for slumber,
his tortoise tight in his arms. In fact, he was carefully watching.
The son of Leto and Zeus was not tricked for a moment: he knew
225   the beautiful nymph of the mountains and also her dear little boy,
a crook, always sticking his fingers in all sorts of knavish devices.
Apollo's eyes pried into the great house's every corner.

He drew out a gleaming key, and opened three locked storage cupboards,
only to find them full of nectar and fragrant ambrosia.

230 There was, indeed, ample store in the house of gold and of silver,
and dresses of crimson and silver, belonging to Maia, the nymph,
the sort of thing one expects in the homes of the blessed immortals.
At last the son of Leto, having snooped into every corner,
gave up the hunt and addressed his words to the noble Hermes:

235 "Look, kid, you who are lying so innocent there in your cradle,
tell me, where are the cows? if you won't talk, there'll be trouble.
I'll grab you and fling you down to the windy darkness of hell,
a miserable end, and one that you'll never succeed in escaping.
Neither your Mama nor Dada can bring you back to the light,
but you'll wander under the earth, with only moppets to boss."

Hermes replied to all this with words that were carefully chosen:
"Tell me, great son of Leto, just why are you talking so tough?
and why come into the house for beasts that live out of doors?
I never saw them, I never heard of them, nobody told me about them.

245 I couldn't tell you a thing, or collect a fee as informer.
Do I look like a rustler of cattle, a brawny and muscular fellow?
That just isn't my style. I'm busy with other grave matters—
especially sleeping, and feeding on milk from the breast of my mother,
and blankets over my shoulders, and splashing in nice warm baths.

250 I hope that no one will ask you just how this argument started,
for even the gods would wonder, if you told them a newly born baby
walked right in the front door with a herd of wide-ranging cattle.
You claim what doesn't make sense! Only yesterday was I born,
my feet are still so tender and the ground beneath is so hard!

255 All right; if you insist I will take a terrible oath,
by the head of my father, and swear that I myself am not guilty,
nor have I seen any other who was driving your cattle away—
whatever 'cattle' may be, for I know of them only by hearsay."

So he spoke, but kept glancing from under half-closed lids,

260 as he raised his eyebrows and watched his audience all around,
sometimes with a long low whistle, as if at a too tall story.
Apollo, who works from afar, laughed gently and spoke to him thus:
"Rascal, deceiver, and knave, how skillful you are at persuasion!
Of course, I know full well that you spent the nighttime in burgling

265 many a solid house, taking lots of poor men to the cleaner's,
noiselessly carrying off whatever you found in their households.
O, what a plague you will be to many a poor rustic shepherd,
out in the wilds of the mountain, when you feel a hunger for meat
and happen to smell out his pen of cattle and thick wooly sheep!

270 But now, unless you long for the longest and deepest of slumbers,
GET OUT OF THAT CRADLE, QUICK! you partner of inkiest night!
From now on all the immortals will give you the infamous function
of championing all the bandits, whose ruler you will be titled."
So speaking, Phoebus Apollo took up Hermes to carry him off.

275 But the mighty slayer of Argus was forming a different plan.
The moment he felt himself lifted, he emitted a terrible portent,
a hard-pressed slave of his belly, a messenger lacking good manners,

then sneezed to cover it up.° Apollo heard with disgust,
and dropped the glorious Hermes out of his hands to the ground.
280   He squatted down by the child, though eager to be on his way,
and addressed to dear little Hermes the following menacing words:
"All right, my diapered friend, the son of Zeus and of Maia,
by these very omens of yours I shall presently sniff out my cattle,
and you yourself will lead me and guide me where they are hidden."
285   At this Cyllenian Hermes sat up in great indignation.
With both his hands he seized the blanket wrapping his shoulders
and pushed it back from his ears, demanding this information:
     "Where are you taking me now, O you who work from afar,
hottest tempered of gods? Has all this fuss over cattle
290   made you so cross that you feel you must take it out on poor me?
I tell you, I wish the whole tribe of cattle would utterly perish.
I didn't steal your cows, and I didn't see any rustler
(whatever 'cows' may be; I know them only by hearsay).
Let us take the matter to law and appeal to Zeus, son of Cronus."
295   First the sheep-tending god and the glorious offspring of Leto
pettifogged over details and stubbornly sidestepped agreement.
Apollo, speaking the truth, did his best to trap noble Hermes,
while he of Cyllenê maneuvered to entrap the lord of the archers
by a show of rhetorical skill and all the tricks of a shyster.
300   Hermes, of course, knew them all, but he found his opponent did too.
     So Hermes changed his tactics and led down the sand-covered prairie,
himself going first, with the son of Zeus and Leto behind him.
The handsome sons of Zeus reached the fragrant peak of Olympus,
the home of their father, Cronus' son. The balance of justice
305   was set before the pair, the jury filled snowy Olympus,
and the deathless gods assembled just after golden-throned dawn.
At the knees of Zeus stood Hermes and Apollo with silvery bow.
Zeus who thunders on high thus addressed his glorious son:
"Phoebus, whence comest thou hither, driving prodigious booty,
310   this newly born child, who resembles ambassadors ancient and wise?
A matter of weight, forsooth, is brought to the council of gods."
     To him replied Lord Phoebus, he who works from afar,
"Father, soon will you hear a matter of serious import;
do not reproach me as being the only one greedy for booty.
315   This little child, who in fact is really a larcenous bandit,
I found at the end of a tedious trip in the hills of Cyllenê,
a cheat more plausible far than any I ever have seen,
god or human or swindler, who walks on the face of the earth.
Stealing my cattle at evening from out the meadow, he drove them
320   straight to Pylos, along the shore of the thunderous sea.
They left two remarkable tracks, of a sort to leave one astonished,
the work of a clownish goblin. The tracks of the cattle were clear,
preserved in the blackish dust, facing the asphodel meadows.

---

278. *cover it up:* That is, Hermes farted. A sneeze—when breath leaves the body—was considered
to be an omen demanding attention.

But the animals' unknown driver crossed over the sandy ground
325   at the side of the path, lifted neither on feet nor on hands.
Some other miraculous scheme he employed to cover the journey,
as if he were walking on stilts he had fashioned of sapling oaks.
    As long as he followed the cattle over the patches of sand,
all the footprints were clear and easy to see in the dust.
330   But once he had finished his weary journey over the prairie,
the marks of cows and master were lost on the iron-hard ground.
One poor mortal alone chanced to notice him hurrying onward,
straight down the road to Pylos, driving the broad-faced herd.
Hermes then shut in the cattle, scrambled the marks of his path,
335   made his way home to his cradle, and lay as still as the darkness,
in a dim and windy cave; not even a sharp-sighted eagle
would have noticed the baby there. He kept on rubbing his eyes
with two chubby fists, and meanwhile planning a wily new scheme.
When I had come in, he looked me straight in the eye and declared:
340   'I never saw them; I never heard of them; nobody told me about them.
I couldn't tell you a thing, or collect an informer's reward.'"
    Having thus finished his speech, Phoebus Apollo sat down.
Hermes arose in his turn and spoke these words in reply:
"O Zeus, my father, I promise to tell the truth, plain and simple.
345   for I am an innocent child, one quite untrained in deceit.
Early this morning, just as the sun was beginning his rising,
this fellow came to our house to hunt for his shambling cattle.
He brought not a single eye-witness, not one of the blessed gods,
but tried to make me own up by threatening horrible torments,
350   namely, that he would hurl me to the lowest levels of Hades.
Now he's in the vigorous flower of handsome and glorious youth,
but I—well, I'm sure he knows I was born only yesterday morning,
and don't even look like a rustler, a brawny muscular fellow.
So please believe my story, if your claim to paternity is true:
355   I didn't drive off his cattle—if I did, may I never be wealthy!
I never crossed our threshold, and all my story is truthful!
I have the highest regard for Helius and all the immortals,
and you, indeed, I love. But Apollo here fills me with terror.
You yourself know very well how perfectly harmless I am,
360   and I'm ready to take a great oath, corroborating my word—
not guilty! I swear by all these terribly costly surroundings.
And mark you, some day he'll pay for harassing me without mercy,
powerful as he is. But for now, be clement to me, a poor infant."
    So the Cyllenian slayer of Argus spoke, surreptitiously glancing
365   to left and right, as he measured the persuasive effect of his words,
tightly holding his blanket over his infantile shoulders.
Zeus gave a cynical laugh at the sight of his plausible child,
how skillfully he rebutted the charge of rustling the cattle.
In the best paternal fashion he told them to be at one,
370   to go and hunt for the cows, with Hermes leading his brother,
and, laying aside his mischief, to show the secret enclosure
in which, so shortly before, he had hidden the cows he had stolen.

So the son of Cronus decreed, and glorious Hermes obeyed him,
for the will of Zeus, lord of the aegis, quickly won his assent.

375   The pair then hurried away, these handsome children of Zeus,
and came to sandy Pylos, by the ford of the river Alpheus.
At last they reached the pastures and high-roofed sheltering barn
in which the beasts were sheltered against the darkness of night.
Hermes went into the cave and was driving the cows to the light,

380   when out of the edge of his eye Apollo noticed two cowhides
up on the face of a rock. He demanded of glorious Hermes:
"How were you able, you crook, to skin and dress these two oxen?
Right now you're only an infant, but I worry how strong you will be.
You don't need to grow very big, Cyllenian, offspring of Maia!"

385   At that, in his hands he braided a cord both pliant and tough,
eager to tie up Hermes with powerful willow-strip bonds,
but the willow strips did not hold. They fell to earth at a distance,
and right where they landed rooted themselves at once in the earth.
The willows entwined together and covered the wandering cattle,

390   by design of thieving Hermes, while Apollo watched in surprise.
Then the mighty slayer of Argus pretended to gaze at the ground,
but his eyes were twinkling with fire, . . . trying to hide [? the shell]°
He easily softened the heart of the glorious son of Leto,
strong though he was, into doing exactly what Hermes desired.

395   With the lyre on his left elbow, he plucked each string with a pick,
so that it boomed and resounded. Apollo laughed with delight
as the wonderful sound of music stirred in the depths of his heart,
and longing possessed his soul as he listened. The great son of Maia,
plucking away on the lyre, took courage and stood to the left

400   of Phoebus Apollo. He presently lifted his voice in a song
with a sweet and melodius voice, of the start of created things,
of immortal gods and the earth, its face first covered with darkness,
how first they came into being and how each was given his share.°
First of the gods he honored Mnemosynê, mother of Muses,

405   who inspired the son of Maia. In their order of generation,
the glorious son of Zeus expounded the birth of each one,
honoring every immortal, and plucking the lyre in his arms.
Passionate longing attacked the heart in the breast of Apollo;
opening his mouth, he addressed straightforward words to his brother:

410   "Cow-killer, confidence-man, operator, a joy at a banquet,
this song of yours is worth far more than fifty fat cattle.
Moreover, I'm sure that our trifling quarrel is easily settled.
But tell me, son of Maia, you of so many great talents,
have you played like this from birth? or is this a gift of a god,

415   or even some mortal man? Either way, I can hardly believe it,
this wonderful gift of whoever taught you such heavenly song.
This beautiful music I hear, whose like has never been sounded
by any mortal man, or immortal who dwells on Olympus,

392. *shell:* Something is wrong with the Greek text here.   403. *share:* The subject of his song is
very like Hesiod's *Theogony.*

what sort of art is this? what charm for incurable sorrow?
420 What path presenting three choices, joy, sleep, or sweetness of love?
I too am the faithful servant of the Muses who dwell on Olympus,
whose greatest delight is the dance and the shining pathway of song,
the intricate joy of rhythm, the passionate thunder of pipes.
But none of these arts of the feast have ever so shaken my heart.
425 And furthermore, son of Zeus, I'm astonished how sweetly you play.
After all, you are only a moppet, prodigy though you may be,
so just sit still; pay attention to the words of a wise older brother.
From now on you will be hailed as famous among the immortals,
you and your mother as well. This future, I tell you, is certain.
430 I swear by my cornel-wood staff, I will make you a glorious leader
among the immortal gods, and a fortunate leader as well.
I shall give you glorious gifts, and I promise not to deceive you."
    Hermes responded to this with shrewd diplomatical phrasing:
"How tactfully, worker from far, you make your suggestion to me!
435 I haven't the slightest objection to your having a share in my music
and shall prove this very day how I long for friendly relations,
in fact, not only in words. As you sit with the gods, son of Zeus,
you can collect information to be quietly filed away.
You are powerful, strong, and rightly favored by plan-making Zeus,
440 who showers favors upon you. They tell me that right from his mouth
you learn, far-worker, the proper ritual owed to each god,
and all the pronouncements of Zeus, disclosed in oracular speech.
From sources like this, I imagine that you garner blackmail enormous,
since inside information is at hand whenever you need it.
445 But now, since your heart is eager to master the lyre's sweet music,
take it from me as a gift. Go right ahead: play, sing, and frolic;
the merriment you will enjoy is quite sufficient reward.
You will warble a wonderful song to this nice party girl in your arms,
for you already know all the answers, you always say the right thing.
450 Take her along to a spirited dance or a frivolous dinner,
or even a glorious revel, where nighttime is turned into day.
If anyone asks the right questions, in a way both clever and wise,
she will teach him curious matters, a joy and delight to his heart.
But be sure to handle her gently, for she loathes dull serious force.
455 If any dullard should tax her with questions insistent and stupid,
she would give him a stupid answer of silly chattering nonsense.
But you're not a bit like that: you can easily learn what you please,
so I'll give you this lyre as a present, O glorious son of great Zeus.
The two of us, worker from far, on mountain or horse-feeding prairie,
460 will graze our wandering cattle on whatever pasture may please us.
The lusty bulls will cover the cows, and abundance of heifers
and bullocks will then be calved. You see, there is really no reason
to fly into a temper; you bargain too shrewdly for that."
Then side by side the pair of them drove the cattle back homeward,
465 to the holy meadow, then hurried away to snowy Olympus,
these good-looking sons of Zeus, delighters both in the lyre.
    Zeus, the giver of counsel, rejoiced to have made them such comrades,

and down to this day Apollo, son of Leto, and Hermes are friendly,
as is shown by the gift of the lyre that Hermes gave the far-darter,
470   which Apollo so skillfully strums, embracing it in his arms.
And as for himself, it was Hermes who invented a clever technique,
producing the sound of the pipe,° whose reedy notes echo far.

Homeric Hymn to Hermes (1–512)

472. *pipe:* The Pan-pipes, a group of reeds of different lengths bound together side by side.

Apollo and Hermes, according to the hymn, are social and political opposites: Apollo, with his fine herds of cows, rich and established; Hermes seemingly a helpless infant huddled in a cave. He has nothing and is nobody, a god's bastard. The mark of the aristocrat in the sixth century B.C. was the lyre with which he entertained his friends in the symposium before holding a girl on his arm, as Hermes describes to Apollo; Apollo, usually represented with a lyre, was the aristocrat's god. The aristocrat had learned alphabetic writing in school and had memorized poetry from written texts for performance to the accompaniment of the lyre. But who invented poetry in the first place? Who made the lyre that made the poetry possible?

Hermes stands for those in Greek society who could actually do things, beginning with the oral poets who, without good birth, could make Greek song. They first possessed the lyre, which they presumably invented. That in which the aristocrat most took pride came from the very social class that he despised. As a people, the Greeks valued intelligence highly; although the rustler threatens the basis of aristocratic wealth, his cleverness commands a grudging respect and even admiration.[9] Apollo stands for the *aristoi,* the "best men," and Hermes for the *kakoi,* the "bad guys." The radical Athenian democracy arose from a century of attempts to minimize these distinctions, during the very period when this poem seems to have been composed. As gods opposite in interests but belonging to the same family were reconciled in the poem, so should the social classes of the *aristoi* and *kakoi* look past their differences to seek a common political interest. This poem may have been composed in Athens. Making fire, which Hermes invented, may be dirty work, but it is nice to have cooked meat, which the rich man's wealth provides.

Until now Hermes has claimed our sympathy as he struggled to win a place in the established order by his ingenuity against Apollo, but the rest of the poem seems to have been composed by somebody with an aristocratic bias who wanted to reinstate the unquestioned position of Apollo. In this portion of the Hymn, Hermes promises, in return for Apollo's gift of the caduceus, never again to steal anything from Apollo. The major forms of divination will remain Apollo's, but Hermes is granted the minor power of divination from casting pebbles (perhaps a form of shooting craps).

The part we have given of this delightful tale sums up all of Hermes' qualities, not least his irreverence for established forms and law.

---

[9]Just as Americans insist that the law be obeyed but admire and make heroes of those, such as Jesse James or Al Capone, who most boldly or cleverly subvert it.

Pan and the Pastoral Tradition

In the reign of the emperor Tiberius, about the time of the crucifixion of Jesus, a ship heading from Greece to Italy was startled to hear a great voice shouting to one of the crew, "Thamus, when you reach land, proclaim that 'Great Pan is dead!'" Thamus did so and was answered by a groan from all the mountains. Pan was the first Greek god who was said to have died in historical times.

But Pan was not dead. An author of the early fifth century A.D. explained that Pan was in fact the totality (*pan* = "all") of Nature, a notion appealing to a learned city-dweller of late antiquity. At roughly the same time a Christian bishop, exulting over the fall of the demons—that is, the pagan gods—complained that among the illiterate peasantry Pan's worship was still vigorous: Pagan comes from the Latin *paganus,* "rustic." Vergil had written that "he too is blessed who honors the farmer's gods, Silvanus, old Pan, and their bevy of nymphs," another reflection of the peasant's enduring feeling for the powers that ruled the countryside and the wilds.

Long after the end of antiquity, Pan and other rustic spirits continued to appear in the pastoral tradition of European literature and painting, which celebrated country life as an idealized antidote to the refined but corrupt ways of the city. John Milton (1608–1674), describing the Garden of Eden, evokes the mood in his epic poem on the fall of humankind, *Paradise Lost:*

> . . . In a shadier bower
> More sacred and sequester'd, though but feign'd,
> Pan or Sylvanus never slept, nor nymph
> Nor Faunus haunted.

John Keats (1795–1821) evokes the myth of Pan and the nymph Syrinx in his poem "I Stood Tip-toe upon a Little Hill," when he admires the poet

> . . . who pull'd the boughs aside,
> That we might look into a forest wide,
> To catch a glimpse of Fauns and Dryads [= "oak-nymphs"]
> Coming with softest rustle through the trees; . . .
> Telling us how fair trembling Syrinx fled
> Arcadian Pan, with such a fearful dread.
> Poor nymph,—poor Pan,—how did he weep to find,
> Nought but a lovely sighing of the wind
> Along the reedy stream; a half-heard strain,
> Full of sweet desolation—balmy pain.

French poet Stéphane Mallarmé (1842–1898), in *L'Après-midi d'un faune* ("The Afternoon of a Faun"), presented the monologue of a faun who meditates on his life, sleeping in the noonday sun, playing music, pursuing nymphs, and loving beauty. The poem inspired Claude Debussy's haunting musical *Prélude à l'après-midi d'un faune* ("Prelude to the Afternoon of a Faun," 1894), which Sergei Diaghilev later made into a renowned ballet.

Pan, the Goatherd's God

The two sides of Hermes—the guardian of flocks and herds and the master of theft, lies, and skullduggery—appear in his sons. One of these, Autolycus, the greatest liar and thief of his day, could make himself, and the things he stole, invisible. Odysseus the trickster was his grandson. That is one side of Hermes' nature. The other, his concern for pastures and fertility, is represented by **Pan,** one of the few deities in Greek myth whose form is not entirely human. He had the hoofs and legs of a goat, pointed ears, a little tail, and horns.[10]

The god's name probably comes from an Indo-European root meaning "to feed"; from it comes English pastor and pastures. As "the feeder," Pan is the power that makes the shepherd's flocks get fat. His parents are usually given as Hermes and the nymph Dryopê ("oak tree"), but there are many other accounts. At birth Pan was so ugly his mother ran off in terror. Pan was considered especially lustful, like a lecherous goat, and the nymph Syrinx, whom he desired, also ran from him, until she was changed into a reed. Pan slashed down the whole reed bed hunting for her, then made himself musical pipes by joining together fragments of reeds of unequal length (this version of the origin of the Pan-pipe, or "syrinx," conflicts with that in the *Hymn to Hermes,* where Pan's father, Hermes, is the inventor).

He did not live on Mount Olympus in Thessaly, but wandered about the wild hills of Arcadia, the only region of Greece with no seacoast. There he lived in caves and danced across the mountains, leading choirs of nymphs. At noontime, when the Greeks believed a strange silence falls over the world, he slept. If a shepherd woke him, Pan gave a terrifying shout, which inspired *pan*-ic, the feeling of irrational terror that can overcome one in remote and desolate country.

Pan also loved the nymph Echo, once an attendant of Hera; Echo entertained Hera with endless chatter while Zeus pursued other nymphs, until Hera punished her with a curious impediment: She could never begin a speech, but only repeat the words of others. Eventually she faded away to a mere voice, an "echo."

Latin writers identified Pan with Faunus and Silvanus, rustic deities who were among the last to succumb to the attacks of Christianity. These spirits were often spoken of in the plural, as pans, fauns, and *silvani*—really, they are interchangeable. From pictorial representations of such figures seems to come our horned, hoofed, pointy-eared, lustful devil.

KEY TERMS

[10]See the lower central figure in Titian's *Bacchus and Ariadnê,* Fig. P 10.1.

FURTHER READING

Borgeaud, P., *The Cult of Pan in Ancient Greece* (Chicago, 1988). Discusses the evolution of this god through Greek history.

Brown, N. O., *Hermes the Thief* (New York, 1969; reprint of original edition of 1947). Perhaps the best book on the *Homeric Hymn to Hermes* (although quasi-Marxist), arguing that Hermes represents the emerging mercantile classes against the established aristocracy, represented by Apollo.

Fontenrose, J., *Python, A Study of Delphic Myth and Its Origins* (Berkeley, Calif., 1959). An in-depth study of the dragon-slaying myth in the Hymn to Apollo, its origins in the Near East, and its meaning.

———, *The Delphic Oracle* (Berkeley, Calif., 1978). A scholarly examination of the evidence for the nature of the oracle at Delphi, opposing many long-held views, especially that the Pythia was a medium and that the oracle was deliberately ambiguous.

Merivale, P., *Pan, the Goat-God: His Myth in Modern Times* (Cambridge, Mass., 1969). The survival of this pagan god of the wild.

Parke, H. W., and D.E.W. Wormell, *The Delphic Oracle* (Oxford, U.K., 1956). A standard introduction to traditional views.

CHAPTER 8

MYTHS OF THE OLYMPIANS
THE FEMALE DEITIES

The race of gods and men is one, and from one mother
we both draw our breath. Yet all the difference in our powers
holds us apart, so that man is nothing,
but the brazen floor of heaven
is eternally unshakable.

PINDAR, *Nemean* 6

T HE MALE OLYMPIANS have fairly clear spheres of operation, although sometimes they overlap or have outlines that are inexplicable (what is the nature of Poseidon's relationship with horses?). The female Olympians, by contrast, seem more to be aspects of a single concept: the fecund forces in life, both natural and human. Thus Demeter is the force that makes grain sprout from the seed. Hestia is the life of the house, where the fire burns and sustenance is prepared. Aphrodite is the horrific power of sexual attraction, indifferent to human happiness as it ensures the creation of a new generation. Artemis is the wealth of the wild, where game abounds. Only Athena has no clear relationship with fertility, but she is know-how in female crafts, especially weaving, in which Greek women spent their lives while not rearing their children. However, in studying male and female gods in Greek myth we must remember that all such portraits are the creations of Greek males, whose complex relationships with the other sex are a central theme of Greek myth. We know almost nothing about how Greek women viewed any gods, male or female.

DEMETER, MISTRESS OF WHEAT

Whereas Gaea/Earth was the female power who presided over the birth of the world, Demeter (de-**mē**-ter) was the mother-goddess who oversaw the fruitfulness of agriculture, especially wheat. The *-meter* part of her name means "mother," but the *De-* has never been explained convincingly; we wish it could mean "wheat" so that Demeter is the "wheat mother," but the etymology seems impossible. Surely wherever wheat was grown, her religion was strong, especially at the town of Eleusis near Athens and in Sicily. Both in myth and in cult Demeter was closely linked to her daughter Persephonê; the two were called simply "the goddesses." We devote all of Chapter 9 to discussing the important myths of Demeter and Persephonê and other related stories.

HESTIA, THE HEARTH

Hestia was the eldest child of Cronus and Rhea, the first swallowed and the last regurgitated. Her name means "hearth." She is the Roman Vesta and the most colorless of the Olympians, being nothing more than the fireplace in every house: There was her shrine and her presence, protectress of the home. She defined the internal space of the female world, for it was the duty of the woman in the family to tend the domestic fire. By extension Hestia was also protectress of the city, the enlarged family, which sometimes kept a central hearth, even as today in Paris the French burn an eternal flame beneath the *Arc de Triomphe*. In Athens, she was associated with a special building where the magistrates of the city dined together as members of the civic family. Few stories are told about her. She was always virgin and never left Olympus, as did the other gods. There she was the center of the divine household, even as the hearth was the center of the human family. Her Roman counterpart, Vesta, was treated as the chief symbol of the city; her shrine, tended by six virgins, contained an undying flame.

Aphrodite, Goddess of Sexual Love

Aphrodite (later identified with the Roman Venus) embodies the overwhelming power of human sexual attraction (see Fig. 5.3); her constant companion was Eros, "love" or "desire" (the Roman Cupid), who emerged from Chaos at the same time as Gaea/Earth and Tartarus, according to Hesiod. In later myths, however, Eros was the son of Aphrodite by Ares, Hermes, or Zeus. In art he is shown as a winged boy with bow and arrows or a flaming torch (a figure still familiar on Valentine's Day; see Fig. 2.11), a mischievous, irresponsible child, showering his arrows randomly and without regard for the harm born from the sexual passion he arouses.

Hesiod derives Aphrodite by false etymology from the Greek word *aphros,* "foam," but the name must in reality be a distortion of the name of the Eastern goddess of fertility, variously called Inanna, Ishtar, or Astartê. The goddess evidently came to Greece through Cyprus, a frequent point of transmission of Eastern culture to the West. At Paphos, in southwestern Cyprus, she was worshiped as early as the twelfth century B.C. in the form of a polished conical stone. Her cult was also important on the island of Cythera, south of the Peloponnesus, where Phoenicians had a settlement; here, as in many parts of the Mediterranean, they processed purple dye from a shellfish.[1] Other important temples were built to her in Sicily, where there were Phoenician colonies, and in Corinth, a gathering place for seafarers of various nationalities. Greek myth preserves a clear sense of Aphrodite's connection with Cyprus and Cythera. According to Hesiod, it was in these places that the goddess first came to land after rising from the sea foam, and she was often referred to in myth as Cytherea (si-the-**rē**-a) or **Cypris** (**si**-pris).

A striking feature of the worship of Aphrodite and Inanna/Ishtar/Astartê was temple prostitution. Women, often of good birth, voluntarily served in her temples, where they had intercourse with men who paid in the form of offerings to the goddess. Such service guaranteed the favor of the goddess and ensured large families to the woman, once she married. The sometimes prudish Greeks did not like the practice at all, but it did occur in temples to Aphrodite at Corinth and Cythera.

Sappho, who lived in the late seventh or early sixth century B.C. on the island of Lesbos and who was celebrated as "the tenth Muse," wrote one of the prettiest poems about Aphrodite, the only complete poem to survive from Sappho's large corpus of nine books. Nothing certain is known about Sappho's life or about the audience for her poetry. She is famous for her erotic celebration of women, but the social environment in which such poetry was performed has been the topic of controversy since ancient times. Not until after classical times was her poetry considered to be homoerotic (hence our word *lesbian*). Some of her poetry must have been performed at weddings, the one occasion in which it was possible to celebrate publicly a young woman's erotic appeal. In her hymn to Aphrodite, she declares the love-goddess' power to sway the hearts even of the unwilling, while, ironically, leaving no doubt that the present situation has occurred many times before:

> O deathless Aphrodite, fancy-throned
> daughter of Zeus, weaver of deceit, I beg you,
> do not conquer me with pain and sorrow,
> O mistress, deep in my heart
>
> but come here, if ever once hearing my voice,
> acquiescing you came
> leaving the golden home
> of your father,
>
> yoking your car. Beautiful, swift
> sparrows brought you over the dark earth,
> whirring their wings, down from heaven,
> through the air

---

[1]This was the most precious dye of the ancient world. Roman senators were distinguished by wearing a purple stripe on their togas; Roman emperors dressed all in purple, hence the purple robes of the pope today. *Phoenician* seems to mean "the red ones" because the hands of these Semitic traders from the Levant were always stained from this celebrated dye.

and swiftly you arrived. You, O blessed goddess
smiling with deathless eyes
asked what *now* I suffered
and why had I called,

and what *now* did I wish to happen,
maddened in my heart. "Who now shall I persuade
to lead you back to her love? Who, O Sappho, has
done you harm?

for if she flees, swiftly she shall pursue;
if she denies your gifts, she shall give;
if she does not love, swiftly she shall love,
even if she wants it not."

Come to me, again, free me
from harsh agony, fulfill for me
all that my heart longs to fulfill. You, yourself,
be my helpmate!

SAPPHO, fragment 1 (Diehl)

Hermaphroditus and Priapus

In addition to her affair with Ares, Aphrodite had an affair with the messenger god Hermes, by whom she gave birth to **Hermaphroditus** (her-ma-fro-**dī**-tus), a boy of remarkable beauty. Ovid tells a famous story about him: One day a nymph, Salmacis (**sal**-ma-sis), noticed him wandering in the woods, fell hopelessly in love, and urged that they sleep together. Innocent Hermaphroditus ran away in confusion. Later, when Hermaphroditus dipped into a spring for a bath, Salmacis leaped in and clung to him tightly, praying that they never be separated. They were fused into one being with a woman's breasts but a man's genitals. The slightly titillating bisexual Hermaphroditus was a common subject of art in late antiquity.

Another child of Aphrodite, whose father was reputedly Dionysus or Hermes, was **Priapus** (prī-**ā**-pus), an amusing Asiatic garden deity and symbol of fertility with an enormous erect phallus who warded off the evil eye. His name is not Greek and he does not appear until late Hellenistic times. He was especially popular among the Romans, who suspended little tablets with clever, highly obscene poetry from the god's phallus (Fig. 8.1).

Pygmalion

Except for the love between Aphrodite and Ares, all important stories about Aphrodite are set outside Greece, reflecting her Eastern origins. Her strong connections with Cyprus and with Eastern myth appear in traditions about the Cypriote royal house, best known through Ovid's story of **Pygmalion,** king of Cyprus, who had become disgusted with the profligate ways of the Cypriote women. In many respects,

Fig. 8.1. Priapus, the garden god, weighs his phallus against a bag of gold (it seems an even contest!), c. A.D. 70 Priapus wears a Phrygian cap (Phrygia is home to fertility cults). His association with Dionysus is indicated by the wand (thyrsus) to his left, his power over gardens by the bowl of fruit at his feet.

(House of the Vetii, Pompeii; Deutsches Archaologisches Institut, Rome)

the story is a remaking of Hesiod's story of Pandora, set not on the early days of the world but in the age of heroes:[2]

[243]   Pygmalion observed these women leading their shameful lives;
       horrified by the vices of which nature has planted such plenty
245   in the mind of their sex, he started by living a celibate life,
       sharing his bed with no one. He presently carved himself a statue
       with delicate skill, of ivory, pure white, possessing a beauty
       greater than any mortal woman could ever hope to attain—
       and promptly conceived a passion for the product of his own hand.
250   The figure was that of a maiden so real you might think it alive;
       perhaps she wanted to move, and only decorum restrained her;
       the skillful sculptor employed his skill in concealing his skill.
         Pygmalion gazed at his work, his heart inflamed with love
       for the counterfeit girl he had made. Again and again his hands
255   uncertainly fondled the work—is it ivory, or is it real flesh?
       At last he persuaded himself that the statue was ivory no longer;
       pressing his kisses upon it, he was sure each kiss was returned.
       Whispering, he hugged closer—did his fingers sink in the flesh?
       Has he been so rough that bruises appeared wherever he touched?

[2]This widely known story was inspiration for the modern play *Pygmalion* by George Bernard Shaw, in which a professor of linguistics breaks English barriers of class by teaching a girl who sells flowers in the street to speak correctly. The play was the basis for one of the most successful musicals of all time, *My Fair Lady*.

260　He kissed the hurt places. He gave her presents girls all adore—
　　　sea shells and well-polished stones, parakeets in their cages,
　　　bouquets of a thousand colors, lilies, bright painted balls,
　　　tears of the Heliad nymphs.° He clothed her in elegant dresses,
　　　gems sparkled on her fingers, long looping chains on her neck;
265　from her ear lobes dangled light earrings, ribbons over her bosom.
　　　All in the best of taste, but without them she looked even nicer.
　　　He tenderly laid her down on a bed of Sidonian purple;°
　　　murmuring "Share this, my couch!" he pillowed her drooping head
　　　on a cushion of softest down, as if it could feel what he wanted.
270　　　　　Venus' feast day arrived, beloved by the people of Cyprus;
　　　victims with gilded horns bowed snowy necks and were slaughtered
　　　as incense fumed in each shrine. Pygmalion, his duties completed,
　　　bashfully stayed by the altar, and bashfully uttered his prayer:
　　　　　"Since you gods, as piety tells us, can grant any human request,
275　I beg that my wife may be—" (not daring "my ivory maiden,"
　　　he gulped and went on) "someone just like my ivory statue."
　　　Venus the Golden herself was there at her very own feast day.
　　　Knowing full well the intent of Pygmalion's stumbling prayer,
　　　she gave him a sign of good will: a flame leaped up on the altar,
280　not once, but three times.
　　　　　　　　　　Pygmalion returned to his workshop,
　　　and hurried to seek the graven image of his true love.
　　　Throwing himself beside it, he smothered the statue with kisses.
　　　How's this? it seemed to get warm! His mouth returned to her lips,
　　　his hand to her breast. At his eager groping the ivory softened;
285　the chill of her flesh passed off; it gladly yielded to his touch
　　　and softened, as does the wax of the honey bees of Hymettus,°
　　　which, warmed by the sun and kneaded, is soft and easily shaped,
　　　better to handle, the more it is handled. Pygmalion, astonished,
　　　was unable to make up his mind; rejoicing, he still hesitated,
290　and kept his rejoicing in check, for fear it was all an illusion.
　　　Again he became the lover, with hands roving over the body—
　　　for body indeed it was! whose veins throbbed under his fingers.
　　　The grateful hero of Paphos poured out his praises of Venus,
　　　then pressed his lips to the lips no longer a statue's, but real.
295　As she felt his kisses, the maiden blushed and raised timid eyes;
　　　the love light and light of heaven together fell on her sight.°
　　　The goddess herself was a guest at the marriage she had arranged.
　　　Nine times the horns of the new moon rounded out to a circle,
　　　when the one-time statue gave birth to a daughter, named Paphos,
300　whose name the island preserves.

OVID, *Metamorphoses* (10.243–297)

263. *tears of the Heliad nymphs*: Amber. For the Heliades, sisters of Phaëthon, see Chapter 4.　267. *Sidonian purple*: Sidon was a city of the Phoenicians.　286. *Hymettus*: A mountain near Athens, still famous for its honey.　296. *sight*: The Latin *lumen* may mean "light," "sight," or "eye."

Paphos, for whom Aphrodite's sacred city is named, gave birth to Cinyras (**sin**-i-ras), whose wife boasted that their daughter **Myrrha** (or Smyrna) was more beautiful than Aphrodite. Aphrodite punished the arrogance by causing Myrrha to fall in love with her own father, Cinyras, whom she lured into a darkened chamber, where she slept with him for twelve nights. Cinyras, drunk, thought he had slept with a concubine while his wife was out of town. When he discovered the truth, Cinyras pursued his pregnant daughter with a sword, but the gods transformed her into the myrrh tree. Her tears of sorrow became the precious resin myrrh, burned on the altar in Aphrodite's cult and other religious cults.[3] Cinyras killed himself for shame over the incestuous union. After nine months, the myrrh tree split open, and the beautiful hero Adonis emerged (compare Fig. P8.1c), whose story we consider in Chapter 9.

Aphrodite and Anchises

Another tale of Aphrodite's ominous love is found in the *Homeric Hymn to Aphrodite*, from the early seventh century B.C. Aphrodite, the irresistible, often dangerous compulsion of sexual love, became victim to her own power when, thanks to Zeus, she fell in love with a mortal, **Anchises** (an-kī-sēz), a prince related to the Trojan royal house. Although male gods regularly pursued mortal women, it was considered shameful for a goddess to consort with a mortal man, and there are few examples of such liaisons. The hymn nicely compares Aphrodite with the great goddesses Athena, Artemis, and Hestia (all of whom remained virgin):

[1]   Sing me, O Muse, the story of Aphrodite the golden,
    the Cyprian, she who arouses the sweetest desire in immortals,
    who conquers the races of mortals, even the birds on the wing,
    and all the numberless creatures supported by earth or by sea;
5   all that has life is concerned in the work of the fair Aphrodite.
    Three hearts alone Aphrodite can neither persuade nor deceive:
    gray-eyed Athena is one, the daughter of Zeus of the aegis,
    who plays no part in the works of Aphrodite the golden;
    rather, her joy is in war and the savage workings of Ares,
10   battles and fights, though she cares for glorious craftsmen as well,
    for Athena first taught mortal workers the art of building a chariot
    with fittings of bronze. It is she, moreover, who teaches
    soft-skinned maidens the arts of the house, revealing her knowledge.
    And Artemis, mistress of arrows, sounding the cry of the huntress,
15   is immune to Aphrodite and her plots to ensnare men with love.
    Her delight is rather the bow, the killing of beasts in the hills;
    the lyre and dance as well, but chiefly the cry of the hunter,
    sounding in shadowy woodlands, by the cities of fair-minded men.
    Finally, Aphrodite and all her works are repugnant
20   to the lady Hestia, first-born of Cronus, who then, by Zeus's design,
    was born again as his last.° The lady was wooed by Poseidon,

21. *Hestia:* The first born of the children of Cronus and Rhea, the first swallowed by her father, and the last to be vomited back to the light.

---

[3]The three kings who brought gold, frankincense, and myrrh to Christ's nativity (Matthew 2.12) often are explained as symbols of royalty, divinity, and sacrificial death.

then wooed by Apollo as well, but both she firmly rejected
and swore an unbreakable oath, her hand on the head of great Zeus,
the father who holds the aegis, to remain forever a virgin,
25   honored among the immortals. Instead of wedlock, Zeus granted
a noble reward to the goddess: she sits in the midst of his palace
by his side at the head of the table, picking the finest of morsels.
In all the temples of every god she is suitably honored,
and men owe due veneration to Hestia, first of immortals.
30   The hearts of these three Aphrodite can never trick or inveigle;
no other, blessed god or mortal, is able to flee her enticement.
She even beguiles the mind of Zeus, who delights in the thunder,
mightiest of all the gods, the holder of mightiest power;
whenever the humor so moves her, she fools even his wily spirit,
35   and leads him to couple with women, evading the sharp eye of Hera,
his sister as well as wife, fairest of all the immortals.
Cronus the schemer begat great Hera, his comeliest daughter,
on Rhea, his consort; then Zeus, eternal in wisdom, received her,
and made her his modest wife, well versed in arts of the household.
40   On Aphrodite herself Zeus cast a sweet spell of desire,
of lust for a mortal man: no more could she shyly dissemble
her knowledge of love of a mortal, experience in a man's bed.
Never again could she claim, when immortals were gathered together,
with a softly innocent smile, that she alone drove them to couple
45   with mortal women, who bore them sons who were destined to perish,
and deathless goddesses too she had driven to mate with mere humans.
Thus Zeus put into her heart a sweet desire for Anchises,
who, high on the slopes of Ida,° mountain of bubbling streams,
at that time was tending his cattle—a man with the form of a god.
50   No wonder that Aphrodite was smitten as soon as she saw him,
or that sweet pangs of desire seized on her heart and her spirit.
Off she hurried to Cyprus, to Paphos, her sweet-scented temple,
into its sacred precinct with its altar fuming with incense.
Behind her she closed the brazen doorway, gleaming and polished.
55   The Graces washed and anointed her flesh with ambrosial oil,
divine, sweet-smelling, that glows on the skin of bodies immortal;
of this she treasured a store, of fragrance greater than earthly.
Then Aphrodite, lover of laughter, dressed in her finest array,
decked her body with gold, and, abandoning redolent Cyprus,
60   hurried her flight to Troy, through clouds and over the mountains.
At last she arrived at Ida, mountain of freshets, the mother
of animals wild and savage. Over the foothills she hastened,
to the hut of Anchises. Behind, there came a once man-eating bevy
of now-fawning dusky wolves, of lions still savagely glaring,
65   bears, and swift-footed leopards, insatiate killers of deer.
The goddess rejoiced at the sight: into their hearts she injected
the spell of amorous desire; all of them, couple by couple,
lay down together to mate, throughout all the shadowy forest.
The goddess soon drew near the shepherd's stoutly built cabin.

48. *Ida:* In northwestern Asia Minor, near Troy.

70   She found the hero Anchises, left all alone by himself.
       His comrades had led out the cattle to graze in rich grassy meadows,
       while he strolled about alone, strumming a tune on his lyre.
       The daughter of Zeus, Aphrodite, stopped in front of the hero,
       disguising her height and form, to resemble an unmarried maiden,
75   lest her godhead frighten Anchises as he opened his amorous eyes.
       But the moment the Trojan saw her he viewed her form in amazement,
       wondering at her stature, her beauty, her glorious garments.
       She was wearing a long red dress, gleaming more brightly than fire,
       lovely, embroidered in gold. And over her tender young bosom
80   it shone as fair as the moonlight, a wonder indeed to one's eyes.
          Anchises, insane with love, addressed these words to the goddess:
       "I greet you, lady, whatever goddess you are, who have happened
       to come to my cabin—Artemis? Leto perhaps? or the golden
       Aphrodite? Thetis, lofty of birth? or even the gray-eyed Athena?
85   Could you be one of the Graces who accompany all the immortals,
       immortal themselves, we are told? or maybe a nymph who has wandered
       down from the pleasant woods where they dwell, or one who inhabits
       the rising springs and the rivers, the grassy meadows and plains?
       See, I shall build you an altar on a crag, to be seen from afar
90   and offer you rich oblations at every season of year.
       This only I ask in return: with a kind and benevolent spirit,
       grant that I grow in importance, a leader and prince of the Trojans.
       Give me a fruitful posterity, keeping my name and my blood.
       And last, for myself I pray that my life may be long and contented,
95   seeing the light of the sun, respected by all of my fellows,
       and so live on, till I come to the threshold of gloomy old age."
          To him Aphrodite, daughter of Zeus, made this modest reply:
       "Anchises, noblest of humans born on the face of the earth,
       no goddess, of course, am I; why liken me to the immortals?
100   I am no more than a woman; the mother who bore me was human.
       You may have heard of my father, Otreus, that glorious hero,
       ruler of all the dominion of Phrygia,° well-fortified region.
       You notice that I speak your Trojan as in my own Phrygian:
       a Trojan nurse took me over, when I was no more than an infant,
105   from my own dear mother's hands, and brought me up in the palace.
       Thus I became as fluent in your language as in my own.
       Just now golden-staffed Hermes, the famous slayer of Argus,
       caught me up from the dancers of Artemis, gold-arrowed huntress.
       Many of us together, both nymphs and girls fit for marriage,
110   were dancing, while all around a crowd uncountable watched us.
       From such a throng gold-sceptered Hermes, the slayer of Argus,
       bore me, past endless cornlands worked by the labor of mortals,
       by endless acres unworked, unclaimed, the haunt of wild creatures,
       of savage man-eating beasts who roam about in the forests.
115   Nevermore, so it seemed, would my feet touch the life-giving earth.

---

102. *Phrygia:* In the legend of the Trojan War, Otreus came to the aid of Priam, king of Troy, to fight against the Amazons. Phrygia is the territory comprising the western flank and part of the central plateau of Asia Minor.

But Hermes insisted that I was to share the bed of Anchises,
be named as his wedded wife, and bear you magnificent children.
All this the slayer of Argos narrated in every detail,
then made his way once again to the deathless gods on Olympus.
120 So I am come before you, as unswerving necessity orders.
In Zeus's name I implore you, and that of your glorious parents
(surely no common mortals could engender so splendid a son!),
take me, a maiden unwedded, and quite unpracticed in love;
present me to your dear father, to your mother, wise and sagacious,
125 to brothers born to your house—no embarrassment will they find me,
but a daughter of high repute. Send a messenger quickly to Phrygia,
land of the speediest horses, to my grieving father and mother.
They will return you a treasure of gold and well-woven garments,
for you to take as an ample—nay, a magnificent—dowry.
130 When all this business is done, set up a magnificent banquet
to celebrate our wedlock, honored by gods and by mortals."
  The goddess's words injected sweet longing into his heart.
Desire took hold of Anchises, and thus he spoke in reply:
"If you are indeed a human, if a mortal woman once bore you,
135 if Otreus, as you say, that famous man, is your father,
if you are here by the will of Hermes, the leader immortal,
and if you are willing forever to bear the title of wife—
then I tell you that nobody, nobody, be he immortal or human,
can hold me back in my passion, until we have bedded in love,
140 no, not if archer Apollo from his silver bow should let fly
his deadly unfailing arrows. Indeed, divinest of women,
I would gladly go down to Hades, if first I had entered your bed."
  At that he took hold of her hand. Aphrodite, the lover of laughter,
coyly averted her face, and, drooping her beautiful eyelids,
145 modestly feigning resistance, crept to the soft-covered bed.
This was warm and well covered with furs of beasts which the hero
had slain high up in the mountains, the pelts of lions and bears.
Once they lay down on the couch, solidly built and uncreaking,
the hero stripped from the goddess her pretty gewgaws and brooches,
150 her necklace and earrings as well. Anchises then loosened her girdle,
and everything else, and tossed them onto a chair made of silver.
So this mortal lay down by the side of a goddess immortal,
not by his own design, but by fate and divine intervention.
  At the hour shepherds return their flocks from flowery meadows,
155 driving their sturdy sheep and cattle back to the shelter,
Aphrodite arose, poured drowsy sleep on Anchises,
and dressed herself once again in all her beautiful raiment.
Then, fully clothed, the goddess stood by the couch in full glory,
her head as high as the roof tree. Beauty shone from her features,
160 beauty such as belongs to the golden-crowned goddess alone.
Then she awakened Anchises from slumber, addressing him thus:
  "Up, son of Dardanus! Tell me, why do you slumber so soundly?
Look at me now, and answer: do I seem to resemble the woman
on whom you first cast your eyes no more than a few hours ago?"
165 So she teased him. Anchises awoke with a start and looked up.

As soon as he looked on the neck and the lovely face of the goddess,
in shame and terror he turned his eyes away from the vision,
lifting his shepherd's cloak and concealing his handsome young face.
In tones of humble entreaty he spoke these words from his heart:

170 "As soon as my eyes beheld your comeliness, beautiful goddess,
I recognized you as divine; it was you who then led me astray.
I implore you in Zeus's great name, the father wielding the aegis,
have pity, abandon me not, unmanned, among men. For the mortal
who mates with a goddess undying can never again be a man."

175 To his reproach Aphrodite, the daughter of Zeus, gave her answer:
"Pluck up your courage, Anchises, noblest of all mortal men;
you need have no fear whatever of suffering harm at my hands—
certainly not from mine, nor those of a godhead undying,
for you are cherished indeed by all the blessed immortals.

180 You shall father a son, to be ruler over the Trojans,
and generations from him shall be born, one succeeding another,
Aeneas, after my terrible° guilt at bedding a human.
Of all the races of men, the closest and dearest to gods
in beauty and charm is that from which you and he are descended.

185 For example, Zeus the planner abducted the fair Ganymede
for his beauty, and kept him to live with him among the immortals,
pouring their drink in the house of Zeus, a wonder to see,
honored by all the gods as he draws the deep ruddy nectar
from a golden bowl. But aching grief held the heart of Tros,°

190 who knew not where the tempest of Zeus had carried his son.
Day and night he lamented, until Zeus repented at last,
giving him high-pacing horses, the sort that carry the gods,
a gift in exchange for his son. And, moved by Zeus's commandment,
the guide, the slayer of Argus, told Tros in every detail

195 how his son would never perish, but be ageless as an immortal.
When Tros understood the promise of Zeus, he ended his grieving,
but afterward traveled in joy, drawn by his storm-footed horses.

182. *terrible:* The Greek is *ainos,* punning on Aeneas.   189. *Tros:* Another early king of Troy, father of Ganymede.

Here Aphrodite tells the story of Eos' love for Tithonus as a second mythical parallel to her own passion for Anchises (see Chapter 4). She then continues:

[248] "For my part, I cannot bear to have you face such a future,
to be, like him,° immortal, but aging through days never-ending.

250 If you could live on forever, keeping the face and figure
which now you enjoy, and if you bore the name of my husband,
then my prophetic heart would not be darkened by sorrow.
But well I know that grim old age will soon be upon you,
pitiless, bringing the future which lies in wait for all humans,

255 a future deadly and grinding, one even the gods must abhor.
And what of me? Shall I not suffer unending reproaches
among the deathless gods, forever, on your account?
Till now they always have dreaded my schemes and the wily devices

249. *him:* Tithonus, who had eternal life but not eternal youth.

260   by which I have driven them all to couple with mortal women;
       immortal they might be, but my workings subverted them all.
       Never again dare I mention such topics among the immortals,
       for I have strayed in my folly, wretched and out of my mind,
       bedding a mortal man and conceiving his child in my womb.
       As soon as the boy is greeted by the light of the glorious sun,
265   deep-breasted mountain nymphs will undertake his upbringing,
       they who inhabit the slopes of this great and sanctified mountain.
       They live by neither the ways of gods nor those of humans:
       for centuries they live on, eating the food of immortals,
       treading along with immortals the steps of their lovely dance.
270   Sileni° and even the sharp-eyed slayer of Argus himself, Hermes,
       mate with them, in recesses of a cool and convenient cavern.
       When one of the nymphs is born, firs and lofty-crowned beeches
       spring from the fertile earth, luxuriant, beautiful trees
       high on the slopes of the mountains. Men say such places are holy,
275   sacred to the immortals, and touch them not with their axes.
       But when the fatal day has come for a nymph of the mountain,
       her tree first withers and sheds its foliage over the earth,
       the shriveling bark peels off, the branches break from the trunk,
       and tree and nymph together depart from the rays of the sun.
280   These nymphs will tend my son, watching over his childhood,
       until he begins to display the first signs of developing manhood.
       Then they will bring him hither, to show him off to his father.
       Now let me explain the plan of the future I am designing:
       five years onward from now I shall come back with my son.
285   You will rejoice as your eyes first fall on him whom you fathered,
       to see him so like a god. Then bring him to windy Ilium.°
       If anyone there inquires, 'What mother bore this, your dear son,
       carrying him under her girdle?' remember to tell him this story,
       as I tell it now: "This child was born of a flower-faced nymph,
290   who lives on a forest-clad hill.' But if, instead, in your folly
       you boast of coupling in love with beautiful-crowned Cytherea,
       Zeus in a rage will blast you with thunderbolts lurid and smoking.
       Now I have told the whole story; bury it deep in your heart.
       Beware of speaking my name, or dread the wrath of the gods."
295   Ending with this injunction, she soared to the windy heaven.
       Hail, O goddess who rules as queen of well-built Cyprus!
       With you I began my song; now I turn to sing of another.

Homeric Hymn to Aphrodite (1–197; 248–297)

270. *Sileni:* Woodland spirits.   286. *Ilium:* Another name for Troy.

Other sources tell how Anchises did reveal who was the mother of his child. Zeus struck him in the thigh with a thunderbolt, and ever after he was lame; so did Anchises suffer the fate he feared, to be unmanned among men for having intercourse with the Great Goddess.

Aeneas (ē-**nē**-as), son of Anchises and Aphrodite, is one of the few Trojan heroes to survive the conflagration of the city, escaping with his lame father and his young son to the far west, where they founded the race of the Romans (see Chapter 22).

ARTEMIS, MISTRESS OF ANIMALS

The name *Artemis* is not Greek, and her cult shows signs of reaching back into the Paleolithic Period, when hunting was a principal source of food; Homer calls her *Potnia Therôn,* "mistress of the animals," a title we associate with representations in art dating back to the Bronze Age showing a woman, sometimes winged, between a pair of wild animals (see Fig. 3.3). As such, Artemis is closely associated with the Phrygian Cybelê, who is also shown in the presence of animals, usually lions. In origin, then, Artemis was evidently a mother-goddess, protectress of the young, animal and human, making fecund the whole of nature. Her early role was never forgotten at Ephesus in Asia Minor, her most important cult center and the site of one of the largest temples ever built by Greeks, one of the Seven Wonders of the Ancient World. There a cult image represented her with what seem to be dozens of breasts stacked like grapes on her chest (or they may represent bulls' testicles, hung on a primitive idol after sacrifice) (Fig. 8.2). Much later, when St. Paul tried to speak in Ephesus, for two hours he was drowned out with shouts of "Great is Diana of the Ephesians!" and that night, in fear of his life, left town.

Despite her origins as a mother-goddess, in classical Greek religion Artemis paradoxically is the preeminent *virgin* goddess. She is not mannish like Athena, who is really asexual, but dangerously alluring: Eternally virgin, she is eternally ready for impregnation. Her pure, remote, and untouched woodland can safely be entered only by those clean in body and spirit. If Artemis is an alluring virgin, she is also a deadly huntress, wandering the wild, untamed places with her train of virgin nymphs, qualities emphasized in a *Homeric Hymn to Artemis:*

[1]   I sing the praises of Artemis, lady of golden-tipped arrows,
      her of the loud-ringing cry, virgin whom all men revere,
      slayer of stags, the goddess whose greatest joy is in hunting,
      sister of Phoebus Apollo, him of the golden sword.
5   Over the shadowy hills and wind-blown peaks of the mountains,
      she leads the hunt, delighting in drawing her bow, all of gold,
      and shooting her deadly shafts. The hilltops are shaken by terror,
      the dark of the woods resounds with the terrified screaming of beasts;
      the earth and the fish-laden ocean tremble in fear at her coming.
10   She roves over all, fearless-hearted, slaying all races of creatures.
      But when the huntress, delighter in arrows, has sated her longing,
      rejoicing in heart, she loosens the string of her well-curved bow,
      and returns to the mighty palace of Phoebus Apollo, her brother,
      in the fertile country of Delphi, to join with the Muses and Graces
15   in treading the maze of the dance. She hangs up curved bow and arrows
      to lead off the chorus, decking her body with loveliest raiment.
      With heavenly voices they carol, how Leto of beautiful ankles
      bore her children, most famous by far for wisdom and action,
      of all who sit in the council on high, among the immortals.

Homeric Hymn to Artemis

At home a lover of music like her brother, abroad she is venomous and without mercy, a hunter of human prey who uses her bow to strike down women in child-

Venus: Images of Beauty

The *Birth of Venus* (the Roman name for Aphrodite) is the theme of one of the most famous paintings of the Italian Renaissance, by master artist Sandro Botticelli (1445–1510) on the walls of a rich patron's villa near the brilliant city of Florence (Fig. P 8.1a). At this time, artists rejected the earlier preference for flat, stylized religious art and grew enthusiastic about nature, naturalistic representation, and classical myth. Botticelli's presentation is especially striking because nude women were almost unknown in medieval art. However, such expressions of ancient myth were always understood in allegorical, neoplatonic terms (see Chapter 23).

The goddess, in a pose derived from classical statues of Venus, symbolizes the spiritual beauty to which every soul aspires, the airy floating object of the soul's contemplation. She stands on a scallop shell wafted over the sea by the breath of the winds. Hesiod says nothing about a shell, a sea-creature from which a delectable meat emerges, in this case the human soul encased within the shell of the body, which lives in the sea of matter. Hesiod says nothing about the winds, here Zephyr ("West Wind") and Aura ("Breeze"), male and female, but the winds are the

FIG. P 8.1a. Sandro Botticelli (Italian), *The Birth of Venus,* c. 1482, oil on canvas.

(Galleria degli Uffizi, Florence; Art Resource, NY; Erich Lessing photo) divine spirit (*spiritus* = "wind"), God's expressive will that drives every event. Rose petals, flowers of love, fall on the whitecaps stirred by the winds, because God's will is an expression of divine love. A Hora, Spring, spreads out a brocaded blanket to receive the goddess; even so does the body, obedient to the rhythms of life's seasons, symbolized by the grove of trees, enclose the soul. At birth unblemished and innocent, the soul is now encased in gross and vulgar matter, the robe cast by the nymph.

Born in Florence, Piero di Cosimo (1462–1521), a younger contemporary of Botticelli, is known for his imaginative, even bizarre, unorthodox, and poignant treatment of pagan and Christian subjects. Homer tells the humorous and salacious story of *Aphrodite and Ares* in the *Odyssey* (8.266–366) but focuses on the chagrin felt by the captured lovers and the trick by which they were taken. Piero, by contrast, influenced by the landscape art and realism of Flemish artists, sees the story as an allegory expressing the true nature of love: It is stronger than strength (Fig. P 8.1b). In the painting there is no hint of Hephaestus' trap. Simply, two lovers lie in the meadow after making love. Mars, on the right, is sound sleep, exhausted by love, whereas Aphrodite/Venus, who is Love, is wide awake, contemplating the fruit to come, the child in her arms and the fecund rabbit on her hip. The black and white doves on the ground between them must symbolize the same duality as Mars/Venus, yet both are doves, the birds of Venus. Winged cupids, the children of Love, play with the war god's armor in the background, useless except as playthings in the conquering ambience of Love.

Veronese, Titian, and Tintoretto were a triumvirate of the greatest painters of the late Renaissance in Venice. Ovid tells the story of the lovers Venus and Adonis in the *Metamorphoses* (see Chapter 9): how when scratched accidentally by an arrow of her own son Cupid, Venus herself fell in love with the beautiful Adonis, born of an incestuous relationship; how happily they hunted the fields together and one afternoon, after hearing Venus' story of the huntress Atalanta, Adonis fell asleep on

FIG. P 8.1b. Piero di Cosimo (Italian), *Venus and Mars,* 1498, oil on panel.
(Staatliche Museen, Berlin)

FIG. P 8.1c. Veronese (Paolo Caliari, Italian), *Venus and Adonis,* oil on canvas.
(Museo del Prado, Madrid; Scala/Art Resource, NY)

a couch of grass under a canopy of poplar; how Venus flew to heaven, but Adonis'
hounds awakened him to hunt the boar that killed him. Veronese (1528–1588, so
called after his native Verona, really Paolo Caliari), devoted to realistic presentation
even of mythical scenes, here illustrates and expounds upon Ovid's story (Fig. P
8.1c). Venus, anticipating what must come, warns away the barking hound in the
lower left, restrained by her son Cupid, the cause of her infatuation, while Adonis
sleeps soundly. Not an allegory as such, the story tells the popular moral that true
love is ever fleeting; Ovid himself had intended as much.

FIG. P8.1d. Velázquez (Spanish), *The Toilet of Venus,* oil on canvas. (National Gallery, London Art Resource, NY; Erich Lessing photo)

The Toilet of Venus is the only surviving female nude by the most important Spanish painter of the seventeenth century and one of the great painters of all time, Velázquez (1529 – 1660). Mysteriously, it passed censure by the vigorous Spanish Inquisition; the commission for the painting must have come from the king himself or someone near him. Called *The Rokeby Venus* from a hall in Yorkshire where it was long kept (Fig. P 8.1d), during the Napoleonic wars this painting belonged to the prime minister and effective ruler of Spain. It does not illustrate a myth as such, but the goddess of love in her naked glory; just such a statue was Praxiteles' *Aphrodite* (see Fig. 5.3), a tradition that began in the ancient world. Venus is shown engrossed in beholding an image of her own beauty; the mirror was the ancient symbol for feminine self-love (although the motif of Cupid holding it is Venetian). Velásquez has made the image in the mirror larger than it should be, and a close look reveals that the image is beholding the spectator, so that Venus is watching herself watching you. In 1911 a suffragist slashed the painting as being a symbol of men's exploitation of women. In Renaissance Italy, however, similar paintings were prepared for the bedrooms of married couples to inspire lovemaking and the production of beautiful children; birth defects, it was thought, resulted from the mother seeing ugly things.

FIG. 8.2. Artemis of Ephesus, marble, second century A.D. Portrayed in the likeness of the great statue of Artemis in her temple at Ephesus, she wears a zodiac around her neck. The bulls, griffins, and sphinxes that decorate her body and headdress stand for her rule over the animal kingdom. (Ephesus Museum; 718 Art Resource, NY; Erich Lessing photo)

birth or those who transgress against her terrible law. When a woman died suddenly without explanation, she was said to be "struck by the arrows of Artemis," even as a man was "struck by the arrows of Apollo."

Homer tells perhaps the best-known story illustrating this theme about **Niobê** (nī-o-bē), wife of Amphion, the legendary cofounder of Thebes. Niobê boasted of her superiority to Leto: She had six sons and six daughters, whereas Leto had only two children. Artemis and Apollo took bloody revenge (Fig. 8.3). Homer places the story in the mouth of Achilles near the end of the *Iliad*, who offers it as an *exemplum*, a model for human behavior, a common use of myth in Greek society. Achilles has offered food to Priam, king of Troy, who, too broken by grief to eat, has come to beg for the body of his son Hector:

FIG. 8.3. Death of the Niobids, Attic vase, c. 450 B.C. Apollo and Artemis shoot down the children of Niobê. A boy and girl lie dead among the rocks. To the right, a boy attempts to flee but is struck in the back. To the left, a boy attempts to pull an arrow from his stomach. The artist has abandoned the single groundline usual in vase painting, probably imitating contemporary wall painting.   (Musée du Louvre, Paris; University of Wisconsin Photo Archive, Madison)

[600]   "At dawn, old sir, arise and take your son's body home.
         But now we need some refreshment, as fair-haired Niobê did,
         who had seen her children butchered before her, watching in horror,
         twelve of them, six fair maidens, and with them six handsome sons.
         The sons were shot by Apollo with shafts of the silver bow,
605   while Artemis, lover of arrows, brought down all Niobê's daughters,
         angered at Niobê's folly—comparing her children to Leto's.
         'She has born only two,' said she, 'but I have born a great many.'
         But those two, few as they were, annihilated her dozen.°
         Nine days they lay in their gore; for nobody buried the corpses;
610   Cronus' son had turned the people to puppets of stone.
         On the tenth day at last the gods from heaven entombed them;
         weary with hunger and sorrow, their mother swallowed a morsel.
         Even now on a cliff of Sipylus,° haunted by eagles,
         where they say the nymphs who race Acheloüs° dwell in their lair,
615   poor Niobê, turned into stone, broods over the miserable fate

608. *dozen:* Traditions vary about how many children Niobê had, ranging from four to twenty. 613. *Sipylus:* A mountain in Asia Minor, near Smyrna. A female image, said to be that of Niobê, was carved on the rock cliff. When it rained, the water seeped through the porous limestone, making it appear as if the figure was weeping. In fact the image (which is still barely visible today) was of Cybelê, the Great Mother goddess of Asia Minor.   614. *Acheloüs:* A stream on Mount Sipylus. A far better-known river of the same name flowed through northwestern Greece.

assigned her by the immortals. So come now, noble sir,
let the two of us also remember our need of food and refreshment."

HOMER, Iliad (24.600–619)

Orion, Actaeon, and Callisto

Most myths of Artemis are descriptions of the humans and animals she killed, and
usually they are associated with hunting. One of the most famous is the story of the
giant **Orion** (ō-rī-on), a son of Poseidon, an inescapable hunter and a devotee of
Artemis. His father had given him the power to walk on water. Orion had long
courted the daughter of Oinopion, "wine-face," a king of the island of Chios, but impatient at the king's reluctance to give her up, he raped her. For revenge, Oinopion
put out Orion's eyes while he slept. Orion hoisted a boy to his shoulders and set out
toward the east. When he reached the eastern horizon, the blazing sun cured his
blindness. He tried to track down and kill Oinopion, but could not find him; he
therefore began an affair with Eos, the dawn goddess. Either because of this or because he had attempted to rape the goddess herself, Artemis placed on his head a
scorpion, which poisoned and killed him. As a reward for its service, the scorpion
was transformed into the constellation Scorpio. Orion became the constellation that
still bears his name, forever fleeing Scorpio (although placed opposite in the heavens). It is the earliest named constellation (in the *Odyssey*).

The Theban **Actaeon** (ak-tē-on) also fell victim to the wrath of Artemis, and
again for a sexual transgression. Early versions of the story tell us that he wanted to

FIG. 8.4. Actaeon devoured by his own hounds, Attic vase, c. 470 B.C. Although the
stories ordinarily say that Actaeon was transformed into a stag, the vase painters
usually represent him in human form, with the hounds attacking, while Artemis
draws her bow.   (Museum of Fine Arts, Boston; 10.185)

marry his aunt Semelê; later explanations report that while hunting on Mount Cithaeron near Thebes, Actaeon accidentally came on Artemis bathing naked in a spring. Ovid tells that story, one of the best-known Greek myths (Fig. 8.4).

[138]   The cause of Cadmus'° sorrow, when all things were going so well,
    was his grandson, upon whose forehead great antlers suddenly sprouted,
140   whose hounds were horribly sated on the flesh and blood of their master.
    If you look at the matter closely, bad luck was really to blame;
    No fault can be charged, for no blame can be placed on innocent error.
    The hill of his hunt by this time was dyed with blood of his victims,
    and the sun, halfway to his goal, had diminished the shadows of noon.
145   Actaeon called to his fellows, who accompanied him through the forest:
    "Our nets and knives are crimson with blood of beasts we have slain;
    enough of good luck for today. When Dawn in her yellow-wheeled chariot
    brings back her light to the earth, then back to the hunting we love!
    Half Phoebus'° journey is finished; his rays have heated the meadows,
150   so abandon our work for today, and roll up our nets till tomorrow."
    The young men did as he ordered and gladly relaxed from their labor.
       A nearby glade was hidden by thickets of pine trees and cypress,
    Gargaphië, a sacred spot of Diana the huntress.
    At its further end is a cave, in an open space in the forest,
155   made by no human hands, for nature herself was its maker.
    She had carved it from living rock and arched it over with tufa.°
    On its right there babbled a trickling fountain of cold limpid water,
    its spreading basin encompassed by a soft green border of grass.
    When Diana, goddess of woodlands, found herself wearied with hunting,
160   it was here she refreshed her maiden limbs in the cool of the waters.
    To one of her nymphs she entrusted her javelin, quiver, and bow;
    another held out her arms for the mantle the goddess discarded;
    two more unfastened the bindings that laced the boots to her ankles.
    Theban Crocalê skillfully braided her loose-flowing tresses
165   (more dexterous she than the others); Nephelê, Hyalê, Rhanis,
    with Psecas and Phialê, poured great basins of water above her.
    But today, as the daughter of Titans was enjoying her usual bath,
    the grandson of Cadmus appeared, postponing his usual hunting;
    alone and with innocent steps he joyfully strolled through the woodlands
170   until then unknown, for such was Destiny's order.
       The moment Actaeon entered the dewy cave of the fountain,
    the nymphs filled the grove with screams and beat on their naked bosoms,
    shielding Diana's body with their own from the young man's sight.
    But Diana was taller and towered above them, full head and shoulders.
175   The color which tints the clouds across from the sun in the heavens,
    or that of the purple dawn, arose to the face of the goddess,
    embarrassed at being thus viewed without the protection of clothing.
    Even though she was surrounded by so great a cohort of comrades,
    she turned away to the side, but fixed her eyes on the stranger,

138. *Cadmus:* Founder of Thebes.   149. *Phoebus:* Ovid identifies Apollo with the sun.   156. *tufa:* A soft volcanic stone, easily worked for building.

180 as if she had arrows to aim. The best thing at hand was the water.
She scooped some up in her hands, and, throwing it over Actaeon,
she shouted this sentence prophetic of the destiny waiting to strike:
"Now you can boast you have gazed on Diana naked of clothing.
Go right ahead—that is, if you still are able to boast."
185 So much for the menace of words. From his forehead antlers erupted,
the horns of a terrified stag, just where the water had spattered.
She forced his neck to grow long and crowned it with pointed ears;
she turned his hands into hooves and traded his forearms for forelegs;
his body she veiled to the view with a spotted velvety deerskin.
190 To crown it, she gave him the heart of a deer. Autonoë's son°
was astonished to find how nimble he was, how speedy of foot,
But O! what a horror to see his antlers reflected in water.
"Can that be your face, Actaeon?" was what he attempted to utter.
Not a word would come out. He groaned; that was all he could manage.
195 Tears dropped down from a pair of eyes no longer his own.
Yet still the mind of a human was left. "What can I do?" he debated,
"Shall I flee to my father's house and the apparatus of power,
or hide in the forest?" but shame blocked one and terror the other.
Hesitant, thus he delayed, till his hounds were drawn to the scent.

190. *Autonoë's son:* Autonoë was sister to Semelê, mother of Dionysus.

[The next twenty lines give the names of Actaeon's hounds, thirty-five in number.]

[225] This pack, all eager to join in the kill, pursued its terrified master
over crags and hillsides, in places no human could follow,
wherever the track was rugged, where no track whatever existed.
He did his best to escape in places he often had hunted,
poor master, now fleeing his servants! He tried to call the pack:
230 "See, it is I, Actaeon; have you forgotten your ruler?"
but his mind no more ruled his words; he could not utter his plea.
Now the whole heaven reechoed the triumphant baying of hounds.
Blackhair was first, who sank his teeth in the back of his master,
with Beastblaster right at his heels. Mountainbred buried his fangs
235 deep in his master's shoulder. These had been slow at the start,
but had taken short cuts on the mountain to be first at the kill.
The rest of the pack came together to rip with their slavering jaws;
soon not an inch remained unmangled, unlacerated.
Actaeon gave a last groan, whose sound was not that of a human,
240 but was equally not a cry that a real stag ever had uttered,
whose mournful complaint reechoed on the hillsides he knew so well.

OVID, *Metamorphoses* (3.138–239)

Other versions tell how Actaeon's hounds then wandered the mountains howling, looking for their lost master. The myth may reflect primitive human sacrifice, the gift of a man to the goddess to ensure success in the hunt. In legends of the Trojan War, the Mycenaean king Agamemnon sacrificed his own daughter to Artemis because his brother Menelaüs had killed a stag in Artemis' sacred grove. In Roman gladiatorial combat, descended from Etruscan ritual human sacrifice, men dressed as wild animals were hunted down and killed.

The motif of human sacrifice emerges again in the story of Artemis' favorite follower, **Callisto,** a nymph or daughter of the wicked Arcadian king Lycaon, who himself practiced human sacrifice and offered Zeus a cannibal banquet (see Chapter 5). Callisto took a vow of chastity, and many hours did the goddess and girl spend hunting in the wilds of Arcadia. One day Zeus spied Callisto resting beneath a tree. Taking the form of Artemis herself, or of Apollo, Zeus disarmed the girl's suspicions and possessed her. Months later, Artemis and her band of nymphs disrobed to bathe in a spring. Callisto hesitated, then revealed her pregnant condition. Wild with anger at the apparent betrayal of her vows, Artemis changed Callisto into a bear. Eventually Artemis herself shot and killed the animal, but the child Arcas, "bear," for whom the Arcadians are named, survived. Near Athens, at a place called Brauron, small girls dressed up as bears in a cult dedicated to Artemis—they were called "little bears"—and many commentators see in Callisto a form of Artemis herself, the dying but fecund spirit of the wild, master of young girls, *parthenoi*, before marriage.

ATHENA, MISTRESS OF THE CITY

Athena (whom the Romans called Minerva) seems to take her name from the city of Athens rather than the other way around. In origin she was not Greek, although she was established in Greece at an early date. Her name is mentioned in the Linear B tablets (c. 1200 B.C.). In Mycenaean times she may have been the protectress of the fortified Athenian hill known as the Acropolis and of the king's house built on it. Here, in classical times, the Athenians built the all-marble Parthenon, "house of the virgin," in honor of the virgin goddess, one of the most beautiful and celebrated buildings in the world (Fig. 8.5; compare Fig. 2.1).

Athena's emblem is the owl, at home in palace rafters, and the domestic olive tree, which she gave to Athens; thus Athenian coins have an owl and a sprig of olive stamped on them. Her common epithet is *glaukôpis*, which means either "owl-eyed" or "gray-eyed." She is sometimes shown with a snake, leading some commentators to identify her with a Minoan goddess who held snakes in her hands. In classical times she was the protectress of all cities (although she had her favorites) and of the crafts and arts that city life makes possible, never more so than in Athens, the city named for her. In this sense she was the goddess of wisdom—the know-how needed to run a city properly. She protects especially the woman's craft of weaving, but also the male craft of carpentry: She directed the building of the ship Argo in the legend of Jason and was behind the building of the Trojan Horse.

Athena is always represented in armor, wearing a helmet, often carrying a spear, and usually holding a shield. As a breastplate she wears the aegis, given her by Zeus. Another story makes the aegis the skin of a giant named Pallas, whom she flayed alive in the Gigantomachy (Fig. 8.6). From the giant, too, she may have taken her epithet *Pallas*, a name of unclear etymology. If Greek, *Pallas* could mean "maiden" or "weapon-brandishing," but it may be pre-Greek.

FIG. 8.5. The Parthenon, built all of marble, 447–433 B.C., from the northwest. In the pediment (the triangle between rooftop and roofline) was portrayed the myth of the contest between Athena and Poseidon for rulership of Athens; the east pediment had the myth of the birth of Athena. The Parthenon was virtually intact, having been a Christian church and Turkish mosque, until 1687, when the Venetians were at war with the Turks, who used the Parthenon as an ammunition dump. The Venetians lobbed a shell through the roof, blowing out the roof and most of the south side. Most of the Parthenon's sculpture—the so-called Elgin Marbles—was removed during the Napoleonic wars by Lord Elgin, the British ambassador to Turkey, and is now in the British Museum, perhaps the best-known original works of art to survive from the high Classical Period.   (Author's photo)

Born from Zeus's head, not from woman's womb, Athena, always virgin, was a faithful servant of her father and a protectress of male heroes. She watched over Perseus, Heracles, Odysseus, and Jason. In the *Iliad* she encouraged the Greeks to glorious deeds, assisting them at critical moments in the fray. The leaders marshaled their troops

[446]   and with them went Athena, she of the steel-gray eyes,
wearing the dreaded aegis, shield which is ageless, immortal.
From it a hundred tassels, all woven of gold, hang free,
each worth a hundred oxen. Sparkling, bright with its gleam,
450   Athena marched down the ranks, arousing their will to attack.
In every heart she injected new courage to fight to the end,
and suddenly war seemed sweeter than sailing in hollow ships
and making a safe return to their own dear native land.

HOMER, *Iliad* (2.446–456)

In myth, Athena also takes an interest in individual women when their interests as women are at stake. Woman's work (apart from childrearing) is preeminently the manufacture of textiles and their care, and in the *Odyssey* Athena appears to the vir-

FIG. 8.6. Athena on a Panathenaic vase, c. 460 B.C. Such vases, filled with olive oil, were given as prizes to winners in the panathenaic festival and usually have the same scene: Athena with shield, snake-edged aegis, and spear between two pillars, in front of one of which is written "I am one of the prizes from Athens." (British Museum, London; B 134)

gin Nausicaa and encourages her to clean her clothes in anticipation of the wedding that must surely come:

[15]   She went to the room, decorated beautifully,
       where slept a young girl like the immortal goddesses
       in loveliness, Nausicaa, the daughter of generous Alcinoüs;
       nearby slept two hand-maidens, made beautiful
       by the Graces, one on either side of the door.
20   The shining doors were shut. Like a breath of air
       the goddess sped to the bed of the young girl,
       and stood above her head, and spoke, taking the form
       of the daughter of Dymas, famed for his ships,
       a girl of the same age as Nausicaa, and dear to her heart.
25   Athena, flashing with her eyes, said:
       "Nausicaa, surely your mother bore a careless girl!
       Your clothes are uncared for, yet your marriage is near,
       when you will need to have fine clothes, and for bridesmaids too.
       That's how you gain a good reputation among men,
30   and make your mom and dad very happy.
       So let us go and wash them at the break of day.
       I will follow with you and help and move things along.
       You won't be a virgin much longer now!"

HOMER, *Odyssey* (6.15–33)

However, Athena's real intention is to assist her favorite, Odysseus, asleep near the seashore, by bringing him and the princess together. Nausicaa does save Odysseus but remains unmarried when Odysseus must continue his journey home.

Athena represents reason's control over elemental force. Poseidon sired the horse Arion, but Athena built the first chariot, which controls the horse. Poseidon rouses the waves, but Athena built the ship that rides on them. Hermes protects the flocks in distant mountains, but Athena taught how to spin the wool from which clothing is made. In war Ares is unrestrained violence; Athena teaches strategy and disciplined tactics. Vengeance has ruled from time immemorial; Athena established law and justice. Not until the late Classical Period did she become the goddess of wisdom in the abstract sense. Her province is the practical know-how that separates humans from beasts and protects them from the arbitrary or indifferent violence of the natural world. Her achievements may be compared to those of Prometheus.

In Athens an annual festival to Athena, the Panathenaea, celebrated her birthday. The festival was of special grandeur every fourth year, when a procession of highborn youths and maids carried sacred implements, led sacrificial animals, and rode in chariots to the Acropolis, bearing a freshly woven robe for the statue of Athena. The procession is shown on the inner relief sculpture of the Parthenon.

Arachnê

Ovid made famous the story of **Arachnê** (a-**rak**-nē), a young woman of Lydia who boasted that her skill in weaving was equal to Athena's. Although a typically Ovidian story of divine envy for human achievement, the story reflects Athena's sponsorship of excellence in the female craft of weaving:

[5]   Minerva° called to mind the fate of Maeonian° Arachnê,
    who, she had heard, had claimed to equal the goddess herself
    in the arts of the working of wool. Her rank and descent were the humblest,
    but in skill she held the first place. Colophonian° Idmon, her father,
    was a dyer of soft white fleeces with the juice of Ionian murex;°
10   her mother, now dead, had been born of the same low rank as her husband.
    Although humble of rank and dwelling in a little town called Hypaepa,
    Arachnê had gained by her skill applause and a great reputation
    through all the land of Lydia, and in all its affluent cities.
    To see her incredible work, the nymphs would abandon the vineyards
15   on the slopes of Tmolus, the Naiads would leave Pactolus' waters.°
    Not just the cloth that she made, but watching it made was a pleasure,
    and the grace she brought to her art—now rolling raw wool into balls,
    now twisting thread in her fingers, now drawing wool from the distaff
    and smoothing the knots of the fleece into yarn as soft as a cloud.
20   Sometimes her nimble fingers would be weaving the yarn into fabric,
    tossing a slender spindle with expert hand, or embroidering:
    whatever she did, you would swear that Pallas Athena had taught her.
    Arachnê indignantly scoffed, "If she is so good she could teach me,

5. *Minerva:* Athena.   5. *Maeonian:* Homer calls Ionia "Maeonia."   8. *Colophonian:* Colophon was a Greek colony in Asia Minor.   9. *murex:* The shellfish of the eastern Mediterranean that produces deep purple dye.   15. *Pactolus' waters:* A stream, small but gold-laden, that ran down Mount Tmolus in Lydia, near Sardis.

maybe she'd dare compete; if I lose, I shall pay her a forfeit,
25   anything she might demand."
       Pallas heard this boast, and, disguised as a feeble old woman,
with hair turned a straggly gray, with a cane for hobbling old footsteps,
chided the girl in these words:
                                "Old age still has a few blessings—
experience comes with the years. So listen, my dear, to my counsel:
30   your greatest glory must come from human spinners and weavers.
Yield to a goddess, rash girl, and humbly beg for her pardon.
If you repent and confess, the goddess will surely forgive you."
       Arachnê glared at the goddess, laid down her half-finished task,
and was ready to slap Minerva. Her fury shone from her face,
35   as she hurled a reply to Pallas, not knowing to whom she was speaking:
       "You gaga old granny, your trouble is that you've been living too long!
Get out and go talk to your daughters, or even your daughters-in-law,
who might be silly enough to attend to your tedious sermons.
I have the brains to look after myself; I don't need you to advise me,
40   and certainly won't change my ways. And as for that goddess of yours,
Why doesn't she come herself? perhaps she can't stand competition?"
       "She has come herself," shouted Pallas, casting off her disguise,
no longer a feeble old woman, but revealed as a goddess.
The nymphs bowed down in worship, as did the Maeonian women;
45   Arachnê alone was defiant, though she jumped to her feet in surprise;
a blush stained her cheek for a moment, but as quickly vanished again.
So the morning sky turns crimson as a sign that dawn is at hand,
but after a few brief moments turns bright with the sun's new light.
Firmly she stood by her offer, and foolishly hurried to her fate,
50   in hopes of the prize of the victor. For her part, Jupiter's daughter
offered no further warning, nor tried to delay any longer.
       A pair of looms was set up, each facing away from the other,
and the slender threads of the weft were interlaced with the warp.

                    Ovid, *Metamorphoses* (6.5–54)

Each wove a robe to demonstrate her skill by illustrating mythical scenes. Minerva made a tapestry showing her contest with Neptune (Poseidon) for the overlordship of Attica and, appropriately, added pictures of the punishment of mortals who challenged gods. Arachnê, too foolish to be frightened, brazenly embroidered stories of the sexual scandals of the gods. When Arachnê had finished her work

[129]   Not Pallas, not Envy itself, could find a fault in the weaving.
        The furious golden-haired goddess tore off the robe with its pictures
        of the escapades of the gods, and, seizing a shuttle of boxwood,
        again and again she slashed it across the face of Arachnê.
        The poor girl refused to be shamed, but hanged herself in a slipknot.
              When Pallas saw her suspended, she took some pity upon her.
135   "Well, poor sinner," said she, "you may live, but still you must hang
        with this condition, to keep you from feeling safe in the future:
        my order shall stay in force for all your descendants as well."

Then as she left she sprinkled the girl with one of Hecatê's poisons.°
The instant she felt the venom, the hairs of her head disappeared,
140   and with them her nose and ears. Her head shrank down to a vestige
of what it had formerly been, and the rest of her body grew tiny.
Long skinny fingers stuck out as legs; all the rest became belly,
from which she turns out the thread for her old occupation—a spider.

OVID, Metamorphoses (6.129–145)

138. *Hecatê's poisons:* Hecatê, although tradition made her a Titan, is the evil counterpart of Artemis—the dark of the moon, a deity of darkness, fear, and death. She was especially concerned with witches and poisoners, who searched out her baneful herbs in the dark of the moon, cut them with a bronze sickle, and used them for the most dreadful purposes.

From this story comes the modern scientific term *arachnid* to refer to spiders, scorpions, mites, and ticks.

KEY TERMS

Hestia, 193	Artemis, 204
Aphrodite, 193	*Potnia Therôn*, 204
Cypris, 194	Niobê, 205
Hermaphroditus, 195	Orion, 207
Priapus, 195	Actaeon, 207
Pygmalion, 195	Callisto, 210
Myrrha, 197	Athena, 210
Anchises, 198	Arachnê, 213

FURTHER READING

Baring, Anne, and Jules Cashford, *The Myth of the Goddess: The Evolution of an Image* (New York, 1993). The female in religious imagery from the Paleolithic to the modern Gaea hypothesis.

Delcourt, Marie, *Hermaphrodite: Myths and Rites of the Bisexual Figure in Classical Antiquity* (London, 1961). Explores the taste for this mythical form in the Hellenistic Period and later.

Shearer, Anne, *Athene: Image and Energy* (New York, 1998). Feminist interpretation of the goddess.

Smith, P. M., *Nursling of Mortality: A Study of the Homeric Hymn to Aphrodite* (Frankfurt, 1981). Scholarly study.

Stehle, Eva, *Performance and Gender in Ancient Greece: Nondramatic Poetry in Its Setting* (Princeton, N.J., 1996). Good discussion of Sappho (and much more on early Greek poetry and society).

CHAPTER 9

MYTHS OF FERTILITY

DEMETER AND THE GREAT GODDESS

Three times blest are those mortals who behold those rites [at Eleusis]
before going down to the house of Hades.
They alone have true life there;
to the rest, everything there is misery.

SOPHOCLES, fragment 837 (Pearson–Radt)

ACCORDING TO THE GREEK MYTHS OF CREATION, as we saw in Chapter 4, female
Gaea, Mother Earth, came after sexless Chaos, and from Gaea sprang the world:
first Sky, Sea, and Mountains and, ultimately, the Olympian gods and human beings.
But it was not only the creation of the world that the Greeks traced back to a female
source; the continual pattern of renewal seen in plant and animal life, the ever-re-
curring creation of new offspring, was also made possible by a female power. Thus
the Greeks associated such diverse phenomena as the fertility of the soil, the repro-
ductive capacities of wild animals, and sexual attraction between men and women
with divine beings who were female.

In this respect Greek myth followed a pattern found in the ancient Near East.
In Mesopotamia, the widely honored goddess known as Inanna, Ishtar, or Astartê
presided over fertility and sexuality. Similar powers were ascribed to the Phrygian
goddess Cybelê (**sib**-i-lē) and the Egyptian goddess Isis (ī-sis). Despite the multitude
of names, these goddesses have much in common, representing a religious figure
whose cults and myths spread across racial and linguistic lines to exert enormous influence throughout much of the ancient world and to have influence today. To em-

phasize the unity of the type, modern scholars often refer to this figure as the Great Mother, or the Great Goddess.

Greek myth differed from that of the ancient Near Eastern cultures not in neglecting the Great Goddess but in dividing her functions rather sharply among a group of goddesses: Artemis controlled the fertility of wild animals, Aphrodite presided over human sexuality, and Hera protected marriage and the family. But the Greek figure whose myths are most closely related to those of the Great Goddess found in other parts of the Mediterranean world is **Demeter** (de-**mē**-ter), goddess of the grain and the rich harvest. In this chapter we examine the myth of Demeter and her daughter **Persephonê** (per-**sef**-ō-nē), as told in one of the oldest of the Homeric Hymns. Before we turn to this myth, however, let us examine several earlier stories that originated in the far older cultures of Mesopotamia and Egypt. We find in these stories a close association between the female, the underworld, the death of the male, and a focus on the cyclical processes of life forms, which die only to be born again.

INANNA AND DUMUZI

Of all Mesopotamian myths, perhaps the one with the most influence on later religion and myth is that of **Inanna,** "queen of heaven," goddess of love and war (Fig. 9.1), and her lover, the shepherd god **Dumuzi.**

FIG. 9.1. A female head from Uruk, c. 3500–3000 B.C., of white marble, perhaps of the goddess Inanna. The head probably was set on a wooden statue, its eyes inlaid with lapis lazuli and shell and its eyebrows and hair of bitumen plated with gold. (Iraq Museum, Baghdad; Hirmer Fotoarchiv, Munich)

One day Inanna decided to descend to the underworld. Either she wanted to become queen of the dead—she was already queen of the living—or she wanted to bring the dead back to life. She dressed in her best clothes, adorned herself with jewels, and set off for the "land of no return." Fearing her sister, Ereshkigal (er-esh-kē-gal), who ruled over the underworld, Inanna left instructions with her prime minister, Ninshubur: If she did not return within three days, Ninshubur was to go to the city of Nippur, the city of the storm god Enlil, and beg him to intercede on her behalf. If Enlil refused, Ninshubur was to go to Ur, city of the moon god Nanna, and there beg for Inanna's life. If unsuccessful there, he was to go to Eridu, city of the clever god Enki, who "knows the food of life" and "the water of life."

Inanna entered the underworld and soon came to the temple of Ereshkigal, made all of lapis lazuli:

> "Gatekeeper, let me in! Open your gate for me!
> Open your gate and let me in!
> If you don't open the gate and let me in,
> I will smash the gate and splinter the bolt!
> I will smash the doorjambs and knock down the doors.
> I will raise up the dead, who will devour the living:
> the dead will outnumber the living!"
> The gatekeeper demands: "Who are you?"
> "I am Inanna from the place of sunrise."°
> "If you are Inanna from the place of sunrise,
> why have you come to the land of no return?
> Upon the road down which no traveler returns;
> how did your heart lead you?"

sunrise: That is, she is the goddess of the morning star.

Inanna gave the doorkeeper a false explanation, but before admitting her, the gatekeeper went inside to consult Ereshkigal. Ereshkigal's face grew dark, she slapped her thighs, she bit her lips. Then she instructed the gatekeeper to lead Inanna inward through the seven gates of the underworld, but he was to follow "the ancient rites." At each gate, guards forced Inanna to remove a piece of her clothing or jewelry. At the first gate she gave up her crown:

> "O keeper of the gate, why have you taken my crown?"
> "Enter, my lady; these are the rites of the Mistress of Earth."
> At the second gate, she gave up her earrings:
> "O keeper of the gate, why have you taken my earrings?"
> "Enter, my lady; these are the rites of the Mistress of Earth."

At the third gate she gave up the beads around her neck; at the fourth, the brooches at her breast; at the fifth, the girdle of birthstones around her waist; at the sixth, the bangles on her wrists and ankles; at the seventh gate she took off her beautiful dress. When she came into the presence of Ereshkigal, she was stark naked and complained bitterly of her treatment, but was told:

"Be quiet, Inanna! This is the way of the underworld.
Do not question the rites of the underworld."

Undaunted, Inanna pulled Ereshkigal from the throne and sat down herself, but the Annunaki gods, the seven dread judges of the underworld, condemned her to death. She turned at once into a side of meat, green with decay, and was hung on a stake. Meanwhile, on earth, all sexual activity came to a halt:

No bull mounted a cow, no jackass mounted a jenny,
no young man had intercourse with a girl in the street;
the young man slept by himself in his room,
the girl slept with her friends.

When Inanna did not return, her minister, Ninshubur, did as he was told. Rejected by both Enlil and Nanna, he finally went to the clever Enki, who agreed to help. From the dirt beneath his nails Enki fashioned two mysterious sexless creatures, called *kurgarra* and *kalaturra*. He gave them the food of life and the water of life and told them what to do when they came to Ereshkigal.

Buzzing over the gates of the underworld like flies, or slipping under the gates like lizards, the *kurgarra* and *kalaturra* came to Ereshkigal's chamber. They found the queen of the dead sick with grief for the little children of the world who had died before their time. They joined her in lamentation. In gratitude for their sympathy, Ereshkigal offered them anything they wanted (the folktale motif of the hasty oath); they immediately replied that they wanted the green piece of meat hanging in the corner. The goddess tried to dissuade them, offering instead the river in flood, or the field of grain, but they insisted. Ereshkigal had no choice. Casting over the meat the food of life and the water of life, which Enki had given them, the *kurgarra* and *kalaturra* brought Inanna back to life.

Inanna was allowed to leave the underworld, but only if she found someone to take her place (the folktale motif of the substitute sacrifice). Demons followed her, to make sure she complied. Ninshubur was first to meet them, but Inanna could not bear to give up the minister who had just saved her. In the first two cities they reached, the local gods were draped in sackcloth, groveling in the dust—mourning for Inanna, who certainly could not give them over to the demons. At last they came to the country of Dumuzi, Inanna's husband. Instead of mourning her disappearance and wasting away from grief, he was dressed in finery and seated on a throne. Inanna looked at him a look of death; she shouted out a word of wrath to the demons who had followed her: "Take this one!"

In terror Dumuzi cried out for help to Utu, the sun god, lord of justice, Inanna's brother and his own brother-in-law (see Fig. 3.4). Despite the intercession of Utu, the demons at last trapped Dumuzi in his sheepfold. The first demon struck him on the cheek with a piercing nail, and the second hit him with a shepherd's crook. As the other demons entered the sheepfold, the butter churn was knocked down and the cup fell from its peg and was smashed. Dumuzi fell dead and his sheepfold was given to the wind. Dumuzi, the lover of Inanna's youth, would dwell in the underworld. One day each year, however, he could return to the world above, where rituals would be performed in his honor—apparently a reference to a rite of the month "Dumuzi" (June/July), when a statue of the god was washed, anointed, and allowed to lie in state in the city of Nineveh.

Observations: The Dying God and the Sacred Marriage

The story reflects the Mesopotamians' experience with irrigation agriculture. The impregnating water is allowed to flow in channels across the receptive, life-giving earth. From the earth grow the life-sustaining crops, cut down at harvest only to grow again. The cycle of life, death, and renewal of life is embodied in the figure of Inanna, who is both the fertile female, goddess of life, and the sister of Ereshkigal, goddess of death, whose realm Inanna covets; Tiamat, too, had both favored and opposed new generation (Chapter 4). Inanna's descent to the underworld is her death and the end of fertility on earth. Her return to the upper world is her resurrection, the return of life on earth. But renewed life can be purchased only at the price of another's death, in this case of her consort Dumuzi. Herein lies the logic of ritual (even human) sacrifice.

The metaphor water/earth = semen/womb, which appears repeatedly in Mesopotamian thought, underlies the myth: Water sinks into the earth, as semen into the womb. The shepherd Dumuzi is connected with milk in many descriptions, and in the story his butter-churns are overturned as he is killed. The milky white stuff is like semen, or like the water that makes the earth fruitful by flowing across it, impregnating the female's womb. When fertilization is complete, the fluid ebbs away beneath the earth, even as after human intercourse the penis wilts, the semen drains away, but the womb swells with new life. Inanna is the earth, now fruitful, now barren, now fruitful again; Dumuzi is like the necessary but expendable substance that fructifies it.

Of course the myth is a story, but the implied association between human sexuality and agricultural productivity was acted out in an important ritual of Mesopotamian religion. During the sacred marriage (= Greek **hieros gamos**), the king took on the identity of Dumuzi and a priestess acted the role of Inanna. Within the temple on top of the ziggurat, the artificial mountain at the center of Mesopotamian shrines, "Dumuzi" really did have intercourse with "Inanna" so that their human intercourse might guarantee a rich natural harvest.[1] Similar rites are found all over the ancient world, including ancient Greece, and the passage from the *Iliad* describing Zeus making love to Hera on Mount Ida (Chapter 6) may depend on the *hieros gamos*. Although religion and myth exist independently, the language of one easily crosses over to become the language of the other.

ISIS AND OSIRIS

A second example of the Great Goddess in ancient religion and myth appears in the central myth of Egyptian culture, which supported from early times the powerful

---

[1]Magic based on the principle that like action produces like result is called sympathetic magic.

FIG. 9.2. Isis and Osiris, from the temple to Osiris at Abydos, built by Sethos II, Nineteenth Dynasty, 1304–1290 B.C. Osiris on the right, wrapped in mummy clothes and wearing an elaborate headdress of feathers, cobras, and ram's horns, receives an offering from a priest. He carries the shepherd's staff in one hand and the crook and flail, also emblems of royal power, in the other. Both hands grip the magical *was*-scepter. A table of offerings bearing flowers and beer stands before him. The priest cass beads of incense on a cup-brazier, from which smoke arises. Behind him stands Isis, who appears as the divine musician and accompanies the ritual by shaking the sistrum, a rattle used in her cult, and rattling the *menat,* a metal necklace-counterweight. She wears the solar disc embraced by cow horns and a vulture headdress (sacred to the mother-goddess). Both Isis and Osiris wear the uraeus serpent on their brows, sign of royal power. The inscription near the priest reads "Burning incense for the King Men-Maat-Re [= the dead Sethos I, identified with Osiris] who is endowed with life." Near Isis: "Shaking the sistrum before your beautiful face, for ever, and ever." Over the priest: "The incense is coming, god's perfume is coming, his incense is come to you, Lord of the Two Lands, Men-Maat-Re."   (From the Temple of Sethos I at Abydos, the Osiris chapel; Hirmer Fotoarchiv, Munich)

Egyptian religion of magical resurrection (Fig. 9.2). In Egyptian the name *Isis* seems to mean "throne," and her name was written with a throne-shaped hieroglyph. Some scholars think she is in origin simply the personified seat of **Osiris** (ō-sī-ris), her husband and brother, whose own name may mean "the seat of the Eye," the eye being the symbol of royal power. In any event, Isis gradually became the greatest goddess of Egypt, absorbing all other Egyptian goddesses (and there were many). In Greece, she was identified with Demeter at least from the time of Herodotus, about 430 B.C. Her religion was especially influential in Rome, and the cult remained vigorous in Egypt until the sixth century A.D. The image of Isis suckling the baby Horus was adopted by early Christians to represent the Virgin Mary and the baby Jesus and is still seen today in churches all over the world. The Virgin's blue dress, crescent moon, and title *Stella Maris,* "star of the sea," were taken from the Roman form of the cult of Isis.

Our fullest account of the myth of Isis and her brother Osiris is that given by the Greek writer Plutarch, about A.D. 120; curiously, the Egyptians themselves never tell the story but only allude to it. In Plutarch's version, the goddess Rhea, pregnant by Cronus, gave birth to five children, including Osiris, Isis, and Typhoeus.[2] Osiris had united in love with his sister Isis while still in the womb, and in the fullness of time he married her and became king of Egypt. Together they led the Egyptians out of their crude and backward way of life: Osiris abolished cannibalism, established laws, and showed the people how to grow crops and revere the gods, while Isis taught the women how to spin and persuaded the men of the advantages of married life. Osiris then set out to travel over the world, teaching the virtues of civilized life wherever he went, and leaving the rule of Egypt to Isis.

When Osiris returned, the evil Typhoeus, who had enlisted seventy-two collaborators, plotted to kill him. Typhoeus secretly measured the body of Osiris and made a beautiful box (a mummy case) of exactly the same size. At a banquet Typhoeus promised the box to whoever could fit inside it. Everyone tried, but only Osiris was the right size, and, as he lay in the box, the conspirators ran up, slammed down the lid, and threw the box into the Nile.

The coffin floated down river into the sea and across it to Byblus in Phoenicia. There it washed up beside a tamarisk tree, which quickly grew to surround it. When the king of Phoenicia ordered the tree cut down for use as a pillar in his palace, the coffin was taken with it.

Isis, grieving and desperate, hunted everywhere for her brother and husband. At last she came to Byblus and, in disguise, sat by a well, weeping piteously. Isis spoke to no one except the queen's maids, whom she delighted by braiding their hair and breathing a wonderful perfume on them. Hearing this, the queen brought Isis to the palace to care for her little boy. Isis suckled the child by putting her finger in his mouth. At night she placed him in the fire to burn away his mortal parts, while she herself turned into a swallow and fluttered around the pillar that contained Osiris' coffin, crying piteously. One night the queen saw the child in the fire, screamed aloud, and so deprived the boy of immortality. The goddess revealed herself in her

---

[2]Plutarch uses Greek equivalents for the Egyptian sky goddess Nut (= Rhea), the earth god Geb (= Cronus), and Seth, god of storm and disorder (= Typhoeus).

majesty and demanded the pillar that contained the coffin, which she brought back to Egypt. Other sources report that on the return voyage, she opened the coffin and, in the form of a hawk, hovered over her husband's penis, inflaming it to life and taking its seed within her.

When she returned to Egypt, Isis hid the coffin in the marshes, but Typhoeus, hunting on a moonlit night, stumbled upon it. He tore the corpse into fourteen pieces and scattered them all over the country. Isis set out in a papyrus boat to search for them, and she built a temple to Osiris wherever she found one. She recovered all the pieces except for the penis, which was eaten by three different species of fish, whose eating was ever after taboo. As a substitute, she made a phallus of wood, which was worshiped in many of the temples of Osiris.

Osiris presently arose from the underworld to prepare his son Horus, whom Isis had now borne, to do battle with Typhoeus and avenge his murder. After many days of fighting, Typhoeus' allies deserted him, and Horus delivered him in chains to Isis. Instead of killing him, however, she turned him loose. In a fury Horus ripped off her royal crown. The god Hermes[3] replaced it with a helmet shaped like a cow's head. Although dead, Osiris appeared to Isis once more and begot another child on her, "Horus the child," a god represented as an infant sucking his own finger.[4]

Much in this myth is etiological for features of Egyptian society and religion. It explains why there were so many temples to Osiris and why two gods with the same name—Horus—were represented differently. The myth also provided a context for the Egyptians' understanding of their pharaohs. Every reigning Pharaoh was Horus, the hawk, son of Isis and Osiris; the dead father of every Pharaoh was Osiris. As Horus avenged the cruel death of his father, Osiris, so does Pharaoh, in life, guarantee that justice and equity prevail in the land of Egypt. As Osiris rose from the underworld to give birth to Horus, so does the dead pharaoh, who is Osiris, guarantee that the living Pharaoh, Horus, will be potent and in death himself become Osiris. As Osiris was brother and husband to Isis, so could the pharaohs maintain political power within a single family through brother–sister marriages.[5]

Beside its etiological function for these features of Egyptian society, the myth of Isis and Osiris incorporates elements found in non-Egyptian myths of the Great Goddess. Like Tiamat or Inanna/Ishtar/Astarté, Isis is curiously ambivalent. When Osiris dies, she mourns him, finds him, cares for him, reassembles him, makes a new phallus, and even conceives a child by him. She resurrects his power and ensures that the royal succession will pass to their son, Horus. On the other hand, she frees the evil Typhoeus after Horus has vanquished him in battle. Prominent is the theme of the death that ensures well-being. Osiris died, but around his coffin grew a wonderful tree. From the other world the dead Osiris watches over this world and, through his son, guarantees its prosperity.

---

[3]The Egyptian Thoth, ibis-headed god of magic and writing, equated by the Greeks with Hermes.
[4]The Egyptians were unclear whether Horus the hawk and Horus the child were the same; in a way they were, in a way they were not.
[5]Brother–sister marriage probably was not common in the early period, but the pure Greek Ptolemies, who ruled Egypt for almost 300 years, adopted the practice regularly. The (almost) final result was Cleopatra.

In the myth Osiris lived, then died, then through his resurrected phallus lived again. In nature, the Egyptians identified Osiris with the Nile, which rose annually to fructify the black, cultivable land, then subsided, then a year later rose again. Isis was the cultivable land, impregnated by the semen of the river. Typhoeus was the hostile, waterless desert, where the corpses of the dead were buried, where no life was possible.

CYBELÊ AND ATTIS

The Greeks were from an early time in direct contact with the Indo-European peoples who lived in the uplands of Anatolia near the Aegean coast. The Phrygians especially made a dramatic impression on Greek culture through the religion of their Great Goddess, **Cybelê,** and her youthful lover, **Attis.** Cybelê was primarily a goddess of fertility, but she could also heal (and send disease), give oracles, and give protection in war. She was the goddess of mountains and a mistress of wild nature. In art she was shown wearing a peculiar crown representing city walls (exemplifying her protective function) and attended by lions (reflecting her association with the wild). By the fifth century B.C. the Greeks had identified her with Demeter or Rhea but often referred to her by her Phrygian name. In the third century B.C., her cult was introduced to Rome on the advice of an oracle during a military and political crisis; thereafter she was called *Magna Mater,* "the Great Mother."

We have no direct knowledge of the original Phrygian myths associated with Cybelê. However, one important myth about her and her consort, Attis, was preserved by Arnobius (*Adversus Nationes* 5.5–7), a Christian writer of the fourth century A.D. writing in Latin who, like most Christian writers, was hostile to the myth he told. In his story, Cybelê was born from a great rock in Phrygia, the very one from which Deucalion and Pyrrha took the stones that became human beings. Zeus, seeing Cybelê asleep atop the rock, approached in a blaze of lust. She resisted him until he spilled his seed on the rock, which became pregnant. Presently the rock bore a son, Agdestis, whose strength and violence were so great they could not be resisted. His bestial lust raged crazily toward both sexes. Fearing neither god nor man, he asserted that earth, sky, and stars held no one mightier than he.

Finally Dionysus, god of wine and of the life force, undertook responsibility for the situation. He poured a powerful dose of wine into the fountain where Agdestis slaked his thirst after becoming heated by hunting. After Agdestis had drunk and fallen asleep, Dionysus made a noose of braided hair and slipped it over Agdestis' feet, at the same time making a vine grow over the monster's genitals. When Agdestis sobered up, he staggered to his feet, ripping the genitals from his body. From the blood that spurted onto the earth grew a fruited pomegranate tree.[6]

Now Nana, daughter of Sangarius (either a river god or a king), astonished at the sight of the tree growing from the blood, plucked a pomegranate from it, slipped

[6]The pomegranate is a fruit the size of an apple with a rough skin; its interior is a mixture of a bright, bloodlike juice and seeds, an obvious sign of life in the present (blood) and life in the future (seeds).

the fruit into her dress, and soon found herself pregnant. Her father, disgraced, locked her up to die of starvation, but Cybelê, the Great Mother, kept her alive with fruit and grain. Nana in time gave birth to a boy named Attis.

The Great Mother doted on Attis because of his lovely face, and the castrated Agdestis became the boy's guide in hunting. But Midas (**mī**-das),[7] king of Pessinus, capital of Phrygia, arranged for Attis to marry his daughter. To keep ill-wishers away from the ceremony, he walled off the town. Agdestis, furious that the boy had been taken from him and had transferred his affections to a woman, bewitched all the wedding guests and drove them mad. "Worship Attis, you Phrygians!" they shouted in their madness. A man named Gallus grew so crazed that he sliced off his genitals; the daughter of his mistress cut off her breasts. Attis seized Agdestis' flute and flung himself down at the foot of a pine tree. "Take this, Agdestis—" he cried; "this is what you wanted when you drove us crazy!" With these words he ripped off his genitals and with them poured out his blood and his life.

The Great Mother sadly took up the severed organs of Attis, washed them, and buried them under the pine tree. From his blood grew violets that wreathed the tree. The maiden who was to have been his bride covered the dead boy's breast with soft wool and, weeping, killed herself above his body. As she died, her blood was turned to violets too. Cybelê buried them both in a common grave, from which grew an almond tree, to signify the bitterness of their fate. Cybelê joined her laments to those of Agdestis, who pleaded with Zeus to let Attis return to life. Their pleas were in vain: Zeus granted only that Attis' body should not decay, that his hair should continue to grow, and that his little finger should stay alive and in constant motion.

This bizarre tale, seemingly of great antiquity, is a mixture of traditional mythical elements with depictions of real rites in honor of the Great Goddess. Zeus's impregnation of the rock recalls the Hittite "Song of Ullikummi," in which Kumarbi had intercourse with a rock, a variation of the myth that human beings were made from earth. The rock is earth itself, the mother: Not only do Deucalion and Pyrrha take their stones from this rock, but Cybelê herself comes from it. Agdestis, like Ullikummi and Typhoeus, is a monster who threatens the order of the world. But the means of the monster's undoing, his castration, is explained by the etiological function of the myth as a whole. The castration of Agdestis leads to the self-castration of Gallus and Attis, which in turn reflects actual practice by the *Galli,* real Phrygian followers of the Great Goddess who castrated themselves in her honor. The Gallus of the story is the eponym for these followers, and his act provides a precedent and explanation for their practice.[8]

Ritual self-castration strikes us as extraordinary, but we must remember that for many peoples, sacrifice was necessary to appease the divine powers that rule the world. Human beings were in debt to the gods and to the angry ghosts, who had to be bought off at any price. The value of sacrifice was gauged by the pain it caused. Many ancient cultures (perhaps including the preclassical Greek) practiced human sacrifice, where the sense of loss is greatest. One of the charges against the kings of

---

[7]This is the same Midas as in the famous story of "Midas and the golden touch" (see Chapter 10).
[8]Probably Gallus is connected with the Gallu, demons of the underworld who accompanied Inanna when she returned to the upper world to find a substitute.

Judah was that they "made their sons pass through the fire"—that is, killed them to the god Moloch.[9] Even Christianity, according to the formulation of St. Paul, accepted as a fundamental principle the sacrifice of God's son to atone for human sin. Animals eventually replaced human beings as ransom to the angry gods (except in times of crisis), as suggested in the biblical story of the ram substituted for Isaac, son of Abraham, and in numerous Greek stories. Castration was yet another form of substitution, and the myth of Cybelê and Attis explains its value. From the blood of Agdestis, spilled like semen on the ground at his castration, comes new life: the pomegranate, ripe with bloody seeds, which in turn impregnates Nana with Attis. Blood is life: When the woman's periodic discharge stops, the child grows. Likewise, from the castrated Attis' genitals, planted by Cybelê, violets grew around the pine, a tree that, from its seed-filled cones and erect straight growth, was an emblem for male sexuality, conspicuously in the Greek cult of Dionysus. Finally, from the bodies of Attis and his betrothed, Cybelê grows yet another tree. Although dead, Attis is still alive in a way: His hair continues to grow and his little finger, like a phallus, continues to wiggle. His sacrifice placates the goddess and allows for life's renewal.

APHRODITE AND ADONIS

A similar mythic pattern appears in Greece. We have already seen Aphrodite in the guise of Cybelê, the Phrygian mountain mother, in the *Homeric Hymn to Aphrodite* (see Chapter 8), where she seduces Anchises on Mount Ida in Phrygia: Wild animals, forgetting their wildness under the goddess's influence, follow in her train, as they do in the story of Cybelê. In the story of Aphrodite and **Adonis** (a-**don**-is) appear other themes about the Great Mother prominent in Eastern myths; the very name *Adonis* is Semitic for "lord" (in modern Judaism, *Adonai,* "my Lord," is still used as a word for God).

As we have seen (Chapter 8), Paphos, the son of Pygmalion and Galatea, was father to Cinyras, whose daughter Myrrha, pregnant by her father, was turned into a myrrh tree. After nine months the tree split open and Adonis emerged. When Aphrodite saw him, she fell in love and spent all her time with Adonis, who cared only for the hunt (see Fig. 8.1c). Aphrodite warned him against pursuing big game, but he ignored her advice, and one day a boar gouged him in the thigh. He bled to death from the terrible wound and from his blood sprouted the blood-red anemone. Ovid tells the story:

[708] Venus thus solemnly warned him and made her way through the sky,
    drawn by her team of swans. But his courage rejected the warning.
710   Chance led his hounds to the recent scent of a savage wild boar;
    they roused the beast from his lair, and as it tried to evade them
    by flight through the woods, the son of Cinyras wounded its hide
    with a glancing blow of his lance. A sidelong twist of the snout
    knocked the weapon away, smeared with the blood of the victim,
715   a sight which enraged the boar. In fury it turned on the hunter,

[9]For example, Manasseh, in 2 Kings 21.6; "Moloch" means "king," as Zeus was king of the gods.

H.D.'s "Adonis"

An important poet of the twentieth century, H.D., who identified herself with Sappho, received little attention until after her death in Switzerland in 1961. Born Hilda Doolittle in Bethlehem, Pennsylvania in 1886, she went to Europe in 1911 for a short visit but practically speaking never returned. In London she joined the expatriate community of writers that included Ezra Pound and T. S. Eliot, a literary group composed of modernists who sought the spirit of the twentieth century in myth, psychoanalysis, and, in H.D.'s case, feminism.

Concerned with the modern voice, H.D. nonetheless often wrote poems on mythical subjects; one scholar lists eighty-nine poems with classical titles. Viewing the classical world through modern eyes, she used myth in a personal way to explore and reveal character. In particular, she was interested in Helen of Troy, writing a monumental epic *Helen in Egypt,* published in the year of her death. Another mythological poem by H.D., "Adonis," was published in 1916. In this remarkable poem the Adonis myth is taken to reflect recurring aspects of human experience:

1.

> Each of us like you
> has died once,
> each of us like you
> has passed through drift of wood-leaves
> cracked and bent
> and tortured and unbent
> in the winter-frost,
> then burnt into gold points,
> lighted afresh,
> crisp amber, scales of gold-leaf,
> gold turned and re-welded
> in the sun-heat
>
> each of us like you
> has died once,
> each of us has crossed an old wood-path
> and found the winter-leaves
> so golden in the sun-fire
> that even the live wood-flowers
> were dark

2.

> Not the gold on the temple-front
> where you stand
> is as gold as this
> not the gold that fastens your sandal,
> nor the gold, reft
> through your chiseled locks,

is as gold as this last year's leaf,
not all the gold hammered and wrought
and beaten
on your lover's face,
brow and bare breast
is as golden as this.

each of us like you
has died once,
each of us like you
stands apart, like you
fit to be worshipped.

The god is a symbol for each individual's winter and spring, death and rebirth.
In the first stanza *gold* symbolizes the eternal: The leaf that dies is turned to gold,
which never dies. In the second stanza, the dead leaves, turned gold, are more alive
than the living flowers. In the third stanza (part 2) the dead leaf, a thing of nature,
is more golden than the real gold on the god's temple, on his sandal, in his hair, and
on classical sculptures of his lover Venus/Aphrodite. We, too, have a dying nature,
but like Adonis have eternal, divine gold within, are even "fit to be worshipped," a
startling conclusion.

who tried to avoid its charge. In vain; the animal buried
his tusks in Adonis' groin, and tumbled the boy, as he perished,
full length on the yellow sand.
    Born in her weightless car, propelled by the wings of her swans
720   through the mid-air of the heavens, Cytherea° had not yet arrived
in Cyprus, her goal, when she shuddered to hear the gasp of Adonis
breathing his last. She wrenched her white birds back in their courses
to the very place they had left, and soon, from high in the ether,
she gazed on the newly dead body, still twitching in its own blood.
725   Down she jumped from her car. Tearing her hair and her bosom,
she beat at her breast with hands unfit to perform such an action,
and railed, "Not everything, Fate, will always succumb to your power!
Forever, Adonis, this token of grief at your death will continue,
this hint at the way that you died, this annual sign of my sorrow:
730   your blood shall turn to a flower. Was not Persephonê granted
the power of turning the flesh of a maiden to sweet-smelling mint?°
Who out of envy refuses the same for Adonis, my hero?"
With this she perfumed his blood with fragrant droplets of nectar.
The mixture swelled like a bubble when rain falls down from the sky.
735   An hour had not fully passed, when a flower the color of blood
rose from the blood-stained sand, like those the anemone bears,
concealing its seeds beneath the pliant red outer rind.
Even this protection soon passes: the light seeds soon fall away
and are blown away by the breezes from which they receive their name.

OVID, *Metamorphoses* (10.708–739)

720. *Cytherea:* Aphrodite.   731. *mint:* Persephonê, queen of the dead, was allowed to turn her
dead follower Mentha—a name cognate to our word *mint*—into the plant that bears her name.

Adonis, like Dumuzi, usually is understood as a dying god of vegetation. In Hellenistic times his cult spread from Asia into Greece and Rome. Thus women planted seeds in shallow earth, allowed them to die, then tore their hair and lamented the death of beautiful Adonis (Chapter 5). The Bible refers to the practice: "He next took me to the entrance of the north gate of the Temple of God where women were sitting, weeping for Tammuz [= Dumuzi/Adonis]. He said, 'Son of man, do you see that? You will see even filthier things than that'" (Ezekiel 8.14–15).

DEMETER AND PERSEPHONÊ

The myth of Demeter and her daughter Persephonê is the subject of the oldest of the Homeric Hymns, which bears many striking resemblances to the myths we have just examined, although it has important differences: In the myths of Cybelê and Isis, the fertility goddess loses her consort, but in the myth of Demeter the goddess loses her daughter. Although the -*meter* of Demeter means "mother" (the *De-* is mysterious), the name of Persephonê has no clear etymology, and she is often simply called **Korê** (kō-rē), "daughter" or "girl"—she is a *parthenos*. Many regard the goddesses as two aspects of a single figure, for they were often called the Two Demeters or the Two Goddesses—the permanently fertile earth and the seasonal giver of grain. Despite differences, the myth of Demeter and Persephonê is a variation on the Sumerian myth of Inanna's descent into the underworld, telling how Hades, lord of death, abducted Persephonê, daughter of Demeter and Zeus, and carried her away to be his bride. Demeter, enraged, refused to allow the grain to grow until a compromise was reached by which Persephonê spends a third of the year in Hades' house and two thirds in the world above. The hymn is also etiological for the origin of the extremely important cult of Demeter at Eleusis, fourteen miles west of Athens:

[1]   I shall begin my song to the fair-haired holy Demeter
and her daughter with lovely ankles, her whom Hades abducted,
whom thundering all-seeing Zeus had given his brother to marry.
The girl was playing one day, she and the daughters of Oceanus,
5   far from gold-sickled Demeter, ripener of bountiful harvests.
In a soft grassy meadow she gathered roses, violets, crocus,
hyacinths, iris, and, fairest of all, a glorious narcissus
which Earth had sent up as a favor to him who swallows whole armies,°
in accord with the counsels of Zeus, a lure to the blossoming maiden.
10   Shining and wondrous to see, a marvel for gods and for mortals,
up from its root there sprouted a hundred sweet-scented blossoms,
at sight of which the high heavens all burst into laughs of delight
and were joined by the earth beneath and the salty waves of the ocean.
Astonished, the girl reached her hands to gather the lovely delight;
15   at once the wide-spreading earth split apart in the Nysian plain.°
Out rode the swallower of hosts, drawn by his deathless horses—
her uncle, Cronus' son, he who holds rule over many,

8. *him who swallows whole armies:* Hades.   15. *Nysian plain:* Scholars have been unable to identify the Nysian plain.

he who is known by a myriad of names. He hustled her, screaming,
into his car, and carried her off, disregarding the protests
20   which she cried aloud to her father, Zeus, who is highest of gods.
But nobody, mortal or god, gave ear to her shouts for assistance,
nor even the fair-fruited olive trees. Only the daughter of Perses,
Hecatê,° she of the shining tiara, thinking inexpressible thoughts,
from her cavern heard her appeal to her father, Zeus, son of Cronus.
25   Lord Helius too, mighty son of Hyperion, heard her lamenting.
But Zeus had delayed in his temple, thronged with pious believers,
to hear their requests and receive the reverent offerings of mortals,
far, far away from the gods.° Thus, then, by Zeus's decree,
Persephonê's father's full brother, receiver and ruler of many,
30   the many-named son of great Cronus, with his span of horses immortal,
carried her off to his kingdom. As long as she gazed on the earth,
the starry heavens above, and the rolling fish-laden ocean,
still in the light of the sun, she could hope that her reverend mother
and all the rest of the race of eternal gods might behold her.
35   For that short space of time she nourished her hope of salvation.
But once carried under the earth, she wailed aloud her despair.
The tops of the mountains, the depths of the ocean reechoed the cries
of her deathless voice. At last she captured her mother's attention.
Pain seized Demeter's heart; her hands tore the dark purple veil
40   off her ambrosial hair, and she wrapped a dark garment of mourning
over her shoulders, then swooped like a bird over dry land and sea.
    Nobody, mortal or god, was willing to say what had happened;
no bird would approach her, reporting reliable news of her daughter.
For nine whole days mighty Deo° wandered the face of the earth,
45   holding in either hand a pair of bright-blazing torches,
refusing to taste of the nectar or ambrosia, sweet to the taste,
nor would she moisten her body with water, so great was her sorrow.
But when there broke in the sky the tenth day's light-bringing dawn,
Hecatê came out to meet her, with a shining torch in each hand,
50   and thus she addressed Demeter, to bring her news of her daughter:
    "Lady Demeter, bringer of seasons, bestower of riches,
which of the gods immortal, or who of the race of mankind,
has carried Persephonê off and tormented your spirit with worry?
I heard her voice, yes, but I could not see for myself
55   just who it was. But this much, I faithfully promise, is true."
    So Hecatê spoke, and the daughter of Rhea with beautiful tresses
did not even stop to reply, but taking her torches in hand,
leaped to her feet and set out, with Hecatê leading the way.
Together they sought out Helius, watchman of gods and of mortals.
60   Standing before his chariot, the glorious goddess addressed him:
    "Helius, pity my plight, for I too, like you, am a god;

23. *Hecatê:* Perses was the son of Helius, brother of Circê, uncle of Medea, and father (in this account) of Hecatê, at first a great goddess with power over the sky, earth, and sea, a giver of riches, later goddess of crossroads and witchcraft.   28. *away from the gods:* Zeus allowed Hades to carry off Persephonê, but was careful to avoid the appearance of responsibility.   44. *Deo:* Another name for Demeter, probably a diminutive.

perhaps I have warmed your heart by what I have done or have spoken.
The daughter I bore, that sweet flower, charming and lovely to see—
I heard her heart-rending cry in the air, the voice of a victim
65   abducted by violent power, though I could not see for myself.°
Now you and your piercing rays look down from the glorious heaven,
over all earth and sea: if you chance to have seen my dear daughter,
tell me, I beg you, the truth. Who dragged her far from her mother?
who was it who seized her by force? Some human, or was he immortal?"
70   So she addressed the son of Hyperion; this was his answer:
"Lady Demeter, fair-braided Rhea's daughter, this you must know,
for the honor I bear you, as well as the pity I feel for your sorrow
as you weep for your fair-ankled daughter. Of all the immortal gods,
Zeus, the driver of clouds, alone must be held to account,
75   who gave the maid to his brother, Hades, as blooming young bride.
Hades is her abductor; he swept her into his chariot,
ignoring her protests, and carried her down to the wind-haunted darkness.
But, goddess, give up your anguish; do not cherish profitless grief,
one which you can never avenge. What shame is it to a goddess,
80   to receive as son-in-law Hades, receiver of so many spirits?
He is, after all, your full brother, and he at the first allotment
received as his share the empire of those who surround him below."
Having thus spoken, the son of Hyperion turned to his horses,
who promptly drew up his chariot, faster than long-winged birds.
85   But deeper, more painful sorrow now settled over the goddess.
In rage at the dark-clouded son of Cronus, she left the immortals
who gather together in council on the broad expanse of Olympus,
and traveled down to the cities and farmland of men here below.
Hereafter her form was disguised, and nobody, low-waisted woman
90   or man, discerned at a glance the divinity hidden within her,
until at last she arrived at the palace of lofty-souled Celeus,
who in those years was the ruler and lord of fragrant Eleusis.
She rested, grieving at heart, by the road at the Well of the Maiden,
a spring which the village women frequented for fetching fresh water. [Fig.
9.3]
95   There she sat in the shade, beneath an olive tree's branches,
the very type of a grandmother, long past childbearing age,
long cut off from the gifts of garlanded Aphrodite,
the pattern of women who raise the children of low-giving rulers,
or tend the household affairs of the busy echoing palace.
100   There she was seen by the daughters of Celeus, son of Eleusis,
who came bearing great bronze jars to carry freshly drawn water
back to their father's house. They were four, in the flower of youth,
like goddesses in their beauty: Callithoë, eldest among them,
Callidicê, lovely Demo, Clisidicê—four handsome sisters.
105   They had no idea that Demeter herself was seated before them,
for gods are not easily known against their will to us mortals.
But as they approached, they spoke in words flying straight to the point:

---

65. *could not see for myself:* A few lines above it was Hecatê, not Demeter, who heard but did not see
Persephonê; good storytellers often sacrifice accuracy of detail for the sake of dramatic speed.

FIG. 9.3. The Well of the Maiden at Eleusis, where Demeter sat down to rest, situated near the elaborate classical entrance to the sacred enclosure. The fine polygonal masonry probably dates from the sixth century B.C.   (Author's photo)

"From what long-settled land do you come, O reverend lady,
avoiding our town, and refraining from entering into its houses?
110   There in the shadowy chambers are women of your generation,
and younger women as well, to respect you in speech and behavior."
Thus they politely inquired, and the mighty goddess replied:
"Thank you, dear girls. Of course I shall gladly tell you my story,
since you are so kind as to ask, though I know not who you may be.
115   The name that my dear mother gave me is Doso, and I have come hither
against my will, from Crete, brought over the surge of the ocean
by pirate men, who by force carried me off from my homeland.
Their swift ship landed at Thoricus,° where they permitted us women
to walk in a group on the shore, as they themselves prepared supper,
120   and busied themselves by the moorings. But I felt no longing for food,
not even the finest of meals, but quietly fled from my captors,
brutes that they were, who wanted to sell me and pocket my price,
refusing all hope of a ransom. I wandered along the dark seashore
and finally reached your village, without the slightest idea
125   what country this is I have come to, or who its people may be.
Now I pray that the gods on Olympus may grant you vigorous husbands,

118. *Thoricus:* A coastal village southeast of Athens, north of Cape Sunium. It was one of the towns later incorporated by Theseus in the federation of Attica.

and a generation of children as fine as those all parents desire.
But, ladies, one more favor: would you be so kind as to show me
whose house—be it man's or woman's—I first should approach for
    employment,
130   the sort of work I do well, what is fit for old women like me.
I could dandle a newly born child in my arms to comfort its wailing;
tend the affairs of the household; spread the bed of my master
in an alcove off the great hall; and teach the women their duties."
Thus the goddess proposed. To her Callidicê answered,
135   Callidicê, maiden unmarried, the fairest daughter of Celeus:
    "Whether we like it or not, old mother, mankind must put up
with whatever fate the immortals may give; they are stronger than we.
So let me tell you by name the men whose power and honor
are greatest here in our village, men of note with the people,
140   a crown of defense to the town, by counsel and virtuous judgment.
Such are Polyxenus, canny Triptolemus, Diocles also;
Dolichus, noble Eumolpus, but chiefly our own lordly father.
The wives of all these leaders rule the affairs of the households,
and none, after even a glance, could fail to see you as worthy,
145   or refuse you a place in her home. No—they would give you a welcome,
for your features indeed are very like those that belong to a god.
Now if you agree, wait here, while we find Metaneira, our mother,
and tell her your story; she surely will urge you into our household,
rather than hunting another. For here in our well-fitted palace
150   she nurses a late-born son, long prayed for, her joy and delight.
If you take care of his childhood till he reaches years of discretion,
no woman exists who could look upon you without feeling envy,
such boundless reward would he give as a recompense for his rearing."
    So spoke the fair Callidicê, and the goddess nodded assent.
155   Delighted, the girls filled up their shining jars with the water,
and with them quickly ran home to their father's glorious palace,
to relate to the lady their mother all they had heard and had seen.
Without hesitation she told them to return and invite the old woman
to take the place and to offer a bountiful wage for her service.
160   They ran like deer or heifers in the sparkling weather of spring,
who gambol about in the meadow, champing the fresh juicy grass.
So the maidens ran off, tucking up the lovely folds of their dresses,
hurrying down the track, with braids bouncing over their shoulders,
fair as the bright yellow flower of blossoming crocus in spring.
165   They found the venerable goddess still seated beside the road,
just where they last had left her, and led her back to their home,
the house of their father. She followed, though aching in spirit,
hiding her head with a veil, while her dark robe covered her ankles.
They presently came to the palace of Celeus, favored of Zeus,
170   and, passing on through the courtyard, they found Callidicê's mother
seated beside a pillar supporting the strongly framed rooftree,
her new-born child at her breast. The girls ran up to their mother,
but the goddess stopped by the door. Her head rose up to the lintel,
and her glory, divine and effulgent, blazed through the open doorway.
175   Awe overcame Metaneira, but pallid terror as well;

yielding her throne to the goddess, she bade her sit down beside her.
But Demeter, bringer of seasons, bestower of wonderful gifts,
politely declined to be seated on the shining throne of the queen,
but quietly stood by the doorway, her lovely eyes fixed on the ground,
180 till Iambê tactfully brought her a stool and a silver-fleeced cover.
On it she sank, but held to her face the veil of her mourning.
For long she sat there in silence, her heart tormented with sorrow,
speaking no word to a soul, displaying no recognition,
unsmiling, tasting no crumb of bread and sipping no goblet,
185 wasting away in longing to regain her slim-waisted daughter.
But finally clever Iambê, with salt-flavored joking and satire,
won over the reverend lady to smile, to laugh, to be merry;
from that time on Demeter delighted in hearing her jesting.°
Metaneira filled for Demeter a beaker of wine that sweetens the heart,
190 but the goddess rejected the cup: it was impious, so she explained,
to drink the ruddy vintage, and she asked them for barley and water,
to compound with fresh pennyroyal, to be drunk off as a potion.
The queen mixed up this *kykeon*° and handed it to the goddess,
who took the cup and drank, as ritual practice demanded.
195   Afterwards slim-waisted Metaneira spoke thus to the goddess:
"I greet you, my lady, assured that you are of no common descent,
but noble indeed, for grace and dignity shine in your features,
such as we find in the faces of rulers, dispensers of justice.
We humans are forced to accept whatever heaven may offer,
200 however painful the gift, for this yoke weighs down on our shoulders.
Now since you have come to my country, you must share whatever I have.
Be nurse to this child of mine, born long after hope had departed,
a gift of the gods, whom they granted in answer to endless prayer.
If you take care of his childhood till he reaches years of discretion,
205 no woman exists who could look upon you without feeling envy,
such boundless reward will he give you in recompense for his rearing."
    To this offer fair-crowned Demeter gave a straightforward reply:
"I heartily thank you, my lady; may the gods repay you with blessings.
I will happily take your child to bring up, just as you ask me.
210 Be sure no slackness of mine will allow him to suffer black magic,
for I know remedies stronger by far than the deadliest venom,
and antidotes of great power against a sorcerer's malice."
    So saying, Demeter received the child in her fragrant bosom,
into her deathless arms, and his mother rejoiced in her heart.
215 In the palace she cared for the manly son of the wise-hearted Celeus,
Demophon, whom the fair-girdled queen Metaneira had born him.
The baby grew like a god, not eating, not nursed by his mother.
Demeter instead would anoint him, as if he were child of a goddess,
with ambrosia, food of the gods, and breathed her sweetness upon him
220 while dandling him in her bosom. And every night she would plunge him

188. *jesting:* Iambê is the eponym of Greek iambic poetry, characterized by insult and obscene abuse; later authors report that Iambê made Demeter smile by pulling up her dress and exposing her private parts, a version too unrefined for the poetry of this hymn.   193. *kykeon:* The kykeon, literally a "mixed drink," was drunk by initiates into the cult of Demeter at Eleusis, evidently a sort of beer mixed with spices.

like a firebrand into the flames, all unknown to his own dear parents.
To them it came as a marvel how swiftly the baby was growing,
resembling the gods. Indeed, he would have been ageless and deathless,
had Metaneira his mother not secretly spied on the goddess,
225 and left her own room in her folly, to see what was done to her child.
In terror she shouted aloud and slapped her thighs in distress,
anxious for her small son, but badly misled in her spirit.
Screaming for grief, she shouted words flying straight to the mark:
    "O Demophon, dearest child, this stranger woman has plunged you
230 deep in the flames, and is causing me terrible sorrow and anguish."
Thus she cried in her grief. The glorious goddess Demeter,
she of the beautiful crown, enraged at the sound of her voice,
with her own immortal hands dragged the infant out of the fire,
the boy his mother had borne in the house when hope had departed,
235 and flung him down on the ground in a terrible passion of spirit.
Meanwhile her anger erupted on the head of well-girt Metaneira:
    "O short-sighted mortals and stupid, you who can never foresee
the destiny, blessed or evil, advancing before your eyes!
What terrible hurt, Metaneira, your folly has brought on your head!
240 I swear the dread oath of the gods, by the terrible water of Styx,
that I would have made your son an immortal, honored forever.
But now that never can be; his death cannot be avoided.
True, he will always be honored; he has sat on the knees of a goddess
and fallen asleep in her arms. As his years advance in their courses,
245 the men of Eleusis will endlessly battle each other in warfare.°
Know that I am Demeter, everywhere honored, the greatest
comfort and joy to all, both mortal men and immortals.
Therefore let all the people erect in my honor a temple,
and beneath it build me an altar, by the steepest wall of the city,
250 by the Well of the Dance,° where I rested, on a high and projecting bluff.
I myself will establish your rites, so that forever thereafter
my blessing will rest upon you if you piously carry them out."
    At this, the goddess transformed herself in size and appearance:
vanished was wrinkled old age, and beauty breathed all around her.
255 Delicious aromas exhaled from the fragrant folds of her garments,
and a radiant halo surrounded the deathless flesh of the goddess.
The golden hair of her head floated down to cover her shoulders,
and flashes like lightning illuminated the firmly built palace.
The goddess then disappeared. The knees of poor Metaneira
260 crumpled beneath her; for long she lay there speechless and fainting,
forgetting her newly born son, to pick him up from the ground.
His sisters heard the piteous wail of the child and came running,
leaving their warm soft beds. One picked up the boy, to cuddle
him safe in her arms, while another quickly rekindled the fire;
265 a third sped on hurrying feet to revive and comfort their mother,
lifting her up from the floor and helping her out of the chamber.

---

245. *warfare:* Nothing is known of the civil war here predicted.   250. *Well of the Dance:* Here called *Kallichoron,* "Well of the Beautiful Dance," in lines 93–94 it is called *Parthenion,* "Well of the Maidens" (unless a different well is meant); see Fig. 9.3.

The girls all gathered around, to bathe her and comfort her sorrow,
but the grieving heart of the child they were quite unable to solace,
for these new nurses of his by no means equaled the old.
270   All the rest of the night they prayed to the glorious goddess,
still trembling with fear. But then, at the very first light of morning,
they told the whole story to Celeus, whose power spread near and far,
expounding Demeter's commands, as the fair-haired goddess had ordered.
Celeus called an assembly, attended by numberless freemen,
275   to bid them rear a rich temple for the goddess, fair-haired Demeter,
with an altar, high on a hillside. At once they heard and obeyed,
building the temple, thereafter to enjoy the goddess' favor.
       At last the work was completed, the time to relax was at hand;
each workman went to his rest. But as for fair-haired Demeter,
280   far from the rest of the blessed she stayed, though withering away
with longing and grief for her daughter, girl of the slender waist.
She sent men a terrible year, a plague for the earth and its harvest:
the land did not foster the seed, for fair-crowned Demeter forbade it.
The oxen tugged the curving plows through the furrows, in vain,
285   and plentiful grains of white barley fell on the ground without fruit.
Demeter might well have destroyed the whole of mankind by a famine,
and robbed the gods on Olympus of the honor of proper offerings,
had Zeus not considered the matter and pondered it well in his heart.
First he sent golden-winged Iris° to summon the fair-haired Demeter.
290   Iris obeyed the order of cloud-driving Zeus, son of Cronus,
plunging on nimble feet down through the air of mid-heaven.
Reaching the fragrant town of Eleusis, she sought out Demeter,
and found her there in her temple, wearing a dark robe of mourning.
She spoke to the goddess in language that flew direct to the mark:
295   "Demeter, Zeus the father, whose decision can never be altered,
has summoned you to attend, with all the other immortals.
So hurry. Do not make any mission from Zeus be effort misspent."
       So she politely requested, but resentful Demeter refused.
Once more the father made envoys of the blessed gods, the immortals.
300   In turn they approached, addressed her, and offered glorious gifts,
and honors which even a god might well be happy to welcome.
But none could make an impression on the mind and heart of Demeter.
Raging in spirit, she sternly rejected attempts at persuasion:
never, she said, would she mount to the fragrant halls of Olympus;
305   never allow the corn to rise from the bountiful furrows,
until with her own eyes she looked on her fair-faced daughter.
       When Zeus, who thunders aloud, whose eye encompasses all things,
heard their report, he ordered the golden-staffed slayer of Argus
down to the darkness of Hades, to win him with words of persuasion
310   to bring back holy Persephonê, back from the wind and the darkness,
into the land of light, the home of the other immortals,
all this in the hope that the mother, seeing the daughter once more,
might abandon her stubborn decision and no longer cling to her wrath.

289. *Iris:* Iris, or "rainbow," was a messenger of the gods, like Hermes. The blue, brown, green, or hazel ring around the pupil of the eye bears her name.

Hermes obeyed him at once; he left his place on Olympus
315 and plunged down under the earth. Within he discovered the ruler,
seated in state on a throne, and beside him his reverend consort,
still resisting his suit and longing to see her dear mother,
while she, far away, was planning to outwit the other immortals.
    The mighty slayer of Argus stopped by the couple and spoke:
320 "Hades, with long dusky ringlets, the ruler over the dead,
Zeus, her father, has ordered that I bring back Persephonê,
the reverend lady, from Erebus° back to the place she deserves;
all this, that her mother, rejoicing to see her daughter returned,
may abandon her grudging resentment against the immortal gods.
325 For she plans a terrible scheme, to wipe out the frail human races
born and sustained by the earth, by hiding the seeds in the ground,
ending the offerings that men now make to the gods in the heavens.
She is gripped by a terrible anger; she speaks no more to her fellows,
but sulks, alone and far off, in the scented depths of her temple,
330 new-built for her, high on a rocky spur in the town of Eleusis."
    To this, the lord of the dead smiled grimly, Hades the mighty,
arching his eyebrows, but did not reject the command of King Zeus.
Without hesitation, he spoke to Persephonê, woman of prudence.
    "Depart now, Persephonê, to the side of your dark-robed mother,
335 with kindly feelings toward me and better will in your heart.
Please, do not feel too resentful—no more than the others who come.
Even among the immortals you will find me a suitable husband;
am I not the full brother of your own father, great Zeus?
Even from here below, you rule all that has motion and breath;
340 together we two will be granted the highest of possible honors.
Our vengeance will fall forever on all the doers of evil,
those who fail to appease your pride with their ample offerings,
who neglect to give what is due us, a sacrifice proper and pious."
    So he spoke, and the prudent Persephonê warmed at the message.
345 At once she leaped up for pleasure. But Hades, peering about
to be sure that no one was watching, casually gave her a seedlet
of a luscious and sweet pomegranate to eat,° thus making it certain
she could not remain forever by the side of dark-robed Demeter.
Then Hades, ruler of many, harnessed his deathless horses
350 to the pole of his golden chariot. Persephonê mounted the car,
while the mighty slayer of Argus took reins and whip in his hands.
Out from the palace they galloped, and the horses soared in delight.
Quickly they covered their journey; not sea, not torrents of rivers,
no grassy meadow or hilltop checked the rush of the galloping horses
355 as high above they sped, traversing the measureless heaven.
    Hermes halted at last and brought the girl to her mother,
fair-crowned Demeter, in front of the well-scented temple. She looked,
then leaped as a maenad° leaps through the hills, through the forests.

---

322. *Erebus:* "Darkness," that is, the underworld.   347. *eat:* Among almost all peoples, eating a
meal—a slice of pizza on a date, a piece of cake at a wedding, or the food and drink after a funeral—
creates a bond between those who share it. The pomegranate is also important in the myth of Cybelê and Attis.   358. *maenad:* An ecstatic follower of Dionysus.

Rossetti's *Proserpina Holding the Pomegranate*

The year 1848 saw the publication of Karl Marx's *Communist Manifesto* and the worst of the Irish potato famine: Millions died. In the same year in England, a group of artists organized the Pre-Raphaelite Brotherhood. Although they used techniques provided by realistic painting, they turned away from a disturbed and hungry Britain and the everyday subjects favored by contemporary realistic painters to find their inspiration in history, literature, and myth. They wanted to return to a time, as they believed, before art was corrupted by the technical skill of the Italian master Raphael (1483–1520), hence their appellation *Pre-Raphaelites*. They were fascinated by death and the hereafter.

Dante Gabriel Rossetti (1828–1882) was a leader of the Brotherhood, son of an Italian immigrant to England. Educated at Oxford, Rossetti was fluent in French, Italian, and German and wrote poems in these languages, which he often illustrated by his paintings. Both his poems and paintings are noted for their gloom and sensuous beauty. When his wife, suffering from depression and tuberculosis, committed suicide, Rossetti in a fit of grief buried with her a manuscript of poems, then several years later dug up the body to recover and publish them!

The dreary pessimism of his group and the morbid state of Rossetti's mind, worsened by addiction to alcohol and chloral, is reflected in his *Proserpina Holding the Pomegranate* (= Greek Persephonê) of 1874 (Fig. P 9.2). Proserpina, unlucky maiden and bride of death, appears as a beautiful but melancholy woman in dark, sensual robes, standing in a dark-walled room. Behind her is an open window through which comes a blaze of light, the land of the living. Her lips are pursed and moist in an expression of hopeless despair. She holds a pomegranate from which she has taken a bite, a sign of surrender to the mysterious lure of the underworld. The curling vine beside her face, like the lighted window beyond, suggests the lifeforce that balances death, as does the smoldering lamp on the table before her. Tacked on the wall is a small piece of paper bearing an Italian sonnet by Rossetti, which may be roughly translated as follows:

> How far away that light, shining above the wall!
> It scarcely flashes through. Then, in a moment,
> it will lead me from this gloom, to the gate above.
> How far away those flowers on Enna's hills°
> from this fruit of your gloomy shades, O Tartarus!
> that brought me my bitter future. And O! how far
> that open sky from this eternal gloom
> that must cover me—forever.
> And O! how far the nights
> still to be passed, from days that once have been.
> How far am I removed from my old self! In aimless search

Enna's hills: In central Sicily, where a variant tradition placed Persephonê's rape.

I listen for the word one pitying heart
might breathe to another's soul. Its broken voice
will someday murmur condolence in my ear,
"O poor Proserpina, even we lament your fate."

FIG. P 9.2. Dante Gabriel Rossetti (1828–1882), *Proserpina Holding the Pomegranate,* 1874, oil on canvas. (Tate Gallery, London/Art Resource, NY)

The Pre-Raphaelite painters were more concerned with the Middle Ages than with antiquity, which usually appears in their work after it was filtered through Dante. The group soon broke up, but their romantic interest in tales of long ago and far away remained important in British art down to World War I.

Persephonê too, as she looked on the beautiful eyes of her mother,
360   jumped down from the chariot and horses and hurried up to embrace her,
flinging her arms round her neck. But even while hugging her daughter,
the heart of the goddess suspected a trick and trembled in worry.
Taking her arms from the girl, she asked the ominous question:
"Daughter, when down below, I hope that you tasted no morsel?
365   Tell me the truth, that we both may know for sure what has happened,
that, freed from gloomy Hades, you may stay with me and your father,
Zeus, the son of great Cronus, by whom the rain-clouds are gathered,
honored by all the gods. But if you have tasted a morsel,
back you must go to the depths, to spend a third part of the year;
370   the rest you may stay here with me and with the other immortals.
For when earth blossoms again with fragrant flowers of springtime,
once more you will rise, a wonder to gods and the race of mankind.
Now tell me, how did the mighty receiver of many deceive you?"
Persephonê, beautiful maiden, at once replied to her mother:

375   "Mother, I promise to tell you all the details of my story.
      Hermes the helper appeared, swift messenger of the immortals,
      with word from my father, Cronus' son, and the dwellers in heaven,
      to leave the darkness of Hades, that, seeing me with your own eyes,
      you might abandon your grudging resentment against the immortals.
380   At this I leaped up for joy. But Hades stealthily forced me
      to eat, though against my will, a honey-sweet pomegranate seed."

Here Persephonê retells how Hades carried her off.

[399]   So the pair passed all the day, each one consoling the other,
400   soothing each other's sorrow, till at last their hearts were assuaged
      in giving and taking comfort for all their misery and torment.
      Presently Hecatê, lady of glittering veil, came to greet them,
      to embrace with delight the maiden daughter of holy Demeter,
      whose helper and friend she had been. And far-seeing thundering Zeus
405   sent fair-haired Rhea, his mother, to summon the dark-robed Demeter
      before the assembly of gods and to promise her choice among honors,
      which she would receive in the presence of all the gathered immortals.
      Demeter consented to this: her daughter thereafter would spend
      a third of each circling year below, in the wind-smitten darkness,
410   but the rest of the time with her mother and all the other immortals.
      Back Rhea came once more, down from the heights of Olympus,
      back to the Rarian plain,° before this the richest of plowlands,
      but now quite barren of life, its greenery withered and shriveled,
      its white barley hidden in earth by design of fair-ankled Demeter.
415   This was the day, at the very beginning of bountiful springtime,
      when fields should groan at the weight of swelling long-beared ears,
      when the new-cut barley should load the plain's rich furrows with sheaves,
      when the reapers labored to bind the newly cut grain into bundles.
          There first Rhea alighted, flying down from unharvested skies;
420   the goddesses greeted each other, and each rejoiced in her heart.
      Rhea the silken-veiled addressed these words to Demeter:
          "Hear, O my child, what Zeus the far-sighted Thunderer offers:
      you must return to the gods, but he has promised to grant you
      whatever honors you choose to possess among the immortals.
425   He decrees that your child must spend a third of the circling year
      down in the windy gloom, but the rest with you, her dear mother,
      and all the other immortals. Thus he decrees it shall be
      and has ratified his decision with the fateful nod of assent.
      Now take my advice, my daughter: do not go too far in your anger
430   with Zeus, who rules the black clouds, but hurry to earth at once,
      to assure the crops will flourish, the source of life to mankind.
          Thus Rhea urged and fair-crowned Demeter gladly obeyed her;
      she sent the crops to the light from every deep-furrowed plowland,
      and all the face of the earth burst out in leafage and flowers.
435   Demeter herself explained the rites of her cult to the kings,
      the givers of justice—Triptolemus, Diocles, lasher of horses,

---

412. *Rarian plain:* Around Eleusis. This was the first land to be sowed and harvested.

mighty Eumolpus as well, and Celeus, ruler of people.
To them she revealed the observance and carrying-out of her rites,
things which are reverend, holy, which no one must ever describe,

440 into which no one may inquire, which no one may ever reveal;
deep reverence for the divine restrains the tongues of the careless.
    Blessed the man who in life has viewed the mysteries' ritual.
But the uninitiated many, who have no part in their teaching,
will have no share in a future like his when they pass below,

445 when they descend to the gloom and the moldering shadow of death.
    Now when the glorious goddesses explained all this to the kings,
they made their way to Olympus, to join the other immortals.
There they dwell beside Zeus, beside him who rejoices in lightning,
august, revered. How happy is he among earth-dwelling mortals,

450 whom the goddesses bless and favor! They send as permanent comrade
to live in his palace, Plutus,° bestower of riches on mortals.
    Hail, goddesses, ruling the folk of the fragrant town of Eleusis,
of Paros,° girt by the sea, and the rockbound region of Antrum!°
The ruler, the giver of gifts, season-restorer, Queen Deo!

455 and with her you too, her beautiful daughter, Persephonê.
Benevolent ones, reward my hymn with heart-warming riches,
and I in turn shall recall your deeds on another occasion.

Homeric Hymn to Demeter (1–381; 399–457)

451. *Plutus:* "Wealth."   453. *Paros:* One of the Cycladic islands and site of an important cult to
Demeter.   453. *Antrum:* A town in Thessaly.

Observations: The Myth of Demeter and Persephonê

The myth of Demeter and Persephonê is one of the most perplexing of all Greek myths. In ancient times the story was interpreted as an agricultural allegory, in which Hades was identified with earth and Persephonê (or Korê) with grain buried in the earth. Korê's return from the underworld was interpreted as the growth of the new wheat crop. However, this allegorical interpretation does not correspond with the facts of Greek agriculture. In the hymn, Korê returns in the springtime (1.415: "This was the day, the very beginning of bountiful springtime"), whereas in Greece the wheat seed is placed in the ground in the autumn, sprouts soon after, and grows through the wet winter. It does not sprout in the spring at all. What must be meant, then, some argue, is that the seed, Korê, is placed in underground containers during the four hot, sterile summer months, until it is brought forth for the autumn planting. Although this interpretation accords with Korê spending one third of the year in the house of Hades and two thirds on earth, it disagrees explicitly with the Hymn and with how the ancients themselves understood the story. Probably we should reject the allegorical approach and search for other ways to understand the myth.

    Persephonê is a *parthenos* and, on one level, the hymn is a human story that exemplifies the experience of Greek *parthenoi* and their mothers. Persephonê's fate resembles that of Greek girls who, at age fourteen, were married to war-hardened men twice their age, whom they scarcely knew. Like the narcissus she could not resist,

FIG. 9.4. Persephonê, queen of the dead, enthroned beside her husband, Hades; clay plaque from the southern Italian colony of Locri, c. 480–450 B.C. Persephonê holds in her left hand a stalk of wheat, appropriate to the daughter of the grain goddess, and a cock in her right. Hades holds a branch of celery and a sacrificial bowl (*phialê*). The cock is also shown at the side of the throne, apparently sacrificed in rituals to Persephonê, whose religion was strong in southern Italy.   (Museo Archeologico Nazionale, Reggio Calabria; 601.3272; Hirmer Fotoarchiv, Munich)

Persephonê is ripe to be plucked (so we say "deflower," to take a girl's virginity). The sudden loss of virginity is a death to childhood, an end to playing with friends in the sweetly scented meadow; Greek *parthenoi* dedicated their dolls to Artemis just before marriage. Because she ate the pomegranate's seed, she can never return to her former state; Greek brides carried an apple or quince into their bridal chambers. A father had the right to give his daughter to whom he chose, even as Zeus gave Persephonê to her uncle, a common form of marital union in Greece to prevent the division of a family's property. Marriage was literal death for many Greek women, who died in childbirth. Yet Persephonê's fate is different from that of real *parthenoi*, who at marriage permanently entered the sphere of their husband's house, where they bore children and became mothers in their own right. Persephonê, by contrast, lives in two worlds, belonging wholly to neither. She is forever Korê, forever childless, never fulfilled. When a Greek girl died unmarried, she was said to be Hades' bride, and a wedding vase was placed over her grave as a memorial. The pomegranate seeds eaten by Persephonê are symbolic of her sexual union with King Death. He offered her seeds, she took them within her body, but the seeds will never bear fruit. Never again can she return permanently to her mother's home. She is Death's proper mate, and with him she will rule the land of the dead (Fig. 9.4).

Demeter's experience more closely exemplifies the real-life experience of Greek mothers, who must give up their daughters to a stranger's household. In many ways her grief is greater than that of her daughter; in art Persephonê is shown consoling Demeter. Nor was the daughter entirely the innocent victim. She voluntarily reached for the flower, even as other women in myth are undone through curiosity about their sexuality. She accepted the pomegranate. Persephonê's curiosity brought division between herself and her mother.

Viewed more broadly, however, Demeter represents the loss that a mother feels for any child, as Greek mothers lost so many children to war and disease. Her loss causes her first to grieve and to rage, but eventually, as mothers must, she accepts that the world will go on, despite her irreparable sorrow. In popular Christianity, the Virgin Mary, whose cult derives from pagan cults of the Great Goddess, is also *Mater Dolorosa,* "the grieving mother," weeping over her dead child.

Parallels with Near Eastern myths suggest further interpretations. In each of these stories the earth goddess seems to represent the permanent fertility of the world. In each story someone dies: Dumuzi is slain by demons, Attis tears off his own organs, Osiris is murdered by his brother, and the dark lord Hades carries off Persephonê. But death of the victim always leads to new life: Inanna restores fertility to the world, Osiris' phallus is made anew and he begets a child, from Attis grows a tree, and Persephonê returns to the upper world. The mythic pattern reflects the theory and practice of blood sacrifice in religious ritual. The gory genitals of the Galli were pleasing to the Great Goddess, who in return brought fertility to the land. The giving of Persephonê to Hades, her sacrifice, creates the seasonal pattern of the growth and harvest of the life-nurturing grain.[10]

Seen in this context, the myth of Demeter offers a mythical explanation, or etiology, for the presence of death in the world, explaining why the fertility of the earth cannot be separated from the inevitable presence of death. There can never be a world (except in the imagination of poets) in which there is only life and never death because life comes out of death, one feeding on the other. Life *depends* on death. The Two Goddesses are a mythic image of the intimacy between the two realms.

[10]Actual prehistoric maiden sacrifice may stand behind the curious practice of temple prostitution in Eastern cults devoted to the Great Goddess: Rather than being killed, the girl's virginity became a substitute, a ransom to the goddess. In place of her life, the flower of her maidenhead was plucked "in honor of the goddess," even as the Galli sacrificed their genitals in her honor.

THE ELEUSINIAN MYSTERIES

The promise of regeneration through the Great Goddess was the premise of one of the most famous religious cults of the ancient world, the **Eleusinian Mysteries,** whose founding the *Homeric Hymn* celebrates. In the seventh century B.C., when the *Homeric Hymn to Demeter* was written down, the city of Athens was growing rapidly. At about 600 B.C. Athens absorbed the nearby village of Eleusis, and ever after the mysteries were the property of the city of Athens. Eventually they were visited by the whole Greek world, then by the Romans.

The word *mystery*, which entered our language from this Eleusinian cult to Demeter, comes from the Greek *mystês* (plural *mystai*), meaning "one who closes the eyes" in order to enter the temple or during the sacred rites. From the Latin translation of the word, *initiatus,* comes our word *initiate,* literally "one who has gone in," that is, into the temple of Demeter to participate in the secret ritual.

To divulge what happened within the temple, called the Telesterion ("hall of initiation"), was punishable by death, and all modern commentators on the Eleusinian Mysteries must begin by confessing that we do not know what happened there. Most of our information comes from unfriendly and unreliable sources, especially the founders of the Christian church. Yet archaeological investigation and careful examination of the surviving sources, including the *Homeric Hymn to Demeter,* have enabled us to form a more accurate picture of the events.

In origin the Mysteries seem to have been an agrarian festival designed to promote the growth of the grain. They were certainly functioning by 1500 B.C. Two principal families were in charge: the Eumolpids, whose ancestor Eumolpus, according to the *Hymn,* received them from Demeter herself, and the Kerykes, "heralds," descendants of Eumolpus' son Keryx ("herald"). The high priest, always a Eumolpid, was called the hierophant (hī-**er**-ō-fant), "he who reveals the *hiera,* 'sacred things.'" The Kerykes provided the torchbearer and the herald. For their services, members of these families received a fee from the initiates. We also know that there was a priestess of Demeter, who, like the hierophant, lived permanently in the sanctuary.

The principal ceremony of the mysteries was held annually in the fall. In classical times, a truce was called (and usually observed) for fifty-five days. Heralds were sent to neighboring cities inviting participation. On the day before the festival, the *hiera* were removed from the Telesterion and carried to Athens in a majestic procession led by priests and priestesses. On the next day began the festival proper, which lasted for eight days. All who could speak Greek (except murderers) were eligible for initiation, including women and slaves.

On the fifth day, following various preliminary rites, the grand procession back to Eleusis, bearing the *hiera,* took place. At night, carrying torches and chanting prayers and hymns, they reached Eleusis. The initiation proper took place on the next two days. The initiates had fasted, but now they drank the *kykeon,* the sacred drink offered to Demeter in the Hymn. Although many have thought that a drug may have been taken, a barley drink mixed with pennyroyal has no druglike effect.

The initiates entered the Telesterion, a building unique in Greek architecture. The ordinary Greek temple, elaborately decorated with sculpture, was meant to be viewed from the exterior, whereas the interior merely held the cult statue. By con-

FIG. 9.5. The Telesterion at Eleusis, constructed on the southeastern slope of a small hill overlooking the bay of Eleusis. The ancient town was on the top of the hill. During the Classical Period, steps at the northern end of the hall were carved into the living rock, visible in the picture. Remains of the columns that supported the roof are visible. The author stands at the site of the Anaktoron, the small room in the center of the building that only the hierophant could enter; from this room, according to one account, a bright light flashed at the culmination of the ceremony. (Author's photo)

trast, the Telesterion was built to hold several thousand people under its great roof, supported by a forest of columns (Fig. 9.5). Inside, off center, stood the Anaktoron, a rectangular stone building with a single door at the end of one of its long sides, probably representing an ancient hut from the earliest days of the cult. Beside the door was a stone chair for the hierophant, who alone could enter the Anaktoron. A huge fire burned on top of the hut, its smoke passing through a hole in the roof.

Except for the flickering light from the fire and torches, the crowd was shrouded in darkness. Terrifying things were shown. A flash of light burst from the Anaktoron, and the hierophant "appeared from out of the Anaktoron in the radiant nights of the mysteries" (Plutarch, Prof. virt. 81 e). More than that we do not know, although some have thought that a dramatic reenactment of the myth took place. Evidently the *hiera* were shown and something was said, but what the *hiera* were or what was said we do not know. The myth speaks of the joy of reunion between daughter and mother, and the message of Eleusis, however communicated, must lie in the emotion excited by the return of the divine Korê. The initiates were blessed with hope not for immortality as such (never mentioned in connection with Eleusis), but for a pleasurable existence after death.

Barely mentioned in the *Hymn* is **Triptolemus** (trip-**tol**-e-mus), one of the princes of Eleusis to whom Demeter taught her secret rites. After the fifth century B.C. his role grew in importance (Fig. 9.6). He was said to have mounted a chariot drawn by dragons and traveled over the whole world—like Osiris—teaching the art of growing grain. The myth was a popular subject of Athenian art, giving support to Athens' claims to cultural supremacy.

The Eleusinian Mysteries advocated no doctrine. As a group experience, it fostered a feeling of community among Greeks. As a magical rite, it ensured the growth of the grain. As a personal experience, it promised a happy afterlife. A high moral tone surrounded the cult, which emphasized ritual purity, righteousness, gentleness, and the superiority of civilized life based on agriculture. The Eleusinian Mysteries were the most honored cult of Greek religion, giving hope and comfort to untold thousands from all over the Mediterranean world and commanding veneration until they were finally suppressed at the end of the fourth century A.D. Some of the ideas associated with the cult, even before then, found their way into Christianity and are reflected in the words of St. Paul:

FIG. 9.6. Demeter and Persephonê send forth Triptolemus to teach the growing of grain, on a marble relief from Eleusis, c. 440 B.C. Demeter is on the left, in a restrained pose, wearing a matronly dress (called a Doric peplos), a staff of authority in her left hand. With her right she hands Triptolemus a grain of wheat (originally probably in gold, now lost). On the right Persephonê, wearing clothes appropriate to a *parthenos* (an Ionic chiton and a cloak), seems to place a grain of wheat (originally gold, now lost) on Triptolemus' head, while with her other hand she holds a torch. The Two Goddesses often are shown with torches, like those used in the nighttime procession from Athens to Eleusis to celebrate the mysteries but also emblematic of resurrected life.   (Archaeological Museum, Athens; 126; Author's photo)

But some one will ask, "How are the dead raised? With what kind of body do they come?" You foolish man! What you sow does not come to life unless it dies. And what you sow is not the body which is to be, but a bare kernel, perhaps of wheat or of some other grain. . . . Lo! I tell you a mystery."

1 Corinthians (15.35–37, 51)

KEY TERMS

Demeter, 217	Cybelê, 224
Persephonê, 217	Attis, 224
Inanna, 217	Adonis, 226
Dumuzi, 217	Korê, 229
hieros gamos, 220	Eleusinian Mysteries, 244
Osiris, 222	Triptolemus, 246

FURTHER READING

Clay, Jenny Strauss, *The Politics of Olympus: Form and Meaning in the Major Homeric Hymns* (Princeton, N.J., 1989). Contains a good essay on the *Homeric Hymn to Demeter* and the other Homeric Hymns.

Ferguson, John, *The Religions of the Roman Empire* (Ithaca, N.Y., 1970). Treatments of Isis and Magna Mater.

Foley, H. P., ed., *The Homeric Hymn to Demeter: Translation, Commentary, and Interpretive Essays* (Princeton, N.J., 1993). Facing Greek/English text with excellent essays focused on gender.

Frankfort, Henri, *Kingship and the Gods, A Study of Ancient Near Eastern Religion as the Integration of Society and Nature* (Chicago, 1978; reprint of 1948 edition). Penetrating analysis of Egyptian and Near Eastern myth and society.

Friedman, Susan Stanford, *Psyche Reborn: The Emergence of H.D.* (Bloomington, Ind., 1981). Authoritative study by a leading critic of H.D.

Hart, George, *Egyptian Myths* (Austin, Tex., 1991). Admirable survey, originally published by the British Museum.

Hinds, Stephen, *The Metamorphosis of Persephonê: Ovid and the Self-Conscious Muse* (New Rochelle, N.Y., 1987). Discusses Ovid's important treatment of the myth of the rape of Persephonê.

Mylonas, G. E., *Eleusis and the Eleusinian Mysteries* (Princeton, N.J., 1961). The best book on the topic, a thorough summary of the literary and archaeological evidence.

Neumann, Erich, *The Great Mother, An Analysis of the Archetype,* 2nd ed. (Princeton, N.J., 1970). An in-depth analysis from the Jungian point of view, with excellent photographs.

Richardson, N. J., ed., *The Homeric Hymn to Demeter* (Oxford, U.K., 1974). The standard scholarly edition of the Greek text, with introductory essay in English and copious notes.

Roller, E., *In Search of God the Mother: The Cult of Anatolian Cybele* (Berkeley, Calif., 1999). The widespread worship of Mata Kubileya in Phrygia, Kybele in Greece, and Magna Mater in Rome.

Vermaseren, Maarten J., *Cybelê and Attis: The Myth and the Cult* (London, 1977). Scholarly treatment of this Anatolian myth and its religious background.

CHAPTER 10

MYTHS OF FERTILITY

DIONYSUS

I feasted on raw flesh for the Mountain Mother.° I brandished
her torch; sanctified, I was hailed as Bacchus of the Curetes.°
My dress is a robe all white. I flee from childbirth and touch
not coffined corpse. Hungry, I hold myself from tasting flesh.°

EURIPIDES (from a lost play, quoted by Porphyry,
On Abstinence 4.19)

DIONYSUS (dī-ō-nī-sus), god of wine, the life force, and the instinctive side of personality, stands somewhat apart from the other Olympians: He was admitted to
Olympus later than the others and, according to some writers, displaced Hestia to
become one of the twelve.

Few Greek myths have influenced the poetic and religious imagination of the
West more than those of Dionysus (Fig. 10.1). To the ancient Greeks, Dionysus (also
known as Bacchus) was the god who taught the art of turning the juice of grapes into
wine, the everyday drink of the ancient Greeks. But this complex and multifaceted
deity was much more than a god of wine. At the center of his mythic character was
his identity as a male principle of fertility, complementary to the female principle
embodied in the Great Goddess and Demeter (Chapter 9). As a god of fertility,
Dionysus encouraged the burgeoning of everything alive: plants, animals, and hu-

1. *Mountain Mother:* The Great Mother goddess of Phrygia.   2. *Curetes:* The young male followers of Rhea who banged on their bronze shields to drown out the cries of the infant Zeus, hidden
in a cave in Crete.   4. *tasting flesh:* As a cultic act the initiate eats raw flesh but otherwise is a veg-
etarian.

FIG. 10.1. Dionysus in ecstasy, Attic vase, fifth century B.C. The god, maddened by his own power, tears apart a live goat, his sacred animal, before eating its raw flesh. The leopard skin around his shoulders and the ivy that crowns his hair are both emblems of the god.   (British Museum, London; PS 124093)

man beings. Thick, luscious ivy was a sign of his presence. He wore a leopard skin, and panthers pulled his chariot. The phallus and the horns of a bull were his emblems (Fig. 10.2). Through his cult this fertility god also came to stand for a distinctive form of human experience, a divinely inspired madness in which one's ordinary sense of self is lost, and with it the accepted norms of decent and rational

FIG. 10.2. A hetaira (prostitute) carries a giant phallus, symbol of Dionysus' power, perhaps at the Athenian festival of the Haloa ("threshing"), dedicated to the fertility gods Demeter and Dionysus, on a vase for mixing wine, c. 450 B.C. (Staatliche Museen, Berlin; V.I. 3206)

conduct. Some features of the cult of Dionysus were later to find striking parallels in the new religion of Christianity.

The myths of Dionysus must be pieced together from many different sources. Homer has little to say about him; the aristocratic epic poet lacked sympathy for this god of drunkenness and sexual license. Two Homeric Hymns (eighth to sixth centuries B.C.) survive, one of which we give below; the other is only a fragment. Apollodorus has the most extended single account of his adventures, and Ovid tells some important myths. Our best-known source, however, is the *Bacchae* (**bak**-kē), a play by Euripides written about 406 B.C., just before Athens, beaten and demoralized, fell to Sparta.

In this chapter we first consider the mythical biography of Dionysus, including his birth, his travels in the East, and his reception in Greece, specifically in Thebes. We then discuss the meaning of these magical and contradictory but deeply moving tales and examine the cult with which they were associated.

THE BIRTH AND EARLY YOUTH OF DIONYSUS

Philandering Zeus fell in love with **Semelê** (**sem**-e-lē), princess of the house of Thebes and daughter of the Phoenician immigrant king Cadmus (see Chart 17.1). Zeus came to her disguised as a mortal man, and Semelê was soon pregnant. Hera, Zeus's queen, inflamed with jealousy, disguised herself as an old woman and hurried to Semelê's door; her hair was straggly and her skin furrowed with wrinkles. For a while the two women chatted. When Semelê revealed her affair with Zeus, the disguised Hera suggested that his claim to be king of the gods might be only a ploy; perhaps he was an ordinary mortal who made up the story to bring Semelê to his bed.

The old woman departed, and Semelê doubted. When Zeus next came, she asked for just one wish. Zeus swore by the underworld river Styx that he would give whatever she asked. "Appear to me as you appear to Hera, when you make love to her!" Semelê asked. Sorrowful, yet true to his word, Zeus appeared in all his glory, burning Semelê to a crisp. Hermes saved the fetus and carried it to Zeus, who sewed it into his thigh. Three months later he removed the stitches, and Dionysus was born again. He was the twice-born god.

Hermes then carried the child to **Ino** (ī-nō), queen of Orchomenus (or-**ko**-men-us), the Bronze Age capital of northern Boeotia, just as Thebes was capital of the south. Ino was Semelê's sister and wife to King Athamas (**ath**-a-mas); she plays an important part in other Greek myths (see Chart 18.1). On Hermes' instruction, Ino disguised the divine child in girl's clothing, hoping to protect him from Hera.

Hera was not deceived. She drove Ino and Athamas insane. Athamas shot one of his two sons, mistaking him for a fawn. Ino seized the other, Melicertes, and boiled him alive in a pot. Mad, she ran with the pot in her hands down to the Gulf of Corinth and leaped. She and the dead child were transformed into sea deities, saviors of distressed mariners (including the legendary Odysseus). Ino's name became Leucothea (lū-ko-**thē**-a), the "white goddess."

To save Dionysus from further persecution, Zeus changed the child into a young goat, and in this form Hermes delivered him to the **nymphs of Nysa** (**nī**-sa), a mountain in Thrace, or in the Far East, India, or Ethiopia; no one knew for sure (Fig. 10.3).

FIG. 10.3. The birth of Dionysus, on a South Italian vase, c. 380 B.C. Dionysus' nurse, Ino, holding a thyrsus, reaches to receive him, while Hermes, with his caduceus, waits in the bottom right to carry the baby to the nymphs of Nysa, shown on the left lounging about with Pan (above Zeus, with pan-pipes) and satyrs (lower right). Apollo and Artemis (off the photo) stand behind Zeus. (Museo Archeologico Nazionale, Taranto; 8264 A)

THE WANDERINGS OF DIONYSUS

In Nysa the young Dionysus discovered the vine and the art of making wine. Hera now struck the god with the same madness he was later to bring to others. In a delirium, Dionysus wandered to Egypt, Syria, then Phrygia in west-central Asia Minor.

Here he met the Phrygian goddess Cybelê, the Great Mother, whom the Greeks identified with Rhea (see Chapter 9). Cybelê, whose own followers danced to the wild music of tambourines and flutes and abandoned themselves to orgiastic rites, cured Dionysus of his madness, and she revealed to him her secret rites. From Cybelê Dionysus acquired his long robes, an effeminate style of dress that offended the manly Greeks.

From Phrygia Dionysus now headed east again, followed by a band of devotees. His female followers were called **Bacchae** ("women possessed by Bacchus")[1] or **maenads** (**mē**-nads, "the raging women"). They carried the thyrsus, a staff wound with ivy leaves and crowned with a pine cone. Male followers were **satyrs** (**sā**-ters), half-human creatures with erect phalli, sometimes of enormous size, and the tails and ears of horses (see Fig. 10.5); later they acquired goatlike legs. *Silenus* (sī-**lē**-nus; plural, Sileni, sī-**lē**-nē) is either a general term for any old satyr or the name of one satyr in particular: an ugly, drunken, extremely fat one, given to the telling of tall tales. He is shown in art with thick lips and pug nose, riding on an ass, so drunk he can barely maintain his balance.

Like Cybelê, Dionysus traveled in a chariot drawn by panthers. He and his band crossed the Euphrates river on a bridge made of grapevines and ivy. They swept east as far as India, to the sound of drums and cymbals, overcoming all who opposed them. Returning west, the god and his train paused again in Phrygia. There Dionysus rewarded the local king **Midas**,[2] son of Gordias and Cybelê, for his generous hospitality by granting a single wish. The king asked that everything he touched be turned to gold, and so it was: his food, his drink, even his little daughter. In desperation, Midas begged Dionysus to take back his gift; the god told Midas to bathe in the headwaters of the Pactolus river, which flows near the citadel of Sardis, the capital of Lydia. The river carried away the cursed gift. The gold settled in the sands, which made Lydia one of the richest kingdoms in the ancient world (the Lydians invented coins).

Dionysus took **Ariadnê** (ar-i-**ad**-nē), a daughter of King Minos, as his wife. He found her on the island of Naxos in the midst of the Aegean sea, where Theseus, hero of Athens, had abandoned her (see Chapter 16). While Ariadnê gazed across the sea to the distant sails of Theseus' receding ship, Dionysus came up behind her through the wilderness, accompanied by his crowd of maenads and satyrs, a scene described vividly by the Roman poet Catullus (84–54 B.C.):

[254]　　All around, on dancing feet the maddened Bacchantes thundered,
255　　　　"Ee-vo-ee!" they shrieked, "Ee-vo-ee," tossing their heads.
　　　　Here, one waved a thyrsus, a vine stem tipped by a pine-cone;
　　　　　　there, bare-handed, they ripped apart a bellowing calf.
　　　　Shouting delirious cries, they tossed its limbs to each other;
　　　　　　still others braided their hair with hissing venomous snakes.
260　　　　Here they gathered to hail the mystical basket of secrets,
　　　　　　truths forever unknown to the uninitiate mass.

[1]A variant is Bacchantes (bak-**kan**-tēz), applied to male and female followers alike. Sometimes the Bacchae were also called Thyiades (**thē**-ya-dēz), "frenzied ones."
[2]He was a real man. His unrobbed tomb, an enormous artificial mound built around 700 B.C., has been found, with Midas' bones within it.

Titian's *Bacchus and Ariadnê*

Dionysus and his wife, Ariadnê, have been depicted by many Western artists, including Titian (c. 1488–1576), a leading painter of the Italian Renaissance in Venice (compare Fig. 6.1a). In his *Bacchus* and *Ariadnê* (Fig. P 10.1), Titian follows closely the narratives of Catullus and Ovid, depicting the youthful god, soft, pudgy, and effeminate, naked except for a cloak loosely draped around him, as he leaps from his panther-drawn chariot. Ariadnê has been gazing out to sea at Theseus' receding ship, barely visible to the left of her shoulder. She turns, startled by Bacchus and his train of satyrs and maenads, who clash cymbals, brandish the thyrsus, and toss parts

FIG. P 10.1. Titian (Tiziano Vecelli, c. 1488–1570), *Bacchus and Ariadnê,* c. 1520.
(National Gallery, London)

of animals. The pose of the satyr in the lower right, twisted with snakes, is modeled after the ancient statue of Laocoön (see Perspective 20.1). In the upper left shines the constellation of the Crown.

In choosing a subject from classical myth, Titian was following the Italian Renaissance's powerful interest in pagan humanism. Whereas medieval art served primarily to exemplify the religious values of an age of faith, art in the Renaissance turned toward the natural and human worlds, focusing on the importance of the individual. At the same time, the revival of the Greco-Roman literary tradition brought with it a renewed interest in myth, especially as presented in Ovid's *Metamorphoses*, which offered to artists a whole new world of subjects to portray. Here Titian focuses on the emotion and surprise of Ariadnê in the midst of a natural setting: She has been abandoned by one man, only to be discovered and restored by the godman Dionysus.

> These with delicate fingers beat rhythm from rumbling tom-toms;
>   those drew a ringing clang from hollow cymbals of bronze.
> For many the horn blared out its brazen dissonant clamor,
> 265   or strident Phrygian flutes shouted their barbarous song.

CATULLUS, Poem 64 (254–264)

The god married her and, for a wedding gift, gave Ariadnê a wonderful crown of gold and precious stones, the work of Hephaestus. Later the crown was raised into the sky to become the constellation *Corona Borealis*, as Ovid reports in his *Metamorphoses:*

> [176]   To her, deserted and grieving,
> Bacchus brought his loving embrace, and for manifesting her glory,
> brilliant among the eternal stars, he transported the garland,
> raised from her brow, to the sky: through the filmy heaven it passes,
> 180   turning its gems, as it flies, into stars of magnificent luster.
> Retaining the form of a crown, it takes its place in the heavens
> between the Kneeler° and the Serpent-holder.°

OVID, Metamorphoses (8.176–182)

182. *Kneeler:* The constellation Hercules.   182. *Serpent-holder:* The constellation Ophiuchus.

Ariadnê then accompanied Dionysus to the island of Lemnos and bore him several children.

RESISTANCE TO THE GOD

Many of the myths about Dionysus tell of the resistance he met when he returned from his travels in the East, bringing his new religion. In the oldest surviving story we have about the god, from Homer's *Iliad*, Dionysus crosses the Hellespont into Thrace and is opposed by **Lycurgus** (li-**kur**-gus), king of the Edonians (a tribe in Thrace):

[130]   Lycurgus, Dryas' son, dared fight with the gods of the heaven,
         but his life was not long. He tried to expel from holy Mount Nysa
         the Bacchanal nurses who follow the maddening god Dionysus.
         Dropping the thyrsus behind, they scattered in abject terror,
         struck by the murderous blows of the ox-goad wielding Lycurgus.
135   In craven fear, Dionysus ran off, diving under the billows,
         where Thetis took him shivering in her arms to quiet his panic,
         while he trembled in cowardly terror at the man's tempestuous yelling.
         But the gods who live in bliss thereafter detested Lycurgus:
         Zeus struck him blind; soon he died, despised by all the immortals.

Homer, Iliad (6.130–140)

Other ancient authors report that Lycurgus went mad and attempted to rape his own mother. With a double-bitted ax he pruned off the legs of his son, whom he took for an ivy plant, sacred to the god. These impious acts made the land sterile. An oracle announced that the king must die. The Edonians carried Lycurgus to nearby Mount Pangaeum ("bloody") and staked him to the ground, to be eaten alive by wild horses.

In Orchomenus in the Boeotian plain, once the home of Ino and Athamas, celebrated for its wealth and power, Dionysus encountered further resistance. Although the city's inhabitants quickly accepted the god, the three daughters of King Minyas, the **Minyads** (**min**-yadz, "daughters of Minyas"), refused to join the new, ecstatic religion. Instead, like proper women they sat in their chambers, dutifully worked their looms, and spoke critically of those who had gone to the mountains to rage as Bacchae. They told sentimental stories of nymphs in love. Dionysus himself appeared to them in the shape of a young girl, but the foolish Minyads refused his warning.

Enraged, Dionysus took on the form of a lion, a bull, a panther. The room filled with the sound of drums and the trill of flutes, the clashing of cymbals and the scent of myrrh. The threads of the loom turned into vines. Nectar and milk dripped from the furniture as darkness filled the room.

Suddenly hungering for human flesh, the Minyads cast lots for their own children. They tore one child into bits and ate him. Joyful, they danced from the palace into the mountains to join the other Bacchae. (Dionysus later turned them into bats, which love the darkness and reject the light.)

In Argos, the god again met resistance from three daughters of a king, this time the daughters of King Proetus (**prē**-tus).[3] Because the **Proetids** (**prē**-tids, "daughters of Proetus") refused to accept the rites of Dionysus, they were afflicted with a gruesome itching on their heads, a leprosy that soon covered their flesh. They went insane, thought they were cows, and wandered into the mountains of Arcadia. Proetus summoned Melampus, a seer famous for his knowledge of incantations and herbs, who agreed to cure them on condition that he receive a third of the kingdom. When Proetus refused to pay the price, the daughters began to eat their suckling infants. The disease spread to other women, who left their houses, killed their children, and wandered in the wild. Proetus again summoned Melampus, but now the prophet demanded two thirds of the kingdom, one third for himself and one third for his

---

[3]A great-uncle to the hero Perseus (see Chart 13.1).

brother. Proetus hastily agreed. Melampus took the strongest young men of the town and by shouting and dancing drove the women north to the coast. There one daughter died, but the other two, once cured, married Melampus and his brother.

DIONYSUS AND THE PIRATES

Another story tells of Dionysus' encounter with a band of pirates. The god was standing on a promontory beside the sea, perhaps on the small island of Icaria near the coast of Asia Minor, when a ship of Etruscan pirates passed below him. What happened is told in a *Homeric Hymn to Dionysus* from the seventh century B.C.:

[1]   I call to mind Dionysus, Semelê's famous son,
        how he appeared one day by the shore of the barren sea,
        on a point reaching into the water, like a good-looking boy,
        maybe sixteen years old. His long dark hair hung loose,
5   and a dark blue jacket covered his muscular shoulders.
        From the benches of their ship, a speedy Tyrsenian° pirate,
        the crewmen disembarked, doomed to a terrible fate.
        They saw the boy, gave a signal, ran up, and dragged him away,
        and took their place in the ship, satisfied with their luck.
10   Thinking him some lord's son, they tried to make him secure,
        but the ropes dropped useless away, off his hands and feet,
        while he sat grinning, and mockery shone from his dark eyes.
        The helmsman understood, and calling the others, he asked:
        "Messmates, what sort of god is the boy we have caught
15   and tried to secure? He's strong! Our ship is well built,
        but it can't carry this burden. He must be Zeus himself,
        the silver-bowed Apollo, or Poseidon. One thing is certain—
        he's like no mortal man, but a god who lives on Olympus.
        So come on, let's let him go, right away, here on the dark shore.
20   And don't lay a hand upon him, or he'll fly into a temper
        and raise up a terrible storm, a regular hurricane!"
        So he advised, but the skipper angrily cut him short:
        "Mind your own business! Just keep your eye on the wind
        and lend a hand when you're needed to heave away on a line.
25   Slave-drivers have to be tough! As for this fellow here—
        maybe he's headed for Egypt, or maybe the island of Cyprus,
        or maybe the ends of the earth and a hundred miles beyond;
        sooner or later he'll tell us about his friends and family,
        the ransom they can pay. To us he's good luck from nowhere!"
30   At that he stepped the mast and set the sail on the ship.
        The strong wind bellied the sail as the crew hauled in on the sheets.
        But as she gathered way, all sorts of wonders appeared.
        The first was sparkling sweet-scented wine that gurgled
        deliciously through the ship, dark, with a heavy bouquet.
35   The terrified seamen gaped as a vine grew out of the topmast

6. *Tyrsenian:* Etruscan.

and snaked along the sail to the yardarms to port and to starboard,
loaded with ripened clusters. Along with the vine, dark ivy,
blooming with flowers and heavy with rich luxuriant berries,
drooped down over the oars, crowning the groaning oarlocks.
40 The sailors panicked to see this and cried aloud to the helmsman
to run at once for the shore. Dionysus then changed his form,
turning into a lion that roared at them from the bows.
Another portent: he raised a shaggy-necked bear amidships,
rearing to growl at the men, while forward the lion glared.
45 In terror the sailors ran aft, crowding around the helmsman,
the only sensible man. Then, with a sudden spring,
the lion pounced on the master, while the horrified sailors looked on.
To escape their fate they dived into the shining sea
and at once were turned into dolphins. And as for the helmsman,
50 Dionysus kept him aboard, and calmed his heart with this word:
  "Courage, my friend, my spirit's greatest joy and delight.
I am thundering Bacchus, born of Semelê, fathered by Zeus!"
  Farewell, O son of beautiful Semelê. He who forgets you
never learns to compose sweet verse of harmonious measure.

Homeric Hymn to Dionysus

It is easy to see how this poem was performed in the symposium, a tribute to the god of wine. The Athenian master painter Exekias seems to have illustrated the story on a black-figured vase, one of the most famous paintings to survive from the ancient world (Fig. 10.4).

DIONYSUS IN THEBES

The best-known resistance to Dionysus takes place in Thebes, the city of his birth. In Euripides' play the *Bacchae*, the god tells us that he returned to Thebes not just to spread his cult of ecstatic experience, but to take vengeance on his mother's sisters, **Agavê** (a-gā-vē), Autonoë (aw-**to**-no-ē), and Ino (although Ino had been Dionysus' nurse; in this version, she is still alive). The sisters had denied Semelê's claim that she slept with Zeus, alleging that her lover was a mortal and that Semelê had been destroyed for telling so outrageous a lie. To punish this slander against his mother, Dionysus cast a spell of madness over the sisters. As the play opens, they are roaming with their followers over Mount Cithaeron (si-**thē**-ron) behind Thebes. Only the stubborn king **Pentheus** (**pen**-thūs or **pen**-thē-us), championing reason against disorder, opposes the god, ensuring his own horrible end. There are two groups of Bacchae in Euripides' play: the maddened women of Thebes, punished for their slander, and the Asian Bacchae, loyal and sane followers of the god who make up the chorus. The following excerpts attempt to give some idea of the play's extraordinary poetry.

[1] *Dionysus* I have come back to this, the land of the Thebans,
  I, Dionysus, whom Semelê, daughter of Cadmus,
  once bore to Zeus, with lightning flash as midwife.

FIG. 10.4. Dionysus and the pirates, interior of Attic wine-cup, c. 550 B.C. The god lounges amid ships surrounded by dolphins, perhaps once the crew. The yardarms have turned to ivy and vines from which hang bunches of grapes. When the wine in the cup was swirled, the dolphins would appear to swim.　(Staatliche Antiken-sammlungen und Glyptothek, Munich; 2054)

> Changing my form, no more divine but human,
> 5　I show myself by Ismenus' spring and Dircê's.°
> See there, the place where Semelê's body lies,
> struck by the thunderbolt, down by the house
> whose ruins smolder with still-living fire,
> witness of Hera's violence to my mother.
> 10　Cadmus was right, who made this place taboo,
> his daughter's grave, which I have hidden deep
> in green and succulent tangles of my vines.

5. *Ismenus, Dircê:* The rivers of Thebes.

I left the golden sands of Lydia
and Phrygia, then Persia's high plateau,
15   scorched by the sun. Onward I marched,
passing the walls of Bactria and traversing
the grim and icy country of the Medes.°
I reached the blessed land of Araby,
then back the long road through Asia, to the salt sea,
20   lined by towered cities thronged with Greeks
and men of other races, all together,
teaching my dances, establishing my rites,
to make these lands know my divinity.
Thebes is the first of all the towns of Greece
25   to hear my followers' ecstatic cries.
I flung the fawn skin on their eager shoulders;
I thrust the thyrsus, ivy-twisted dart,
into their hands. For here my mother's sisters
spread the slanderous lie that Dionysus
30   was not—as Semelê claimed—the son of Zeus,
but that she gave her maidenhead to some mere man,
and laid the blame of fatherhood on Zeus.
Her wedlock they called a lie made up by Cadmus,
fiction to hide his daughter's fall from grace,
35   which Semelê spread abroad, to Zeus's fury,
for which he killed her.
        For this I drove the sisters from their homes,
forcing them, brainstruck, to wander on the hills
and made them wear my Bacchic orgies' gear.
40   Then each last woman of the Cadmean race
I drove in frenzy out from her quiet home.
Now they are banded with old Cadmus' daughters,
resting beneath green pines, by soaring cliffs.
        This city, uninitiate in my rites,
45   must learn, like it or not, that I am here
to show my mother's glory, manifesting
myself to men as the god she bore to Zeus.
Cadmus himself abandons pride and power
to Pentheus, child of one of these, his daughters.
50   Pentheus, a godless man, resists my ways;
he drives me off from his solemnities;
he skips all mention of me in his prayers.
Well, for all this I soon shall make it clear
to him and all the people of the Thebans
55   that I indeed was born divine.
        That well and truly done, my steps will turn
to another land, another epiphany.
And if the Theban city takes up arms
and tries to drive the maenads from its hills,

---

17. *Medes:* Bactria, roughly northern Afghanistan, was part of the ancient Persian empire; the Medes are here equated with the Persians.

FIG. 10.5. A maenad and a satyr, interior of Attic wine-cup, c. 480 B.C. The satyr, with erect phallus, attacks the maenad, who strikes his genitals with her thyrsus, a fennel stalk wrapped with ivy leaves. She wears the leopard skin around her shoulders and has ivy in her hair. The satyr has a pug nose and horse's tail. Although they often attack maenads, satyrs are never successful: Their sexual excitement is no doubt emblematic of their condition of being filled with the god.   (Staatliche Antikensammlungen und Glyptothek, Munich 2654)

60   I and my Bacchae will meet force with force (Fig. 10.5).
      With this in mind, I have taken mortal shape,
      disguising myself beneath a human form.

(Dionysus turns and calls offstage)

        You women who left the Tmolus,° Lydia's wall of defense,
        band of my devotees, whom I brought from barbarian homelands
65   to follow my steps and travel along with me in my mission,
        take up your pipes and your drums, your native Phrygian music,
        inventions of me, Dionysus, and of Rhea, Great Mother of gods.
        Come here—beat out your rhythms around the palace of Pentheus;

63. *Tmolus:* A mountain in Lydia.

let the whole city of Cadmus know well that my maenads have come.
70   I for my part will return to the shady woods of Cithaeron,
the haunt of my Bacchae, to join with them in ecstatical dancing.

After an interlude in which the aged prophet Tiresias and the creaky old king Cadmus, founder of Thebes, ludicrously make ready for the cult by decking themselves in fawnskins and ivy, the scoffer Pentheus enters:

Pentheus   I happened to be absent from the country,
when word was brought that strange new-fangled cults
210   had seized the city: women had left their homes
for bogus bacchanals, held in the dimlit hills,
in which they worshiped this new deity,
this so-called Dionysus, with indecent dances.
They tell me, right in the middle of their covens,
215   they keep the wine bowls constantly refilled;
first one, then another woman sneaks off to the woods,
to the nest she serves for some young lusty fellow.
All this beneath the mask of maenad priestesses—
of Aphrodite, rather more than Bacchus.
220   All that I catch are handcuffed and given over
to warders, who keep them in the city jail.
Of course, some get away. I'll catch them yet
when I turn my bloodhounds loose into the hills—
Ino and Actaeon's mother (you know, Autonoë)
225   even Agavê, Echion's wife, my mother.
I'll chain them up in good strong iron cages
and end their Bacchic nonsense once for all.
They also say some wandering Lydian guru
has just appeared. He has curly yellow hair
230   that stinks of perfume; in his wine-dark eyes there glows
all Aphrodite's magic. Day and night
he always hangs around, proffering his cult
of ecstasy to all these silly girls.
Just let me catch him here inside the palace!
235   I'll end his pounding with his leaf-topped staff.
I'll stop that showoff tossing of his hair
by chopping his pretty head from off his body.
That fellow, they call him Dionysus?
That's the one Zeus once sewed up in his thigh?
240   the one who was vaporized by thunderbolts
along with his mother, self-styled "bride of Zeus"?
Whoever he is, he well deserves the gallows
for making such a blasphemous claim as that.

Tiresias and Cadmus attempt to persuade Pentheus to accept the new religion, but he has no patience for their argument:

[343]   *Pentheus*   Don't paw me with your dirty hands! Go dance,
if dance you must; don't smear pollution on me!

As for your guru here, who taught this nonsense,
355   he'll share your punishment.
    Quick, somebody, hurry to his place of prophecy,
    there, where he sits when he consults his birds.
    Dislodge it with a crowbar, toss it over,
    till everything you see is one big mess.
360   Dump his regalia out to the wind and rain—
    nothing I do will irritate him more.
       The rest of you, go back into the town,
    hunt out that pretty girl-faced foreigner,
    the one who brings our women new contagion,
365   and fouls their marriage beds. Then, when you catch him,
    bring him back here in chains. He'll die by stoning
    and find that revelry is tough in Thebes.

    Pentheus goes into the palace, Tiresias and Cadmus to the hills to join the Bac-
chae. A servant enters, leading Dionysus in bonds. Pentheus, who does not recognize the prisoner as the god himself, comes back on the stage:

[451]   *Pentheus* All right, untie his hands. He's caught in a net.
    He may be nimble, but I don't think he'll escape.
       You're quite good looking, stranger, to some women,
    and they, of course, are why you've come to Thebes.
455   Your hair is nice and long, not like a wrestler's,
    but curling sexily beside your chin.
    Your skin—peaches and cream, untouched by sunburn,
    but pale with hunting love in amorous shadows.
    First question: just who are you? what's your family?
460   *Dionysus*   No need to shout; you want a simple answer.
    No doubt you've heard of Tmolus' flowery hills?
    Pentheus Yes, it encloses the great city of Sardis.
    Dionysus That's where I come from. Lydia is my home.
    Pentheus And where did you get these rites you bring to Greece?
465   *Dionysus* Dionysus, Zeus's son, passed through our land.
    Pentheus You have some sort of Zeus, who breeds new gods?
    Dionysus No, the same one who wedded Semelê here.
    Pentheus Did he recruit in a dream or face to face?
    Dionysus We viewed each other when he gave his rites.
470   *Pentheus*   Tell me the form of these mysterious rites.
    Dionysus To uninitiates they may not be told.
    Pentheus What value do they have for worshipers?
    Dionysus Their worth is priceless—but you may not hear.
    Pentheus Hocuspocus, to arouse my interest!
475   *Dionysus* Your cynicism makes you mock our rites.
    Pentheus You saw the god so clearly; just how did he look?
    Dionysus However he pleased. I didn't make his choice.
    Pentheus You ducked that nicely, making no real reply.
    Dionysus Speak sense to a fool, he thinks it's only nonsense.
480   *Pentheus* Is Thebes the first place where you brought this god?
    Dionysus All other lands already dance in his rites.

	Pentheus	Their wits are feebler far than those of Greeks.
	Dionysus	In this, far stronger. All laws are not the same.
	Pentheus	Do you worship him by night, or in the day?
485	Dionysus	Mostly by night, for darkness fosters awe.
	Pentheus	But night seduces women into vice.
	Dionysus	If one should seek by day, she'd find it then.
	Pentheus	You deserve punishment for your clever speech.
	Dionysus	And you for your ignorant slander of the god.
490	Pentheus	This Bacchic priest speaks rash and slippery words.
	Dionysus	What dreadful torture, then, do you propose?
	Pentheus	First, to cut off your pretty curling hair.
	Dionysus	My locks are sacred; I tend them for the god.

(Pentheus cuts off the prisoner's hair.)

	Pentheus	Hand over that thyrsus you've got in your hands.
495	Dionysus	You take it from me; it belongs to the god.

(Pentheus snatches it.)

	Pentheus	We'll chain your body up in a cell, inside.
	Dionysus	The god himself will free me when I ask.
	Pentheus	Only when all your Bacchae join your prayer.
	Dionysus	No, he is close at hand and sees me suffer.
500	Pentheus	Indeed? Just where? My eyes don't see a thing.
	Dionysus	Right here with me. Your folly makes you blind.
	Pentheus *(to jailer)*	Take him away for mocking Thebes and me.
	Dionysus	I warn you triflers, trifle not with me!
	Pentheus	I warn you that I will, for I am the stronger.
505	Dionysus	What gives you power? What are you doing? Who are you?
	Pentheus	Pentheus, Agavê's son, fathered by Echion.
	Dionysus	A name of evil omen; it fits you well.°
	Pentheus	Take him away. Chain him up by the horse troughs.

Let him enjoy the black and murky darkness,
510 and dance his fill. Those women he brought with him,
accomplices in crime—perhaps we'll stamp them out,
perhaps we'll keep their hands from thumping drums,
by using them as slaves, bound to their looms.

507. *of evil omen:* Because Pentheus' name may mean "man of grief."

The guard takes away Dionysus, but a clap of thunder is heard, the earth quakes, the palace collapses. Dionysus reappears, freed of his bonds. Pentheus, in a towering rage, enters from the ruins of the palace:

[642] Pentheus   Humiliated! and that vagabond escaped,
who, so I thought, was well and safely bound.
But—wait a minute! Surely that is he.
645 What's happening here? *(to Dionysus)* How could you escape,
get out, and swagger right before my house?

Dionysus Relax now; trample down your angry passion.
Pentheus How could you slip your shackles and get away?
Dionysus I said—or are you deaf—someone would free me.
650 *Pentheus*   Who? for you tell me things I never heard.
Dionysus He who grew many-clustered vines for mortal men.
Pentheus [A fit accomplice for your break from jail.]⁴
Dionysus You slander Dionysus' greatest gift.
Pentheus (to guards) Orders: lock up the city's gates—at once!
655 *Dionysus* Why? Can't the gods jump over them at a bound?
Pentheus My, but you're shrewd—except where shrewdness counts.
Dionysus Where shrewdness matters, there indeed I'm shrewd.

*(Enter a messenger from Cithaeron, the mountains behind
Thebes)*

Now listen to this man and heed his words.
He has just come from the hills with news to tell.
660 Don't worry; I'll not run, but stay with you.
Messenger Pentheus, ruler of this Theban land,
I come from Cithaeron, where the sun's bright ray
can never melt the drifts of winter's snow.
Pentheus What vital news has brought you in such haste?
665 *Messenger* I saw the mystic Bacchae, women of Thebes,
barefoot, ecstatic, stamping out their dance.
To tell you and all Thebes their miracles,
yes, things surpassing wonder, I have come.
But first from your own lips I wish to hear
670 if I should speak my mind, or bridle my tongue.
Your bile is quick to rise, my lord, and I
must dread your anger, too tyrannical.
Pentheus Speak out; from me I swear you shall be safe.
No one should storm at those who tell the truth.
675 Moreover, the worse the tales you tell about these Bacchae,
the readier I shall be to punish him
who taught these women all their shameful arts.
Messenger Our herds of cattle were setting out to pasture,
plodding their way to the hills, just when the sun
680 began to shed his rays to warm the land. And as I looked,
three bands of dancing women met my eye: Autonoë led one,
your mother Agavê the second, Ino the third.
Exhausted in body, they lay there fast asleep,
some resting heads against a fir tree's trunk,
685 some pillowed in oak-leaves, sprawling anyhow—
but all was decent, not the way you think!
Not one of them, drunken with wine or song,
went chasing Aphrodite through the bush.
Hearing the lowing of our horned beasts,
690 your mother first jumped up and gave a cry

---

⁴A line has dropped out of the text, but something of this sort must be meant.

to rouse their sluggish bodies up from sleep.
They wiped refreshing slumber from their eyes
and jumped up, wide awake, in ordered ranks—
young women, grannies, maidens yet unwed.
695   First they let down their hair upon their shoulders,
then fixed disheveled fawnskins with fresh ties
of snakes, which licked their cheeks. And some of them,
whose newborn children had been left at home,
picked up a fawn, or cub of an untamed wolf,
700   offering white milk from a still flowing breast,
then crowned the cub with ivy, oak, and yew.
One seized her thyrsus and with it struck a rock:
out sprang the dewy water's limpid spring.
Another thumped her staff upon the ground:
705   for her the god sent up a spring of wine.
And those who felt an urge for whiter drink
scratched at the earth: a stream of milk gushed up!
Sweet honey drippings poured from ivied thyrsi.
Had you been there yourself and seen all this,
710   you would now reverence the god you scorned.
Shepherds and cowherds muttered to each other,
discussing, arguing the wondrous things
the women were performing. One of us,
a city boy, blessed with a slippery tongue,
715   made this suggestion: "Hey, you who spend your days
here in these dark mysterious mountain glades,
how about snatching Agavê, Pentheus' mother,
from out the revels, to do the king a favor?"
We all thought this a fine idea, and hid
720   ourselves in ambush, crouched in undergrowth.
    When the moment came, each woman waved her thyrsus,
in sign of revel, and all with one voice called
on Iacchus, on Bromius,° son of Zeus.
The hills returned their cry, the beasts responded,
725   nothing could stay unmoved by their wild rush.
Agavê led them, close by where I hid;
I jumped out from my cover to bear her off,
but she let out a shout: "My hunting hounds,
a pack of men dares to pursue our band.
730   So follow me, follow; the thyrsus be your sword!"
We took to our heels, and so escaped the fate
of being torn to pieces by the Bacchae.
A herd of cattle was browsing in the wood;
the women seized them with unweaponed hands.
735   And then—you could have seen one woman brandish
in either hand limbs of a bellowing calf.

723. *Iacchus, Bromius:* Iacchus, "Lord of Cries," an epithet drawn from Eleusinian cult, where Iacchus personified the shouting of the procession from Athens to Eleusis; Bromius, "Roarer," was an epithet of Dionysus.

Others would rip apart a heifer as trophy;
then you would see its ribs, its legs, its hoofs,
tossed through the air, and, dangling from a fir tree,
740 dripping its life-blood to the gore-smeared earth.
Arrogant bulls, that charged with slashing horns,
were tripped to the ground by countless women's hands,
and stripped, O king, of skin and flesh before
you could blink the eyelids on your royal eyes.
745 Like flocks of birds that rocket from the ground,
they swooped across Asopus'° fruitful vineyards,
like raiders plundering Hysiae and Erythrae,
hamlets nestled beneath Cithaeron's cliffs.
Wherever they lighted, they ravaged wantonly,
750 even abducting babies from their homes.
They set their loot, unfastened, on their backs,
where even bronze and iron stayed, not falling
down to the earth. Upon their heads they piled
hot coals, yet not a single hair was singed.
755 A few brave peasants, stung to a valiant rage,
charged out against the arms the Bacchae bore.
I shudder, lord, to tell what happened next:
their pointed spears drew not a drop of blood,
but the Bacchae, tossing thyrsi at their foe,
760 disabled some and forced the rest to flee—
women subduing men, through some god's aid.
Then back they came to the place from which they started,
to springs of milk and honey sent by the god.
They washed themselves, while tongues of dappled snakes
765 licked from their cheeks the spatterings of blood.
    Whoever, lord, he is, this deity
you must receive in Thebes. While all his powers
are great indeed, greatest of all, they say,
is this: he gave the sorrow-drowning wine
770 for us poor men. Without it, love could not survive
nor any other pleasure for our race.

746. *Asopus:* A river in Boeotia.

Still, Pentheus is not persuaded. He summons his troops for action against the Bacchae, but Dionysus, seemingly casting a spell over Pentheus, proposes an alternative course of action:

[810] *Dionysus*   Wait! Would you like to watch their gathering in the hills?
Pentheus I would indeed, though it cost an enormous sum.
Dionysus What makes you feel so eager for the sight?
Pentheus Disgust at seeing all these women drunk.
Dionysus Would you really enjoy a thing that so disgusts you?
815 *Pentheus* Yes, if I hid, unnoticed, under a tree.
Dionysus Even if you sneak up they'll track you out.
Pentheus That's true, they will. Your point is taken well.
Dionysus Shall we get started? Are you ready for the road?

	Pentheus	Yes, yes. You lead; I'm impatient with this delay.
820	*Dionysus*	Well then, conceal yourself in this linen gown.
	Pentheus	How's that? Must I now turn woman, man no more?
	Dionysus	If you don't, they'll kill you, knowing you're a man.
	Pentheus	You're right again. You think of everything.
	Dionysus	Dionysus shows me everything I know.
825	*Pentheus*	How can we make this scheme of yours succeed?
	Dionysus	I'll go now, inside, to help you with your dress.
	Pentheus	Dress? In a woman's dress? I will die of shame!
	Dionysus	What, you no longer want to watch the maenads?
	Pentheus	All right. Then what concealment hides my face?
830	*Dionysus*	First you must wear a wig, long curling hair.
	Pentheus	Yes; what's the second part of my disguise?
	Dionysus	A skirt down to your ankles and a bonnet.
	Pentheus	What else would you suggest, besides all this?
	Dionysus	A thyrsus in your hand, and a spotted fawnskin.
835	*Pentheus*	But this is women's gear. I'd die of shame!
	Dionysus	When you meet the Bacchae, blood will surely flow.
	Pentheus	Good! Should we first spy out the terrain?
	Dionysus	Yes; trickery is less a crime than murder.
	Pentheus	How can I pass unnoticed through the city?
840	*Dionysus*	We'll go through empty streets. I'll lead the way.
	Pentheus	Anything, so these women do not mock me.
		So in we go. I'll work out what is best.
	Dionysus	Just as you please. You're safe, with me at hand.
	Pentheus	Forward. Maybe I'll take up arms . . .
845		or else I'll do exactly as you say.

Pentheus and Dionysus go into the palace, then return, Pentheus wearing a long dress, fawnskin, and blond wig, waving a thyrsus:

[912]	*Dionysus*	You who are so desirous of forbidden sights,
		so eager for things you should never want to see—
		yes, Pentheus, I mean you—come here, before the house
915		and let us look you over, dressed as a woman,
		a maenad, yes, one of the crazed Bacchantes,
		to spy on your own mother and her attendants.
		My, you're as pretty as one of Cadmus' daughters!
	Pentheus	I see—do I really see it?—not one, but a double sun.
920		and look—a pair of Thebeses, the seven-gated town.
		And you—why, you're a bull who leads me forward!
		whose horns have sprouted out upon your head.
		—have you ever been a beast?—I'm sure that you're a bull.
	Dionysus	The god is here beside you, your onetime enemy,
925		now your good friend, who makes you see the truth.
	Pentheus	How do I look to you? am I not just like Ino,
		or do I more resemble Agavê, my own dear mother?
	Dionysus	Looking at you, I think I'm looking right at them.
		But wait: this lock of hair has come astray,
930		not quite the way I tucked it in your scarf.

Pentheus Oh dear! I must have shaken it too hard,
when I tried out my dance's wilder steps.
Dionysus There now, I'll put it back where it belongs,
like a good maid. Just hold your head up straight.
935 *Pentheus* Yes, you fix it. Whatever you say, I'll do.
Dionysus Your sash is loose, and makes your dress's folds
a bit uneven, down there at the hem.
Pentheus Yes, so they are. But only on the right.
On the other side it falls just to the foot.
940 *Dionysus* You'll understand how good is my advice,
when, in surprise, you see the modest Bacchae.
Pentheus Should I hold the thyrsus up in my right hand,
or in the left, to make me look more like them?
Dionysus The right; be sure you raise it up in time
945 with your right foot. I'm glad you've changed your mind!
Pentheus Won't I be strong enough to lift Cithaeron
with all its glades, and with the Bacchae too?
Dionysus Of course, if you wanted. Your thought was all unsound,
till now, when you think exactly as you should.
950 *Pentheus* Will we need crowbars? or are my hands enough
to rip off cliffs cracked by my arms and shoulders?
Dionysus You surely won't destroy the home of the nymphs,
or the place where Pan relaxes with his pipes!
Pentheus You're right: mere courtesy demands restraint
955 in fighting women. I'll hide beneath a tree.
Dionysus You're best concealed, in the most concealing way,
coming concealed as a spy upon these maenads.
Pentheus That way, of course, I'll catch the little pigeons
billing and cooing, snuggled in their nests.
960 *Dionysus* Exactly, you are sent to guard their morals.
You'll catch them at it—unless they catch you first.
Pentheus Lead me, then, onward through the land of Thebes,
the only man with courage thus to act.
Dionysus The only man in Thebes to take such pains,
965 for pains are waiting, of that you may be sure.
So follow me. I shall bring you safely there,
other hands will bring you back—
Pentheus   My mother's!
Dionysus—your name will be a byword—
Pentheus   That's why I'm here!
Dionysus You will be carried back—
Pentheus   O luxury!
970 *Dionysus*—in your own mother's arms.
Pentheus   O greatest joy!
Dionysus Such joys await you.
Pentheus   O worthiest ambition!
Dionysus Shrewdest of men, you face the shrewdest trial;
you will reap a fame to sting the hearts of heaven.

As often in Greek tragedy at a moment of high tension, the chorus sings a rapid
lyric, here, ironically, on the joy of the Bacchae and the greatness of justice. When

the song and dance end, a messenger enters and describes in gory detail the death of Pentheus. When the king and Dionysus, he reports, had gone out to view the maenads, Pentheus could not see them clearly. Dionysus magically made a pine tree bend low, and Pentheus climbed up on it. Dionysus let the tree snap upright, then disappeared:

[1078] *Messenger* From heaven a voice resounded (Dionysus', I suppose)—
"Bacchae, I bring your enemy and mine,
1080 who mocks our sacred orgies. Avenge our wrongs."
So spoke the voice. A holy light flashed out
to paralyze for a time all heaven and earth.
The air fell silent, the forest leaves fell still,
the very beasts were quiet in the wood.
1085 The women heard the voice, but only faintly,
and stood erect, with darting, waiting eyes.
Again the summons of the god rang out.
This time Cadmus' daughters heard its call,
the voice of Bacchus. Swift as rocketing doves,
1090 they raced with drumming feet in hot pursuit. . . .

(Agavê directs the women to tear down the tree with their bare hands.)

Crying in terror, down from his high perch,
down to the earth poor Pentheus plunged,
now fully conscious that his end was near.
His mother first began this pious murder,
1095 flinging herself upon her fallen son.
He tore away his headdress, in the hope
that poor Agavê might restrain her hand.
His hand reached out to touch his mother's cheek;
"See, mother!" he implored, "I am your son,
1100 your Pentheus, whom you bore to Echion.
Pity me, mother; do not slay your child,
whatever, in your eyes, my guilt may be."
  She only rolled deluded bloodshot eyes,
demented, stung by madness from the god.
1105 She caught his left arm, just below the shoulder,
and bracing against his ribs, she ripped it out
from the shoulder socket, with violence not her own,
for the god had given power to her hand.
Ino wrenched hard at Pentheus' other arm,
1110 and tore his flesh apart. The other Bacchae,
led by Autonoë, rushed up for the kill.
  Then everything became one screaming clamor:
the poor man groaning while his breath remained,
the women screaming in triumph. One waved an arm,
1115 one waved a foot, whose boot hung by one lace.
His ribs were stripped of flesh by grasping claws;
each bloodied hand played a mad game of ball

FIG. 10.6. The dismemberment of Pentheus, a wall painting from Pompeii, 54–79 A.D. Agavê, on the left, seizes her son's hair and prepares to strike him with her thyrsus, which she holds poised in her right hand, while on the right Autonoë, Pentheus' aunt, seizes his arm to pull it from his shoulder. The other Theban women swarm in, carrying thyrsi and rocks to kill the intruder.   (Museo Archeologico Nazionale, Naples; Deutsches Archäologisches Institut; 77-35-99)

with Pentheus' flesh.
His mangled body lay, scattered and torn,
part on the jagged flints, part in the bushes,
a gruesome task to gather up to bury.
His wretched head fell to Agavê's hands.
She waved it proudly, on her thyrsus' point,
believing it a mountain lion's head.

1120

1125 Leaving her sisters with the maenad crew,
   she marched, exulting, from Cithaeron's height,
   down to the city walls, hailing the Bacchic god
   as "fellow-hunter," "comrade in the chase,"
   and "glorious in victory."

                 Euripides, *Bacchae*

  Agavê enters with the head of Pentheus stuck on her thyrsus;[5] Cadmus and attendants carry the mangled body of Pentheus on a stretcher. Agavê boasts of her exploits and offers the head of Pentheus to her father, who gradually brings her back to her senses, until with horror she realizes what she has done. Dionysus appears and sentences Cadmus and his daughters to exile, although Cadmus and his wife eventually are admitted to a blessed life in Elysium (see Chapter 11).

  Euripides' theme in the *Bacchae* was old: We know of several earlier treatments in plays now lost. In his play Euripides joined the wild irrationality of ancient Phrygian and Thracian religion with the theological skepticism of his own contemporary Athens. Posthumously produced, probably in 405 B.C., the play won Euripides his last of only five first prizes, from a jury of men like those who, a few years later, would condemn Socrates to death for impiety and for corrupting the young.

DIONYSUS' JOURNEY TO THE LAND OF THE DEAD

Several stories, less well known but no less important, describe the end of Dionysus' career on the earth. Having introduced his cult to Greece and to the East as far as India, he prepared to ascend to Olympus to take his place with the other immortals. But he did not want to leave his mother, Semelê, in the house of Hades, and he decided to bring her back. He himself did not know the way, but in Argos he encountered a shepherd who led him to the gloomy, bottomless Alcyonean lake near the swamp of Lerna. Plunging into its depths, the god presently emerged in the lower world and persuaded Hades to restore his mother. By the time they reached the upper world, the shepherd had died. Dionysus selected a branch of a fig tree and from it carved a phallus, the first of the many found all over the world, which he placed on the grave.

  When they came to Olympus, Dionysus changed his mother's name to Thyonê, "she who receives the sacrifice." Although born a mortal, she became a god like her son, and they joined the other Olympians.

Observations: The Myths of Dionysus

Dionysus' name is perplexing. The *Dio-* part derives from the same Indo-European root as the name *Zeus,* but *-nysos* has not been explained. It might mean "son," so

---

[5]When the Parthians (a people from Persia) captured and killed the Roman general Crassus in 51 B.C., they brought his head back to their capital just in time for it to be used as a stage prop for a performance of the Bacchae!

that Dionysus would be the "son of Zeus." It might also refer to the otherwise un-known place whence come the "nymphs of Nysa," so that Dionysus would be the "god from Nysa." Again, *Nysos* could simply be another name for Dionysus himself, which would explain why his followers sometimes were called *Nysai*, as the Bacchae were named from Bacchus; the "nymphs of Nysa," then, would mean simply "the follow-ers of Dionysus."

Many of the names and words associated with Dionysus are of Eastern origin. Some scholars have thought that Semelê's name, certainly non-Greek, is the same as *Semelô*, a Phrygian name for the Great Goddess attested on inscriptions. If so, in the Greek myth an Eastern goddess has been downgraded into a mortal woman involved in an adulterous intrigue, a figure of religious importance recast in an all-too-human role. The word *thyrsus* may be related to Hittite *tuwarsa*, "vine." Even the name *Bac-chus* itself may be derived from the Lydian name of the god: A Lydian inscription equates the name *bakivali* with Dionysus.

The myths of Dionysus also suggest Eastern origins. The god is usually said to have arrived in Greece from Thrace, the coastal area between Macedonia and the Hellespont, or from Phrygia and Lydia farther east, the hill country in Anatolia be-tween the west coast of Asia Minor and the ancient centers of Hittite power in cen-tral Anatolia. This tradition accords nicely with the apparent Eastern origin of *Semelê*, *thyrsus*, and *Bacchus*. Certainly Dionysiac or similar religions were strong in Thrace and Phrygia in the Classical Period.

Scholars used to think that the tradition of Dionysus' Eastern origin reflected a historical fact, the late introduction of his cult into Greece from Asia Minor about 800 B.C., at the beginning of the historical period. They pointed out that Dionysus plays only a small role in Homer's epic poems, composed about 800–750 B.C. How-ever, Dionysus' name has now been found on two fragmentary Linear B tablets from Late Bronze Age Pylos (thirteenth century B.C.), perhaps in association with wine. Important myths about him are localized in Orchomenus, in Thebes, and on the Ar-give plain, all Bronze Age strongholds. And although it is true that Homer seems to have little interest in Dionysus, several passing references prove that he was familiar with Dionysiac cult. For these reasons, scholars now consider Dionysus to be a god who was known and worshiped in Greece at an early date. His religion no doubt un-derwent revivals from time to time and was certainly influenced by foreign cult, but he was established in Greece long before the beginning of the historical period.

This conclusion leads to an important question of interpretation. The tales of his travels to Egypt and India might be etiological to explain the spread of vine grow-ing throughout the world, and stories of military conquest could serve as propa-ganda for the god, who claimed universal sway. But why is Dionysus portrayed as a strange and foreign god, if he was known in Greece at such an early date? Let us re-turn to this question after first considering the general character of his myths and his role in Greek religion.

Many elements in the story are familiar from folktale. For example, "the short-sighted wish" appears in Semelê's request to see Zeus in his full glory and Midas' de-sire to have all that he touches turn to gold. Hera, who persecutes her stepson Diony-sus, acts as "the vengeful stepmother." Two folktale motifs appear in the story of Proetus and Melampus: "a portion of the kingdom as reward," in Proetus' payment to Melampus for curing his daughters of madness, and "the short-sighted fool," in Proetus' purchase of the same service for twice the price first asked. As in many other Greek myths, these folktale elements contribute entertainment to the story.

To move to deeper levels of interpretation, we need to recall that in religion Dionysus was first a god of fertility, closely associated with certain plants and animals. Many of his epithets refer to power over fruitfulness in plant life and over the moisture that makes plant life possible. In some areas Dionysus was known as "he of the trees" (*dendritês*). The fig, from the lushness and sweetness of its rich, seed-filled fruit, was thought exemplary of the god; it was from a fig branch that Dionysus carved the phallus he implanted on the grave of the shepherd who guided him to the lake of the underworld.[6] The pine, which remains green in winter and oozes a rich pitch used in the making of wine, was also close to Dionysus; a pine cone, filled with seeds, was mounted on one kind of thyrsus.

Dionysus was "god of blossoms" (*anthios*), specifically the vine blossoms that presage the grape. From the juice of the grape comes wine, an "enspirited" drink that contains, through a mysterious transformation, something wonderful, unique, divine. Ivy is complementary to the vine as emblem of the god. On artistic representations, ivy entwines the god's hair, or he is worshiped as a staff entwined by ivy, surmounted by a mask (Fig. 10.7). Like Dionysus, ivy is tenacious, strong, and luxuriant in growth. Unlike the "hot" grape, which loves bright sun and yields a fiery wine, the "cool" ivy flourishes in shade and remains green all winter. One version told how ivy vines protected the unborn Dionysus from the lightning blast that destroyed his mother.

In the animal kingdom, Dionysus loved creatures noted for their strength, ferocity, or sexual vitality. As a child Dionysus was changed by Zeus to a goat, an animal whose male is renowned for its sexual power and whose female yields most of the necessities of life—milk and cheese, wool, hide, and meat. Thus he was known as the goat god (*melanaigis*, "he of the black goatskin"), but more often he appears as a bull. The Thracian king Lycurgus pursued Dionysus into the sea with an ox-goad, appropriate if Dionysus is himself the bull. In Euripides' *Bacchae*, Pentheus falls into a trance and mistakes the god for a bull. The followers of Dionysus sometimes wore horns and were even called "bullherders" (*boukoloi*). Finally, Dionysus was close to cats, especially the lion and the panther. Like the god, they are fecund, lithe, beautiful, and terrible. In art he is often shown in their company.

In his role as a fertility deity, Dionysus can be compared to Demeter. Demeter gives the grain, which is precious to human beings but by nature dry and passive. Dionysus, on the other hand, represents a wet and active substance, the "juice" that gives life to things. Water is the natural element closest to Dionysus. Many stories tell of Dionysus returning to water: Lycurgus drives him into the sea, to the protective arms of the sea goddess Thetis. Dionysus descends through the Alcyonean lake to bring back his mother from the underworld. His encounter with the Etruscan pirates takes place at sea, and Ino, his nurse and victim, becomes a sea goddess. It is fitting that this watery god would also be associated with the wet components of living things: semen, sap, milk, and blood. The coincidence in color between wine and

---

[6]In Italian today, *fico*, "fig," is an obscene term for *penis*.

FIG. 10.7. The Athenian festival of the Lenaea, from an early fifth-century B.C. drinking cup. The Lenaea took place at the end of winter and seems to have been a procession and dance by Athenian women dressed as maenads, or *Lenai*. Later, comedies were performed at the festival. Here the central figure, before which is an altar, is a wooden pillar draped with robes to the top of which is fastened a clay mask of Dionysus. Offerings to the god are pushed onto the vines behind the figure. The women dance to the sound of the double flute (really an oboe), said to inspire ecstasy.   (Staatliche Museen, Berlin; 2290)

blood no doubt aided the identification, in Dionysus, of a single power that makes plants bloom and die and animals breathe, procreate, and kill.

Dionysus' associations with both the life force and with death give him the appearance of a dying god of the Dumuzi type (see Chapter 9). Like Attis and Osiris, he can be viewed as a companion to the Great Mother: He was the son of Semelê (compare the Phrygian *Semelô*), an initiate of Cybelê, and husband to Ariadnê, whose name, "very holy one," suggests her own close relation with the Great Mother. Several stories tell of his death and rebirth. He is "killed" by the thunderbolt that destroys Semelê, then "born again" from Zeus's thigh. He descends to the underworld to find his mother, then returns with her to the realm of the living. Departure and return, death and resurrection—these are recurring themes in Dionysiac myth.

But what makes Dionysus unique in Greek myth are the many stories of resistance to him and his cult and of the vengeance he took on those who rejected his divinity. Lycurgus scattered the maenads and drove Dionysus himself into the sea, then went mad and pruned off the limbs of his child. The Minyads were afflicted horribly for their resistance and feasted on their own children. The Proetids suffered a similar fate. The Etruscan pirates, who failed at first to recognize the god's power, were driven insane so that they threw themselves into the sea. King Pentheus, who tried to arrest the gods, grows delirious and marches eagerly to his own doom. Agavê, Ino, and Autonoë deny the god at first, then dismember Pentheus in a fit of Dionysiac madness. No one in these stories ever blames Dionysus for taking revenge on his opponents. The Greeks did not question Dionysus' right to destroy any more than they questioned the right of a thunderstorm to knock down a building.

Those who resist Dionysus are not the only ones who suffer madness and destruction: Even those who welcome and assist him can meet a similar fate. His mother, Semelê, was burned to ashes. Ino, his nurse, was driven insane and boiled her child alive. When Dionysus comes, disaster follows. He can bring death and madness to those who favor him as well as to those who resist.

Dionysus brings destruction, but paradoxically resurrection and life as well. After leaping into the sea, Ino becomes a beneficent sea goddess. Semelê, although burned to a crisp, eventually joins Dionysus and the other gods on Mount Olympus. Called "the destroyer of men" and "he who eats raw flesh," he is also "the god of many joys," "the giver of riches," "the benefactor." Like living nature itself, this contradictory god is the master of both life and death, carrying his creatures to an inevitable destruction, then bringing new life. Madness is not merely a punishment; it is the god's gift to those who follow him, offering the loss of the burdensome sense of self.

It is not surprising that this god of madness and destruction should be represented as "foreign" in the myths of the ancient Greeks. To the rational, conscious mind, which values order and balance above passion and spontaneity, Dionysus must appear the antithesis of all that is good and right. The reluctance to embrace this foreign being, the unwillingness to acknowledge his power, is an understandable human response. To many ancient Greeks (who invented rationalism), he must have seemed, by his very nature, to be something especially strange, something new. Wherever Dionysus and his cult originated, the persistent portrayal of him as a new god, and likewise the many stories of the resistance he encountered, must reflect the Greeks' aversion to the violent, irrational side of human existence, their reluctance, and ours, to accept the power of unreason.

THE CULT OF DIONYSUS

Like the cult of Demeter, that of Dionysus is reflected in the myths told about him. The evidence we have makes clear that the Dionysian religion was quite different from those devoted to other ancient deities. The original Olympian gods were separated from human beings by a great gulf symbolized by the poetic conception of Zeus and his court as ruling from the high peaks of Mount Olympus. These gods were known through their works, helpful or harmful, but were rarely directly manifest to ordinary human beings. Dionysus was different. Most stories about him take place on earth, in the midst of human beings. The Greeks believed they could feel his presence in a direct way, and the cultivation of this experience was a central focus of his religion. Many features of the myths of Dionysus are best understood as reflections of the practices of his cult.

He was "the god who comes," and the myths tell of his sudden and violent arrival in Greek cities. The intense emotion felt by individual followers must have come in a similarly abrupt and decisive manner. The god's presence in his followers was called *enthousiasmos*, "being filled with the god" (the origin of our word *enthusiasm*).

His followers experienced *ekstasis*, "standing outside oneself" (hence our word *ecstasy*). When Dionysus was present, his devotees lost their sense of personal identity and became one with the god. So strong was this sense of oneness that the follower was called Bacchus too. With the loss of identity came a willingness to transcend ordinary standards of decent and rational conduct. Appropriately, Dionysus was known as *lysios*, "deliverer": Through their enthusiastic and ecstatic communion with the god, his devotees were temporarily released from everyday life and united with a cosmic force.

The presence of a crowd of witnesses fostered the experience of Dionysian ecstasy, as suggested in myth by the band of followers who always surround the god, the maenads and satyrs. Continuous dancing to the beating of drums and the playing of flutes, and the consumption of wine, led devotees to direct experience of the god. So did the communal tearing apart of an animal (*sparagmos*) and the eating of its raw flesh (*ōmophagia*). In prehistoric times this practice may have taken a cannibalistic form, with human beings as victims. In the myths, Pentheus is torn limb from limb (although not actually eaten) by the god's crazed followers, Ino boils her son in a pot, and the Minyads eat their own children. The myths no doubt exaggerate the more sensational forms of the cult; cannibalism and human sacrifice were abhorrent by the Archaic and Classical periods. Still, we have inscriptional evidence that Dionysus' followers really did practice the "eating of raw flesh" as late as the Hellenistic Period.

The cult of Dionysus appealed especially to women, whose social responsibilities were to preserve the stability of the family. Some explain this by saying that women are more emotional than men and thus more likely to embrace a religion centered on intense feeling; others suggest that women formed an oppressed class in Greece who longed for the ecstatic release that Dionysian religion could provide. Whatever the correct explanation, in myth Dionysus is surrounded by women: his nurse, Ino; the nymphs of Nysa; the maenads; and his wife, Ariadnê. The nymphs of Nysa in particular, as nourishers and followers of the god, were mythic models for the bands of female devotees. Although Euripides (who liked to defy his audience's expectations) describes the Bacchae's behavior as chaste, sexual profligacy was undoubtedly a feature of the real religion. It is not surprising that Hera, protectress of the family, would oppose the raging god who excited married women to madness and caused them to forget their duty to husband, family, and community.

Greek and Roman religions in general lacked creeds and claimed little moral authority, but they did develop local priesthoods, which eventually became integral parts of the institutions of the state. In this way the savage features of Dionysiac religion disappeared from the festivals of the Classical Period. Nevertheless, on several occasions the worship of Dionysus was felt to be a political threat. In Rome his cult grew to such proportions during the long and painful war with Carthage that in 186 B.C. an alarmed senate, after many executions, brought it under severe restrictions.

In the Christian Period Dionysus came to be viewed as an evil demon. From his religion and the cult of Pan (Chapter 7) derive the goatish qualities of popular representations of the devil and the attribution to the devil of ritual indulgence in intoxicants and sex. Yet the Dionysian notion of the identification of god and worshiper became central to Christian doctrine and is sometimes expressed in terms strikingly similar to those current in Dionysiac cult. For example, from the *Book of Common Prayer of the Church of England* (A.D. 1549, still used in churches of the Anglican Communion):

> Grant us therefore, gracious Lord, so to eat the flesh of thy dear Son Jesus Christ, and to drink his blood . . . that we may evermore dwell in him and he in us.

Paradoxically, the pagan god of drunkenness and sexual license served as one model for the early Christians in their attempts to understand their relationship to their own dying god. Sarcophagi with scenes from the stories of Dionysus often were reused for Christian burials. In the eleventh or twelfth century A.D. an unknown Byzantine author, no doubt inspired by parallels between Pentheus' interrogation of Dionysus and Pontius Pilate's of Christ, put together a work called *Christus Patiens* (*The Suffering Christ*), the story of the crucifixion told as a Greek tragedy. *Christus Patiens* is made up entirely of lines taken from ancient drama, especially the *Bacchae*.[7]

DIONYSUS, GOD OF THE THEATER

Dionysus also played an important role in Greek culture through his association with the theater. Many of the best-known Greek myths are preserved as the plots of tragedies performed in his honor. Beginning in the sixth century B.C., tragedies were performed at a spring festival of Dionysus in Athens known as the Lenaea (le-nē-a), "festival of the maenads."[8] Others were performed at the more important City Dionysia, probably reorganized in the mid–sixth century B.C. by the popular leader Pisistratus and again near the end of the century by the democratic leader Clisthenes. During the City Dionysia, held on consecutive days in the Theater of Dionysus on the south slopes of the Acropolis (Fig. 10.8), each of three tragedians presented a group of three tragedies and one satyr play. The satyr play (a burlesque of a mythic theme) had a chorus of satyrs (compare Fig. 10.5). On a fourth day, comedies were performed, a genre noted for ribaldry, obscenity, and verbal license. The production costs for all these plays were paid for by a wealthy citizen as a public service. Some elements in Greek drama seem to be traceable to the cult of Dionysus, in whose honor these festivals were held, but more than a hundred years of intensive scholarship have been unable to clarify the precise relationship between the cult and Greek drama.

Aristotle, writing two hundred years after the event, offers the earliest theory of the development of tragedy (*Poetics* 3–5). According to him, tragedy originated from "those who led off the dithyramb." The dithyramb was at first a hymn to Dionysus, and later any hymn with a heroic subject.[9] The early tragic chorus was composed (Aristotle says) of satyrs, followers of Dionysus who had some of the physical char-

[7]Portions of the end of the *Bacchae*, lost from the manuscripts, have been recovered from this work.
[8]*Lênai* is still another name for the maenads, meaning something like "those of the wine vat" (see Fig. 10.7)
[9]For example, Bacchylides' poem on Theseus (see Chapter 16) is said to be a dithyramb.

FIG. 10.8. The Theater of Dionysus in Athens, built on the southern slope of the Acropolis. All extant Greek tragedies were performed in this theater. The horseshoe-shaped orchestra, constructed in the Roman Period, has replaced the original round dancing place, or *orchêstra*. Foundation stones from the ancient stage building can be seen behind the orchêstra.   (Author's photo).

acteristics of goats (*tragoi;* the word *tragedy,* Greek *tragoidia,* means "goat song").[10] At first the stories were light-hearted and the tone ludicrous; later, they became longer and the tone more serious.

In modern times, three influential theories about the origin of tragedy have been proposed. The first is based on Aristotle: Tragedy evolved from the dithyramb, that is, from a ritual celebration of the god Dionysus. The second is based on anthropological evidence: Tragedy grew out of a religious mystery performance, such as that of Eleusis (see Chapter 9). The third is based on the internal evidence of the many formal laments for the dead in surviving plays: Tragedy grew out of a cult of the dead, a ritual mourning of a hero's ghost.

All three explanations have in common the desire to see in Greek tragedy something sacred to the god Dionysus, coming from and belonging to a religious realm. However, there is a strong possibility that the origin of tragedy had more to do with

[10]In fact, in art of the fifth century satyrs were horselike; only later did they acquire the attributes of goats.

Nietzsche's *The Birth of Tragedy*

The figure of Dionysus played a prominent role in the writings of influential German classicist and philosopher Friedrich Nietzsche (1844–1900), particularly in *The Birth of Tragedy,* an early work in which Nietzsche sharply criticized the prevailing view of Greek art and civilization. Before Nietzsche, Greek culture was understood as embodying the calm, rational values of balance and harmony; Greek art was worth studying and emulating, people thought, because it embodied "a noble simplicity and a quiet grandeur," as art historian Johann Winckelmann wrote in the eighteenth century. According to Winckelmann, Apollo was a perfect expression of these ideals. But Nietzsche's analysis of the origin of tragedy led him to a different view, that the creative spirit of the Greeks was Dionysus, who represented wild, exuberant emotion, the desire to break through norms, the longing to unite ecstatically with one's fellows and with nature itself.

Nietzsche used classical Greek tragedy to bolster his argument. Greek tragedy consists not only of dialogue between characters but of commentary by the chorus. Nietzsche viewed dialogue as the Apollonian, intellectual part of the genre, but historically earlier was the chorus, whose members were closely connected with the cult of Dionysus: in origin (according to Aristotle) the chorus were dressed as half-goat, half-human satyrs, devotees of the god. This Dionysian element, Nietzsche thought, was essential. Greek tragedy therefore reflects a tension between opposite forces, a synthesis of Apollonian and Dionysian principles. If we overlook the Dionysian element and emphasize the Apollonian, Nietzsche argued, we reach a distorted understanding of Greek tragedy and Greek culture itself.

Nietzsche considered his discovery to be important not only for classicists, but for everyone concerned with the rejuvenation of modern culture, dominated for too long by intellectuals following the rationalist Greek philosopher Socrates. What the modern world needed was a reawakening of the Dionysian spirit:

> Yes, my friends, believe with me in Dionysian life and the rebirth of tragedy. The age of the Socratic man is over; put on wreaths of ivy, put the thyrsus into your hand, and do not be surprised when tigers and panthers lie down, fawning, at your feet. Only dare to be tragic men; for you are to be redeemed. You shall accompany the Dionysian pageant from India to Greece. Prepare yourselves for hard strife, but believe in the miracles of your god.
>
> NIETZSCHE, *The Birth of Tragedy,* Sec. 20.

Nietzsche's later works developed the notion that modern Western culture, dominated by a "slave mentality" fostered by Christianity, was in a decadent state and required radical reform. Proclaiming himself "the last disciple and initiate of the god Dionysus," Nietzsche, in *Beyond Good and Evil* (1886), called for the appearance of a new vitality, a new spirit embodied in a superior man who transcended the petty morality of bourgeois life, much as Dionysus crossed the boundaries of space and convention in Greek myth.

Nietzsche's life ended unhappily. He went insane after contracting syphilis and spent the last ten years of his life in the care of his family. In his deteriorated mental state, he identified more closely with the Greek god who had inspired him and sometimes signed his confused, incoherent letters with the name *Dionysus*.

literary invention and politics than religion. In discussing the origins of tragedy, Aristotle noted that a man named **Thespis** (late sixth century B.C., none of whose works survive) added to a preexisting chorus "a prologue and a speech." We may interpret his remark as a remembrance that as a literary form, tragedy was the invention of a single man, a new way to tell a story. Before tragedy, characters in myth were described from the outside, in the third person. That is the way Homer tells a story, and this was the natural form of storytelling at the aristocratic symposium. Thespis' radical innovation was to have an actor take on the role of a mythical character and speak in the first person as that character. The chorus, too, consisting of perhaps twelve dancers, always speaks as a character in a dramatic situation (Fig. 10.9). Aristotle also tells us that Thespis introduced "the first actor," by which he must mean someone speaking in the first person who presented a crisis in the career of a mythic figure, perhaps a moment of fateful decision. Thespis' innovations—and the use of

FIG. 10.9. A half-chorus of dancing youths, on an Attic vase for mixing wine, c. 500–480 B.C., probably illustrating a lost play of Aeschylus, *The Youths*. The play may therefore be older than any surviving Greek tragedy (our oldest is Aeschylus' *Persians,* 472 B.C.). Aeschylus' "Youths" were followers of Dionysus and, in the story, may have had something to do with the punishment of Lycurgus. Their arms are outstretched as they dance barefoot toward a typically stepped altar, an important prop in Greek tragedy. They wear light masks and embroidered outfits with a similar design. A suppliant sits on the altar.   (Antikenmuseum, Basel; BS 415)

masks—made possible the presentation on stage of visible, direct conflict between characters prominent in traditional tales. Later, says Aristotle, Aeschylus added a second actor and lessened the role of the chorus, and Sophocles added the third actor.

Thespis must have made his fateful invention some time in the reign of the Athenian tyrant Pisistratus. To please the *dêmos*, the Athenian people from whom Pisistratus derived important political support, Pisistratus reformed an old festival of Dionysus and made of it something popular and well attended; Dionysus was a god of the *dêmos*. Pisistratus seems to have sponsored Thespis' new form of storytelling, one no longer confined to aristocratic symposia but presented before all "the people" in the citywide drinking party that was the City Dionysia. In this way drama, which Aristotle described as the "imitation of an action," the public presentation of personalities locked in conflict, was born. Thus political motives could have had more to do with the origins of tragedy than religious ones.

We know little for certain about the origins of tragedy, but the origins of comedy, "revel-song," are still more obscure, although the genre may be far older than tragedy. Aristotle's remarks on the origins of comedy are lost, but presumably, at some unknown time, a dramatic element was added to the Dionysian *kômos*, "revel," a sort of parade of drunken men singing songs. Almost everything we know about comedy contemporary with the surviving tragedies, called Old Comedy, is derived from the plays of Aristophanes (c. 450–388 B.C.; see Perspective 5.1). Unlike the plots of tragedy, those of Attic comedy were not mythical but based on some fantastic notion. In Aristophanes' *Birds*, birds band together to take over the world; in his *Lysistrata* (li-**sis**-tra-ta), the women of Greece withhold sex from their husbands to stop the war between Athens and Sparta. There was always a strong political element in comedy: Contemporary politicians or civic policies were held up to scorn and ridicule. Myths and conventional theology also were ridiculed, but Athenian comedy holds far more importance for historians than for students of myth.

KEY TERMS

Semelê, 250
Ino, 250
nymphs of Nysa, 250
Bacchae, 252
maenads, 252
satyrs, 252
Midas, 252

Ariadnê, 252
Lycurgus, 254
Minyads, 255
Proetids, 255
Agavê, 257
Pentheus, 257
Thespis, 280

FURTHER READING

Carpenter, Thomas H., and Christopher A. Faraone, eds., *Masks of Dionysus* (Ithaca, N.Y., 1993). The relationship of Dionysus to tragedy and his influence on the modern world; essays by leading scholars.

Detienne, Marcel, *Dionysos at Large* (Cambridge, Mass., 1989). A study by the eminent French interpreter, using the methods of comparative social science.

Dodds, E. R., introduction to *Euripides' Bacchae,* 2nd ed. (Oxford, U.K., 1960). The best short discussion of the religion and myths of Dionysus.

———, *The Greeks and the Irrational* (Berkeley, Calif., 1951; reprinted 1973). A classic investigation of the importance of unreason among the Greeks, the discoverers of reason.

Else, Gerald F., *The Origin and Early Form of Greek Tragedy* (New York, 1972). Presents Thespis as the inventor of Greek tragedy.

Lewis, Ian, *Ecstatic Religion, A Study of Shamanism and Spirit Possession,* 2nd ed. (London, 1989). Excellent general study.

Nietzsche, F. W., *The Birth of Tragedy out of the Spirit of Music,* trans. W. Kaufmann (New York, 1968). The German edition of this book, published in 1871, set the stage for the modern appreciation of the role of the irrational in Greek culture.

Otto, W. F., *Dionysus, Myth and Cult* (Bloomington, Ind., 1965; originally published in Germany in 1933). Despite its romantic style, Otto judiciously summarizes the ancient evidence and argues for Dionysus as an indigenous Greek god.

Pickard-Cambridge, Arthur W., *Dithyramb, Tragedy, and Comedy,* 2nd ed., ed. by T.B.L. Webster (Oxford, U.K., 1962). Thorough treatment of the evidence; indispensable to the study of the subject.

West, M. L., *Ancient Greek Music* (Oxford, U.K., 1992). The definitive study.

Winkler, John J., and Froma I. Zeitlin, eds., *Nothing to Do with Dionysos? Athenian Drama in Its Social Context* (Princeton, N.J., 1990). Collection of modern essays addressing diverse aspects of Athenian drama.

Winnington-Ingram, R. P., *Euripides and Dionysus* (Cambridge, Mass., 1948). A detailed examination of Euripides' *Bacchae.*

CHAPTER 11

MYTHS OF DEATH

ENCOUNTERS WITH THE UNDERWORLD

You will die and be silent. No memory will be left of you,
no regret when you are gone. You have never touched the Muses' flowers.
Shadowy forever in Death's realm,
you will be wafted on a ghost's fluttering wings,
one of the black dead.

SAPPHO, fragment 58 (Diehl)

THE GREATEST MYSTERY IN LIFE is death, to which we are all subject. The Greeks, like all peoples, held complex attitudes toward death and the dead, and many stories reflect them. The myths of fertility we have just examined are themselves deeply concerned with the meaning of death and its place in the natural and human order. But death and the afterlife can be conceived in different ways. The Greeks' bleak conception of the afterlife (so different from that of the Egyptians) contributed importantly to their conviction that happiness must be achieved in this world. Some mythical figures actually escaped death, either by becoming gods or by achieving immortality in a paradise somewhere at the edge of the world. A recurring theme in Greek myth is descent into and return from the world of the dead; we have already seen it in the myth of Demeter and Persephonê (Chapter 9). In this chapter we look at the principal ancient conceptions of death and the dead and examine accounts of the underworld in Homer's *Odyssey* and Vergil's *Aeneid*.

THE GREEK VIEW OF DEATH

We think of death as a natural process, but the notion is modern. No doubt "natural death," as we conceive of it, was uncommon in the ancient world, and to the early

Greeks and other early peoples, death did not seem to come inevitably in the course of things. It was felt to be caused by a hostile force from the natural world (a storm, an animal attack), from a human being (an enemy soldier), or from the invisible and inexplicable realm of gods, ghosts, and priests. Today we suppose that only human beings can make decisions and carry them out, but the ancients attributed powers of choice and action to everything that exists. They believed that human beings are the constant victims of these choices. Even when death was caused by an obvious external event, such as a storm or a human or animal attack, it could still be the result of a god's will; in Homer's *Iliad* the gods stand beside their favorite heroes and guide their weapons or in other ways bring about the death of their opponents. There were stories of men who never died, who had somehow escaped the dangerous forces that, for most, made death inevitable.

Any god could cause the death of a mortal, but one played a special role. **Hades** (**hā**-dēz), apparently "the unseen one," was the general agent of death, removing the dead from the sight of the living. The dead were buried in the earth, and Hades was appropriately associated with a realm beneath the earth's surface. The brother of Zeus and Poseidon, he received the underworld as his lot when rule over the universe was divided. Thus he was also called **Pluto,** the "enricher," because from beneath the earth comes mineral and agricultural wealth. The Romans borrowed this latter Greek name, although they also called him Dis or Dives (**dī**-vēz), Latin for "rich"; the Romans called the death god's realm Orcus, which probably means "the place that confines." Hades was often referred to by his epithets, such as *Polydegmôn,* "receiver of many," and *Polyxenos,* "host to many." Just as many people today avoid the words *die* and *death,* the Greeks often regarded Hades as a god too dangerous to call by his real name.

In spite of rationalist doubters, always important in Greece, most ancient Greeks believed that individual human beings continued to exist after death, although in an attenuated form. The buried body might decay, or the cremated body turn to ash, but the soul survived as a sort of "image" (*eidolon*) dwelling thereafter in a separate realm ordinarily unseen by the living. Traditionally, the soul was associated with the breath, the invisible, barely tangible natural element that animates the living body. The connection can be seen in the derivation of the Greek and Latin words for "soul": The Greek *psychê* originally meant "breath," and the Latin *anima* is related to the Greek word *anem-,* "wind."[1] Similarly, the Latin word *spiritus,* "spirit," means "breath." In Sanskrit and Hebrew, too, the word for "wind" or "breath" (*atma* and *ruach*) is the same as that which designates the immaterial part of a human being. No doubt the Greeks and Romans, like many other early peoples, observed that breathing is what distinguishes the living from the dead. We breathe continually for as long as we live—even in sleep, when we appear to be doing nothing else. The ancients logically inferred that breath is the basis for all the other activities of a living human

---

[1]From *psychê* comes psychology = "study of the soul" and psychoanalysis = "a breaking down of the soul." From the Indo-European Sanskrit *atma,* "breath," comes *Mahatma,* "great-souled," as in *Mahatma Gandhi.* In the Bible, we are told that "the Lord God formed man of dust from the ground and breathed into his nostrils the breath of life (*ruach*); and man became a living being" (Genesis 2.7.5). The word *ruach* is also used for the "spirit" of God that moved over the face of the waters (Genesis 1.2).

being, such as sensing, thinking, and moving. The body performs these functions only as long as the breath or soul is present within it. The body is thus only the material part of a human being; the soul is the warm, invisible force that animates the body for the duration of the person's life. Such observations, when refined by Plato and Christian theologians, were to form the basis for deep philosophical speculations about the relationship of the human to the divine.

Most peoples agree that the soul retains its airlike nature even after it has departed the body. The dead exist as ghosts, as bodiless breath-souls that are invisible, intangible, elusive, and ordinarily known only through their effects. We may dismiss the fear of ghosts as superstition (although some are wary of cemeteries in the dark of night), but the existence of ghosts is a logical inference from the comparison of live with dead bodies: They are superficially the same, but one breathes, the other does not. Obviously the breath, the ghost, has escaped from the dead body and is abroad in the world, invisible, probably unhappy, and certainly dangerous. In the living body the ghost is present not only in the breath, but in the blood as well. That is why the shedding of blood brings death.[2] These disembodied spirits usually lead a dark, shadowy existence in the underworld realm of Hades. Occasionally, however, they emerge to haunt the world of the living, especially when not properly "laid" through appropriate ritual. Some ghosts work to protect human interests; for example, Hesiod tells us that when the men of the Gold and Silver races died, they became beneficent spirits. More often, however, the ghosts of the dead aim to bring misfortune to human beings. They long to rejoin their former bodies and are envious of the living, who still know the pleasures of food, sex, and wealth. Some are bent on revenge, as were the Greek **Erinyes,** or Furies, mythical portrayals of the ghosts of slain members of one's own family. Precautions had to be taken to ensure the safety of the living without infringing on the rights of the often malevolent dead.

Many customs of the ancient Greeks originated as ways of warding off the angry, threatening ghosts. Some were designed to persuade the spirit that the surivors had not benefited from a person's death; thus the person's most valued possessions, weapons and jewelry, were buried with the corpse or burned on the pyre. Dark and gloomy clothes showed the survivors' sadness, and the loosening of the hair and the scratching of the face and breasts by mourning women showed how they too suffered. To further mollify the envious and vindictive spirit, a special house might be built for the dead (the tomb), sometimes imitating the houses of the living. The Etruscans built elaborate houses underground for their dead, then buried the ashes in house-shaped urns. There the ghost lived on, as a hero or family ancestor, and could appear to well-wishers as a friendly snake (called *agathos daimon,* "good spirit"), eat honey-cakes set out for it, then slither back into the tomb. Respect might also be given through mourning songs and eulogies and, at least in myth, even sexual companionship provided by the sacrifice of female slaves over the tombs of the mighty; thus the Trojan princess Polyxena was sacrificed over the tomb of Achilles (see Fig. 20.5). The famous pyramids of the ancient Egyptians were an exaggerated expression of ghost cult, symbolic buildings in which dwelt the powerful ghost of the de-

---

[2]Consider the biblical injunction against eating blood: "For the life of the flesh is in the blood of it" (Leviticus 17.14).

parted pharaoh. Because the breath-soul required a body to function properly, the Egyptians mummified the corpse (unlike Homer's Greeks, who ensured complete separation of soul from body by cremation). In case the corpse was nonetheless destroyed, the Egyptians made lifelike stone statues as substitute bodies—the origin of large-scale sculpture to imitate the human form. The early Greeks, copying Egyptian usage, put statues on graves.

Some peoples banished or "laid" the ghost by cutting the corpse to pieces, burning it on a pyre, or imprisoning it beneath a large stone (one origin of the tombstone). Another precaution was tying up the corpse; the feet of the baby Oedipus, exposed on the mountain to die, were pinned together to prevent the royal infant's ghost from walking. Because ghosts were considered stupid and readily confused, they might easily lose their way to the other world and thereafter bring misfortune to the living who would like to be rid of them; fortunately, Hermes was prepared to lead them to Hades' house and relieve this world of the burden of their presence. In this capacity Hermes is called **psychopompos** (si-ko-**pom**-pus) "soul-guide" (see Fig. 11.1). Ghosts were thought to be frightened by loud noises. The wails of mourners not only were flattering, but drove the ghosts away, as do noisemakers at weddings, where ghosts flock, attracted by the spectacle of human happiness and sexual pleasure that death has cruelly taken from them. Yet another strategy to appease the ghosts was to allow them one or two nights a year when they could mingle freely with the living. Thus ghosts were invited to the Athenian spring festival of the Anthesteria, "the festival of the sending up [of vegetation]," but on the last day expelled with the cry, "Out the door you go, you souls of the dead! The Anthesteria is finished!"[3]

The common view of the breath-soul was eventually questioned by Greek intellectuals. The invention of alphabetic writing made it possible to record traditional ideas and analyze them in new ways. Many Greek philosophers came to doubt that the soul survived after death as a ghostly shadow in Hades' realm. The philosopher Epicurus (341–270 B.C.) denied that the soul survives death, which is the soul's end as well as the body's, a view widely held by modern philosophers. Still, the traditional view persisted among most ancient Greeks and Romans, and on this view were based several of the best-known classical myths.

ODYSSEUS' JOURNEY TO DEATH'S REALM

The earliest testimony to popular Greek belief about the dead comes from Homer's *Odyssey*. The Greek hero Odysseus tells the strange story of his journey to the other world at a banquet given by the king of the island of Phaeacia, where he has been shipwrecked on his way home to Ithaca. Lost on the high seas after sacking Troy, Odysseus was instructed by the witch Circê to seek advice from the ghost of **Tiresias** (ti-**rē**-si-as), in life the most famous seer in Greek myth and an important character in Euripides' *Bacchae* (Chapter 10). Tiresias was descended from one of the Sparti ("sown-men"), the five founders of the ruling families of Thebes, who sprang from

---

[3]A similar manner of thinking gives rise to Halloween ("All Hallows' Eve," the night before All Saints' Day, November 1), when the ghosts are allowed to come forth from their tombs and beg for food. If refused, they will do harm ("trick or treat!").

the teeth of a dragon killed by Cadmus (Chart 17.1). According to post-Homeric accounts, when still a young man, Tiresias saw a pair of serpents coupling and killed the female. As a punishment, he was turned into a woman. After seven years he (or she) again saw a pair of serpents coupling. This time he was careful to kill the male and was turned back into a man.[4]

To inquire of the prophet, who had died a generation before, Odysseus set sail for the shores of Ocean, the mythical river thought to surround the world.

[11]   We carefully checked the gear in every part of the vessel,
        then all of us took our places. Wind and helmsman sped her along,
        and all day long her bellying sail drew the ship on her voyage.
        The sun set at last, and darkness had fallen all over the world,
15   when we finally reached the edge of the deep-tided current of Ocean,
        to the land and city where dwell the Cimmerians, shrouded in mist,
        sunken in endless dark clouds. The sun never looks down upon them,
        with his radiant beam—not when he climbs to the stars in the heaven,
        not when he turns once more to the earth, and the perils of darkness
20   once more enfold wretched men.
            We beached the vessel, and from it unloaded its cargo of sheep,
        then out we set on foot along the shore of the Ocean,
        until we arrived at the place described in Circê's directions.
        Two of my men, Perimedes and Eurylochus, tethered the victims,
25   while I drew my sharp-edged sword from my side and dug out a pit
        a foot and a half each way, into which I poured our oblation
        of drink for the dead to consume: first honey mingled with milk,
        then sweet wine, and last of all water thickened with barley.
        I promised the strengthless ghosts that, safely landed in Ithaca,
30   I would offer there in my palace a heifer that never had calved,
        my best, and would load an altar with good things for them alone.
        I also promised a ram, the best of the rams in my flock,
        for Tiresias all by himself. So I promised the crowds of the dead,
        then slit the throats of the sheep so the blood ran into the hollow.
35   Up from Erebus sallied the bodiless souls of the dead—
        brides and unmarried young men; feeble rheumatic old gaffers;
        maidens once happy but now broken-hearted; men killed by the spear;
        young soldiers, still in their armor—all crowded around the pit,
        with indescribable screaming, till cold fear seized on my heart.
40   I hastily ordered my comrades to flay the sacrificed sheep,
        dead by my sword, and to burn the bodies with prayer to the gods,
        to mighty Hades and awesome Persephonê. Meanwhile I waited,

---

[4]Shamans sometimes dress themselves in clothes of the opposite sex and imitate their behavior, and that is probably the origin of this story. The Greeks spun a typical joke around the transformation of Tiresias. Zeus and Hera were battling furiously over who got the greater pleasure from sexual intercourse, men or women. Because Tiresias was the only person who had both experiences, they put the question to him. Tiresias replied without hesitation that of ten parts in the enjoyment of sex, women receive nine, and men but one. In a rage at this impertinent reply Hera blinded Tiresias. Zeus compensated him with the gift of prophecy and a lifetime extending through seven generations of men.

drawing my keen-edged saber, a menace to frail nerveless spirits,
keeping them off from the blood till I could question Tiresias.

45   The first to approach was the ghost of my good comrade Elpenor,
whose body was not yet buried under the broad-stretching earth.
We had left it, unmourned and unburied, back in the palace of Circê,
for other labors were calling. My eyes filled with tears as I watched
and spoke these words of pity, words which flew straight to the mark:

50   "Elpenor, how did you come down here to the echoing darkness,
traveling faster on foot than I in our dark-sided vessel?"
Such were my words. With a groan my comrade Elpenor responded:
    "Noble son of Laërtes, Odysseus the wise and resourceful,
an evil fate sent from heaven, and too much wine and too potent,

55 fuddled my wits and brought on my death in the palace of Circê.
From my bed on the roof I stumbled to find the long downward ladder,
but plunged headlong to the ground and broke the bones of my neck.
My soul fluttered down to Hades. Now hear my last supplication:
I beg you, by those you have left behind in the land of the living,

60 by your wife, by the father who raised you, tiny child that you were,
by Telemachus, your only son, whom you left at home in the palace—
since I know that you will go back once more from the house of Hades,
to Circê's isle of Aeaea in your speedy and well-built vessel—
when you arrive there, my lord, remember my final entreaty:

65 when again you set out for home, do not leave me unwept and unburied,
abandoned, hateful to gods. But lay me to rest with my weapons,
with everything that is mine, in a grave on the coast of the sea,
the tomb of a poor hapless man, a reminder to those who come after.
Grant me that favor, and this: mount on my tomb the same oar

70 that I swung in the land of the living, seated alongside my fellows."
    So Elpenor requested, and at once I gave him my answer:
"Of course I shall do what you ask, poor fellow, in every detail."
    Thus then the two of us sat, discussing a matter so gloomy,
I on one side of the blood-filled pit, with my vigilant weapon,

75 the ghost of my friend on the other, showing what he wanted done.
    Presently up there came the ghost of my long-dead mother,
Anticlea, the daughter of Autolycus,° mighty of spirit.
Her I had left, still alive, on my way to Troy's holy city.
My tears welled up when I saw her, and pity filled all my heart;

80 but, grieved though I was, I dared not let her come up to the blood,
until I should learn the future from Tiresias, wisest of prophets.
The ghost of Tiresias the Theban, golden staff in his hand,
was next to appear; he recognized me, and thus he addressed me:
    "Son of Laërtes, descendant of Zeus, pray tell me, poor fellow

85 why have you left the light of the sun and come down to the dead
in their grim and joyless land? Step back, I pray, from the pit;
hold your weapon aside, so that I may drink your oblation,
and afterward tell you the truth."

HOMER, *Odyssey* (11.11–96)

---

77. *Autolycus:* A famous trickster and thief, the son of Hermes, from whom Odysseus doubtless inherited his wily intelligence.

After drinking the blood, Tiresias warns Odysseus about the dangers that lie ahead, the suitors who besiege his home, and the nature of his death.

The Cimmerians (sim-**mē**-ri-anz) were a real people who in Homer's day lived north of the Black Sea—seemingly, to the Greeks, at the very end of the world. Homer mythologizes the Cimmerians and places them in the extreme west beside the river Ocean, which bounds the earth and separates the living from the dead (for some reason, ghosts are unable to cross water). This region where the sun never shines is not presented as the land of the dead as such but as a place where the dead can be approached. The honey, milk, wine, water, barley, and blood that Odysseus pours into the pit are to feed the strengthless shades and allow them to speak. In the story, Odysseus plays the role of a necromancer, a magician who summons spirits of the dead to question them and gain knowledge. His ordinary sword functions as a magical weapon, restraining the thirsty, disembodied ghosts from the life-restoring vapors of the fresh blood.

Elpenor (el-**pē**-nor), ghost of one of Odysseus' own companions (Fig. 11.1), is first to appear at the pit of blood. He is able to speak without drinking because his

FIG. 11.1. Odysseus and the ghost of Elpenor, Attic vase, c. 460–430 B.C. On the left Elpenor rises from the ground, attracted by the pit of blood; the skins of the sacrificed rams are heaped at his feet. Odysseus holds his sword in his left hand and thoughtfully supports his chin with the other. Hermes psychopompos is at the right, wearing winged helmet and boots and carrying the caduceus. (Museum of Fine Arts, Boston; 34.79)

ghost, not yet "laid," is still abroad in the land of the living. Elpenor begs for proper burial, but the need to lay the ghost is, in origin, in the interests of the living.

After hearing Tiresias' prophesy about his own fortunes, Odysseus asks him how he might be able to speak with the ghost of his mother, Anticlea (an-ti-klē-a):

[141] "Tiresias, yonder I see the ghost of my dear dead mother,
waiting in silence beside the blood, not daring to face me,
her son though I am, nor address me in words. Now tell me, my lord:
how can she know it is I, how recognize me as her son?"
145 Thus I questioned the seer, who promptly replied to my question:
"The answer to that is easy; store my reply in your heart.
Whichever of these dead folk you allow to draw up to the blood,
will tell you the truth, but those you refuse must retire within."
With that Tiresias' ghost sank back again to the dwelling
150 of Hades, once he had finished revealing what destiny ordered.
But I stood waiting in silence, while my mother, approaching the pit,
drank of the dark-clouded blood and recognized me as I waited.
She heaved a sigh from her heart and asked the natural question:
"My son, how is it you come, still alive, to this echoing gloom?
155 No easy task for the living to find what is here in the darkness!
Great rivers and horrible torrents swirl between in the journey,
and chiefly the Ocean itself, which no one can ever pass over
on foot, but must make his voyage on the deck of a well-built ship."

HOMER, *Odyssey* (11.141–159)

Anticlea tells of her death from grief over Odysseus' long absence. Odysseus, longing to embrace her, three times reaches out his arms; three times she flutters away like a dream or a shadow:

[210] "Dear mother, why do you shrink away and avoid my embrace?
Even in Hades, can we not put our arms round each other
and give full play to our grief? Has Persephonê sent an illusion
to deceive me and make me sorrow the more in my aching grief?"
To my plea the lady my mother replied, "Alas, my poor son,
215 miserable, more than all men, this is no deceit of the goddess
Persephonê, daughter of Zeus, but the fate of all who have perished.
No more do the sinews hold their flesh and bones in their places,
but the burning heat of the pyre overwhelms and crumbles our flesh.
Once the soul has abandoned the body, the poor homeless spirit
220 must flutter about like a dream, then vanish forever. So hurry!
Fight your way back to the light, to tell your wife your adventures."

HOMER, *Odyssey* (11.210–222)

Persephonê, queen of the dead, sends other spirits up to drink of the blood— first the women of olden times, then the heroes who died at Troy. Agamemnon, king of Mycenae, murdered by his wife, Clytemnestra, when he came back from Troy, appears and complains bitterly; he warns Odysseus to trust no woman, not even his

faithful wife, Penelopê. Achilles, greatest of all the Achaeans, is next to come to the
pit and address Odysseus:

[473]   "Noble son of Laërtes, Odysseus, the wise and resourceful,
        man with a heart of steel, what harder task can you dream of?
475   How did you summon the courage to descend to the palace of Hades,
        down to the half-conscious dead, the shades of men who have perished?"
            So Achilles inquired, and I gave him an honest reply:
        "Achilles, Peleus' son, by far the bravest Achaean,
        I have come down to inquire of wise far-sighted Tiresias,
480   if he could direct me home to Ithaca, rugged and stony.
        For never have I drawn near to the coast of the land of Achaea,
        nor landed in my dear homeland, but am always dogged by misfortune.
            "No one, Achilles, of all men past or yet to be born
        has been more blessed than you. We Argives gave you honor
485   equal to that of a god, and, now you have migrated hither,
        you govern the dead. Don't mutter complaining of death, Achilles!"
            I scolded him in these words, but Achilles quickly retorted,
        "Don't you attempt to instruct me on death, O learned Odysseus!
        Better to be a peon on some poor landholder's acres,
490   a man who is landless and hungry himself, than here to be ruler
        of all these shriveled-up dead."

                                    HOMER, *Odyssey* (11.473–491)

The famous reply of Achilles sums up the pessimistic view the Greeks held of the afterlife. Achilles goes on to ask about his son Neoptolemus and joyfully departs on
learning of the young man's achievement. Next comes Ajax, who committed suicide
when Odysseus, rather than he, was awarded the armor of the dead Achilles. Even
in death he bears his grudge: Too angry even to speak, his silent ghost disappears
among the crowd of spirits.

At this point Homer forgets that Odysseus is on the shore of Ocean. Without explanation he shifts the hero into the underworld itself:

[566]   Next I beheld King Minos, the glorious son of great Zeus,
        seated, with scepter of gold, as arbiter over the spirits.
        They crowded, seated or standing, before the wide portals of Hades,
        pleading their cause before Minos, who served them as ruler and judge.
570   Behind him I noticed the form of mighty Orion, the giant,
        beating the bushes for game all through the asphodel° meadows.
        Some he slew with his bludgeon, off in the desolate mountains,
        his club of unbreakable bronze, which he swung in his powerful hands.

                                    HOMER, *Odyssey* (11.566–575)

571. *asphodel:* A pale weed growing wild in Greece and southern Italy, associated with the dead and
to this day often planted on graves.

Homer describes Minos (**mī**-nos) as a judge; a better English word would be *ar-
bitrator.* He decides quarrels in accordance with existing custom, but they are fresh

quarrels, not carried over from the litigants' life on the earth. His sentences are not punishments of moral shortcomings but decrees designed to maintain the existing order of society. The Cretans were legendary lawgivers: In later accounts we find Minos assisted by his brother Rhadamanthys (rad-a-**man**-this) and by Aeacus (**ē**-a-kus), king of Aegina, across the Saronic Gulf from Athens. Minos acts like other kings in Homeric society. Orion, son of Poseidon, a famous hunter in life (see Chapter 8), continued to hunt after death. In Homer, for most people of high rank, life below is much like life on the earth.

A few notorious offenders against the dignity of the gods suffer endless torment in the underworld:

[576] Tityus too I saw, son of Gaea, who lay there extended
over a plain, who covered a full nine acres of ground.
A vulture sat tearing his liver, pecking away at his entrails,
where his hands could make no defense. He had assaulted Leto,
580 the noble partner of Zeus, who was making a journey to Pytho,°
through the fair plain of Panopeus.°
    Tantalus also I saw, who was suffering terrible torments.
He stood in a swampy lake, whose water reached up to his chin.
Strain as he might in his thirst, he never could drink of the water,
585 which soaked down into the mud that gurgled between his feet,
sent by some demon. From trees that arched up over his head
drooped fruit of the richest and ripest: clusters of juicy fat pears,
pomegranates, sweet-fruited quinces, ripe olives, delectable figs.
But whenever he tried to reach them, to pull them down with his hands,
590 a gust of wind would blow them away to the shadowing clouds.
    Sisyphus too I observed, down there in his terrible torment,
pushing his boulder before him, straining with every limb
to shoulder it over the crest of the hill. But just as it tottered,
mocking gravity pushed it back, back again to the plain.
595 Once more he strained; once more the sweat poured down from his limbs,
and clouds of dust arose from around his head as he struggled.

HOMER, *Odyssey* (11.576–600)

580. *Pytho:* Delphi. 581. *Panopeus:* A village on the way through Boeotia to Delphi.

Tityus (**tit**-i-us) had attempted to rape the goddess Leto, mother of Apollo and Artemis; the liver, which is devoured, was thought to be the seat of sexual passion. His punishment was similar to that assigned to Prometheus, who stole fire from the gods. **Tantalus** (**tan**-ta-lus) and **Sisyphus** (**sis**-i-fus), too, were guilty of violence against the gods, although Homer is more interested in their punishments than in their crimes (Fig. 11.2). Tantalus, once a friend to the gods, tested their omniscience (like Lycaon) by serving them his own son Pelops (**pē**-lops) at a banquet. They instantly knew the truth, except for Demeter; mourning for Persephonê, she absent-mind-edly ate Pelops' shoulder. The gods reassembled the unfortunate Pelops and made him a new shoulder of ivory. From Tantalus' punishment comes our word *tantalize*. Sisyphus was famed for his cleverness: He seduced Anticlea, Odysseus' mother, on her wedding night and, according to this tradition, was the true father of Odysseus.

FIG. 11.2. The tortures of the damned, from a fresco representing scenes from the *Odyssey,* in a Roman copy of a Greek original, c. 40 B.C. In the center of the picture a great rock looms over Tityus, as if about to fall upon him. He lies spread-eagle and tied down while two vultures pick at his liver. In the foreground the Danaïds (not mentioned by Homer) attempt to fill a trough with vases that have no bottoms. In the upper left, Orion hunts through eternity, while Sisyphus pushes the rock that ever rolls backward. (Vatican Museum, Rome; II.19.17)

Sisyphus' troubles began when he informed the river god Asopus that Zeus himself had abducted his daughter Aegina, eponym of the island near Athens. In anger Zeus sent Death to carry Sisyphus away, but Sisyphus imprisoned Death in chains. No one could die until Ares released Death and gave Sisyphus to him. As Sisyphus was being carried off, he instructed his wife not to perform the proper funeral rites. Hades therefore allowed Sisyphus to return to the upper world to correct what appeared to be his wife's careless omission. Once returned, Sisyphus remained until he died of old age. Going a second time to the underworld, Sisyphus was allotted his terrible punishment.

The tortures of the damned really are tortures of the living, transposed to the other world. Tityus suffers endless physical pain. Tantalus can never satisfy his gluttonous desires for food and drink. Sisyphus labors endlessly without result. It is a fixed list: No one new is added (until much later). The offenses are against the honor of the gods.

Now Odysseus spies Heracles, but it is an "image" (*eidolon*) of him: The real Heracles, when he died, was raised to heaven as a god (see Chapter 14). Odysseus might have seen still more heroes, but

[632]   before I was given a chance
          an endless cloud of specters ran up with a scarce-human mutter.
          Cold fear clutched at my heart, that haughty Persephonê
635   might send from the House of Hades some Gorgon-headed destroyer.
          I hurriedly ran to the ship and ordered my trusty companions
          to embark and cast off the cables which moored the prow to the beach.
          Quickly they jumped on board and seated themselves in their places.
          The surge of the current bore us down the waters of Ocean;
640   then first we tugged at the oars, till a stern wind freshened behind us.

                              Homer, *Odyssey* (11.632–640)

At the end of the poem Homer describes another journey to the underworld,
that of the suitors who had been infesting Odysseus' palace and were killed by him:

[1]   Cyllenian Hermes° summoned the crowding ghosts of the suitors
          with the rod of gold° in his hand, with which he closes the eyelids
          of those whom he picks for sleep, or wakens others from slumber.
          With it he threatened and led them; they followed after him, squeaking
5   just as gibbering bats swoop and whirl through a dark cave's recesses
          when one of them falls from a cluster clinging high up on a wall:
          just so the ghosts came squeaking and flitting about after Hermes,
          conductor of souls along the moldering highway to Hades.
          They passed the tides of the Ocean,° on past the chalky White Rock,
10   by the Gates of the Sun and the Region of Dreams, and then at the last
          they came to the asphodel meadow, where dwell the ghosts of the dead,
          the insubstantial shadows of those who have ended their toil.

                              HOMER, *Odyssey* (24.1–14)

1. *Cyllenian Hermes:* Named for his birthplace, a cave in Mt. Cyllenê.   2. *rod of gold:* The caduceus.
9. *Ocean:* Odysseus had to cross the stream of Ocean to get to the misty land of the Cimmerians.

A blessed few end up in a special afterworld, **Elysium** (e-**liz**-i-um), or the Elysian
Fields. In Book 4 of the *Odyssey*, the Greek hero Menelaüs, stranded on a desert island while returning from Troy, asks the sea god Proteus about his fate. Proteus
replies,

[561]   "It is not your destiny, Menelaüs, friend of the gods,
          to die in horse-raising Argos and meet man's usual fate.
          No, the immortals will send you off to the Field of Elysium,
          to the very ends of the earth, where rules fair-haired Rhadamanthys.
565   There at the last you will find the most blessed fate for a mortal:
          snow never falls, nor destructive storms or violent cloudbursts,
          for the ocean constantly sends the whistling breezes of Zephyr,°
          to brace and refresh the spirits, however fevered, of mortals.
          This is your lot as Zeus's son-in-law, husband of Helen."
570   At this the old man of the sea plunged into the depths of the Ocean.

                              HOMER, *Odyssey* (4.561–570)

567. *Zephyr:* The west wind.

No ordinary man or woman in Homer's time could hope to see the Elysian Fields as a reward for virtue or fear the torment of Tartarus for his or her sins. Menelaüs had married Helen, daughter of Zeus and Leda, and for this reason he will go to Elysium: Family connections count even after death. Those destined for Elysium do not descend to the underworld but continue a blessed life in a remote part of the earth. The word *Elysium* may be of pre-Greek Cretan origin and perhaps reflects a Minoan notion of a happy other world, like that of their trading partners, the optimistic Egyptians.

PLATO'S "MYTH" OF ER

A great spiritual ferment appeared in many places in the sixth century B.C. It was the age of the Orphics (discussed later in this chapter), the mystical philosopher Pythagoras, many of the Hebrew prophets, Zoroaster in Persia, Gautama the Buddha in India, and Confucius in China, although it is hard to trace a direct connection between these still influential teachers and their schools of thought. In the Mediterranean world this was the age of increased concern with the morality of the individual and the effect of right action on a future life. Morality implies choice between what one knows to be good and what one knows to be wrong. Although the wicked may flourish for a while, an effective moral system requires that wrongdoers be punished later in this life or in a life to come, or that one's descendants suffer—that the sins of the fathers be visited on the children.

In the fourth century B.C., the philosopher Plato (428?–347 B.C.) advanced such a moral system of reward and punishment. No one more than Plato is responsible for our modern notion of a myth as a fictitious, untrue story or version of events. So hostile was he to traditional tales that he banned poets from his ideal city. However, Plato did not object to making up his own myths to promulgate his views. For example, he invented the "myth of Atlantis," a description of a once powerful world sunk beneath the waves. In Plato's dialogue *The Republic*, Socrates attempts to arrive at a definition of justice. Opposing popular views that injustice is rewarded, Socrates maintains that it is punished not only in this world, but in the next.

To prove his point, Socrates describes to his interlocutor, Glaucon, the experience of a man named **Er** ("springtime," the season of rebirth) who came from the land of Pamphylia (a real place in southern Anatolia, but meaning "land of all races" or "everyman's land"). Er was killed in battle, but ten days afterward, when the bodies were placed on a funeral pyre, he was found still alive and able to tell his story. He and all the other dead found themselves, he said, in a place where openings on either side led up to heaven or down into the earth. The souls were judged and sent under the earth, or into the heaven, to be punished or rewarded tenfold for the evil or good they had done. For a thousand years they suffered torment or enjoyed bliss. After this they returned to the place of judgment and were offered a choice of new lives to live when they returned to earth. A herald took a number of lots (prepared by Clotho, one of the Moerae or Fates), from the knees of Lachesis (another of the Fates) and proclaimed, "Souls of a day, here you begin a new period of life. Nobody will choose for you. You must make your own decision. Do not blame the god for it;

the responsibility will be your own." The souls then picked what they wanted. The famous singer Orpheus chose to be a swan; an ugly warrior who fought at Troy, Thersites, chose to be a monkey; Agamemnon, king of the Greek forces at Troy, chose to be an eagle; Odysseus, whose former life had taught him the folly of ambition, hunted for a long time before he found what he wanted: a quiet, obscure life, one that everyone before had rejected.

The destiny each soul chose was confirmed by the third of the Fates, Atropos. Then they all journeyed to the Plain of Forgetfulness (*Lethê*) through a burning, choking, stifling heat, for it was bare of trees and plants. There they camped at eventide by the River of Unheeding, whose waters no vessel can hold. They were all required to drink some of the water, but those who were not saved by their reason drank more than the measure. Each one, as he drank, forgot everything and went to sleep. It was the middle of the night, there was thunder and a quaking of the earth. Suddenly they were carried away, one this way, one that, up to their birth like shooting stars. Er himself was not allowed to drink the water, he said, yet how he returned to the body he did not know. Suddenly recovering his sight, he saw himself at dawn, lying on the funeral pyre.

> And so, Glaucon, his story has been preserved, and it would save us if we believed it. We shall safely cross the River of Forgetfulness (*Lethê*) and keep our souls undefiled. But if we are persuaded by me, we shall believe that the soul is immortal and able to endure every extreme of good and evil. Thus shall we shall hold always to the upward path and always pursue justice with wisdom, so that we may be friends to ourselves and to the gods both during our time here and afterward, like victors in the games who go to collect their prizes. Thus both here and in that journey of a thousand years, which I have described, we will fare well.
>
> PLATO, *The Republic* (621a–d)

The "myth" of Er is not a traditional tale but a philosophical and intellectual recasting of ancient traditional accounts of life after death and of the underworld to teach that the soul is immortal and that a moral law governs the world. Plato's principal contribution was to allow for a purification of the soul before it returned to another human life—for the presence, in more modern terms, of a Purgatory ("place of purification") as well as an Inferno and a Paradise. Although not a myth, Plato's vision of Er influenced other myth-makers, especially the Roman poet Vergil in his highly influential account of the descent of Aeneas in the sixth book of the *Aeneid,* so slippery does the category "myth" become!

AENEAS' DESCENT TO THE UNDERWORLD

Many popular conceptions about the other world still current today lead back directly to Vergil's description, which incorporates both Greek and Roman myth, religion, and philosophy.

Aeneas, who has escaped from the burning wreckage of Troy, travels to the far west to found a new race, the Romans. Before his purpose is complete, he must descend to the underworld through an opening near mephitic Lake Avernus, north of the Bay of Naples, to consult his father, Anchises.[5] (Avernus was thought to mean "birdless" because the foul vapors kill even birds that fly over it.) To do so he must consult the Sibyl of Cumae (an early Greek colony near Avernus), once loved by Apollo, to whom the goddess Hecatê had revealed the nether realms; now an old woman, the Sibyl will be his guide. First Aeneas plucks a magical golden bough from a sacred wood, a sign that he is chosen by fate. Vergil's report of Hades, which we summarize as follows, repeats much of that in the *Odyssey*, but with many minor changes and some major ones.

After sacrificing to the gods beneath the earth, Aeneas and the Sibyl set forth at the earliest rays of the rising sun. At the entrance to the underworld hovers a crowd of personified abstractions, a tree filled with deceptive dreams, and beyond it a crowd of monsters. Hesiod has a few allegorical creatures like these, but their use was far more common among the Romans:

[268] They groped a desolate way through the shadowy gloom of the night,
       through Dis'° echoing house, through a region devoid of the living,
270   like those who traverse a forest under the sinister light
       of a half-seen overcast moon, when Jupiter buries the heavens
       in scudding clouds, and darkness robs all the world of its color.
       There by the very gateway, at the gaping entrance of Orcus,°
       lurked Griefs and torturing Worries; beside them lay waxen Diseases,
275   with hopeless Old Age, with Terror, with Poverty driving to crime.
       The loathsome forms of others sat by: Death; inescapable Toil;
       Somnolence, brother of Death; and criminal Gloatings of Soul.
       Right across the way couched War, the slayer of thousands;
       the Furies, chambered in iron; and the maniac raving of Discord,
280   her poisonous serpentine hair besmeared with drippings of blood.
          In the gnarled and tortuous branches of a dark and ancient elm
       was the roost (so rumor assures us) of treacherous cheating Dreams
       clinging in hiding beneath every leaf. And there at the portal
       lurked nightmare, horrible shapes of beastly hybrids and monsters—
285   Centaurs were there, and Scylla,° Briareus of the hundred arms,°
       the screeching Hydra of Lerna, Chimera belching her fires,
       Gorgons and Harpies, and Geryon, ghost of a three-bodied horror.

VERGIL, Aeneid (6.268–289)

269. *Dis:* Hades.   273. *Orcus:* The underworld.   285. *Scylla:* A flesh-eating monster faced by Odysseus, female from the waist up but with six snarling dogs from there down. Milton (*Paradise Lost* 2.650) compares Sin to Scylla:

> woman to the waist, and fair,
> but ended foul in many a scaly fold. . . .
> About her middle round
> a cry of Hell-hounds never ceasing barked.

285. *Briareus:* One of the Hundred-handers.

Their journey soon brings them to the river **Acheron** (**ak**-er-on, "sorrowful"), the boundary proper of Dis's realm. If the dead have the fare, they are soon taken aboard

[5]For Anchises' union with Aphrodite, who bore Aeneas, see Chapter 8.

Michelangelo's *The Sibyl of Cumae*

A belief that the truest mouthpiece for prophecy is an inspired, often aged woman is very ancient: She appeared to the Greeks as the Pythia, Apollo's voice at Delphi; in the Bible as the Witch of Endor, who summoned the ghost of Samuel to foretell the grim future facing King Saul; and in Vergil's *Aeneid* as the Sibyl of Cumae, Aeneas' guide to the world below, said to be still alive in the early Roman Empire. But there were other Sibyls in the ancient world, as many as ten.

Michelangelo Buonarroti (1475–1564), a poet as well as architect, sculptor, painter, and engineer, lived at the end of a century and a half of extraordinary artistic and intellectual ferment in Italy. His most famous painting is in the Sistine Chapel in the Vatican, residence of the Pope, where in four years (1508–1512) he decorated in wet plaster the enormous ceiling and upper third of the side walls. Taking the creation, fall, and redemption of humankind as his topic, Michelangelo covered the ceiling with more than 300 figures in a sweeping drama of human existence. On the side panels he represented prophets of Christ's coming. Here, curiously, he includes the old and muscular Sibyl of Cumae (labeled *CUMAEA;* Fig. P 11.1), who looks into one of her prophetic books while two *ignudi,* "nude youths," look on.

FIG. P 11.1. Michelangelo Buonarroti (1475–1564), *The Sibyl of Cumae in the Sistine Chapel,* c. 1510, fresco. (Vatican Museum, Rome)

Such an absorption of pagan motifs into Christianity was a logical outgrowth of the allegorical interpretations placed on classical myth by Renaissance intellectuals. Thus according to neoplatonic principles (compare Perspective 8.1), the Sibyl represents the physical body, the first youth behind her stands for the intellectual faculty by which humans contemplate divine truth, and the second youth is the immortal soul itself. In this way the three figures correspond to Plato's division of the soul into three parts: appetite, intellect, and spirit. A contemporary of Michelangelo understood Michelangelo's sibyl in this fashion, and of course she is a true prophet whose books foretell Christ's coming. Within this intellectual ambience it was easy for artists to incorporate pagan images and themes, even in the private chapel of the Pope.

the boat of the grim ferryman **Charon** (kā-ron; Fig. 11.3); if not, they must wait a hundred years to cross:

[295]   From there the downward way led them to Acheron's waters,
         whose black and sluggish current eddied in whirlpools of mud.
         A filthy old guardian boatman kept watch on the banks and the river,
         Charon, whose red flaming eyes peered over a greasy gray beard,
         dressed in a dirty old scarf looped around and over his shoulder.
300   Scorning the help of a crew, he alone handles punt pole and sail,
         and loads the dead to the gunwales of his rusty, leaky old hull—
         an old man now, but old age in a god is green and resilient.
         Great crowds of the dead swarmed out and rushed on down to the water,
         to the slimy banks of the Styx° in an endless torrent of humans—
305   mothers of children, their husbands, great-hearted heroes,

304. *Styx:* "Hateful," one of the rivers of the underworld. An oath sworn by the gods and witnessed by this river could not be broken (as when Zeus swore to Semelê).

FIG. 11.3. Charon and Hermes psychopompos, Attic vase, c. 380 B.C. Charon, wearing a rough cloak and cap, punts the bark of the dead, while Hermes psychopompos, wearing his winged cap and carrying the caduceus, leads the ghost of a woman recently dead. Such *lekythoi* (oil vases) were made expressly to bury with the dead. (Staatliche Antikensammlungen und Glyptothek, Munich; 2777 vas)

schoolboys, unmarried maidens, young men scarcely mature,
but laid on the funeral pyre before the eyes of their parents.
A crowd like swirling leaves that fall from the branches in autumn,
when nipped by the first cold blast, or like the flocking of petrels,
310   when icy winter drives them in flight from the open sea
in search of a warmer climate. Just so the dead, passing number,
came stretching their hands in longing to cross to the opposite shore.

VERGIL, Aeneid (6.295–314)

Among those who hold out their hands in longing for the further bank is Palinurus, the helmsman of a ship of Aeneas; Palinurus, overcome by sleep, had fallen
overboard. Like Elpenor in Homer's *Odyssey*, he begs to be buried properly. (But
Homer has no Charon and no underworld river to be crossed.) Aeneas and the Sibyl
embark in Charon's skiff. Having human bodies, they very nearly swamp it:

[384]   Having completed this part of the journey, Aeneas and Sibyl
385   drew near the bank of the stream. The pilot, from out in the river,
noticed them making their way through the silent gloom of the forest
and hurrying down to the shore. He raised a threatening clamor:
"Whoever you are, approaching in arms the bank of my river,
stop right there where you are! Speak up; say why you have ventured
390   to a place belonging alone to dreams, to night, and to shadows.
I may not carry the living across in my Stygian ferry . . ."
            . . .To this the Sibyl replied,
"Although you remain unimpressed by this man's feelings of duty"°
(drawing the golden bough from her cloak, she showed it to Charon),
395   "even so you will recognize this."
    Anger died in his swelling heart as he looked down in silence
at the awesome gift of the Sibyl. At last he slowly directed
his gloomy prow to the shore, drove out the rows of the spirits,
and cleared a way for the pair. When mighty Aeneas was boarding,
400   the rickety vessel creaked and groaned at the weight of the hero
and was nearly swamped by the water that lapped in over its gunwales.
But Charon finally landed the prophet and hero in safety,
to splash their way through the mud and drifted weeds of the river.
    From his triple throat the snarls of Cerberus rang to the sky
405   as he crouched, immense, by his cave, straddled across their pathway.
The Sibyl glanced at his neck, already bristling with vipers,
and threw him a morsel of honey and dough made narcotic with drugs.
Stretching three ravenous jaws, he snapped at the bait in the air;
at once his taut-muscled back went slack on the ground where he lay,
410   filling with his huge bulk the entire width of the cavern.
As the beast lay snoring, Aeneas hastily ran for the portal
and hurriedly ran on beyond the stream no mortal recrosses.

VERGIL, Aeneid (6.384–425)

393. *duty:* The Latin word is *pietas,* duty to family, country, and gods, which Augustus was eager to
inspire in the Romans. Aeneas was its great exemplar: At the command of Jupiter he has come down
to the underworld to ask his father about the destiny of Rome.

The Sibyl and Aeneas next come to the region of the great mass of the dead, who are divided into various groups. The first is that of those who have died too soon: infants, those wrongly convicted of crime, suicides, and those who have died for love. These last include the Phoenician queen of Carthage, Dido, whom Aeneas had abandoned. Next to these are soldiers who fell in battle, especially the dead of the Trojan War.

Now they come to a fork in the road. The way to the left leads to Tartarus, place of eternal torment:

[548]   Aeneas chanced to look up. Beneath the cliff to his left
          his eye fell upon a grim fortress, enclosed in three circling walls,
550   all closed in by the torrent of Phlegethon,° river of hell,
          blazing with roaring fire as it twists its way through its gorge.
          Its gate stood heavy and solid, flanked by two adamant columns;
          no power fashioned by man, no warlike armies of heaven,
          could shake that tower of iron that raises its head to the sky.
555   There at the head of the gate Tisiphonê,° ragged and bloodstained,
          keeps her unsleeping watch at the portal by night and by day.
          The tortured sounds from within, the screams of the pitiless lashes,
          join with the grating screech and rattle of dragged iron chains.
          Aeneas halted in panic at the racking unbearable clamor:
560   "What sort of crime demands this? Speak out, O Sibyl, and tell me,
          what torment is here exacted for offenses that cry out to heaven?"
              To this the Sibyl replied, "O noble lord of the Trojans,
          no mortal soul may pass beyond this crime-darkened threshold.
          but when Hecatê put me in charge of the sinister grove of Avernus,
565   she taught me the sentences ordered by the gods, in every detail.
          Rhadamanthys the Cretan is king of this grim and implacable empire;
          he hears every plea, he questions, he forces the culprits to speak
          the truth about ancient offenses—deceits in the land of the living
          over which they have gloated, delaying too long a proper repentance,
570   till death caught them unawares. And then—how Tisiphonê mocks them,
          that guilty crowd, while mangling their tremulous limbs with her lash!
          brandishing venomous snakes, calling her fierce-minded sisters.
          Imagine those cursed gates had swung on their screeching old hinges;
          what horrible form would you see sitting as guard on the doorway?
575   The monster with fifty black mouths,° Tisiphonê's master in cruelty,
          dwells just within the portal; there Tartarus stretches his body
          twice as far down to the shades as Olympus rises to heaven.

                                    VERGIL, *Aeneid* (6.548–579)

550. *Phlegethon:* "Flaming," sometimes called Pyriphlegethon (pi-ri-**fleg**-e-thon), "flaming with fire."
555. *Tisiphonê:* "Punisher," one of the Furies.   575. *monster . . . mouths:* Tartarus, treated both as a monster and a place.

In Tartarus are the great sinners, including those that Homer described: Tityus, Tantalus, Sisyphus. The Titans are there too, sent to Tartarus by the thunderbolts of Zeus, according to the account in Hesiod's *Theogony*. Another famous sufferer is **Ixion** (ik-**sī**-on), who was a king of the Lapiths in Thessaly. He lusted after Hera. Zeus,

Dante's *Inferno*

Dante Alighieri (A.D. 1265–1321) was a citizen of the powerful and independent state of Florence. In 1301 he was convicted on political grounds of corruption and spent the rest of his life in exile, writing poetry in his native Tuscan dialect instead of the traditional Latin, one of the first modern poets. So influential were his works that they are regarded as founding the modern Italian language: Until Dante's time it appeared that the Provençal dialect of southern France would become the speech of northern Italy.

His great work was the *Divina Commedia,* comprising the *Inferno,* the *Purgatorio,* and the *Paradiso.* An allegory of the soul's progress from sin to redemption, the poem is a highly complex and learned exploration of morals, politics, theology, cosmology, and philosophy. From the time of its publication it has gripped the imagination by its vivid images, narrative power, and beauty of language, and in spite of its difficulty has always been a popular work.

The *Inferno* is deeply indebted to classical myth as transmitted by the Roman poets (Greek texts were not available to Dante and he did not know Greek). Vergil, especially, was his literary model. In the poem, the Roman author guides Dante through the underworld, which Dante thinks of as an enormous inverted cone divided into nine layers, each layer assigned to the punishment of some category of sin. Many of the scenes are modeled on those in Vergil, just as Vergil modeled his scenes on the *Odyssey* and on Plato. At the very bottom stands Lucifer, with three heads and three mouths, chewing eternally those who sinned against their masters: Brutus and Cassius, who killed Julius Caesar, and Judas, who betrayed Christ.

A persistent mythical image is the infernal river one must cross to reach the world of the dead. For Odysseus, this water was the river Ocean, which encircles the world and which Odysseus himself navigated. For Vergil, it was the river Acheron, over which the boatman Charon ferried the souls of the dead. Although a "Christian" Hell, Dante's is bounded by Acheron, and, as in Vergil's *Aeneid,* Charon fears to transport a living man across it. In this passage Dante describes the moment when Charon sees Dante and Vergil, his ghostly guide, at the river's edge, surrounded by the souls of the damned, who await transport to the other side:

[82]   And there I saw, poling his punt toward us,
        an ancient boatman, his hair grown white with years.
        "You're out of luck, you wicked souls," he screamed,
85   "who have no hope of ever seeing heaven.
        I'm here to ship you to the other side,
        to burning, freezing, to eternal darkness—
    but you," (he looked at me) "you're still alive!
        Get out; you don't belong; all these are dead!"
90   When he looked again and saw I had not moved,
    "Go, take another path, another vessel,"

he cried to me. "To reach the other shore
you'll need a nimbler boat than this of mine."
My leader told him, "Charon, don't get excited.
95   This was decreed where will translates to power.
Accept it, then, and question it no more."
The pilot through that death-hued leaden swamp
clamped shut his bearded jaws and angry tongue,
though red flame still glared from his savage eyes.
100   Then all those poor exhausted naked souls
Turned pale and shook with trembling chattering teeth,
hearing the bitter words that told their fate.
They cursed their god, their parents who begat them,
their race, the time and place of their conception;
105   they cursed the day on which they saw the light.
And now together, crowded in one mass,
they drew with screams of pain to the cursed shore
that waits for every man who fears not God.
The demon Charon, glaring with hot red eyes,
110   drives them ashore and herds them in together,
belaboring the stragglers with his oar.
Just as, in autumn, the leaves drop one by one;
at last the naked branch looks sadly down
to see the rustling pile upon the ground,
115   So from the bank there plunged the cursed seed
of Adam, one by one, as falcons drop,
when the huntsman gives the whistle to return.

DANTE, *Inferno* (3.82–117)

Dante, overcome by the spectacle of the herds of the damned crowding into Charon's boat, faints and does not revive until he is on the other side.

Here is a clear example how ancient stories and images are recast to acquire utterly new meanings; Michelangelo did the same with the Sibyl in the Sistine Chapel (Perspective 11.1). For Homer Hell is a dismal, dull realm, dark, beneath the ground—a vision built on primitive fears of ghosts and our own sure end. For Vergil Hell can be happy because it holds the spirits who will be Romans, who will fulfill Rome's mission in history. For Dante Hell is the vicious, unending pain of those who have chosen deliberately to reject God's love when they might have chosen to accept his love. Homer is spooky and nostalgic, Vergil political, and Dante moral.

not believing that anyone could really desire his wife, for sport made an image of Hera out of cloud. Ixion pounced on it and his seed tumbled through the cloud to the earth. Up sprang Centaurus, father of the Centaurs. Zeus bound Ixion to a wheel of fire that turns slowly through the eternal mists.[6] The crime of most of Vergil's sufferers, like Homer's, is impiety against the gods, but Vergil also adds those guilty of crimes against human morals and law, something we do not find in Homer. As in

---

[6]Sinners not mentioned by Vergil or Homer but common in later accounts are the Danaids (dan-ā-idz), the "daughters of Danaüs," who killed their husbands on their wedding night. Their punishment was to fill a vat by carrying water in jugs that had no bottoms (see Fig. 11.2).

Plato's story about Er, their torment is hidden: Even the Sibyl was not allowed to see, but she learned about them from Hecatê:

[608]   Here are those who in life detested and envied their brothers;
         those who attacked their fathers, who cheated and swindled dependents,
610   who refused to offer to others a part of their chance-given riches,°
         but in avarice hoarded it all; of the greedy the number is legion.
         Here were the men who were slain in the very act of adultery;
         and faithless breakers of oaths° who fought for a criminal cause—
         all these, loaded with chains, lie dreading the penalty waiting. . . .
615   Sadly they cry a warning in a voice that rings through the shadow,
         "Be warned by my words; learn justice; do not belittle the gods."
         Here is the traitor who peddled his country and set up a tyrant,
         who for a bribe would establish bad laws and abolish the good;
         here the incestuous man who corrupted the bed of his daughter—
620   darers of horrible crimes, who enjoyed the fruit of their daring.
         If I had a hundred mouths, I could not exhaust their offenses,
         nor could I even begin to expound the torments they suffer.

                                          VERGIL, *Aeneid* (6.608–627)

> 610. *chance-given riches:* Magnanimity or liberality ranked high as a virtue in the ancient world and miserly greed as a great vice.   613. *breakers of oaths:* That is, the opponents of Augustus in the wars with Mark Antony.

Aeneas leaves the golden bough as an offering to Proserpina (= Persephonê) before the gate to Pluto's palace, and he and the Sibyl hurry on to Elysium, where dwell the ghosts of heroes who died in battle—many more than we find in Homer— and of many other sages and poets. Vergil's description owes much to Plato's vision of the mythical dead gathered for reincarnation:

[638]   They passed to the happy region of green and flowering glades,
         the groves where the favored dwell, the blessed haunt of the heroes.
640   A purer ether enfolds them and clothes them in larger soft light;
         a sun of their own shines above, their own stars call them to slumber.
         Some find delight in wrestling in rings made soft by the grass;
         some exercise well-trained muscles in arenas of golden sand.
         Others delight in the steps of the dance or the singing of verses;
645   Orpheus, dressed as a bard, fits musical notes to the epic,
         sweeping the lyre with his fingers, or plucking with ivory plectrum.
         Here dwell the noble descendants of Teucer,° a glorious lineage,
         great-hearted heroes, the men of an earlier, happier age—
         Ilus, Assaracus, back to Dardanus, founder of Ilium.
650   Aeneas gazed at their ghostly weapons, their hurrying chariots,
         no longer loaded with fighters; at spears, just stuck in the ground;
         at their horses, now grazing in peace. Yet the joy of their owners
         in chariots, horses, and weapons, which once they enjoyed while alive,

> 647. *Teucer:* The first king of Troy; Ilus, Assaracus, and Dardanus were among his successors (see Chart 19.3). Aeneas himself belonged to this house, and from his son Iulus sprang the Roman Julii, including (by adoption, and by a bad etymology) Augustus, Vergil's patron.

655 remained with these fortunate spirits, whose bodies lay in the earth.
And others Aeneas observed, relaxing at ease in the meadows,
picnicking, singing, or dancing, or raising a paean in chorus,
all through the perfumed thickets of laurel, watered by brooklets
bickering down through the woods, from great Eridanus on earth.°
Here were those who alive had shed their blood for their country,
660 and those who all through their days were pure and reverend prophets,
wise men, uttering oracles worthy of Phoebus himself.
Here were those whose talents have rendered life more attractive,
and all who deserve our remembrance as generations roll onward.

VERGIL, *Aeneid* (6.638–664)

658. *Eridanus on earth:* The Po. Because the lower world is a sort of copy of that above, its rivers presumably have the same source.

At the end of Book 6 Aeneas at last meets his father. Just as Odysseus reached out to his mother three times, but his arms passed through her, so does Aeneas reach out to his father, with the same result. Anchises then shows to his son the great procession of souls awaiting their return to earth, naming those who are to be the mighty heroes of Rome. Anchises prefaces this account with a cosmology (a theory of the universe) that accepts the cyclical nature of things: Everything that is happening now has repeatedly happened in the past and will happen again and again in the future.[7] When the souls of the good, corrupted by a life in the flesh, descend to the underworld, there they are purified so that (as in Plato), after a thousand years, they might return to a new life in a new body. This is philosophy, not myth, but it is philosophy aided by images drawn from older traditional myth.

At the end of Book 6, we are told that there are two gates of dreams: one of horn, through which true dreams emerge, the other of ivory, through which the false ones pass. Anchises directs Aeneas, and with him the Sibyl, to depart back to the upper world through the gate of ivory; no one has ever explained why.

ORPHEUS AND EURYDICÊ

Odysseus and Aeneas were not the only figures in classical myth to journey alive to the land of the dead; **Orpheus** (**or**-fūs or **or**-fe-us), the son of a Thracian named Oeagrus and a Muse, did so as well. Orpheus was famous for his sweet singing to the lyre, an instrument some say he invented. His music enchanted wild animals, stopped birds in flight, and uprooted trees and rocks, drawing them all into the magic circle of his song. He was one of the Argonauts (Chapter 18), but the most important myth of Orpheus described his tragic love for his wife, **Eurydicê** (ū-**rid**-i-sē). A beekeeper named Aristaeus (a-ris-**tē**-us, husband of Autonoë and father of Actaeon) disrupted the wedding of Orpheus and Eurydicê, pursuing the bride across a field, intending to rape her. As she fled, she was bitten on the heel by a snake and died. Overwhelmed by grief, Orpheus determined to bring her back from the dead. He entered the other

[7]The Latin motto on the American dollar bill, *novus ordo seclorum*, "a new cycle of the ages," is a paraphrase of another line of Vergil, referring to his cyclical conception of history and time.

world and, sweetly singing, entranced the ghosts and even softened the icy hearts of Hades and Persephonê. They agreed to release Eurydicê on a single condition: While climbing the paths that lead to the upper world, Orpheus must not look back. All went well until they neared the entrance, when an agonizing doubt seized Orpheus. He looked around in time to see Eurydicê recede into the shadows. He tried again to enter the underworld, but Cerberus turned him away. Inconsolable, Orpheus wandered over the world, playing his lyre (Fig. 11.4). Wanting nothing to do with any other woman, he invented male homosexuality. He met his end in his wild homeland of Thrace, where Bacchae tore him to bits, either because he promulgated homosexuality, because he neglected Dionysus, or because he excluded women from his sacred mysteries. The Bacchae threw the pieces of his corpse into the river Hebrus, the principal river in Thrace, and they were washed down to the sea; the head continued to sing and prophesy even after it was washed ashore on the island of Lesbos. At last Apollo, envious of its powers, commanded it to be silent.

The story of Orpheus and Eurydicê was popular in the Hellenistic and Roman periods. One of the best-known versions is that of Vergil in the *Georgics* ("poems about farming"). Aristaeus, who had attacked Eurydicê, was punished by the loss of all his bees. He sought out the prophetic sea god Proteus, who in explaining the consequences of Aristaeus' act tells the story:

[457]   "Running from you in terror and splashing her way through a stream,
         the poor girl, fated to perish, failed to see that a monstrous viper
         lurked in the long thick grass on the bank just over the river. . . .
460   Only his hollow lyre gave Orpheus some consolation:
            "'O dear lost bride!' he murmured, pacing the shore all alone;
         her name was his theme at daybreak, his theme as the sun sank down.
         At last in despair he entered Taenarum's° grisly approaches,
         the deepest portal of Dis and the grove of black shadows and fear.
465   Passing the legions of ghosts, he sought the implacable ruler,
         whose pitiless heart never learned to be softened by human entreaty.
         His song fetched even the phantoms from the lowest circles of hell,
         and the wraiths of unhappy spirits deprived of the blessing of light.
         They flocked, as many in number as the migrant birds of the autumn,
470   driven together by darkness or the whistling storms of the winter.
         Mothers of children, grown men, soldiers fallen in battle,
         small boys, maidens unmarried, young men laid on the pyre
         under the grieving eyes of anguished father and mother.
         Black mud closes them in, and the rotting sedge of Cocytus,°
475   with its sluggish disgusting fens, through which the Stygian water
         meanders in ninefold looping, cutting off any escape.
         Yet even the lowest hell, the deepest circle of Hades,
         even the Furies with livid vipers entwined in their hair,
         gaped in surprise; even Cerberus silenced his triple-jawed barking,
480   and Ixion's wheel stood still as the wind that drove it fell silent.
            "When at last his prayer was granted, Orpheus, shunning ill luck,

---

463. *Taenarum:* A peninsula near Sparta, the southernmost tip of Europe (except for Gibraltar), where certain caves were thought to lead to the underworld.   474. *Cocytus* (kō-sī-tus): "Moaning," another river of the underworld.

FIG. 11.4. Orpheus in Thrace, Attic vase, c. 440 B.C. Orpheus, sitting on a rock, sings and plucks the lyre, while Thracian warriors listen, entranced. (Antikenmuseum, Staatliche Museen, Berlin; V.1.3972)

was preceding his newly recovered Eurydicê up to the light,
Eurydicê followed behind him, for thus Proserpina ordered.
But just as she came in reach of the fresh sweet wind of the heaven,
485   madness seized the incautious lover—forgivable, yes,
but only if death knew how to forgive. He halted his step,
forgetful, besotted by love, and turned around in his folly,
back to his bride, just before Eurydicê entered the daylight.
    "A second too soon! for now all his labor was fruitlessly wasted;
490   he had broken the stern condition of the iron ruler's decree;
as witness, three crashes of thunder resounded all through Avernus.
'What folly' the girl sobbed out, 'has sentenced poor wretched me,
and you, my Orpheus, as well? a cruel fate now recalls me.
Farewell, farewell! my eyelids are drowned by my final slumber,
495   the darkness enfolds and abducts me; in vain do I stretch out my arms,
which now will never embrace you.' No more. From out of his sight
she vanished, as smoke disperses when touched by a whisper of wind.
He eagerly clutched at the darkness, longing to bid her goodbye;
but she no longer was there to see his frantic endeavor.
500   He tried to follow her down, but the grim-faced porter refused him
another passage across the marshes, now wider than ever.
    "What could the poor man do? where hunt for a twice-vanished wife?

Marcel Camus's *Black Orpheus*

Ancient Greek artists were able to handle the fantastic elements in myth—the intervention of gods, the appearance of nonhuman and monstrous beings, transformations of shape—with some success. Modern filmmakers, by contrast, have found it difficult to represent mythical topics on the screen. Even when assisted by sophisticated special effects (as in the 1981 movie *Clash of the Titans,* really the story of Perseus), the medium of film is evidently too realistic, too visually specific, to allow the free play of imagination that contributes to the power of myth. The most successful film versions of Greek myth recast an ancient tale into modern guise, and none has done this better than the classic Brazilian–French movie *Black Orpheus* (*Orfeo Negro,* 1957), directed by Marcel Camus.

In this film, set to an enchanting musical accompaniment by A. C. Jobim and Luis Bonfa, all of the actors and characters are of African descent. The movie begins with Orfeo, a handsome, guitar-playing streetcar conductor, playing to the rising sun. Orfeo is engaged to a striking but overbearing woman, but when he sees Eurydicê, beautiful and soft in manner, who has come to Rio to escape a mysterious stranger, he forgets his fiancée and pursues this new love. It is Carnival, the Brazilian equivalent to Mardi Gras ("Fat Tuesday," the day before Lent, when you say goodbye to meat: *carne* = flesh; *vale* = farewell). Music is everywhere, and the streets are filled with merrymakers dressed in outlandish costumes.

A mysterious stranger appears wearing a skeleton-like suit and mask. Orfeo briefly thwarts the threatening stranger, who, of course, is Death. Orfeo makes love to Eurydicê, then loses her in the crowds. Death seizes her and takes her to the streetcar terminal, where Eurydicê is electrocuted. She disappears in an ambulance. Desperate to find her, Orfeo goes to the Bureau of Missing Persons. A porter advises him to visit a Voodoo priestess and medium, a grotesque, ugly woman with a dog named Cerberus. While Orfeo looks away, the priestess falls into a trance and from her mouth comes the voice of Eurydicê. Orfeo thinks she is in the room, turns to see, and at once the trance is broken.

Orfeo finally finds Eurydicê's body at the morgue. While he bears her away in his arms, he is himself killed by his angry former fiancée, who smashes his head from behind with a rock, knocking him from a cliff. As a new dawn approaches, two young boys run to Orfeo's shack high on the hills over Rio, to find and play his wonderful guitar. Only the sound of music can make the sun rise again.

In ancient myth, and in modern adaptations (including many operas and ballets), Orpheus is the type of the master musician, embodying the mysterious power that music holds over the human soul, even to bring souls back from the land of the dead.

What plea could avail with the spirits, what piteous cry to the gods?
Eurydicê's stiffening body already was crossing the Styx.

505   "They tell us that Orpheus lamented Eurydicê seven long months,
under a windy crag of the lonely bank of the Strymon,°
chanting his story aloud to the icy caves of the northland,
breaking the savage hearts of even the man-eating tigers,
moving the rooted oak trees to follow and hark to his song.

510 As a nightingale mourns its young, whom a callous peasant has stolen,
unfledged as yet, from the nest, she perches high in the branches
and all night long pours out the voice of her sorrow. So Orpheus
wept for his loss; no new love, no marriage offered him solace.
Alone he gazed at the ice of the Arctic, at snow-drenched Tanaïs,

515 at endless Scythian plains,° whose snow lasts all through the summer,
mourning Eurydicê's loss and the empty concession of Pluto.
The women of Thrace were enraged, who, worshiping wild Dionysus,
rent Orpheus limb from limb in ecstatic orgies, and scattered
his flesh through the plains of their Thrace. Only his death-pale head

520 they tore from his neck, to hurl in Oeagrian Hebrus'° current.
Yet even as Hebrus carried the head out into the sea,
the ice-cold stiffening tongue gasped Orpheus' last invocation:
'Alas! my lost Eurydicê!' it cried with his final breath;
'Eurydicê!' back came the echo from Hebrus' sorrowing shores."

VERGIL, Georgics (4.457–527)

506. *Strymon:* A river of Thrace.   515. *Scythian plains:* Tanaïs is the modern river Don, flowing through the Ukraine into the Black Sea. Scythia, modern southeast Russia, lies to the east.   520. *Oeagrian Hebrus:* Oeagrus was Orpheus' father; the Hebrus is the largest river in Thrace. *story:* Here Clement quotes from an Orphic hymn.   *Pallas:* On the assumption that *Pallas* means "beating" (a possible but improbable interpretation).   *Parnassus:* That is, Delphi.

ORPHISM

In the sixth century B.C., religious teachers began to claim the mythical Orpheus as the promulgator of special teachings about the nature and destiny of human beings. Like the Eleusinian Mysteries, these "teachings of Orpheus" offered ordinary Greeks hope for salvation, a means of ensuring a more comfortable life after death. Unlike other Greek religious teachings, however, the Orphic doctrines were recorded and transmitted in written form, in the so-called *Hymns of Orpheus,* a collection of writings from different times by many different authors. These hymns were supposed to contain the knowledge that Orpheus gained in the world below and later taught while he wandered through Thrace. Although these stories incorporate material from various myths, they are no more traditional tales than is Plato's "myth" of Er but rather made up by the Orphic poets; Plato was to pick up the practice. Although most of the Orphic hymns are now lost, we can draw some conclusions about their central doctrines from surviving fragments and other sources.

    Dionysus figures prominently in these pseudo-myths. Our knowledge about one important Orphic myth is derived from comments by an unfriendly Christian writer from about A.D. 200, Clement of Alexandria, who ridicules beliefs he finds absurd and offensive:

The mysteries of Dionysus are utterly savage. While he was an infant, the Curetes danced around him in full armor but the Titans sneaked in, distracted the baby's attention with toys, and tore him limb from limb. The poet of initiation, Orpheus, tells the story:°

> Tops and hoops and dollies,
> With moving feet and hands;
> Pretty golden apples,
> From singing western lands.

To make you laugh, let me list the silly symbols of that rite of yours: knuckle-bones, ball, top, apples, wheel, mirror, fleece.

Well, Athena stole the heart of Dionysus and, because it was still palpitating, she received the name of Pallas.° Meanwhile, the Titans who had torn Dionysus to pieces set a pot on a tripod. They tossed in his limbs, which they first boiled up, then put them on spits and held them over the fire. Afterward Zeus appeared (if he was really a god, he had doubtless caught a whiff of roasting meat, which those gods of yours claim as their due). He blasted the Titans with a thunderbolt and gave the remains of Dionysus to his son Apollo to bury. Apollo would not dream of disobeying Zeus, so he took the mangled corpse to Parnassus° and buried it there.

Clement of Alexandria, Protrepticus (2.15)

The story appears to reflect an initiation rite common in preliterate societies. A young man (Dionysus) is approached by older men (the Titans), symbolically "killed," then brought back to new life in the adult world. Some accounts tell how the Titans smeared their faces with gypsum, an actual practice in initiation rites, where older men take on the role of the ghosts of tribal ancestors.

Other Orphic myths report that Zeus created human beings from the ashes of the blasted Titans. Thus, although human nature has an evil, Titanic aspect, it also has within it a spark of divinity because the flesh of Dionysus, whom the Titans had earlier devoured, was mingled with the Titans' ashes. A human being therefore possesses a divine Dionysian spark encased in a gross Titanic body, and the goal of human striving should be to free the immortal soul from its bodily prison. This view is succinctly expressed in an Orphic slogan: The body is a tomb (*sôma sêma*).

The Orphics also taught metempsychosis, or the reincarnation of the soul. According to this doctrine, the souls of the dead do not remain forever in the realm of Hades but repeatedly return to the earth for a new life in a different body (Plato, as we have seen, accepted this view, and so did Vergil after him). It is only with great effort, and with the help of Orphic teachings, that the soul can at last be purified and the cycle of rebirth broken.

The soul's escape from its entanglement with matter required a life of ascetic purity, including abstention from such animal products as meat and woolen cloth, from beans (for unknown reasons), and from sexual intercourse. Magical formulas could also be useful in the world below. A number of gold plates have been found in tombs in south Italy and on Crete that contain Orphic instructions to be used by the dead.

The religious teachings advanced in the cult of Orpheus show strong influence from shamanism, a religious practice highly developed in Siberia and found across

Asia down into Thrace, Orpheus' legendary homeland. The training of a shaman involves arduous rites, including a symbolic dismemberment and reconstitution of his body (remarkably similar to the Orphic story about Dionysus). In this context, the myth of Orpheus becomes more than a simple folktale, the story of a man who went to the other world and returned. Orpheus can be viewed as a shaman in his own right, returning from the underworld to teach the truth about human nature and destiny.

Although the origin and exact nature of the Orphic teachings are, like Hades' realm, shrouded in mist, they seem to be connected with the doctrines of **Pythagoras** (sixth century B.C.). Pythagoras is best known for the philosophical claim that the essence of reality is to be found in mystical relations between numbers, proportions, and measures. Pythagoras also believed in metempsychosis, and he taught his followers to lead ascetic lives based on principles much like those of Orphism. Plato's dualistic conception of human nature—the soul as a divine spark entombed in an earthly body—parallels Orphic teaching and probably depends on it, as do his views on metempsychosis and the virtues of an ascetic life. Through Plato, Orphic doctrines influenced the fathers of the Christian church. Much of what we think of as Christianity is Platonic philosophy, some of it Orphic in origin. The early Christians themselves recognized the affinity, and paintings in catacombs sometimes show Christ as Orpheus.

Both Orpheus and Dionysus journeyed to Hades. Although Orpheus failed to bring back Eurydicê, he did bring back knowledge of death and its sequel, teachings spread through his followers. In his myth the master singer drew close to Apollo, god of musical harmony and prophecy, and away from Dionysus, god of ecstasy. He finally met his end at the hands of maenads, followers of Dionysus—according to some accounts, while paying tribute at dawn to Apollo, the rising sun.

KEY TERMS

Hades, 284	Tityus, 292	Charon, 299
Pluto, 284	Tantalus, 292	Ixion, 301
Erinyes, 285	Sisyphus, 292	Orpheus, 305
psychopompos, 286	Elysium, 294	Eurydicê, 305
Tiresias, 286	Er, 295	Pythagoras, 311
Elpenor, 289	Acheron, 297	

FURTHER READING

Bremmer, Jan, *The Early Greek Concept of the Soul* (Princeton, N.J., 1983). History and prehistory of Greek thinking about the soul.

Burkert, Walter, *Ancient Mystery Cults* (Cambridge, Mass., 1987). Lectures on the promise of salvation offered by various pagan cults, especially in the Hellenistic Period.

Garland, R., *The Greek Way of Death* (Ithaca, N.Y., 1985). Covers burial customs, attitudes about the dead, and hero-cults.

Linforth, I. M., *The Arts of Orpheus* (New York, 1973; first published in 1941). This important study rigorously examines our slender evidence for Orphic teachings; fundamental to all later studies, including M. L. West's (below).

Rohde, E., *Psyche, the Cult of Souls and Belief in Immortality among Ancient Greeks,* 8th ed., trans. W. B. Hillis (Chicago, 1987; first published in German, 1925). Pathbreaking study of ancient Greek conceptions of death and the soul.

Vermeule, Emily, *Aspects of Death in Early Greek Art and Poetry* (Berkeley, Calif., 1979). A stimulating review of how the Greeks looked at death, including burial and mourning rites, visions of the underworld, conception of the soul, and historical connections with the Bronze Age and other Mediterranean cultures.

West, M. L., *The Orphic Poems* (Oxford, U.K., 1983). The most modern review of our evidence for "Orphic" religion and literature. Although it was written for scholars, the general reader can follow most of the argument.

CHAPTER 12

INTRODUCTION TO HEROIC MYTH

I N DIVINE MYTHS the principal characters are gods and goddesses, but in legends—the second major category of myth examined in this book—the protagonists are human characters. Gods and goddesses often play a role, but legends are chiefly stories about heroes, stories that purport to narrate events from the human past.

We use the term *hero* very broadly to refer to the principal character in a play or film, to celebrate a neighbor who saves a cat in a tree, or to express admiration, as in the phrase "my hero." For us, a hero (or a heroine) is someone who stands out from others, someone distinguished by prominence, bravery, or merit. For the ancient Greeks, however, the term *hero* had a much more specific meaning. Homer used it to mean any "noble" or "well-born" figure, but later the term was applied exclusively to noble figures from the distant past, some of whom had come to be worshiped as powers dwelling beneath the earth, both male and female.

These hero-cults, centered around tombs surviving from the Bronze Age, were an important element in ancient Greek religion, but our concern is with the myths that recounted the lives and deeds of these legendary figures. Not all ancient cultures produced such heroic myths. There are no heroes (in the Greek sense of the word) in the myths of ancient Egypt and none in the Bible except for Samson. Even the ancient Romans had no true heroes of their own devising. But the ancient Mesopotamians did tell a series of stories about one such hero of their own, the great king **Gilgamesh.** The so-called epic of Gilgamesh is not an oral poem, like Homer's poems and Hesiod's, taken down in dictation, but rather a scribal exercise meant to be read and studied by other learned scribes. Still, the Gilgamesh stories have many elements in common with the legends of Greece, and the parallels are more than mere coincidence. We cannot be sure how these stories passed from East to West, but somehow they did. Before turning to the Greek legends themselves, therefore, we first examine the ancient Mesopotamian tales of Gilgamesh.

Gilgamesh seems to have been a real king of the Sumerian city of Uruk (ū-ruk; biblical "Erech"), and his example is strong evidence that legendary characters did live at one time. According to the surviving king lists inscribed on clay, he lived for 126 years sometime about 2600 B.C., the grandson of a certain Lugalbanda. He became the greatest of the Mesopotamian heroes (see Fig. 3.4), best remembered for building the city walls of Uruk. Fragments telling of his life and deeds survive recorded in Sumerian, Akkadian, Hittite, and other languages and scripts. On twelve tablets from the library of Assurbanipal in Nineveh (seventh century B.C.) survives something close to a connected tale, recording a version of the story that may go back a thousand years earlier. The story had many separate episodes, which in the tablets from Nineveh have been pieced together to form a whole.

GILGAMESH AND ENKIDU

The poem begins with a summary of Gilgamesh's career:

> The man who saw everything to the ends of the earth,
> who experienced everything, considered all!
> He saw what was hidden, he disclosed the undisclosed.
> He brought back a story of times before the flood.
> He went on a long journey. He was wearied; he rested.
> Everything he did he engraved on a monument made of stone.

Many have noticed how the first lines of the Greek *Odyssey* seem to echo this opening of Gilgamesh, a clue to continuity from East to West in the mythical tradition:

[1]
> Sing to me, O Muse, of the wily man,
> who wandered far after he had sacked the holy city of Troy.
> Many were the men whose cities he saw and he learned their mind
> and many the hurts he felt in his heart upon the sea,
> 5 trying to win his own life and the return of his comrades.

> HOMER, *Odyssey* (1–5)

Described as two thirds divine and one third mortal (just how this is possible is not clear), Gilgamesh was destined to die. He became king of Uruk but was proud and mighty and abused his royal power. All who challenged him he overcame, and he slept with every virgin of the city before her wedding night (the medieval *droit du seigneur*, the aristocratic male's right to be first to sleep with any woman).

At last the people of Uruk could bear no more and begged the gods for relief. Aruru, mother of the gods, pinched off a piece of clay and fashioned a rival to Gilgamesh, someone who could temper his spirit. Her creation was **Enkidu** (en-ki-doo), a primitive man who wore his locks long like a woman. His body was matted with hair, and he lived in the wild, ran with gazelles, ate grass, and drank at the water holes.

One day a trapper saw Enkidu. Terrified, the trapper reported to the city that there was a wild man on the steppe, destroying his traps and releasing his game. Meanwhile, Gilgamesh learned in a dream about the coming of one who would be his best friend:

> Gilgamesh says to him, the trapper:
> "Go, my trapper, and take a whore with you.
> When he [Enkidu] comes to water the beasts at the water hole,
> she will pull off her clothing and lay bare her ripeness.
> When he sees her, he will approach her.
> Then will his beasts, raised on the plains, reject him!"

For two days the trapper and the whore waited beside the water hole. On the third day Enkidu came. The whore bared her nakedness. For six days and seven nights Enkidu made love to her until, satisfied at last, he arose and went back to the wild, sadly changed:

> Enkidu was lessened, he could not run so fast,
> Yet he had acquired discernment, was wiser.
> He returned, sat at the feet of the whore.

The whore explained to Enkidu that now he was like a god and that he should follow her. From the shepherds he learned how to eat bread, drink wine, and wear clothes. A report came from the city that on that night Gilgamesh would deflower a virgin about to be married. Enkidu leaped up and declared that he would challenge the tyrant.

Enkidu entered the city. Crowds gathered around him, admired his strength, and compared him with Gilgamesh. As Gilgamesh came down the alley, Enkidu threw up a challenge. The two mighty men wrestled. Walls shook, doors broke. At last Enkidu was thrown to the ground. The rivals got up and, filled with mutual admiration, embraced one another warmly and began a lifelong friendship.

GILGAMESH AND HUMBABA

Gilgamesh proposed that he and Enkidu go together to the Land of the Living, also called the Land of the Cedars, ruled over by the sun god Shamash (**sha**-mash, = Sumerian Utu). Enkidu hesitated; he had already been there and feared Humbaba, the guardian of the forest. Gilgamesh brushed aside his friend's fears: Even if they perished, their names would live on. The heroes made careful preparations. They took with them mighty swords, axes, and bows. After crossing seven mountains, they came to the edge of the cedar forest, which extended one thousand miles in every direction:

> They stood, they admired the forest,
> stared and stared at the high cedars,
> stared and stared at the entrance to the cedars,
> where Humbaba left tracks as he paced on his rounds.
> The paths were worn, the road was good,

they admired the Cedar Mountain, dwelling of gods.
The cedars gleamed on the side of the mountain.
Their shade was delicious, bringing happiness.
The undergrowth was thick, blanketing the forest.

But when Enkidu touched the gate of the forest, his hand was at once paralyzed. Gilgamesh helped him to overcome his fear. They entered the forest and traveled far. At night they had ominous dreams, for Humbaba knew of their presence.

Then Gilgamesh took up his ax and chopped at the forest.
When Humbaba heard the noise,
he was angered. "Who has come,
who has injured the trees
which grow in my mountains?
Who has felled the cedar?"

The sun god Shamash urged Gilgamesh to attack Humbaba, but suddenly Gilgamesh was overcome with sleep and fell down on the ground as if dead. Enkidu could not stir him. Then Gilgamesh came to himself, stood up, and put on his armor. Overcome, with tears in his eyes, Humbaba begged for his life, even taking Gilgamesh by the hand like a friend. Gilgamesh struck Humbaba on the neck with his sword. Enkidu struck him too, and down fell Humbaba, dead. They offered his head to Enlil, the storm god, but Enlil was furious that they had killed the guardian of the forest.

GILGAMESH AND ISHTAR

When they arrived back in Uruk, Gilgamesh put away his dirty clothes and combed out his long hair. Ishtar (= the Sumerian goddess Inanna) saw how handsome he was and promised that, if he would only pour his seed into her, she would give him rich rewards. Gilgamesh sneered at the great goddess and abused her as follows, one of the best known passages in Mesopotamian literature:

"You are a charcoal grill which goes out in the cold!
You are a back door that lets in the squall and the storm,
a fortress which smashes down the brave,
pitch which fouls its bearers,
a siege engine that wrecks the enemy's land,
a shoe that pinches its owner's foot!
Which lover did you love forever?
Which of your shepherds pleases you for all time?
Listen, I will name your lovers:
To Tammuz [= Sumerian Dumuzi], lover of your youth,
you have given moaning year in, year out.
You loved the spotted shepherd-bird,
then struck him, breaking his wing.
Now he sits in the woods crying "Oh—my wing!"
You loved a lion, the perfection of power;

> twice seven pits you dug for him,
> Then you loved a stallion, a charger in war;
> what is his lot? the whip, the spur, and the lash."

Gilgamesh gave other examples of those who had suffered after yielding to the goddess of love, including her father's own gardener: When he brought her baskets of dates, she turned him into a frog!

Ishtar burst into a fury and stormed off to her father, Anu, king of heaven. She demanded that Anu send down the Bull of Heaven to destroy Gilgamesh. If Anu refused, she would crack open the gates of the underworld and release the legions of the dead (Inanna makes the same threat in the story of Inanna and Dumuzi, Chapter 9). Anu agreed, and Ishtar entered Uruk, leading the Bull of Heaven. The bull snorted, a chasm opened, and a hundred young men of Uruk fell in, then two hundred, then three hundred. The bull snorted again and a second chasm opened; in fell a hundred young men, then two hundred, then three hundred:

> When the bull snorted a third time a chasm opened,
> and Enkidu fell in,
> but leaped out and seized the Bull of Heaven by the horns.
> The Bull of Heaven shook spittle into his face
> and with its fat tail threw dung all around.

Enkidu, blinded with dung, called out to Gilgamesh, who plunged his sword into the monster's neck (Fig. 12.1). The heroes cut out its heart for the sun god Shamash. Ishtar, enraged, appeared on the towers of the city. Enkidu cut off the bull's genitals and threw them in her face. If he had the chance, he would lash the bull's guts to her body!

FIG. 12.1. Gilgamesh kills the Bull of Heaven. Terracotta votive relief, 2250–1900 B.C. Such votives were placed in temples as offerings or carried in camels' saddlebags to gain the gods' protection. (Musées Royaux d'Art et d'Histoire, Brussels; 0.1054).

The two friends held a great celebration, but the gods were deeply offended by Enkidu's behavior. One of the pair would have to die. Enkidu had terrible dreams. He knew that he would die. He dreamed that he had gone down

> to the house which is never left, once entered,
> on the trail of no return,
> to the house where the dwellers live in darkness,
> where dust and clay is food.
> They are clothed like birds, have wings for garments,
> and never see the light, dwelling in darkness.

Enkidu fell sick and for twelve days lay in bed. Then he died. Gilgamesh mourned, hovering over the body, waiting for it to revive. On the seventh day a maggot crawled from Enkidu's nose. Gilgamesh realized that, for Enkidu, the end had come.

The Quest for Eternal Life

Gilgamesh roamed the open country, terrified of the death that would one day be his lot as well. He decided to search for **Utnapishtim** (ut-na-**pish**-tim; "he saw life" = Sumerian Ziusudra, Akkadian Atrahasis, and Hebrew Noah). Utnapishtim and his wife were the only mortals to have survived the flood, for the gods had transported them across the sea to a place where they enjoyed everlasting life. Gilgamesh set out to question Utnapishtim about the living and the dead.

On his long journey Gilgamesh (like Heracles) killed ferocious lions lurking in the passes, then came to the high mountains of Mashu, where the sun rises. At the gate of the mountain, Scorpion Men, whose glance was death, stood guard. Somehow (the tablet is broken here) he persuaded them to let him pass. He entered a tunnel of darkness, where no one could see ahead or behind. For twelve leagues of darkness Gilgamesh traveled on the path of the sun. At last he saw light and emerged into the garden of the gods at the edge of the sea (perhaps the Phoenician coast of the Mediterranean). Gorgeous plants made of precious stones grew there.

In the garden lived **Siduri** (si-**doo**-rē), the divine beer maid. Siduri advised Gilgamesh to give up his search, accept mortality, eat good food and drink strong liquor, wear fine clothes, and love his family; no one, except Shamash, had ever crossed the lethal waters of the sea. But she could not persuade him and Gilgamesh set off, punting across the waters of death. On the other side, Utnapishtim came up, complained about Gilgamesh's uncouth appearance, then delivered a speech about death:

> No one sees Death,
> No one sees the face of Death,
> No one hears the voice of Death.
> Brutal Death just cuts you down.
> We may build a house, we may build a nest:
> our brothers divide it when we die.
> There may be hostility in the land,
> but then the river rises in flood.°

rises in flood: That is, death settles all disputes.

Dragonflies drift upon the water,
they turn their gaze upon the sun.
From the beginning there has been no permanence.
The sleeping and the dead are the same.
There is no picture of Death.

How did Utnapishtim escape the lot of other mortals? Utnapishtim answered this question by relating the story of the flood. He and his wife had escaped death because of Enlil, but who would intercede for Gilgamesh?

To prove Gilgamesh's innate mortality, Utnapishtim suggested a trial. Let Gilgamesh stay awake for six days and seven nights, the length of time of the flood. If he could not conquer Sleep, the brother of Death, how could he conquer Death himself? Gilgamesh thought the trial easy, but promptly fell asleep and awoke seven nights later. Although he denied that he had slept, Utnapishtim pointed to seven loaves in progressive stages of decay that his wife had baked and placed, one each day, at the hero's side.

There was still a chance that Gilgamesh might escape at least the ravages of old age. Utnapishtim told him of a prickly herb that grew deep in the sea. Its flower, which looked like a rose, would restore youth to an old man. Gilgamesh tied stones to his feet and dropped down deep into the water, found the plant, and plucked it, although its thorns tore his hands. He cut the ropes that held the stones, bobbed to the surface, and came ashore. Gilgamesh set out for home. On the way he stopped to bathe in a cool well. A serpent that lived in the well emerged and ate the plant. That is why serpents can renew their youth.

Gilgamesh realized that immortality could never be his. He sat down and wept. He returned to Uruk and admired its great city walls, his true achievement. He engraved his tale on a stone, grew old, and died. He was given a splendid burial.

Observations: The Hero Caught between Nature and Culture

The Gilgamesh epic is the longest and most ambitious literary epic recorded in cuneiform writing. A central theme is the contrast and hostility between the natural world and the cultural world of humans. Enkidu is the "natural man"—his hair is long and he eats grass with the beasts of the field. After intercourse with a woman, he becomes "wise" and is separated from the natural world, the lot of all humankind. Similarly, Adam and Eve, after eating from the Tree of Knowledge, see that they are naked (discover their sexuality) and must leave the Garden of Eden (the natural world). When Enkidu is dying, he bitterly blames the world of culture for his undoing. He blames the trapper who found him and the whore who tamed him. Sympathizing with Enkidu's resentment, Gilgamesh puts on animal skins and wanders through the wild on a quest to the ends of the earth. When the quest fails, he returns from nature to the world of culture, dons clean clothes, and rejoices in the city walls, the symbolic divide between the human and natural worlds.

Although gods occasionally die, their ordinary lot is to live forever. Only a mortal like Gilgamesh can suffer anguish from speculating on the meaning of action and of life and on his hopeless future in a stale, dank afterlife where clay is food and good people and bad, kings and ordinary mortals, are treated alike. This very torment is an essential part of his nature as a hero and explains our interest in him: We, too, live between nature and culture, and we, too, are destined to die.

The deep concerns and speculations that underlie this story developed specifically in Mesopotamia, a dangerous land with mysterious beginnings. Egyptians did not fear death and so did not seek a way to escape it; they had already found that way. The hostility toward the female stands out strongly in this story: We have already seen the heirs of this attitude in Hesiod's story of Pandora and in the biblical story of Adam and Eve, and we will see more in the chapters to come. Ishtar is sexual attraction, irresistible force, and death all wrapped into one. Here for the first time appears the story of the journey in search of truth. We receive this story directly from the immensely influential Greek *Odyssey,* from which the West has taken its self-image as a restless inquiring being, spinning restlessly on across the prairies, even into space. But this story is not Western in origin at all.

FOLKTALE MOTIFS IN HEROIC MYTHS

Like other ancient legends, the story of Gilgamesh does have some connection with historical fact. We noted earlier that Gilgamesh was in fact a king of the Mesopotamian city of Uruk, a real place where his name has been found on clay tablets. We know nothing about him or his reign, but we can imagine that the real king Gilgamesh might have been a great ruler who accomplished much in his lifetime. It is easy to believe that he or his followers would have been eager to see his reputation enhanced and his memory preserved for posterity (just as the story itself tells of Gilgamesh's longing to be remembered in reputation and in words graven on stone). The Mesopotamian legend of Gilgamesh, like many ancient Greek legends, probably began in such a wish to preserve a memory of the words and deeds of a real man who accomplished great things during his lifetime.

In the fluidity of oral tradition, however, such stories about past heroes can easily mix with other elements having no real connection to any particular historical figure. The hero's name is preserved, but the stories told about him come to incorporate patterns drawn from other stories, many of them motifs known to us from folklore. We see a number of these motifs in the story of Gilgamesh:

- The hero's birth is miraculous or unusual, but of his childhood we know little (Gilgamesh was partly divine).

- The hero has great strength and is a menace to his compatriots as well as to others (Gilgamesh abused the people of Uruk).

- The hero's truest companion is another male (Enkidu).

- The hero falls under an enemy's power and is compelled to perform impossible labors (Gilgamesh destroys Humbaba).

- The hero breaks a taboo, and a terrible price is demanded (Enlil was angry that Gilgamesh and Enkidu killed Humbaba, lord of the forest).

- The hero resists the temptations of an irresistible but dangerous woman, whom he curses and derides (Ishtar).

- The hero is responsible for his best friend's death (Enkidu dies after he and Gilgamesh kill the Bull of Heaven).

- The hero goes on a long journey to discover the secret of eternal life (deathless Utnapishtim lives beyond the waters that separate this world from the next).

- The hero returns home and accepts his limitations (Gilgamesh returns to rule Uruk).

- The hero is rewarded with something of great value (at his death Gilgamesh receives full honors).

Many of the same elements recur, with slight variations, in the legends of the ancient Greeks, as we will see in the following chapters.

KEY TERMS

hero, 313	Utnapishtim, 318
Gilgamesh, 313	Siduri, 318
Enkidu, 314	

FURTHER READING

Dalley, Stephanie, *Myths from Mesopotamia: Creation, the Flood, Gilgamesh, and Others* (Oxford, U.K., 1989). The most recent translations, with commentary, of the Mesopotamian myths of Atrahasis, Gilgamesh, the descent of Ishtar, and other important myths (see also Further Reading for Chapter 3).

George, Andrew, *The Babylonian Gilgamesh Epic* (Oxford, U.K., 1992). New research on the Gilgamesh epic, including previously unpublished fragments.

Sandars, N. K., *The Epic of Gilgamesh* (Baltimore, Md., 1972). Readable, inexpensive compilation, with a good introduction, of the many fragments (written in several languages) that make up the epic.

West, M. L., *The East Face of Helicon: West Asiatic Elements in Greek Poetry and Myth* (Oxford, U.K., 1997). Powerful argument that Greek literature is really Near Eastern literature.

CHAPTER 13

PERSEUS AND MYTHS
OF THE ARGIVE PLAIN

The son of Abas remained, Acrisius, cousin of Bacchus,
whom he churlishly drove away from the well-walled city of Argos.
Acrisius warred with the god, denying that Zeus was his father;
Perseus too he disclaimed, the child of the shower of gold
that quickened Danaë's womb. Yet mark you the power of truth:
Acrisius was forced to repent of both these arrogant gestures,
violence toward the god, disowning the child of his daughter.

OVID, *Metamorphoses* 4.607–614

THE **ARGIVE PLAIN** (**ar**-jīv; see Map II) is the richest province in Greece in its physical remains from the Greek Bronze Age and in its wealth of myths. Even today, the ruins of Mycenae are some of the most impressive in Greece. Almost the only large sculpture to survive from the Bronze Age, two lions rampant on either side of a Minoan column, loom over the great entrance way, framed by enormous stones (see Fig. 13.1). Around the citadel are nine beehive tombs, domes constructed underground to house the remains of Mycenaean kings. The so-called Treasury of Atreus has the largest dome ever constructed until the Romans built the Pantheon fifteen hundred years later. Graves excavated in the nineteenth century contained an enormous quantity of golden objects of extraordinary quality. In the Bronze Age, Mycenae was a populous city of enormous wealth and power. In myth, it was first the city of **Perseus** (**per**-sūs, or **per**-sē-us), later that of Atreus and his son Agamemnon, who led the Greek forces against Troy (Chapters 19 and 20).

Five miles away stands **Tiryns** (**ti**-rinz), smaller than Mycenae, a fortress sur-

FIG. 13.1. Victorian visitors at the Lion Gate at Mycenae. Nearly the only surviving large sculpture from the Greek Bronze Age stands in the "relieving triangle," a device that reduces structural weight, over the lintel of the main gate. The central pillar in the sculpture, beside which two lions stand heraldically, is carved in same style as pillars found in Crete. Through the gate one can see the lower retaining wall of the citadel, which rises to the right to the top of the hill.   (Deutsches Archäologisches Institut, Athens)

rounded by amazing walls of immense stones carefully fitted together. Tiryns was the birthplace of Heracles, although relations between Mycenae and Tiryns are confused in myth, as they may have been in reality. Argos itself, between Mycenae and Tiryns, was capital of the Argive plain in the Classical Period. It was not important in the Bronze Age, but in the mythical tradition it was often confused with Mycenae.

In this chapter we consider stories of the founding of settlements on the Argive plain and the famous hero Perseus, whose stories are closer to folkatle than those of any other Greek hero, a measure of these myths' great age. But the story of Perseus begins generations before his birth.

IO AND HER DESCENDANTS

The Wanderings of Io

Melia, nymph of an ash tree, was an Oceanid, daughter of Oceanus and Tethys (Chart 13.1). She united with Inachus (īn-a-kus), god of the river that flows through the Argive plains, and bore two sons and a daughter, **Io** (ī-ō), ancestor of three great dynasties: the houses of Argos, Thebes, and Crete.

In the best-known version, Io was a priestess of Hera[1] after whom Zeus lusted.

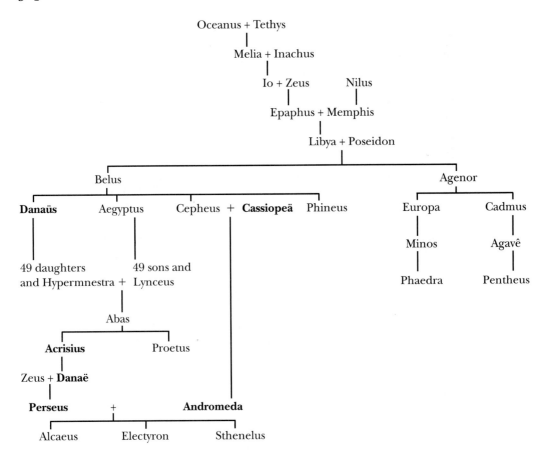

CHART 13.1. The Descent of Perseus

He surrounded her with a mist and within it had his way with her. Hera, seeing a mysterious cloud on an otherwise bright and sunny day, came to investigate. Zeus barely had time to disguise his philandering by changing Io into a cow. Not that Hera was deceived—she admired the handsome animal and asked for it as a gift. Zeus was reluctant to turn his transformed lover over to his wife, but he feared her anger and complied. Hera tethered the cow to an olive tree in a grove near Mycenae. To keep her away from Zeus, she set up the monster Argus, a child of Gaea, who had a hundred eyes and never slept.

    To free Io from his wife's malice, Zeus sent Hermes, god of stealth and thieves, but even Hermes could not at first get past Argus' ever-vigilant watch; while some of the monster's eyes were asleep, the rest were always awake. Then Hermes, disguised

[1]Evidently in a predecessor to the classical Heraeum, the holiest classical temple to Hera in mainland Greece, constructed on a Bronze Age site on the northern edge of the Argive plain, not far from Mycenae.

FIG. 13.2. Hermes slays Argus, hence his name Argeïphontes, "Argus-killer," Attic pot, c. 490 B.C. Hermes, with his characteristic traveler's cap (*petasos*) and cape thrown back, prepares to stab the monster Argus, shown as a naked bearded man with eyes all over his body. Io, shown as a steer, watches; over her is written the word for "beautiful woman."   (Museum für Kunst und Gewerbe, Hamburg; 1966.3h)

as a shepherd, sang a lullaby, and one by one Argus' eyes grew heavy. When all were closed, the god moved in and cut off Argus' head, which is why Hermes is called Argeïphontes (ar-jē-i-**fon**-tēz), "Argus-killer" (Fig. 13.2). Hera placed Argus' eyes in the tail of the peacock, one of her favorite birds.

Io was free, but now Hera sent a gadfly to torment her. Stung constantly, she wandered through Greece, to the northwest—the Ionian Sea was named after Io—then across the Pindus range to Macedonia, and through Thrace to the straits that divide Europe from Asia.[2] Ever since, these straits have been called the Bosporus, "cow-crossing." Io wandered through Scythia, north of the Black Sea in what is today southern Russia, or, according to other accounts, across Anatolia in what is now central Turkey. She ended up in the Caucasus Mountains at the eastern end of the Black Sea. There she found Prometheus, pinioned by Zeus to a mountain crag because he refused to divulge the name of the woman whose offspring would be greater than his father (see Chapter 5).

The principal surviving account of the myth of Io appears in Aeschylus' play *Prometheus Bound*. Io tells Prometheus the story of her seduction and persecution:

[2]Site of the later Greek colony Byzantium, renamed Constantinople after the first Christian emperor, who ruled A.D. 307–337; now the Turkish city of Istanbul.

[645] Night after night foul dreams surged over my virginal bed,
seducing me with their whispers: "You lucky, fortunate girl!
Why are you still a virgin, when the greatest suitor of all
is eager to enter your bed? Zeus burns and itches with lust—
his heart is asking for you; why, then, must you be so coy?
650 Come, girl, show some sense, and don't be so scornful
of lustful philandering Zeus. Steal down to the meadows of Lerna,°
down past the sheepfolds, past the pens where your father keeps cattle;
there you can bring satisfaction to the lecherous craving of Zeus."
Every night I was bothered, poor girl, by such endless phantoms,
655 until I gathered my courage and told my father the nightmares.
He sent long strings of inquirers to Delphi, and even Dodona,°
to ask what words or actions the gods would find to their liking.
All they reported were mere conundrums, riddles, enigmas.
Finally Inachus heard a command that was, at least, clear in its menace,
660 bidding him drive me out of the bounds of my home and my country,
an exile destined to wander to the very ends of the earth.
If he refused, a thunderbolt, blazing with fire from heaven,
would fall on the land and annihilate all the race of mankind.
Reluctantly he obeyed the command of prophetic Apollo,
665 driving me out forever, homeless, abandoned, reluctant,
forced as he was to yield to great Zeus's imperious orders.
At once my outward form and the soul within me were altered:
horns, as you see, grew out; stung by a fire-mouthed deerfly,
in maddened torment I plunged in the cooling stream of Cerchnia,
670 the fountain of Lerna. But Argus, the shepherd, the child of the Earth,
malignantly followed my steps with his baleful hundred eyes,
till a fate he never expected deprived him of life and of breath.
Plagued by his ghost in the form of a deerfly, the vengeance of Hera,
I wander from land to land, all over the face of the earth.

AESCHYLUS, *Prometheus Bound* (645–686)

651. *Lerna:* A swampy plain near Argos.   656. *Dodona:* Zeus had an oracle there.

Prometheus predicts to Io what wanderings still lie ahead, a magical journey
through a geography whose hopeless confusion reflects Greek ignorance and fancy
about distant places, even in the fifth century B.C. Io is horrified by the prospect of
these endless wanderings, but Prometheus comforts her: In Egypt she will regain her
human form after Zeus touches her with his hands. She will then be pregnant with
Epaphus (**ep**-a-fus), "he who has been touched," future king of Egypt. And a descendant of hers in the thirteenth generation (Heracles) will set him, Prometheus,
free.

The story of Io has the same general structure as that of the daughters of Proetus (Chapter 10): In both a god causes the transformation of an Argive princess into
a cow, who wanders aimlessly through the countryside. In some versions Hera, not
Dionysus, transformed the Proetids as well. In origin Io may be Hera herself, whose
animal was the cow and whom Homer regularly calls *boôpis*, "cow-eyed," just as Callisto, whom Artemis turned into a bear, looks like a doublet of Artemis (Chapter 8).
The Greeks identified Io with the Egyptian goddess Isis, sister of Osiris and a mother-

goddess in her own right; not only does *Isis* seem to have the same word root as *Io*, but the Egyptians often represented Isis as a cow or with the head or horns of a cow (see Fig. 9.2).

The Crimes of the Danaïds

Epaphus became king of Egypt and married Memphis, eponym of the Egyptian capital of the Old Kingdom at the juncture of the delta and the river, roughly the site of modern Cairo.[3] Memphis was the daughter of Nilus, eponym of the river. Epaphus and Memphis had a daughter Libya, eponym of the country west of the Nile, who by Poseidon had two sons, Agenor, father of Europa (see Chart 13.1), and Belus. Belus became king of a vast territory on either side of the Nile, married another daughter of Nilus, and by her had the twin sons Aegyptus (ē-**jip**-tus) and **Danaüs** (dan-**ā**-us; see Chart 13.1).

Belus set up Aegyptus as king of Arabia[4] and Danaüs as king of Libya. Aegyptus conquered a people called the Melampods ("blackfeet") in the Nile valley and named the kingdom after himself.[5] By numerous wives Aegyptus had fifty sons and Danaüs fifty daughters, the **Danaïds** (**dan**-a-ids). When Aegyptus suggested to his brother Danaüs that the fifty girls marry his fifty sons, Danaüs suspected that Aegyptus' true motive was to add Libya, birthright of the Danaïds, to his own kingdom of Arabia. With Athena's help, therefore, he built one of the earliest ships and fled with his daughters across the sea to Argos in the Peloponnesus, the home of his ancestress Io. There Danaüs, an eponym of the Danaäns (dan-**ā**-ans), became king.

The fifty sons of Aegyptus soon arrived across the sea in hot pursuit of the Danaïds and demanded that Danaüs give his daughters to them.[6] Eventually Danaüs agreed to his brother's demands, but on the wedding night he gave each of his daughters a dagger and instructed them to murder their husbands. Next morning forty-nine of the daughters presented their father with the heads of their husbands. Only Hypermnestra had spared her husband, Lynceus—the folktale motif "all but one"—because Lynceus had spared her virginity. The heads were buried in the swamp of Lerna and the bodies given a funeral outside the city. For defying her father's orders, Hypermnestra was imprisoned, but later released and allowed to remain with Lynceus. From Lynceus and Hypermnestra descend the House of Argos.

Understandably, after this incident Danaüs had difficulty finding suitable husbands for his daughters. At last he held a foot race and gave them away as prizes, offering fancy shields as an added inducement.

---

[3]President Andrew Jackson named Memphis, Tennessee, after the Egyptian city because it, too, stands at the juncture of two waterways, the Wolf and Mississippi rivers.

[4]*Arabia* was often used to include Africa east of the Nile.

[5]In fact, *Egypt* is a corruption of an Egyptian phrase meaning "the house of the *ka* [vital force] of Ptah," the name of an Old Kingdom temple in Memphis dedicated to the creator god Ptah.

[6]This part of the myth is the subject of a surviving play by Aeschylus, the *Suppliants* (unfortunately, the second and third plays of the trilogy are lost).

FIG. 13.3. Poseidon and Amymonê, on an Attic oil-jar, c. 430 B.C. Such scenes of pursuit were common in Attic art of the fifth century and seem to have been a metaphor for courtship. Here Poseidon raises his trident, a tool used to spear tuna-fish in the Mediterranean from the earliest times (other vase-painters show the trident actually penetrating her thigh). Although Amymonê is running away, her gestures indicate the bride's submission: Her gaze meets Poseidon as the bride first meets the gaze of her husband on the wedding night. Her left hand, raising her garment in the traditional bridal "unveiling," indicates the moment of highest sexual tension, as Amymonê prepares to submit. Such vases were given as gifts to young brides.   (Metropolitan Museum of Art, New York, Rogers Fund; 17.230.35)

Observations: Springs and the Dangers of Woman

The myth of the Danaïds appears to be a conflation of different traditions. One explanation suggests that in an early form the burial of the heads of the sons of Aegyptus was an etiological tale to explain the origin of the great swamps in Lerna at the southern edge of the Argive plain, "which have fifty heads." There are fifty Nereids, too, spirits of the water, and there are many magical uses of fifty, the number of phases of the moon per year.[7] The Danaïds' connection with freshwater springs emerges from another story: When the Danaïds arrived in Argos, the land was waterless, cursed by Poseidon because the local inhabitants chose Hera as presiding divinity rather than him. One of the Danaïds, Amymonê, went in search of a spring. She threw a spear at a deer, missed, and struck a sleeping satyr, who leaped up and tried to rape her. Poseidon appeared, chased away the satyr with a cast of his trident, then raped Amymonê himself (Fig. 13.3). When he pulled the trident from the rock, out sprang the springs of Lerna.

[7]The Jewish/Christian feast of "Pentecost" (= Greek "fiftieth") came fifty days after Passover/Easter.

The story of the Danaïds carrying water in the underworld in leaky vessels to fill a trough (Chapter 11, Fig. 11.2), first attested in the Hellenistic Period, further associates them with freshwater springs, although the story is a late invention apparently inspired by Orphic teachings about the miseries of the underworld. Whatever their original association with springs and water, an undisguised theme of the story has become the resentment of the female at submitting to the male in lawful marriage. In early versions of the myth, the Danaïds were not punished for their crime, no doubt because they had saved their people from the wicked sons of Aegyptus, the Egyptians. The association between Egypt and the Danaäns who lived on the Argive plain suggests to some that the story of the Danaïds may go back to the end of the Bronze Age, about 1200 B.C. Texts from this time inscribed on Egyptian temples report that dangerous seaborne invaders called Danuna, one of the Peoples of the Sea, had attacked Egypt, bringing with them their families and possessions. But the Egyptians destroyed them all. Remnants seem to have settled in Gaza, where they are remembered as the biblical tribe of Dan. *Danaän*, then, was the name of an early Greek tribe, one of the Sea Peoples. By Homer's day the name was used interchangeably with *Argives* and *Achaeans* for the Greek forces at Troy. In Homer's time, the later name *Hellenes* meant the people of a small district in Thessaly.

THE LEGEND OF PERSEUS

Danaë and the Shower of Gold

Lynceus ruled Argos after Danaüs died. His son, Abas, had twin sons **Acrisius** (a-**kris**-i-us) and Proetus, the second set of hostile twins in the house of Argos (after Danaüs and Aegyptus). These twins hated each other so much that, like Jacob and Esau in the Bible, they quarreled even in the womb.[8] When grown, Acrisius drove Proetus from the land. Proetus crossed the Aegean Sea to Lycia (in southern Turkey), took refuge with the local king, and married his daughter. Proetus then returned to the Argive plain with an army of Lycians at his back and seized Tiryns; the Cyclopes built for him its massive walls. Acrisius remained king of Argos. Each brother married and had daughters: Proetus fathered the Proetids (for their madness and fate, see Chapter 10), and Acrisius fathered **Danaë** (**dan**-a-ē).

However, Acrisius wanted a male heir. He consulted the oracle and was told that he would have one in the son of Danaë, but that this grandson would also kill him. Attempting to forestall fate, Acrisius constructed an underground chamber of bronze and imprisoned Danaë in it. But Zeus fell in love with her and came in the form of a shower of gold that fell from the roof of the chamber into her womb (Fig. 13.4). In this way was Perseus ("destroyer"?) conceived: Heroes have special conceptions and are often part divine.

When Perseus was several years old, Acrisius heard a child's shout from inside the chamber and knew the truth. He refused to believe that Zeus was the father. Afraid to kill his daughter and grandson outright, he ordered a wooden box built

[8]Genesis 25.22. So Isis and Osiris hated their brother Seth even in the womb.

FIG. 13.4. Danaë and the shower of gold, Attic vase, c. 490–480 B.C. Danaë prepares for bed, untying the band that binds her hair, when the shower of gold, falling like rain, surprises her. This is the earliest surviving representation of the myth.   (Hermitage Museum, St. Petersburg; 15.1602A)

(Fig. 13.5), placed them both within it, and cast the box into the sea. Simonides, a lyric poet of the sixth and fifth centuries B.C., wrote a charming choral poem describing Danaë's anxiety for her young son as they drift over the high seas. A fragment survives:

[1]   She huddled down in the stout-walled box,
       which the wind drove on, and the surges tossed.
       Terror whitened her tear-stained cheek,
       but she clung to Perseus with guardian arms.
5   "Heaven save us both in this hour of peril," she murmured,
       "and you, dear innocent, warm and well-fed, sleep on,
       locked in our wooden prison with nails of bronze,
       shrouded in darkness visible, blue-black night.
       The crash of the breakers over your head,
10   the driving waves and the hurrying wind,
       mean nothing to you.
                    So snuggle down
       in your warm dark blanket, upon my breast.
       My heart would break if you knew that this storm
       was a threat to you, if your baby ears
15   might understand my terrified words.
       So sleep, my baby; and sleep, you winds,

FIG. 13.5. Danaë and Perseus about to be locked in a box, Attic vase, c. 490 B.C. Acrisius, to the left, oversees a carpenter who is drilling a hole in the box with a bow drill. Danaë stands behind the box, which will soon imprison her, with an imploring gesture. The nurse to the right holds the infant Perseus. Two breathing holes seem to be drilled in the side of the box.   (Museum of Fine Arts, Boston; 13.200)

and sleep, you trouble that knows no end.
O Father Zeus, send a blessed relief!
With humble and righteous heart I implore you!"

SIMONIDES, fragment 38 (p. 37B)

Instead of drowning, mother and child were saved when a fisherman named Dictys (**dik**-tis), "netman," caught the box in his net off the island of Seriphos (se-**rī**-fos), a poor and miserable place, little more than a cliff jutting up from the sea. Danaë and Perseus lived with Dictys, and the boy grew to manhood. Then Dictys' brother, **Polydectes** (pol-i-**dek**-tēz, "much-receiver," a common epithet of Death), the king of the island, fell in love with Danaë and wanted her to become his mistress. Danaë was unwilling and Perseus defended her refusal. Polydectes therefore pretended that he wanted to marry Hippodamia[9] and demanded a wedding gift of a fine horse from every young man on the island. Perseus had no horses, but boasted that he would instead bring anything else Polydectes wanted—even a Gorgon's head! "Fine, get that," Polydectes agreed, seeing an easy way to get rid of the young man: Now the hero has found his adversary, the monster he must overcome.

[9]The daughter of Oenomaüs (see Chapter 19).

Perseus the Gorgon-Slayer

No one had ever returned alive from an encounter with the three death-dealing **Gorgons:** Stheno (**sthē**-nō, "strength"), Euryalê (ū-**rī**-a-lē, "far-leaper"), and **Medusa** (me-**dū**-sa, probably a shortened form of *Eurymedousa,* "wide-ruling"). The Gorgons had enormous tusks and wide, staring eyes that turned anyone who saw them into stone, bronze hands, snakes for hair, and golden wings; they could not be approached on foot because they lived at the edge of the world. Only Medusa was mortal, but even if one succeeded in killing her, escape from her swift-winged sisters would be impossible.

Athena appeared to Perseus and gave him exact instructions. He must extract essential information from the **Graeae** (**grē**-ē), daughters of Phorcys and Ceto (**sē**-tō) like the Gorgons themselves (see Chart 4.3). The Graeae, two or three in number, were hideous hags (although they had beautiful cheeks) and lived near the place where Atlas supported the world. They had only one tooth and one eye between them, which they passed to whichever wanted to see or eat.

With Athena's help, Perseus traveled almost to the edge of the world and found the Graeae in a cave. He grabbed the eye as it was being passed and demanded that the Graeae reveal to him where certain nymphs could be found. Then he gave them back the eye (or, just to be mean, threw it into nearby Lake Tritonis).

Perseus found the nymphs and from them received several objects essential to his success: the cap of Hades, which made the wearer invisible; winged sandals, which enabled him to fly through the air; and a special leather pouch, called a *kibisis,* in which he could conceal the Gorgon's head. Hermes also gave him a distinctive steel sword, a kind of scimitar. Finally, the nymphs instructed him how to find the Gorgons: Heroes need assistance to overcome the monster.

Perseus flew to the river Ocean. There the Gorgons lay, sound asleep, surrounded by the twisted, petrified forms of those who had earlier come too near. Because looking directly at them meant death, he crept past Stheno and Euryalê, using his polished bronze shield as a mirror, and slashed off the head of Medusa. Medusa was pregnant by Poseidon, and as the head came free, out sprang the winged horse Pegasus[10] and a giant, Chrysaör (kri-**sā**-or), "he of the golden sword" (Fig. 13.6). Perseus quickly pushed the snaky head into the *kibisis* and flew away on his winged sandals. Although Stheno and Euryalê awoke and pursued him, they could see nothing, thanks to the cap of Hades (Fig. 13.7).

Meanwhile Polydectes, sure that Perseus would never return, pressed his wooing of Danaë with violence. When Perseus arrived back at Seriphos, he found his mother and Dictys cowering at the altar of the gods for protection from Polydectes. Perseus walked into the palace where Polydectes was reveling with his friends and announced that he had returned with the Gorgon's head. Of course, no one believed him. He turned his eyes aside as he pulled the Gorgon's head from the *kibisis* and Polydectes and his friends at once turned to stone. Perseus established Dictys as king of the island, gave his magical implements to Hermes to take back to the

---

[10]From Greek *pegai* = "springs" of water: A spring was said to burst forth where he struck the ground with his hoof. Pegasus later fell into the hands of Bellerophon and ended as a constellation.

FIG. 13.6. Perseus slays Medusa, from a relief-decorated amphora from Boeotia, early seventh century B.C. He turns his face aside to avoid being turned to stone. Over his shoulder he carries the scabbard for his sword and the leather pouch. He wears the cap of Hades and the magical sandals. Medusa does not yet have the form typical later of a woman with a Gorgon's head but is represented as a skull-faced woman with a mare's body attached at the waist. Mysterious plants frame the scene. The meaning of the salamander is not clear. (Musée du Louvre, Paris, LA 45998; Giraudon/ Art Resource)

nymphs, and delivered the Gorgon's head to Athena, who ever after wore it on her breastplate or shield or attached it to the aegis that she draped around her shoulders (compare Fig. 8.6).

The professional poet Pindar told the myth of Perseus and Medusa in an ode he wrote to celebrate the victory of one Midas, a resident of the Greek colony of Acragas (modern Agrigento) in Sicily, in the flute contest[11] at Apollo's sanctuary at Delphi in 490 B.C. In an amazing image Pindar suggests that Athena invented the first flute because she was inspired by the wailing of Stheno and Euryalê when they beheld the death of their sister, a good example of the flexibility of myth in the hand of Greece's finest poets. The poem ends with some general reflections about the uncertainty of human life:

[1]   City delighting in splendor, fairest city of men,
       loved by Persephonê,° dweller high on your columned hill

2. *Persephonê:* For some reason her cult was strong among the Greeks living in Sicily and southern Italy.

[11]The instrument ordinarily translated as "flute" had a vibrating double reed, like a modern oboe. In the hands of the effeminate Phrygians it maddened the followers of Dionysus; in those of the warlike Spartans, it aroused their spirits to battle.

FIG. 13.7. A Gorgon pursues Perseus, Attic vase, c. 490 B.C. Winged, with snakes in her hair, she has a fearsome face and huge mouth from which protrude boar's teeth and a thick, lolling tongue. Perseus, shown on the other side of the vase, wears winged sandals and magic hat and carries a scimitar and *kibisis* over his shoulder. The Gorgon's head alone, often represented in ancient art, is called a gorgoneion.
(Staatliche Antikensammlungen und Glyptothek, Munich; Hirmer Fotoarchiv)

      smiling over the banks of Acragas, feeder of sheep—
         hear me, my lady;°
5   join the gods' applause, the praise of men of good will;
      accept this Pythian crown, this glory of Midas;
      welcome Midas himself, in Athena's music
         champion of Hellas.
      This art of intricate song the goddess developed
10   from the gloomy dirge, sung by the arrogant Gorgons,
      who poured its sound of woe from their serpent heads,
         mourning their sister.
      Perseus heard it, slaying the first of the maidens;°
      again, when he brought their doom to the lords of Seriphos;
15   again, when he stole the eye of the daughters of Phorcys,°
         and when Polydectes
      was forced to curse his feast and the gifts he called for—

---

4. *my lady:* That is, the city of Acragas.   13. *the maidens:* The Gorgons.   15. *when he stole the eye . . . .:* Pindar is not worried by the chronological order of Perseus' adventures.

Danaë's servitude, his forcing her to marriage,
his charge that Medusa's head be fetched by the hero,
20   golden-rain fathered.
The maiden goddess° canceled her servant's duty°
and set herself to arrange the ringing flute-notes,
mimicking shrill sounds of hungry Euryalê,
     lamenting Medusa.
25   The goddess adapted the sound for the use of mortals,
naming it "the song of the many-headed serpents,"
the song which fires men to heroic action
     defending their nation.
Its music spurts from the brazen mouth of the woodwind,
30   which growls from the vibrant reeds of the Graces' city,°
by the holy stream Cephisus,° whose nymph and guardian
     watches the dancing.
No bliss which mortals know can fall to our portion
without hard work, and a god, at a moment's notice
35   may end that bliss. No mortal man can escape from
     destiny's orders.
To all a time will come like a bolt from heaven,
of fortune, far beyond all his expectation,
granting one a wish beyond bounds of dreaming—
40   denying another.

PINDAR, Pythian 12 (1–29)

Perseus and Andromeda

In a later addition to the myth, Perseus did not return directly to Seriphos, but flew first over Ethiopia, or Joppa on the Palestinian coast.[12] The land was ruled by Cepheus (sē-fūs), who like Aegyptus and Danaüs was a son of Belus and hence a distant relative of Perseus himself. Looking down, Perseus saw Cepheus' daughter **Andromeda**[13] (an-**dro**-me-da) chained to a rock and about to be devoured by the sea-monster Ceto.[14] This situation had come about because Andromeda's vain mother, **Cassiopeä** (ka-sī-o-**pē**-a), had boasted that she was more beautiful than the Nereids. The infuriated sea-nymphs complained to Poseidon, who sent a flood over the land. An oracle revealed that only the sacrifice of the king's daughter would prevent the land's destruction. As he flew over, Perseus immediately fell in love with the lovely

---

21. *maiden goddess:* Athena.   21. *duty:* That is, assisting Perseus to overcome Medusa.   30. *Graces' city:* Athens.   31. *Cephisus* (se-**fī**-sus): A stream that runs through Athens.

---

[12]Also called Jaffa, it is the only part, and barely that, between Egypt and Phoenicia, at the southern edge of the modern city of Tel Aviv.

[13]Something is wrong with the genealogy here. As daughter of Cepheus, Andromeda should have lived four generations before Perseus; see Chart 13.1.

[14]Hence our words *cetacean,* "referring to whales," and *spermaceti,* "whale-seed," the waxy substance in the head of sperm whales.

Vasari's *Perseus and Andromeda*

Architect and painter Giorgio Vasari (1511–1574) is best known today for his history of Italian art, *Lives of the Best Italian Architects, Painters, and Sculptors.* Written in 1550 in the late Renaissance, the book is invaluable not only for the attributions of works to artists and anecdotes about them but for its account of the theories of art in Italy. A close friend of Michelangelo and Titian, Vasari traveled throughout Italy to interview other artists and study their works for his book.

In Vasari's well-known painting, based on Ovid's account (Fig. P 13.1), Perseus frees the naked Andromeda, who is chained to a rock. Perseus is wearing the Cap of Hades, which makes him invisible, and the winged sandals, which enable him to fly. At his feet is the polished bronze shield that he used as a mirror to avoid looking at Medusa. In the lower left is Pegasus, who sprang forth when Medusa's head was cut off. At the lower center is Medusa's head, whose terrifying power petrifies the leaves beneath it. Sea nymphs on the right examine the new substance of coral. In the middle ground to the left of Perseus is the dying sea-monster Ceto. The people moving from the left to the gates of the fine Renaissance city in the upper right probably are the followers of Phineus.

FIG. P 13.1. Giorgio Vasari (1511–1574), *Perseus and Andromeda,* 1570. (Fresco in the Studiolo, Palazzo Vecchio, Florence; Alinari/Art Resource, NY)

Vasari painted *Perseus and Andromeda* in 1570 as part of the larger project of adapting the immense Palazzo Vecchio in Florence as living quarters for the family of Cosimo de' Medici. Vasari himself decorated the Studiolo, a small, secret room in the Palazzo surrounded by cupboards where the prince kept his collection of minerals. On the ceiling was Prometheus surrounded by the elements and along one wall were paintings of aquatic activities with appropriate mythical subjects, including Perseus and Andromeda. Vasari justified the mythical theme in his notebook, explaining, "Although they are false gods, it is lawful in this to imitate the ancients, who under these names hid allegorically the concepts of philosophy."

Completely unheard of in the Middle Ages, the morally dangerous practice of drawing from live naked models began in the early fifteenth century; by the second half of the century it was a regular part of an artist's training. Our first Western treatise on the art of painting, written in 1435 by Leon Battista Alberti, already assumes the basis of academic training in art to be a scientific study of the nude. Alberti advises artists to "begin with the bones, then add the muscles, and then cover the body with flesh." Vasari noted that Antonio Pollaiuolo, who painted the *Labors of Heracles* for the Medici Palace in 1460, was modern in his treatment of the nude because "he dissected many bodies to examine their anatomy." For moral reasons, dissection, like nudity, had been impossible in the European Middle Ages.

girl. Ovid tells the story in the *Metamorphoses*, explaining, on the way, the origin of reptiles in the Sahara Desert and coral in the sea:

[615]   Bearing the glorious trophy, the head with a garland of serpents,
he sped through the yielding air, borne on his murmuring pinions.
But while the victor was hovering over the deserts of Libya,
drops of venom rained down from the bleeding head of the Gorgon.
Quickened by these, the earth gave birth to poisonous reptiles,
620   making the region a desert of noxious vipers and asps. . . .
His winged sandals swept through the gentle wind of the heavens;
below and behind he left the countless nations of mortals,
till off in the distance there lay Ethiopia, kingdom of Cepheus.
Ammon, strict god, had ordered that Cepheus' innocent daughter,
625   Andromeda, there must pay for the haughty tongue of her mother.°
The descendant of Abas gazed on her charms, secured to the rocks.
Only her hair, tossed gently by the wind that blew from the sea,
and her piteous streaming tears, as she wept for her imminent fate,
persuaded the hero that this was no marble statue, but warm, live woman.
630   He checked his flight as the fire of love blazed up in his heart.
So taken was he by her beauty, his wings for a moment were still. . . .

624–625. *Ammon . . . her mother:* According to Ovid's version, Cepheus had consulted the oracle of Ammon, a powerful Egyptian god, about the flood and sea-monster, and Ammon had ordered Andromeda to be offered to the monster.

Perseus swooped down to Andromeda's weeping parents, who expected the monster to appear any moment. He offered to save the girl if he could marry her. They hastily agreed and promised him the kingdom as dowry. Then the sea-serpent appeared:

As Perseus' shadow fell on the waters, the monster rose to the bait.
Like Zeus's eagle whose eye has lit on a glittering serpent
sunning itself in a meadow: he plunges down from behind it,
635 and before the snake can reverse his poisonous fangs to attack,
the eager talons impale the scale-covered nape of the viper.
So the Inachean hero° plunged headlong down from the ether,
and sank his curving blade in the writing neck of the monster.
Struck by that deadly wound, it arched its back to the heavens,
640 then dived beneath the waters, as a wounded but still savage boar
twists and turns to hear the barking of hounds who entrap him.
Perseus evaded its snapping jaws with a twist of his pinions;
wherever he saw an opening, he darted a thrust of his saber,
now at the back, encrusted with ancient barnacle remnants,
645 now at the sensitive ribs, now where ribs turned into a fishtail.
The monster vomited up a clot of its life-blood mingled with water,
and Perseus' feathery wings grew heavy and damp with the spray.
No longer dared he entrust his life to the feathers thus sodden,
but made for a reef whose crest was dry if the waters were quiet,
650 submerged if the winds arose. His left hand clung like a limpet,
but again and again his saber drove at the monster's entrails.
The cheers of the watchers resounded along the seacoast beyond him,
and echoed all through the homes of the gods on Olympus above.
Cassiopeä and Cepheus, Andromeda's mother and father,
655 hailed him in joy as son, as helper, as stay of the household.
Andromeda, cause of the struggle, prize of the victor as well,
free of her chains now approached as the victor drew himself water
to wash his victorious hands. To keep from abrading the head
crowned with poisonous vipers, with the grating sand of the ocean,
660 he gathered a leafy blanket of seaweed that floats in the depths
and on it he gently laid the head of the daughter of Phorcys.°
The succulent fresh-cut foliage, still alive and absorbent,
drank up the monster's venom, but hardened to rock at its touch,
gaining a stony hardness spreading through leaf and through stem.
665 The nymphs of the sea kept testing this new and remarkable substance;
in all the weed, they discovered, the wondrous change kept recurring.
The mutant seeds were dispersed by the tossing waves of the sea,
and down to this very day the coral in this is peculiar:
Its stiffness comes from the air; the plant in water is supple,
670 but hardens into a stone when torn from the sea of its birth.

OVID, *Metamorphoses* (4.615–620, 667–677, 712–752)

637. *Inachean hero:* Perseus is so called after the river Inachus (Io's father) near Argos.
661. *daughter of Phorcys:* Usually called a sibling, here Ceto is child of Phorcys.

Unfortunately, when Cepheus agreed to Perseus' proposal, he neglected to mention that Andromeda was already engaged to Phineus, Cepheus' brother. Cepheus held a splendid banquet during which, according to Ovid, Perseus described his adventures. Phineus burst into the banquet hall with a small army behind him. While the cowardly Cepheus quietly withdrew, Perseus, cornered and with only a handful of followers, warned his supporters to look away, pulled out the Gorgon's head, and, in a doublet of his action on Seriphos, turned Phineus and his men to stone.

According to this version, Perseus remained in Ethiopia for a year, where Andromeda bore a son, Perses, ancestor of the Persians. Only then did he return to Seriphos to free his mother.

The Death of Acrisius

Wanting to meet his grandfather Acrisius, Perseus now took his wife and mother with him and traveled to Argos. When Acrisius heard he was coming, he remembered the oracle that his grandson would kill him and fled north to Thessaly. Perseus left Andromeda and Danaë in Argos and followed. The Thessalian king was holding athletic games when Perseus arrived. Unrecognized, Perseus entered the games and threw the discus, but the wind blew it astray. Acrisius, who was standing in the sidelines, was struck in the foot(!) and died. Thus the oracle was fulfilled: Heroes can be a threat to civil society.

A mournful Perseus buried his grandfather with full honors, then returned to Argos. Ashamed to inherit the rule of Argos from the man he had killed, his own grandfather, he traded Argos for Tiryns with a son of Proetus (named Megapenthes) who was king of Tiryns. Perseus also founded the nearby city of Mycenae and surrounded it with magnificent walls. He and Andromeda lived there for many years. She bore him a daughter and several sons. At their deaths, Athena placed Perseus and Andromeda among the stars along with Cepheus, Cassiopeä, and the sea-monster Ceto. Like many heroes, Perseus returned after his dangerous quest to rule over his people, beget a dynasty, and be remembered forever.

Observations: Perseus and Folktale

We have drawn attention to some of the motifs in the story of Perseus that were anticipated in the story of Gilgamesh, but the tone of the two stories is utterly different. Gilgamesh is a harsh, tragic tale of the defeat of our deepest aspirations. The stories of Perseus are like children's tales, with hideous monsters, ugly hags, magic implements, and distressed maidens, and they all lived happily ever after. One of our earliest representations of Perseus and Medusa is on a large pot (at Eleusis) that contained the body of a child, as if the Greek child might enjoy the story even after death.

Of all Greek legendary cycles, that of Danaë and Perseus is closest to folktale. The early part of the story is not about Perseus but about his mother, and it follows a folktale pattern sometimes called the girl's tragedy, which contains these elements: prohibition, seclusion, violation of the prohibition, threat of punishment or death, and finally liberation. Because of an oracle, Danaë is forbidden to marry (*prohibition*). She is locked in a chamber to keep her from men (*seclusion*), but nonetheless becomes pregnant (*violation*). A wicked relative, her father Acrisius, places her and the child in the box (*threat of death*), but she is saved by Dictys (*liberation*).

Classical Myth and the Stars

A surprising number of figures from the myth of Perseus became constellations—Perseus, Andromeda, Cassiopeä, Cepheus, and Ceto—no doubt because he is the only Greek hero to fly through the heavens (Fig. P. 13.2). On this sixteenth-century woodcut by the great German artist Albrecht Dürer you can make out these constellations in the upper central portion: Ceto (unnamed) is to the immediate right of the constellation Aries ("Ram") and threatens Andromeda, in a horizontal position. Perseus is to the left of the soles of Andromeda's feet, holding a scimitar in one hand and the head of Medusa in the other. Below Perseus and Andromeda is Cassiopeä, and beneath her, near the center of the diagram, Cepheus.

Far more than we, ancient peoples needed to use the heavens as indicators of times and seasons, and especially the heavens by night, when the stars and planets are visible. This need led to the organization of the night sky into various configurations or bodies, many of which received mythical names. Looking at the heavenly realms, one sees a chaos of disorganized points of light, but myths provided an intellectual framework for combining stars into groupings so they could be examined systematically.

To an observer on the earth, most of the stars appear to be fixed in their relative positions. Ancient astronomers theorized that they were fastened to the inside of a great sphere that revolved around the earth. We can only see one end of the axis of the heavens, the star Polaris, which never moves. But they noted that not all stars are fixed in their places. The seven *planets* (= Greek "wanderers") known to the ancients seem to follow a different path and to move at different speeds relative to each other. These seven—including Sun and Moon as well as Mercury, Venus, Mars, Jupiter, and Saturn—pass along a group of twelve constellations, the zodiac (= Greek "animal show") in an apparently irrational way. Dürer has placed them around the circumference of his map. From Hellenistic times the Greek gods have been associated with the planets (the Sun = Apollo and Artemis = Moon), capable of purpose and action. Astrology, which arose in Mesopotamia in the eighth century B.C., not in Greece, is based on the assumption that careful study can reveal profound laws about the influence of the planets, who are gods. Astrology is the "science" of the stars, their true and essential nature, as opposed to astronomy, the study of their arrangement.

The names we use for individual stars include many of Arabic as well as Greek and Latin origin; Dürer's map is based on Arabic celestial maps, but he has translated the figures into their Greco-Roman mythical forms. Sometimes the connection is far-fetched: The zodiac includes Aries, said to be the ram that saved Phrixus and Hellê, whose skin became the Golden Fleece; Taurus is the bull that carried off Europa; Gemini are the twins Castor and Pollux; Cancer is the crab that kept snapping at Heracles as he fought the Hydra; Leo is the Nemean Lion of Heracles' first labor. The other names of signs are obscure or improbable: Virgo is Astraea ("jus-

FIG. P 13.2. Albrecht Dürer (1471–1529), *Map of the Northern Hemisphere,* 1503, woodcut. The map has a Latin title that means "Figures of the northern sky with the twelve signs of the Zodiac." Note Hercules, beneath and to the right of center. In the corners are famous astronomers: Aratus of Cilicia (third century B.C., upper left), Ptolemy of Egypt (second century B.C., upper right), Asophi the Arab (that is, Al Sufi, really Abdul Rahman, tenth century A.D., lower right), and Marcus Manilius the Roman (first century A.D., lower left). (Metropolitan Museum of Art, New York, Harris Brisbane Dick Fund, 1951; 51.537.1)

tice"), the last of the gods to leave the earth in the wicked Iron Age; Scorpio was produced by Earth to kill the hunter Orion, who had boasted that there was nothing he could not kill; Sagittarius ("arrow-man") is a Centaur named Crotus, devotee of the Muses with a fondness for hunting; Capricorn ("goat-horned"), son of Amalthea, is the goat who nursed the infant Zeus and was raised to the heavens as reward; Aquarius is the same as Ganymede, cupbearer to the gods. For Pisces ("fishes") the ancient astrologers had recourse to a non-Greek myth about a Syrian goddess, Derceto, equated with Aphrodite. Libra ("balance," "scales") also had no good mythical model but in the Roman Empire was said to be the spirit of Julius Caesar, famous for his fairness and clemency.

The slow change of the planets' position against the zodiac (the sun moves through the whole circle in about 24,000 years) gave rise to the notion of "ages" governed by the sign on the eastern horizon at sunrise. About the time of the birth of Christ, the sun moved from Aries into Pisces, which is one reason the fish became a special Christian symbol. In the nearly worldwide youth movement of the late 1960s, a hoped-for new era was greeted as the "Age of Aquarius."

Perseus' own story follows closely the folktale pattern of the quest, elements of which heroic legend often incorporates. The folktale quest may contain these elements: A member of a family is threatened, the hero is sent on a quest, he acquires the use of a magical agent, he reaches his goal in a faraway land, he combats a villain, he is temporarily overcome, he vanquishes the enemy, he is pursued but escapes, he arrives home and is recognized, the villain is punished, and the hero is married and ascends the throne. In the case of Perseus, Polydectes wants to marry Danaë (*threat*), which leads to Perseus' boast that he will bring back the Gorgon's head (*quest*). The hat, sandals, *kibisis*, and scimitar make his task possible (*magical agent*). He reaches the river Ocean (*faraway land*) and beheads Medusa (*combat and victory*); conspicuously missing from this story is the hero's temporary defeat. The immortal Gorgons come after Perseus (*pursuit*), but he escapes. On Seriphos (*arrival home*) he proves his greatness by holding up the Gorgon's head (*recognition*) and petrifying Polydectes, whose name may tie him to Death's realm (*villain punished*). He frees Andromeda and takes the kingship of Tiryns (*marriage and ascent to throne*). His victory over Ceto and petrifying of Phineus and his followers repeat some of these motifs.

Obviously folktale, which is a system of patterns and motifs, has a lot in common with heroic myth, which is a story about a great man. When we investigate folktale, we are interested in recurring patterns, ways of telling a story; when we investigate heroic myth, we are interested in the meaning attached to a hero's deeds. In the stories of Perseus, the hero himself has little or no personality; he is just someone who does special things. We might say that there is no internal conflict. Conspicuously absent is the hero's conflict with woman, but that is an adult theme, of no interest to children, and Perseus is a children's story. It was never told in an epic poem, as far as we know. In the stories of Heracles we will meet a very different kind of hero.

Medusa's Head

The beheading of Medusa, one of the most discussed incidents in all Greek myth, has attracted many psychological interpretations, although in ancient accounts the event is passed over briefly. Sigmund Freud, the creator of psychoanalysis, offered a bizarre explanation of the Gorgon's head as representing the female genitals, in particular those of the mother. Freud supposed that the young boy's glimpse of his mother's genitals inspired him with the fear of castration—he could become like her, without a penis. However, the phallic snakes reassure the boy about his own penis, as does "being turned to stone," which Freud thought refers to the boy's erection. Later psychoanalytic commentators have developed Freud's thesis, arguing that the myth grows out of a social system in which mothers control the lives of young boys, as they did in ancient Greece. To behead the Gorgon is to overthrow the negative power of the mother, as the Greek boy did when he left his mother's care at puberty and joined the society of men. The positive, nurturing aspect of the mother, by contrast, is represented by the figure of Danaë (for more about psychological interpretations of myth, see Chapter 23). For those who depend on the historically unlikely theory of a primordial matriarchy replaced later by patriarchy (for Bachofen's theories of matriarchy, see Chapter 23), the Medusa represents the power of women in society, overthrown by the power of the male, a reflection of social history in myth.

In fact, the Gorgon originally did not belong to the myth of Perseus at all. Our earliest information is in Homer, who on several occasions refers to "Gorgo" as a fearsome demon with staring eyes, unconnected to the myth of Perseus. Gorgo is represented on the shield of Agamemnon, leader of the Greek host, together with allegorical figures:

> Round about it ten circles of bronze, and on it twenty bosses of tin,
> shining and white, surrounding a boss of metallic dark blue.
> As a crown was the face of Gorgo, fearful for man to behold,
> glaring terribly; with her, as companions, Terror and Panic.
>
> HOMER, *Iliad* (11.33–37)

Gorgo also appears in the *Odyssey*, when Odysseus is describing his visit to the underworld (Chapter 11):

> Cold terror seized me
> lest noble Persephonê rise to me from the mansion of Hades
> displaying the head of Gorgo, that dreadful monster.
>
> HOMER, *Odyssey* (11.633–635)

Gorgo, then, is a bogey with staring eyes, a terrifying demon. The origin of the Gorgon in Greek art as a head with large staring eyes, boar's teeth, and snakes for hair (see Fig. 13.7) is obscure. Some associate this iconography with Eastern monsters, and others trace it back to the Bronze Age and the Minoan cult of the snake goddess (see Chapter 16). In any event, the Gorgon's head is often used as an *apotropaic* ("turning away") device, a magical means to deflect "the evil eye," according to the magical principle that like is effective against like. Belief in the evil eye, the notion that an unfriendly look can harm, is universal, and apotropaic eyes are found in many cultures to deal with this fear. Until the seventeenth century the English word *fascinate* meant "to fix with the evil eye." Gorgons often appear on the interior of Athenian wine cups, evidently because intoxication makes one vulnerable to magical harm. The outsides of these cups sometimes have two large, goggly eyes so that as the drinker raises the cup, the eyes reflect back any unfriendly stare (a few examples have an erect phallus for a base, allowing the drinker to "give the finger" to his companions as he drinks!). Apotropaic Gorgons also appear on early Greek temples, as gargoyles do on medieval cathedrals.

Evidently a folktale told how Perseus slew one of three wicked sisters, a monster named Medusa, "wide ruler," but her appearance was not well defined (see Fig. 13.6). Only later did Greek artists borrow the iconography of Gorgo, an apotropaic bogey that turned away the evil eye, and attribute it to Medusa. The presence of a horse (Pegasus) and a small man (Chrysaör) together with Gorgo in temple sculpture from the seventh century B.C. show that Gorgo had by then been drawn into the myth.

KEY TERMS

Argive plain, 322	Danaë, 329
Perseus, 322	Polydectes, 331
Tiryns, 322	Gorgons, 332
Io, 323	Medusa, 332
Danaüs, 327	Graeae, 332
Danaïds, 327	Andromeda, 335
Acrisius, 329	Cassiopeä, 335

FURTHER READING

Lloyd-Jones, Hugh, *Myths of the Zodiac* (London, 1978). Interesting, sometimes obscure myths associated with the zodiac signs.

Siebers, Tobin, *The Mirror of Medusa* (Berkeley, Calif., 1989). Good material on Medusa and the evil eye.

Woodward, Jocelyn M., *Perseus: A Study in Greek Art and Legend* (Cambridge, U.K., 1937; reprinted New York, 1976). Gathers together the most important Greek representations of the Perseus myth, with commentary.

CHAPTER 14

HERACLES

Tarantara! Lord Heracles, all hail, handsome in your victories!
Yourself and Iolaüs, a pair of invincible spearsmen!
Lord Heracles, all hail, glorious in your victories! Tarantara!

ARCHILOCHUS, fragment 119

HERACLES, called Hercules by the Romans, was the greatest of Greek heroes. His image and career are strikingly similar to those of Gilgamesh, and his stories certainly owe much to importation from the East. Like Gilgamesh, Heracles is strong and willful. He lusts for adventure and experience. He understands loyalty and friendship. The contrast and hostility between the natural world and the cultural world of humans, a central theme in the story of Gilgamesh, is also strong in stories about Heracles. He shows his sympathy with the natural world by toting a primitive club, by shooting with bow and arrow (when shield and spear were "modern" weapons), and in his bad manners and unruly behavior. Yet he rid the civilized world of dangerous animals and dangerous men.

After a life of suffering, victory, and defeat, Heracles was taken to Olympus, where he became a god, a fate that Gilgamesh only longed for and that Perseus never imagined. No town claimed his grave. He is among the earliest mythical figures in Greek art, as early as the eighth century B.C. His Twelve Labors were the theme of the sculptural art on the temple of Zeus at Olympia, where the cult statue by Phidias was one of the Seven Wonders of the Ancient World. His story inspired epic poetry (although none survives), lyric, and tragedy. We have no continuous literary account of his career, but mentions of Heracles and his deeds are so many that we can construct a complete biography. We must remember, however, that in this form the myth of Heracles is a modern reconstruction assembled from many pieces.

THE BIRTH OF HERACLES

About Heracles' special birth, appropriate to a great hero, we hear a complex tale. Perseus' son Electryon married his own niece, and they had a daughter, **Alcmena** (alk-**mē**-na), and nine sons (Chart 14.1). Of Electryon's other brothers, Sthenelus had a son, **Eurystheus** (ū-**ris**-thūs), and Alcaeus had a son, **Amphitryon** (am-**fi**-tri-on). Electryon became king of Mycenae but soon was attacked by pirates. In the battle all but one of Electryon's sons were killed. Electryon, bent on revenge, prepared to leave on campaign, entrusting the kingship and care of his daughter Alcmena to his nephew Amphitryon, understanding that Amphitryon would respect her chastity. But before Electryon could leave, Amphitryon killed him in a quarrel and so was banished.

Taking Alcmena, Amphitryon fled north to Thebes, where Creon, king of Thebes, purified him of blood-pollution. Amphitryon now married Alcmena, but she would not sleep with him until he avenged the deaths of her brothers, as her father Electryon had planned. Amphitryon gathered allies, including Creon himself, and set out against them. He was soon victorious over the pirates and set out for home, eagerly anticipating sexual relations, so long deferred, with Alcmena.

However, Zeus also admired Alcmena's beauty, and before Amphitryon arrived Zeus took on Amphitryon's likeness and appeared at Alcmena's door. He displayed booty, proof of victory over the pirates, and demanded the sexual favors he had earned. On the next morning the disguised Zeus took his leave, just before the real Amphitryon appeared. To Alcmena's considerable confusion, the real Amphitryon proudly displayed to her his booty, proof of victory, and demanded the long-awaited sexual favors. Once again Alcmena retired to the wedding bed and in this way re-

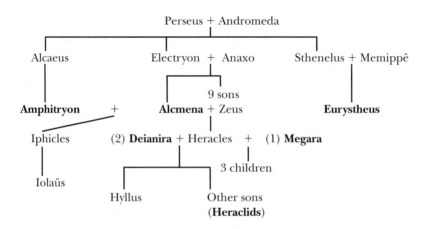

CHART 14.1. The Descent of Heracles

ceived two kinds of seed, mortal and divine, in a single night. From Zeus's seed came Heracles, the greatest Greek hero, and from Amphitryon's seed came Iphicles (**if**-i-klēz), a man of humbler stature. The potentially humorous myth is told in an epic poem called *The Shield of Heracles,* attributed in antiquity to Hesiod but probably composed considerably later by an unknown oral poet:

[1]   Or like Alcmena, the daughter of Electryon, shield of his people.
        Leaving her country behind, with Amphitryon, valiant in battle,
        she journeyed to Thebes. The fairest was she of all generations
        of women who suckle children, in beauty of face and of figure.
5   Of all the mortal women who have slept in the beds of immortals
        and borne them a race of children, there was none to rival Alcmena
        in wisdom and prudence of mind. From her brows and lustrous eyes
        an aura of charm breathed out as from Aphrodite the golden.
        Yet all her devotion was given to her wedded husband alone,
10   such an affection as never another woman has offered.
           Now he had quarreled, alas, with his excellent father-in-law,
        over a herd of cattle, and slain him in violent anger.
        He therefore left his country and came as a suppliant exile
        to Thebes, where he made a home with the Cadmeans,° bearers of shields.
15   But he and his modest wife forswore the sweetness of passion:
        he might not enter the bed of Electryon's slim-ankled daughter,
        till he avenged the death of his great-hearted brothers-in-law
        by burning the towns of the heroes, the Taphians and Teleboans.°
           This he had promised to do and called the gods as his witness.
20   Dreading their wrath, he labored at the task commanded by Zeus.
        His allies obeyed his call to warfare and terrible conflict—
        horse-spurring men of Boeotia, shield-bearers, panting with rage.
        Locrians, hand-to-hand fighters, and valorous Phocians followed;°
        all these obeyed the orders of the mighty son of Alcaeus.
25   But the father of men and gods contrived quite another contrivance:
        to beget a son to defend both gods and bread-eating mortals
        from all the evil that threatens the common safety and comfort.
        From Olympus he came one night, deep in profound meditation;
        burning, as well, with lustful desire for the beautiful woman.
30   Zeus, most skillful of planners, descended at Typhaonium;°
        on the Hill of the Sphinx he rested, plotting wonderful things.
        Disguised as her husband, that night he enjoyed the bed of Alcmena.
           But on that self-same night came Amphitryon, guard of the people.
        His task accomplished, he hurried in such an amorous frenzy
35   to enter the bed of Alcmena that he greeted no mortal whatever,
        not even the rustic herdsmen and peasants who worked on the land.
        As a wanderer thanks his star for escape from terrible danger,
        from fever and deadly disease or the anguish of lying in prison,

---

14. *Cadmeans:* The Thebans.   18. *Taphians and Teleboans:* The pirates, who also claimed to be descended from Perseus.   23. . . . *Phocians followed:* Locris and Phocis are territories bordering on Boeotia.   30. *Typhaonium:* On the outskirts of Thebes, named after Typhoeus, the father of the Sphinx; the "Hill of the Sphinx" was the place where she propounded her riddle and from which she hurled herself when Oedipus solved it (see Chapter 17).

Amphitryon, now delivered from all the pangs he had suffered,
40   returned again to his home, overflowing with love and delight.
The rest of the night he lay in the arms of his reticent partner,
delighting himself with the gifts of Aphrodite the golden.
    Alcmena, having submitted to a god and the best of mankind,
in Thebes of the seven gates gave birth to a pair of twin brothers—
45   brothers, but by no means alike in thought or in vigor of spirit.
The one was by far the weaker, the other a much better man,
terrible, mighty in battle, Heracles, hero unconquered.
Him she bore in submission to Cronus' cloud-ruling son,
the other, by name Iphicles, to Amphitryon, powerful lancer.
50   Of different sires she conceived them: the one of a human father,
the other of Zeus, son of Cronus, the ruler of all the gods.

Pseudo-Hesiod, Shield of Heracles (1–56)

    Although destined to become a god, Heracles was not to be king of Mycenae or Tiryns but became the slave of his abject cousin Eurystheus. For when Alcmena was about to give birth, Zeus swore that on that very day a descendant of his own seed would be born, who would rule over Mycenae. Hera, jealous once more over Zeus's infidelities, delayed the birth of Heracles while hastening that of Eurystheus, the child of Menippê and Sthenelus, also a son of Perseus, hence Zeus's grandson. The story is told in the *Iliad,* in the context of a warning against foolish action:

[91]   We are all victims of Blindness,° the oldest daughter of Zeus,
who leads us on to our ruin. Her soft feet never make contact
with stones and dust of the earth; she does her damage to humans
by flying over their heads, now humbling one, now another.
95   She once, indeed, snared Zeus, strongest of gods or of humans,
when Hera (a woman, of course!) entrapped him in subtle deception.
This happened upon the day that Alcmena hoped to deliver
Heracles, mightiest of men, in the fair-crowned city of Thebes.
    Then Zeus arose and boasted in the midst of all the immortals,
100   "Listen to these my words, all gods and goddesses present,
while I tell you the news my heart and my spirit bid me declare.
Eileithyia, ruler of childbirth, today will bring to the light
a man who will rule these regions—a mortal, but born of my flesh."
    Hera, just like a woman, dissembled and gave him this answer:
105   "O yes, but you will see to it that this does not come about.
Do you dare, Olympian, to swear me a great and terrible promise,
that the child, descending today between the knees of his mother,
human, but your own blood, is destined to rule the regions?"
    Such was her challenge. But Zeus overlooked her secret deception
110   and swore a mighty oath, which would bring him sorrow thereafter.
Hera sprang from her place and sped from the peaks of Olympus,
down to the land of Achaea, to the famous city of Argos,
where she knew that the buxom wife of Sthenelus, Perseus' child,

---

91. *Blindness:* The Greek *atê* means roughly "failure to see the consequences of your actions." It is sometimes rendered as "folly" or "madness."

115   had conceived a son, and by now was fully seven months pregnant.
      This child Hera brought to birth, prematurely and well before normal,
      but checked Alcmena's delivery, delaying the birth of her child.
          She then reported the news in these words to Zeus, son of Cronus:
      "Zeus, thou wielder of thunder, let me drop a word in your hearing:
      a splendid man-child is born, who must rule the people of Argos—
120   Eurystheus, Perseus' grandson, and therefore your very own offspring!
      Who has a better right, pray tell me, to rule the Achaeans?"
          Thus lady Hera gloated, but anguish struck Zeus to the heart.
      Blindness he took by the hair that circled her shining forehead
      and hurled her forth in his rage, swearing a powerful oath
125   that never again should Blindness return to lofty Olympus,
      or view the starry heavens—Blindness, deceiver of all.
      Screaming these words, he whirled her around with his mighty arm
      and flung her down from the heavens, down to the works of men.
      Ever since he has groaned at the terrible deeds of Blindness,
130   seeing his dear son labor at the shameful command of Eurystheus.

                            HOMER, *Iliad* (19.91–133)

Ovid adds an amusing detail to the story. Alcmena had been in the birthing
room for seven days and was nearly dead from exhaustion. She cried out to the birth
goddess Eileithyia (Roman Lucina) to help her. Eileithyia came, but at Hera's instructions sat outside in the antechamber with her legs crossed tightly together and
her fingers intertwined. By magical sympathy she thus prevented the birth, and she
muttered dark spells under her breath.

Alcmena's terrible screams brought all the serving girls to her side, including
the clever and loyal Galanthis (ga-**lan**-this). Noticing the strange old woman sitting
outside the birthing room in an odd posture, the suspicious Galanthis realized what
was happening and suddenly proclaimed: "Hooray! Alcmena's prayers are answered!
A child is born!" "What!" shouted Eileithyia and jumped up, breaking the spell. In
this way Heracles and Iphicles were born. Galanthis laughed, but the angry Eileithyia
turned her into a weasel.

Observations: Twins and Divine Birth

Many early peoples viewed twins (about one birth in eighty) with superstitious awe
and either killed them or regarded them with wonder. One logical explanation for
fraternal twins is two fathers: one mortal, the woman's human consort, and one divine, an invisible being present at the moment of conception. Twins in Greek mythology tend to be either very close friends or bitter enemies. There are four such sets
in the legend of Perseus and his descendants, two of deadly enemies (Danaüs and
Aegyptus, Acrisius and Proetus) and two of the closest friends (Heracles and Iphicles, Castor and Polydeuces[1]).

---

[1]Polydeuces' Roman name is *Pollux;* we will use both names, according to whether the context is
Greek or Roman.

The notion of simultaneous intercourse of man and god with a queen is old and was developed prominently in the Egyptian religious fiction that Pharaoh, king of Egypt, was born not to a mortal, but to the god Amun, who came to the queen in the guise of her husband (just as Zeus, later equated with Amun, took on the shape of Amphitryon). Some would trace the story of Heracles' birth to the Egyptian tradition, which is portrayed in reliefs showing sexual union between god and queen in Egyptian temples. A charming poem inscribed on the funerary monument of Queen Hatshepsut (1490–1468 B.C.) accompanies such a relief, telling of Amun's appearance to Ahmes, wife of Tuthmosis I, to beget the divine child Hatshepsut. Thoth, god of writing and magic, leads Amun to the queen's chamber:[2]

[1]   The glorious god came,
        Amun himself, the lord of the two lands,
        in the guise of her husband.
        They° found her resting in the beautiful palace.
5   She awoke when she breathed the perfume of the god,
        and she laughed at the sight of his majesty.
        Inflamed with desire, he hastened toward her.
        He had lost his heart to the queen.
        When he came near to her,
10   she saw his form as a very god.
        She rejoiced in the splendor of his beauty.
        His love went inside all her limbs.
        The god's sweet perfume
        suffused through the palace,
15   the perfume of Punt, the land of incense.
        The greatness of this god
        did to the woman what he pleased.
        She kissed him
        and delighted him with her body.

Egyptian Hymn on the Birth of Hatshepsut

4. *they:* Amun and Thoth.

If the story of Zeus and Amphitryon does descend from the Egyptian, it is a good example of the "downgrading" of a traditional tale, which in an earlier culture had important political and religious meaning, to a Greek heroic vignette rich in comic potential. A comedy, the *Amphitruo* of the Roman playwright Plautus (second century B.C.), exploits this potential: Zeus appears in the guise of Amphitryon and makes the night last three times its ordinary length, so great is the god's pleasure in Alcmena's body. All the while the clownish Amphitryon stands outside the house, prevented by high jinks from getting inside.[3]

---

[2] Ordinarily the child would be a boy. That Hatshepsut was born a girl was an embarrassment to the Egyptian theory of monarchy, according to which the pharaoh was the incarnation of the male hawk god Horus, son of the sun god Re. In art Hatshepsut is shown dressed in male garb, including the ceremonial beard, and Egyptian texts use the masculine pronoun to refer to her.

[3] Just before World War II the French playwright Giraudoux wrote on the theme and named his play *Amphitryon 38* for the number of previous versions.

HERACLES' YOUTHFUL DEEDS

Amphitryon knew that he was father to one of the twins, Zeus to the other, but was not sure which was which. Only when Hera sent serpents to destroy the son of mighty Zeus did Amphitryon learn the truth, as Pindar relates in an ode for the winner in the chariot race at Nemea (near Corinth) in 476 B.C. The ode presents a bird's-eye view of Heracles' whole career:[4]

[33]   When I arouse the memory of ancient stories,
        as I wander among the mountain tops of prowess,
35   most eagerly I cling to one of Heracles.
    The story tells how this child of Zeus sprang out
    to the glorious light of day, from his mother's womb,
    along with his twin half-brother, Iphicles,
    and left their mother's pangs of birth behind.
40   The story goes on that, though swaddled in saffron,
    he did not escape the suspicion of golden-throned Hera.
    Enraged in her heart, she promptly dispatched
    a pair of venomous serpents.
    Through the open door they crawled to the nursery,
45   with slavering fangs, all frenzied to mangle the infants.
    But Heracles lifted his little head,
    and made his first trial of battle.
    Both serpents he seized with his two mighty fists (Fig. 14.1),
    till the passing moments cut off breath from their coils.
50   Uncontrollable terror struck at the women
        who were tending Alcmena.
    She herself leaped up, half-dressed as she was,
    from the blankets over the bed where she rested from labor.
    On flying feet she ran to ward off
55   the attack of the serpents.
    Bronze-clad Cadmean chiefs, seizing their weapons,
    crowded to help. Amphitryon brandished his naked sword,
    snatched from the scabbard. Sharp terror shook his heart,
    for everyone fears a threat to himself;
60   concern for others' worries soon subsides.
    But he gaped with wonder, scarce to be born,
    and exultant pride, when he saw the mysterious power
    and courage of his son. For the deathless gods
    had disproved the messengers' tale.
65   He summoned Tiresias, dweller in Thebes,
    truth-telling seer, great prophet of Zeus the Highest.
    To the king and the army Tiresias foretold
    what the future held for the boy.
    What rebellious monsters, on land and by sea,
70   would Heracles slay: the fiercest° was one who walked

70. *fiercest:* Probably the Giant Antaeus (see later in this chapter).

[4]The deed of Heracles is cited as a mythic parallel of the chariot-driver's greatness.

FIG. 14.1. The infant Heracles strangles the serpents, fresco from Pompeii, c. 65 A.D. In the Roman representation, the baby Heracles strangles the serpents sent by Hera, while Alcmena, to the right, flees and Amphitryon looks on pensively. To the left, a nurse raises her hand in horror, while an eagle, the bird of Zeus—Heracles' real father—looks on.　(Museo Archeologico Nazionale, Naples; University of Wisconsin, Madison Photo Archive)

in the tortuous paths of envious men,
whom the boy would deliver to death.
He told how the gods and Giants would meet
on the plain of Phlegra, where the hair of the fallen Giants
75 　　would be fouled as they writhed in the blood-stained dust,
slain by Heracles' arrows.
He would rest at last from his mighty toil,
and receive as reward eternal peace.
Taking Hebê as bride at a marriage feast
80 　　in the halls of the blest, he would sit beside Zeus,
great Cronus' son, and justify his holy ways.

PINDAR, *Nemean* 1 (33–72)

Many of the stories told of Heracles were humorous, or are raw jokes in the spirit of "Hey, did you hear about the time that. . . ." For example, a story told how Zeus ensured Heracles' greatness by placing the infant at Hera's breast so that he could imbibe the divine milk. Heracles bit down sharply, and Hera screamed bloody murder and dashed the child from her: The spurting milk became the Milky Way!

Another example concerns Heracles' fine and aristocratic education as he grew up tall and strong, his torso rippling with muscles. Amphitryon taught him how to drive the chariot and brought in the finest tutors. Autolycus (aw-**tol**-i-kus), famed for his roguery and thievery (the father of Odysseus, whose mother hastily married another man), taught him wrestling; Eurytus (**ūr**-i-tus), greatest of archers, showed Heracles how to shoot; Castor, brother of Polydeuces (and of Helen of Troy), showed him how to fight in heavy armor; and Linus (**lī**-nus), a brother of the great Orpheus, instructed him in playing the lyre. Heracles quickly mastered the martial arts, but his big, clumsy fingers broke the lyre's strings, and he could not get the notes right. Linus complained so often that one day Heracles smashed his lyre over Linus' head, killing him on the spot. Tried for murder, he was acquitted on a claim of self-defense!

Another humorous story is just as easy to place within the all-male Greek aristocratic clubs. After the death of Linus, Amphitryon decided to remove his boisterous son from town until things cooled down. He sent Heracles to the country to tend cattle on the slopes of Mount Cithaeron (in southwestern Boeotia). There Heracles grew until he was eight feet tall! He defeated the local boys in throwing the javelin, shooting the bow, and similar activities. When eighteen years old, he hunted an enormous lion that ravaged the flocks of Thespius (**thes**-pi-us), king of the nearby town Thespiae (**thes**-pi-ē). For fifty days he hunted the beast. Each night, exhausted from stalking, he stayed in Thespius' house. Seeing how tall, strong, and handsome was Amphitryon's son, Thespius determined to have grandchildren by him. Each night he sent one of his fifty daughters to Heracles' bed. Heracles thought it was the same woman each night, and so begot his first fifty sons. Another tradition reports that Thespius got Heracles drunk and in a single night sent in all fifty daughters, one after the other—Heracles thought it was one woman the whole time and impregnated them all! Eventually Heracles killed the lion.

Heading back to Thebes, Heracles met the heralds of Erginus (er-**jī**-nus), king of the Minyans, whose city was nearby Orchomenus.[5] Defeated in a dispute, Thebes had been forced to pay tribute of one hundred cattle each year to Erginus. When Heracles learned of the heralds' mission, in a fury he attacked them, cut off their noses, ears, and hands, hung them on strings around their necks, and told them to take *these* as tribute to Erginus. Erginus was outraged and attacked Thebes. The Minyans had earlier forced the Thebans to disarm, but Heracles found old swords, armor, and other weapons hanging as dedications in the temples of the gods. He armed the Thebans and led them against the Minyans, killed Erginus, and forced the Minyans to pay twice as much as they formerly levied on the Thebans.

---

[5]Home of Athamas and Ino, in the Bronze Age Orchomenus was Thebes' greatest rival for power in the Boeotian plain, and important ruins are still found there.

CHART 14.2. Heracles' Wives and Offspring

MARRIAGE, MADNESS, AND MURDER

Heracles is often a buffoon or a sexual genius, but in his excess he soon went too far. In a crisis the hero is great, set against savage lion, invading horde, or dragon of chaos, but in peacetime he can be a danger to others and to himself.

Amphitryon was killed in the Minyan war. The new king of Thebes, Creon (**krē**-on), gave Heracles his daughter **Megara** (**me**-ga-ra) in marriage (Chart 14.2). Heracles settled down and fathered three children, but one day he simply went mad—Hera was behind it—and without warning murdered his wife and children. The myth is the subject of a play by Euripides, the *Heracles Insane* (414? B.C.). In the following excerpt a messenger describes the terrible crime. After destroying a pretender to the Theban throne, Heracles is about to perform a sacrifice, but suddenly he imagines he is traveling to Mycenae to kill the cowardly Eurystheus (who compelled him to undergo the Twelve Labors, which in Euripides' version took place *before* this incident):

[925]   The fair-faced group of children took their place;
       his father too, and Megara. The sacred basket
       was passed around the altar° as we watched
       in reverent silence. Waiting to take the torch
       in his right hand, to quench it in the font,°
930   Alcmena's son jerked to a sudden halt
       and stood without a word, without a step.
       At this delay the children turned their gaze
       to see their father change before their eyes.
       His bloodshot eyes rolled wildly in their sockets;
935   foam trickled down his heavy-bearded chin,
       and thus he screamed, convulsed with manic laughter:
       "Father,° why light the purifying flame,
       doubling my work, before I slay Eurystheus?
       A single blow will set the matter right;

926–927. *basket . . . altar:* In sacrificial ritual a basket was circulated containing barley and the sacrificial knife.   929. *font:* Onlookers were purified by water sprinkled from a basin in which the sacrificer had quenched a torch.   937. *Father:* Amphitryon. In Euripides' version, Amphitryon is still alive.

940 I'll fetch his skull, include it along with these
of men already dead—then purify my hands.
Pour out the holy water, toss the basket away!
Here, someone, get my bow! somebody else, my sword!
I'm off to smash Mycenae. All I need is a pick,
945 perhaps a crowbar; I'll turn those walls to rubble,
walls the Cyclopes framed by square and chisel;
one twist of an iron bar, and down they go!"
Then out he charged to a nonexistent chariot,
climbed its imagined rails, and with his hand
950 stabbed out, to goad the horses that weren't there.
    What should we servants do—chuckle or shiver?
Each glanced at the other with a muttered question,
"Is this the master's joke? or has he gone crazy?"
Heracles meanwhile prowled upstairs and down.
955 Charging into the quarters of the men,
he shouted, "Here I am, in Nisus' town!"°
From there he went on in, not changing clothes,
squatted by the door, and had them pack a lunch.
After a little wait, he next announced
960 his passage through the Isthmus' wooded vales.°
Presently, stripping off his buckled cloak,
he wrestled furiously with himself alone,
demanded silence, crowned himself the victor.
He next imagined himself back in Mycenae,
965 bursting with rate against Eurystheus.
    Touching his mighty hand, his father pled,
"My boy, whatever has gone wrong with you?
On what mad journey have you now embarked?
I pray the blood of these, your recent victims,
970 has not destroyed your wits." But crazy Heracles
took him to be the father of Eurystheus,
a trembling suppliant clutching at his hand.
He shook him off, plucked arrows from his quiver
to aim at his own sons, blindly supposing
975 that he was slaying the family of Eurystheus.
    The frightened children rushed, now here, now there:
one sought his terror-stricken mother's skirts,
one hugged a pillar's all too slender shade,
one fledgling trembled at the altar's side.
980 Megara screamed, "To these you once gave life;
will you, their father, be their cause of death?"
The old man and the slaves joined in her cries.
    But Heracles, unheeding, stalked the boy
who hid behind the pillar's treacherous bulk.

956. *town:* Megara, between Thebes and Mycenae. Because Heracles is about to kill his wife, Megara, Euripides avoids introducing the confusing name of the city, although he doubtless assumed his audience would recognize it.   960. *wooded vales:* The narrow strip of land connecting the Peloponnesus with the mainland, where athletic games were held, similar to those at Olympia.

985	Cornered, the boy turned round to face him,
	and Heracles stabbed. The child fell back,
	his life-blood spurting out upon the walls.
	The madman screamed a boast of victory:
	"One of your brood, Eurystheus, lies here dying,
990	part payment of the debt his father owes."

985 Cornered, the boy turned round to face him,
   and Heracles stabbed. The child fell back,
   his life-blood spurting out upon the walls.
   The madman screamed a boast of victory:
    "One of your brood, Eurystheus, lies here dying,
990 part payment of the debt his father owes."
   An arrow he aimed at the second, crouched by the altar,
   hoping, in vain, to hide there unobserved.
   Before the arrow could fly, the poor boy reached for a hug,
   but fell, and vainly tried to clutch at his father's knees.
995   "O dearest Daddy," he cried, "Daddy, please don't hit me!
   I'm not Eurystheus' son, I'm your own little boy!"
   Heracles only rolled his wild and Gorgon eyes.
   The child was too close as a mark for his deadly bow;
   like a blacksmith at his anvil, Heracles whirled his club
1000 down on the boy's fair hair and shattered the bones beneath.
    The second child dispatched, he stalked the third,
   to make him a fellow-victim to join the others.
   But Megara saw his plan: she snatched the child,
   and bolted the doors behind. As though storming Cyclopean walls,
1005 Heracles pried at the doors, ripped their framing apart,
   and with a single arrow slew both his wife and child.
    This done, he savagely charged to Amphitryon's murder.
   But a ghostly form appeared before our horrified eyes—
   Pallas herself, with crested helmet and brandished spear,
1010 hurled a great stone which struck right on Heracles' chest,
   to end his murderous madness and put him into a coma.

EURIPIDES, Heracles Insane (925–1008)

Athenian playwrights, above all Euripides, were fascinated by such descriptions of irrational behavior, a counterweight in popular entertainment to the glorification of reason heard in the streets of Athens. At the height of happiness Heracles suddenly lost control and committed a terrible crime; such is the uncertainty and the terror of human life. In 416 B.C. the island of Melos revolted and tried to leave the Athenian empire. The Athenians crushed the uprising, killed every adult male in Melos, and enslaved the women and children. Euripides' play—if it was staged after 416, as many think—may refashion an old myth to dramatize the horror of this contemporary event.

THE TWELVE LABORS

After murdering his wife and children, Heracles (according to the usual sequence of events) went to Delphi to learn what he must do to atone for the deed. The oracle replied that he must leave Thebes and travel to Tiryns, his parents' home. There he would serve as bondsman to his cousin Eurystheus, king of Mycenae and Tiryns, and perform for him Twelve Labors.[6] The Greek word is *athloi*, which really means

---

[6]Or, according to some accounts, ten.

contests, for which the victor wins a prize. Heracles' prize would be immortality, the oracle said, and several of his contests were to be waged against Death himself.

In fact, Heracles completed far more than twelve tasks. Ancient commentators divided his deeds into two categories: the Twelve Labors, accomplished mostly by Heracles at Eurystheus' command, and the Deeds (Greek *praxeis*), various other exploits, sometimes military. Later a third category was added: the Side-Deeds (Greek *parerga*), subsidiary adventures in the course of the Twelve Labors. In this account, we discuss the Labors and Side-Deeds together, then some of the better-known Deeds.

1. The Nemean Lion

The first task Eurystheus demanded was to kill a savage lion ravaging the country around Nemea, northwest of Mycenae. Heracles fired at the lion with bow and arrow, then realized, when his arrows bounced off, that the beast had an impenetrable skin. Heracles chased the lion into its lair. Because his weapons were useless, he seized the beast in a wrestler's grip, threw it to the ground, and through brute strength snapped its powerful neck (Fig. 14.2). When he tried to skin the lion, Heracles discovered his weapons could not break the skin. Sometimes as clever as he was strong, he took one of the lion's own claws and with this unbreakable tool cut the uncuttable pelt. Ever after, he wore the skin around his shoulders, its gaping jaws em-

FIG. 14.2. Heracles and the Nemean lion, Attic water-jug, c. 510 B.C. This is the single most common theme in all Greek art; more than 500 examples are represented on pottery alone. The hero has hung his cloak and quiver in a tree. To the left, Iolaüs, Heracles' nephew, and to the right Athena, carrying a shield with her special owl as emblem, reach out protectively. Heracles is shown as the ideal Greek athlete.
(Museo Civico, Brescia; M 667–6731)

FIG. 14.3. Heracles and the Erymanthian boar, Attic water-jug, c. 510 B.C. Heracles, left foot poised on the edge of Eurystheus' underground bronze bowl, threatens to drop the boar on him. Eurystheus makes a deprecating gesture, and even Athena turns away in fear. On the right, Hermes, holding the caduceus, raises his other hand in surprise. (Musée du Louvre, Paris; F 59)

bracing his head like a helmet (see Figs. 14.3–14.7), and he always carried the club he had cut at Nemea.

Heracles brought the dead lion back to Eurystheus, but in the comic vein of many tales about Heracles, the king skulked in a corner of the palace, bellowing out orders that Heracles never again be allowed into the city. Henceforth he would have to announce his results to the herald Copreus (**ko**-prūs), "dungman." To be on the safe side, Eurystheus also had an enormous bronze jar set into the ground in which he could take refuge when Heracles was anywhere near (Fig. 14.3).

2. The Lernaean Hydra

Heracles' second labor was to destroy an enormous serpent, the **Hydra** ("water serpent") with many heads, which lived near the swamps of Lerna southeast of Mycenae, where it ravaged the fields and livestock. Even its breath was death. Iolaüs (ī-ō-**lā**-us), Heracles' nephew (Chart 14.1), accompanied him to the springs; he is the hero's companion, like Enkidu (but the motif is much supressed in stories about Heracles). Heracles soon drove the monster from its lair by shooting burning arrows, then moved in close with a sword. But the Hydra wrapped its coils around one of his feet while a giant crab attacked the other. Every time Heracles cut off one head of the Hydra, two others grew, and the central head was immortal.

Although he smashed the crab, the outcome was uncertain. Iolaüs brought firebrands to cauterize the stump of each head. Heracles cut off the immortal one and buried it beneath a rock, then ripped open the fiend's body, spilling a filth of deadly bile. He dipped his arrows in the black liquor, so poisonous that a trace would kill the strongest man. (Little did Heracles know he was preparing his own death.) The crab became the constellation Cancer ("crab"; see Fig. P 13.2).

3. The Ceryneian Deer

His next task was to bring in a deer living in Ceryneia (se-ri-**nē**-a), a remote mountain in the northern Peloponnesus. This magical animal, although female, had golden antlers and brazen hoofs and belonged to Artemis. He tracked her for a full year until in Arcadia he wounded her with an arrow, threw the deer over his shoulder, and headed for Mycenae. On the way he met Artemis and Apollo. Apollo reproached Heracles for capturing his sister's sacred animal. The hero apologized, saying that he was under orders. Artemis allowed him to show the deer to Copreus, after which Heracles let it go.

4. The Erymanthian Boar

The **Erymanthian boar** lived on Mount Erymanthus in Arcadia in the cental Peloponnesus, and Heracles was to capture it.

Side-Deed: Pholus. While trying to pick up the boar's trail, Heracles stopped to visit a Centaur named **Pholus** (**fō**-lus), who lived in a remote cave. Pholus wanted to be hospitable and offered Heracles cooked meat (he himself only ate raw). When Heracles asked for wine, pointing to a cask in the cave, Pholus explained that the wine belonged to all the Centaurs and he ought not to open it. Heracles assured Pholus that there would be no problem, but when the scent from the aged liquor wafted across the mountain tops, the neighboring Centaurs gathered, carrying stones and ash trees as weapons.

Alarmed at their aggressive manner, Heracles threw torches and fired arrows. They fled to the one wise Centaur, **Chiron** (**kī**-ron), who had migrated from northern Greece. Unlike the other Centaurs, Chiron was immortal, but in the melee he was wounded by one of Heracles' poisoned arrows, so that the venom that always killed coursed through the veins of a being that could not die, the sort of paradox in which the Greeks took delight. Prometheus, chained on the Caucasus, eventually traded his mortality for Chiron's agonizing immortality, allowing Chiron to die (although Chiron is somehow still alive a generation later to tutor Achilles).[7] The other Centaurs, including Nessus (**nes**-us), later instrumental in the death of Heracles, scattered to the four winds.

After the battle, the friendly Pholus picked up a stray arrow, astonished that a puny thing could bring down a large, powerful Centaur. He let the arrow slip, it struck his hoof, and Pholus, too, fell dead.

Heracles at last drove the boar from the bush, ran it down in a snow bank, and carried it to Eurystheus, who beheld it in terror from the bottom of his bronze jar (see Fig. 14.3).

---

[7]We usually think of Prometheus as immortal, but he evidently was not so originally.

Daumier's *Hercules in the Augean Stables*

Honoré Daumier was a caricaturist, painter, and sculptor considered by many to be the greatest social satirist of his day. He was an early master of the technique of lithography (drawing directly on stone, from which multiple copies of an image can be printed). He contributed cartoons regularly to the weekly *La Caricature;* in 1832 his parody of Louis Philippe (king of France, 1830–1848) as Gargantua, a character in a famous satire by Rabelais (1490–1553), earned him a six-month term in prison. From 1835 on, the journal *Charivari* published many other satiric lithographs, four thousand in all, whose subjects were mostly contemporary urban industrial life.

Daumier also did a series of parodies of Greek myth and Roman history called *Histoire ancienne.* Such traditions of satire go back to the ancient world. For example, in the *Iliad* Hera takes the arrows of Artemis and, like a comic-book buffoon, slaps Artemis around the ears with them. In antiquity Heracles was often shown in comic plays and on pots as a greedy, drunken bully; one pot shows him as a drunken satyr dancing around the tree of the Hesperides, from which hang golden wine goblets instead of apples. In Daumier's lithograph of *Hercules in the Augean Stables* (Fig. P 14.1), from *Histoire ancienne,* the great hero is shown as a lumpy and disgruntled peasant, naked except for his deep boots and a tawdry lion skin, in the midst of the dung, shovel over his shoulder and mop in hand. The horse behind him is contributing to his task.

FIG. P 14.1. Honoré Daumier (French, 1808–1879), *Hercules in the Augean Stables,* c. 1848.
(From *Histoire ancienne*)

5. The Augean Stables

Augeas, a son of Helius, was king of the district of Elis in the northwestern Peloponnesus. His father had given him many herds, but Augeas never cleaned his stables. After years of neglect, they were several feet deep in dung. Eurystheus, wanting to humiliate Heracles, ordered him to clean the stables. Without revealing that he was under orders, Heracles bargained with Augeas, who agreed that if he cleaned the stables in a day—an obvious impossibility—he would receive one tenth of Augeas' cattle (Perspective 14.1).

Heracles easily accomplished the task by diverting a nearby river through the stables. But when Augeas learned of Heracles' obligation to Eurystheus, he refused to pay. Later, as one of the Deeds, Heracles returned to Elis, killed Augeas and his sons, and instituted the Olympic Games.

6. The Stymphalian Birds

In Arcadia around a lake called Stymphalis swarmed mighty flocks of death-dealing birds with arrow-firing wings and armor-piercing beaks. Heracles drove them from their cover in the thick forest around the lake by clanging bronze castanets. As they flew into the sky, he shot them down with his arrows (Fig. 14.4).

7. The Cretan Bull

So far the hero's tasks have been confined to the Peloponnesus, but now Eurystheus ordered Heracles to capture the **Cretan bull,** a magnificent animal summoned from the sea by Minos (see Chapter 16). Heracles sailed to Crete, seized the bull by the horns, tossed it in the sea, then rode it like a cowboy back to the Peloponnesus. After Copreus inspected it, the bull got away and wandered north across the Isthmus to the plain of Marathon, where the Athenian hero Theseus killed it (Chapter 15).

FIG. 14.4. Heracles and the Stymphalian birds, Attic water-jug, c. 530 B.C. In this version he hunts them with a slingshot. Some fly, some are shot, and others go about their business. (British Museum, London; PS 014235)

8. The Horses of Diomedes

Next Hercules was to capture the horses of Diomedes, a son of Ares and king of a savage tribe in Thrace. These horses, which were not ordinary animals, dined on human flesh.

Side-Deed: Alcestis. As we saw earlier (Chapter 7), Apollo's son Asclepius, the great physician, brought back Hippolytus, son of Theseus, from the dead after he was dragged to death (for his death, see Chapter 15). In anger at Asclepius' presumption, Zeus killed him, and in revenge for Asclepius' death, Apollo killed the Cyclopes, Zeus's armorers. Then Zeus punished Apollo by forcing him to serve for a year King **Admetus** (ad-mē-tus) in Pherae (**fer-ē**), a town in Thrace. Admetus treated the god so well that Apollo gave this boon: Admetus need not die if he could find someone else to die in his place.[8] Only his dutiful wife **Alcestis** was willing (see Fig. 2.12).

While traveling north toward Thrace, Heracles stopped in the court of Admetus. His visit is the subject of one of Euripides' best-known plays, the *Alcestis* (438 B.C.). Heracles notices that the house is in mourning but is not told why, except that a "neighbor" has died. Seeing no reason the death of someone unknown should affect his own amusement, Heracles demands wine, gets drunk, bawls out a song, and lectures a servant for going around with a long face. He should seize the day, Heracles advises, and enjoy its pleasures, a point of view natural to the rambunctious son of Zeus:

[773]   Hey, you, why are you giving me that sour look?
        Slaves have no business eyeing guests like that.
775   They ought to greet them with a great big smile.
        But you—when you see an old friend of your master's,
        you raise your eyebrows, greet him with a snarl!
        Why so excited at some one else's pains?
        Just listen, now, to me, and learn some sense.
780   Have you a notion how human nature works?
        I don't believe so. Listen, while I tell you.
        Everyone born is bound some day to die,
        and nobody human ever knows for sure
        whether tomorrow's dawn will see him living.
785   Luck, good or bad, cannot be prophesied.
        It can't be taught, no art can comprehend it.
        All right, now listen—learn the truth from me:
        drink up, enjoy yourself, and count today
        the only day you own; the rest belongs to luck.
790   Pay greatest honor to the sweetest goddess
        mortals can know—the kindly, gentle Cypris.

                        EURIPIDES, *Alcestis* (773–791)

Soon Heracles learns that the house is in mourning for the queen. Regretting his thoughtless behavior, he takes a characteristically bold course: If she must die, he

---

[8]Cf. the motif of the substitute sacrifice in the story of Inanna and Dumuzi (Chapter 9).

will bring her back from the other world! He goes to the place (off-stage) where the body awaits its funeral, meets Death (*Thanatos*), wrestles him down, and takes back Alcestis.

When Heracles reached Thrace, he promptly captured the horses of Diomedes. Because they enjoyed human flesh, he fed them their master, Diomedes. After Copreus saw them, they escaped and returned north to Mount Olympus, where they were eaten by wolves.

9. The Girdle of Hippolyta

Theseus and Dionysus fought the Amazons; so did Heracles. Eurystheus ordered him to bring back the girdle of the Amazon queen **Hippolyta** (hip-**pol**-i-ta, "horse-tamer," or Antiopê) for his daughter. The girdle was a belt that women wore above their hips: To loosen it was to offer oneself sexually, to take it forcibly was rape. This labor is a sexual one, directed against the queen of the man-hating Amazons.

Heracles gathered some companions and set out on the long journey to the river Thermodon on the southern shore of the Black Sea. When he arrived, Hippolyta gladly offered him the belt, so great were Heracles' charms. An angry Hera disguised herself as an Amazon and ran through the city proclaiming that Heracles had abducted their queen. The Amazons attacked, and Heracles, fearing treachery, strangled Hippolyta, removed her girdle, and sailed away. He gave the girdle to Eurystheus.

10. The Cattle of Geryon

For his tenth labor Heracles had to capture the cattle of the monster **Geryon** (**jer**-i-on), who had three bodies joined at the waist and lived on the island of Erythia (e-ri-**thē**-a), "red land" (perhaps named from the colors of the sunset), somewhere in the far west near the river Ocean. He possessed a wonderful herd of red cattle, watched over by Eurytion and his demonic two-headed dog, Orthus.

Heracles trudged through the sands of northern Africa, finally reaching the narrows where the Mediterranean Sea opens into the Atlantic Ocean. He set up pillars on either side, known today as the Rock of Ceuta in Tangiers and the Rock of Gibraltar in Spain. To the ancients they were the Pillars of Heracles, the geographical boundary between the human world and the unknown vastness of outer space.

As Heracles traveled the African sands, it got so hot that, in exasperation, he fired an arrow at Helius, the sun. Helius admired his boldness and lent him the cup by which he traveled every night underground from the western to the eastern horizon (Fig. 14.5).[9] With this cup, Heracles crossed the waters to Erythia.

Heracles landed, bashed in Orthus' brains, and killed the herdsman Eurytion. He rustled the cattle and was driving them across a river when Geryon himself attacked. Heracles felled him with a shot from his bow, herded the cattle into the cup, and bobbed back to the known world. He landed on the Atlantic coast of Spain, then returned the cup to the sun god.

[9]The image is taken from Egyptian religion, where the sun god Re makes this daily journey in the bark of the sun.

FIG. 14.5. Heracles in the cup of Helius, Attic wine-cup, c. 480 B.C. Only his torso with lion skin shows. He grips his club and bow and stares across the great unknown. Fish and octopods play in the waves. (Vatican Museum, Rome; XXXII. 92.17)

Heracles drove the cattle across what is now Spain, then southern France, then for some reason turned south into Italy.

Side-Deed: Cacus. Near the future site of Rome, **Cacus** (kā-kus), a three-headed fire-breathing monster, stole some of the cattle and hid them in a cave on the Palatine, one of the seven original hills of Rome. Heracles heard their lowing, climbed the hill, tore away the rocks at the top of the cave, leaped down inside, and demolished Cacus with his club. Vergil (70–19 B.C.) tells the story in his epic poem the *Aeneid.* The speaker is Evander, an early Greek settler on the future site of Rome, who is explaining to Aeneas the origin of an important sacrificial ritual:

[190]   First look up at this crag overhanging the fallen debris,
       how falling rocks of the mountain have left its caverns exposed,
       how the tumbled face of the cliff was left as a great pile of rubble.
       This used to be the cave in whose dark and sinister recess,
       never touched by the sun, dwelt the bestial half-human Cacus.
195   The ground used to stink with blood, and over its arrogant portal
       were nailed the bloodless heads of his victims, green with decay.
       This creature was sired by Vulcan; Vulcan's fire would blaze
       from his maw as he wandered, deadly, threatening, enormous.
       But finally came the day of deliverance, answering our prayers,
200   the presence and help of a god, the greatest of all avengers.
       Alcides,° proudly driving his booty of great-muscled cattle,
       the spoil of his glorious conquest of Geryon, triple of body,

201. *Alcides:* "[Grand]son of Alcaeus," another name for Heracles. Alcaeus was the father of Amphitryon, Heracles' (human) father, and Anaxo, Heracles' maternal grandmother (see Chart 14.1).

approached to encamp with his loot here in our valleys and hills.
Cacus' mind was enraged that a deed either cruel or treacherous

205   should remain undared, unattempted. He stole to the pastures,
and stealthily drove away four of the mightiest bulls
and an equal number of heifers, the finest of all the herd.
To keep from leaving tracks, he dragged them away by the tail,
and thus reversing the hoofprints,° hid them down in his inky den.

210   Time passed; Amphitryon's son was ready to move with his booty.
Rested and bored in the pens, impatient to start on the journey,
the cattle began to complain and to fill the forests and hillsides
with bovine lugubrious bellows, although leaving so pleasant a spot.
    A heifer from the depths of the cavern promptly responded:

215   with the sound of a mournful "Moo!" she wrecked the ambition of Cacus.
The blackest bile blazed up in the liver of raging Alcides;
with his mighty fists he reached for his knobby ponderous bludgeon,
and swift as the wind he thundered up to the mountain's peak.
That was the first time our peasants saw Cacus' arrogant eyes

220   rolling in fear, as he hastened, faster than winds of the east,
to seek the seclusion a cavern grants; fear hurried his feet.
The instant he got inside, he broke the chains and let tumble
the massive boulder which hung on hooks put there by his father,
and propped it against the doorway, to block the angry intruder.

225   Raging, gnashing his teeth, the baffled Tirynthian hero°
rolled his eyes at the doorway, trying to find a way in.
Three times, boiling with rage, he studied the Aventine mountain;
three times he tried to smash the gateway's threshold of granite;
three times he had to retreat, exhausted, into the valley.

230   From the ridge above the cavern there arose a pillar of flint,
conspicuous, sheer on all sides, fit nest for fowl of ill omen.
The pinnacle, leaning a bit, overhung the left bank of the river,
so Heracles pushed to the right.° Ripping it up by the roots,
he hurled it down with a blow like that of a bolt of thunder.

235   The banks of the river parted, its terrified water surged back.
The cave of Cacus lay naked, as big as the vault of a palace,
and the dark recesses behind it were opened up to the light.
    Imagine the crust of the earth has been peeled by some mighty power,
baring the region beneath, pale realms abhorred by the gods.

240   Down below in the pit you would see the terrified phantoms,
shrinking away in terror at the sudden influx of light.
Like them Cacus was trapped by the sudden glare and retreated
deep in his hollow of rock, with screams like none heard before.
    Alcides pressed his advantage: he shouted for all his weapons,

245   and even grabbed broken branches and millstones, mighty and massive.
Cacus, all hope being gone of ever escaping his peril,
belched (believe it or not) from his jaws a cloud of black smoke.

---

209. *hoofprints:* Compare Hermes' trick with the cattle of Apollo (Chapter 7).   225. *Tirynthian hero:* Heracles, whose parents came from Tiryns.   233. *to the right:* One speaks of the left or right bank of a river from the point of view of looking downstream. The Aventine is to the east of the Tiber, which here runs roughly south.

250

The cavern at once was shrouded in the inky blackness of night,
which stripped the eyes of their sight, and under the rocky roof
mixed choking sinister darkness with lurid flashes of fire.
But Alcides did not submit: one jump, he was over the flame,
into the cave, where the smoke was pouring its murkiest billows.
In vain did Cacus belch out his flames to lighten the darkness:
the hero, catching his neck, squeezed till his eyes started out,

255

till blood no longer was pulsing in the arteries of his throat.
    The black den's gates lay open, the stolen cattle restored,
the theft and the trick to conceal it now lay exposed to the day,
and the monster's ugly cadaver was dragged away by the heels.

VERGIL, *Aeneid* (8.190–269)

After other adventures, Heracles brought most of the cattle to Mycenae, where Eurystheus sacrificed them to Hera.

11. The Apples of the Hesperides

Heracles' next task was to bring back the **apples of the Hesperides** (hes-**per**-i-dēz), "the nymphs of the West." These apples grew on a magical tree with golden bark and golden leaves, which Zeus gave to Hera as a wedding present and Hera planted in a garden at the foot of Mount Atlas.[10] Because the Hesperides liked to pilfer from the tree, Hera set a ferocious hundred-headed serpent named Ladon as guard over it.[11]

Heracles did not know where to find the Garden of the Hesperides (just as Perseus did not know where to find the Gorgons). He had first to find and seize the sea god Nereus, who changed into every kind of shape until at last he gave Heracles the directions.

Side-Deeds: Antaeus, Busiris.   Heracles again crossed north Africa. There he was attacked by **Antaeus** (an-**tē**-us), a giant who wrestled passersby to death and built a house of their skulls. Heracles lifted him up and threw him to the ground again and again, but every time Antaeus hit the dirt he came back stronger. Heracles remembered that Antaeus was a son of Gaea, and therefore became stronger every time he touched his mother Earth. He clasped the monster tightly, held him high in the air, and soon strangled him.

Although the Hesperides were in the far west, Heracles seems to have become confused and headed east. At least his next Side-Deed takes place in Egypt, against **Busiris** (bū-**sī**-ris), a son of Poseidon and one of Epaphus' daughters (hence a cousin of Perseus). Some years before, when Egypt was barren, a seer told the king that to restore abundance, he must sacrifice a foreigner. The king began with the seer himself, and ever after sacrificed every foreigner he could. Heracles allowed himself to be bound and led to the altar. Then, impatient with the silly, tiny, effete Egyptians

---

[10]Hence the name *Atlantic Ocean*, that is, the great expanse of water that surrounds the world, near Mount Atlas. Although the Titan Atlas was said to have become a mountain when Perseus showed him the Gorgon's head, he was still alive generations later in the days of Heracles.

[11]Compare the hundred-eyed monster Argus sent to watch over Io (Chapter 13).

FIG. 14.6. Heracles kills Busiris, on an Attic water-jug, c. 470 B.C. Heracles swings a shaven-headed Egyptian priest by both legs, as if he were a club by which he will kill other priests cowering on the other side of the altar. His ordinary club leans against the altar.   (National Museum, Athens; 9683)

and their foolish airs, he burst his bonds, seized Busiris and his sons, and cut their throats across the altar (Fig. 14.6).

Busiris is a Greek corruption of the Egyptian *Bu-Osiris,* meaning "the place of Osiris," the name of a temple dedicated to the Egyptian judge of the dead. Heracles' sacrifice of Busiris, then, is Death overcome.

Side-Deed: Prometheus.   Still trying to find the Hesperides, Heracles came to Prometheus, nailed to a rock in the Caucasus. He killed the eagle that tormented him and set Prometheus free, as Hesiod reports in his *Theogony:*

[525]   Heracles at last, mighty son
              of fair-ankled Alcmena, slew the eagle and saved the child
              of Iapetus° from his torment. Zeus, of course, consented,
              he who governs the world from high on Olympus,
              that the glory of Thebes-born Heracles might be greater
530   than ever before through all the abundant earth.
              Considering all this, he honored his son and his fame;
              furious though he was, he gave up his long-held anger
              that Prometheus had dared contest the plans of mighty Zeus.

                              HESIOD, *Theogony* (525–534)

527. *child of Iapetus:* Prometheus.

It must be at this time that Prometheus exchanged his mortality for the wounded Chiron's immortality, allowing the wise Centaur to die.

At last Heracles came to the western edge of the world, where Atlas held the heavens upon his shoulders (see Fig. 5.1). On the advice of Prometheus, Heracles persuaded Atlas to fetch the apples from the magic tree, a mission too dangerous even for Heracles. While Atlas was away in the Garden of the Hesperides, Heracles himself held up the sky. The Titan returned but, exultant with his freedom, declared he would himself take the apples to Eurystheus; Heracles could go on holding up the world. Heracles agreed, asking only that Atlas take the sky back for a moment so that he might place a pad on his head to cushion the immense weight. Stupid Atlas put down the apples and hoisted the sky. Heracles grabbed the fruit and hurried away.

He gave the apples to Eurystheus, but they were too dangerous to keep. Eurystheus returned them to Heracles, who gave them to Athena, who restored them to the Hesperides.

12. Cerberus

As his twelfth labor Heracles was ordered to descend to the underworld and bring back its many-headed guard dog, **Cerberus.** He traveled to the entrance to Hades at Taenaron, a system of caves near Sparta. As he came down from the upper world, the ghosts fled before him. He seized one of Hades' cows (Hades, like Geryon, is a cattleman) and sacrificed it to Lord Death. He appeared before the king and queen of the dead and requested permission to take Cerberus. Hades agreed, so long as Heracles did not use any weapons. Protected by his lion's skin and breastplate, he seized the hell-hound by the throat, although Cerberus' snake-tail lashed and bit him. Heracles passed a chain around the beast and dragged it, foaming and snarling, to Eurystheus (see Fig. 4.3), then released it to the world below.

Observations: Heracles' Labors

Gilgamesh overcame a great bull, as did Heracles, and he destroyed the mysterious Humbaba. Heracles began his heroic career as an animal-slayer, then proceeded further afield to take on new adversaries. As Gilgamesh crossed faraway waters to consult with Utnapishtim, the man who never died, and Perseus went to the edge of the world to defeat a demon whose glance was death, so did Heracles descend to the underworld and bring back its guardian.

Scholars have wondered when and how originally separate and disorganized tales were organized into a group of twelve. Our earliest accounts show no trace of a standard list or number. In a genealogical passage, explaining the parentage of important mythical monsters, Hesiod refers only to Geryon, the Hydra, Cerberus (although not explicitly connected with Heracles), and the Nemean lion from the list later to become standard:

[287]　　Chrysaör° bedded Callirhoë, daughter of far-famed Ocean,
　　　　on whom he fathered Geryon, three human bodies conjoined.

287. *Chrysaör:* Sprung from the severed neck of Medusa, along with Pegasus.

Geryon was herding his slow-moving cattle in rich Erythia
290   when mighty Heracles slew him, plundered the herds as his booty,
and drove them across the ocean to the holy city of Tiryns,
first stilling Orthus the hound and Eurytion, Geryon's cowherd
in the windy pastures beside the coast of the far-famed Ocean.
Callirhoë bore to Chrysaör another, like neither men nor immortals,
295   Echidna, divine, strong-minded, born in a hollow cave.
Down to the waist a soft-cheeked maiden, glancing demurely;
below, a speckled serpent, terrible, monstrous in size,
feeding on human flesh in the sacred depths of the earth. . . .
They say that Typhoeus, the creature of cruelty, terror, unreason,
300   bedded this soft-eyed maiden, who bore him terrible children.
First came Orthus the hound, Geryon's servant and watchdog.
Cerberus next she conceived, an unspeakable flesh-eating horror,
the bronze-voiced watchdog of Hades, fifty-headed and ruthless.
The third of her spawn was the Hydra of Lerna, plotter of evil,
305   whom white-shouldered Hera brought up in her anger at Heracles.
Yet Zeus's son slew the beast with the edge of his pitiless sword,
Heracles, son of Amphitryon, and his warlike friend Iolaüs,
all in accord with the plans of Athena who gathers the booty.
And Echidna bore the Chimera, breathing unquenchable fire. . . .
310   who, yielding to rape by Orthus, conceived a bane to the Thebans,
the terrible Sphinx, and her brother, destruction to mortals,
the savage Nemean lion, whom Hera, consort of Zeus
raised from a cub and settled among the vales of Nemea,
as tyrant over Nemea, Tretos, and Apesas.°
315   But he too fell to the valor and power of Heracles.

HESIOD, *Theogony* (287–332)

314. *Apesas:* Tretos and Apesas are mountains near Nemea.

The earliest evidence for the canonical cycle of Twelve Labors is found not in literature but on the twelve stone panels, called metopes (**me**-tō-pēz), mounted above the columns of Zeus's temple at Olympia, built about 470 B.C.[12] The cleaning of the Augean stables was included on the temple in the twelfth position, evidently to honor Pisa, the site of the temple, in the territory of the legendary Augeas. This labor is different from the others, which pit Heracles against dangerous enemies, and cannot belong to an earlier list. The number twelve may be an accident: The sculptor had twelve spaces to fill, and the fame of these sculptures made the selection canonical.[13]

By Hellenistic times the same twelve adventures always appear in roughly the same order. There is a logic to their organization. The early adventures are set in the Peloponnesus in an ever-widening circle around Mycenae. Of the first seven, six are simple combat between man and animal (once again, the cleaning of the Augean

[12]Metopes alternated with stone imitation roof-beams at the level of the roof on Doric temples.
[13]Twelve is also a magical number and suitable for a collection: There are twelve Olympians, twelve Titans, and twelve months in the year.

FIG. 14.7. The Roman emperor Commodus (A.D. 180–192) as Hercules, marble, c. A.D. 192. Alexander the Great had shown himself as Heracles, and the tradition lasted among rulers until the end of antiquity. Here Commodus, son of the emperor–philosopher Marcus Aurelius, shows himself absurdly wrapped in the skin of the Nemean lion, with foppish hair and petulant smile. Toward the end of his reign Commodus, like Heracles, seems to have gone insane. He murdered many, performed as a gladiator in the ring, called himself the Roman Hercules, and was strangled shortly after this portrait was done.
(Museo Capitolino, Palazzo dei Conservatori, Rome; Deutsches Archaologisches Institut, Rome)

stables does not fit). Later adventures carry Heracles south to Crete (Cretan bull), north to Thrace (horses of Diomedes), east to the land of the Amazons (girdle of Hippolyta), and west to Erythia (cattle of Geryon), and the last are set in paradise (Garden of the Hesperides) and hell (Cerberus). The deliberate arrangement must reflect a lost poem, although we do not know whether the poem came before or after the designer of the metopes at Olympia.

Heracles' geographical exploration ever further afield made him a natural model for the many Greeks living overseas, especially those in the distant and dangerous west, in Sicily and Italy. Ninety percent of surviving illustrated Greek pots (of which some are illustrated in this book) come from graves in Italy, and the abundance of scenes illustrating the adventures of Heracles no doubt reflects the western Greeks' reverence for him. Heracles had traveled into the Atlantic Ocean and faced Death himself, and he easily overcame every foreign people. Heracles was the colonists' favorite hero, and in fact became a god. Alexander the Great, who claimed descent from Heracles, is also identified with the mythical hero. When Alexander is shown on coins wearing the skin of the Nemean lion, he is evoking the image of Heracles as he seeks to impose his will on all foreigners who might stand against him (Fig. 14.7).

VARIOUS DEEDS

Heracles was released from his servitude to Eurystheus and settled in Tiryns. He wanted to marry again and heard that Eurytus, king of Oechalia (a town somewhere in Euboea), who had been Heracles' own archery instructor, had offered his beautiful daughter **Iolê** (ī-ō-lē) as a prize in an archery contest. However, it was rumored that Eurytus loved her himself and did not want anyone else to have her. Heracles traveled to Oechalia and easily defeated his old master. But Eurytus would not give up Iolê, fearing, he said, that she and her children might share Megara's fate.

Heracles stalked off in a huff. Shortly afterward, Eurytus discovered that twelve fine mares were missing. He thought Heracles had taken them, but Eurytus' son Iphitus (**if**-i-tus), who admired Heracles, insisted that so great a man could never stoop so low. Iphitus said he would go to Tiryns and place the matter before the hero.

In fact, the mares were in Heracles' herd, either because Heracles had taken them or because he had gotten them from someone else. Heracles welcomed Iphitus to Tiryns and invited him to the top of the stone ramparts, then for his nosiness pushed him to his death. For a second time Heracles had violated a sacred social code, this time *xenia*, "guest-friendship," whereby a host never for any reason harmed his guest.

Heracles went to the Delphic Oracle to learn how to atone for his crime. The Pythia refused even to answer, disgusted with a man twice accursed and blood-polluted. Heracles broke into the temple, seized the Pythia's holy tripod, and ran down the road, shouting that he would set up his own oracle. Apollo came down from Olympus and seized a leg of the tripod. Back and forth they tugged, until Zeus separated them with a thunderbolt.

Apollo agreed to purify Heracles on these conditions: He must serve a woman for three years as her slave, and he must give everything he earned to Eurytus as blood-money. Hermes led the hero, a base commodity, to the slave market, a rope around his neck. **Omphalê** (**om**-fa-lē), queen of Lydia, liked the hero's physique and bought him on the spot, thinking he would make a fine lover.

Omphalê and Heracles spent the next three years in idle pleasure. The liked to wear each other's clothes. Omphalê lugged Heracles' club, smothered in his lion skin, while Heracles pranced in her negligee before settling down at her feet to spin thread.

One day they went to the wild for a little fun. When night fell, they entered a cave. Pan, goat god of shepherds and flocks, saw them and in the night sneaked into the cave, bent on having his way with Omphalê. Feeling a negligee drooping from the bed, he leaped on his prey. Heracles (for they had exchanged clothes) awoke with a roar and smashed the miserable Pan against the stony walls. Never since has Pan worn clothing!

During his Lydian period Heracles captured the **Cercopes** (ser-**kō**-pēz), two ruffians who robbed passersby and treated them cruelly. One day they saw Heracles sleeping beside the road and sneaked up, hoping to rob him, but instantly Heracles seized them in his massive hands, suspended them from the ends of a pole, and went down the road with the pole on his shoulders (Fig. 14.8). But the ruffians, although hanging upside down, continued to crack jokes. Seeing Heracles' buttocks burned

FIG. 14.8. The Cercopes, on a metope from Selinus in Sicily, c. 530. The evidently trivial tale is the subject of artistic representations from Corinth, Sparta, Attica, south Italy, and Sicily over a span of two hundred years, between the sixth and fourth centuries. (Museo Nazionale, Palermo; University of Wisconsin, Madison Photo Archive)

black from his journeys across deserts and through foreign lands, one shouted, "O, beware the great black buttocks! Beware the great black buttocks!" And the other giggled, "That must be what Mama meant!" Years before their mother had warned them: Only "Black Buttocks" could defeat them. Heracles was amused by their carryings-on (as we are meant to be) and let them go. Zeus later turned the Cercopes into monkeys.

After his three years of servitude were completed, Heracles left Lydia, gathered an army, and set out to settle a few scores. He started with Troy, where he was badly treated on an earlier adventure. Heracles killed the king Laomedon and all his sons except for one, named Podarces. Before giving the king's daughter away as warbooty, he permitted her to save one prisoner. She chose Podarces, who thereafter was called Priam (**prī**-am), which means "the ransomed one." Priam was king of Troy during the Trojan War.

THE DEATH OF HERACLES

Gilgamesh died peacefully in Uruk, and of Perseus' death nothing is known. Heracles, by contrast, died horribly at the hands of a woman scorned in love; even so had Ishtar destroyed Gilgamesh's beloved friend Enkidu when Gilgamesh rejected her.

Heracles first heard of **Deianira** (dā-ya-**nī**-ra, "man-killer") when he was in the underworld. The ghost of her brother Meleager (mel-**ē**-**ā**-jer), hero of the Calydonian Boar Hunt (see Chapter 18), had suggested to Heracles that he marry Deianira

Carracci's *Hercules at the Cross-Roads*

Although "The Choice of Heracles" or "Heracles at the Crossroads" is widely known, it is not a myth, a traditional tale, but a philosophical allegory consciously designed in the fifth century B.C. by Prodicus of Ceos, a contemporary and acquaintance of Socrates. Heracles, like Paris, was wooed by goddesses, says Prodicus, but his goddesses were Virtue and Wickedness. Each urged him to follow her: Wickedness, surrounded by every delight, offered pleasure and happiness; Virtue offered a hard road with an uncertain end. Heracles chose Virtue and earned immortality. This "myth" of Prodicus was later taken over by the philosophical school of the Cynics to illustrate the choice everyone must face. The Cynics were so called because their most famous member, Diogenes of Sinopê, was nicknamed *kuôn,* "the dog": He snarled at worldly power and possessions. According to the Cynics, who often lived as beggars, wandering the world and mocking its pretensions, the virtuous man scorned comfort, social propriety, and conventional social entanglements; Heracles was their ideal.

FIG. P 14.2. Annibale Carracci (Italian, 1560–1609), *Hercules at the Cross-Roads,* c. 1596, oil on canvas.   (Museo di Capodimonte, Naples)

Annibale Carracci presents the story here (Fig. P 14.2). In the center, a meditative Heracles is leaning on his club. Wickedness, the white-clad goddess on the right, stands in a lush wood, symbolizing the delights of nature, accompanied by tragic and comic masks—the delights of art. The violin represents the pleasure of song. To the left, Virtue points up a narrow barren road to a mountaintop, where a wild horse perches—the harsh, steep road to excellence. At her feet a demonic creature reads from a book, perhaps a prophecy of the suffering that Heracles must endure before achieving immortality.

should he escape from Death's realm. Now he set off to Calydon, capital of Aetolia in the southwestern corner of the mainland, where she lived. The river god **Acheloüs** (ak-e-lō-us), who is usually represented as a bull but can take on other forms (Fig. 14.9), also wanted Deianira. Heracles wrestled Acheloüs and broke off one of his horns. In Sophocles' play *Women of Trachis* (**trā**-kis; c. 430? B.C.), whose subject is the downfall and death of Heracles, the chorus gives a good description of the fight:

[503]   Tell me, who were the real heroes
                 who advanced to fight for this girl as bride,
505   in contests with no holds barred, no times out?
         One of them had the strength of a rushing river,

FIG. 14.9. Heracles wrestles with Acheloüs, Attic vase, c. 520–510 B.C. Here the river god has the shape of a Triton, a sea spirit with the pug nose and pointed ears of a satyr. Acheloüs' fish body suggests the stormy water of the untamed stream. Heracles is about to break off his horn.   (British Museum, London; LX1-C42)

resembling a long-horned, solid-set bull
    that was Acheloüs of Calydon.
The other came from Thebes, the town of Bacchus,
510   brandishing bow and spear and bludgeon,
        the son of Zeus himself. The two together
        entered the ring, both eager for the girl.
The referee? Aphrodite the coupler
        was there to see to fair play.
515   First came the thud of fists, then the twang of bows,
        then a noise like the combat of bulls in rut.
            They twisted and grappled, with the sound of butting heads,
        and the angry screams of them both.
But the fair-faced kindly girl for whom they fought
520   sat quietly apart, on a distant bank—
    (I tell you this, as if I myself were her mother)—
    waiting to learn whose bride she was to be.
        A piteous sight!
        After that, she left her mother.
525   Like a deserted calf, she slowly walked away.

SOPHOCLES, *Women of Trachis* (503–530)

Taking his bride, Heracles headed for Trachis, a city built in a gorge above a plain northwest of Thermopylae, whose king had offered him hospitality. On the way he had to cross the river Evenus, where the Centaur Nessus ferried travelers for a small fee. Nessus had lived in the Peloponnesus near the cave of Pholus until Heracles drove him out. Deianira got on the Centaur's back while Heracles easily swam to the other side, but in the middle of the river Nessus assaulted the young woman. When Heracles saw, he shot the Centaur with a poisoned arrow (Fig. 14.10). Nessus staggered ashore and with dying words instructed Deianira to collect his blood and semen, a powerful love potion, should she ever need it.

Heracles and his new bride stayed at Trachis. Still resenting his treatment at the hands of Eurytus of Oechalia, who had cheated him of Iolê, Heracles organized a military campaign. He sacked the town, killed Eurytus, took the girl, and retired to a cape on the long island of Euboea to prepare a sacrifice to his father, Zeus, in thanks for his victory. He sent a messenger, Lichas, across the strait to Trachis to bring a clean cloak for the sacrifice. Deianira, learning about Iolê, remembered the love potion:

[555]   Preserved in a bronze container for many a year,
    I keep an old gift of the ancient Centaur,
    which, still a maid, I took from the shaggy Nessus,
    as he lay dying, weltering in his blood.
    He used to carry people in his arms
560   for a trifling fee, across Evenus' river,
    in his arms, not bothering with oars or sails.
    He carried me too, held up against his shoulder,
    when first I followed Heracles as wife,
    so ordered by my father. Out in midstream

FIG. 14.10. Heracles and Nessus. Avenging the attack on his wife, Heracles seizes the Centaur's hair, presses his left foot into his side, and prepares to bury his sword in the monster's chest. Heracles wears a simple cloak crossed with a telamon ("shield strap"); note his neatly trimmed mustache against the shaggy, unkempt beard of the Centaur. This is an early mythic scene, about 600 B.C., painted on the neck of a large amphora used to mark an Attic grave. The belly shows one of the earliest representations of Perseus beheading Medusa.
(National Archaeological Museum, Athens; A1002)

565   he fondled me with his lubricious hands.
I screamed aloud, the son of Zeus spun round
and from his hands let fly a feathered arrow,
which whistled into his lungs. The dying Centaur
gasped out a few last words: "Child of old Oeneus,°
570   you are the last I shall ever bring across.
So listen carefully, and profit from my labors.
Take in your hands a blood-clot from my punctured lungs,
black with Hydra's bile, which Heracles
smeared on his arrows. This charm will never fail
575   to bind his heart: he will never look again
at another woman, to love her more than you."
    With this in mind, my friends, since Nessus died
I have kept the venom, safely locked away.
Now I have brought it out, to stain this shirt.
580   All is made ready, as the living Centaur directed.

SOPHOCLES, *Women of Trachis* (555–581)

569. *Oeneus:* Deianira's father, Oeneus ("wine man"), was king of Calydon.

She gave the shirt to Lichas. In the *Women of Trachis,* Hyllus (**hī**-lus), oldest son of Heracles and Deianira, tells his mother what happened:

[749]   Since you insist, I'll tell the whole sad story.
750   When Heracles had sacked the town of Eurytus,
      away he marched, with trophies and great loot.
      There is a Cape Ceneium, washed by the waves,
      at the very tip of Euboea, where he dedicated
      an altar and grove to his ancestral Zeus.
755   After my separation, I was overjoyed
      to find him there, about to offer up
      a splendid sacrifice. But just as all was ready,
      his faithful herald Lichas came from home,
      bringing your deadly gift, the envenomed shirt.
760   He put it on, according to your command,
      then offered up a dozen perfect bulls,
      the best of all the booty, and made ready,
      a hundred victims of every sex and age.
      At first, poor man, his heart rejoiced at the show,
765   and he prayed with fervor, wearing your recent gift.
      But then, as the blood-fed fires of the sacred rite
      blazed up and joined the resinous firewood's heat,
      and his whole body broke into a sweat,
      your shirt, as tight as any builder's mortise,
770   clung to his ribs, and then to every limb.
      On every bone came cramping, torturing, fire,
      as the serpentine and deadly venom gnawed.
      He screamed in pain to bring him hapless Lichas,
      who had no share at all in his distress.
775   "What scheming made you bring this deadly garment?"
      Poor man, what did he know? he kept repeating
      the gift was yours alone, he just the bearer.
      As Heracles was listening to his words,
      a wrenching torment tore apart his lungs.
780   He seized poor Lichas by one ankle joint
      and dashed him down against a wave-washed reef.
      The white stuff of his brain, marbled with blood,
      burst from his shattered skull and soaked his hair.
      No bystander but gasped and groaned in horror,
785   at Heracles' torment, Lichas' death,
      yet not a soul dared to approach the hero,
      now squirming in anguish, groveling on the earth,
      now starting up in sharp spasmodic pain.
      The cries of Heracles reechoed from the rocks
790   on every side—Locrian cliffs and headlands of Euboea.
          At last, exhausted, he collapsed to the ground,
      cursing and groaning at the bitter wedlock
      with you, the marriage bargained from old Oeneus,
      which poisoned his life. At last he raised his eyes
795   uncertainly from the thick and clinging smoke,

and saw me weeping in the stricken crowd.
    "Come near, my son," he called, "don't run away,
though it may mean you join me in my death.
Lift me, carry me out, where none can see my pain.
800   If you have any pity, take me across the water
far from this place, and let me not die here."
    At this command, we laid him in a ship
and painfully rowed him here in his distress,
screaming in torment. When you see him next
805   he may still be alive; more likely not.

SOPHOCLES, *Women of Trachis* (749–806)

Years before, Zeus warned Heracles that no living man could kill him, but that he would die by the hands of the dead: The bile from the dead Hydra, coursing in the veins of the wounded Nessus, killed him (folklorists call this the dead-hand motif). Seeing what she had done, Deianira stabbed herself. Writhing in death's agony, Heracles commanded Hyllus to marry Iolê, dragged himself to the top of Mount Oeta behind Trachis, made an enormous pyre, and lay down on it. No one dared to light the pyre, remembering the fate of Lichas, until a passing shepherd, Philoctetes (fi-lok-**tē**-tēz), dared to do it. In gratitude, as his last human act, Heracles gave Philoctetes his bow.[14]

A cloud gathered around the pyre, thunder cracked, and Heracles was raised into heaven—his *apotheosis* ("the process of being made a god"). When the ashes cooled, only his armor was found, no trace of bone. His spirit was led in high procession to the halls of Zeus on Olympus, where he became a god and married Hebê (**hē**-bē), "youth." Although Odysseus saw him in the underworld, it was not the real Heracles, but a shade, a phantom:

[601]   My eyes fell next, after him, on Heracles' apparition,
    a mighty form but a ghost, for he himself sits in the midst
    of the banquet of deathless gods, with Hebê, fair-ankled maiden,
    daughter of glorious Zeus and Hera of golden sandals.
605   From around him rose the terrified din of the gibbering phantoms,
    who fluttered away as he came, an image of blackest night.
    He carried his bow at the ready, with an arrow upon its string.
    His eye glanced fiercely around, always preparing to shoot.
    He wore an enormous game-bag strapped to his mighty chest
610   and a golden sword-belt as well, that pictured wonderful actions:
    hunts of savage bears, wild boars, and fierce glaring lions;
    hand-to-hand fighting, battles, murder, and sudden death.
    Skilled as he was, this maker of Heracles' wallet and sword-belt
    could never hope to design another such wonderful work.
615   Heracles knew me at once, as soon as his eyes fell upon me.
    Sadly shaking his head, he spoke words flying right to the mark:
        "Son of Laërtes, descendant of Zeus, inventive Odysseus,
    are you too forced to endure some destiny loaded with trouble,

---

[14]Later important in the Trojan War.

like that which I had to bear, alive in the light of the sun?
620 Although a child of Cronian Zeus, I carried limitless burdens,
for a man far worse than myself, who exacted impossible tasks.
At last he ordered me here, to return with the hound of Hades—
no labor, or so he thought, would be harder for me to accomplish.
Yet I carried Cerberus up and away from Hades' domain,
625 with Hermes to show me the way, and gray-eyed Athena to help me.

HOMER, *Odyssey* (11.601–626)

THE RETURN OF THE HERACLIDS

When Heracles died, Eurystheus was determined to kill the many sons, fathered on many women, whom Heracles had left behind, called the **Heraclids** (**her**-a-klids). They fled, first to Trachis, then to Athens, where they took refuge at the Altar of Mercy. The Athenians bravely refused to surrender the refugees, took up arms, and defeated Eurystheus and killed five of his sons, although the king himself escaped in a chariot. Hyllus gave chase and ran him down, cut off Eurystheus' head, and brought it to Alcmena, who, laughing, poked out its eyes with large bronze pins.

The Heraclids now entered the Peloponnesus and conquered it, but soon a plague struck the land. At the command of an oracle, they withdrew back across the Isthmus to Marathon. Another oracle declared that they could return to the Peloponnesus after "the third harvest," which Hyllus took to mean "in three years." To his surprise, Hyllus was defeated by the new king of Mycenae, Tisamenus (tis-**am**-en-us), son of Orestes (see Chapter 20). The oracle, when questioned, explained that "third harvest" did not refer to the fruit of the earth, but to the generations of men. True enough, under one Temenus, Hyllus' great-grandson and the great-great-grandson of Heracles, the Heraclids were victorious. Hyllus and Tisamenus, last of the House of Atreus (see Chapter 19), were both somehow still alive and both fell in battle.

The classical Greeks identified the legendary return of the Heraclids with the Dorian invasion that caused the collapse of the Mycenaean world about 1200 B.C. The Dorians of the Peloponnesus always claimed to be direct descendants of Heracles and made of Heracles their special hero. But Heracles was never a local or tribal hero: At all times he belonged to all the Greeks.

Observations: Heracles *Kallinikos*, "Handsome in Victory"

Heracles' name, which seems to mean "the glory of Hera," appears puzzling.[15] Why should he be named after Hera, when she persecutes him relentlessly? In the Greek Bronze Age, when parts of this myth may have taken form, Heracles was perhaps a common name, like John or Paul, applied to the common folktale hero who suffered

[15]Hence the title of Philip Slater's book *The Glory of Hera;* see Further Reading in this chapter. The name may also mean "lordly glory," as does our *Albert.*

greatly, then was saved at the end. His origins remain obscure, and we do not know where his legends first appeared in Greece. The Argive plain, where he served Eurystheus, and Thebes, where he was born and first married, have equally strong claims. His character is complex and hard to summarize. Although often called the archetypal Greek hero, to the Greeks of Homer's day he was already very old-fashioned, evoking the image of a bygone age when violence could solve every problem. The historical period that begins with Homer was a tamer time (although still murderous) in which the stories of Heracles served as examples of the dangers of excess, though often with a humorous twist, as we have seen.

Heracles does everything too much. He commits terrible crimes, which are followed by humiliating expiation. He violates the most sacred human obligations, killing his wife, children, and his guest-friend Iphitus, after which he must live in degrading bondage first to the cowardly Eurystheus, then to a woman as her sexual plaything and slave. A passing reference in Homer speaks of the time when Heracles shot Hera in the breast with an arrow. Here is the hero's essence: reckless, fearless, sometimes tricky, getting away with things others cannot, attacking the very gods. Another passing reference in Homer mentions that he shot Hades "in the Gate, among the dead."

Of course, other heroes challenge Death—Gilgamesh inquires of Utnapishtim, Perseus slays the Gorgon, Odysseus and Aeneas descend to the underworld—but none so often or explicitly as Heracles, and no other is rewarded at the end with immortality, Heracles' reward for completing the Twelve Labors. After death, Heracles

FIG. 14.11. The Hercules of Farnese, marble Roman copy of Greek original by Lysippus, fourth century B.C. The once elegant, aristocratic hero has become a muscle-bound, ridiculous brute as he leans against his club covered by the lion skin. This is the Heracles parodied by the comedians, somewhat like the modern stereotype of the stupid athlete, all brawn and no brain. (Museo Nazionale, Naples; Art Resource, NY; Erich Lessing photo)

married Hebê, "youth," on Mount Olympus: He never got old. In life he journeyed to the underworld and brought back Cerberus. The triple-bodied Geryon lives across water (where death's realm lies) in the far west (where the sun dies daily), and from there Heracles returned. The souls of the dead often are pictured as birds: Heracles slays the death-dealing species that hovers around Stymphalus. Busiris is the Egyptian lord of the dead, but Heracles kills him. The apples from the Hesperides' garden grow on the tree of eternal life; they fall, although temporarily, into Heracles' hands. In one version, his pursuit of the Ceryneian deer also takes him to this garden, for the deer is the magical but dangerous animal that appears in folktales, leading the hunter from the everyday world to the other side of the mirror, the land of dreams and of the dead.

As the best-loved of all Greek heroes, Heracles was *alexikakos,* "the averter of evils," summoned as a god to turn away disease, human and animal attack, and every kind of harm. A common oath in Greek was "By Heracles!"—just as we might say, "By God!" He was the paradigm of heroic tragic existence, but in many humorous tales, and on the comic stage, his reputation for womanizing and gluttony made him a figure of fun (Fig. 14.11). He embodied the Greeks' naive eagerness to try anything without fear of the result, which too often proved disastrous. He destroyed evil, sinned greatly, loved unwisely, fathered a whole race, and died shamefully at a woman's hand, yet he received his triumphant reward. Heracles is not a hero who fights other heroes, like the warriors before the walls of Troy and Thebes. Like Gilgamesh, he is the tough guy, the strongest man on the earth, another folktale type, the animal-slayer who made the world safe by destroying dangerous beasts.[16]

KEY TERMS

Heracles, 345	Admetus, 362
Alcmena, 346	Alcestis, 362
Eurystheus, 346	Hippolyta, 363
Amphitryon, 346	Geryon, 363
Megara, 354	Cacus, 364
Nemean lion, 357	apples of the Hesperides, 366
Hydra, 358	Antaeus, 366
Ceryneian deer, 359	Busiris, 366
Erymanthian boar, 359	Cerberus, 368
Pholus, 359	Iolê, 371
Chiron, 359	Omphalê, 371
Augeas, 361	Cercopes, 371
Stymphalian birds, 361	Deianira, 372
Cretan bull, 361	Acheloüs, 374
horses of Diomedes, 362	Heraclids, 379

[16]The biblical Samson, too, killed a lion and was destroyed by a woman.

FURTHER READING

Brommer, Frank, *Heracles: The Twelve Labors of the Hero in Ancient Art and Literature,* trans. and enlarged by S. J. Schwarz (New Rochelle, N.Y., 1986). The best succinct review of Heracles in literature and art.

Dale, A. M., ed., *Euripides: Alcestis* (Oxford, U.K., 1954). The introduction to the Greek text has a good analysis of the myth and how Euripides used it.

Galinsky, Karl, *The Heracles Theme* (New York, 1972). Surveys the development of the figure of Heracles from ancient through modern times.

Slater, Philip E., *The Glory of Hera: Greek Mythology and the Greek Family* (Boston, 1968). A psychoanalytic interpretation of Heracles' career and other Greek myths.

Small, Jocelyn Penny, *Cacus and Marsyas in Etrusco-Roman Legend* (Princeton, N.J., 1982). The Italian background to the story of Cacus.

CHAPTER 15

THESEUS AND THE MYTHS OF ATHENS

Our city is not ruled
by orders of a single ruler: no, it is free.
In yearly terms of office, men succeed
each other; the rich receive no more
consideration than the worthy poor.

THESEUS SPEAKING TO A THEBAN HERALD, FROM
EURIPIDES, *Suppliant Women* 405–408

IN THE CLASSICAL PERIOD Athens was preeminent for achievement in literature, philosophy, and the arts, but the city's legendary history is unusually confused: Several characters bearing the same name turn up in different generations of the early kings, probably because later Greek mythographers ("writers about myth") tried to fill in gaps and fashion a coherent genealogy. In particular, many additions to the legends of Athen's greatest hero, **Theseus,** were made in the sixth and fifth centuries B.C., when Athens became an important military power and cultural center. Let us first examine the stories of the early kings of Athens, then Theseus' heroic career (except for his Cretan adventures, presented in Chapter 16), and, finally, how Athenian politics shaped and used Athenian myth.

CECROPS, ERICHTHONIUS, AND THE DAUGHTERS OF CECROPS

The stories of the first kings of Athens are complicated and even self-contradictory. The Athenians made three claims about their origins: that they were descended from

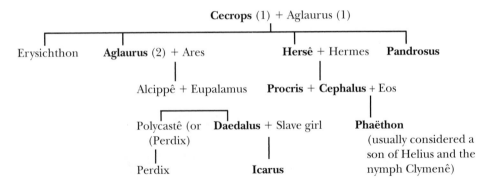

CHART 15.1. Cecrops and His Descendants

a mortal named **Cecrops** (sē-kropz; Chart 15.1), that they were autochthonous (aw-**tok**-tho-nus), "sprung from the earth";[1] and that they were descended from Athena, after whom the city was named (even though Athena was a virgin goddess). The claims of autochthony and descent from Cecrops are brought together in the story that Cecrops simply sprang from the earth, with the form of a snake beneath the waist, a man above. The snake often symbolized origin from the earth: The Giants, also born from the earth, were represented in Greek art with the tails of snakes.

The reign of Cecrops was a golden age. He brought to the people the arts of civilization and taught them to worship Zeus, to abandon human sacrifice (although Erechtheus, a later king, sacrificed his own daughter), to build cities, and to bury the dead properly. He introduced monogamous marriage. In his reign Athena and Poseidon competed for recognition as patron of the city, Athena offering the olive and Poseidon a spring of salt water on the Acropolis; Athena was chosen (Fig. 15.1). The choice reminds us that the land (producer of olives) was for a long time more important to the Athenians than the sea, a preference lasting down to the early fifth century, when the wily Themistocles (them-**is**-to-klēz, c. 524–460 B.C.) persuaded the people to spend the proceeds of newly discovered silver deposits on building a great fleet. This fleet defeated the Persians in 480 B.C. at the battle of Salamis near the harbor of Athens and made Athens the greatest sea power of the eastern Mediterranean.

The theme of Athenian autochthony was reinforced by the story about **Erichthonius** (er-ik-**thō**-ni-us), another early king of Athens (Chart 15.2), who came to the throne after Cecrops died. Erichthonius was born in this way: Athena had gone to Hephaestus' smithy for repair of her weapons. Missing his ex-wife Aphrodite, whom he had divorced for adultery, Hephaestus took one look at the goddess and pursued her lustfully across the Acropolis. Although lame, Hephaestus caught up with her and ejaculated semen onto her leg. Athena wiped it off with disgust on a piece of wool, which she threw to the ground. Up sprang Erichthonius, whose name probably means "the man of wool and earth" (Fig. 15.2).

[1]Like grasshoppers; certain high officials wore golden grasshopper pins in their hair in celebration of this claim.

FIG. 15.1. The Erechtheum, or House of Erechtheus, built about 420 B.C. during the Peloponnesian War (the Parthenon is visible on the far right). A door led into the shrine of Poseidon/Erechtheus through the porch on the left, as did a stairway down from the Porch of the Maidens (right of building). The maidens, used in place of columns, are called caryatids and may represent the *Arrephoroi,* the girls who carried Athena's sacred basket. On the east of the temple (not visible) was the old temple of Athena, the predecessor of the Parthenon, where, many believe, stood the ancient wooden statue of Athena, supposedly fashioned by Erichthonius. In front of the temple grows the sacred olive (a modern planting), Athena's gift to the *polis;* a hole was left open in the ceiling and floor of the porch to show where Poseidon had struck the rock with his trident.   (University of Wisconsin, Madison Photo Archive)

Athena took the infant, whom she wanted to make immortal, placed him in a basket, and gave the basket to the daughters of Cecrops—Aglaurus (a-**glaw**-rus), "shining," Hersê (**her**-sē), "dew," and Pandrosus (**pan**-dro-sus), "all-dew"—warning them on no condition to look inside. Pandrosus obeyed, but her two sisters could not resist. They saw something in the basket that drove them mad: a serpent, which sprang at them, or a child with serpent's tail instead of legs, or a child entwined by a serpent. Aglaurus and Hersê leaped from the Acropolis to their death and Athena took back the child and raised him herself. When he grew up, Erichthonius became king of Athens. In honor of his "mother," Athena, he set up a wooden image of her on the Acropolis, where Pandrosus and Aglaurus also had shrines.

Observations: The Festival of the Dew Carriers

The story of the daughters of Cecrops is a good example of a myth that appears to reflect a ritual,[2] in this case one performed annually at year's end on the Acropolis

---

[2]See Chapter 23 for theories about myth and ritual.

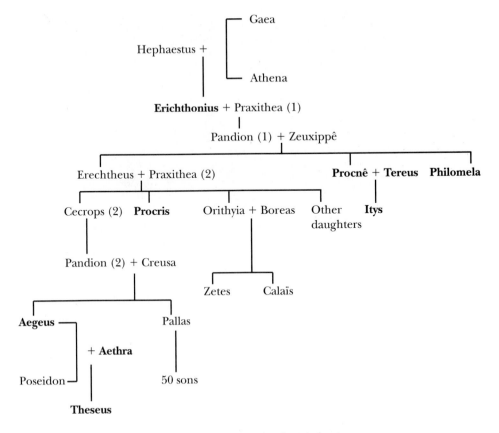

CHART 15.2. The House of Erichthonius

at a festival called the Arrephoria (probably "festival of the dew carriers"). Two young girls, the *Arrephoroi*, lived all year long in a special house on the Acropolis, playing and weaving a robe offered each year to the statue of Athena. When the festival came, the priestess of Athena sent them at night into a grove of Aphrodite on the north edge of the Acropolis. There they took baskets on their heads, carried them down a secret stairway cut in the rock, and left them at the bottom. They then climbed back with a covered basket containing some mysterious thing (compare Fig. 15.3).

The ritual and the myth associated with it are built on the motif of the maiden's sacrifice, with its prominent sexual overtones. Entrance into the grove of Aphrodite represents the virgins' loss of sexual innocence, as does their nocturnal descent underground, where Hades carried the virgin Persephonê to make her his bride. In the myth, Aglaurus and Hersê literally die; in the ritual the girls die symbolically to the virgin's life of sexual innocence.

In the myth, two of the sisters die after looking at a terrifying thing in a basket, possibly a serpent. We can take the serpent as an emblem of the phallus, and thus the literal death of the maidens in the myth reflects the death of sexual innocence—an experience, enacted at the Arrephoria, which every *parthenos* must undergo to

FIG. 15.2. The birth of Erichthonius, on an Attic wine-cup, c. 435 B.C. Cecrops, with a snake's body from the waist down, looks on while Gaea, with crown and scepter, rises from the earth to give the infant Erichthonius to Athena. Behind her stands Hephaestus, "father" of the child, and behind him Hersê rushes forward.   (Antikenmuseum, Staattliche Museen, Berlin; F2537)

FIG. 15.3. Athena and Erichthonius, on an Attic wine-jug, c. 440 B.C. Athena watches as Erichthonius bids her goodbye, secure in his basket encircled by serpents.   (British Museum, London; E 372)

become a woman (*gynê*). The phallus also engenders life, as the basket in the myth contains new life in the form of the infant Erichthonius. The loss of virginity, the death of the daughters, brings the promise of new life, and the daughters of Cecrops bear names related to the shining dew that appears on the ground in the morning after darkness, the moisture from the dark heaven that nourishes the coming day.

PROCRIS AND CEPHALUS

Ovid makes very different use of the story of the daughters of Cecrops, and tells a sensational tale about the harm, to guilty and innocent alike, of uncontrolled sexual passion in the next generation of Athenian rulers. In his version, the daughters survived the viewing of the infant Erichthonius. Years later, Hermes noticed Hersê in a procession and fell in love with her. When he hunted for her on the Acropolis, Aglaurus offered to lead him to Hersê's bed in return for gold. Hermes gave her the bribe, but Athena, still angry that Aglaurus had looked inside the basket, inspired a ferocious jealousy in her. When Aglaurus tried to prevent Hermes from coming to Hersê, Hermes angrily turned Aglaurus to stone and went to Hersê anyway. Hersê became pregnant and bore **Cephalus** (**sef**-a-lus), who grew up and married **Procris,** daughter of Erechtheus, usually called the grandson of Erichthonius (the chronology does not fit very well in the desperately confused genealogy of the House of Athens). Eos, the lustful goddess of dawn (= Latin Aurora), carried Cephalus away to Syria, where she bore Phaëthon by him.[3]

At first the marriage of Cephalus and Procris was happy—too happy. Cephalus could not believe his good fortune and began to give way to irrational suspicion. To test Procris' love, he came to her in disguise, tempting her with ever greater rewards to sleep with him. At last he offered her a golden crown and she agreed. In a rage, he revealed who he really was, and Procris, shamed and frightened, fled to the court of Minos in Crete.

There she attracted the amorous king's attention. Unfortunately Minos could not consummate his passion, for his wife, Pasiphaë (pa-**sif**-a-ē), had placed a curse upon him: Instead of semen, he ejaculated spiders and scorpions, which devoured the genitals of his mistresses! Procris cured him with a root she received from Pasiphaë's sister, the witch Circê. In return, Minos gave her a magical hound named **Laelaps** that always caught what it chased and a magical spear that never missed its mark. Procris, fearing the anger of Pasiphaë, soon regretted her behavior and fled with the gifts back to Athens, disguised as a boy.

Although Cephalus still mourned his beautiful wife and the marriage he had thoughtlessly ruined, he coveted the pretty "boy's" wonderful hound and unerring spear. The disguised Procris offered to give them up if he would sleep with him/her. Cephalus at last agreed, so convicting himself of the same weakness he had discovered in his wife. They were reunited and for a while lived happily together again.

But Procris feared that Cephalus was still meeting Eos/Aurora, his former mistress, especially because every morning he arose at the crack of dawn to go hunting,

[3]Phaëthon is more commonly called the child of Helius, the sun.

a perfect chance to meet one's lover. One morning Procris followed him, with fatal results. Ovid tells this story twice, in the *Metamorphoses* and in another poem, the *Ars Amatoria* ("The Art of Love"), from which the following selection is taken. In Ovid's Latin version, Aurora is replaced by Aura.[4]

[686]   Don't you believe all you hear! the peril of trusting in gossip
        is clear from the sad example of Procris' wretched fate.
      Close by the purple slopes of Hymettus'° flowering foothills
        there bubbles a sacred spring in a copse of soft green turf.
690   Young saplings join in a grove, the ground is thick with arbutus;
        rosemary, laurel, dark myrtle breathe out their sweet perfume.
      Heavy-leaved box-trees abound; tamarisks, fragile and slender;
        sweet clover's rambling shoots; pine clumps, planted by man.
      At the Zephyr's gentlest whisper, each life-giving sigh of the wind,
695   every grass-tip trembles, every leaf springs to life.
      To Cephalus quiet meant bliss. His hounds and huntsmen forgotten,
        he loved to relax his weary frame in that magical spot.
      "Come, gentle gale, who so often has cooled the heat of my bosom,"
        thus would Cephalus murmur to summon the whispering wind.
700   A gossipy friend heard the prayer and dutifully passed it along
        to the jealous ears of his wife, repeating it, word for word.
      When Procris heard the name, she shivered with silent horror.
        Had Cephalus gone astray with a painted hussy named Gail?
      She paled, as a vine-leaf, clinging after the season of vintage,
705   turns a shivery white, touched by the wintry frost;
      as ripening quinces pale, whose weight depresses their branches;
        as cornel-berries whiten while still not ready to eat.
      When Procris revived from her faint, she tore open the delicate bodice
        covering her bosom; her nails tore at her innocent cheeks.
710   No time to reflect: like a crazy maenad stung by the thyrsus,
        her hair astream, she raced up the road that led to the hill.
      What did you hope to accomplish by your mad attempt at an ambush,
        poor Procris? what hope had risen in your delirious heart?
      Did you really think this "Gail," whoever she was, would be waiting
715   for you to appear and denounce her sin with your furious tongue?
      One moment you blushed for shame, hoping you wouldn't catch him,
        the next you were glad you knew; love drove you opposite ways.
      Whatever made you do this? the place, the name, the suggestion?
        These, and the human worry that what we fear must be so.
720   She noticed a place where grass had been crushed by a weary body.
        Her bosom quaked with horror that rose from her fevered heart.
      Now as the sun of noon drew in to a sinister twilight,
        as the morning of hope descended in gloomy and hopeless night,
      Cephalus, Mercury's son, returned from the hunt in the forest
725   to splash his burning face from the icy depths of the spring.

    688. *Hymettus:* A mountain near Athens.

---

[4]The basis for a bad Latin pun between *aura* = "breeze" and *Aura* = a girl's name, here rendered by *gale/Gail*.

Breathless, Procris, you waited. Nearby, her husband, reclining,
  panted, "O breeze, refresh me and you, O delectable gale!"
The silly misunderstood pun flashed on the heart-broken woman,
  whose common sense returned, whose pallor turned to a blush.
730 Starting up to her feet, she eagerly parted the bushes,
  and, true wife that she was, ran to her husband's embrace.
But he in his childish error imagined a boar or a panther.
  He leaped erect and poised the spear in his swift right hand.
Stupid, what are you up to? No wild thing, that. Drop your weapon!
735   Alas, too late! for your spear flies out and pierces her breast.
"Alas!" she sobs, "my love has stabbed the heart of his lover,
  the heart so often wounded by the folly and haste of the head.°
Before the dawn I shall die, but not of being supplanted—
  this, at least, will make the earth lie light on my bones.°
740 My spirit departs with the gale, which once I wrongly suspected
  for its name alone. Dear hands, now close my fainting eyes."
Close to his broken heart he lifted the form of his lady,
  washing with hot salt tears the gaping wound in her breast.
Slowly, her life ebbs away from her all too credulous bosom;
745   her final gasp is received on her husband's sorrowing lips (Fig. 15.4).

OVID, *Ars Amatoria* (3.686–746)

737. *haste of the head*: Another pun: The name *Cephalus* = "head."   739. *make the earth . . .*: A common inscription on Roman graves was "may the earth lie light on your bones," usually abbreviated as S.T.T.L. (*Sit tibi terra levis*).

FIG. 15.4. The death of Procris, on an Attic wine-mixing bowl, c. 440 B.C. Procris, dressed as a young man, her eyes half-closed in death, attempts to pull the spear from her side: Her soul (*psychē*) flies away as a human-headed bird from her head. Her father, Erechtheus, runs toward her from the right, while Cephalus, on the left, holding Laelaps by a leash, strikes his head in a tragic gesture.   (British Museum, London; E 477)

For the unintentional murder of his wife, Cephalus was tried by the Areopagus, the court in Athens where capital crimes were heard, and exiled for life. He went to Thebes, at that time persecuted by a wild vixen fated never to be caught. Each month the desperate Thebans, to forestall worse disaster, exposed the son of a prominent citizen for the fox to devour. The hero Amphitryon (the mortal father of Heracles), then resident at Thebes and under obligation to its king, Creon, offered Cephalus a great treasure for the loan of Laelaps. Thus the hound that always caught its prey chased the fox that could never be caught. Zeus, impatient at the contradiction, turned them both into stone.

PROCNÊ AND TEREUS

When Erichthonius died, his son Pandion (pan-**dī**-on) became king. Pandion had two daughters, **Procnê** (**prok**-nē) and **Philomela** (fil-ō-**mē**-la), and twin sons, Butês and Erechtheus. When war broke out with neighboring Thebes, Pandion summoned to his assistance **Tereus** (**te**-rūs), king of the Thracians, a son of Ares, to whom Pandion gave Procnê in marriage. She soon bore him a son, **Itys** (**it**-is). What happens next is told in one of Ovid's best-known stories of metamorphosis, another sensational tale about the harm of uncontrolled sexual passion:

[424] Tereus came to Pandion's aid and smashed the enemy armies,
425   thus winning a great renown for his glorious victory.
       Pandion, impressed by his wealth, the number of his retainers,
       and his glorious ancestry (which he traced back to Mars himself),
       gave him Procnê as wife. But Juno, patron of wedlock,
       avoided the feast, and Hymen;° no Graces attended their marriage.
430   Only the Furies were there, with torches snatched from a tomb.
       Furies prepared their bed, and owls hooted high on the roof,
       mocking the solemn rites. So Procnê and Tereus married,
       shadowed by gloomy omens, and under these ominous portents
       she soon bore a son. All Thrace, of course, was delighted.
435   Pouring out thanks to the gods, they consecrated the days
       when Tereus married Procnê and Itys her son was born—
       so far did their real advantage lie hidden from their eyes.
          Titan° had led the seasons five times from autumn to autumn,
       when Procnê asked for a favor: "If indeed you think I deserve it,
440   either send me off to visit my sister or have her come here.
       My father will surely consent, if you promise her speedy return.
       For me the finest of presents would be seeing my sister again."
       Tereus agreed to invite Philomela, and summoned his galleys.
       With oars and a following wind he sped to the harbor of Athens.
445   Cordially greeting each other, the kings began their discussion:
       why Tereus was there, what Procnê had asked, and the promised return.
       As they conversed, Philomela appeared, in luxurious garments,

429. *Hymen:* Mythical embodiment of the marriage song; the god of marriage.   438. *Titan:* That is, Hyperion, the sun.

but lovelier far for herself. Enchanted at sight of the maiden,
Tereus' heart caught fire, like dry straw touched by a spark.

450 Fair she was, it is true, but her beauty served only to kindle
the inborn lust of the man, the child of a lecherous race,
who burned with his people's vices, and added them to his own. . . .
  He repeated Procnê's request;
masking his own desire, he pleaded the longing of Procnê.

455 But love gave him eloquent words, and whenever his plea grew too eager,
"That," he exclaimed, "is exactly what Procnê so eagerly wishes."
He even would burst into tears, as if Procnê ordered that too.
Ye gods, what blackness of night confuses intelligent mortals!
All his duplicitous scheme won him praise as a dutiful husband,

460 the more so when Philomela implored the same favor as he.
Stroking Pandion's hands, she begged she might visit her sister,
not knowing the horror in store, thinking alone of the pleasure.
  Tereus watched, and squirmed with fantasy at the caresses
lavished upon her father—her kisses, arms round his neck—

465 all of them goading him on, torches and tinder to passion.
As she put her arms round her father, he wanted to be her father,
but not with a father's feelings toward his innocent child.
Pandion soon gave way to the fervent pleas of his daughter,
and gratitude blended with joy in poor Philomela's delusion,

470 gloating over a triumph concealing the ruin to come. . . .
  No sooner had Philomela embarked in the bright-sided galley,
the oars driven into the waves, the shore out of sight astern,
than barbarous Tereus exulted, "Success! I have what I wanted!"—
gloating, not trying to hide the glee of his lecherous spirit,

475 an eagle loosing his talons from the terrified hare he has taken
up to his aerie on high, hopeless, contorted with fright,
the captor silently gloating at the pleasure soon to be his.
  The voyage at last is done. From wave-battered vessels they land.
The tyrant drags Philomela to a hunting-lodge deep in the forest.

480 Trembling, weeping, she begged him, "Tell me, where is my sister?"
But snarling with bestial lust, he raped her, virgin, alone. . . .
  Consciousness slowly returned. She tore her dishevelled tresses,
beat at her breast with her fists, and hurled a bitter reproach:
"Cruel uncivilized savage, what you are is shown by your deed!

485 Had my father's pleas no effect? or even his tears of farewell?
Did my sister matter so little? my innocence? even your marriage?
Go ahead, cut my throat, round out your wicked achievements—
I wish you had cut it before you dirtied my soul with your filth!
If heaven decides this matter, if the gods indeed possess power,

490 if all that I am or can do does not perish along with my breath,
some day—mark my words!—you will reap the reward of your crime.
Modesty thrown to the winds, I will trumpet your deed of shame,
through cities of men if I can; if not, through forest and hills.
Your crime I accuse to the sky, to whatever gods are in heaven!"

495 Tereus reddened with fury, from fear no less than from anger.
Goaded by both, he whipped the knife at his side from its sheath.
Seizing the girl by her hair, he twisted her arms behind her,

and bound her immobile, secure. Offering her throat to the blade,
her heart conceived a new hope of a rapid and merciful death.
500 But no—as she vainly struggled to call the name of her father,
he seized her tongue with pincers and sliced it off at the root.
The stump convulsively twitched, as the rest lay writhing about,
trying to add its protest to the dark and blood-stained ground;
like half of an injured snake, it jerked in its mistress's track.
505 And then—the story goes on, scarcely deserving of credit—
the sadist returned in his lust again, and again, to his victim.
 After all this, the king in his insolence went in to Procnê.
Before she asked for her sister, he wept with fraudulent tears,
narrated a fictional death, winning Procnê's trust by his sorrow.
510 The queen ripped off her shoulders the veil with a wide gold hem
and put on the garments of sorrow. She erected an empty tomb,
made sacrificial offerings to the ghost of one still alive,
and mourned the death of a sister, not ready thus to be mourned.
 A year passed by as the sun moved through the Zodiac's signs.
515 Philomela stayed locked in a cell of inescapable granite,
guarded on every hand. Her tongueless mouth could tell nothing.
What could the poor girl do? Great pain may mother invention
and cleverness come to the aid of those in profoundest distress.
She set up the threads of the warp, and with a barbarian shuttle
520 wove in its pure white threads and the purple strands of the weft
the tale of Tereus' crime. She gave it, complete, to a servant,
revealing by her gesture that she wanted it brought to the queen.
The slave girl in innocence took it and handed it over to Procnê.
 The wife of the barbarous tyrant unfolded the damning indictment,
525 and on it deciphered the tale of woe Philomela had woven.
Procnê spoke not a word in her grief, too deep to be spoken.
No adequate words arose in her mind as she tried to express it.
Wasting no time on tears, she rushed to a mission of vengeance,
heedless of right or wrong, determined on punishing Tereus.
530 The season had come for the women to celebrate Dionysus
in their sacred biennial rites, observed under cover of darkness.
All night the slopes of Rhodopê° reecho with clanging of cymbals;
the queen goes out of her house, dressed for the bacchanal orgy.
She bears the signals of madness: a vine-leaf crown on her head,
535 a fawn skin hangs from a shoulder, a javelin rests on the other.
So Procnê with her mad crew run screaming over the woodland,
a terrible vision to see. Bacchus, she feigns, is her master;
in fact, it is you, O Furies of pain, who drive her along.
At last the Bacchanals come to the lodge hidden deep in the wood.
540 She shouts and cries the "Ee-vo-ee!" she smashes the doorway in.
She seizes her sister and on her drapes the insignia of Bacchus,
hides her features in ivy, and brings her, amazed, to the palace.
 Philomela soon understood she had come to the cursed household.
The poor girl bristled in fear, her face turned pallid in terror.
545 But Procnê, once they were safe, tore off the ivy of Bacchus,

532. *Rhodopê:* A mountain of Thrace, sacred to Dionysus.

unveiling the mortified face and wretched plight of her sister.
She tried to embrace her sister, whose eye clung fixed to the ground,
for shame at having been forced to defile the marriage of one so close.
Longing to swear to the truth, summoning gods to bear witness,
550   with hands replacing her voice she told of her rape and disgrace.
     Procnê blazed with anger, and checked Philomela's lament:
"Weeping will do us no good. We must have recourse to the dagger,
or anything else you conceive more lethal to him than the steel.
I am fully ready to go to the furthest limits of vengeance—
555   to set the palace on fire over Tereus' criminal head,
to hack out tongue, eyes, whatever crushed your soul in disgrace.
Shall we watch his guilty life drain off through a thousand cuts?
No matter. Whatever we do, our revenge must make people tremble."
     As Procnê pondered her crime, little Itys came up to his mother.
560   His innocent face suggested the blackest vengeance of all.
Gazing with pitiless eyes, "How like you are to your father!"
she murmured. No further word, but seething in hot-blooded anger
Procnê prepared for her crime. And yet, and yet—
when her tiny son toddled up, little arms outstretched for a hug,
565   mixing his eager kisses with the lisping words of a child,
his mother's purpose was shaken, her murderous anger grew still,
her eyes overflowed with tears welling up from her aching heart.
At once she knew too great affection had weakened her purpose.
Turning away from her child, once more she regarded her sister.
570   "How can I choose, when the one babbles his childish endearments,
the other, bereft of her tongue, can nevermore utter a word?
Philomela cannot call me sister, whom Itys addresses as mother.
Consider, O Pandion's daughter, the sort of man you have married.
Has the daughter fallen away from the spirit shown by her sires?
575   Crime toward a husband like Tereus is the truest virtue of all."
     Delaying no more, she seized little Itys and dragged him away,
like a tigress of India's dark jungle seizing a suckling fawn [Fig. 15.5].
She hurried him off to a murky unfrequented part of the palace.
There Itys saw what was coming. Hugging his mother for comfort,
580   "Mommy, Mommy!" he wailed. She stabbed where flank meets breast,
fixing her eyes on her target. Although that one blow was enough,
Philomela again took the dagger and slashed it across his throat.
     Together they carved the flesh, still warm with traces of life.
Some boiled in a big brass pot, some hissed and spat on a skewer.
585   The room grew slimy with blood. At last, when all was made ready,
Procnê invited her husband to join in a ritual dinner.
Alleging an ancient custom that no one, her husband excepted,
might join the meal with a matron, she had the attendants depart.
Tereus sat there in state, high on the throne of his fathers,
590   greedily stuffing his belly with his own flesh and blood.
Blinded in soul, he shouted, "Let Itys be brought inside!"
No longer could Procnê conceal the cruel joy of her vengeance;
No longer need she delay announcing her murderous message.
     "It is Itys you want? but Itys is already inside—inside you!"
595   In puzzlement, Tereus repeated his wishes again and again,

FIG. 15.5. Philomela and Procnê prepare to kill Procnê's son, Itys—a somewhat different version of the story (and 500 years earlier than Ovid), Attic wine-cup, c. 490 B.C. On the left Philomela gestures, unable to speak because her tongue has been cut out. A sword, the murder weapon, hangs at her side. In the potter's version, Procnê, not yet convinced, seems to hang back, as if protecting her son.   (Musée du Louvre, Paris, G 147; Giraudon/Art Resource, New York)

Till Philomela sprang in, her hair bespattered with blood,
and flung the head of Itys straight in his father's face.
    "O, that I still had a tongue, to tell my delight at your fate"
(she thought), "in words you deserve!" Tereus shouted in horror,
600   kicked back the table, and called in pain on the Furies of Hades.
Gladly, could he have done so, would he have opened his entrails
and brought back into the light the grisly meal he had eaten.
All he could do was groan, "Wretched me, the tomb of my son!"
He draws his sword. He charges, pursuing Pandion's daughters.
605   But look! who would imagine that these, descendants of Cecrops,
could fly off, born as on feathers? Yet fly on feathers they did.
The one took off to the forest, the other nests among men—
yet still they bear on their bosoms the bloody tokens of murder.
Tereus, swiftened by grief that struggled with lust for revenge,
610   was transformed into a hoopoe, a bird with a feathery crown;
his beak resembles a sword, and he goes as if armored for battle.

OVID, Metamorphoses (6.424–676)

Ovid is not clear about which woman becomes which bird, but most other sources agree that Procnê, the mother, became the nightingale with its haunting nocturnal song; tongueless Philomela became the songless swallow. Nonetheless, later poets, confused by the obscure line in Ovid and depending on a dubious etymology of *Philomela* = "song-lover," made Philomela the nightingale: Such is its meaning in classical English poetry.

Observations: Ovid's Literary Myth

A deeply human instinct is to feel kinship with the natural world, to think of animals and plants and even stones as inhabited by intelligence somehow like our own. The mutability of nature, and of ourselves who are destined to die, suggests that the same being can take on more than one form, human or inhuman. Much religious cult is based on efforts to communicate, and negotiate, with the humanlike powers in nature. In theory we reject this interpretation of the natural world, but many who own pets treat them as equals (or superiors!), and the popularity of Bugs Bunny, Mickey Mouse, the Lion King, and other cartoon characters shows how easy it is for us to accept that animals can behave and think as we do.

But Ovid does not tell stories about metamorphosis to appeal to an instinct within us to explain nature by humanizing it. Ovid is a highly urbane and literate poet, unlike Homer, Hesiod, and the singers of the Homeric Hymns, and he created his poems in writing to be read aloud to upper-class Romans, women as well as men, who could themselves read and write and who were intimately familiar with the monuments of Greek literature. He gave contemporary relevance to old stories, which contained primitive elements, by embellishing them with the rhetorical display familiar to the Romans from their education (as in the highly wrought speeches of Philomela and Procnê). In the *Metamorphoses,* he does not focus on the metamorphosis itself so much as the events leading up to it, punctuated by elaborate descriptions of states of feeling. He concocts melodramatic situations and images (Philomela's tongue is compared to an injured snake twitching in the grass). His stories have homespun morals. The story of Tereus, Procnê, and Philomela proves that one should not give in to irrational desire, as if we needed to be told that: We are never sure how far Ovid is mocking the reader's expectations and using simplistic morals to justify his touching or lurid descriptions. Although Ovid's humans pay for their mistakes, we often have the sense that the god or goddess metes out an excessive punishment, that humans are the innocent victims of petty but divine emotion—did Actaeon really deserve to be torn apart by his own dogs? When Ovid does describe the psychology of metamorphosis, his focus is on the anguish of the human being trapped inside the beast, where its human mind continues to think and feel as it did before the transformation.

One type of Ovidian story tells of a deity having intercourse with a mortal woman, who is then turned into an animal (so Io became a cow) or of a human who inadvertently offends a god (as Actaeon was turned into a stag after seeing Artemis naked). Procris and Cephalus and Procnê and Philomela are examples of another type of Ovidian story, where the conflict is not between men and gods but within a human family. Still, Ovid concentrates on the rhetorical and moral aspects of the tale. Procris and Cephalus is a tale of lovers who love too much until suspicion destroys them; lovers should trust one another. In Procnê and Philomela, the initial acts of impiety are horrendous, but the punishment is equally savage and the avengers as twisted as their attacker. Metamorphosis into birds is nearly an afterthought, a device allowing Ovid to attach the tale to his general scheme. The gods do not figure in the action. Humans of their own will commit crimes against each other, making their lives a misery. When human passions are allowed to run unchecked, innocent and guilty are destroyed alike. In the elegant high society of Ovid's Rome, where men and women with equal legal rights to property mixed freely, where love affairs and sexual passion were a principal preoccupation of the great and the idle, such stories no doubt had a special appeal and poignancy, as they did in similar later epochs.

THESEUS

The Begetting of Theseus

When Pandion died, **Erechtheus** (e-**rek**-thūs) became king. (*Erechtheus* is probably a variation of *Erichthonius*.) Erechtheus married and had several children, including a second Cecrops, Procris (who married Cephalus), and Orithyia (or-ĭ-**thī**-ya), with whom Boreas, the winged north wind, fell in love and whom he carried off. Orithyia gave birth to Zetes (**zē**-tēz) and Calaïs (**cā**-la-is), winged warriors who figure in the legend of Jason and the Golden Fleece (Chapter 18). It was during the reign of Erechtheus that Demeter came to Eleusis (Chapter 9).

Erechtheus fought a savage war against Eleusis; although his daughters' patriotic voluntary self-sacrifice brought him victory, Erechtheus soon died. The second Cecrops became king, then the second Pandion, who was driven out of Athens and became king of Megara. There he married one Creusa (crē-**ū**-sa), who bore him four sons, including **Aegeus** (**ē**-jūs) and Pallas (**pal**-las). When the second Pandion died, his sons regained power in Athens. Aegeus had the upper hand over Pallas and his brothers, but his power was threatened because none of his several wives was able to bear him a son and heir. Pallas, who had fifty sons, despised the sterile Aegeus.

Aegeus went to the Delphic Oracle to learn how he could have an heir. "Do not open the swelling mouth of the wineskin until you come to the height of the Athenians," the oracle said. Aegeus could not understand the reply and went out of his way to Troezen (**trē**-zen) at the northeastern tip of the Peloponnesus, across the Saronic Gulf from Athens, to consult with Pittheus (**pit**-thūs), the local king, a son of Pelops[5] and famous for his wisdom. Pittheus understood the oracle right away: Aegeus was destined to beget a child when next he had intercourse with a woman. Realizing that a child who joined the blood of Erechtheus to that of Pelops would be destined for glory, Pittheus plied Aegeus with much wine and sent in his daughter **Aethra** (**ē**-thra) to him.

After having intercourse with Aegeus, Aethra, instructed by a dream, rose and went to offer sacrifice on a nearby island, but Poseidon appeared from the sea and possessed her. Thus was Theseus conceived, at once the son of the mortal Aegeus and of the immortal Poseidon. The story of Heracles' divine birth (Chapter 14) probably was the inspiration for the story: Alcmenê too slept with man and god on the same night (although Theseus has no twin).

The next morning Aegeus, suspecting that Aethra was pregnant, ordered her to

---

[5]The stories of Pelops, founder of the House of Atreus, are told in Chapter 19.

raise their child in secret. He placed a sword and a pair of sandals under a large rock. When Theseus had grown strong enough to lift it, he should take the objects beneath the rock and travel to him in Athens.

The Labors of Theseus

When Theseus grew to manhood, Aethra showed him the rock. Exerting his full strength, he lifted it and removed the sword and sandals, tokens that he was the true son of King Aegeus (Fig. 15.6). With these he set off to Athens. Aethra and Pittheus, fearing the infamous bandits and monsters along the route, begged him to go by sea, but Theseus insisted on the land route. In imitation of the Twelve Labors of his cousin Heracles, Theseus performed six famous deeds of strength on the coastal road (Fig. 15.7):

- At Epidaurus he killed Periphetes (per-i-**fē**-tēz), nicknamed "clubber." Periphetes, a son of Hephaestus, liked to bash passersby with his iron club. Theseus took the club, killed Periphetes with it, and thereafter carried it himself.

- At the Isthmus of Corinth he slew Sinis (**sī**-nis), a giant and a son of Poseidon, nicknamed "pinebender" because he used to force travelers to help him bend a pine tree to the ground. He would then unexpectedly let go, catapulting the victim through the air (some say he would tie the victim to two bent trees pegged to the ground, then cut the ropes to rip the victim apart). Theseus gave Sinis the same treatment he had given others.

FIG. 15.6. Theseus discovers the tokens of the sword and the sandals. Roman relief from the late first century A.D.   (British Museum, London; D 594)

FIG. 15.7. The labors of Theseus. Center: Theseus drags the dead Minotaur from the Labyrinth, indicated by the vertical band of meanders. From top clockwise: Theseus wrestles Cercyon; with a double-bladed ax Theseus cuts Procrustes down to size; Theseus about to strike Sciron with the foot-basin while the monstrous turtle waits at the bottom of the cliff; Theseus subdues the Marathonian bull; Theseus is about to release the pine tree to which Sinis clings; and the old woman Phaea tries to protect the Crommyonian sow, while Theseus attacks with a sword. The painter omits the adventure with Periphetes but includes the Bull of Marathon instead, Attic vase, c. 430 B.C., found at Vulci in Italy.   (British Museum, London; E 84)

- North of Isthmus, at a place called Crommyon (**krom**-mi-on), he killed an enormous pig, the Crommyonian sow.

- Near Megara he turned the tables on Sciron (**sī**-ron), a rascal who made way-farers bend over to wash his feet, then kicked them down the steep slope to the rocks below, where a giant turtle devoured them. Theseus forced Sciron to wash his feet, then kicked him down the precipitous slope.

- At Eleusis, he crushed to death Cercyon (**ser**-si-on), a powerful wrestler.

- Finally, Theseus killed **Procrustes** (pro-**krus**-tēz), who had a house by the road with two beds, one large and one small. Procrustes used to offer travelers a place to sleep for the night, putting the big people in the little bed and the little people in the big bed. Because he enjoyed symmetry, Procrustes sawed off the protruding parts of the big people and stretched out the little ones. Theseus forced Procrustes to fit into one of his own beds (from him comes the English term *procrustean*, of an arbitrary standard to which exact conformity is forced).

FIG. 15.8. Aegeus greets Theseus, on an Attic drinking cup, c. 475 B.C., as the hero enters Athens. Behind the hero a young woman reaches to crown him for his victory.   (Musée du Louvre, Paris; G 195)

Arrival at Athens

A choral poem by the poet Bacchylides (fifth century B.C.) survives, nearly dramatic in form, that portrays Aegeus awaiting the approach of Theseus. Aegeus does not know that it is his own son who comes. He and the chorus imagine that a god must be within this monster-slayer but fear that he may be a monster more dreadful than those he has destroyed (Fig. 15.8):

[1] *Chorus of Athenians*   King of holy Athens, lord of the lavish Ionians,°
      why do brass-belled trumpets scream new songs of war?
      Does an enemy warrior thrust at our borders,
      or do hostile raiders with violent hands
5   drive off the sheep of protesting herdsmen?
      What harasses your heart? Speak, for of all men
      you have the bravest defenders and soldiers.
          Tell me, O son of Creusa and Pandion.
      Aegeus   Newly come is a messenger whose flying feet
10   have run the long road that traverses Isthmus,
      telling wonderful works of a man of great might.
      Proud Sinis he slew, of all mortal men
      the strongest by far, son of Cronus' child,
      earth-shaking Lytaeus.° Far off in the wood
15   he slew the man-slaying wild sow of Crommyon;

1. *Ionians:* The Athenians belonged to the Ionian branch of the Greek people (the other two being Aeolian and Dorian).   14. *Lytaeus.:* That is, Poseidon, who was said to have smashed open a mountain to let the river Peneus flow to the sea: *Lytaeus* = "looser."

arrogant Sciron died by his sword.°
The wrestling of Cercyon he ended forever;
Polypemon° the Mauler abandoned his mallet,
meeting the menace of a far better man.
20   I dread where such exploits will finally finish.
    Chorus   Who is this man? and whence does he come?
What following force do they say that he brings?
Does he lead a great army, in hostile array,
or advance alone, with a few attendants,
25   like a traveler seeking an unknown country?
Who is as strong, courageous, yes, rash,
as he who puts down from their seats mighty men?
A god must impel him to make law for the lawless;
one as busy as he must at times meet misfortune,
30   yet over the years the gods' will comes to pass.
    Aegeus   The messengers tell me only two stand beside him.
From his brawny shoulders, they say, hangs a sword.
In his hands are a pair of well-polished lances;
on his flaming hair a Laconian° cap.
35   A sea-blue tunic wraps over his chest;
over all a Thessalian tunic of wool.
From his eye there flashes red Lemnian fire.°
He looks like a boy just entering manhood,
yet he seems to delight in bronze-ringing war,
40   as forward he strides to our glorious Athens.

BACCHYLIDES 18

16. *sword*: Bacchylides does not seem to think of Sciron as the foot-washer, as in most accounts.
18. *Polypemon*: Another name for Procrustes.   34. *Laconian*: Spartan.   37. *Lemnian fire*: There were said to be volcanoes on the island of Lemnos. Or, because this island was a favorite haunt of Hephaestus, Lemnian fire may mean "a flame like a forge."

Theseus entered Athens a conqueror, but Aegeus did not recognize him. The king had fallen under the influence of the sorceress Medea (me-**dē**-a; see Chapter 18), who had cured Aegeus' infertility by magic and drugs. Recognizing Theseus and fearing him as a rival to the child with whom she was pregnant, she persuaded Aegeus to send the young stranger against a bull wreaking havoc on the plain of Marathon, the very bull that had begotten the Minotaur on Crete; Heracles had brought it to the mainland as one of his labors. Theseus attacked the bull, chained it up, and sacrificed it to Apollo (even as Gilgamesh and Heracles had overcome dangerous bulls; Fig. 15.9).

Medea, the dangerous female antagonist in myths about Theseus, now planned to poison her rival. At a banquet in the stranger's honor, Theseus was raising the fatal goblet to his lips when Aegeus recognized the sword hanging at his side; leaping across the table, he knocked the cup to the ground. Medea fled in disgrace to her homeland in Asia, where she gave birth to Medus, ancestor of the Medes (that is, the Persians, Greece's greatest enemy). When the fifty sons of Pallas, Aegeus' brother, learned that Aegeus now had a proper successor, they laid an ambush to kill Theseus, but Theseus killed them instead.

FIG. 15.9. Theseus and the Marathonian bull, interior of a wine-cup, c. 450 B.C. On the outside, the hero overcomes the sons of Pallas. (Elvehjem Museum of Art, University of Wisconsin, Madison; 1979.3)

At this time took place Theseus' famous adventure with the Cretan Minotaur, told in Chapter 16.

Theseus and Antiopê

When Theseus returned from Crete, he became king of Athens through a tragic lapse of memory. He had promised his father that if he were successful in overcoming the Minotaur, he would change his black sail to white before his ship approached Athens. If he perished, his companions would leave the black sail up so that Aegeus could know the truth before the ship docked. But in his excitement Theseus forgot to change the sail. In despair Aegeus threw himself to his death into what is now known as the Aegean Sea.

Upon becoming king, Theseus instituted many government reforms. He brought together the peoples in the outlying demes of Attica into a single federal system, called in Greek a *synoecism,* with Athens as capital of the new state. He instituted the Panathenaic festival, symbol of Attic unity, where in the Classical Period tragedies and comedies were performed before the *demos.* He founded the popular assembly, where the people could debate and vote on decisions of state.

Longing for adventure, Theseus then sailed to the land of the Amazons to abduct their queen, Antiopê (an-tī-o-pē; sometimes called Hippolyta). To his surprise, the tribe of warrior women received him in a friendly way and offered many presents. When Queen Antiopê brought the presents to his ship, Theseus hoisted sail and carried her away captive to Athens.

The abduction of Antiopê provoked the **Amazonomachy** (a-ma-zon-**o**-ma-kē), "battle with the Amazons." The Amazons invaded Attica, quickly overran the countryside, and set up camp on a hill northwest of the Acropolis, where they sacrificed to their ancestor Ares. Ever since, the hill has been called the Areopagus, "hill of Ares," site of the oldest and most renowned law court in Athens.[6] After some initial setbacks, the Athenians utterly defeated them. The Amazons' graves were shown in classical times near the agora.

Observations: The Amazons

The Amazons are important and recurring figures in Greek myth. Many Greek heroes fought against them: Bellerophon, at the command of the Lycian king; Heracles, at the command of Eurystheus; Achilles at Troy; and even the god Dionysus. Their homeland was usually placed on the slopes of the Caucasus mountains between the eastern end of the Black Sea and the Caspian or in Scythia, the southern steppes of what is today Russia, north of the Black Sea. They were descended from Ares and the nymph Harmonia. They hated men and would tolerate them only as slaves to perform the most menial tasks.

To preserve their race, the Amazons periodically came together with strangers and for a short time engaged in indiscriminate intercourse. When boy babies were born, they were killed or blinded and maimed. The Amazons were said to cut off the right breasts of young girls so that when they grew to maturity they might better draw the bowstring and handle the spear, a detail constructed on the false etymology of Amazon from *a-* (= no) + *mazos* (= breast). They followed Artemis and, according to some accounts, constructed the enormous temple of Artemis at Ephesus, one of the Seven Wonders of the Ancient World (compare Fig. 8.2).

The Greeks themselves never questioned the historical reality of the Amazons. The historian Herodotus, for example, speaks of a tribe of female "mankillers" who roamed the Scythian steppe (although he does not call them Amazons), and modern archaeologists have found burial mounds there for women dressed as warriors. In fact, however, there never was a tribe of warrior-women. The Amazons are a good example of mythical inversion, in which a conspicuous feature of social behavior is turned upside down, in this case the values traditionally assigned to Greek, especially Athenian, women.

A good Athenian woman of the fifth century B.C., as we have seen (Chapter 2), was expected to be submissive, sexually chaste, productive of male heirs, and zealous to preserve the stability of the family. The Amazons, by contrast, were brazen, licentious, and murderous to males and did not live in families. Amazons defied their destiny as women and lived like males, fighting, hunting on horseback, ruling themselves, and having sexual intercourse when they pleased. They lived in a perennial confusion between childhood and maturity, neither girls nor women, neither male nor female, at the edge of the world in a twilight zone between civilization and bar-

---

[6]The name may really mean "hill of curses" because the Erinyes had a shrine there. Ares himself was tried here for committing the first murder (of a man who had accidentally killed Ares' daughter by Aglaurus), as was Cephalus for killing Procris, Daedalus for killing Perdix (see Chapter 16), and Orestes for killing his mother (Chapter 20). St. Paul preached before the court of the Areopagus (Acts 17.18–34).

barism. In myth they are a perversion of all that is proper and correct, a threat to the family, the basis of Greek society. The myth of the Amazons is a refinement of the traditional heroic motif of female hostility, but the threat is directed against all society; thus are they always an army, and they do not tempt the hero with their sexuality (although this motif is submerged in Heracles' need to acquire the belt of the Amazon queen). Their incursion into the civilized world is the encroachment of darkness into light, and Greek heroes always overcome them just as they defeat other denizens of the nightmare realm, ruthlessly and without mercy.

The Athenian myth of the Amazonomachy became especially vigorous after the astounding victory of Athenian hoplites over the Persian invaders in 490 B.C. at the battle of Marathon. After this time the Amazons were represented in Greek art as Persians, wearing long leather trousers and with Persian leather caps (Fig. 15.10). Theseus' victory over the Amazons symbolized and justified Athens' superiority—moral and political—not only over the Persians, but over all peoples who would oppose its imperial democracy. The Amazonomachy was represented on a metope frieze of the Parthenon (begun in 460 B.C.), on the shield of Phidias' celebrated gold and ivory statue of Athena that stood in the Parthenon, and on the frieze in a temple to Hephaestus that still stands just off the Athenian agora.

Theseus and Hippolytus

Antiopê bore a son, **Hippolytus** (hip-**pol**-i-tus, perhaps "breaker of horses"), but Theseus later cast her off to take a new wife, **Phaedra** (**fē**-dra), daughter of Minos and

FIG. 15.10. Theseus and a companion, perhaps Pirithoüs, defend themselves against an attacking Amazon, Attic wine-mixing bowl, c. 450 B.C. The Amazon is mounted and dressed in Persian garb and a Persian leather cap. (Museo Etrusco Gregoriano, Vatican Museum, Rome; xxxv-10-94)

sister of Ariadnê (see Chart 16.1). When Hippolytus grew to manhood, he became a devotee of the virgin huntress Artemis. As his mother had despised men, he despised women, denied his own sexual nature, and cared only for the hunt and the wilderness. The Cretan Phaedra, like her sister Ariadnê and her mother, Pasiphaë (next chapter), was unable to control her sexual desires; she fell in love with her stepson.

The story is the subject of Euripides' play *Hippolytus,* performed in 428 B.C. Aphrodite (whose statue stood on one side of the stage, across from that of Artemis) summarizes the plot in the play's prologue. Her speech is a vivid depiction of the relentless and calamitous power of sexual desire:

[1]   All mortals know me, Cypris,° great in every land,
       a mighty goddess, great in heaven as well.
       From darkest Pontus° to the Atlantic shore
       they know my strength, all men who view the sun:
5   those who respect me and my power I cherish;
       those who disdain me trip and are brought low.
       For the race of gods shares this with humankind:
       honor from others feeds their self-esteem.
       I soon shall prove the truth this maxim holds.
10   The son of Theseus, born of an Amazon,
       is named Hippolytus, whom Pittheus reared.
       Alone of all the dwellers here in Troezen,°
       he flouts me as the most corrupt of gods,
       scorns love's delights, disdains the marriage bed.
15   Apollo's sister Artemis, child of Zeus,
       he hails in honor, "Goddess of all most great!"
       He and his maiden huntress range the greenwood,
       trying, with their swift hounds, to wipe it clean
       of all its creatures. O, how he preens himself,
20   that he has found a more-than-mortal friend!
       Well, if he likes it, why should I object?
       But he has offended me in other ways
       for which today his punishment is due.
       My plans are laid, but little work is left.
25   Hippolytus once returned to Pandion's land,
       from Pittheus' house, to view the holy rites.°
       His father's well-bred bride, Phaedra of Crete,
       saw him. Her heart stood still—at my command!—
       trapped by forbidden love.
30   Even before she came across to Troezen,
       she built me a shrine, next to Athena's rock,°
       from which she gazed across the sea for him
       she loved from far away. Ages to come
       will call it Aphrodite-by-Hippolytus.°

1. *Cypris:* Aphrodite.   3. *Pontus:* The Black Sea.   12. *Troezen:* Where Theseus was then living in temporary exile; see ll. 35–38.   26. *the holy rites:* The Eleusinian Mysteries.   31. *Athena's rock:* The Acropolis.   34. *Aphrodite-by-Hippolytus:* That is, "[the shrine of] Aphrodite by [the tomb of] Hippolytus." But the phrase could also mean "[the shrine of] Aphrodite who overthrew Hippolytus." The shrine has been found in modern times.

35   Later, when Theseus left the land of Cecrops,
    fleeing pollution for his murdered cousins,°
    he brought his bride and settled in this country
    to spend a year abroad in expiation.
    Weeping and sick at heart with passion's sting.

40   she pines—in silence; none in the house know why.
    But not of unspoken love will Phaedra die:
    Theseus will learn the truth, and all the world.
    Then will his father kill this priggish boy,
    who so disdains my ways. Poseidon, lord of the sea,

45   once promised Theseus that, ask what he would,
    three times his prayers would not go unfulfilled;
    by Theseus' curse Hippolytus will die.
    Phaedra? her reputation will survive,
    but she herself must die. I cannot value

50   her misery higher than my own revenge
    on those who hate me. They must pay the price
    that shall to me seem best.
    Enough! for I see this son of Theseus
    has left the toil of hunting and drawn near.

55   I therefore must depart, for all around him
    a pack of yelping huntsmen dog his steps,
    barking their hymns to honor Artemis.
    That Hades throws wide its gates they do not know;
    this day which now is breaking will be his last.

                        EURIPIDES, *Hippolytus* (1–57)

36. *his murdered cousins:* The sons of Pallas, whom Theseus killed. Because they were blood relations, Theseus had to go into exile and be purified. He chose to go to Troezen.

Hippolytus comes on the stage and deposits a wreath before the statue of Artemis, a token of his devotion. He leaves and Phaedra is carried on the stage, near death from lovesickness, contemplating suicide. Phaedra's old nurse twists the truth from her, that she has fallen in love with her stepson, and Phaedra rises from the couch to deplore the war between sexual passion and a woman's desire for respectability:

[373]   Women of Troezen,° nearest to us of all
    who live in Pelops' land, in years gone by

375   I used to lie awake, through the long nights
    wondering what most corroded human life.
    Not from an inborn weakness of our reasoning
    do we go wrong. Most of us know full well
    how we should act. No, we must think of this:

380   with mind and soul we know just what is right,
    but lack the character to make it real.°

373. *Women of Troezen:* The chorus.   381. *make it real:* Medea in Ovid, trying to decide whether to obey her father or to run off with Jason, has a similar line: "I see the better course, and I approve it—but I then pursue the worse." See Chapter 18 for the story of Medea and Jason.

Some of us act thus out of laziness;
some put some pleasure far ahead of duty,
and life holds many pleasures—that precious curse,
385   our hours of idle talk, being one of them. . . .
Now let me show you the line of my own reason.
I fell in love. I had to find a way
by which most honorably to bear the wound.
My first idea was this: keep my mouth shut,
390   suppress the whole affair. But who can trust the tongue?
How cleverly it admonishes human thoughts—
that is, the thoughts of others. But if it talks
about its owner, what damage it can bring!
So next I tried to moderate my folly,
395   to conquer it by reasoning it away.
Of course, I could not thus control my passion.
Then what was left? to die. No one denies
that this was much the best course open.
For me, while my honor stands, all may applaud.
400   but if that falls, then let it fall unwitnessed.
Both act and inclination to the act bring disgrace
(I am a woman; this I know for sure)
in all men's eyes.
      Yes, cursed be she who first
405   defiled her husband's bed with other men.
Some woman, married within a noble house,
infected all her sex with this corruption,
for once such vice wins favor with the high-born,
it soon is modish in plebeian eyes.
410   How I detest those moral-sounding women,
who privately delight in viciousness!
How, lady Cypris, mistress of the sea,
dare they to look into their husbands' faces?
Do they not shudder at the pandering darkness,
415   and dread indictment by the bedroom walls?
      O closest friends, this is what tortures me:
the shame my guilt would bring upon my husband,
upon the children whom I bore. May they live free
and confident, freemen of glorious Athens,
420   rejoicing in their mother's fair renown.

EURIPIDES, Hippolytus (373–423)

The nurse is at first horrified at Phaedra's secret and considers suicide herself. She soon has second thoughts (a recurring theme in this play). Speaking like an Athenian rhetorician in a court of law, the nurse turns black into white through ingenious speech, using examples from myth to prove her point that passion, being irresistible, should not be resisted:

[431]   Mistress, just now the troubles of your heart
        gave mine a sudden pang of senseless fear,

but second thoughts show me how dull I was—
and everyone knows that second thoughts are wiser.
435   Your pain is nothing strange, nothing unheard-of.
Hit by a thunderbolt, you fell in love.
What else is new? That's happened many times.
Do you really want to cut your throat for that?
Will lovers now and henceforth learn from you
440   that they must die of unrequited love?
If Cypris strikes at once with all her force,
no one can stand the shock. If you give way a bit,
she walks beside you like a gentle friend.
But her who arrogantly stares her down
445   she takes in hand and humbles to the dust.
Cypris walks through the air, Cypris walks over the sea,
all things arise from Cypris, who plants desire within us;
all of us here on the earth are born of desire she sends.
All those who search the books of long ago,
450   whose lives are spent in commerce with the Muses,
can tell how love-struck Zeus wed Semelê,
how bright-rayed Dawn abducted Cephalus,
and all for love. They keep their place in heaven
and never dream of fleeing from the gods.
455   Struck with love's dart, they shrug, and keep their love.
If gods can bear their lot, then why can't you?
So you don't like the rules? Perhaps your daddy
should have begotten you on special terms
or made a contract with some other gods.
460   Tell me, how many husbands—sensible, shrewd men—
seeing their wives' first passion cooling down,
politely turn their eyes another way? How many fathers
procure new loves for bored and straying sons?
The wisest proverb humans can observe
465   is this: don't stir up ugly sleeping dogs.
People ought not to ask too much of life
or tear the house down if a rafter creaks.
No doubt you're floundering in a sea of troubles;
just ask yourself, "How can I swim ashore?"
470   You're human, and you should be quite content
if your good luck barely outweighs the bad.
So, dearest Phaedra, stop our gloomy mutter
which only harms yourself. The height of arrogance
is hoping to be stronger than a god.
475   You've fallen in love? bear up. Some god planned it.
Treat your illness rightly, you'll drive your illness off.
Charms abound and potions; somewhere we'll find a cure.

                 EURIPIDES, *Hippolytus* (431–479)

    Phaedra allows the nurse to approach Hippolytus on her behalf, but the prud-
ish sportsman is horrified, revolted at the offer of adulterous union with his own stepmother. He delivers a tirade against women, who only bring emotional and financial

ruin. Like Hesiod, he wishes that Zeus had devised some other way to propagate the species:

[616]   Why, why, O Zeus, did you ever bring to life
        and settle on mankind this false-faced breed of women?
        If all you wanted was to spawn our mortal race,
        there was no need for women. A man might have gone
620   into your temples, laid down the proper mass
        of bronze or gold or iron, and in exchange
        at a price to fit his station, bought himself a brood
        and lived in a quiet home thereafter, free of women.
        Why is it clear that women are a curse?
625   The man who fathered her, who brought her up,
        must pay still more to free himself from her,
        in dowry, from a purse already strained.
        The fool who bought her takes the creature home;
        he loves to pay outrageous bills for clothes
630   to deck his ugly idol. "No one's wife
        has nicer clothes than you!"—till he goes bankrupt.
        A pauper has no trouble of this sort,
        but a silly woman is a plague° at best.
        And how I loathe the clever of that sex!
635   Never may a woman knowing more than woman ought
        infest my house. For Cypris stirs up mischief
        much more in clever women; the stupid doll
        is saved from folly by her witlessness.
        No woman needs a clever serving-maid;
640   better a dumb and snarling animal
        with nothing to say, nothing she wants to hear.
        But as things are, women contrive their schemes
        within the house, and the servants bring them forth.
        Thus, you old bitch, you sidled up to me.
645   with an unholy offer, to share my father's wife,
        whose person should be sacred in my eyes.
        Bring holy water; I'll pour it in my ears,
        to wash away your foul polluting bargain.
        What made you think that I could be so vile,
650   I, whose purity shrinks at the very thought?

EURIPIDES, *Hippolytus* (616–655)

633. *plague:* The Greek word *anopheles,* here translated as "plague," means "not helpful"; it is the (modern) name of the genus of mosquito that transmits malaria.

Phaedra overhears his speech. Terrified that Hippolytus will tell Theseus and desperate to preserve her honor, she hangs herself in the bedroom. She leaves behind a note pinned to her bosom, saying that she killed herself for shame, that Hippolytus had assaulted her. Theseus, away consulting an oracle, now comes home. He places Phaedra's charges before Hippolytus, but the noble young man is unable to defend himself because he had sworn to the nurse, before she propositioned him, never to reveal her words. Disgusted, Theseus uses one of the three wishes given him

Boccaccio's *Misfortunes of Famous Men*

Giovanni Boccaccio (1313–1375), fired with Renaissance enthusiasm for the classics, is best known for his *Decameron,* a collection of stories that has had immense influence in the development of modern literature. But he also liked to recount Greek myths, giving his mythical characters the thoughts and feelings of his own contemporaries. He sometimes attempted to explain the complex meanings to be discovered in these stories.

In one work, *De Casibus Virorum Illustrium,* "Concerning the misfortunes of famous men," Boccaccio gathers together stories about the disasters that befell famous men and women in myth, history, and the Bible. One of the stories he retells is that of Theseus, Phaedra, and Hippolytus. Finding a moral for everyone, Boccaccio chastises Phaedra for slandering her stepson and Hippolytus for jumping to hasty conclusions. *De Casibus,* translated into Italian, French, German, and English, was immensely popular all over Europe. Shown here (Fig. P 15.1) is an illustration

FIG. P 15.1. *Phaedra Killing Herself,* from a manuscript of Boccaccio's *De Casibus Virorum Illustrium,* 1470. (The British Library, London)

from a French manuscript of *De Casibus* from 1470, showing the suicide of Phaedra. In Boccaccio's version of the story, Phaedra first confesses her slander to Theseus (to the left, on his throne), then stabs herself in the belly. Neither Boccaccio nor the illustrator could conceive of the appearance of ancient people and places in terms other than those suggested by their own experience, even as today many condemn the past for not holding ideals obvious to us. Little was known of real Greek costume, architecture, and daily life until the eighteenth century, and not until this century have we begun to see clearly who the ancients were and how they lived.

by Poseidon (a folktale motif) to curse his son. As Hippolytus races his chariot along the sea, an immense bull, sent by Poseidon, comes out of the sea and frightens the horses. They rear and throw him from the chariot. Tangled in the reins, he is dragged to his death over the rocks. Too late, Theseus learns the truth from Artemis.

Euripides' innovation in his *Hippolytus* is to cast the woman as a sympathetic character, Aphrodite's helpless victim caught in a divine plan to destroy Hippolytus. His audience expects to see the wicked woman vilified and the virtuous youth exalted; that is the tradition. Instead, Euripides portrays his Phaedra as a highly moral woman struggling against the shame of her passion, while Hippolytus is an intolerant prig. Thus Euripides, fond of overturning his audience's expectations, changes basic assumptions of an old story. His is a morality play: To think you can live without sex is a destructive illusion. Hippolytus, like the Amazons, refuses his biological and social obligations to marry, have sexual relations, and engender a new generation. Like the Amazons, he follows the virgin Artemis. Although he foolishly hopes to dam the deluge of sexual desire, the waters of passion sweep everything away, destroying innocent and guilty alike.

Observations: The Folktale of "Potiphar's Wife"

The story of Phaedra and Hippolytus is one version of the common folktale story-type about family life called "Potiphar's Wife." Named after the biblical story of Joseph, the story is far older than that, surviving in a Nineteenth Dynasty Egyptian papyrus (about 1250 B.C.), the "Story of the Two Brothers," the oldest recorded folktale on planet Earth. In the story, the wife of Anubis (also a god's name) propositioned her husband's handsome brother Bata, and when he refused, she used fat and grease to make it appear as if she had been beaten. She told Anubis that Bata had wished to sleep with her and, when she refused, had beaten her up. Anubis hid behind the door of the shed, intending to kill Bata, but Bata ran away. Here the story drops its realistic guise and becomes an exploration in symbolic form of ever-renewed vitality, in this case the vitality of pharaoh, who embodied Egypt: Repeatedly Bata dies and is reborn. Death is repeatedly brought by a woman's treachery, but always overturned through Pharaonic vitality. The folktale is a political myth.

The later biblical tale, perhaps about 600 B.C. in the form preserved to us, reads like a historical account, moralizing how with God's help the Jewish Joseph survived the foreign devil:

Joseph was taken down to Egypt, and Potiphar, an officer of Pharaoh, the captain of the guard, an Egyptian, bought him from the Ishmaelite who had brought him there. The Lord was with Joseph, and he became a successful man in the house of his master the Egyptian, and his master saw that the Lord was with him . . . and left all that he had in Joseph's charge. . . .

Now Joseph was good-looking and attractive. After a time his master's wife cast her eyes upon Joseph, and said, "Lie with me." But he refused and said to his master's wife, "Lo, having me, my master has no concern about anything in the house, and he has put everything that he has in my hand. . . . How then can I do this great wickedness, and sin against God?" And although she spoke to Joseph day after day, he would not listen to her, to lie with her or to be with her. But one day, when he went into the house to do his work, and none of the men of the house was present, she caught him by his garment and begged him, "Lie with me." But he left his garment in her hand, and fled and got out of the house. And when she saw that he had left his garment in her hand . . . she called to the men of her household and said to them, "See, he [Potiphar] has brought among us a Hebrew to insult us; he [Joseph] came in to me to lie with me and I cried out with a loud voice; and when he heard that I lifted up my voice and cried, he left his garment with me, and fled and got out of the house." . . . Then she laid up his garment by her until his master came home, and she told him the same story. . . . And Joseph's master seized him and put him into the prison.

GENESIS 39

Joseph is finally freed when he interprets Pharaoh's dreams: The folktale is a religious myth, glorifying Yahweh's protection of his people.

An example of the same folktale appears in Homer's *Iliad,* told about the Corinthian hero **Bellerophon** (bel-**ler**-o-phon). After Bellerophon rebuffed the wife of a King Proteus while residing at Corinth, the king sent him to his father-in-law in Lycia, carrying sealed tablets with instructions, "kill the bearer" (the only reference to writing in Homer). The king of Lycia sent Bellerophon on impossible tasks. First, he was to kill the dread Chimera (compare Fig. 4.4), but Bellerophon mounted the winged horse Pegasus, which sprang from the neck of Medusa as Perseus cut it off, and killed the monster. Then he was to fight the Amazons and perform other tasks, but he was always successful and in the end married the princess and received a portion of the kingdom: The folktale is now a heroic myth, with the familiar ingredients of dangerous woman, treacherous king, conquest of a monster, victory, marriage, and kingship. But Bellerophon came to a bad end. Arrogantly flying to heaven on Pegasus, he fell to his death.

The story type, given such different meaning by Egyptians, Jews, and Greeks, appeals to the same male fear of woman's power that underlies tales about the Mesopotamian Aphrodite, the vindictive Inanna/Ishtar/Astartê who attempted to seduce Gilgamesh, then sent the Bull of Heaven. When a respectable woman charges rape, nothing will save the man, guilty or innocent.

The Exploits of Theseus and Pirithoüs

Pirithoüs (pī-**rith**-o-us), a son of Ixion, was king of the **Lapiths,** a Thessalian tribe. Having heard of Theseus' prowess, he decided to test him, so he came into Attica under cover of darkness and raided Theseus' flocks on the plain of Marathon. Theseus caught him red-handed. They were about to come to blows when Pirithoüs, admiring Theseus' physique, apologized and volunteered to become Theseus' slave. Theseus was equally impressed by Pirithoüs and suggested that, instead of killing one another, they swear eternal friendship (like Gilgamesh and Enkidu).

Pirithoüs married a woman named Hippodamia (hip-po-da-**mī**-a; there were several in Greek myth) and invited the monstrous **Centaurs,** half men and half horse, to the wedding feast. The Centaurs were cousins of Pirithoüs because Centaurus, their forebear, had sprung from the seed of Pirithoüs' father, Ixion, when he ejaculated into a cloud that looked like Hera (Chapter 11). Being wild, uncivilized, and unaccustomed to wine, the Centaurs lost control of themselves after a few drinks. They attacked the bride on the altar and tried to rape her attendants too. Theseus joined the fight to rescue Hippodamia. Thus began the famous war between the Lapiths and the Centaurs. Like the Amazonomachy, the Centauromachy came to symbolize the struggle between civilization and barbarism, between Greek and foreigner. Like the Amazonomachy, it was often represented on Greek temples, including the celebrated west pediment of the great temple to Zeus at Olympia.

After Phaedra and Hippodamia died, Pirithoüs and Theseus decided to look for new wives together. Because they were famous and of high birth, they could be satisfied only with daughters of Zeus. Helen, a daughter of Zeus and Leda, although not yet of marriageable age, was said to be good-looking. The two companions traveled to Sparta and snatched her up as she was performing a ritual dance to Artemis (just as Hades snatched Persephonê as she played in the meadow with her virgin friends). Although pursued by the Spartans, they escaped to the Isthmus, then drove

FIG. 15.11. Heracles and Pirithoüs in the House of Hades, on an oil-jar, c. 475 B.C. Heracles pulls Theseus from the stone seat where he is imprisoned, while Theseus pushes down hard with his two spears.   (Staatliche Museen, Berlin; 30035)

hard along the Megarian coast to Athens, where they stopped to cast lots for Helen. The lot fell to Theseus, but because Helen was too young for intercourse, he took her to an outlying village and left her with his mother, Aethra.

Pirithoüs now revealed which daughter of Zeus he wanted to marry: Persephonê! Reluctantly, Theseus accompanied his friend into the underworld. Hades listened politely to their request, then invited them to sit down to a meal. They sat in stone chairs and immediately their flesh clung firmly to their seats and their limbs were bound with serpents. Later, when Heracles came to the underworld to fetch Cerberus, Theseus cried out to him as the conqueror of Death. Heracles seized Theseus by the arm and wrenched him from the chair, leaving a good part of Theseus' backside attached (that is why the Athenians have such slender hips; Fig. 15.11). Heracles also tried to save Pirithoüs, but when the earth trembled he backed away, and Pirithoüs remains there to this day.

The Death of Theseus

When Theseus returned to the upper world, he found Athens in turmoil. The Dioscuri (dī-os-**kū**-rē, "sons of Zeus"), Castor and Polydeuces (pol-i-**dū**-sēz), Helen's brothers and mighty heroes in their own right, had come in his absence and taken Helen back, along with Theseus' mother, Aethra.[7] A certain Menestheus, the first demagogue of Athens, had taken over the city, decrying Theseus as a tyrant. (Menestheus would later lead the Athenian contingent to Troy.)

Theseus fled to the island of Scyros (**sī**-ros), east of Euboea, hoping for hospitality. But the local king, envying Theseus, led him to a cliff to see the view and pushed him off. Thus, Theseus died not gloriously as a hero, but shamefully and by treachery. His father, Aegeus, betrayed by his careless son, also plunged from high rocks to his death.

Observations: Myth and Propaganda

By the fifth century B.C., the golden age of Greece, the days of Aeschylus, Sophocles, Euripides, Pericles, and the Parthenon, Theseus had become the official hero of Athens and its empire, celebrated in sculpture and song. It was not always so. Just a hundred years before, he was scarcely known, except for the adventure of the Labyrinth (see Chapter 16) and his participation in the Centauromachy; these are his oldest myths. No important family claimed him as its ancestor, no town or village was named in his honor. In the *Iliad* and the *Odyssey* of about 800 B.C., he is mentioned only three times, always in passing, and Menestheus commands the Athenians at Troy. Only in the sixth century B.C. did Theseus rise to prominence, when a festival was named after him and he began to appear more often in Athenian art. Before the end of the sixth century, an epic called the *Theseïs*, now lost, was composed, which must have given form to what became the standard cycle of legend recounted here.

---

[7]She appears in the *Iliad* as Helen's slave, who had gone with Helen to Troy.

The popularization of the legends of Theseus, including the composition of the *Theseïs*, took place under the sponsorship of **Pisistratus** (pi-**sis**-tra-tus), the famous leader of Athens, who first came to power in 561 B.C. and governed Athens off and on until his death in 527, when his sons, Hippias and Hipparchus, succeeded him. The dynasty began to come apart in 514 B.C. after Hipparchus was assassinated in a homosexual intrigue. Like Theseus, Pisistratus unified Attica under the political and cultural rule of Athens and fought for Athens' interests overseas, in Ionia and on many islands. Parallels were constantly drawn between the accomplishments of Theseus and Pisistratus. Theseus was often given credit for Pisistratus' important deeds, such as the unification of Athens. Such parallels strengthened Pisistratus' reputation as a benevolent and powerful leader.

By the fifth century B.C., Theseus was claimed as the founder of Athenian democracy, but it was Pisistratus who, in the sixth century B.C., encouraged the individualism and cultural enlightenment that made the democracy of the fifth century possible. In myth, Theseus founded the Panathenaic games, which celebrated the unity and glory of Attica; in reality, Pisistratus gave this old festival its special character, including a festival of special magnificence every fourth year, when the entire *Iliad* and *Odyssey* were recited. Theseus defeated a wild bull on the plain of Marathon; Pisistratus returned from temporary exile in 546 B.C. on this same plain, from which he drew much of his support, and shortly afterward Athenian vase painters began to portray the Bull of Marathon. Coinage, one of the most important economic innovations of the sixth century B.C., was attributed in myth to Theseus, but Pisistratus probably was the first Athenian to strike coins in Athens, and his coins bore a bull's head. In myth Theseus stopped at the island of Delos after escaping from the Labyrinth; in history it was Pisistratus who exerted powerful influence over this strategic island, site of the ancient cult of Apollo and Artemis. Theseus destroyed the bandits living on the edge of the gulf from Troezen to Athens; Hippias, Pisistratus' son, rid the Saronic gulf of pirates. Scenes showing Sinis, the Crommyonian sow, Sciron, and Procrustes appear in sculpture and painting soon after Hippias' achievements.

After the murder of Hipparchus, Hippias' rule became oppressive, and he was soon driven out. One might have expected the myths of Theseus, which glorified the Pisistratids, to decline in popularity, but the opposite occurred. Old cults were remade in Theseus' honor, and he was ever more commonly represented in art. From the model for benevolent autocratic rule by the Pisistratids, Theseus became the hero of the Athenian democracy, founded in 510 B.C. by Clisthenes (**klīs**-then-ēz). Attic drama celebrated Theseus' kindness to such suppliants as Oedipus, Adrastus, the sons of Heracles, and Orestes, all refugees from cities hostile to Athens in the fifth century B.C. Theseus was said to have renounced autocracy in favor of democracy (although there was no democracy in Greece before the reforms of Clisthenes). The new style of government, a drastic departure from traditional forms, was legitimized by modifying the traditional tales.

In 490 B.C. a badly outnumbered Athenian citizen army under the leadership of Miltiades (mil-**tī**-a-dēz) turned back the Persian host on the plain of Marathon. Once again, the act of a mortal was given prominence by being linked to an act of Theseus. Eyewitnesses reported that the ghost of Theseus rushed up before the

Athenian lines: On the plain of Marathon Theseus had captured the bull. Earlier myths telling of Theseus' rape of the Amazon queen (Heracles had performed a similar deed) were altered to emphasize the Amazons' invasion of Attica and Theseus' destruction of their army. Theseus was transformed from the swashbuckling adventurer and loverboy to the magnanimous and stalwart defender of homeland and freedom, and Miltiades was his successor.

Cimon (**sī**-mon), the son of Miltiades, further politicized the myths of Theseus. An aggressive general and politician like his father, Cimon led an alliance of Greek states formed after the Persian invasions to victory after victory, sponsored trade, captured slaves, and took booty that enormously enriched the city of Athens. He, too, made use of Theseus' story when, after an outbreak of piracy in the northern Aegean, he occupied the pirates' hideout on the island of Scyros, where Theseus had died. An oracle directed Cimon to find the bones of Theseus, a task proper for the son of one who, aided by the ghost of Theseus, had led the Athenians to victory at Marathon. On Scyros Cimon saw an eagle clawing at a mound of earth. He dug down and found an enormous skeleton, bronze spear and sword at its side (did Cimon find a Bronze Age tomb?). These were obviously Theseus' bones, and Cimon proudly brought them home to Athens. A new Festival of Theseus was added to the calendar and a shrine constructed in the agora to house the relics. The shrine was decorated with scenes from the Amazonomachy, the Centauromachy, and Theseus' dive into the sea to retrieve the ring of Minos (Chapter 16). Such activity redounded to the credit of Cimon, the new Theseus who brought fresh glory to a new Athens.

When the threat of Persia receded and Athens and its often unwilling allies began to square off against Sparta, the myths underwent further transformation. Theseus now stood for the Ionians under Athens' leadership, while the Dorian states under Sparta claimed Heracles as their hero. Parallels between the two cycles of myth were drawn carefully; the Labors of Theseus surely were designed on the model of older stories about Heracles.

Such developments furnish a good example of the use of myth as propaganda. The legends of Theseus encapsulated, symbolized, and justified Athenian policies: ascendancy at sea, suppression of marauders, and determined resistance to the barbarian. It took only about a century for Theseus to become the official hero of Athens because Pisistratus, Miltiades, and Cimon all consciously, for political gain, made Theseus their model. To accomplish this goal, they often had to remake or reform the traditional legends. The Athenians pioneered use of myth for political ends, but today such use can be found in every country.[8] In our own day stories of the exemplary lives of George Washington and Abraham Lincoln inculcate values useful to a modern democracy but bear small resemblance to the actual deeds and thoughts of these men. History and myth are a perennial tangle; humans are myth-making animals, retelling ancient stories to fulfill present needs.

---

[8]See Chapter 22 for political myth in Rome.

KEY TERMS

Theseus, 383

Cecrops, 384

Erichthonius, 384

Cephalus, 388

Procris, 388

Laelaps, 388

Procnê, 391

Philomela, 391

Tereus, 391

Itys, 391

Erechtheus, 397

Aegeus, 397

Aethra, 397

Procrustes, 399

Amazonomachy, 402

Hippolytus, 404

Phaedra, 404

Bellerophon, 412

Pirithoüs, 412

Lapiths, 412

Centaurs, 413

Pisistratus, 415

FURTHER READING

Bagg, Robert, trans., *Euripides: Hippolytus* (Oxford, U.K., 1973; reprinted 1992). Modern translation with a good interpretive essay.

Hurwit, Jeffrey M., *The Athenian Acropolis: History, Mythology, and Archaeology from the Neolithic Era to the Present* (Cambridge, U.K., 1999). Superb review of Athenian traditions, including myth, focused on Athens' most prominent landmark.

Knox, Bernard M. W., "The Hippolytus of Euripides," in *Oxford Readings in Greek Tragedy*, ed. E. Segal (Oxford, U.K., 1989). Enlightening essay about the forces that drive the play, by a leading modern critic of ancient literature.

Powell, B. (no relation to the author), *Athenian Mythology: Erichthonius and the Three Daughters of Cecrops* (Ithaca, N.Y., 1906; reprinted Chicago, no date). Scholarly (although dated) summary, with interpretation, of all the variants of this perplexing myth.

Tyrrell, William Blake, *Amazons. A Study in Athenian Mythmaking* (Baltimore, 1984). Argues that Amazons take their character from an inversion of traditional Greek values.

Ward, A., ed., *The Quest for Theseus* (New York, 1970). Abundantly illustrated, has chapters on the development of the myth of Theseus, archaeological background, and survival of the myth into medieval and modern times; the essay by Robert Connor on the political uses of the myth of Theseus is excellent.

CHAPTER 16

THE MYTHS OF CRETE

There is a land called Crete, in the midst of the wine-dark sea,
where a countless number of men inhabit a full ninety cities.

HOMER, *Odyssey* 19.172–174

T HE STORIES OF THE HOUSE OF CRETE, closely related to those of Athens, are a
complex of folktales about brave men, tricksters, lascivious or victimized women,
and monstrous beasts. In contrast to the myths of Athens, which were told by Athenians as well as being about Athens, the myths we have about Crete were told by
Greeks living on the mainland, most of them in Athens itself. Until about 1450 B.C.
the Cretan upper classes were, of course, not Greeks (see Chapter 2), but archaeology has revealed that in the second millennium B.C. Crete was a great sea power and
that bulls and goddesses, personifications of fertility, played important roles in their
religion. The powerful kings, served by a hereditary caste of scribes, oversaw and collected the agricultural produce of rich inland and coastal plains. They lived in enormous, complex palaces, which they decorated with remarkably realistic frescoes. The
richness and power of seafaring Crete have survived in story, but the king has become a folktale figure: the evil persecutor finally overthrown by a wandering hero
who wins the love of a princess. The elaborate buildings became in story a prison-
maze constructed by a trickster–artist, and the bull of Cretan fertility religion has
turned into a half-human monster, demanding human sacrifice. The myths of Crete
appear to be a clear example of history becoming myth, but unfortunately we have
only the myths; there is Cretan archaeology, but no Cretan history.

Many myths about Crete took on a nearly official form in the works of Greek

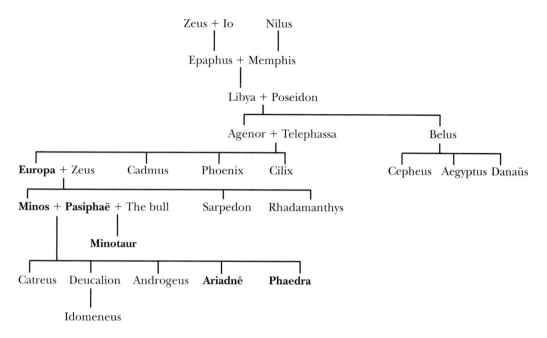

```
              Zeus + Io        Nilus
                   |              |
              Epaphus + Memphis
                      |
              Libya + Poseidon
           ┌──────────┴───────────────────────────────┐
           Agenor + Telephassa                      Belus
    ┌──────────┬─────────┬──────────┐         ┌────────┬──────────┬────────┐
 Europa + Zeus   Cadmus   Phoenix   Cilix   Cepheus  Aegyptus  Danaüs
    |
 Minos + Pasiphaë + The bull      Sarpedon   Rhadamanthys
    |         |
         Minotaur
 ┌─────────┬──────────┬──────────┬──────────┐
 Catreus  Deucalion  Androgeus  Ariadnê    Phaedra
    |
 Idomeneus
```

CHART 16.1. The House of Crete

dramatists—both Euripides and Sophocles wrote tragedies about Europa and the bull—but almost all their works have been lost. For most Cretan legends we rely on Roman writers who hark back to the Greek classics but prefer to emphasize the erotic, the rhetorical, and the bizarre.

EUROPA AND THE BULL

Agenor (a-**jē**-nor, = Semitic "leader of men") was descended from Zeus (Chart 16.1). While his brother, Belus (**bē**-lus, = Semitic "lord," biblical Baal), ruled Egypt, Agenor traveled to the coast of the eastern Mediterranean. There, in the land later called Phoenicia, he settled, married, and had a daughter, **Europa** (ū-**rō**-pa, perhaps simply the eponym of Europe), and three sons: Cadmus, Cilix (**sī**-lix), and Phoenix. Zeus fell in love with the beautiful Europa and came to her in the form of a bull (Fig. 16.1). The most famous account of the story is found in Ovid's *Metamorphoses,* in which the divine bull is a handsome seducer and Europa the innocent but not unwilling virgin. As in Roman love poetry, addressed to an upper-class urban audience familiar with sexual escapades, the seducer needs a helper to overcome obstacles to the satisfaction of his lust. The passage begins with Jupiter/Zeus summoning Mercury/Hermes, go-between of the gods, to help his wooing:

[834]   When the grandson of Atlas° heard this, he left behind the land
835   which takes its name from Pallas,° arising into the air

834. *grandson of Atlas:* Mercury.   835. . . . *name from Pallas:* Athens.

FIG. 16.1. Europa and the bull, Attic vase, c. 490 B.C. Europa wears a himation (a kind of robe) over a sleeved chiton (a kind of shirt), bracelets, and diadem in her hair, while she touches the magnificent bull by the horn. (Museo Archeologico Nazionale, Tarquinia; 53237)

on flying wings. His father beckoned, concealing the truth,
that love demanded his help. "My son, my messenger trusty,
fly down at once, the way you know so well, to the country
left of the seven stars of your mother, the Pleiades,°
840 called by its natives Phoenicia. Seek out the herd of the king,
and drive it down to the sea."
> Down from the hills flew Mercury;
the cattle flocked to the shore, where the sovereign's daughter
used to play with her Tyrian friends.° Now grandeur and love
rarely go well together; Zeus—father and ruler of gods,
845 whose right hand is armed with triple fire, whose menacing scowl
shakes the firm earth—put off his scepter, and donning the mask
of a bull calf, he joined the heifers. Beautiful in their eyes,
he wandered softly mooing and champing the tender grass. . . .
No anger wrinkled his brow; no fierceness glared from his eye;
850 his face just begged to be fondled.
> Agenor's daughter, entranced,
cooed, "What a lovable creature! he wouldn't hurt even a fly!"
(Yet for a while she stayed a little way off from the creature.)
At last she dares to approach with flowers to that mild face.
His heart leaps up, but for now he only licks at her fingers,
855 as he waits for pleasures to come. Now closer, closer they draw:
in sport, he writhes and squirms about in the succulent grass;
his snowy flanks lie churning the warm yellow sand of the shore.

839. *the Pleiades:* The mother of Mercury/Hermes was Maia, one of seven daughters of Atlas. Orion the hunter fell in love with them and pursued them for five years, until they were turned into doves (*Pleiades* = "doves"). Zeus raised them into the sky as the star-cluster in the constellation of Taurus, still called Pleiades.   843. *Tyrian friends:* Tyre was an island close to the shore, one of the two principal cities of Phoenicia, the other being Sidon.

Europa's fears shrink away as he offers his mighty dewlaps
to be stroked by her virginal hand, his horns for garlands of flowers.
860 Soon the innocent princess, not knowing what lay in her future,
dares climb up and sit on his shoulders. Slowly the god arises,
slowly moves down to the shore and dips his feet in its ripples.
Then—just a few steps further, and off he goes with his prize.
The girl begins to worry, looks back at the shore she has left;
865 her right hand clutches a horn, the other clings to his back
while her thin and fluttering dress is blown by a gathering breeze.
    At last the god abandons his treacherous masquerade,
as they reach the coastline of Crete.

OVID, *Metamorphoses* (2.834–3.2)

When Agenor discovered that his daughter was missing, he instructed his three sons, Cadmus, Phoenix, and Cilix, to search for Europa and not to return without her. They traveled over the wide world but, finding nothing and afraid to return home, settled in various lands: Phoenix near his first home in the land ever since called Phoenicia, Cilix in Cilicia (si-**li**-sha),[1] and Cadmus in Thebes, in central Greece.

Zeus and Europa meanwhile had several children: Minos, Sarpedon (sar-**pē**-don), and Rhadamanthys (rad-a-**man**-this). For protection, Zeus gave Europa Laelaps, the wonderful dog that always caught its prey, and Talus (**tā**-lus), a gigantic bronze robot that ran around the island three times each day and pelted with enormous boulders any ship that attempted to land (later important in the story of Jason).

MINOS AND PASIPHAË

After Zeus tired of Europa and returned to Olympus, a local Cretan, Asterius, married her and looked after her three sons. When they grew up, they all fell in love with the same boy. They quarreled furiously until **Minos** succeeded in driving out his two brothers. Sarpedon went to Lycia, in southwest Anatolia, and Rhadamanthys to Boeotia, the plain northwest of Attica. When Rhadamanthys died, he became a judge of the dead, as did Minos and Aeacus, a king of the island of Aegina and grandfather of Ajax (see Chapter 11).

When Asterius died, Minos claimed the kingship for himself, boasting, as proof that he deserved the rule, that the sea god Poseidon had promised him the throne. He asked that a bull should rise from the sea as a sign; this he would sacrifice to the god who sent it. A magnificent bull did rise from the sea, but one so splendid that Minos could not bear to give it up. Instead, he sent it to his herds and in its place sacrificed another. Thus Minos became the powerful king of Crete, oversaw the land, and promulgated laws. He married **Pasiphaë** (pa-**sif**-a-ē, "all-shining"), a daughter of Helius (the sun), who bore him many children, among them Ariadnê, Phaedra, and the prince Androgeus (an-**drō**-jūs).

Poseidon, angered that Minos had not sacrificed the bull, contrived a terrible punishment: Pasiphaë, his wife, fell hopelessly in love with the creature and was de-

[1]Phoenicia is, roughly, modern Lebanon; Cilicia is in southern Turkey, northwest of Lebanon.

termined to satisfy her uncontrollable passion for him. Pasiphaë confided her passion to an Athenian then living on Crete, **Daedalus** (dē-da-lus), the greatest craftsman of all time, a consummate architect and the inventor of statues. A descendant of Cecrops (Chart 15.1), Daedalus had been exiled from Athens for hurling his nephew and student Perdix from the Acropolis.[2] This he had done in a fit of jealousy because Perdix, not he, invented the saw, in imitation of a fish's backbone. To help Pasiphaë, Daedalus constructed a hollow wooden cow and covered it with a cow hide. Little wheels mounted in the legs enabled him to roll it into a pasture where the bull from the sea liked to graze. Pasiphaë climbed inside; the bull, snorting with desire, mounted the wooden cow and impregnated the queen, who stood hunched over inside. The fruit of this union was the dread **Minotaur** ("the bull of Minos"), a man-eating monster with the head of a bull and the body of a man (Fig. 16.2).

Ovid describes Pasiphaë's bizarre passion in his brilliantly amusing *Ars Amatoria*, which pretends to be a handbook on how to seduce one's beloved:[3]

[275]   Men and women alike delight in counterfeit coolness,
      but men soon blurt what they feel, girls pretend to be coy.
  If we males refused to show interest and let the girls make advances,
      be sure they would start an affair, setting the pace for the suit.
  Look at the beasts of the field: the cow moos her amorous passion,
280   the stallion is always entrapped by the whinnying voice of the mare.
  Humans alone can claim that their passion is kinder and gentler;
      the fire in a masculine breast is ruled by custom and law. . . .
  Once in the shadowy glades on the wooded slopes of Mt. Ida,°
      as pride and joy of the herd, there sported a snowy white bull.
285   Except for a tiny black spot between the horns, on his forehead,
      his coat was a milky white, faultless, unblemished, unmarked.
  Every cow in the kingdom of Cnossus° or western Cydonia,°
      longed to tremble, half-crushed by his thrusting weight on her back.
  Pasiphaë shouted for joy when the animal made her his mistress;
290   but scowled with jealousy' pangs at a shapely heifer's approach.
  All of you know the old tale; all Crete, with a full hundred cities,
      where every man is a liar,° must still acknowledge its truth.
  The queen herself, so they say, with hands not used to such labor,
      plucked him the tenderest leaves, the softest grass of the field.
295   She follows the herd; no thought of her husband keeps her from going;
      Minos must now wear horns,° cuckolded now by a bull!

283. *Mt. Ida:* There are two mountains named Ida, one is near Troy; this is the Cretan Ida.   287. *Cnossus:* The main city of Crete, near modern Heraklion in the middle of the north coast.   287. *Cydonia:* The modern Chania, in the northwest of the island.   292. *liar:* The Cretans had a reputation as liars. For example, the Cretan philosopher Epimenides is quoted by St. Paul (letter to Titus, Bishop of Crete, 1.12): "One of their own kind, one of their own prophets, said, 'the Cretans are always liars, evil beasts, dull bellies.'" (But because this statement was made by a Cretan, can it be true? The paradox of the Cretan liar was a favorite plaything of ancient logicians.)

---

[2]According to one version, Perdix was turned into a partridge, which in Greek = *Perdix*.
[3]The emperor Augustus, who wanted to reform the sexual behavior of the Roman upper classes, was so offended by this poem (and by some other unknown act of Ovid) that in A.D. 8 he banished Ovid to the remote town of Tomis on the Black Sea; there the lonely poet died in A.D. 17.

FIG. 16.2. Pasiphaë with the baby Minotaur, on the interior of an Etruscan wine-cup, c. 340 B.C. Pasiphaë is shown within her boudoir, indicated by the basket hanging from the wall and the pet goose at her feet. She gazes somewhat disheartened at the monster she has begotten. (Bibliothèque Nationale de France, Paris; 1066)

Pasiphaë, what is the use of your color-coordinate costumes?
    Your bull-friend isn't aware that richness is better than rags.
What use to you is a mirror, as you plod through mud to your pasture?
300   Why waste time on your hair, endlessly changing its braids?
Can't you believe your mirror's assurance that you're not a Holstein?
    How long will you ache for horns to bud and sprout from your brow!
If you are content with Minos, why seek an adulterous lover?
    If a manlier man you prefer, at least find a man you can love.
305 Slipping away from the palace, Pasiphaë runs to the woodland,
    like a Bacchanal driven along by the maddening Aonian god.°
Again and again she glares at a sweet and innocent heifer:
    "What on earth can my lover see in that ugly old cow?
Just look at the way she goes slinking before him, there in the meadow;
310   I suppose she's silly enough to believe she's prettier than I!"
So she would sneer, but at once would order her innocent rival
    to be dragged from the herd, to labor tugging the yoke and the plow.
Better yet, she would slay her as sacrificial oblation,
    gleefully rubbing her hands in the entrails, steaming and hot.
315 So she appeased the immortals, and with each envy-born murder
    she muttered, "Go back to my lover; see what he thinks of you now!"
One moment she longs to become a Europa, another an Io;
    one of whom was a cow, the other seduced by a bull.
Well, the lord of the harem, deceived by a wooden plush-covered dummy,
320   got Pasiphaë pregnant. The child looked just like his dad.

OVID, *Ars Amatoria* (1.275–282, 289–326)

296. *wear horns*: The cuckold, a man whose wife has been unfaithful, was for some reason thought to grow horns (in modern Italian a cuckold is *il cornuto*, "the horned one"), hence our slang term *horny* for someone in need of sexual gratification.   306. *Aonian god:* Dionysus. Aonia was a district in Boeotia, whose capital was Thebes, where Dionysus was born.

Picasso's *Minotauromachia*

Pablo Picasso, a versatile explorer of many fields of art, was prolific and influential throughout his long life. Although Spanish-born, he lived mostly in France, leader of the so-called School of Paris. Picasso drew imaginatively on Greek art in his monumental nudes and monsters, and the Minotaur was a favorite mythical symbol for his own artistic fecundity, imagination, and brutal sexual vitality, and for these qualities in all of us. In a dreamlike print called *Minotauromachia* of 1935 (Fig. P 16.1, alluding to a series of prints of bullfights by his predecessor Goya, called *Tauromachia;* see Perspective 4.1), Picasso lets free the symbol-making power of the unconscious mind to present a complex image of danger, fear, cruelty, hurt, hope, and opposition.

On the left a man in a loincloth climbs a ladder while looking over the scene. In a darkened room to his right are two women with doves, the bird of peace. They

FIG. P 16.1. Pablo Picasso (1888–1973), *Minotauromachia,* 1935, etching.   (Indiana University Art Museum, Bloomington)

look down at a candle held by a small girl, who clutches a bouquet. Between the girl and the Minotaur leaps a mare, whose entrails, ripped out, spew onto the ground. Across the mare lies a female matador, evidently wounded. With his left hand the Minotaur touches her extended hand, which holds an executioner's sword. At first glance, the Minotaur appears to be holding the sword, or he is covering a wound in his shoulder; in fact he hoists a large sack on his back. With his right arm he shields his eyes, as if in terror, from the candle's light. In the distance, between the Minotaur's knee and the horse's tail, sails a ship on a peaceful sea.

The Minotaur is evil but may not see well, and he is frightened by the light in the hand of the innocent girl, who reminds us of Ariadnê in the Greek story; there she holds the life-saving clue of thread. Theseus killed the monster, but here the man on the ladder, shown like Christ taken down from the cross, with a Christlike face, flees away. The women of peace, with their doves, look down, dispassionate and uninvolved, as spectators watch a bullfight, where horses really are gouged by the bull's horns. Everything in this scene is topsy-turvy and contradictory: The matador is a woman, the bull is half-man, the child is unafraid, the hero is in flight, the women of peace sit in darkness, the Minotaur has a burden to bear.

The symbols in Picasso's etching are like terrifying images in a dream, hinting at meaning but never revealing it. The artist owes a good deal to his Spanish background, evoking emotions that surround the bullfight; he owes still more to a revolutionary social, intellectual, and artistic movement important in the early twentieth century called surrealism, "beyond the real," which rejected the authority of the conscious mind and the science that served it. That was half the picture; the other was the dark, dream-time world of raw desire and raw impulse, the source of all artistic inspiration and probably of life itself. Picasso designed the first cover to a famous surrealist publication, called appropriately *Minotaure* (in French), showing now a heroic Minotaur holding out a defiant dagger. He often painted bulls too; the best-known example is in his painting *Guernica,* inspired by the German saturation bombing of the small Basque town of Guernica on April 26, 1937. The beast, Minotaur or bull, could be evil, but it was also the ocean of power and thrilling force that gave life meaning and made art possible. It was also Picasso himself, as the artist often claimed, and biographers of Picasso have identified real people behind the female characters in *Minotauromachia,* although even they, in the surrealist vision, had become symbols of unspeakable things we can acknowledge and draw pictures of but never really understand.

Although shamed by his wife's behavior, Minos hesitated to kill the Minotaur, who, after all, was family. He ordered Daedalus, who built the cow, now to build a prison capable of holding the monster. So Daedalus designed a complex maze of windings and turnings, and in the center of this **Labyrinth** (**lab**-e-rinth) the Minotaur was imprisoned. No one who entered could find a way out but was doomed to be eaten by the monster within.

MINOS AND SCYLLA

In a story made famous by Ovid, Minos' son Androgeus, an athlete of exceptional prowess, traveled to Athens to participate in the Panathenaic games, held each year on Athena's birthday. Defeating every contender in every contest, he so annoyed Aegeus, king of Athens, that Aegeus ordered him to fight a wild bull that was ravaging the plain of Marathon. The ferocious animal killed him.[4]

Minos learned of his son's death while sacrificing on the island of Paros. He immediately collected a fleet and set sail to attack Athens. On the way he besieged the coastal town of Megara, between Corinth and Athens, ruled over by **Nisus** (**nī**-sus), brother of Aegeus. Nisus was invulnerable as long as a certain purple lock grew on his head. His daughter **Scylla** (**sil**-la), standing on the ramparts of the city, saw the handsome Minos in the distance and fell instantly in love with him. She sent a secret message to the invader saying that she would cut away her father's purple lock if, when Minos captured Megara, he would marry her. Minos agreed, but when the city fell, he spurned the treacherous daughter.

Scylla's love turned to hate as she watched the ships leaving without her; she could neither stay at home, in the city she had betrayed with the father she had ruined, nor join the man for whom she had done all this. She dived into the sea and swam after the ship, overtook it, and clung to the stern. Nisus, turned to an osprey, swooped down on her with talons extended; she fell back into the waves, turned into a bird called in Greek "the shearer" (Ciris) because she had sheared her father's hair, and thus escaped.

THESEUS AND AMPHITRITÊ

Having taken Megara, Minos turned to Athens, but could not capture it even after a long siege. He prayed to Zeus for help. The god heard him and sent plague and famine on the city. The Athenians died in enormous numbers; in desperation they sacrificed the four virgin daughters of a Spartan who had settled in Athens, but still the plague raged unabated. An oracle instructed them to capitulate to the Cretan king. Minos ordered as punishment for the death of Androgeus that every nine years (or every year) they should send seven boys and seven girls to be devoured by the Minotaur.

Several bands of youths had already met their gruesome deaths when Theseus volunteered to join the band of sacrificial youths. A curious poem by Bacchylides (fifth century B.C.) describes a sort of boasting contest during the fateful voyage to Crete, which makes much of Theseus' descent from Poseidon and his special relationship with the sea. Although called in the papyrus that preserved it a dithyramb, a poem in honor of Dionysus, in fact (to judge from the last lines), the poem must have been sung and danced in a festival to Apollo on the island of Delos.

Minos, captain of the ship, was attracted by the beauty of Eriboea (er-i-**bē**-a), one

---

[4]Apparently the same bull that impregnated Pasiphaë, now transported to the mainland by Heracles (see Chapter 14); Theseus will kill this bull (Chapter 15).

FIG. 16.3. Theseus and Amphitritê, Attic wine-cup, c. 500–490 B.C. The boy Theseus, protected by Athena, reaches out to the sea goddess Amphitritê in her underwater realm, indicated by the three dolphins behind Theseus. A small, bearded Triton, with a serpent's body, supports him in the water. Because Poseidon is father to both Triton and Theseus, they are half-brothers. Amphitritê holds her gift, a wreath, in her left hand (not visible in the photo). (Musée du Louvre, Paris; Hirmer Fotarchiv)

of the Athenian *parthenoi,* and made a pass at her. Theseus warned him off and boasted that his ancestry was as glorious as that of Minos, son of Zeus: He was himself a son of the sea god Poseidon (in this version Poseidon was Theseus' true father). Minos accepted the challenge by asking Zeus for a sign; a bolt of lightning flashed from a clear sky. When Theseus demanded a chance to prove his own claim, Minos threw a ring into the sea and ordered Theseus to retrieve it. Theseus dove and soon brought back a wreath from Amphitritê, wife of Poseidon (Fig. 16.3), as proof that he too was of divine descent. For some reason, nothing further was heard of the ring (perhaps bringing it back would indicate Theseus' submission to Minos):

1   Over the sea between us and Crete the dark ship drove forward,
    with Theseus, ignoring the crash of waves, and seven sad couples
    of the handsomest maidens and boys of all the Ionian city.°
    You could see the white of her sails bellying out in the breezes
5   that whistled down from the north, sent to the ship by Athena,
    she who wears the terrible aegis that rouses men to do battle.
    The mystic gift of the Cyprian lady crowned with desire
    tormented Minos' heart.° No more could he hold back his hands
    from the girls in the ship, but caressed Eriboea's pale features.
10   In fright, the girl screamed out to Pandion's bronze-armored son.°

3. *of all the Ionian city:* The Athenians belonged to Ionian stock.   8. *heart:* Aphrodite's "gift" is lust for Eriboea.   10. *Pandion's bronze-armored son:* Theseus. Strictly speaking, this Pandion is Theseus' grandfather; see Chart 15.2.

Theseus saw what was happening. Hot fury goaded his spirit,
angry eyes glared under his brow as he snarled out his challenge:
  "So, son of mighty Zeus, you can't even keep decent control
over the lust of your spirit? Control your heroic passion.
15   What ineluctable fate has decreed, whatever is the will of the gods,
however the scales of Justice incline, in our favor or not,
remember, my lord, we all must fulfill our destiny's orders
when the moment to act has come. So forget your dirty intentions.
The lovely daughter of Phoenix° bore you, O mightiest of men,
20   having lain, no doubt, with Zeus, high up by the brow of Mount Ida,
a girl both modest and mortal. But what can I claim for myself?
Poseidon, lord of the sea, loved wealthy Pittheus' daughter;°
I was the son that she bore. The Nereids, nymphs of the waters,
dark-haired and sleek, embroidered a golden veil at my birth.
25   This, O war lord of Cnossus, gives me the right to advise you:
control your arrogant lust, which will bring you trouble and grief.
Never again may I see the gladdening light of the morning,
if you violate one of these girls; first we will duel it out;
some higher power, I trust, will decide the issue between us."
30   So spoke the hero, who knew so well the test of the spear,
and all the ship's company gaped at the man's incredible courage.
The heart of the son-in-law of the Sun° was seething with anger,
but quickly he formed a new plan and cried aloud to the heavens:
"Listen, O mighty Zeus, my father! If the white-shouldered maiden,
35   the daughter of Phoenix, in fact bore me with you as my father,
now hurl from the heavens a bolt of thunder with tresses of fire,
as an undeniable proof to all men. But, Theseus, if Aethra,
the woman of Troezen, really conceived you as son by Poseidon,
the shaker of all the earth—go, throw yourself into the waters,
40   into the sea, your father's home, and return to me with this ring,
this golden pride of my hand, back from the salty abysses.
Then we will learn if thundering Zeus, the planner of all things,
has accepted my prayer."
                              Zeus heard, and answered.
Eager, for Minos' sake, to display an omen portentous,
45   he sent a sign, till then unheard-of: a flash of his lightning.
The hero Minos, that stout-hearted man of war, gazed on the omen;
raising his hands to the ringing heaven, he shouted aloud:
"Theseus, gaze on the evident token of Cronus' son!
and you, for your part, now dive into the thundering deep.
50   Lord Poseidon, your father (like Zeus a son of great Cronus),
will doubtless grant you the highest glory that earth can know."
So he crowed. But Theseus' spirit knew no hesitation.
From the stern he dived to the waves that offered their watery welcome.
Minos' heart was aghast; he muttered, "Hold to our course;
55   and run on, straight down the wind!" But Destiny did not agree.

---

19. *Phoenix:* According to Bacchylides, Phoenix was the father of Europa; other sources name
Agenor as her father.   22. *Pittheus' daughter:* Theseus' mother, Aethra.   32. *son-in-law of the
Sun:* Pasiphaë, Minos' wife, was daughter of Helius.

Driven by northerly blasts, the ship drove on to the southward.
    The young Athenians trembled when the hero dived in the sea;
flowerlike eyes shed tears at the thought of what was lying before them.
But the dolphins, folk of the sea, escorted great Theseus down

60   to the house of his father, lord of horses, the dwelling of gods.
Trembling, he gazed at the famous daughters of Nereus the rich,
whose lovely flesh sent out a light like the light of a fire.
Gold-braided glittering ribbons sparkled and gleamed in their tresses
as they danced on spray-wet feet, hearts athrob with delight.

65   There in that wonderful house Theseus beheld Amphitrîtê,
his father's beloved wife, the lady with great soft eyes.
Over his shoulders she draped a robe of the sea's richest purple;
and in his luxuriant hair set the diadem, golden, refulgent,
which Aphrodite, mistress of wiles, had given at her marriage,

70   a crown decked with roses of crimson.
    No action done by a god should startle a man in his senses:
miracle! Theseus burst up beside the slim contours of the vessel.
What astonishment then disturbed the mind of the Cnossian captain
as the hero sprang, quite dry, from the sea, a wonder to all!

75   On his limbs shone the gifts of the gods. The Nereids shouted
in sheer delight from their throne, and the sea raised a cry of applause;
aboard the ship young men and maids raised a clear-voiced paean.
    Lord of Delos,° be warmed in heart by the dance of the Ceans;°
grant us a victor's garland, a god-sent token of fortune!

BACCHYLIDES, *Dithyramb* 17

78. *Lord of Delos:* Apollo.   78. *Ceans:* Inhabitants of the island of Ceos, one of the Cyclades, home of the poet.

The dive into deep water is a common motif in myths from all over the world. Often the diver is a creator god, who fetches the first earth from the bottom of the primordial sea, and Bacchylides' poem may have such a story as its basis. His miraculous reception by Amphitrîtê at the bottom of the sea and his subsequent return to the surface associate him directly with divinity and portend his coming victory over the Minotaur. Performed on Delos, where Athens exercised strong influence, the happy story of Athens' hero would awake in the spectators, many of them Athenian, a feeling of participation in Theseus' wonderful strength. For Theseus, *anything* was possible.

THESEUS AND THE MINOTAUR

When Theseus arrived on Crete, Minos' daughter Ariadnê saw him and immediately fell in love, just as Scylla had fallen in love with Minos (and Ishtar with Gilgamesh). She promised to show Theseus how to subdue the Minotaur if he would take her away and marry her. Following instructions given Ariadnê by Daedalus, Theseus tied the end of a ball of thread to the door of the labyrinth and unrolled it behind him as he penetrated the mysterious corridors (our word *clue* originally meant "a ball of thread"; its common metaphorical use is taken from this very story). Theseus found

FIG. 16.4. Theseus kills the Minotaur, interior of an Attic vase, wine-cup, c. 470 B.C. While holding a horn with one hand, with the other he decapitates the beast, his feet propped the frame of the painting. The rocks indicate the labyrinth; a hat hangs from the wall.   (Museo Nazionale, Florence; 70800 Deutsches Archaologisches Institut, Rome)

the Minotaur in the innermost recess of the Labyrinth and killed it with his sword (Fig. 16.4), then followed the thread back to the entrance. That night he and Ariadnê fled in his ship, soon landing on the Cycladic island of Naxos.

A famous literary description of these and earlier events of the legend is found in the work of the Roman love-poet Catullus. In the poem that follows, Catullus' subject is actually the wedding of Peleus and Thetis, the parents of Achilles, but he devotes more than half the poem to the story of Theseus and Ariadnê embroidered into a coverlet spread on the wedding couch:[5]

[76]   Long ago, says the legend, a plague forced the city of Cecrops
      to atone at a terrible price for the murder of Cretan Androgeus:
      each year the city must send, as meat for the Minotaur's banquet,
      a chosen group of young men and the flower of unwedded maidens.
80   The little town was groaning as the day of the tribute drew near,
      when Theseus offered himself on behalf of his well-loved Athens:
      better that one should die than a dozen fall prey to the monster.
      So the light ships, driven by oars and a following breeze,
      soon reached great-hearted Minos, in arrogance there on his throne.
85   Ariadnê, just out of childhood, gazed from the scented nursery
      where she lived, till now secure in the sweet embrace of her mother. . . .
      She could not tear her eyes from their longing gaze on the hero,
      till the flame that gaze enkindled was searing her inmost heart.
      O Cupid—must I call you holy?—mixer of heaven and hell,
90   and Venus, who rule over Golgi and wooded Idalia in Cyprus,°

90. *Golgi, Idalia:* Towns in Cyprus.

---

[5]This kind of story within a story, called an *epyllion,* "little epic," was a favorite device in Greek literature of the Hellenistic Period and its Roman imitators.

what a tempest you two churned up in Ariadnê's emotions
of endless sighing for Theseus, the fair-haired wonderful stranger!
What fear tormented her soul, what pallor shone in her features,
when Theseus announced he was ready to battle the furious monster,
95   be the outcome glorious death or life with a garland of glory!
Ariadnê's vows were not petty, and the prayer of her silent lips
rose up to heaven like incense, to win the assent of the gods.
      The monster slashed with his horns at the unresisting breezes,
but Theseus' sword brought him low in a thunderous earth-shaking crash,
100   like an oak laid low by a storm on the rocky summit of Taurus.°
Led by the slender thread he had laid to guide his returning,
to keep him from losing his way in the labyrinthine turnings,
unharmed, the victor retraced his steps to safety and glory.
      Must I leave my song's first theme for its tragic continuation?
105 Ariadnê fled the face of her father, the arms of her sister,
the anxious tears of her mother, who wept for the girl she was losing—
above all these she treasured the honeyed endearments of Theseus.

CATULLUS 64 (76–120)

100. *Taurus:* The high mountain range in southern Anatolia, modern Turkey. But there is also a pun: Latin *taurus* = "bull."

The eloping Theseus and Ariadnê sailed to the island of Naxos, sometimes called Dia. Theseus, disgusted by Ariadnê's treachery to her father, abandoned her and returned to Athens:[6]

[52]   From Dia's wave-beaten shore Ariadnê looks out on the ocean,
watching the flight of Theseus with all his swift-running vessels.
Passion tortures her heart; she cannot believe what she sees,
55   for only a moment ago she had shaken off treacherous slumber,
to find herself wretched, abandoned, alone on a desolate shore.
      Theseus, his eye on the weather, urges his men at the oars,
forgetful of poor Ariadnê; embarrassed, he tries to speed homeward,
leaving his empty promises blowing like scraps in a tempest.
60   Minos' daughter wades out, till the seaweed swirls at her ankles,
watching with horror-struck eyes, the form of a graven Bacchante.
Waves of trouble, as savage as those of the sea, fall crashing upon her.
The wind has blown the soft head-scarf free of her soft yellow hair;
lost is the silken blouse that covered her milkwhite bosom;
65   no more did a thin-woven girdle encircle her swelling breasts.
All her beautiful clothing was tumbled about by the waves,
swirling around by her ankles. But she gave it never a thought.
Stunned by her lot, to Theseus she directed heart, mind, and soul.

CATULLUS 64 (52–70)

[6]The order of events in the poem is different: Catullus first describes Ariadnê's abandonment, then what happened before (in a flashback). Ovid liked the story of "Ariadnê on Naxos" so much that he told it three times: in the tenth letter of the *Heroïdes* ("famous women"), in *Ars Amatoria* (1.527–564), and in *Metamorphoses* (8.174–192).

Catullus gives a vivid portrait of the betrayed and love-stricken Ariadnê loudly lamenting her fate. She ends by cursing Theseus in what she is sure is her last breath:

[192] "You Furies, avengers of crime by stern and appropriate torment,
       who bind your hair and foreheads with vipers hissing your anger,
       come to my help, I implore you. Hear the bitter complaints
195   I blindly pour from my heart in its poverty, passion, and fury.
       Since these complaints are just and spring from deep in my being,
       never, I pray you, allow that my misery be forgotten.
       Careless of all save himself, Theseus deserted and left me;
       may Theseus' careless mind be a curse to himself and his kin!"
200   From a heart tormented by anger burst out these furious curses;
       the ruler of highest heaven displayed his assent with a nod,
       commanding the earth and wild ocean to shake together in terror,
       striking the dome of the sky, shaking the stars in their courses.

CATULLUS 64 (192–206)

Catullus then narrates Theseus' tragic return to Athens and Ariadnê's unexpected rescue by Dionysus (see Perspective 10.1).

Many versions report that, before returning to Athens, Theseus stopped on the island of Delos, which was, with Delphi, the greatest sanctuary of Apollo in classical times. There in the temple he dedicated a statue of Aphrodite that Ariadnê had given him. He and the youths and maidens he rescued danced a complicated dance in a circle that mimicked the turns of the Labyrinth, called the crane dance.[7]

DAEDALUS AND ICARUS

Minos was enraged when he learned of Theseus' escape and his daughter's treachery. In revenge, he imprisoned Daedalus and his son **Icarus** (**ik**-a-rus), born to a Cretan slave girl, inside the Labyrinth that Daedalus had himself built, sealing off every escape, for Daedalus had started the chain of disaster, first constructing the wooden cow for Pasiphaë, then devising the trick of the clue. Ovid tells the story of Daedalus' escape twice, once in the *Metamorphoses* and again in the *Ars Amatoria*. Here is the version from the *Ars Amatoria*, which Ovid introduces in order to compare the unrestrainable Daedalus with the unrestrainable Cupid, troublesome winged spirit of sexual desire:

[25]   "Mercy," Daedalus begged, "O Minos, justest of mortals!
           Grant that the land of my fathers receive my ashes as well!
       Envious Fate has forced me to live far off from my homeland;
           back in my homeland, I pray, allow me to finish my days.
       At least let my boy return, though return is denied to his father;

---

[7]Some think that the poem of Bacchylides, quoted earlier, may be connected with this dance because that poem mentions Delos. However, nothing certain is known about this dance or its relationship to Bacchylides' poem.

30   or pity the father's fate, though you grudge return to the son."
        Such was his prayer, and he might have added additional reasons.
            All would have been in vain; Minos denied his request.
        Daedalus had to agree, but thought, "Just what, pray, is lacking?
            All that I need I have, plus the wits to put it to use." . . .
35 Adversity sharpens the mind. Would anyone think that a human
            could follow the path of a bird, soaring on wings to the sky?
        Daedalus picked out feathers, the weightless oars of the eagle,
            and bound a delicate frame with slender fetters of thread.
        The lower stubs he anchored in wax, made soft by the fire,
40   and thus he finished his careful work on the new device.
        Icarus stroked the wax and the gleaming feathers it bonded,
            not yet aware that the pinions were made for his slender arms.
        "This is our ship of hope, in which we shall fly to our country,"
            Daedalus smiled at the boy, "by which we can baffle the king.
45 Minos has blocked all our ways, but he cannot cut off the heaven;
            the wings my wits have invented will waft us wherever we will.
        But remember this: do not climb toward Helicê, maid of Tegea,°
            or Orion with flashing sword, Boötes'° trustworthy friend.
        Soar on the wings I have given along the way that I lead you;
50   your only task is to follow in safety your trustworthy guide.
        Consider: too close to the sun, too high in the fiery heaven,
            the wax on which we depend will droop and melt in the heat.
        But if we direct our wings too low, down by the threatening waters,
            our dampened feathers will droop, heavy with salt-laden spray.
55 So fly on between the two, bewaring the squall and the tempest;
            wherever a gentle breeze directs you, that way in safety set sail."
        So he instructs his son while fitting the wings to his shoulders,
            showing the boy their use, like a bird with a fledgling chick.
        Next he adjusts the pinions on his own muscular torso,
60   carefully poising himself to embark on the perilous trip.
        Lastly, before taking off, he presses a kiss on the stripling,
            unable to hold back the tears that dampen his trembling cheek.
        A knoll arose from the plain (too small to consider a mountain);
            from it the father and son started their ill-fated flight.
65 Daedalus plied his own wings, but kept his eyes on the boy;
            smoothly gliding along on the line of the course he had laid.
        The courage of Icarus mounted with joy at the newly found motion;
            higher, more rashly he flew, as he mastered the wonderful art.
        A fisherman, down below, was casting his bait. He looked upward,
70   gaped at the soaring pair, and hurried off home with his tale.
        Samos they saw to their left after passing Naxos and Paros,
            and Delos, island beloved by Apollo, the Clarian god.°
        On the right was the island Lebynthos and shaded woody Calymna;

---

47. *maid of Tegea:* Helicê was a nymph of Tegea, a town in eastern Arcadia, in the central Peloponnesus. After death Zeus transformed her into the constellation Ursa Major, the Greater Bear, also
known as the Big Dipper (see Fig. P 13.2).   48. *Boötes:* The Wagon Driver, a constellation near
Ursa Major but much lower in the heavens (see Fig. P 13.2).   72. *The Clarian god:* Claros was a
town in Ionia with a famous oracle of Apollo.

Astypalaea as well, girded with fish-laden pools.°
75   Then Icarus, overly rash in his adolescent bravado,
    abandoned his father's side and soared up into the sky.
The bindings slacken, the wax gives way as the hot sun grows closer.
    Pull as he will, his wings no longer maintain their grip on the wind.
Shaken by terror, he stares from the upper vaults of the heaven
80   at the rolling sea below, and faints from his gathering fear.
The wax gives way; he thrashes his arms in profitless panic,
    knowing he has no check on his headlong precipitate fall.
"Daddy, Daddy, come help me!" he screams in vain as he tumbles,
    but the livid waves close in and stifle his cry as he falls.

OVID, *Ars Amatoria* (2.25–34, 43–92)

74. ... *pools:* Samos, Naxos, Paros, Delos, Lebynthos, Calymna, and Astypalaea are islands of the Aegean sea. This is an unlikely route for anyone traveling from Crete to Athens, but the poet had to accommodate the story that the Icarian Sea (east and south of Samos) and the island of Icaria, where the body of Icarus was washed ashore, were named for the luckless boy.

The story of Icarus is a mythical illustration of the Greek maxim "Nothing too much," one of the proverbs inscribed over the temple of Apollo at Delphi. Doubtless because overdoing things was a common weakness of the Greeks, their sages were fond of preaching the virtue of the Golden Mean.[8]

THE DEATH OF MINOS

Daedalus seems to have given up his plans to land in Attica; he was flying east when Icarus drowned, but now flew west to Sicily, where he took refuge at the court of **Cocalus** (**kok**-a-lus), king of Camicus (later Agrigentum) on the south central coast of Sicily. Raging for revenge, Minos sought Daedalus everywhere. He carried a spiral conch shell with him and promised a grand reward to whoever could pass a thread through its windings. Minos well knew that only Daedalus was clever enough to accomplish the feat.

He presently came to the court of Cocalus, who, pretending that he could solve the puzzle, took the shell to Daedalus. The master craftsman drilled a hole in one end, attached a thread to an ant by a drop of honey, and allowed the ant to draw the thread through the labyrinthine shell (much as Theseus had done through the windings of the Labyrinth). When Cocalus presented the shell to Minos, the tyrant knew he had found his man and demanded that Cocalus surrender Daedalus. Cocalus agreed, but invited Minos first to join him for dinner. When Minos went to bathe before the feast, Cocalus' daughters filled the tub with hot pitch and burned him to death. Of the further adventures and death of Daedalus, nothing is reported.

[8]Aristotle defined virtue as the mean between opposite extremes. Thus courage is the middle way between cowardice and foolhardy rashness.

Brueghel's *The Fall of Icarus*

Flemish painter Pieter Brueghel was fond of combining scenes of daily activity with landscape. In *The Fall of Icarus* (Fig. P 16.2), he reduces Ovid's story to an inconspicuous pair of flailing legs (lower right, near the ship). Most of the canvas is devoted to a fisherman (lower right), a plowman, and a shepherd (center). In Brueghel's ironic version of the story, no one notices the boy's death, as in the folk saying, "No plow stops for the man who dies."

Modern Anglo-American poet W. H. Auden (1907–1973) was a stretcher-bearer for the Republican Army during the Spanish Civil War. Influenced by his experiences there, he wrote *Musée des Beaux Arts* (= "Museum of Fine Arts," in Brussels, Belgium), a poem inspired by Brueghel's painting, in which Auden speaks of the commonplace nature of suffering:

FIG. P 16.2. Pieter Brueghel the Elder (c. 1525–1569), *Landscape with the Fall of Icarus,* c. 1554–1555, oil on panel. (Musées Royaux des Beaux-Arts, Brussels)

*Musée des Beaux Arts**

About suffering they were never wrong,
The Old Masters: how well they understood
Its human position; how it takes place
While someone else is eating or opening a window or just walking dully
    along;
How, when the aged are reverently, passionately waiting
For the miraculous birth, there always must be
Children who did not specially want it to happen, skating
On a pond at the edge of the wood:
They never forgot
That even the dreadful martyrdom must run its course
Anyhow in a corner, some untidy spot
Where the dogs go on with their doggy life and the torturer's horse
Scratches its innocent behind on a tree.
In Brueghel's *Icarus,* for example: how everything turns away
Quite leisurely from the disaster: the ploughman may
have heard the splash, the forsaken cry,
But for him it was not an important failure; the sun shone
As it had to on the white legs disappearing into the green
Water; and the expensive delicate ship that must have seen
Something amazing, a boy falling out of the sky,
Had somewhere to get to and sailed calmly on.

OBSERVATIONS: ARCHAEOLOGY AND CRETAN MYTH

The long island of Crete lay at the intersection of trading routes from all directions: Egypt to the southeast, Cyprus, Phoenicia, and all of Asia Minor to the east, Greece to the north, and Sicily and Italy to the west. Peoples from many different lands had settled in Crete during its long history (and still do), bringing their religions, myths, and legends with them. According to modern archaeological research, the principal population, whom we call Minoans, may have come from Anatolia as early as 7000 B.C., with a second wave of immigration about 3100 B.C. They used several scripts. The two earliest were pictorial, perhaps modeled on Egyptian hieroglyphic writing. Later these pictographs were schematized into the (still undeciphered) Linear A and into Linear B, used to keep tallies and inventories of commodities.

    Minoan power evidently came to an abrupt end about 1450 B.C., when palaces all over the island were destroyed. From this catastrophic period comes archaeological evidence of ritual cannibalism of children and of human sacrifice, no doubt in an attempt to stave off the impending disaster. Some of the native Minoans escaped to mountain retreats or, perhaps, left the island. Many scholars have thought that an enormous volcanic explosion on Thera caused the universal destruction, but recent evidence indicates that the explosion took place about 1630 B.C., too early to have caused the catastrophe.

After 1450 B.C. only Cnossus was rebuilt, to be destroyed again by fire about 1400 B.C. The third and final destruction came at about 1200 B.C. The conflagration that accompanied the second and third destructions accidentally preserved thousands of clay tablets inscribed in the Linear B writing.[9] In 1953, British architect Michael Ventris deciphered the complicated writing and proved, to the surprise of everyone, that the language behind the writing was Greek. This is how we know that Mycenaeans from the mainland—Greeks—were living in Crete at this time. Mycenaean Greeks seem to have taken over Cnossus after the earlier destruction of 1450 B.C., which, indeed, they may have caused. No details are known, nor do we know what caused the second and third destructions of Cnossus in 1400 and 1200 B.C.: insurrection, perhaps, or internecine struggles among the Mycenaeans themselves. The biblical Philistines, who settled in five cities on the coast of Palestine south of modern Tel Aviv in about 1200 B.C., seem to have been Mycenaean Greeks from Crete; Palestine takes its name from this people.[10]

In thinking about Cretan myths, and about Crete, we must remember that Cretans before about 1450 B.C. were Minoans, racially, linguistically, and culturally distinct from Cretans after about 1450 B.C., who were Mycenaean Greeks, presumably invaders. Gradually Greek language and culture replaced the indigenous Minoan culture, and Greek is spoken on Crete today, but the influence of the complex older world was profound. We do not have any Minoan myths; we have Greek, especially Athenian, myths about Crete.

Even in the ancient world, intellectuals tried to distinguish historical truth from myth in stories about Crete, a problem we referred to earlier, and scholars continue today. In the fifth century B.C. the Athenian writer Thucydides (thu-**sid**-i-dēz), in the introduction to his history of the Peloponnesian War, argued from mythic accounts that the kingdom of Minos was the first thalassocracy, a political order having "supremacy over the sea." Thucydides was a pioneer in efforts to distinguish myth from history:

> Minos was the first whom we know—granted, only by hearsay—to build a navy. He was able to take control of most of the Aegean Sea, to govern the islands we call the Cyclades, and to start colonies in many of them. First of all, he had to drive out the Carians.° He then set up his own sons as rulers, and, as far as he could, wiped out the pirates, no doubt in the hope that their income would thereafter flow into his own pockets.

THUCYDIDES 1.4

Carians: A people of Asia Minor, whom Thucydides assumed to have ruled these islands.

The archaeological record behind myths about Crete lay buried until 1899, when Englishman Arthur Evans, inspired by the German Heinrich Schliemann's discoveries of Troy and Mycenae on the mainland, purchased with his own funds part

[9]Only recently has it been shown that the Linear B tablets come from two different destruction levels.
[10]By c. 600 B.C. they spoke a Semitic language, as proven by recent inscriptional finds.

FIG. 16.5. The palace at Cnossus. Sir Arthur Evans reconstructed portions of the ancient labyrinthine palace at Cnossus. In this photo are visible the typical Minoan wooden columns, thicker at the top than at the bottom. The walls were of masonry cushioned by internal wooden beams, to lessen the shock of earthquake. Behind the reconstructed portion was the central courtyard, where the bull games may have been celebrated.   (Author's photo)

of the north central plain of Crete, where a low mound showed promise of concealing ancient remains. There he gradually uncovered the ruins of ancient Cnossus, an enormous palace complex dating from the earliest European civilization, which flourished from about 3100 to 1000 B.C. (Fig. 16.5). It was Evans who applied the term *Minoan* (after the legendary Minos) to this culture and to the people who fashioned it. Since Evans' day, archaeologists have enlarged his excavations at Cnossus and explored many other palace sites on Crete.

Excavations suggest that the Minoans were a vigorous, pleasure-loving, seafaring people with a taste for vibrant, naturalistic art and elegant, sophisticated living. Their palaces rarely were fortified; they must have had no enemies. Frescoes recently discovered on the nearby island of Thera, a Minoan outpost, show grand flotillas of ships and armed warriors, confirming Thucydides' description of them as the first thalassocracy. In 1992, to the amazement of the scholarly world, Minoan frescoes from about 1800 B.C. were found in the Nile delta, further testimony to the far-reaching power of this extraordinary people.

The tales of Theseus and the Minotaur and the doings of Daedalus also are connected intimately with Athens. Those who trust myth to preserve real history see in these stories a memory of hostilities between Athens and Crete at some time before 1450 B.C., when the Cretan thalassocracy could have exerted direct influence on the mainland. We have never understood how the Greeks came to take possession of the island, and perhaps the story preserves a recollection from a time of actual hostilities. We can neither prove nor disprove the thesis.

Most features of the myth certainly belong to a later time. Athenian supremacy in artistic production after about 900 B.C. must have increased the popularity of stories about an Athenian artist named Daedalus, and the exploits of Theseus are in large part Athenian propaganda generated in the late sixth and fifth centuries B.C. (see Chapter 15), when the sea power of Athens grew until it was unrivaled anywhere. The Athenians were glad to draw mythical parallels between their own sea empire and that of Minos, especially when such a parallel allowed them to show Theseus defeating the Minoan king in a contest requiring intelligence, bravery, and superior moral commitments, and especially chivalry toward women.

In addition to possible historical elements, we can occasionally identify Cretan religious practices in the Cretan stories, although interpretations of Cretan religion are difficult; no contemporary texts illuminate the archaeological evidence. Most scholars agree, however, that the Cretans worshiped a Great Mother goddess represented as a bare-breasted woman with snakes twining up her arms (Fig. 16.6). Ari-

FIG. 16.6. The snake goddess from a deposit in a room sanctuary in the palace at Cnossus, faience, c. 1600 B.C. She may be a priestess and wears the dress, with breasts exposed, characteristic of Minoan women, but the odd feline (perhaps a leopard) on her head and the serpents in her hands suggest that she is the goddess herself.   (Heraklion Museum, Crete; Lauros-Giraudon Art Resource, NY)

adnê, whose name means "the very holy one," may have been a name for this goddess, reduced in legend to a folklore heroine. Her original function as mother-goddess would be reflected in her cult on Cyprus as Ariadnê Aphrodite, in which a young man would lie down and pretend to give birth. The bull was central to Cretan cult and figured in an acrobatic bull game often illustrated in Minoan art (Fig. 16.7). The game was certainly dangerous and may underlie the legend of the man-devouring Minotaur, which means "the bull of Minos," as does, perhaps, the ritual cannibalism for which we have evidence during the period of Crete's collapse. The bull is an embodiment of divine power and in historical religion was the animal of Zeus, to whom the bull was sacrificed in bloody ritual.

Another Cretan religious emblem, often found in shrines, was the double ax, which many scholars take to represent the sacrificial tool by which the bull was felled. A Greek grammarian tells us that the Cretan word for a double-edged ax was *labrys,* so that *Labyrinth* would mean "place of the double ax," the place of sacrifice, where in legend Athenian youths were fed to the bull-man.

Sexual surrender of a female victim as a substitute for her sacrifice is perhaps reflected in the story of Zeus's possession of Europa in the guise of a bull, and some speculate that some such ritual may have been performed in Minoan Crete. A similar pattern appears in the tale of Pasiphaë, who couples with the "bull from the sea" sent by Poseidon, in a sense Poseidon himself, lord of the sea, with whom the Minoans had a special relationship. Once, young women were sacrificed to gods; later, as a substitute for their life, they surrendered their maidenhood in a "sacred marriage" (*hieros gamos*) to a priest or king, who may even have worn a bull's mask.

If such a ritual gave rise to the stories of Europa and Pasiphaë, the religious background had long since dropped away by the Greek Classical Period, when the focus fell on Pasiphaë's bizarre lust. Unfortunately, no classical works treating the House of Crete have survived, but we should suspect a humorous origin to principal features of the myth: Pasiphaë, a queen, inside a cow, waiting for the bull to possess her, can only be pornographic or ludicrous and conforms to a Greek stereotype of women as hopelessly lustful and unashamed. Similar patterns of abhorrent or excessive sexuality characterize the house of Crete in general, also appearing in Ariadnê's willingness to betray family and country to satisfy her passion, in Minos' assault on the Athenian maiden en route to Crete,[11] and in the incestuous love of Pasiphaë's daughter Phaedra for her stepson, Hippolytus (see Chapter 15). For the Athenians of the fifth century, the Cretans had become a type: the lustful, incestuous, violent, tyrannical cousins who live over the hill, who never tell the truth about anything.

The overall pattern of the story belongs to folktale: A wandering hero (Theseus) comes to a strange land (Crete) oppressed by a wicked king (Minos), in league with a man-eating monster demanding human sacrifice (the Minotaur); the daughter of the king (Ariadnê) falls in love with the hero; assisted by her and a trickster–magician (Daedalus), the hero kills the monster; the wandering hero and princess flee, but the hero, abhorring her treachery, abandons the princess and returns to his

[11]Scylla, princess of Megara, although not a member of the House of Crete, is inspired to commit her parallel treachery by lust for Minos.

FIG. 16.7. The bull-vaulting fresco from Cnossus. To the right a woman (indicated by her white skin) holds out her arms to receive a man (dark skin) somersaulting over the back of a bull, while a second woman, to the left, takes holds of the horns of the charging bull. All four of the bull's feet are off the ground in a flying gallop. The naturalistic representation of the animal is characteristic of Cretan art. This perilous game seems to have been celebrated in the large central courtyard of the palace at Cnossus, perhaps the origin of the myth of the Minotaur.   (Heraklion Museum, Crete)

home, where he becomes king (Ishtar, too, was rejected by Gilgamesh because of her treacherous nature). The prominence of such standard traditional narrative elements forces us to be extremely cautious in searching for historical events behind the myth.

Some scholars have emphasized how elements in the story also resemble patterns of male initiation into adulthood. In the story,

- Theseus journeys to a far land.

- He overcomes death and a monster.

- He has an amorous adventure.

- He is elevated to the kingship.

In widespread patterns of ritual male initiation, these corresponding elements appear:

- The young initiate is driven from his native town.

- He undergoes mock death and encounters demons from the other world (often in the form of grotesquely masked men).

- He has some form of sexual experience.

- The initiate returns to society with the full privileges of an adult.

In Athens, Theseus was the protective spirit of male initiates. Called *ephebes* ("on the verge of adulthood"), between the ages of eighteen and twenty they underwent a time of stringent testing after which in an oath they invoked the model of Theseus' career and were admitted to full citizenship. Such parallels are interesting but demonstrate the profound difference between myth and ritual activity: One is a story, with its own internal rules and demands; the other is a pattern of social behavior.

Important in Cretan legend is Daedalus, the trickster–inventor so common in folklore: He invented the tools of carpentry, built the wooden cow for Pasiphaë, designed the Labyrinth, and threaded the conch shell. He is the prototype of the passionate artist, so jealous of his powers that he murdered Perdix, his nephew and only rival, and risked his life to show off by threading the shell. Imprisoned within the maze of his own making, he is the emblem of the artist captivated by his own creation. Although many explain his origin as a late personification from the common Greek adjective *daidalos*, which means "skillfully made," his name may appear on a linear B tablet from Cnossus, and he is mentioned already in the *Iliad*, where Homer describes the design on a wonderful shield that Hephaestus, Daedalus' divine counterpart, makes for Achilles:

> The god of the brawny arms, displaying the skill of the artist,
> Modeled a dancing floor, as Daedalus once did in Cnossus,
> for Ariadnê, the maiden of lovely soft-flowing ringlets.

> HOMER, *Iliad* (18.590–592)

Greek writers of the Roman Period attributed to Daedalus the invention of realistic sculpture and the construction of many famous buildings, including the Bronze Age conical towers on Sardinia and various temples in Egypt. Early Greek sculpture is still sometimes called Daedalic.

KEY TERMS

Europa, 419
Minos, 421
Pasiphaë, 421
Daedalus, 422
Minotaur, 422

Labyrinth, 425
Nisus, 426
Scylla, 426
Icarus, 432
Cocalus, 434

FURTHER READING

Cambridge Ancient History, 3rd ed., vols. I and II (Cambridge, U.K., 1970). The standard reference in English for the Greek Bronze Age, by leading scholars.

Cottrell, Leonard, *The Bull of Minos* (London, 1955). Exciting popular account of the discovery of Minoan Crete.

Doumas, Christos G., *Thera, Pompeii of the Ancient Aegean* (London, 1983). Popular description of the volcanic eruption that destroyed Thera, thought by many (until recently) to have caused the destruction of Minoan civilization.

Evans, Arthur, J., *The Palace of Minos at Knossos* (London, 1939; reprinted 1964). The basic book on Bronze Age Crete by the man who discovered the civilization.

Farnaux, Alexandre, *Knossos: Searching for the Legendary Palace of King Minos,* trans. David J. Baker. Presents the story of the discovery of Knossos by English archaeologist Arthur Evans.

Marinatos, S., and M. Hirmer, *Crete and Mycenae* (London, 1960). Lavish illustrations of the archaeological finds on Crete and the mainland, with an excellent text.

McDonald, W. A., *Progress into the Past* (New York, 1967). A good general book on Bronze Age archaeology, with a section on Crete.

Morris, Sarah, *Daidalos and the Origins of Greek Art* (Princeton, N.J., 1992). Thorough study of the myths and origins of Daedalus, tracing him back to Near Eastern prototypes.

Nilsson, Martin, P., *Minoan–Mycenaean Religion, and Its Survival in Greek Religion,* 2nd ed. (New York, 1950). Authoritative account by one of the greatest historians of Greek religion.

Pendlebury, J.D.S., *The Archaeology of Crete* (London, 1939; reprinted New York, 1965). A standard review of the important sites.

Willets, R. F., *The Civilization of Ancient Crete,* 2nd ed. (New York, 1992). Good general overview.

CHAPTER 17

OEDIPUS AND THE MYTHS OF THEBES

But do not worry about marriage with your mother;
No end of males have dreamed of sleeping with theirs.

SOPHOCLES, *Oedipus the King* 980–982

THEBES, the principal city of **Boeotia** (bē-ō-sha), lay near the chief land route from the northern Balkans south to Attica and the Peloponnesus. It was a center of power in both the Bronze Age and the Classical Period and a focus for a complex cycle of legends next in importance only to those of Mycenae. The site has been occupied continuously for more than five thousand years. Unfortunately for historians, the modern town covers the ancient remains and inhibits archaeological exploration. In Thebes "mortal women were the mothers of gods [Dionysus and Heracles]," as Sophocles put it in a surviving fragment, and there men fought the greatest war in Greek legend, except for the Trojan War: that of the Seven against Thebes. Some of the best-known Athenian tragedies describe the myths and legends of this city, taking many of their stories from an epic poem now lost, the *Thebaïs*, attributed (perhaps rightly) to Homer.

THE FOUNDING OF THEBES: CADMUS AND THE DRAGON

Thebes was unique in Greek legend in that two separate stories were told of its foundation. One of them begins with the story of Europa, the Phoenician princess who

FIG. 17.1. Cadmus kills the serpent, Attic wine-mixing bowl, c. 450 B.C. Beside the dragon sits Harmonia (probably), future wife of Cadmus; her father, Ares, stands behind her. The plants behind the serpent indicate the spring. Cadmus holds the pitcher for the sacrificial water in his left hand, while with his other he makes ready to stone the serpent. Athena stands beside him. (The Metropolitan Museum of Art, New York, Rogers Fund; 07.286.66)

disappeared over the sea on the back of a bull. Her father, Agenor, ordered his sons, including Cadmus, to search for their sister and not to return without her (Chapter 16). They must have had little hope of success, for the brothers Cilix, Phoenix, and Thasos soon gave up the search and settled permanent colonies, to which they gave their own names: Cilicia, Phoenicia, and the island of Thasos in the northern Aegean.

Only Cadmus continued the search, but he too was unsuccessful. He went to Delphi, where the Pythia told him to give up—he would never find Europa. Instead, he should follow a cow with special markings and found a city where the cow became exhausted and lay down. Cadmus did as he was told, came to a hill in southern Boeotia, and on it built the city of Thebes.

Wishing to sacrifice the cow to Zeus (or Athena), Cadmus sent companions to a nearby spring, sacred to Ares, to get water for the sacrifice. When they did not return, he went himself and found that a huge serpent, a dragon, had killed his companions. Cadmus defeated the dragon in a great battle (Fig. 17.1), then at Athena's suggestion knocked out the dragon's teeth, plowed the ground, and sowed half of the teeth into the furrow.[1] Up sprang armed men. Cadmus threw stones among them. Thinking they were being attacked, the newborn warriors battled each other until only five remained, the **Sparti,**[2] "sown men," ancestors of the principal aristocratic families of Thebes.

Ovid has fun telling this story of dragon combat and miraculous birth:

[3]   In panic over Europa, her father gave orders to Cadmus,
        her brother, to search her out and warned him not to return

---

[1]Athena gave the other half to Aeëtes, king of Colchis, who figures in the legend of Jason (Chapter 18).

[2]No connection with the famous city of Sparta. From the same root comes the English words *sperm*, *spore*, *sporadic*, and *diaspora*.

5   until he had found the girl, lest he be banished forever—
       a virtuous order, indeed, but one of a criminal harshness.
       He hunted on land and sea, but in vain: what mortal can ever
       hope to detect the concealments and wiles of an amorous Zeus?
           Abandoning hope of return to the home and wrath of his father,
10   he wandered to Apollo's oracular shrine and humbly inquired
       where he might find a land to live in thereafter.
           "In the lonesome plains nearby," replied the prophet of Phoebus,
       "an ownerless heifer will meet you, one never yoked to a plow.
       Follow wherever she goes, and where she lies down in a meadow,
15   there you must build your walls and name the region Boeotia."°
       Hardly had Cadmus gone down from the lofty Castalian precinct°
       than he noticed an ambling heifer, bearing no scars of a yoke.
       Checking his eager advance, he followed her wandering footsteps,
       silently breathing his thanks to Phoebus, who showed him the way.
20   He passed the stream of Cephisus and left the Panopean plain:°
       the animal halted and, raising her face and beautiful horns
       to heaven above, gave tongue, filling the air with her bellows.
       Coyly turning her head to be sure that the comrades of Cadmus
       were following close behind, she yawned and stretched herself out
25   full length in the juicy grass. Cadmus gave thanks to the gods,
       kissing the new found land, saluting its mountains and plains.
       Then he made ready to bring to Zeus an ample offering.
       He ordered his servants forth, to hunt for a living fountain
       of water fit to employ in the rites which the god had demanded.°
30   An ancient grove lay nearby, untouched by hatchet or billhook;
       within, half-hidden in bushes, there opened the mouth of a cavern,
       a shallow arch, supported by rough fitted pieces of stone.
       Plenty of water poured out—but within lurked a terrible serpent,
       sacred to Mars. Its head bore a crest resplendent and golden;
35   fire shot from its eyes; its body was puffy with venom;
       triple its tongue, and triple the line of its snapping teeth.
           The Tyrian wanderers° entered the grove with ill-omened footsteps,
       but when they lowered a cauldron down in the babbling water,
       it uttered a brassy sound. From within the depths of the cavern,
40   the livid dragon protruded its head with terrible hissing.
       The water-jars fell from their hands, their faces whitened in terror,
       chattering fear seized upon them, they stood there, weakened and trembling.
       The serpent twisted his coils in rolling knotted gyrations;
       enormous, unpredictable, changing his way in a flash.
45   Raising full half his bulk to the sighing breezes of heaven
       (as big, compared with the sky, as the space dividing the Bears°),

---

15. *Boeotia:* "Cowland"; compare Io's crossing of the Bosporus, "cow-crossing."   16. *Castalian precinct:* At Delphi, near where the Pythia gave oracles, was a famous spring called Castalia.   20. *Panopean plain:* North of Delphi. It is watered by the river Cephisus, which rises on Mount Parnassus, flows north and east across the Panopean plain, and ends in a lake north of Thebes. There is another Cephisus in Attica.   29. *demanded:* Apollo, in his instructions to Cadmus.   37. *Tyrian wanderers:* From the major Phoenician settlement.   46. *Bears:* The constellations Ursa Major and Minor.

he glanced at the grove. A few of the men were scrambling for weapons,
more had elected to run, but, paralyzed, most could do neither.
Some he snapped up in his jaws, some in a crushing embrace;
50   the rest he slew with a murderous blast of his poisonous breath.
    The sun, now high in his course, had shrunk the shadows of noonday,
when Cadmus began to wonder at the long delay of his comrades
and set out to follow their track. For defense he put on a hide
ripped from a lion's body; for offense, he carried a javelin
55   and lance with a bright steel head. But no such armor could equal
the hero's stoutness of heart as he entered the forest of death.
Before him on every side lay the grisly remains of his comrades;
behind them, the bloated victor, licking with bloodstained tongue
the mangled remains of his victims, Cadmus' own partners and friends.
60   "You fell giving proof of devotion, loyal right to the end;
I will either avenge your passing or be your partner in death."
So he swore. Then, poising a boulder as big as a millstone,
he let it fly with a force to shake the ramparts of heaven.
The serpent ignored the blow; his scales behaved as a breastplate
65   and his black adamantine hide brushed off the ponderous missile.
But toughness did him no good against the thrust of a javelin
piercing the joints of his spine and the tender entrails beneath.
The dinosaur twisted his anguished head to gaze at the torment,
to bite at the clinging spear (thus enlarging its sad laceration),
70   at last to wrench it away from entrails mangled and screaming,
but even then the point broke off and clung to his backbone.
    This newly experienced pain only roused the furious creature;
the swollen veins of its throat poured pale and venomous foam,
to drool from its lethal jaws. The rattling noise of its scales
75   reechoed over the earth, and the Stygian° breath of its nostrils
(such as it still retained) polluted the breezes of heaven.
One moment it twisted its coils in vast and tangled contortions,
then suddenly stretched itself up, as straight as the mast of a ship.
Now it charged like a torrent swollen with rain in the springtime,
80   leveling acres of forest by its weight and momentum alone.
    Slowly the son of Agenor retreated before the beast's fury,
checking its forward rush with his buckler, the skin of a lion,
and blocking its jaws with the outthrust iron tip of his javelin.
Baffled, the dragon's mouth came clamping down on the spearhead,
85   doing no harm at all, but the poisonous blood from its palate
went spattering over the soil, staining the grass with its venom.
The wound was only a trifle; the dragon recoiled for a moment,
drawing its head from danger, by yielding preventing more damage,
while keeping the son of Agenor from following up his advantage.
90   Now Cadmus took the offensive, driving the steel at its gullet.
Back, back he drove the monster, whose retreat was finally halted
by the trunk of an ancient oak, which blocked all hope of escaping.
Cadmus' javelin flew, transfixing the neck and the oak tree;
the tree bent under its weight, and creaked as the tail of the dragon

75. *Stygian:* From Styx, a river in the underworld.

95 thrashed at its trunk, while the monster vainly struggled with death.
  Amazed by his enemy's bulk, the victor regarded his victim,
  till roused by the sound of a voice—whose or whence, he had no idea.
  But hear it he certainly did, "What, son of Agenor, still viewing
  the snake you have killed? Still alive, in the form of a serpent,
100 you too will become an object of the wondering gazes of men."°
  Shaken with fear and amazement, bereft of poise and of color,
  his hair all a-bristle in terror, Cadmus stood fixed to the spot.
  But see! a divine protectress came gliding down from the heavens,
  no other than Pallas Athena. She told him dig up a furrow
105 and bury the teeth of the dragon as seed for a new generation.
  The hero did as she told him: as soon as a furrow was finished,
  he scattered the teeth in the earth as seed of a new race of humans.
  Faster than eyes could believe, the plowland began to crack open,
  and the first keen tips of spears rose up from the soil of the furrow.
110 Then came the headgear of soldiers, nodding with colorful crests;
  shoulders and chests emerged and stout arms brandishing weapons.
  At last a whole army had grown, of bellicose shield-bearing soldiers:
  As when the curtain is lifted at the end of a play in the theater,°
  the figures painted upon it at first show only their faces,
115 then, in their leisurely rising, the rest of the body emerges,
  till firm-set feet appear at the lower edge of the curtain.
  Alarmed at the sudden appearance of the packed and menacing host,
  Cadmus felt for a weapon. "Don't draw it!" cried one of the soldiers
  newly born of the earth. "Don't meddle in other folk's quarrels!"
120 At that he thrust with his sword at a neighboring son of the earth,
  then fell with a crash at the blow of a javelin thrown from afar—
  whose owner did not survive the man he delivered to Hades,
  but breathed out the last of his breath, drawn but a moment before.
  So the whole regiment perished in crazy internecine struggle;
125 for a moment turned into brothers, each fell by his brother's stroke.
  Strong young men that they were, they lived for only a moment;
  soaking their mother's breast in blood, they groaned, then they died.
  Five of them only were left. At the warning of Pallas Athena,
  Echion, one of their number, had thrown aside all his weapons,
130 giving and asking for peace, which the other four had accepted.
  These were the only supporters to stand by Sidonian° Cadmus
  in founding the city ordained by Phoebus Apollo's instructions.

OVID, *Metamorphoses* (3.3–130)

100. . . .*gazes of men:* A prediction of Cadmus' ultimate fate, to be turned into a serpent.   113.
theater: The Greek theater had no curtain. The Roman had one, often painted, which during the
action lay rolled up at the front edge of the stage. At the end of a play it was raised to conceal the
stage.   131. *Sidonian:* Sidon was another city of Phoenicia.

Cadmus was forced to serve Ares for eight years in penance for the dragon he
had killed.[3] Once purified, he married Harmonia, daughter of the adulterous liai-

[3]Heracles and Apollo also had to serve others in penance for murder, evidently actual social practice in prehistoric Greece.

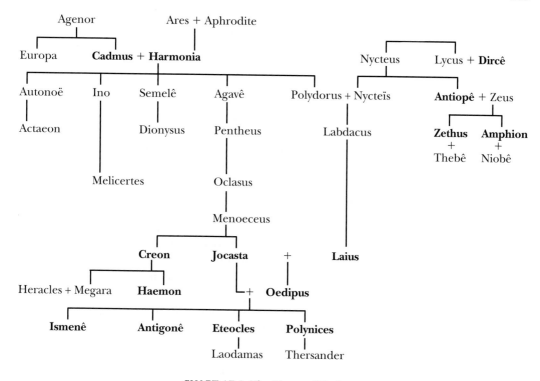

CHART 17.1. The House of Cadmus

son between Ares and Aphrodite (Chart 17.1). Their wedding was one of the two most splendid in Greek myth, the other being that of Peleus and Thetis, the parents of Achilles. The gods attended, sat in golden chairs, and sang songs of praise. For a wedding gift, Aphrodite gave Harmonia a necklace made by Hephaestus himself and a robe that gave its owner royal dignity—objects of wondrous beauty, but a jinx to whoever owned them in later generations. The children of this union were to lead accursed lives: Ino killed her own children, then jumped off a cliff; Semelê was blasted by a thunderbolt; Agavê ripped her son Pentheus to bits; Autonoë's son, Actaeon, was devoured by his own hounds.

Grown old and worn out with grief, Cadmus and Harmonia left Thebes. They wandered across the Pindus range to Illyria (modern Albania). There, too, Cadmus became king. Enfeebled by age, he and his wife were changed into serpents and sent by Zeus to live forever in the Elysian Fields.

The Twins Amphion and Zethus

After Cadmus abdicated, his grandson Pentheus ruled briefly until coming to his gruesome end (Chapter 10). The dynastic succession then becomes confused. A separate tradition reports that an otherwise unknown son of Cadmus, Polydorus, came to the throne, married a woman named Nycteïs, and then on his deathbed turned over the kingship to his wife's father, Nycteus.[4] In the meanwhile, Nycteus' other daughter, **Antiopê** (an-tī-o-pē), was seduced by Zeus and became pregnant. Shamed by her misdeed, Nycteus drove Antiopê from Thebes. Antiopê took refuge with Epopeus, a king of Sicyon in the Peloponnesus, and presently married him.

Still stinging from shame because of his daughter's behavior, Nycteus commanded his brother, Lycus (lī-kus), to avenge the family honor, then killed himself. Lycus followed Nycteus' command and mounted a campaign against Sicyon, killed Epopeus, took Antiopê prisoner, and dragged her back to Thebes. On the way, Antiopê crawled into the bushes on Mount Cithaeron and gave births to the twins she was carrying. Antiopê then returned to her Uncle Lycus, leaving the twins behind. The twins were found and raised by a shepherd, who named them **Amphion** (am-fī-on) and **Zethus** (zē-thus).

When Lycus returned to Thebes, he handed over Antiopê to his wife, **Dircê** (dir-sē), who conceived a particular hatred for the girl, locked her in a cell, and tortured her daily. Eventually Antiopê escaped her tormenters, fled to the mountains, and by chance took refuge in the hut of Amphion and Zethus. Somehow they recognized her, and, eager for revenge, tracked down Dircê, a follower of Dionysus, while she was reveling in the mountains. They tied her to a wild bull, which dragged her to death. They threw Dircê's body into a spring, ever after called Dircê, and then killed Lycus (Fig. 17.2).

While growing up, Amphion and Zethus showed themselves to be utterly opposite in nature. Zethus was a cattle breeder, a man of action and practical affairs. Naturally he scorned Amphion, who spent his time practicing the lyre. But the power of art was revealed when the two brothers set out to build the walls of Thebes, a story that describes in effect a second foundation: The first thing one does in founding a city is to build protective walls. Zethus struggled to carry mighty stones on his back, while Amphion merely strummed on his instrument; the stones rose miraculously from the ground and settled into place.

Despite their different dispositions, the brothers were friendly and ruled together in harmony. Zethus married Thebê, after whom Thebes was named, another indication that the story of Amphion and Zethus is itself a foundation myth. Amphion married Niobê, daughter of Tantalus, who bore him seven sons and seven daughters. She boasted of this achievement and jeered at Leto, who had borne only one of each sex. Apollo and Artemis avenged the insult by killing all fourteen children of Niobê (see Chapter 8).

Observations: The Two Foundings of Thebes

Most Greek colonies had stories of their foundations and the reasons for them, but the old mainland cities lacked such traditions. Why, then, should Thebes alone have two foundation stories? No one has answered this question successfully, but it is clear that separate traditions have been clumsily melded together.

---

[4]*Nycteïs* means "daughter of Nycteus."

FIG. 17.2. Death of Lycus and Dircê, on an South Italian wine-mixing bowl, c. 380 B.C. The scene seems to be inspired by a play of Euripides. To the left Dircê is trampled to death by the bull. Within a cave, the entrance framed by two trees bent together, Amphion and Zethus are killing Lycus, while Antiopê flees to the right. Hermes hovers in the air outside the cave, prophesying that the twins will have a glorious future and that Dircê will be changed into a spring. From above hangs a panther skin, a dedication to Dionysus (Dircê was a Bacchante).   (Antikenmuseum, Staatliche Museen, Berlin; F 3296)

The founding by Cadmus is an adaptation of the ancient Near Eastern myth of creation as dragon combat, whose basic pattern we examined in the story of Marduk's victory over Tiamat (Chapter 4). Cadmus kills a terrible dragon that guards a spring, as Marduk kills the monster Tiamat, who represents the primeval chaotic waters out of which the world was made. To judge from a fifth-century B.C. vase (see Fig. 17.1), the dragon-slayer's prize was a woman, Harmonia, as often in the folktale pattern.[5] Cadmus' sowing of the dragon's teeth is a variation on another Near Eastern motif, whereby the first men grow from the earth like plants. A tale that once described the origin of the world, then, has been "downgraded" to describe the origin of a city. Because the story is Eastern in origin, it is plausible that it was brought to Greece by immigrants from the East. Many have sought a historical basis underlying the legend and wondered whether Phoenicians really did found a colony at Thebes in the Bronze Age, perhaps bringing with them the ancient Mesopotamian myth of creation, an explanation supported by Cadmus' name, Semitic in origin, apparently "the man from the East."

In 1963 an astonishing hoard of forty-two Mesopotamian cylinder seals (compare Fig. 3.4) was found in a basement in the modern town of Thebes on the site of the ancient city. The hoard seemed to provide hard evidence of Eastern settlement. But the seals come from different Eastern lands and belong to different periods, the earliest from about 2500 B.C. and the latest from about 1300 B.C. Apparently a precious collection, which may have been acquired as trade or booty, was kept in a single box when the Mycenaean palace was burned about 1250 B.C. No other evidence for Eastern presence has been found in Thebes.

According to a strong tradition, Cadmus brought with him from the East something more precious than seals, called *Phoinikeia grammata,* "Phoenician scratch-

---

[5]Unless the woman represents the spirit of the spring, as some believe.

ings," or *kadmeia,* "Cadmeian things," early Greek terms for the alphabet. However, this story cannot be accurate because the Greek alphabet (which includes signs for the vowels) was invented on the basis of the Phoenician syllabary about 800 B.C. Cadmus belongs sometime in the middle of the Bronze Age, perhaps about 1600 B.C., according to mythical chronology based on counting generations. Mythographers knew that the model for the Greek alphabet came from Phoenicia, and they knew that Cadmus was a Phoenician; therefore, they reasoned, Cadmus must have introduced the alphabet.

The story of Cadmus and the dragon is a recasting of an ancient Eastern story, but that of Amphion and Zethus is a folktale of the tribulations and eventual triumph of magical twins. Foundlings lost in the world, the twins discover in the nick of time who they really are, just as the "wicked stepmother" Dircê is about to kill their mother. Deservedly, Dircê dies instead. Although on the best of terms, Amphion and Zethus are opposites in temperament, embodying a common contrast between the man of action (Zethus) and the man of intellect (Amphion), the man "good at doing" and the man "good at talking." Rome, too, had a tale about twins who founded the city, also opposites, but hating one another bitterly.

Why Thebes should have attracted two stories to explain its origins, one a creation myth and the other folktale, we cannot say, but the Thebans reconciled the stories by saying that Cadmus had founded the higher city on the Acropolis, called the *Cadmeia* (cad-**mē**-a), whereas Amphion and Zethus had walled the lower city, named after Thebê, the wife of Zethus. In any event, the mighty walls of Thebes had seven gates, about which many tales were told.

OEDIPUS THE KING

Late mythographers tried to tie the story of Amphion and Zethus to the House of Cadmus by reporting that Polydorus and Nycteïs had a son named Labdacus (**lab**-da-kus), whose son, **Laius** (**lā**-yus), fled from the confusion in Thebes to take refuge in the court of Pelops in the province of Elis in the northwestern Peloponnesus. There Laius fell in love with Chrysippus, son of Pelops. On the pretext of teaching him how to drive a chariot, Laius lured Chrysippus outside of town and raped him. For this outrage Pelops cursed Laius, who fled back to Thebes, where Amphion and Zethus had died, leaving the throne unoccupied. Laius, made king by the Thebans, married **Jocasta** (jō-**kas**-ta), a descendant of the Sparti. Learning from an oracle that he would die at the hands of his own son, Laius avoided intercourse with his wife, until one night he got wildly drunk and had intercourse with her anyway.

When Jocasta bore a son, Laius ordered that the child be exposed to die. He pinned together the child's feet with an iron pin (to keep the ghost from walking) and delivered the baby to a shepherd, with orders to leave him on the slopes of Mount Cithaeron near Thebes. However, the shepherd took pity on the child and gave it to a friend, a visitor from Corinth, who delivered the child to Polybus, king of Corinth (Fig. 17.3). His childless wife, Meropê, took the child as her own, calling him **Oedipus** (**ē**-di-pus, **e**-di-pus), which seems to mean "swollen foot."

When Oedipus was grown, some of his envious age-mates taunted him about his

FIG. 17.3. Oedipus the foundling, Attic water-jar, c. 450 B.C. A shepherd, labeled Euphorbos, carries the infant Oedipus to a man who must be Polybus, king of Corinth (not shown in photo). (Bibliothèque Nationale de France, Cabinet des Médailles, Paris)

birth, saying he was adopted. Because Meropê would tell him nothing about this, Oedipus went to Delphi to discover the truth. Instead of answering his question, the Pythia told him that he was going to kill his father and marry his mother. Thinking that the oracle referred to Polybus and Meropê, the horrified Oedipus vowed never to return to Corinth and headed east toward Thebes. At a fork, a man in a chariot came from the other direction and drove him off the road. A wheel of the chariot grazed his foot, and the man in the car struck him with his goad. In a rage, Oedipus leaped onto the chariot and killed the driver, his passenger, and all his retainers, except for one who got away.

Before long Oedipus came to Thebes, a city in turmoil. The Sphinx, a daughter of Typhoeus, had perched on a nearby hill and was devouring the Thebans one by one. Before killing her victims, the monster posed a riddle: "What goes on four legs in the morning, two at midday, and three in the evening?" Only when the riddle was answered would the Thebans be delivered of the Sphinx.

Laius, the king, had gone to Delphi to find out what to do about the situation. When his brother-in-law Creon, who ruled in his absence, heard that Laius had been killed by unknown bandits, he decreed that whoever solved the riddle and freed the city could marry the queen and become the next king.[6]

Quick-witted Oedipus quickly saw that the answer to the riddle was "a human." Infants crawl on all fours in the morning of their lives, walk on two legs in their maturity, and in the evening of their lives, old and doddering, they walk with the aid of a cane. The Sphinx was so chagrined that she threw herself from the cliff and was dashed on the rocks below (Fig. 17.4).

[6]There seems to have been a rule in dynastic succession at the time of the formation of these stories that the surviving female member of the royal line could not rule but determined, through marriage, who did. In Homer's *Odyssey* it is clear that the suitor who marries Penelopê will reign as the next king (see Chapter 21).

Gustave Moreau's *Oedipus and the Sphinx*

The Romantic painters of the late nineteenth century were interested in the myth of Oedipus, and here Gustave Moreau (1826–1898), sometimes called a Symbolist,

sets the scene in a melancholy and darkened wilderness (Fig. P 17.1). Whereas the Greek story celebrated the power of the intellect to unravel the mysteries of irrational nature, Moreau was interested in the struggle of male against female. At the forefront of the picture are the decaying feet and hands of someone who succumbed to her power. With her rear claws she supports herself against Oedipus' inner thighs, emphasizing the sexual threat, while she keeps herself aloft with beating wings. Incongruously she wears an enticing belt around her hips. Her lovely eyes look into his, but his determined lip and fierce counter-gaze show that he will be triumphant over her seduction. Moreau said that in this painting he wanted to show moral idealism pitted against sensual desire.

FIG. P 17.1. Gustave Moreau (1826–1898), *Oedipus and the Sphinx,* 1864, oil on canvas. (Metropolitan Museum of Art, New York, bequest of William H. Herriman)

Thus Oedipus married the queen and became the king. They had two sons, **Polynices** (pol-i-**nī**-sēz) and **Eteocles** (e-**tē**-o-klēz), and two daughters, **Antigonê** (an-**tig**-o-nē) and **Ismenê** (is-**mē**-nē). Our earliest literary source for the story of Oedipus is the *Odyssey*, where Odysseus, reviewing the ghosts of famous dead women, sees the mother of Oedipus, whom Homer calls Epicastê:

FIG. 17.4. Oedipus and the Sphinx, interior of Attic drinking cup, c. 490 B.C. Oedipus is shown as a mature man, fully bearded, wearing a traveler's broad-brimmed hat, his left hand poised pensively beneath his chin, his traveler's staff between his legs. He ponders the riddle of the Sphinx, presented as winged lion with a woman's head perched on an Ionic column, as it is actually found in funeral monuments.   (Museo Etrusco Gregoriano, Vatican Museum, Rome; XXXIV.2.46)

[1271]   Oedipus' mother I saw, Epicastê, famous in story.
          She, all unknowing, committed a great and terrible crime,
          marriage to her own son. Unknowing, he murdered his father,
          then married Epicastê. The gods set the pair as a warning:
1275   in lovely Thebê he reigned, over all the people of Cadmus,
          but suffered terrible things: she suspended a noose from a rafter
          and sank through the iron gate of the house of implacable Hades.
          Clutched by remorse, she bequeathed a legacy grim and undying,
          vengeance his mother's Furies relentlessly wreaked on her son.

                    HOMER, *Odyssey* (11.1271–1280)

Sophocles' *Oedipus the King*, the most famous play from the ancient world, treats this shocking story in clinical detail and seems to have added certain important elements. When the play opens, a plague has fallen on the city. Oedipus, decisive in action and attentive to the needs of his people, learns from an oracle that the plague has been caused by miasma, pollution. In the confusion caused by the Sphinx, no one had taken time to find the murderer of King Laius and punish him, so the ghost of King Laius is angry and vengeful. Oedipus, anxious to find the murderer and lift the plague, declares before the Theban people:

[224]   To all Cadmeans do I now proclaim:
225   If any of you knows by whom your king,
          Laius the son of Labdacus, was slain,
          I order him to tell me all he knows.
          But if he fear that punishment may fall

upon himself, let him remain assured

230   of amnesty: he shall remove the charge
by going into exile, nothing more.
Or, if he knows some wandering stranger guilty
of murder, let him speak the truth, to win
a great reward, and public thanks as well.

235   But if you still keep silent, fearing for yourself,
or for some friend, hear what I next propose.
I order that no dweller in the country
of which I hold the power and the throne,
shall shelter the killer, whoever he may be;

240   shall say a word to him; shall be his partner
in prayer, in sacrifice, in purification.
Rather, all men must thrust him from their homes,
for he pollutes us all. That this is true
the Pythian oracle has just assured me.

245   Taking these measures, then, I prove myself
true ally of both murdered man and god.
I hereby call down curses on this killer—
be he alone, or helped in secret crime—
that horribly, as he is horrible,

250   he may drag out his wretched unblessed days.
This too I pray: though he be of my house,
if I learn of it, and let him still remain,
may I receive the curse I have laid on others.
All this I order, on my own behalf,

255   at the god's orders, for our country's sake,
which now lies helpless, blasted, cursed by the gods.

SOPHOCLES, *Oedipus the King* (224–254)

Thus Oedipus curses himself, for the man he had killed at the crossroads was his own father, and the woman he had married was his mother, just as the oracle foretold. The rest of Sophocles' play is a masterful unfolding of how these terrible events have come to pass. Oedipus summons the blind seer Tiresias, who at first refuses to speak. When Oedipus accuses him of conspiring with Creon, Tiresias blurts out the fantastic truth. Oedipus dismisses it out of hand and turns against Creon, suspecting him of aiming at the throne. But he is shaken by the close correspondence between the death of Laius and his own experience at the crossroads.

A messenger arrives to inform Oedipus that his "father," Polybus, has died, and that he may now succeed to the throne of Corinth. Although grieving for Polybus, Oedipus is relieved at seeming proof that oracles are fallible; he did not kill his father after all. Still, he decides not to return to Corinth for fear that he might somehow marry his mother. He need not worry on that account, the messenger points out, for he is, in fact, not the son of Polybus and Meropê. The messenger himself had given Oedipus, a foundling, to the king to raise, having received him from a shepherd on Mount Cithaeron. Whose son, then, is he?

Jocasta realizes the truth and leaves the stage. Oedipus summons an old shepherd, the only survivor of the massacre at the crossroads, who by an extraordinary chance was the very man to whom Laius once delivered his infant son. Out of pity, the shepherd admits, he gave the child to the Corinthian messenger. Oedipus too sees the truth and rushes into the palace. After a song by the chorus, a messenger reports the fate of the queen and what Oedipus did when he found her:

[1241]   Frenzied, Jocasta rushed inside the house
   and flung herself upon her marriage bed,
   tearing her hair with both her maddened hands.
   She slammed and locked the door by which she entered
1245 and cried the name of Laius, long since dead,
   joined with his son's, the man he once begat,
   at whose hand he then died, leaving her to mother
   sons by her son—a dreadful generation.
   How then she died I cannot know or tell,
1250 for Oedipus burst in with cries of torment,
   preventing us from gazing on her end—
   for all our eyes were riveted on him,
   as he stormed about and clamored for his sword.
    "Where will I find the wife who is no wife?"
1255 he cried, "the womb twice plowed, twice harvested,
   of me at first, then later of my children?"
   Some demon, doubtless, pointed out the way
   to the frenzied king; it surely was none of us.
   With madman's scream he charged the double doors,
1260 led by some guiding instinct, dragged the bolts
   from out their pair of sockets, and ran inside.
    Hanged from the ceiling, there we saw his wife,
   choked by a twisted rope around her neck.
   Oedipus saw her too. With a piteous groan
1265 he loosed the throttling noose around her throat.
   Her huddled body lay there at his feet,
   a piteous sight, but worse was still to come.
   He ripped the golden pins from off her robe,
   raised them on high, and plunged them in his eyes,
1270 choking out words of anguish, such as these:
   "Never again will these eyes ever watch
   me doing or suffering what I have done or suffered!
   Only in inner darkness of my soul
   shall I hereafter see the faces of those
1275 I never should have seen,° nor shall I fail
   to see the missing forms, for which I longed."°
    Cursing himself, again, and yet again,
   he slashed his eyes, and with each frenzied blow
   the bleeding sockets dripped down on his beard,
1280 until at the last the drops became a storm.

       SOPHOCLES, *Oedipus the King* (1241–1279)

1275. . . . *have seen:* That is, his mother as his wife and his children as his brothers and sisters.
1276. . . . *for which I longed:* His father and mother as parents rather than as victims.

Gore streaming from his face, Oedipus returns to the stage and begs to be sent into exile. The actual blinding is not seen by the audience—this would be too horrible—but is reported by a servant.

Observations: Heroic Sufferer for Truth or Victim of Curiosity?

Oedipus usually is called a "hero," although he does not have divine parents, and we need not look far to uncover familiar elements: His unusual birth is expected, as are his journey and his mission to save the world from unruly monsters, as are the deadly danger of woman and his mysterious death. Yet the tenor of the story, focused on parricide and incest, and the difference between being and seeming, is very different from that of stories about Gilgamesh, Heracles, and Theseus. We saw long ago, in the stories Hesiod tells, how the organizers of the cosmos, Cronus and Zeus, overthrew their own fathers to establish the world, while Gaea, mother of the world, was also its enemy; here, in heroic legend, Oedipus kills his father but creates only chaos, whereas the ambiguity of the female receives a surprising twist by being represented within the context of the human family: As Jocasta gave birth to Oedipus, so does her protective love destroy him.

Homer knows the essential elements of the story, that Oedipus killed his father and married his mother, but says nothing about Oedipus' self-blinding. This detail may be Sophocles' own invention, appealing to the Athenian taste for horror and gore. In Homer, Oedipus continues as king after the truth is discovered; in Sophocles' play, he becomes a homeless outcast. Aristotle saw in Sophocles' *Oedipus the King* the perfect tragedy because in it the two essential elements in a good plot come together at the same moment: *anagnorisis,* "recognition," when the identity of someone previously unknown or in disguise is revealed, and *peripeteia,* "a turning around," when the leading actor's fortunes turn from good to bad. When Oedipus recognizes who the murderer really is, his fortunes turn around. He ceases to be the wise king and savior of his people and is revealed to be a man who has violated the deepest taboos of his society.

Earlier critics saw in Oedipus a victim of fate, a plaything of the gods. Whatever he did to escape the oracle's prediction only brought him closer to its fulfillment. But foreknowledge is not fate. Although Jesus predicted to Peter that "Before the cock crows, you will deny me three times," Peter might have chosen otherwise. Nor do the gods compel Oedipus to know what he has done. The power of the story lies in the spectacle of a man who freely chooses to pursue the truth, regardless of the consequences, even his own ruin. Oedipus is a man of high intelligence who solved the riddle of the Sphinx and saved the city. He is a man of action who defended himself at the crossroads and slew his attacker. To our minds, conditioned by two thousand years of Christian ethics, he may appear violent, hasty, and overconfident, but the Greeks would not have seen that. In their eyes Oedipus had no moral fault: He wants to obey the will of the gods, as conveyed through Apollo's instructions, and to save his people. He applies his intelligence and courage to discover the truth for the benefit of the citizens he serves. He freely chooses a course leading to his own undeserved disaster.

Everything that seems true about Oedipus is false, the reverse of appearance. He is a study in the contrast between being and appearance. He thinks he is a Corinthian, but he is Theban born. He is a decipherer of riddles, but cannot solve, until too late, the riddle of his own life. In the city he is judge of right and wrong, but he is the worst of criminals. He is a seer who is blind. He is Thebes' savior and its destroyer. The greatest of men, comparable even to the gods, and an honored ruler, he is also the worst of men, worse than an animal, a despised outcast and object of horror. He who raised himself to the highest rank is reduced to the lowest.

At first unquestioned monarch, Oedipus becomes the *pharmakos,* "scapegoat," a loathsome pariah on whose head all society's sins are heaped. Like the scapegoat in real Greek religious ritual, he is driven from the community of men, carrying with him the pollution that curses all his fellows. He must die neglected, apart from human society. Early in Sophocles' drama, Oedipus accepts his role of *pharmakos,* which the gods have imposed on him:

> My suffering subjects, all too well I know
> how sick at heart you are; but know you this:
> sick though you are, none is as sick as I.
> The pangs that strike you strike one man alone,
> and no one else. But my poor spirit weeps
> at once for city, citizens, and self.

> SOPHOCLES, *Oedipus the King* (59–64)

Here is a riddle: What can walk on four legs, two legs, and three legs? The answer is humans. Here is another: How can someone be brother to his own children and husband to his mother? The answer is Oedipus. Oedipus solves both riddles, first saving Thebes, then destroying himself. He is savior, who thwarted the Sphinx, and destroyer, who brought the plague. Both riddles have the same answer: Oedipus embodies the restless human intelligence, always prying and never letting go until every riddle is solved. That the truth should be horrible is typically Greek in its pessimism; when the riddle is solved, human happiness is shown to be based on illusion.

The power of Greek myth is never clearer than in the story of Oedipus. Writers who knew little about ancient culture have attempted to elucidate it (see Chapter 23), and it has often been recast by artists and literary figures. The old myth has generated new myths, as such interpretations have been called, stories sprung from the human imagination and themselves requiring interpretation. Yet Sophocles' play, one of the masterworks of human culture, remains as mysterious and disturbing as ever.

THE SEVEN AGAINST THEBES

Oedipus' sons, Eteocles and Polynices, agreed to share the power of the city equally, one ruling one year, the other the next. But after the first year Eteocles, whose name means "true glory," refused to relinquish the power and drove his brother Polynices, "filled with contention," from the city. Polynices fled to Argos, taking with him the necklace and robe the gods gave to Harmonia at her wedding.

Adrastus, king of Argos, had learned from an oracle that he must "yoke his daughters to a boar and a lion." He did not understand the meaning of this saying, until one stormy night he heard a loud clamor in the forecourt outside the palace. He rushed out and discovered Polynices fighting with **Tydeus** (tī-dūs), son of Oeneus,[7] who had been exiled for homicide from Calydon (in Aetolia, across the Corinthian Gulf in the southwestern mainland). When Adrastus saw that one man had a boar painted on his shield, the other a lion, he realized the meaning of the oracle, settled the quarrel, and married them to his daughters. Furthermore, he agreed to restore Polynices and Tydeus to their kingdoms. First they would attack Thebes, then Calydon.

Adrastus summoned his chieftains for a great campaign. Among the heroes came **Amphiaraüs** (am-fi-a-**rā**-us), a seer of the first rank. Amphiaraüs, realizing that all the leaders except for Adrastus were going to die, argued vehemently against the war. His efforts were in vain for this reason: Much earlier, Amphiaraüs had accidentally killed Adrastus' father in a riot, a crime for which Adrastus never forgave him. In an attempt to bridge their differences, Adrastus arranged for his sister **Eriphylê** (e-ri-**fī**-lē) to marry Amphiaraüs, and the brothers-in-law agreed in any future quarrel to allow Eriphylê to decide the issue. Still, Adrastus nourished his resentment against Amphiaraüs and now saw his chance to even the score. He told Polynices about the agreement, and Polynices offered Eriphylê the necklace of Harmonia if she would decide the dispute about the coming war in Adrastus' (and his own) favor (Fig. 17.5). Amphiaraüs could only accept the decision, but before leaving he told his sons to avenge his inevitable death.

The army set out. Seven heroes led the way: Adrastus, Amphiaraüs, Capaneus (**kap**-a-nūs), and Hippomedon, all from the leading houses of Argos; Polynices from Thebes; Tydeus from Calydon; and Parthenopeus from Arcadia.

Oedipus at Colonus

In his last play,[8] produced in the year after his death in 406 B.C., Sophocles describes the last days of Oedipus. The army of the Seven is marching toward Thebes when the blind old man, exiled from Thebes and accompanied only by his daughter Antigonê, wanders into the Grove of the Furies at Colonus, a beautiful suburb of Athens. The chorus of inhabitants, learning who he is, warns the accursed Oedipus to leave the grove so that it will not be polluted, and they send for Theseus. Meanwhile, Ismenê, daughter of Oedipus and sister of Antigonê, arrives to tell about the quarrel of the brothers and to report that Delphi has declared that whichever city possesses the bones of Oedipus cannot be captured. For this reason, Creon (representing Eteocles) and Polynices both appear and try to abduct Oedipus, until The-

---

[7]Tydeus was a half-brother to Deianira (Chapter 14) and to Meleager (Chapter 18).

[8]Sophocles, then eighty-nine years old, was sued by his sons, who wanted control of his property, on grounds of mental incapacity. Instead of answering their charges, he read the first chorus of the still-unfinished *Oedipus at Colonus* to the court. The jurors immediately threw out the case.

FIG. 17.5. Polynices bribes Eriphylê with the necklace of Harmonia, on an Attic wine-jug, c. 450 B.C. Leaning on his staff and wearing a traveler's cap, he has removed the necklace from a box and dangles it over her extended hand. Shamelessly Eriphylê meets his eyes: The iconography is the same as when a young man propositions a prostitute. A long-necked bird stands between them. (Museo Provinciale, Lecce; 570 Deutsches Archaeologisches Institut, Rome)

seus orders them to leave. But first the furious Oedipus curses Polynices and his brother and predicts their fate:

[1354]   And as for you, you hypocrite, you who once
1355   held the same power that now your brother holds,
         you drove me out from Thebes—me, your own father!—
         and made me homeless, reducing me to tatters
         that now draw forth your tears, now that you too
         have met with misery as great as mine.
1360   I shall not weep for wrongs so long ago,
         whose burden I must bear until I die,
         never forgetting you, my parricide.
         You are the man who brought me down to this;
         you drove me out; by your doing I must wander,
1365   begging my daily bread from kindly strangers.
         These girls I raised, but not to be my nurses.
         Except for them, I would by now be dead,
         for all you cared. They alone preserve me,
         they stand beside me, sharing all my troubles.
1370   They are true men, not women. As for you,
         the pair of you are bastards, not my sons.
            The gods are watching, with unhurried gaze,
         not as they will, if all those troops of yours

are marching against Thebes. There is no way
1375 for you to take the city; before that day appears,
you will lie weltering in your blood—your brother too.
That curse I laid on the pair of you long ago,°
that curse I now call back to my defense;
that you two may learn that parents must be honored,
1380 blind though your father was, begetting such as you.
Your sisters here committed no such sin.
Not prayers, not royal state, will help you now
against my curse, if ancient justice still
sits in her place beside the laws of Zeus.
1385   Get out! I spit you out and I disown you!
Get out, you slimy thing, bearing this added curse
which I pronounce: your spear will never
win back your homeland, nor will you ever again
see hill-girt Argos. By your own brother's hand
1390 your doom will come, his from you whom he banished.
This is my curse. To bring it all to pass,
I invoke Hell's awful dark to call you home;
I summon the Furies, worshiped in this spot;
and with them Warfare, who stirred up your hate.
1395 Now you have heard me, go. Tell all the Thebans,
tell all your loyal allies, "this is the legacy
that Oedipus is leaving to his sons."

SOPHOCLES, *Oedipus at Colonus* (1354–1396)

1377. . . . *long ago:* Apparently Oedipus refers to the time when his sons failed to give him the best cut of meat from a sacrifice, and he cursed them for it (reported in the lost epic the *Thebaïs*).

Peals of thunder warn Oedipus that his time has come. He withdraws into the grove, blesses his daughters, and in the presence of Theseus disappears mysteriously. A messenger reports his end:

[1647]   So we withdrew. Then presently we turned,
but found the man was nowhere to be seen.
Theseus alone we saw, who raised his hands
1650 before his face, as if to shade his eyes
from some tremendous horror unfit for human view.
A moment passed. We saw him make his prayer
at once to Earth and to the Olympian gods.
    How Oedipus departed from this life
1655 no mortal man could say, save only Theseus.
No fire-blazing bolt came from on high,
no whirlwind from the sea was blowing then,
to take him off. Perhaps some herald
came from the gods; perhaps the earth below
1660 opened in pity doors to its dark pit.
He died unweeping, suffering no pain—
a wondrous death, if ever mortal's was.

SOPHOCLES, *Oedipus at Colonus* (1647–1665)

Tydeus at Thebes

When the Argive army came to Mount Cithaeron, they sent Tydeus ahead to Thebes to persuade Eteocles to step down. What happened next we learn from the *Iliad*. The Greek commander Agamemnon is trying to shame the hero Diomedes, Tydeus' son, into aggressive action by reminding him of his father's deeds in the campaign against Thebes:

[370]   "Well, well! Just look at the son of shrewd and valiant old Tydeus!
        Why are you skulking back here, instead of advancing to battle?
        He never used to cringe like this, away from the fighting,
        but rather would always be first to lead his friends to the fray.
        So those who saw him in action report; I never met him myself,
375   but they say that no one on earth was a better fighter than he.
        For example, in time of peace he once went into Mycenae,
        along with his friend Polynices, recruiting troops for his army,
        in the days when he was assaulting the mighty ramparts of Thebê.
        They asked the city to give them a troop of experienced soldiers.
380   The rulers gladly consented to the terms of the application,
        but Zeus sent signs and portents that changed Mycenae's decision.
        They set out, nevertheless, and were well along on their road,
        having reached the reeds of Asopus,° the river of soft grassy meadows.
        There once more the Achaeans sent Tydeus forth to a parley.
385   Into the city of Thebes he went, to find that all the Cadmeans
        had gathered to feast together in mighty Eteocles' palace.
        Tydeus, leader of horsemen, although a stranger and all alone
        in the midst of a countless number of angry hostile Cadmeans,
        fearlessly challenged them all to competition in wrestling,
390   and easily pinned them all, for Athena helped him, when needed.
        So the vengeful Cadmean horsemen, smarting in humiliation,
        fifty young men all told, laid an ambush, carefully plotted,
        to trap him as he went back. It was led by two noble leaders,
        Maeon the son of Haemon, a man with a godlike appearance,
395   and Polyphontes, the son of Autophonus, dogged in battle.
        But Tydeus brought death and disgrace to all, one only excepted:
        Maeon, whom he sent home, for a god so ordered by portents.
        That was a wonderful man indeed, the Aetolian Tydeus!
        The man he begat is feebler in war, though a far better speaker."

                                           HOMER, *Iliad* (4.370–400)

383. *Asopus:* A river in southern Boeotia.

Homer's story is patterned after the folktale of the mysterious stranger who appears in the king's court, makes demands, defeats all comers in impossible contests, and when ambushed kills all (but one) of his attackers.

The Battle before Thebes

The army arrived before seven-gated Thebes. There were seven heroes on either side, an Argive to attack each gate, a Theban to defend. Aeschylus, in his play *Seven against Thebes* (467 B.C.), placed into a messenger's mouth a description of the arrival of the Argive army and the Thebans' response:

[39]   Eteocles, most noble ruler of the Cadmeans,
40   Fresh from the army I am here with news,
        myself an eyewitness of all that happened.
        Seven aggressive officers met together
        to cut a bull's throat over an iron shield.
        They dipped their hands into the blood he shed
45   and swore an oath, by Ares and his mother,°
        and by the bloodthirsty Panic of the Battle:
        "Either we level Thebes and plunder its ruins,
        or we die and soak this whole land in our blood."
        With their own hands they decked Adrastus' chariot
50   with tokens for their parents back at home,
        stained with their tears. None spoke a word of grief,
        for their iron spirits burned to show their fire,
        hot as the wrath of lions glaring for war.
        No hesitation makes this news grow cold;
55   I left them just as they were drawing lots,
        allowing chance to say against which gate
        each officer should lead his faithful band.
        Since things stand thus, select your bravest men
        and station them at the mouths of the city gates,
60   each with his own command, to guard the town.
        Hurry! for the well-trained Argive army
        is advancing fast. Its dust makes dark the air;
        the foam of its panting horses stains the ground.
        You, like a skilled sea-captain, have the duty
65   to batten down the city's hatches, before
        the hurricane of war can roll her over.
        Just so this war on land screams down upon us;
        let him whose mind is quickest now take charge.

AESCHYLUS, *Seven against Thebes* (39–65)

45. *his mother:* Hera.

Tiresias informed the Thebans that they could win the war only if Creon's son, Menoeceus, were sacrificed to Ares. Overhearing this, Menoeceus willingly killed himself outside one of the gates. The Theban heroes drew lots for the gates they would defend: Eteocles found himself paired with his brother, Polynices.

When the battle began, the Thebans were soon driven back into the city. Capaneus threw a ladder against the walls and climbed to the top, exclaiming that not even Zeus could stop him, but a thunderbolt from the clear sky cast him to his death. For a while the battle turned against the Argives: The Theban hero Melanippus dueled with Tydeus, and each was mortally wounded. Athena loved Tydeus and begged Zeus to give her a potion of immortality, but Amphiaraüs, who hated Tydeus for favoring the war, knew her intention. He quickly cut off Melanippus' head and brought it to the dying, vengeful Tydeus, who broke open his enemy's skull, scooped

FIG. 17.6. Tydeus kills Ismenê, on a Corinthian water-jar, c. 560 B.C. The figures are labeled. We do not have literary versions for all myths represented in Greek art, and the myth depicted here is unexplained in surviving sources. Tydeus, one of the Seven against Thebes, naked and with sword drawn, is about to kill Ismenê, who reclines half-naked on a couch. Periclymenus, one of the Theban heroes who fought the Seven, also naked, runs away, apparently caught in the act of intercourse with Ismenê. On the far left is a mounted youth, labeled Clytus (otherwise unknown).
(Musée du Louvre, Paris; Hirmer Fotoarchiv)

out the brains, and gulped down the blood. He was drooling clots of gray matter when Athena came to his side. In disgust she dashed the potion to the ground, and Tydeus died (but see Fig. 17.6). Amphiaraüs fled in his chariot, but as he was about to be speared in the back, Zeus (who loves seers) caused the ground to open and swallow him alive. In classical times the hero gave oracles from a shrine near where he disappeared.

Eteocles and Polynices met in hand-to-hand combat and each killed the other, as their father had predicted. A passage describing the duel comes from Euripides' *Phoenician Women*[9] (about 411 B.C.), the longest extant Greek tragedy, which recounts the entire Theban saga:

[1359]   Girding their bodies in shining brazen armor,
1360   the pair of sons of poor old Oedipus
  marched out and halted in the no-man's land
  between the armies, each ready to display
  in single combat his prowess with the spear.
    Facing toward Argos, Polynices prayed,
1365   "My lady Hera—mine, since I wed the daughter
  of King Adrastus, and dwell within your land—

[9]So called from the chorus of Phoenician women, uninvolved in the action, who have stopped in Thebes on their way to Delphi.

grant me my wish, that I may kill my brother,
and soak my hand as victor in his blood."
A shameful gift he asked—his brother's murder.
1370   Many an eye shed tears at this mad jest of fate,
as furtive eye met furtive eye of neighbor.
    Turned to the house of golden-shielded Pallas,
Eteocles begged this: "O child of Zeus,
control my audacious spear, that it may fly
1375   straight from this hand into my brother's heart,
and waste the man who came to waste my city."
    The trumpet-blast of the Tyrrhenian horn°
burst on our ears, a blood-red call to battle.
They ran a dreadful race straight toward each other
1380   and clashed like savage boars whetting their teeth,
the white foam slavering down to soak their chins.
Each hurled his spear, then ducked behind his shield,
from which the other's harmless dart would glance.
Whenever either noticed the other's eye
1385   peeping above his shield's rim, he stabbed out,
hoping to get in first with his deadly point.
But both were skillful at dodging the other,
and thus their brandished spears did them no good.
Indeed, from fear their friends might suffer damage,
1390   the watchers sweated more than did the actors.
    A stone beneath Eteocles' foot
rolled as he stepped; he kicked it to the side,
and for a moment lost the shield's defense
for his bare shank. Polynices darted forward,
1395   glanced at the mark thus offered to his spear,
and drove the point clear through his brother's calf,
while all the Argive army jumped and cheered.
But Eteocles, though wounded, saw that his brother
in his eagerness had left a shoulder bare;
1400   he hurled his lance clean through his brother's breast.
The Cadmeans' hearts leaped up—but the point broke off.
Now weaponless, he staggered back a pace,
picked up a rock and threw it at Polynices,
snapping his spear in half. On equal terms
1405   once more, but empty-handed, they faced each other.
    Each took his sword in hand and charged the other;
their shields collided with a brazen clang.
Back, forth, they struggled, fighting hand to hand.
Eteocles remembered a Thessalian gambit,
1410   something he learned while traveling in that land.
He took one backward step onto his left foot,
keeping his eye fixed on his brother's belly,
then swung with his whole weight onto his right.
The sword transfixed the side of Polynices,

1377. *Tyrrhenian horn:* A horn of Etruscan manufacture.

1415 and stuck between his lower vertebrae.
The poor man fell, contorting ribs and belly,
coughing his life out in spouts of crimson blood.
Eteocles, convinced that he was winning—
nay, that he had already won—the battle,
1420 dropping his sword to earth, began to strip
his brother's armor. Intent on that alone,
he took no thought for guarding his own safety,
an oversight that killed him. For Polynices
though gasping out his last tormented breath,
1425 still clutched his sword, and painfully, feebly
(for he himself had been the first to fall),
managed to thrust it through his brother's vitals.
So side by side the brothers fell to earth,
one by the other; thus they shared the realm.

EURIPIDES, *The Phoenician Women* (1359–1424)

Only Adrastus escaped, in his chariot drawn by the magical horse Arion (a-rī-on).[10]

SOPHOCLES' *ANTIGONÊ*

What happened after the battle is the subject of Sophocles' *Antigonê*, his best-known play after *Oedipus the King* and, in nineteenth-century Europe, thought by many critics to be the finest literary creation of all time. Creon, now the king, has cast out the corpses of the attackers, including Polynices, to rot on the Theban plain. They are not to receive proper burial, and anyone defying the edict will be punished by death. Still, Antigonê is determined to bury Polynices. She declares her intention to Ismenê, who cannot believe that Antigonê plans to defy the king's decree and will not help her. Antigonê insists that her first duty is to family and to ancient custom; her duty to the modern state and its capricious decrees comes far behind.

When Creon, cast as a political strongman (a type familiar to Sophocles' audience), learns that someone has cast a handful of dust on the corpse, he immediately suspects a political conspiracy. He is astonished when Antigonê, a *parthenos* and a member of his own family, engaged to marry to his son **Haemon** (hē-mon), is dragged before him as the culprit. True to his vision of the *polis* and its rights, which transcend the archaic emotional attachments of the ancient family, he condemns her to death:

[441] *Creon*   You there, with eyes fixed on the ground for shame,
do you admit this, or deny your guilt?
Antigonê   I admit it proudly; this I don't deny.
Creon   Then tell me this, and keep your story short:
[445] did you know that my decree forbade the deed?
Antigonê   Like everyone else, I knew. Just what did you expect?

[10]Begotten of the union of Poseidon and Demeter. Although the goddess took the form of a mare to escape the lustful sea god, Poseidon changed to a stallion and covered her.

Creon   But still you dared to flout the city's law?
Antigonê   I did indeed; that law was not prescribed by Zeus,
nor are such rules laid down for us by Justice,
[450]   who works with even those dark gods below.
I cannot think your law could have such force
that you, mere man, could negate the unwritten
inviolable statutes of the gods.
They are not of today or yesterday,
[455]   but live forever; none knows when they were given.
I do not so fear one man's selfish plans
that I would pay the price the gods demand
from those who break their laws. Of course I knew,
even without your edict: I must die.
[460]   If I die before my time, so much the better.
Whoever lives in endless pain, like me,
must surely take death as his greatest prize.
I am not worried at my own destruction,
but—leave my brother's rotting corpse unburied?
[465]   that is a thing that really gives me pause.
In your eyes I'm a fool, but—just perhaps—
the fool is he who charges me with folly. . . .
Creon   Remember, to be too rigid risks collapse.
Iron, if smelted in too hot a furnace,
[470]   may snap and shatter. I have seen fiery horses
tamed by a tiny bit. Pride has no place
in slaves obeying what their neighbors order.
This woman knew quite well what she was doing
then, when she broke the law's express command,
[475]   and now she glories in the things she's done!
I am no man; that name belongs to her,
if she can act thus, and get off unharmed.
She is my sister's child, my closest kin
of all who bow before the family altar.
[480]   Yet she and her sister cannot avoid their fate. . . .
Antigonê   You caught me; you'll kill me. What more do you want?
Creon   Nothing at all. With that, I've everything I need.
Antigonê   Why wait, then? I disagree with all you say,
and always will. Our thoughts will always jar.
[485]   But how could I have won a greater glory
than that of laying my brother in his grave?
The citizens of Thebes would all support me,
If fear did not put fetters on their tongues.
But tyrants, who enjoy so many blessings,
[490]   can do or say whatever they may please.
Creon   In all of Thebes, you alone hold this delusion.
Antigonê   The people all agree, but dare not speak.
Creon   Have you no modesty, to fight this stubborn fight?
Antigonê   Where is the shame in honoring my own kin?
[495]   *Creon*   And was his enemy your brother too?
Antigonê   He was indeed, to the same parents born.

Creon   Why, then, shame him by honoring the other?
Antigonê   The dead men's views may differ much from yours.
Creon   Does the patriot win less honor than the traitor?
[500]   *Antigonê*   Not just my slave, but my own brother, died.
Creon   But one invading, one defending Thebes.
Antigonê   Hades applies his equal laws to both.
Creon   How can the good and bad deserve the same?
Antigonê   How can we know what those below find pure?
[505]   *Creon*   No enemy becomes a friend by dying.
Antigonê   Not enmity, but friendship, rules my nature.
Creon   Go seek your friends in Hell, if you want friends!
No woman rules me, not while I'm alive!

Antigonê's sister, Ismenê, enters and wants to share the blame, but Antigonê harshly reproves her for wanting to take the glory once the deed is done. Then:

[544]   *Ismenê*   How can I go on living, lacking her support?
[545]   *Creon*   Don't speak her name. She's now as good as dead.
Ismenê   You really mean to slay your own son's bride?
Creon   Why not? Let him plow in other fields.
Ismenê   But none so fitting, both for her and him.
Creon   Disgusting thought, that my sons take treacherous wives!
[550]   *Antigonê*   Haemon, beloved, do you hear your father's slander?
Creon   I've had enough of you and of your marriage!
Death is at hand to cancel the wedding feast. . . .
Tie up these women, guards, or they'll slip off;
Even the bravest try to run away,
555   when they see Death come marching toward their life.

SOPHOCLES, Antigonê (441–581)

Haemon comes to his father and pleads that he yield, but Creon will not and in anger threatens even Haemon with death, so overriding is the obligation of the leader of the *polis* to uphold the public interest. Creon sends Antigonê to a cave to be buried alive; like Persephonê, she will be the bride of Death.

Tiresias reports unsavory omens in the city and warns Creon to retract his harsh decree. At last relenting, the king goes to the cave to release Antigonê. When he arrives, he finds Haemon clinging to Antigonê's corpse: She has hanged herself. Maddened with anger and grief, Haemon draws his sword and lunges at his father, misses, then buries the blade in his own chest. Creon hurries back to the palace. His wife, hearing of Haemon's suicide, has killed herself as well. "Lead me away. I've been hasty and foolish," Creon concludes, but softens his responsibility by adding: "Savage Fate has ruled my course."

Observations: Revenge of the *Parthenos*

Sophocles' fine drama manages to express all the principal conflicts in the human condition: between women and men, old and young, state and family, the living and the dead, humans and gods. Such conflicts can never be resolved, but only dealt with, and the characters in this play deal with them very badly.

The story takes place at several levels. First, the political. Viewers side with Antigonê, who touches the audience with her fire and righteous indignation, whereas Creon repels with his insistence on law and the rights of society. Although the head of the state, to the contemporary Athenian, Creon is transparent as the sort of tyrant ("I am the law!") against which the Athenian democracy struggled both within and without. In history, such a man was Pisistratus and his sons of the sixth century B.C., whose power was overthrown by violence. The danger was always strong that one man would gain enough personal power to be a king, to end the power of the *demos,* the body of adult male warriors. Civil authority in Athens had almost within memory become transcendent over the family, yet the family remained the basis of society. Its obligations were entirely real. Antigonê's voice is the "voice of the people," what everybody wants. A conservative, she advocates the old ways of family right against the modern authority of the state. It was the family's obligation to bury its own dead, or they would be the first to suffer from an offended ghost, and no decree is going to change that. The play embodies a deep contradiction: If the people's voice is heard, how can progress be made? If the people's voice is drowned, where is freedom? Antigonê is ferocious in her knowledge that she is right and, like all vigilantes, she is proud to take the law into her own hands. Creon, by contrast, advocates civic law supported by a community united through common economic and political interests that transcend the ties of blood. A progressive, he scorns such primitive religious commandments as justify Antigonê's actions but also justify human sacrifice and cannibalism. By forcing Creon to kill her, Antigonê, although weak, female, and a child, places in jeopardy all that Creon stands for. Creon, with his impulsive and artificial laws of the *polis,* must gain his power from those he rules, and he has lost their confidence.

Second, there is a philosophical level to the play: Contemporary debate was heated over the conflict between the laws of custom (*nomos*), whence Creon derives his authority, and the laws of nature (*physis*), whence Antigonê derives hers. It is "natural" to bury one's brother, and she gains her courage from the gods, who will justify her in the other world.

Third, the play is a study in the power of the untamed female. Creon constantly expresses conflict with Antigonê in these terms: She, the female, is determining the action, is acting on the male, while he, the male, is being acted upon. Antigonê, still a *parthenos,* is untamed by the marriage prepared for her, and no power on earth can stop her destructive force—not law, family, persuasion, or threat. Alone and unaided she unravels the state. Creon, the man of tyrannical reason, is wrecked by an indignant and emotional girl more suicidal than unafraid of death. Even today the state is almost helpless against fanatical individuals prepared to die for traditional views.

THE EPIGONI

While Oedipus' family destroyed itself at Thebes, Adrastus escaped to Athens and took refuge at the Altar of Mercy. Theseus took pity on him and his dead companions and led an expedition to Thebes. He forced the Thebans to allow the Argives to bury their dead, an act celebrated again and again by Athenian politicians, proud of their city's righteous mythical past. Evadnê, wife of Capaneus, threw herself on her husband's funeral pyre and was burned alive.[11]

Ten years later the sons of the original seven, called the **Epigoni** (e-**pig**-o-nē), "descendants," organized a second expedition. Eriphylê was bribed again, now with the robe of Harmonia, which had fallen into the hands of Polynices' son, Thersander. She persuaded her sons Alcmeon and Amphilochus to go on the campaign; they obeyed and besieged the city. The ruler of Thebes was now Laodamas, son of Eteocles. On the advice of Tiresias, the Thebans fled by night. Tiresias himself died on the way. Either Alcmeon killed Laodamas, or Laodamas survived to lead his people to Illyria (roughly, modern Albania).

The Epigoni took the city and sacked it. Ten years before, Amphiaraüs had ordered Alcmeon to kill Eriphylê for sending him to his death with the Seven. Encouraged by the Delphic oracle, Alcmeon now carried out his father's orders. Driven insane by this deed and polluted by miasma, he wandered through Greece. Wherever he went, the land became barren. An oracle told him to find a land that did not exist at the time he committed the matricide. When he came to the mouth of the Acheloüs river, where a delta was newly formed, the river god Acheloüs purified Alcmeon of his crime and gave him his daughter Callirhoê as wife. Callirhoê bore Acarnan, eponym of Acarnania, a province of western Greece adjacent to Aetolia. There Alcmeon might have lived happily ever after, but his wife heard about the famous necklace and robe of Harmonia and insisted on having them. While trying to recover these dangerous objects, Alcmeon was ambushed and murdered.

KEY TERMS

FURTHER READING

Berkowitz, Lucy, and T. F. Brunner, trans. and eds., *Oedipus Tyrannus: A New Translation, Passages from Ancient Authors, Religion and Psychology: Some Studies, Criticism* (New York, 1970).

[11]A proper Hindu widow was expected to act in this way, a practice called suttee, common until the British put an end to it in the eighteenth century. There is no other example in Greek myth.

A good overview of the wide range of critical interpretations, ancient and modern, inspired by this play.

Edmunds, Lowell, *Oedipus: The Ancient Legend and Its Later Analogues* (Baltimore, 1985). Collects all the ancient variants of this myth and later examples of similar stories.

Edwards, Ruth B., *Kadmos the Phoenician: A Study in Greek Legends and the Mycenaean Age* (Amsterdam, 1979). Thorough review of the myth: its origins, relations with Eastern sources, and general conclusions about the value of Greek legend for the study of the Bronze Age.

Knox, Bernard, *The Heroic Temper: Studies in Sophoclean Tragedy* (Berkeley, Calif., 1964). Good overall study, with emphasis on character.

——, *Oedipus at Thebes* (New York, 1984). An in-depth study of the social and intellectual background to the play, plus interpretation, by a leading classical scholar.

Mullahy, Patrick, *Oedipus: Myth and Complex* (New York, 1948; reprinted 1955). Interpretations of this myth according to the psychological theories of Freud, Jung, Adler, Rank, Sullivan, Horney, and Fromm.

Steiner, George, *Antigones* (New York, 1981). Reviews treatments of the story of Antigonê throughout European literature.

CHAPTER 18

JASON AND THE MYTHS OF IOLCUS AND CALYDON

No ship has ever come near these moving rocks and escaped them,
for waves of the sea and fiery blasts bring them all to destruction.
Their timbers swirl to and fro with the rotting bones of the sailors.
One vessel alone has sailed through, the *Argo*, famous in story,
sailing over the sea on her way to the land of Aeëtes.
And surely she would have foundered, striking these terrible rocks,
but Hera let her go safely for the sake of Jason, her favorite.

HOMER, Odyssey 12.66–72.

THESSALY, the widest plain in Greece, was the northernmost mainland outpost of the Hellenes before colonization in the Archaic Period carried them further north on the mainland and across foreign seas. In the Trojan War it was best known as the birthplace of Achilles; later it was backward socially but famed for its horses and horse-breeders. The Peneüs (pe-**nē**-us) river flows through Thessaly, issuing as a torrent from the steep Pindus range, the backbone of Greece.[1] Beyond the low mountains at the southeastern edge of the plain lies the Gulf of Pagasae (pa-**ga**-sē), formed by the embracing arm of a scimitar-shaped forested and mountainous peninsula called Magnesia (see Map V, back inside cover). The highest peak of Magnesia is Mount Pelion, original haunt of the Centaur Chiron. At Pelion's foot lay the Bronze Age city of **Iolcus** (ī-**ol**-kus), a name corrupted into that of the modern har-

---

[1]The river later pours forth into the sea through a spectacular landscape framed in ancient poetry as the sylvan Vale of Tempê.

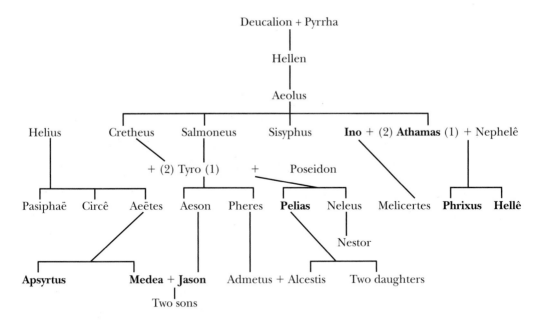

CHART 18.1. The House of Aeolus

bor town of Volos. Although the modern town covers most of the ancient ruins, traces of two Mycenaean palaces have been found there.

From Iolcus Jason and the Argonauts set forth, a generation before the Trojan War. Homer's *Odyssey,* composed in the eighth century B.C., refers to the voyage of the Argonauts as a tale already familiar (see quotation at beginning of chapter). But the most important literary version is the *Argonautica* of **Apollonius** (a-pol-**lōn**-i-us) **of Rhodes** (third century B.C.), whose account of the voyage we generally follow. Euripides' play *Medea* gives the best-known story of Jason's later years.

PRELUDE TO THE ARGONAUTICA

Phrixus, Hellê, and the Golden Fleece

Jason belonged to the family of the Aeolids (ē-o-lids), descendants of Aeolus (ē-o-lus), eponym of the Aeolians, a tribe of northern and central Greece (Chart 18.1). Aeolus was king of Magnesia, in Thessaly, a son of Hellen and grandson of Deucalion (the Greek Noah) and Pyrrha. He had seven sons, including **Athamas** (**ath**-a-mas), one of the unluckiest men in Greek legend.

When Athamas came of age, he migrated south to Boeotia and became king of the town of Orchomenus on the western shore of the enormous Lake Copais, which dominated the geography of Boeotia until it was drained in the nineteenth century A.D. Athamas' first wife, Nephelê (**nef**-e-lē), "cloud," bore him a boy, **Phrixus** (**frik**-

sus), and a girl, **Hellê** (**hel**-lē), but eventually Athamas tired of Nephelê and took a second wife, Ino (**ī**-nō), daughter of Cadmus of Thebes (she was nurse to Dionysus; Chapter 10). Ino bore Athamas two sons and was insanely jealous of Phrixus because she feared that he, instead of one of her own children, might inherit the throne; she therefore contrived a plot to destroy her stepchild. She persuaded the local women to parch the seed grain. The crop failed and famine fell on the land, so Athamas—as Ino had foreseen—sent to the oracle at Delphi to ask what to do. Ino intercepted the messengers and bribed them to report that Apollo had replied that, to restore fertility to land, Athamas must sacrifice his first-born child, Phrixus.

Athamas sorrowfully led Phrixus to the altar, knife in hand, but just as he was about to stab, a golden ram appeared beside the altar.[2] Athamas stood back while Phrixus and his sister, Hellê, climbed up on the back of the animal. The ram soared away to the east; the children were never again seen in Greece.

As the ram passed over the entrance to the straits between the northern Aegean and the Propontis (prō-**pon**-tis),[3] Hellê lost her grip and tumbled to her death in the narrows below, still today called the **Hellespont,** "Sea of Hellê." The ram flew on and at last alighted in the distant town of **Colchis** (**kol**-kis), in the land of Aea (**ē**-a, "earth") at the eastern end of the Black Sea. There the tyrant Aeëtes (ē-**ē**-tēz), "earthman," ruled. Aeëtes was a son of Helius, the Sun, and brother to Circê (the witch who entertained Odysseus; see Chapter 21) and Pasiphaë, wife of King Minos of Crete. Phrixus sacrificed the ram to Zeus in gratitude for his deliverance and gave the skin to Aeëtes, who hung it from an oak tree in a grove of Ares.[4] Aeëtes honored Phrixus by giving him one of his daughters to marry.

Pelias and Aeson

Salmoneus, brother of Athamas, had a daughter named **Tyro** (**tī**-ro), who became the grandmother of Jason. Her story is told by Odysseus, who encountered her shade in the underworld:

[235]   The first of these that I saw was Tyro, daughter of princes,
        child of high-born Salmoneus, as she herself told her story,
        adding that she was the wife of Cretheus, Aeolus' son.
        She had fallen in love with Enipeus, the patron god of a river,
        the fairest of all the waters that run on the face of the earth,
240   and often would wander alone by Enipeus' beautiful current.
        Poseidon, the shaker of earth, disguised himself as the river
        and lay with Tyro in love at the mouth of the eddying stream.
        A mountainous sea-purple wave rose curving over the couple,

[2]Like the ram that an angel showed Abraham as a substitute for Isaac (Genesis 22.13).
[3]The Sea of Marmara: the "lake" between the Aegean Sea and the Black Sea. The straits of the Hellespont are also called the Dardanelles, after the legendary Trojan king Dardanus; just north of them, on the west coast of the peninsula opposite the Troad, is Gallipoli, the site of the catastrophic defeat of the British by the Turks in 1915; Winston Churchill organized the campaign, and Mustafa Kemal ("Ataturk") led the Turks.
[4]The pelts of sacrificed animals often were hung from trees near the altar.

hiding the deathless god who lay with his mortal bride.

245   Then, when the god had ended the bliss of amorous pleasure,
squeezing her hand in farewell, he gave her a fond loving promise:
"Dearest of women, goodbye! When the year has finished its cycle,
you will bear me glorious sons; gods do not love women in vain.
Take them for now in your house and bring them up into manhood,

250   but refrain from naming their father—for I indeed am Poseidon,
the shaker of earth." With that, he dived down into the billows.
Pregnant indeed, she bore twin children, Pelias and Neleus,
who both grew up into manhood as mighty henchmen of Zeus.
Pelias dwelt in Iolcus, land of meadows and cattle,

255   Neleus in sandy Pylos. As for Tyro, queen among women,
other children she bore to Cretheus, her dear wedded husband:
Amythaon, lover of horses, and also Pheres and Aeson.

HOMER, Odyssey (11.235–259)

    Pelias (**pel**-i-as), an arrogant and intolerant man, aspired to supreme power over Thessaly. He drove out his brother Neleus (**nē**-lūs), who migrated to Messenia in the southwestern Peloponnesus, there to found the royal dynasty of Pylos. Pelias kept his half-brother Aeson (**ē**-son), the rightful heir, imprisoned in the palace of Iolcus, took a wife, and fathered many children (including Alcestis, who married her cousin Admetus, the son of Pheres; see Chapter 14).

    Aeson's wife bore a son, but, fearing for the child's life, they spread the rumor that he was stillborn. In fact, they sent him to the wise and civilized Centaur **Chiron** on the slopes of Mount Pelion; Chiron named the boy Jason, taught him the arts, and raised him to manhood. In the meantime, Pelias learned from an oracle that a man with one sandal would one day bring about his downfall.

    When Jason grew to maturity, he came down from the mountains and headed toward Iolcus, determined to claim the throne as his own. It was the time of a festival to Poseidon (Pelias' father). Jason came to a rain-swollen stream, by which an old woman sat crouched. Hurried though he was, Jason hoisted her to his shoulders and carried her across, but lost a sandal in the torrent. Having no time to look for it, Jason set down his burden and hastened to the city, not realizing that the old woman was Hera in disguise.[5] Hera hated Pelias because he did not honor her, and she had decided to destroy him through the wiles of the beautiful sorceress **Medea** (me-**dē**-a), daughter of Aeëtes, king of Colchis. Jason's kind act proved to Hera's mind that Jason was a man capable of bringing Medea to Greece.

    Pelias was busy at sacrifice when he learned that a one-sandaled man was standing in the agora. Straightaway he mounted his chariot and drove into the square. He asked the stranger, "What would you do if you knew someone was going to kill you, someone over whom you had power?" "Why, I'd send him to recover the Golden Fleece," Jason replied. "I shall do as you have suggested," snarled Pelias. "Go!"

---

[5]A similar story is told of St. Christopher, who carried the Christ child across a flooding stream. When he asked the child why he was so heavy, the child replied, "Because I am bearing all the sins of the world."

THE VOYAGE OF THE *ARGO*

Jason summoned Argus (the son of Phrixus, according to some accounts), who constructed an enormous ship, the largest ever made, that could hold fifty men. Athena inserted into its prow a magic speaking beam, cut from Zeus's oracular oak at Dodona. The ship was christened *Argo* after its builder.

Jason sent out a call to the best fighting men of his day, who gathered from far and near (Fig. 18.1). Among them were Heracles; Orpheus; the Dioscuri (dī-os-**kūr**-ī), Castor and Polydeuces, sons of Zeus and brothers of Helen of Troy; the Boreads (**bō**-re-ads), **Zetes** (**zē**-tēz) and **Calaïs** (**kā**-la-is), sons of Boreas (the North Wind); Telamon, father of the Trojan war hero Ajax, and his brother Peleus (**pē**-lūs), father of Achilles; the brothers Idas and Lynceus; Admetus, who married Alcestis and whom Apollo served for a year as a slave; Augeas, whose stables Heracles cleaned; Tiphys (**tī**-fis), the helmsman; and Argus himself. The seer Idmon turns up in many accounts. At the last minute, as they were pulling out, Pelias' own son Acastus ran and leapt into the ship, either defying his father or just looking for adventure.

Before their departure, Idmon read the entrails of a sacrificed animal and saw that they would all return safely, except for him. As the ship pulled out into the harbor, the speaking beam declared its impatience for the adventure. Rowing the harder at this, the Argonauts rounded Cape Magnesia, turned north along the coast, passed Mount Pelion to the west, then Mount Ossa, then Olympus, then headed due east across the Aegean, toward the island of Lemnos (see Map V, back inside cover).

FIG. 18.1. The gathering of the Argonauts (?), on an Athenian wine-mixing bowl, c. 575–550 B.C., found in Etruria. Heracles is easily recognizable in the middle with his club and lion skin. Athena stands on the left, and the man in between, touching the rim of his shield, is probably Jason. Other heroes lounge about or try out their armor.   (Musée du Louvre, Paris; Hirmer Fotoarchiv)

Early Adventures

Only women lived on Lemnos. Years before, the Lemnian women had insulted Aphrodite, who punished them by causing an intolerable smell to come from their bodies. Their husbands refused to have intercourse with them and crossed to mainland Thrace to capture some local women, who bore them children. At last the Lemnian women burst into a jealous rage and, like the Danaïds, in a single night killed every male on the island: husbands, fathers, sons, and brothers, along with the Thracian women and their children. Only the queen, Hypsipylê (hip-**sip**-i-lē), saved her father by hiding him in a chest.

The Lemnian women, who had long feared a punitive expedition from Thrace, were therefore alarmed to see the Argo loom on the horizon. Led by Hypsipylê in her father's armor, an unruly band of wild-haired, sex-starved women swarmed out to meet the ship. When they realized that the Argonauts were not from Thrace, they invited them into their beds (their foul smell seems to have gone away). Jason chose Hypsipylê, who later bore him two sons. Thus the Argonauts' first adventure took place in the bedroom.

Heracles refused to participate in the activity on shore, but remained on the ship, anxious to go and enjoying the company of pretty Hylas (**hī**-las), his boyfriend, whose father he had killed. Finally Heracles sent a sour message, congratulating his companions on their lovemaking. In shame, they straggled back; nine months later a new generation of Lemnians sprang up to replace the old.

The Argonauts set out again, touched at the island of Samothrace, then headed past the Trojan headland through the narrow Hellespont into the Propontis, watery anteroom to the Black Sea. Coasting along the south coast, they came to a sharp headland, really an island attached to the shore by a narrow strip, called Bear Mountain. They put ashore and were warmly greeted by the local king, Cyzicus (**siz**-i-kus), a young man of Jason's age, newly married, who ruled over the Doliones. An oracle told him to be kind to strangers.

After nights and days of entertainment, the crew bid goodbye to Cyzicus and put to sea, working their way around Bear Island. Near dusk, a strong headwind caught them. Without knowing it, they were blown backward and, as night fell, pulled into the nearest harbor. Immediately they were attacked by the inhabitants and fell to hard fighting. Dawn came to reveal dead Doliones everywhere. The Greeks had returned to the harbor whence they set out! In the midst of the corpses lay Cyzicus, Jason's own spear piercing his throat. After a funeral and effusive apologies, the Argonauts made their way back into the Propontis and continued east along the south coast.

Heracles, showing off his gigantic strength, pulled so hard he snapped his oar in two. They had to put in at the coast of Mysia for him to cut another one. While Heracles looked for a good tree, his friend Hylas went inland to look for water. Some lustful water nymphs saw him as he reached to draw the water and pulled him into the spring. Heracles heard the scream and came running, but found nothing: The boy now lived with the nymphs deep in the pond.

The next morning the Argonauts put to sea, not noticing that Heracles and Hy-

FIG. 18.2. The binding of Amycus, from a South Italian water-jug, c. 400 B.C. Here the boxing bully has been tied to a rock, evidently after being defeated by Polydeuces, probably the youth to his left who sits on a pot and holds a strigil, a tool for cleansing the body after a sports event. The other youth is probably Castor. To the far right, a winged Nikê, goddess of victory; to the far left, a maenad and a satyr (for unclear reasons). (Bibliothèque Nationale de France, Cabinet des Mèdailles, Paris)

las were missing. When they discovered their mistake, some wanted to turn back, but Zetes and Calaïs insisted that they go on, a decision for which Heracles later killed them. A sea god rose from the waters and told them to go on their way without worry, for Heracles still had to finish his Labors.

The Argonauts sailed for a day and a night. The put in to the land of the Bebryces (be-**brī**-sēz), ruled over by a braggart named Amycus (**am**-i-kus), an ugly, brutish man who challenged all passersby to box. He had always won, but Polydeuces, although not so big or strong, dodged a killer blow, slipped in behind, and let Amycus have it behind the ear, crushing the bones into the brain. The bully dropped dead (but see Fig. 18.2).

Phineus and the Harpies

The Argonauts reached the eastern end of the Propontis. Sailing into the Bosporus,[6] they stopped at Salmydessus, where King **Phineus** (**fin**-ūs) was in a terrible plight. Apollonius of Rhodes describes the poor man's condition:

[179]   Phineus, son of Agenor, dwelt there on the coast of the sea,
180   tortured beyond all men by gnawing affliction and torment,
         for abuse of oracular gifts which the son of Leto had granted.
         Ignoring the reticence due to Zeus's sacred intention,
         he fearlessly bared the future to the eager hearing of men.
         Zeus therefore gave him the burden of long and painful old age,
185   but took from his eyes sweet light, and also denied him enjoyment
         of the bountiful food his people piously brought to their ruler,
         offering gifts when they came to his house to ask of the future.
         For down from the clouds would sweep a flock of venomous Harpies,
         who snatched the food from his fingers, or even his open mouth,
190   and carried it off in their talons, now not leaving a morsel,
         another time only a crumb, to keep him alive, but in torment.
         Over it all they shed such a stench of putrid decay,
         that none dared even approach, let alone dispose of the remnants.
             Phineus, hearing the tramp of the Argonauts' marching feet,
195   arose to meet the heroes, aware that those who approached him
         were restorers, promised by Zeus, of all his pleasure in feasting.
         He staggered up from his bed, as weak as a bodiless phantom;
         limping on shriveled old feet, he hobbled in with his crutches,
         leaning at times on the walls to rest his feeble old bones.
200   His skin, all filthy with scab, alone kept his body together.
         On trembling shanks he limped down through the court to the threshold
         and sank back into a chair. Black swirling darkness descended;
         silent, helpless, he lay, as the earth spun churning about him.
         The bystanders gaped in surprise as Phineus, gasping in torment,
205   uttered from deep in his heart a dark and prophetical message.

APOLLONIUS OF RHODES, *Argonautica* (2.179–206)

But Phineus' wife, Cleopatra, as a sister of Zetes and Calaïs, the winged sons of Boreas, and the desperate Phineus agreed to give Jason exact information about the future course of the Argo if Zetes and Calaïs would free him from the Harpies ("snatchers";[7] Fig. 18.3). The Argonauts baited a trap, a table set with delicious food. When the Harpies appeared, Zetes and Calaïs drew their swords and rose against them, pursuing them at lightning speed through the air, until they fell from the sky.

---

[6]The Bosporus. Istanbul (a corruption of Greek *eis tēn polin*, "to the city"), once called Constantinople ("Constantine's town," after the Roman Emperor), stands on the European side.
[7]Perhaps in origin spirits of death, who whisk away a mortal's soul.

FIG. 18.3. Phineus and the sons of Boreas, Attic jug, c. 450 B.C. The blind Phineus sits on a throne, holding a scepter. The winged Zetes and Calaïs stand on either side, wearing Thracian clothes. (Museum of Fine Arts, Boston; 1979.40)

The Symplegades

Phineus now revealed the Argonauts' future course in great detail. He warned them especially about the **Symplegades** (sim-**ple**-ga-dēz), the "Clashing Rocks," which until that time had barred access to the Black Sea. These massive rumbling rocks, which lay in an impenetrable mist, smashed together and destroyed anything between. Before attempting to get past, the Argonauts should release a dove. If the dove made it through, so would they; if it were killed, they should forget about their adventure and go home.

When they got near the Clashing Rocks, they released a dove, which sailed through, losing only a tail feather when the rocks smashed together. Now the Argonauts took their chance:

[579]   To port, to starboard, ahead lay the limitless waters of Pontus.°
580   Suddenly over their bows swelled up the crest of a breaker,
        arching as high as a cliff. The men crouched, bowing in terror,
        sure that the wave would break, engulfing and sinking the vessel.
        But Tiphys eased her past, before the breaker could harm her,
        as she labored with straining oars. The wave at last slipped away
585   from under her keel, and in passing lifted her high on its back,
        raising her clear of the rocks, driving her safely on forward.
        Up and down through the benches Euphemus hurried and shouted,
        "Pull! Give it all you've got!" Cheering, they tore at the water,
        but for every yard they gained, the ship drove back twice as far.

579. *Pontus:* The Black Sea.

590 Each hero tugged his oar till it bent like the bow of an archer.
A second cresting wave came rushing, threatening, upon them,
but *Argo* slid over its top and plunged down as if on a roller.
Halfway between the shaking and thundering Clashing Rocks,
the iron grip of the current clutched at the paralyzed hull.

595 But the mighty left hand of Athena held fast to one of the crags,
and a thrust of her powerful right sent *Argo* clear of the danger.
The ship sped out as a feathered arrow speeds to its target,
leaving the envious rocks to smash at each other in fury,
only to clip off the banner that proudly hung from the sternpost.

600 As soon as she knew they were free, Athena rose up to Olympus.
The rocks were rooted forever, unchangingly facing each other,
for so, long ago, the Fates and the blessed immortals had ordered
should be their lot when a sailor could pass between them alive.

APOLLONIUS OF RHODES, *Argonautica* (2.579–606)

Just as the tail feather of the dove was caught by the rocks, so was the banner on the *Argo*'s stern snapped away.

Medea and the Golden Fleece

Jason, although badly unnerved, continued on, and the crew made their way along the south coast of the Black Sea. After various adventures, they landed at the mouth of the river Phasis, which flows through the land of Colchis. On its bank was Aea, city of King Aeëtes. Jason and several companions went up to the palace to make their request. First of the Colchians to see the hero was Medea, the king's daughter, agent of Hera's complicated plan to destroy Pelias. Hera had persuaded Aphrodite to send Eros to prick Medea with such love for Jason that she would help him against her cruel father Aeëtes, who despised foreigners and had no intention of giving up the fleece.

Aeëtes greeted the foreigners brusquely. Although Jason protested that he merely wanted the fleece and would then be on his way, Aeëtes had been warned by an oracle that a foreigner would be his undoing. He hoped to make an example of Jason and his crew. Craftily, he announced that he would gladly let Jason take the fleece once he had yoked two fire-breathing, bronze-hoofed bulls, plowed the ground, sowed the dragon's teeth left over from the monster that Cadmus killed at Thebes, and destroyed the armed warriors who would spring from the teeth.

Jason fell into a deep depression. He could see no escape. Fortunately, Medea, driven by passion for Jason, betrayed her family and country. Secretly she met with Jason and gave him a magic ointment to spread on his sword, shield, and body. Jason thanked her and said he would take her away from all this (if only he were not killed!) and marry her. On the next day,

[1278] The men hauled in on the hawsers that drew the ship to the beach,
and Jason jumped from the stern, armored and ready for battle [Fig. 18.4].

FIG. 18.4. A Greek ship of the Classical Period, from the interior lip of an Attic wine-mixing bowl, c. 520 B.C. (when the bowl was filled with wine, the ship seemed to sail upon it). The ship has a single mast, which can be raised or lowered; there is no jib, so you cannot tack into the wind and much traveling is under oar. Thirteen banks of oars are shown, surmounted by shields. The rowers sit on benches in the un-decked midship. At the rear, on a partial deck, sits the captain. The prow has an animal-shaped ram by which enemy ships could be sunk.   (Cleveland Museum of Art; 71.46)

1280   Along with his spear and shield he carried a glittering helmet,
        brazen, filled with teeth, each one with the point of a needle.
        His sword hung over his shoulder, like that of bellicose Ares,
        but he left his head uncovered, like golden-weaponed Apollo.
        He glanced down into the meadow at the brazen yokes of the oxen
1285   and their plow with adamant share, constructed all in one piece.
        Thither he went and fixed his spear in the earth by its side,
        pushing the butt in the ground and leaning the helmet against it.
        Holding his shield before him, he followed the trail of the oxen,
        which led to a cave in the earth, half hidden in billows of smoke.
1290   The pair of oxen emerged, breathing out flashes of fire,
        looking like bolts of lightning that leap from a sinister sky,
        one gleaming after another from clouds overflowing with rain.
        The heroes shook at the sight, but Jason stood firm and unshaken
        and met the advancing beasts like a granite reef on the seashore,
1295   unmoved by thundering waves driven on by perpetual storm winds.
        He kept his shield before him as the bellowing animals charged,
        and even their slashing horns did not budge him, no, not an inch.
            As bellows under a furnace make fire blaze up in a foundry,
        but must stop to suck back the air, roaring and wheezing in turn,
1300   just so the oxen roared, blowing the flame from their gullets,
        and after the roar came a flash like the blaze of a bolt of lightning.
        Yet Jason went quite unharmed; the ointment afforded protection.

The horns of the right-hand ox he seized in a powerful grip
and twisted, to force the beast to bow its head in submission.

1305 The other he brought to earth by a sudden kick at its fetlock;
tripping, it fell to its knees, downed in a single deft motion.
Jason now freed both arms by tossing his shield to the ground,
and, darting to left and right, clutched at the kneeling oxen,
trusting the ointment's power to keep him safe from the fire,

1310 while Aeëtes stared in amazement at the man's incredible power.
Obeying an old prophecy, the sons of Tyndareus° lifted
the yoke off the ground for Jason to lay on the animals' withers.
He set this over their necks, lifted the bronze-fitted drawbeam,
dropped it between the oxen, and jammed it down on its peg.

1315 Avoiding the flame, the brothers hurried back to the *Argo,*
while Jason retrieved his shield and hung it over his shoulders.
He lifted the mighty helmet, filled with the teeth of the dragon,
and grasped his invincible spear, with which to goad on the oxen,
as a peasant pokes his staff at the tender flanks of his cattle.

1320 With sure and certain hand he controlled the well-fitted handles.
The oxen snorted and raged, pouring out billows of fire;
the noise arose like the sound of a hurricane, terror of seamen,
warning the crew to reef and ease the stress on the mainsail.
But presently, prodded along by Jason's spear, they moved onward,

1325 as the wiry turf of the meadow was plowed and broken behind them,
split by the oxen's might and the massive weight of the plow.
The sod torn out by the plow, in pieces a man could just carry,
fell with a ripping sound along the sides of the furrow.
Jason followed and pressed with all his weight on the plowshare

1330 and scattered the teeth behind him, in the land already prepared,
repeatedly glancing back, to be sure that a crop as destructive
as this of earth-born men would not face him until he was ready.
The oxen meanwhile plodded ahead on bronze-armored hooves,
with only a third of the dying light of the day still remaining,

1335 when weary peasants are longing for the blessed hour's arrival
for oxen to be unharnessed and bedded down for the night.
At last the four-acre meadow was tilled by the tireless plowman;
Jason unfastened the terrified beasts, who fled to the lowlands,
while he himself turned back to revisit the furrows, still empty

1340 of men of the earth-born race. Around him crowded his comrades,
with words of advice and cheer. When he came to the turbulent river,
he drew a helmet of water and quenched the thirst of the soil.
Then lightly he sprang to his feet, enkindling his fiery spirit;
he raged like a furious boar, who whets his tusks for the hunter,

1345 while the dripping foam of his muzzle dampens the ground beneath.
By now the earth-born soldiers had sprouted all over the meadow,
and the field of man-killing Ares bristled with two-ended lances,
the brazen faces of shields, the gleaming crests of the helmets.
The glitter of arms flashed up from earth to the peak of Olympus.

1350 As when a blizzard of snow has folded the land in a blanket:

1311. *sons of Tyndareus:* Castor and Polydeuces.

a west wind harries the clouds, and all the stars of the heavens
shine out again through the murky gloom and darkness of night—
so these men and their weapons broke out and shone from the soil.
Jason recalled the advice of the shrewd and clever Medea:
1355   he picked up a rock from the ground (a discus fit for an Ares!).
No four men, heavy of sinew, could stir it up from its base.
He picked it up with a flourish and tossed it into their midst,
while he himself sat in hiding, his shield concealing his body.
The Colchians shouted in glee, like a wave smashing into a headland,
1360   but silence fell on Aeëtes to see Jason tossing the boulder.
Each earth-man snarled at another, like dogs attacking a quarry,
then, prey to his neighbor's spear, fell to the earth, his mother,
as oaks and firs of a forest fall at the blast of a tempest.
As a fire-star falls from the heavens, leaving a luminous trail,
1365   a portent to humans observing its beam shining out in the darkness—
just so the great son of Aeson ran charging into the earth-men,
pulled out his naked sword, and dealt out wounds left and right.
Part of the victims, still buried up to the flank and the navel,
risen half way into the air, received his terrible slashes.
1370   Some were freeing their shoulders, others were standing upright,
and a few were even advancing with eager step to the battle.
     You know how war may erupt in a hot dispute over boundaries:
how a farmer, in terror of raiders, takes up a new-whetted sickle
and runs to bring in his crop, though it still stands green and unripened,
1375   not daring to wait for the rays of the sun to ready the harvest.
Like that farmer, Jason cut down a crop of the sons of the earth.
     The furrows brimmed with blood, as ditches draining a spring
run overflowing with water. Some men fell down on their faces,
biting the soil as they fell, some on their backs or their hands,
1380   some in a fetal position, as crooked as some sea-born monster.
Many died of their wounds before their feet were yet lifted
out of the ground. They crumpled to earth, a few minutes after
lifting themselves to the heavens. Now back to earth they tumbled
with the deadly sweat on their faces, as damp as Zeus's cold rain.
1385   Bitterest grief came down on the heart of the lordly Aeëtes.
Back he returned to the town, the mighty city of Colchis,
wondering how at one blow to checkmate the Argonauts' planning.
Thus, then, ended the day, and with it the labor of Jason.

APOLLONIUS OF RHODES, Argonautica (3.1278–1407)

     Aeëtes, although foiled in his plan to destroy Jason, had no intention of giving up the fleece and decided to destroy the Greeks at once. Medea, realizing that she was about to be discovered, led Jason to the fleece and put the unsleeping dragon to sleep with a magic potion. (This dragon, larger than the *Argo*, had been born from the blood of the monster Typhoeus.) They snatched the fleece, ran to the *Argo*, and rowed down river toward the open sea (Fig. 18.5).

     Aeëtes gathered his fleet and gave pursuit. The *Argo* made for the mouth of the Ister (= Danube) at the other end of the Black Sea. According to the fantastic geography of Apollonius, the Danube joined with another river that opened into the

FIG. 18.5. The serpent disgorges Jason, interior of Attic wine-cup, c. 470 B.C. The scene seems to preserve a version of the myth absent from the literary accounts. Apparently Jason has been swallowed by the dragon, to emerge again live. A protective Athena stands before him, holding an owl in one hand, spear in the other. Note the *gorgoneion* on her breastplate and the sphinx on her helmet. The Golden Fleece hangs from a tree in the background. (Vatican Museum, Rome; XXXIV-22-7)

Adriatic Sea somewhere near the modern border between Italy and Slovenia. When he came near the Ister's mouth, Aeëtes split his fleet and sent half toward the Bosporus, to come at the Argonauts from the south, and half, commanded by Medea's brother **Apsyrtus** (ap-**sir**-tus), westward up river after the fleeing Greeks.

The two parties met in the Adriatic, where a parley was held. Medea lured Apsyrtus into a trap. Jason killed him, chopped off his fingers and toes, and three times sucked up a mouthful of the blood and spat it out.[8] He then buried the corpse. In another version Apsyrtus was a little boy when Medea kidnapped him, cut him into pieces and dropped the pieces overboard to slow her pursuing father (an instance of the folktale motif of the trail of objects dropped to delay a pursuer, given a bizarre and bloody twist).

Their further course carried them, according to more impossible geography, up the Eridanus (= Po) river to the Rhone, then via southern France again to the Mediterranean, down the west coast of Italy, past Sicily, and across the Ionian Sea to Corcyra, land of the hospitable Phaeacians. No sooner had they arrived than the second Colchian flotilla, which had come through the Bosporus, intercepted them. The Colchians demanded that Alcinoüs, king of the Phaeacians, surrender Medea, but he was willing to do so only if Jason and Medea had not yet had intercourse. Jason hastily arranged a wedding ceremony, led Medea to a cave, and slept with her. The Colchians, defeated and tired of the chase, settled down on the island.

[8]To confuse the ghost.

Libya

The Argonauts set out once more, heading south. A storm drove them to the Syrtis, a "dead sea" filled with seaweed off the coast of Libya. In one of the most fanciful twists in the voyage of the *Argo,* a huge wave threw the ship inland, dropping it amid the burning sands. The desperate sea-roving Argonauts picked up their ship on their shoulders and carried it for nine days until they reached the large, brackish inland Lake Tritonis. Staggering under the weight and overcome by thirst, they set the *Argo* down in the sand and dragged themselves to a nearby grove, hoping to find water. They came instead upon the Garden of the Hesperides—not in the far western seas, but in the middle of the desert! Its nymphs were weeping inconsolably over the snake Ladon, which had long protected the Golden Apples. He now lay dead, killed by Heracles, the former Argonaut, who had arrived just before them in search of the apples.[9] The Argonauts sent out trackers, and even saw the great man tromping away near the horizon, but could not overtake him.

Bedraggled and hopeless, the Argonauts reembarked in the *Argo* and for a long time rowed aimlessly around Lake Tritonis. At last the water god Triton took the prow in his hands and guided them through treacherous waters back to the Mediterranean. They headed north to Crete. As soon as they caught sight of land, huge boulders crashed around them, tossed by the bronze giant **Talus** (tā-lus), whom Zeus had given to Europa. The giant had a single vein of ichor, the liquid that serves as blood for the gods, replenished through a hole in his ankle. Every day Talus ran around the island, looking for strangers to attack. Medea summoned the death-spirits and fixed Talus with her evil eye so that he struck his ankle against a rock and dislodged the plug that held in the divine ichor. Fatally weakened, he stumbled and fell from a cliff into the sea (Fig. 18.6). They rounded Crete, then continued north to the Gulf of Pagasae, whence they had begun. At this point the poem of Apollonius ends.

Observations: Jason, the Deflated Hero

The notion of a sailing quest to the eastern end of the Black Sea to bring back a treasure may echo exploration in the Bronze Age (although no archaeological evidence for this has been found) but must depend principally on historically attested Greek experience in these cold and dangerous northern waters during the late Iron Age, beginning about 800 B.C. After this time Greek colonization in the Black Sea became extensive.[10] To this real history has been added the folktale of the quest that carries the hero, hidden at birth and brought up by a magical animal, to a magical land where he is compelled to accomplish impossible tasks. His reward is marriage with the local princess, but the kingship that came to Gilgamesh, Theseus, and Bellerophon escaped the very unheroic Jason, as we shall see.

Apollonius of Rhodes, unlike the oral poets Hesiod and Homer, composed his poetry in writing, as we do today. He consciously imitated the literary style of Homer,

---

[9]Other forms of the story do not mention that Heracles killed the snake (see Chapter 14).
[10]One of the principal colonizers was the Ionian city of Miletus.

FIG. 18.6. The death of Talus, Attic wine-jug, c. 400 B.C. In this version, the collapsing Talus (painted gold, to simulate bronze), is caught by the mounted Dioscuri, Castor and Polydeuces. (Jatta Collection, Ruvo; Deutsches Archäologisches Instituts, Rome; 64-1046).

never knowing that such distinctive features of Homer's poetry as the use of standard descriptive epithets, such as "swift-footed Achilles" and "Hector of the shining helm," depended on the original oral nature of Homer's verse. Such epithets were a device enabling poets to compose in the presence of a live audience but were mistaken by Apollonius and other imitators (such as Vergil, Ovid, and Milton) as stylistic contributions to epic grandeur. Homer and Hesiod composed orally for live audiences of illiterate warriors and farmers (some of their poems were recorded by dictation), whereas Apollonius composed his poem in writing for a socially elite audience that had learned to read and could appreciate the ways in which he rang clever variations on ancient themes.

Apollonius' poem is curiously modern, presenting Jason as an amorous, indecisive, even incompetent figure. He falls into a deep depression when he is told what he must do. Medea stands behind his success in subduing the dragon and getting the fleece and is by far the braver and stronger of the two. Apollonius is consciously inverting, or perverting, expected patterns of heroic behavior inherited from the preliterate past. Homer or Hesiod would never show a woman wielding so much power directly.

No doubt the voyage of the Argonauts lacks the interest of the sea journey of

Odysseus as told by Homer; Apollonius is more concerned with vivid descriptions of technical seamanship and with Jason's erratic emotional life than in the gutsy heroic society that makes Homer's characters and stories so memorable. The learned and affected taste of Apollonius' day enjoyed such descriptions and explorations of romantic individual emotions, and in his powerful romantic element lies Apollonius' originality and lasting contribution. He profoundly influenced the Roman poet Vergil, who modeled his Carthaginian heroine Dido on Medea (see Chapter 22). Vergil's tragic love story, in turn, became the model and inspiration for countless later tales in European literature and in modern film.

AFTER THE VOYAGE OF THE *ARGO*

The Death of Pelias

Meanwhile back in Iolcus, the rumor spread that the *Argo* had sunk with all hands aboard. Pelias congratulated himself on being the first human to escape the fate predicted by an oracle and decided to finish off his half-brother Aeson; he graciously permitted the old man to kill himself by drinking bull's blood (a deadly poison!) at a sacrifice. Aeson's wife, Jason's mother, ran screaming into the palace, cursed the king, and killed herself with a sword. She left a young son, but Pelias killed him too.

Jason's voyage had lasted four months. When he returned unexpectedly and presented the fleece to Pelias, the haughty king accepted it but showed no sign of relinquishing the throne. Medea saw a way to get rid of him that required the aid of

FIG. 18.7. Medea boiling the ram, from an Attic wine-jug found in Vulci, Italy, c. 510 B.C. Jason stokes the fire while Medea points out the old ram, boiling in the pot, to old king Pelias. One of his daughters stands to the far right.   (British Museum, London; B 328)

his daughters. Pelias, whose power only old age could challenge, could be made young again through her magic, Medea explained. To show what she meant, she cut up a doddering old ram, threw the pieces in a pot, boiled them for several hours, then removed the top (Fig. 18.7). Out popped a feisty spring lamb, gleefully baa-baaing. The daughters were persuaded. That night they sneaked into their father's chamber, chopped him in pieces, and brought the pieces to Medea. She cooked them for several hours, then removed the lid to reveal a thick, gluish, evil-smelling something. She apologized, admitting that she must have omitted an ingredient.

So Pelias met his end, as the oracle foretold, and Hera's plan was fulfilled. However, the Iolcans were outraged by the murder and celebrated splendid games in the dead king's honor. They drove Jason, hero or not, and his foreign girlfriend away from Iolcus forever.

Jason and Medea in Corinth

The star-crossed couple traveled to Corinth and settled there. Jason dedicated his ship at a shrine of Poseidon. They lived happily for several years, and Medea bore two sons. But Jason grew dissatisfied with his irregular liaison with this strange woman from the Black Sea and arranged with King Creon[11] to marry his daughter Glaucê (**glaw-sē**). He needed only to get rid of Medea. This is the subject of the *Medea* of Euripides, a seemingly contemporary tale of the bitter emotions that accompany the breakup of marriage in a monogamous society. The play was performed in 431 B.C., the first year of the Peloponnesian War between Sparta (allied with Corinth) and Athens. As it opens, Medea has just learned of Jason's intention to take a new wife. She appears on the stage to complain about woman's wretched lot, speaking to the chorus of Corinthian women:

[225]   *Medea* An unexpected chance has struck me down
and blasted my heart. I only long to die,
forsaking all the charm that life once held.
There was a time, my friends, when in my heart
my husband stood as type of all good things—
230   alas, that time is gone; he now turns out
to be the wickedest of mortal men.
    Of all the creatures who have heart and soul
we women are the most unfortunate.
All that we have we give to buy a husband
235   and, even worse, a tyrant of all we are.
A dreadful gamble, be he good or bad,
for no escape lies open to a woman,
save in dishonor; she cannot be free.
Blindly she enters a new estate, new ways;
240   untaught at home, she now needs second sight
to learn to deal with him she sleeps beside.
If she succeeds, if her husband is content

[11]No relation to King Creon of Thebes; Creon means simply "ruler."

to dwell without rebelling at his yoke—
then she is blessed; if not, far better dead.
245   Men bored by endless petty household chatter
can take an evening off from household cares;
while we must always worry how he feels.
They tell us what untroubled lives we lead,
while they must stand against the hostile spear.
250   What nonsense!
Better three times to face the foe in battle
than only once to bear the pangs of childbirth.
   But you and I face different situations.
This is your city, this your father's home,
255   here you are used to life, your friends are here.
But I am all alone. I have no home;
my husband scorns me as a worthless chattel
picked up as loot in some barbarian land.
I have no mother, brother, kin, whose aid
260   might shelter and protect me from disaster.
   Only one favor dare I ask from you:
if I can find a way to repay my husband
for all the misery he has laid on me—
with him the king, who bought him with his daughter,
265   and with the girl he miscalls his wedded wife—
if I do this, I beg you, hold your tongues.
Women, no doubt, in other ways are timid;
they dread a fight, and shudder at cold steel.
But when their marriage beds appear dishonored,
270   no other creature has a deadlier heart.

                       EURIPIDES, *Medea* (225–266)

Creon rightly fears this dangerous woman and banishes her from the city. She coaxes him into giving her just one more day to settle her affairs. Euripides' opportunistic Jason comes onto the stage to rail at Medea:

[446] *Jason* This is not new: how often have I seen
the raging anger of hysteria,° which leaves
the witness helpless. You know very well
that if you had shrugged your shoulders and accepted
450   decisions of men stronger than yourself,
you could have lived in quiet in this city
and kept your house and children. But no,
your stupid talk went on—and now you face
immediate exile. Defame me as you please,
455   tell all the world how foul a cur is Jason.
I am not bothered by your silly slander.
But when your words reflect upon the rulers,
think yourself lucky only to be exiled.
I tried to soothe the ruler's rising anger;

447. *hysteria:* = "Trouble with the womb," originally considered a specifically female disorder.

460 I begged him to allow you to remain.
But you still screamed aloud your silly charges
against the king, until he lost his patience.
No wonder you are exiled from the land!
    Still, madam, I admit my obligation.
465 I have come to see you well provided for,
you and the children, not penniless or lacking
what you may need as you go into exile,
for exile brings discomfort in its train.
And keep in mind that, however you may hate me,
470 never could I bear you the least resentment.
    Medea   Most evil of cowards—you deserve that name,
the worst my tongue can give your spinelessness.
Have you no sense of shame? You ruin me
and then come back and justify yourself!
475 It is not just arrogance or self-esteem
to wrong a friend, then look him in the eye,
but plain remorselessness, mankind's worst blight.
Still, I am glad you came. It will ease my pain
to publish your sin and make you blush to listen.
480 To start at the beginning, it was I who saved you,
(as all the Greeks of *Argo*'s crew know well)
when you were sent to break the fire-breathing bulls
under the yoke and sow their field of death.
My sleepless labor saved you from the coils
485 of the dragon who enfolded the fleece of gold—
I killed him, and restored your hope of safety.
My home, yes, my own father I betrayed
and followed you to Pelian Iolcus,
cold-blooded and efficient—but unintelligent.
490 Pelias I murdered by a most painful death
at his daughters' hands and crushed his family's power.
All this, ungrateful man, I did for you,
yet you betrayed me, courting your new bride,
although I had already borne your children.
495 Had you been childless still, you might be pardoned
for so desiring this new marriage bed,
but, as it is, trust in your oath has flown.
Do you believe the ancient gods still reign?
Or have they made new rules for men to obey?
500 How can I learn the answer? This alone is sure:
your guilty conscience knows you lied to me.
My poor right hand! which you so often clasped.
Poor knees! which often felt your false embrace,°
a perjurer's, designed to cheat my hopes.
505 Well, should I talk with you as with a friend,
should I expect a kindly act from you?

503. *embrace:* Holding another's hand or clasping another's knees emphasized the sanctity of a promise, as when we raise our right hand when taking an oath of office.

These very questions make you seem the viler.
Where would you have me turn? to my father's house,
I, who for you betrayed my home and country?
510   Shall I flee, perhaps, to Pelias' poor daughters?
They would gladly welcome home their father's killer.
In short, this is my story: to my old friends at home
I am become a deadly enemy, and those
I least had cause to harm abhor me now
515   for all the ill I did because you asked.
In exchange, of course, you've made me truly blessed
in the eyes of many women here in Greece.
What a splendid faithful husband in you have I!
poor wretch, abandoned, exiled from the land,
520   bereft of friends, alone with lonely children.
A fine reproach for a newly wedded bridegroom,
that she who saved you, and the children whom she bore,
now wander through the world as hungry beggars.
O Zeus, who gave mankind sure ways of trial,
525   to see if gold be true or counterfeit,
why did you set no stamp upon our features
by which we might tell honest men from knaves?
Chorus   Terrible rage, never totally cured,
boils up when lovers turn to enemies.
530   *Jason*   I must display my modest skill at speaking,
and, like a sailor of old and long-tried skill,
close-reef my sail and run before this storm,
the vitriolic blast of your angry tongue.
Now, since you boast too much of your own share
535   in this my enterprise, it seems to me
that Cypris, alone of gods or men, preserved me.
Your mind, I know, is quick and very subtle,
but envious Rumor mutters that it was Love
who forced you on, with his unerring arrows,
540   to save my life. This point I shall not stress,
but rather dwell on benefits to you.
For surely you received far more reward
by saving me, than was the price you paid.
First, you now dwell in no barbarian land,
545   but here in Greece. You know what "justice" means,
and how to live by law, not by compulsion.
All Greece has learned that you are wise and skillful,
and honors you for this; but if you lived hidden
in some unheard-of place at the world's end,
550   no word of you would hither penetrate.
What use a store of gold within a house,
what use a lovelier song than that of Orpheus,
unless one's fortune rings in all men's ears?
For my own exploit, such is my reply.
555   But you go too far, warring with words of spite,
and carping at my marriage with the princess.

First I shall prove that I was wise and prudent,
next moderate and restrained, then finally
how great a friend to you and to my children—
560 no, no; control yourself and let me speak.
When I migrated here from the land of Iolcus,
with me I brought a desperate load of troubles.
What better way for me, a helpless exile,
to free myself, than marriage to this princess?
565 I did so not, as jealous envy prompts you,
from boredom at your bed or lust for a new woman,
nor yet from eagerness to father children—
two is enough; I find no fault in this—
but hoping—mark you well—to live in comfort,
570 wanting for nothing. I have learned the lesson well,
that each man tries to avoid his needy friend.
I could raise children as befits my house,
begetting brothers to the sons you have borne,
and, joining families, live happily together.
575 What need have you of children? but consider:
I can help the living through those yet unborn.
Have I planned so unwisely? You would agree,
but feel humiliated to lose your rank.
Things now have gone so far that you women think
580 that if your marriage prospers, you need no more.
But if some great disaster strikes your wedlock,
what once was beautiful you think a horror.
O that men might have sons some other way,
and that the female sex did not exist!
585 Without it, blest indeed would be mankind!

EURIPIDES, *Medea* (446–575)

Medea concocts a magnificent revenge. She sends Jason's fiancée, Glaucê, a beautiful wedding gift. Soon a messenger reports that the princess and Creon both are dead:

[1133] *Medea*   Now take your time, my friend,
to tell the story. Just how did they die?
1135 You would give me twice the pleasure, if you replied,
"They died in torment."
Messenger   When your two children entered with their father
into the bridal house, we slaves rejoiced,
we who before had grieved for all your troubles.
1140 The word went round that you and he had settled
your long-time quarrels. One servant kissed the hands,
one the fair hair of your two boys, then I myself
followed with joyful steps to the women's quarters.
Our lady, whom in your place we reverenced,
1145 kept her adoring eyes fixed upon Jason,
until they fell upon your pair of boys.
At that she quickly turned away her gaze

and drew a veil over her fair white features,
as though embarrassed by the children's presence.
1150 Your husband tried to calm her angry temper,
and thus addressed her: "Please, don't be offended
at those who wish you well. Forget your anger
and turn again a smiling face upon them;
consider friends those whom your husband loves.
1155 Accept their gifts and mollify your father;
for my sake, let him revoke the children's exile."
Seeing the presents, she did not persist
and promised everything her husband asked.
But scarcely had your children and their father
1160 gone from the house, when she at once unwrapped
the splendid garment and quickly tried it on.
Upon her curls she set a golden tiara
and fixed her hair before a polished mirror,
smiling for joy at her own lifeless likeness.
1165 Then up she rose from her chair and paced the room,
gloating over her gifts, mincing on dainty feet,
gazing delighted at her slender ankles.
Then, all at once, a dreadful sight to see,
she turned dead white, she staggered to the side,
1170 trembling in every limb. Into a chair she crumpled,
barely escaping ruinous collapse.
An old handmaiden, doubtless imagining
a fit from Pan or another god had struck her,
screamed out a cry of terror, even before
1175 she saw the foam come boiling from her mouth,
the eyes protrude, the blood ooze from her flesh.
Another cry at that the handmaid uttered,
this one a dismal moan of suffering.
One maid ran off to the bride's father's dwelling;
1180 another to her newly wedded husband,
to tell the bride's disaster. All the house
resounded with panic running to and fro.
In the time a sprinter runs a hundred yards
and reaches the finish, the poor girl came to,
1185 opened her eyes, and gave a shriek of pain.
A double torment was advancing to attack:
the gold tiara resting on her tresses
poured out an awful stream of gnawing flame,
while her clinging robe, your children's wedding gift,
1190 devoured the tortured woman's milky flesh.
She leaped, ablaze, up from her seat and fled,
desperately throwing her head this way and that,
trying to fling the crown from off her hair.
But the golden links clung firmly, and at each toss
1195 the flames blazed higher. To the floor she fell
writhing in torment, crushed by a dreadful fate,
unrecognizable to all, save to her father.

Her eyes dissolved into a shapeless chaos,
her face's native beauty shriveled away,
1200   a flux of blood came pouring from her scalp,
her flesh dropped peeling from her tortured bones,
scaled by the poison gnawing from within,
like pitch from a burning pine—a dreadful sight.
None of us dared to touch the poor girl's body,
1205   to offer help. Her fate gave us its warning.
        Her father, who had no word of her disaster,
suddenly entered the hall. With a dreadful groan,
he flung himself headlong upon the body,
embraced it in his arms, and cried aloud,
1210   "O my poor daughter, say, what ruthless god
has thus destroyed you? Who made this poor old man,
bereft of you, into a living tomb?
Alas, alas, my child, would I might die with you!"
At last his tears of sorrow were exhausted.
1215   The old man longed to rise and hide himself,
but his body clung as tight to her fine clothing
as ivy does to branches of the laurel.
A grisly wrestling match arose between them:
the father trying to stagger to one knee,
1220   the daughter clinging fast to hold him down.
Each time he pulled, he ripped his ancient flesh
right off his bones. Exhausted, he gave up
the fight he could no longer hope to win,
and breathed his last. Together there they lie,
1225   father and child, asking your tears in death.

EURIPIDES, *Medea* (1133–1221)

To put a fine touch on her revenge, Medea then puts her two sons to the knife, throws them into a chariot drawn by dragons (a gift of her grandfather Helius), and prepares to leave the city (Fig. 18.8). Jason runs in, aghast:

[1323]   *Jason*   Woman most hated, most loathsome to the gods!
loathsome to me, to all the race of men!
1325   You did not scruple to take up a sword,
to murder the children you yourself had borne,
leaving your husband desolate and childless.
Unholy crimes you dared. Dare you still gaze
up to the sun of heaven, down to the earth?
1330   My curse fall on you! My sense at last returns,
lost when I took you from your savage house,
your savage land, and brought you home to Greece,
horror that you are—betrayer of your father
and traitor to the fatherland that bore you.
1335   The gods have hurled on me the curse you earned,
by murdering your own brother by his hearth,°

1336. *hearth:* Euripides gives still another version of Apsyrtus' death.

Seneca's *Medea*

The character of Medea has meant many things to many people. In his tragedy *Medea,* the Roman philosopher, statesman, and dramatist Seneca (c. 4 B.C.–A.D. 65) made her a bloodthirsty sorceress who rules the elements for her own ends by magic and horrible incantation. Euripides' disillusioned heroine coldly plans revenge on her betrayer; Seneca's is driven mad by the apparition of Furies and the ghost of her brother Apsyrtus, dismembered by her own hands. Euripides has her kill her children off stage; in Seneca she butchers them in full view, slowly, gloatingly, one at a time. In the following passage Seneca's Jason appeals to Medea to spare at least one child:

[1002]   *Jason* By every god, by perils we have shared,
        by our marriage bed, its honor still unsmirched,
        I beg you, spare this child! blame what you will,
1005   on me let your blame fall. Take me, O Death;
        butcher this noxious, guilty soul of mine!
        Medea Where most you shrink in pain will I drive the knife.
        Go, run away to your little sweet sixteen,
        and leave real life to women who know its pangs.
1010   *Jason* Is one child not enough for your revenge?
        Medea This hand would not have struck, had that been so.
        No, even two scarcely mollify my pain.
        Jason Then grant me this: either complete the deed,
        or else delay it, moved by my agony.
1015   *Medea* Draw out his torment, my tormented heart.
        A long day lies before me; make the most of the time.
        Jason Kill me, you hag of hell, kill me!
        Medea I, pity you?

   [Stabs child]

        There, that is all, my heart; I have no more revenge
1020   to soothe your pain. Well, Jason, aren't you pleased?
        Lift up your swollen eyes to know your wife
        for what she is.

   [A chariot drawn by two snakes appears behind her]

        This is the way I travel; the sky lies open;
        my team of dragons bows its scaly necks
1025   beneath the yoke.

   [Medea gets into the chariot]

        Here, daddy, take your sons

[Throws him the bodies]

while I fly down the winds in my winged car.
Jason Depart, through highest reaches of the ether;
Where e'er you go, proclaim, "the gods are dead."

SENECA, Medea (1002–1027)

Seneca studied and wrote on science and philosophy. He tried to live by the dictates of Stoicism, living in self-imposed poverty, although he was one of the richest men in Rome. He enjoyed immense status as a chief advisor to Nero but eventually fell out of favor and was forced to commit suicide (he opened his veins while taking a hot bath, to keep his blood from clotting). Seneca wrote eight other tragedies based on Greek myth. These plays, full of psychological improbabilities and gruesome horror, were not meant for theatrical presentation but probably were read aloud without action. However, they were acted in the Renaissance, especially in the universities, before the Greek tragedies became well known. Seneca's plays were widely imitated; Shakespeare's *Titus Andronicus,* for example, is a welter of incest, gore, and mutilation that Seneca would have applauded. Still today we call a blood-and-guts play based on motives of revenge Senecan.

then daring to go aboard the sleek-prowed *Argo.*
So you began. And then you married me
and bore my children. Now you butcher them,
1340   all for the sake of your lost marriage bed.
No women ever born of good Greek blood
has ever dared to dream of such a deed—

FIG. 18.8. Medea stabs her child, on a South Italian water-jar, c. 330 B.C. Without pity, she holds her son by the hair as she plunges a knife under his arm, as he runs for asylum to the altar on the right, surmounted by a statue of Apollo.
(Musée du Louvre, Paris; K 300)

          women whom I rejected, choosing you,
          destructive, hostile, hateful foe of mine.
1345   As wife I chose a tigress, not a woman,
          one with a fiercer heart than Tuscan Scylla.°
          Why waste my time? Ten thousand condemnations
          would leave no mark on your conceited heart.
          Get out, perverted murderess of your children!
1350   All I can do henceforth is groan at fate,
          I, who will have no fruit of my new bridal,
          to whom no child whom I begot and nourished
          is left to say "good-bye" above my grave.
          O lost! O lost!
1355   *Medea*   I could draw out an answer to your speech,
          but Father Zeus already knows full well
          what you received from me, and what you gave.
          Was it your duty to degrade my marriage,
          to live in pleasure while you mocked at me?
1360   Did you suppose your princess or that Creon,
          who offered her in marriage, could drive me out
          and still escape my vengeance? Call me tigress,
          call me a Scylla in her Tuscan cave—
          I still have wrung your heart as it deserved.

                    EURIPIDES, *Medea* (1323–1360)

1346. *Scylla:* A monster perched on one side of the Straits of Messina between Italy and Sicily ("Tuscan" = Etruscan, Italian). She had once rejected the advances of some deity, who persuaded Circê (Medea's aunt) to change her to a monstrous form. Scylla lived by snatching sailors from passing ships (see Chapter 21).

Medea flies away to Athens, where Aegeus, father of Theseus, has promised to receive her (see Chapter 15). So ends the play. Jason never recovered from the disaster. Depressed, ill, old, he sat down one day beneath the prow of his old friend *Argo,* where it lay decaying near the precinct of Poseidon. The rotten prow broke off, fell on Jason's head, and killed him—fitting end to a hero who had too much of everyman in him to fill the part.

The wonderful witch Medea never pays the price for her crimes. After escaping to Athens, she later returns to Colchis with her new son by Aegeus (see Chapter 15), Medus, who kills Aeëtes and takes the power. Medus spreads his realm to the east and becomes the ancestor of the Medes, another name for the Persians, Greece's deadly enemy during the Classical Period. There are no traditions about Medea's death; perhaps she never died. According to one story, she married Achilles in the Elysian Fields.

Observations: Medea, Sorceress and Wife

Circê, daughter of Helius (see Chapter 21), and Medea, granddaughter of Helius, are the best-known sorceresses in Greek myth. Unlike the witches of European folklore, however, they are not ugly hags, but beautiful and sexually alluring. Circê likes to change men into pigs, but Medea is a more realistic figure who uses potions to achieve her ends: protecting Jason from the fire-breathing dragon, putting to sleep the snake that guards the fleece, and, in Iolcus, resurrecting the aged ram (she might have resurrected Pelias too). She impregnates with terrible potions the cloth that kills Glaucê. Although a witch, she is close to the traditional practitioner of herbal remedies, and Euripides presents her as little more than a foreigner who understands exotic medicines. In deemphasizing her powers as magician, Euripides portrays her as almost an ordinary human, a wife betrayed by a callous husband.

Of course, as a foreigner Medea can expect special hardships, but Athenian women also were strangers in their own homes, tied to their husbands' families only by the children they bore. Should these children die, a woman would ordinarily return to her father's house, a possibility not open to Medea. Because women were perpetual outsiders from the "men's club" that was democratic Athens, a man could never be sure of his wife's intentions, of the harm she might do to him and to the established order he represented; marriage was meant to tame the *parthenos,* but marriage was not always successful. The woman's tools were always the same: intrigue and sex. Euripides' *Medea* is the Athenian husband's worst nightmare come true, a ruthless woman who cannot control her violent emotions and her jealousy, who kills even her own children to settle a domestic dispute.

Still, we must not take dramatic presentations of women, written by men for men, as reflecting closely the realities of a woman's life in Athens. Although divorce was easy for a man, the wife was protected legally and financially and her dowry returned (if she was member of the *polis,* which Medea was not). Through exaggeration of a wronged woman's plight Euripides tweaks the audience's self-confidence in the righteousness and superiority of their customs. Jason comforts Medea by reminding her that, although divorced and outcast, at least she is living in Greece where "justice" prevails. The audience could only smirk at such pretension.

THE CALYDONIAN BOAR HUNT

A minor but famous local myth involving some of the heroes who sailed on the *Argo* comes from **Aetolia** (e-tō-li-a), the district north of the entrance to the Gulf of Corinth, whose capital was **Calydon.** The king in the days of Heracles was Oeneus (ē-nūs), "wineman," a descendant of Aeolus and the first man in Greece to grow grapes for wine. His wife, **Althaea** (al-thē-a), sister of Leda (mother of Helen of Troy), bore him **Meleager** (mel-ē-ā-jer; Chart 18.2); a later wife of Oeneus also gave birth to Tydeus, one of the Seven against Thebes (Chapter 17).

On the seventh day after Meleager was born, the three Fates appeared in the room. Two of them promised that the child would be handsome and brave, but the third pointed to a log burning in the fireplace. "When that log is consumed," she said, "the child will die." Althaea leapt from the bed, took the burning log from the fire, extinguished it, and placed it at the bottom of a chest, which she hid in a secret part of the palace.

Meleager grew to manhood. He was handsome and brave and joined the Ar-

Delacroix's *Médée*

The French poet Baudelaire observed that Romantic painter Eugène Delacroix (1798–1863) brought to his works "the feeling which delights in the terrible." Although Delacroix usually chose his subjects from nonclassical or postclassical topics, including events of his own time, occasionally he drew from the classical world. Inspired by the Senecan *Médée* (1635) of the French playwright Corneille, he painted Medea three times. In the illustration shown here (Fig. P 18.2, Delacroix's first version, Medea sits with her dagger, holding (not very firmly) her two sons. The breasts with which she suckled them are bared; the boys are wriggling to get away. Medea herself, wearing the diadem and earrings of a queen, gazes off fearfully through the opening of a cave at the man for whom she has done so much, who has brought her to this.

FIG. P 18.2. Eugène Delacroix (1798–1863), *Medea About to Kill Her Children,* 1838, oil on canvas.
(Musée des Beaux Arts, Lille; P 542)

Corneille's version was written when stage technology was in its infancy, but by Delacroix's lifetime many improvements in scenery and lighting had been made, which allowed the full horror of the gruesome story to fill the stage. The proscenium arch and curtain made possible movable sets, which could be painted as realistically as a director wanted. Gas light came into use soon after 1800 and made possible unheard-of dramatic contrasts: For example, mysterious and gigantic figures could be produced by stretching gauze at the back of the stage, behind which a backlighted actor walked, casting an immense shadow. Romantic caverns could be constructed with a dark background, dim lights by the entrance, and a brightly lit Medea (with interesting shadow effects) killing her sons in the center stage. Delacroix the painter evidently was inspired as much by anonymous stage designers and technicians as by the stories told by Euripides, Seneca, and Corneille.

gonauts. When he returned from Colchis, he married Cleopatra, who bore him a child. Many years before, Oeneus had offended Artemis by forgetting to include her in the harvest sacrifice. She now took revenge by sending an enormous boar against the countryside around Calydon. The boar ran amok, tearing up crops, uprooting trees, killing everyone who stood in its way. As Jason had summoned heroes from far and wide, so did Oeneus. Many who had sailed on the *Argo* also joined the Calydonian Boar Hunt. Accounts differ, but most include the Dioscuri, Castor and Polydeuces, cousins of Meleager from Sparta; Theseus of Athens; Admetus from Pherae in Thessaly; Jason from Iolcus in Thessaly; Pirithoüs, king of the Lapiths, son of Ixion and good friend of Theseus, from Larissa in Thessaly; Peleus, the father of Achilles, from Phthia in Thessaly; Iphicles, twin brother of Heracles, from Thebes in Boeotia; and the seer Amphiaraüs of Argos, who would die in the war against Thebes. Meleager's uncles, his mother's brothers, also joined in the hunt, as well as the Calydonians' usually hostile neighbors, the Curetes (kū-**rē**-tēz).[12]

The famous female athlete **Atalanta** (at-a-**lan**-ta), from Arcadia in the central Peloponnesus, also joined the hunt. Her father, wanting only boys, had exposed her at birth, but a she-bear found and suckled her and hunters raised her. Like her sponsor and model, Artemis, she cared only for hunting. Many objected to a woman coming on the Calydonian Boar Hunt (Jason had turned her away from the *Argo,* fearing a woman's presence), but Meleager was attracted to Atalanta and demanded that she be admitted.

The heroes closed in on the boar. Several went down before its flashing tusks and others died when hit by their companions' spears, gone astray. Atalanta got in close and fired an arrow in the pig's ugly red eye. Amphiaraüs also wounded the creature, and Meleager made the kill (Fig. 18.9) and skinned out the beast. He gave the pelt to Atalanta, ostensibly because she had drawn first blood but also because he wanted to sleep with her. Meleager's maternal uncles loudly protested that a woman should not be given the trophy and took it from her. Meleager tried to get it back and in the scuffle killed his uncles.

When Althaea learned that her beloved brothers were dead, she broke down

---

[12]Unconnected with the Cretan protectors of the crying infant Zeus, who had the same name (see Chapter 4).

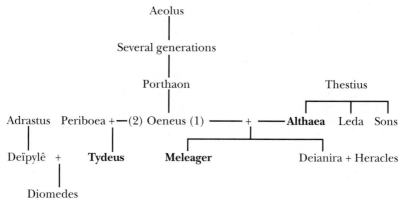

CHART 18.2. The House of Calydon

with grief. In her rage at the son who had killed them, she ran to the hidden trunk, took out the log, and threw it into the fire. So Meleager died.

Bacchylides tells the story in a hymn. Heracles, descending to the underworld to bring back Cerberus, suddenly sees Meleager's ghost. He thinks it is real and draws his bow, but instead of attacking listens to Meleager's tale:

[56]   For once, they tell us, the smasher of gates,°
    invincible son of Zeus, lightning-bolted,
    went down to the halls of fair-ankled Persephonê,
    to drag to the light from Hades' domain
60   the jagged-toothed whelp of dreadful Echidna.°
    There he saw the ghosts of the grief-torn mortals
    who wander in woe on the banks of Cocytus,°
    shaken by sorrow, like leaves in the wind
    that swirls over Ida, pasture of sheep,
65   shaking its sun-whitened headlands.
       Among them most striking he saw the shade
    of Porthaon's son,° that hurler of spears.
    When the mighty hero, the son of Alcmenê,
    saw the gleam of his armor, he strung his bow
70   with a loud-twanging string, took the lid from his quiver,
    and pulled out an arrow, headed with bronze.
    Meleager's ghost, knowing well what he planned,
       floated up, face to face, and spoke to the hero:
       "Son of great Zeus, calm your fiery spirit;
75   do not rush to attack, nor let fly from your hands
    your deadly barbed arrow at the ghosts of the dead;
    it will do us no harm. You have nothing to fear."
    In amazement the hero, great son of Amphitryon,

56. *smasher of gates:* Heracles, who had sacked several cities.   60. *whelp of . . . Echidna:* Cerberus.
62. *Cocytus:* A river of the underworld.   67. *Porthaon's son:* Meleager, son of Oeneus and grandson of Porthaon.

FIG. 18.9. The Calydonian Boar Hunt, on an Attic wine-mixing bowl (the famous François Vase), c. 570 B.C. Moving from left to right are an archer, then Melanion and Atalanta (with white flesh), with a dog named Methepon ("follower"); Peleus, father of Achilles, and Meleager stab into the boar's mouth while the hound Ormenos, "rusher," lies dead beneath the boar's hooves; a warrior lies dead beneath the boar, while Castor and Polydeuces stab it in the rump; other hunters and dogs approach from the right.   (Museo Archeologico Nazionale, Florence; 36890/1)

replied to his words, "What line of the gods,
80   what stock of mere mortals, engendered this man?
In what land was he born? By whose hand was he slain?
Perhaps well-girt Hera will send this man's killer
to bring my head low. But fair-haired Athena
   will see to the matter of my defense."
85   With tears in his eyes, Meleager replied,
"A difficult task for us mortals on earth
it is to deflect the designs of a god!
If this were not so, Oeneus my father,
goader of horses, might have ended the wrath
90   of rose-crowned Artemis, white-armed, revered,
by his humble prayers, by his sacrificing
of numberless goats, of tawny-backed oxen.
But no, she clung to implacable anger.
The maiden goddess sent a wide-ranging boar,
95   berserk in his fury, to Calydon's meadows.
Overflowing with rage, he savaged the vineyards,
disemboweled the sheep, their owners as well,
   if those owners ventured to face him.
      For six days we fought the terrible fight,
100   we, bravest of Greeks, all valiant of spirit.
At last the god gave the Aetolians mastery;
we buried those fallen to the boar's savage rage:
Agelaüs, Ancaeus, both dearest of brothers,
born to Althaea in Oeneus' house.
105   And many more fell by a horrible fate,
for the huntress Artemis, daughter of Leto,
still clung to her anger and drove us to fight
the aggressive Curetes, who claimed the trophy,
   the rough, tawny hide of the boar.
110   I slew many men, the noble Aphares

and Iphiclus too, my mother's swift brothers,
for hard-hearted Ares does not favor one's friends
in the heat of the battle; the spear flies blind
from the hand of the thrower to the heart of the foe,
115   bringing its death at the whim of some god.
                Forgetting all this, my star-crossed mother,
the daughter of Thestius, fearless and clever,
planned my destruction. From its well-carved chest
she drew the stick which the Fates had marked
120   at the time of my birth for a sign of my death
            and threw it into the fire.
                By the towers of Pleuron, his city of refuge,
I had just run down and was poised to kill
Clymenus, noble son of Deïpylus,
125   handsome of body and valiant in battle,
when all at once my dear soul shriveled,
and I groaned at feeling my strength decay.
With my dying breath I mourned for the brightness
    of the youth and joy I was leaving behind."
130   They say that this was the only time
that the son of Amphitryon, fearless in battle,
let tears of pity well from his eyelids,
in his grief for Meleager's sad fate.
"Man's happiest lot would be 'not to have lived,
135   not to have looked on the light of the sun.'
Platitudes! useless as comfort to mourners,
so let us consider practical matters.
Tell me, does warlike Oeneus' house
hold an unmarried daughter as handsome as you?
140   such a one would I have as my glorious bride."
                Brave Meleager's ghost gave an answer:
"Fair-necked Deianira I left in my house,
a maid unacquainted with the man-charming arts
    of the golden witch Aphrodite."

BACCHYLIDES (5.56–164)

At the end of the poem Heracles arranges to marry Meleager's sister, Deianira, once he has returned to the upper world. We learn from other sources that, after killing her son, the remorseful Althaea hanged herself, and Meleager's wife followed suit.

There is more to tell of Atalanta. She returned to her father's house. He wanted her to marry some young man, but she was determined to remain a virgin. At last she agreed to marry whoever could overtake her in a foot race. When a suitor lost (as all did), Atalanta chopped off his head and hung it from a staff at the edge of the stadium. Her method was to give the suitor a head start, then come from behind and skewer him in the back with her spear. Soon skulls in varying stages of decay dangled from staffs around the stadium.

Then came Melanion (sometimes named Hippomenes). Aphrodite favored him and gave him three golden apples from the tree of the Hesperides. As usual, Atalanta allowed Melanion a good lead. As she dashed past, he rolled an apple in front of her. She stopped to pick it up, allowing him to get ahead. In this way Melanion won the race, but the couple could not contain their lust, and in a nearby shrine of Zeus they enjoyed ecstatic intercourse (forbidden, of course, within sacred precincts). For this act Zeus changed them into lions, a fitting end: According to Greek folklore, lions can mate with leopards, but never with other lions.

Observations: Heroic Myths of the Hunt and the Hunter

Meleager's extraordinary birth is part of the heroic pattern, and he is surprisingly like Oedipus in the fatal effects of his own mother's affections. His quest is to hunt the boar, but there things go wrong.

The hero is a hunter, and various features emerge in myths of the hunt: the similarity between hunting and sacrifice, the similarity between hunting and war, the dangers that hunters meet and that they themselves pose to society, and patterns of the dragon combat or ritual initiation.

Only through hunting and sacrifice did the ancient Greeks acquire meat to eat. Both activities were governed by strict prescriptions of behavior, although sacrifice took place in the city and hunting in the wild. Whereas the purpose of sacrifice was to procure good relations with the gods, the purpose of the hunt was to obtain meat or destroy savage animals. In the dangerous wild where the hunt takes place, the hunter sometimes becomes the hunted, and his fate can resemble that of the sacrificial victim. Euripides makes much of the closeness between hunting and sacrifice in his story of Pentheus (Chapter 10), who sets out to hunt the Bacchae, then is himself hunted down and dismembered in a scene closely resembling ritual sacrifice (he is not eaten in Euripides' play, but Dionysus' human victims, or their children, usually are).

Ancient hunting was always close to war and entailed similar dangers. In each activity a human group organized to kill an adversary. The social and technical skills useful in war—solidarity of the group, weaponry, athletic prowess, and bravery—also brought success in the hunt, and in Greek myth martial heroes are accomplished hunters, too. However, there are important differences, because in the hunt one does not negotiate with the adversary, and the quarry of the hunt is eaten, unlike the enemy in civilized warfare. (But Tydeus, half-brother of Meleager, did split open the head of Melanippus to devour his brains; see Chapter 17.)

Although the hunt is conducted for the benefit of society, the hunter can easily give in to passion excited by the chase and become a danger to those he hoped to benefit; this danger haunts the hero always. Hippolytus is so devoted to the hunt that he violates his human sexuality, bringing destruction to himself and to his house (see Chapter 14). The wilderness obeys its own laws, but within the group of hunters social relations are determined strictly by convention. In the eyes of his family, Meleager disobeys the laws of his hunting group by giving the skin of the boar to Atalanta, a thoughtless act that changes the hunt into war and brings about the deaths of Meleager and his relatives. Although the hunter's victory over the animal marks him as a hero, he remains a threatening figure, living at the edge of society; even in the midst of the city, Heracles wears his lion skin and drags around his club, an image of untamed violence.

Hunters who are too successful often come to a bad end, as did Orion and Actaeon, whom Artemis sent to their deaths, and Cephalus, who killed his beloved Procris. Success in the hunt seems to generate sexual excess or misbehavior. Hippolytus, lover of the hunt, tries to put sex out of his life, but his scorn for Aphrodite only excites her special attention. Orion attempts to rape either Artemis herself or one of her numphs. Actaeon sees Artemis naked. Meleager, although married, loves Atalanta. When Melanion defeats the huntress Atalanta, they immediately have sexual relations in a forbidden place, causing their transformation into hunting animals.

The legendary hunt of a single hero against a savage animal has the appearance of the myth of the dragon combat. The hunter–hero is a culture-bearer, and the animal is extraordinarily menacing, a threat even to human survival. The animal's defeat allows human life to return to normal. Gilgamesh's fight against Humbaba, or the bull of Heaven, Heracles' hunt for the Nemean lion, and Theseus' capture of the bull of Marathon are examples of such heroic encounters of one man, using his bare hands, against a prodigy of nature. Collective hunts, on the other hand, such as the Calydonian Boar Hunt, have the earmarks of male initiation, binding together human males as a group; Atalanta does not belong here, and her presence leads to disastrous family conflict. The band is led by the king's son, Meleager, because it is a royal prerogative to keep the land free of monsters and to unite the young males of his realm through camaraderie in the hunt.

Hunting, the killing of animals in the wild, was an important activity in early Greece, as was sacrifice, the killing of animals in religious ritual. Both activities brought great benefits: a chance to consume meat and a neutralization of the hostile forces that surround human communities in the wilderness and in the realm of the gods. Few myths are devoted entirely to the hunt, but few are free of some reference to this primordial activity and to the exemplary qualities or unmanageable feelings that the killing of animals can encourage.

KEY TERMS

FURTHER READING

Bacon, Janet R., *The Voyage of the Argonauts* (London, 1925). Attempts to associate Jason's voyage with ancient trade routes.

Beye, Charles Rowan, *Epic and Romance in the* Argonautica *of Apollonius* (Carbondale, Ill., 1982). Lively study of literary aspects.

Conacher, D. J., *Euripidean Drama: Myth, Theme and Structure* (Toronto, 1967). Euripides' innovations in myth and the relationship of *Medea* to folktale.

Fontenrose, Joseph, *Orion: The Myth of the Hunter and the Huntress* (Berkeley, Calif., 1981). Comparative study of Greek and Near Eastern hunting myths, including Orion, Actaeon, Callisto, Hippolytus, and Atalanta.

Fowler, B. H., *Hellenistic Poetry: An Anthology* (Madison, Wisc., 1990). Has the best translation of the complete *Argonautica,* plus representative selections from other Hellenistic poets.

———, *The Hellenistic Aesthetic* (Madison, Wisc., 1990). Companion volume to her anthology, this book describes attitudes toward love, nature, art, and myth in the Hellenistic period.

Gardner, John, *Jason and Medeia* (New York, 1973). Modern recreation of the ancient myth.

Hunter, Richard, *The* Argonautica *of Apollonius* (Cambridge, U.K., 1995). Scholarly study of poem as literature.

Onians, J., *Art and Thought in the Hellenistic Age* (London, 1979). Good review of the cultural background that produced Apollonius' *Argonautica,* with many illustrations.

Severin, Tim, *The Jason Voyage: The Quest for the Golden Fleece* (New York, 1985). Sponsored by the National Geographic Society, Severin attempts to follow Jason's route, sailing in a twenty-oared galley.

CHAPTER 19

THE TROJAN WAR

THE HOUSE OF ATREUS; THE ANGER OF ACHILLES

So Paris, visitor in the Atreïds'° palace,
dishonored the laws that bind guest and host:
ate the king's bread, then eloped with his wife.
Behind her she left a vengeful clangor of shields,
of citizen spearmen, of seamen in arms.
Bringing as dowry destruction of Ilium,°
gaily she passed through the gate of the city,
daring a crime no human should dare.

AESCHYLUS, *Agamemnon* 399–408

No cycle of stories is better known than those surrounding the Trojan War, and many scholars believe that these stories began with a real historical event: the sack of a Bronze Age city near the Hellespont around 1200 B.C. However, on present evidence we can never know for sure the relationship between stories told by poets beginning around 800 B.C. and historical events hundreds of years before. The songs of Homer and later ancient poets are not about historical events, but about the difficult choices and tragic consequences that face all human beings as they attempt to answer the demands of society and their own desires. In this chapter we consider the events leading up to the war and the story that Homer tells in his *Iliad;* in the next two chapters we consider what happened when Troy fell and the heroes returned home.

Atreïds: The "sons of Atreus," Menelaüs and Agamemnon.   *Ilium:* Another name for Troy.

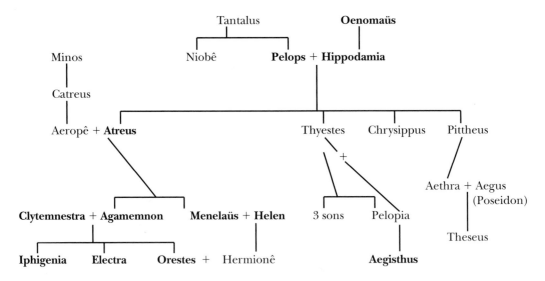

CHART 19.1 The House of Atreus

THE HOUSE OF ATREUS

The kings who led the Greek expedition to Troy came from the House of Atreus (ā-trŭs), which ruled the Argive plain from either Mycenae or Argos. This dynasty is unrelated to that of the earlier Mycenaean king, Perseus, which became extinct after the death of Heracles' persecutor, Eurystheus. The new line went back to Tantalus of Lydia, the arrogant king who dined with the gods, then stole their nectar and ambrosia, then to crown his folly tempted them to eat his own son (Chapter 11). The descendants of Tantalus committed crimes worthy of the founder of their line: hideous crimes of treachery, adultery, cannibalism, incest, rape, and murder. According to the myths that were told about this family, their misfortunes resulted from crimes committed in the early days of the dynasty and the curses that these crimes provoked from their enemies.

Pelops, Oenomaüs, and Hippodamia

Tantalus had invited the gods to a banquet, then chopped up his son, **Pelops** (pē-lops; Chart 19.1), and served the pieces in a stew—to test their omniscience, so the story went. All the gods recognized the dish at once as human flesh and rejected it, except Demeter, too preoccupied with the disappearance of her daughter Persephonê to notice anything amiss. She accidentally consumed Pelops' shoulder. Zeus ordered Hermes to put the pieces back into the pot and boil them some more; out came a fresh child, minus his shoulder. Hephaestus made a new one of ivory, which you could still see in ancient times as a relic in a temple near Argos.

At this time **Oenomaüs** (ē-nō-**mā**-us) ruled as king over Pisa, a village beside the Alpheus river in the district of Elis in the northwest Peloponnesus, in classical times the site of the Olympic Games. Oenomaüs was in love with his own beautiful daughter, **Hippodamia** (hip-po-da-**mī**-a). She refused to sleep with him, but he prevented her from marrying anyone else by offering her as a prize in an unwinnable contest. The suitor had to carry her away in a chariot, was given a head start, and was sent racing toward Corinth. Oenomaüs, who had a team of horses sired by the wind, always caught up with the suitor, speared him from behind, cut off his head, and nailed it to the door of his palace. Hippodamia was so beautiful that these gruesome conditions were no deterrent; soon the door was covered with twelve decaying heads of unsuccessful suitors.[1]

Pelops heard of Hippodamia's beauty and was determined to win the contest. He crossed the sea from Lydia bringing a golden-winged chariot drawn by horses that never tired, gifts from his divine lover, Poseidon. Just to be sure, Pelops also bribed Myrtilus (**mir**-ti-lus), the king's charioteer, promising him the first night in bed with Hippodamia. Myrtilus removed the bronze linchpins[2] from Oenomaüs' chariot and replaced them with wax, so that when Oenomaüs raced toward the Isthmus after Pelops (Fig. 19.1), the heated axle melted the wax and the wheels flew off. Oenomaüs was tangled in the reigns and dragged to death.

Myrtilus, Hippodamia, and Pelops traveled on together. They stopped on a headland so that Pelops could get some water for his new and thirsty wife. When Pelops returned, he found Myrtilus clawing at Hippodamia, eager for his reward. In a rage Pelops threw him from the towering crag into the sea. As Myrtilus fell, he screamed out a curse on Pelops and all his line: Curses on the lips of dying men are particularly effective.

The Banquet of Thyestes

Pelops, purified of his murders of Oenomaüs and Myrtilus, returned to Pisa and became its king. He named the land Peloponnesus, "island of Pelops," and produced many sons, including Pittheus, father of Aethra, Theseus' mother; Chrysippus, raped by Laius, father of Oedipus (for this crime Pelops cursed Laius, which explains the many disasters that befell the House of Cadmus; see Chapter 17); **Thyestes** (thī-**es**-tēz), father of **Aegisthus** (ē-**jis**-thus); and **Atreus,** father of **Menelaüs** (men-e-**lā**-us) and **Agamemnon.**

When Eurystheus, persecutor of Heracles and last descendant of Perseus to sit on the throne of Mycenae, was killed by the Heraclids, an oracle ordered the Mycenaeans to choose a child of Pelops as the new king. The Mycenaeans sent across the mountains to Pisa and asked for Atreus and Thyestes. Which was to be king? Atreus, as the older, was the obvious choice, but Thyestes declared that a token was needed, a sign, and suggested that whoever could produce the fleece from a golden lamb should be king.

---

[1]Cf. the story of Atalanta, Chapter 18.
[2]The linchpin was a cotter-pin at the end of an axle that kept the wheel from falling off.

FIG. 19.1. Pelops flees with Hippodamia, South Italian jug, c. 425 B.C.
He looks over his shoulder to see
whether Oenomaüs pursues, while
Hippodamia raises her right arm
and looks ahead. (Museo Civico,
Arezzo; 1460)

Years before Atreus had vowed to Artemis to sacrifice his finest lamb to her, but
when a lamb with golden fleece appeared in his flocks, he killed it and hid the skin
in a trunk instead of burning the fleece on the altar. The only other person who knew
about this was his wife, Aëropê (ā-**er**-o-pē), a granddaughter of Minos. Unknown to
Atreus, she was carrying on a love affair with her brother-in-law Thyestes and had secretly given him the fleece. When Thyestes proposed that whoever could produce
the skin from a golden lamb should be king, Atreus hastily agreed, only to see
Thyestes produce the very fleece he thought safe in his trunk.

But Atreus was sure that Zeus, god of kings, wanted him to be king, and to prove
it, Atreus declared, Zeus would on the next day make the sun rise in the west.
Thyestes thought this was impossible, but when the sun did rise in the west, crossed
the sky backward, and set in the east, Thyestes withdrew his claim on the throne.
Atreus banished him from the land.

Atreus began to wonder how Thyestes had acquired the fleece and discovered
his wife's infidelity. Burning for revenge, he invited Thyestes, now living abroad, to
return to Mycenae; bygones would be bygones. While Thyestes was entertained in
an outer room, Atreus murdered Thyestes' three little boys, cut off their extremities,
and roasted their trunks in the kitchen, then served the parts to Thyestes. After a
tasty meal, Atreus asked Thyestes whether he knew what he had eaten. He showed
him the heads and limbs of his children.

Thyestes fled, cursing,[3] and traveled to the Delphic Oracle to ask how he could

---

[3]Some attribute the sufferings of the House of Atreus to this curse rather than that of Myrtilus.

even the score with his brother. He learned that he must beget a child by his own daughter, Pelopia (pe-**lō**-pi-a). Ignorant of his daughter's whereabouts, Thyestes left Delphi by night and came to a stream near Sicyon. In the flickering light of a sacrificial fire, he saw a girl go to the water. He saw his chance, jumped from the bushes, and raped her, but in the confusion left his sword behind. He did not know that the girl was in fact Pelopia, nor did she know her attacker.

In the meanwhile, Atreus was searching for Thyestes, sorry that he had let him off so lightly. He came to Sicyon and saw the pretty Pelopia, whom he thought was a daughter of the king. Atreus took her as his new wife. When Pelopia bore a son, Atreus naturally thought it was his own and named him Aegisthus.

Years passed, but Atreus continued to search for Thyestes. At last he sent his two older sons, Agamemnon and Menelaüs, to Delphi to ask Apollo where his brother was. Amazingly, Thyestes was at Delphi too; unable to find his daughter (he thought), he sought new advice from Apollo on how to take revenge on Atreus. Agamemnon and Menelaüs seized Thyestes and dragged him back to Mycenae.

Atreus, delighted that he could finally settle scores with the brother who had seduced his wife, summoned his other "son," Aegisthus, and ordered him to finish off Thyestes. Aegisthus entered the prison house, drew his sword, and prepared to behead Thyestes. Suddenly Thyestes called out, "Where did you get that sword?" "From my mother," Aegisthus replied. "But that's my sword!" cried Thyestes.

Pelopia was summoned in secret. She revealed how she had taken the weapon from a nocturnal rapist, Aegisthus' real father. As she spoke, she realized what had happened—that she had had intercourse with her own father. In horror at the deed, Pelopia seized the sword and plunged it into her heart. Aegisthus, realizing his true paternity, drew out the bloody weapon and carried it to Atreus, seeming proof that his murderous command had been performed. Relieved, Atreus offered sacrifice to the gods, then went to the river to wash his hands. Aegisthus came up from behind and knifed him in the back.[4]

With Atreus dead, the throne of Mycenae was empty, and Thyestes mounted it. Agamemnon and Menelaüs fled and took refuge with **Tyndareüs** (tin-**dar**-e-us), king of Sparta. He was sympathetic to their cause and raised an army. Together they returned to Mycenae to drive Thyestes from the land.

THE HOUSE OF TYNDAREÜS

Leda and the Swan; The Dioscuri

Tyndareüs had married **Leda** (**lē**-da), daughter of King Thestius of Aetolia and sister of Althaea, Meleager's mother (Chart 19.2). Leda's beauty was so great that even Zeus took notice. He appeared to her in the form of a swan, seized her by the nape of the neck (as swans do), and had his way with her. Tyndareüs also had intercourse

---

[4]This complex, detailed, and extravagant myth is a distillation of typical plots of lost plays by Euripides, who must be responsible for the myth's general shape.

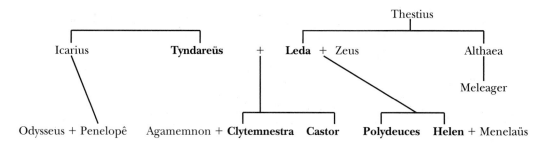

CHART 19.2. The House of Tyndareus

with her on the same night. She gave birth to four children: **Polydeuces** (= Roman Pollux) and **Helen,** fathered by Zeus, were semidivine; **Castor** and **Clytemnestra,** fathered by Tyndareüs, were mortal. According to one version, Leda actually laid a pair of eggs—from one egg hatched Zeus's children, from the other those of Tyndareüs!

As we have seen, Leda's children Castor and Polydeuces are the inseparable Dioscuri, "the sons of Zeus," who traveled on the Argo and joined the Calydonian Boar Hunt. When Theseus carried away a youthful Helen, the Dioscuri went in hot pursuit and brought her back, together with Theseus' mother, Aethra (Chapter 15). When Castor was killed in a cattle raid, the grieving Polydeuces gave up half his immortality to Castor. On alternate days the brothers lived in Hades, then on Olympus. They tend to lurk on the edges of more prominent mythical cycles yet have considerable importance in their own right.[5] To the Romans the Dioscuri were protectors of the Roman state, who appeared to them on horseback during a desperate battle of the early fifth century B.C. The Romans built a grand temple to them in the forum, three columns of which stand today. But in Greek religion, the Dioscuri were preeminently the protectors of sailors in distress (perhaps because of their participation in the voyage of the *Argo*).

The Oath of Tyndareüs

Tyndareüs married Clytemnestra to Agamemnon but was worried about Helen, who had grown up to be the most beautiful woman in the world. The richest and best-born young men from all Greece gathered in Tyndareüs' halls to seek her hand. Among them were Odysseus, son of Laërtes; Diomedes, son of Tydeus who fought against Thebes; Ajax,[6] son of Telamon; Philoctetes (fi-lok-**tē**-tēz), son of Poeas, who had dared to light the funeral pyre of Heracles; Patroclus (pa-**trō**-klus), son of Menoetius, who became Achilles' best friend; Menelaüs, son of Atreus; and many others. Being young, headstrong, and dangerous, the rejected suitors were likely to turn on Tyndareüs once he had made a choice.

---

[5]Some scholars trace their origins back to a very early Indo-European myth about divine horsemen twins (see Chapter 23).
[6]The common Latin form for the Greek *Aias*.

Yeats's "Leda and the Swan"

William Butler Yeats (1865–1939) was born in Dublin and at age 21 dedicated himself to literature. In his life he worked successfully toward the establishment of a national Irish theater, which still exists, but he is best known for his lyric poetry, some of the finest in the modern English language. Yeats's work was much influenced by the Golden Dawn, a secret society dedicated to occultism and magic. His poetry also appealed to contemporary politics and took inspiration from history and, sometimes, classical myth, as in the following sonnet, published in 1924:

Leda and the Swan*

A sudden blow: the great wings beating still
Above the staggering girl, her thighs caressed
By the dark webs, her nape caught in his bill,
He holds her helpless breast upon his breast.
How can those terrified vague fingers push
The feathered glory from her loosening thighs?
And how can body, laid in that white rush,
But feel the strange heart beating where it lies?
A shudder in the loins engenders there
The broken wall, the burning roof and tower
And Agamemnon dead.
    Being so caught up,
So mastered by the brute blood of the air,
Did she put on his knowledge with his power
Before the indifferent beak could let her drop?

*Reprinted with permission of Simon & Schuster from *Collected Poems of W. B. Yeats: A New Edition,* edited by Richard J. Finneran.

In his book *A Vision* (1925), Yeats explains the union of Leda and the swan as symbolizing the opening of a new two-thousand-year age of the Zodiac, that of Sagittarius, which ended with the birth of Christ, at which time began the cycle of Pisces ("fish") now about to end (compare Perspective 13.2). According to Yeats, the union of woman and god was "the annunciation that founded Greece . . . , remembering that they [the Greeks] showed in a Spartan temple, strung up to the roof as a holy relic, an unhatched egg of hers; and from one of her eggs came Love (Helen and Clytemnestra) and from the other War (Castor and Polydeuces)." Yeats here refers to the tradition that Leda's four children did not come from her womb directly, but from two eggs that she laid, fecundated by her union with Zeus and Tyndareüs. Yeats saw history—especially that of antiquity—as a record of the endless struggle of Attraction and Repulsion, Love and Hate, both issuing from the same divine force. However, we might prefer to read his sonnet on Leda more simply, as a metaphor for mortal incomprehension of the divine.

Odysseus understood Tyndareüs' position and realized that he was too poor to be chosen Helen's husband, coming as he did from Ithaca, an obscure rocky island in the western seas. He therefore went to Tyndareüs and offered a solution to his dilemma, if only Tyndareüs would arrange Odysseus' marriage with Tyndareüs' niece, Penelopê (pe-**nel**-o-pē). Odysseus' solution is called the Oath of Tyndareüs, described by Hesiod in a fragment from a poem that cataloged the famous women of olden time:

[78]   Of all the suitors her father° demanded unbreakable pledges,
      making them swear an oath, with libations poured in the fire:
80   "The victor, be he who he may, can rely on my giving support
      in defense of his marriage with Helen, maiden of beautiful arms."
      He ordered the suitors, moreover, to assent to another condition:
      if anyone carried her off, forgetting his own reputation,
      and with it the vengeance to come, then all the suitors together
85   must join in pursuit and exact due punishment from the offender.
      Most of the suitors assented, in empty hopes of the marriage,
      but the son of Atreus was victor, Menelaüs, delighting in battle,
      who offered a price for the bride greater by far than the others.
         Now off in Pelion's forests Chiron was training Achilles,
90   nimble of foot, the bravest of men, though only a stripling.
      Had nimble Achilles come home from the wooded valleys of Pelion
      while Helen still was a maiden, not Menelaüs the warlike,
      nor any man of the suitors would have met success in his wooing.
      But long before then Menelaüs had won and had wedded fair Helen.

HESIOD, *Catalogue of Women,* fragment 204.78
(Merkelbach–West, 78–93)

78. *her father:* Helen's, that is, Tyndareüs.

Helen bore Menelaüs a daughter, Hermionê (her-**mī**-o-nē). But trouble was brewing and had actually begun a long time before, at the wedding of Peleus and Thetis.

THE WEDDING OF PELEUS AND THETIS

Peleus was born on the island of Aegina in the Saronic Gulf. When his father, Aeacus, came to the island, it was uninhabited, until Zeus changed the ants into people, afterward called Myrmidons, "ants." Peleus and his brother Telamon so envied their half-brother Phocus for his superior athletic ability that they murdered him. For this terrible crime Aeacus exiled them, on pain of death if they ever returned. Perhaps because of this stern judgment, Aeacus was believed, by the time of Plato, to be one of the judges of the dead, along with Rhadamanthys and Minos.

Telamon fled to the nearby island of Salamis, just off the harbor of Athens, and became king. There he fathered **Ajax,** a suitor of Helen and one of the greatest heroes in the Trojan war. Peleus traveled much further north to Phthia (**thī**-a) in southern Thessaly.

We saw in our study of Greek cosmogony how Zeus had lusted after Thetis and relented only when Prometheus revealed that Thetis' child would be greater than the father (Chapter 5). To repay the Titan for warning him, Zeus allowed Heracles to shoot the eagle that daily devoured Prometheus' liver; at last the Titan was released from bondage. This story is now attached to that of Peleus because Zeus arranged for Thetis to marry Peleus. Peleus knew where Thetis danced with her nymphs on the seashore at night. He lay in wait, leaped out, and pinned her down. As he clung tightly, she changed into many shapes—fire, a tree, a lion, a bird—but returned at last to her womanly shape. Powerless, Thetis agreed to marry the son of Aeacus (Fig. 19.2).

Hera evidently was grateful to Thetis for not having slept with her husband and was instrumental in providing for Thetis the most splendid wedding ever held, on the slopes of Mount Pelion.[7] Euripides describes this famous wedding in a choral passage from one of his last plays, *Iphigenia in Aulis* (**aw**-lis), probably produced after the poet died in 406 B.C.:

[1036]   What wedding songs rang, what Libyan fluting,
        echoes by lyre-strings, apt for the dance,
        joining the reedy notes of the Pan-pipe
           sounding their strain,
1040   when on Pelion the fair-haired Pierian Muses°
        danced in the banquet given by gods,
        striking the earth with gold-sandaled feet,
           for the marriage of Peleus,
        and lifting their glorious voices for Thetis,
1045   singing her marriage to Aeacus' son
        all through the mountain haunted by Centaurs,
           and the forests of Pelion.
        The child of Dardanus, Zeus's beloved,
        darling delight and sharer of pleasure,
1050   Phrygian Ganymede, poured out the wine
           from craters of gold.
        Weaving their figures on silvery sands,
        fifty maidens, daughters of Nereus,
        linking hands and, singing for joy,
1055   danced for the wedding.
        Up through the pine trees, garlanded green,
        a herd of Centaurs, half man, half horse,
        came to the feast the gods had provided,
           to the crater of Bacchus.
1060   They shouted for joy, "O daughter of Nereus:°

1040. *Pierian Muses:* Pieria, near Mount Olympus, was the birthplace of the Muses.   1060. *daughter of Nereus:* Thetis.

---

[7]For Catullus' poem on this wedding, which also describes the union of Dionysus and Ariadnê embroidered on the wedding bed's coverlet, see Chapter 10.

FIG. 19.2. Peleus wrestles with
Thetis, interior of Attic wine-cup,
c. 500 B.C. Peleus, kneeling, holds
Thetis around the waist. The lion
and three snakes, which seem to attack Peleus, symbolize her many
transformations.   (Antikenmuseum,
Staatliche Museen, Berlin)

> Chiron, versed in the arts of Apollo,
> sends you the message, 'The son you will bear
> will be Thessaly's glory.
> With his Myrmidons,° expert with shield and with spear,
1065   he will ravage the storied country of Priam,
> clothed in the armor made by Hephaestus
> at Thetis' bidding.'"
> Then the gods all sang at the blessed marriage
> of the high-born eldest daughter of Nereus,
1070   and joined her name in the wedding hymn
> with the name of Peleus.

EURIPIDES, Iphigenia in Aulis (1036–1079)

1064. *Myrmidons:* Although Achilles comes from Thessaly, the ethnic title *Myrmidons* descends to
his followers through his father, Peleus, who came from Aegina.

THE JUDGMENT OF PARIS

In the midst of the wedding of Peleus and Thetis, Eris, "strife," appeared at the door
of the wedding tent, resentful because she had not received an invitation (who wants
"strife" at a wedding!). Eris rolled an apple across the floor, crying, "May the most
beautiful goddess take it." (In some versions, the apple had a tag, reading "to the
fairest.") The vain Hera, Aphrodite, and Athena each claimed the apple for herself.
They made such a ruckus in the middle of the party that Zeus ordered them to be
quiet and to present themselves for impartial appraisal before Paris, a son of the Trojan king Priam (Chart 19.3).

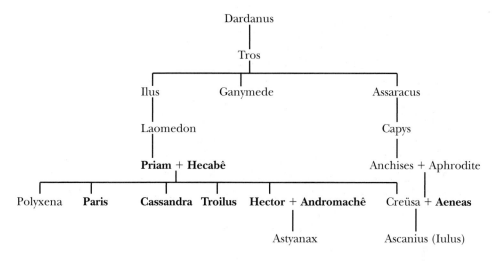

CHART 19.3. The House of Troy

In Homer's account, the Trojans are viewed as a foreign people whose allies, at least, speak foreign tongues (archaeology suggests that in the Late Bronze Age the Trojans may in fact have been Greeks; see Chapter 2). However, Trojans share the same gods and, although Priam has many wives, otherwise behave much like the Greeks, whom Homer calls without distinction *Achaeans* (men from the territory of Achaea), *Argives* (men from Argos), or *Danaäns* (descendants of Danaüs). *Greeks* (Latin *Graeci*) was the name of one of the first tribes the Romans knew in northwestern Greece; *Hellenes* as a term to describe all the Greeks does not appear until after Homer.

Priam was the sole surviving son of Laomedon, whose many other sons Heracles had killed (Chapter 14). Priam married **Hecabê** (**hek**-a-bē),[8] who bore many children, including Hector, destined to be the greatest fighter of the Trojans. When Hecabê became pregnant after Hector was born, she dreamed that she gave birth to a firebrand. A seer explained that the next child would cause the city's destruction. Priam therefore ordered the child exposed on Mount Ida behind Troy, but a shepherd found the child, called him Paris, and raised him as his own. Far more handsome and stronger than the rude hill folk, Paris single-handedly defeated a band of robbers, after which he was also called Alexander, "warder-off of men."

The Trojan Paris, known to have a good eye for a lovely woman, awoke from a nap to find before him the god Hermes, who presented the three feuding goddesses for inspection (Fig. 19.3). One by one they undraped to show their naked bodies to the astonished shepherd. Each also offered a bribe, if only Paris would call her fairest: Hera offered dominion over all the world, Athena offered a glorious military career, but Aphrodite offered the best prize, the most beautiful woman in the world.

---

[8]The Latin form is *Hecuba*.

FIG. 19.3. The judgment of Paris, Attic jug, c. 470 B.C. Paris sits, holding a lyre, beside a ram from his flocks on Mount Ida. A buxom Hera, holding the scepter of authority, stands before him with the Apple of Discord. Behind her are Athena, wearing the aegis and carrying a spear, and Aphrodite, demurely clad in a concealing robe.   (British Museum, London)

Paris declared Aphrodite fairest. As prize she gave him Helen, daughter of Zeus and Leda, who lived in Greece across the sea.

Paris came down from the hills, was recognized in Troy as a lost child of the royal family, and took a ship to Sparta to claim his reward. Menelaüs received Paris warmly, according to the conventions of *xenia*, "guest-friendship." When Menelaüs was called to Crete to attend a funeral, Paris and Helen, irresistibly attracted to one another, gathered up the treasure in the palace and eloped. Thus Helen left behind her lawful husband, her nine-year-old daughter, Hermionê, and her good name—such is the power of Aphrodite.

THE TROJAN WAR

The Gathering at Aulis

When Menelaüs returned from Crete and found that Paris had violated the solemn bonds of *xenia*, he fell into a black rage. To restore the family name, he appealed to his brother, Agamemnon, in Mycenae. The brothers invoked the Oath of Tyndareüs, and soon from all over Greece Helen's former suitors assembled with their armies at the port of **Aulis** on the coast of Boeotia, opposite the long island of Euboea.

However, Odysseus, who had devised the oath, did not appear, and Menelaüs and several companions went to Ithaca to collect him. Recently his wife, Penelopê, had borne a boy, **Telemachus** (tel-**em**-a-kus, "far-fighter," more appropriate to the father than the son); Odysseus had lost his taste for war. When the embassy arrived, they were astonished to find him on the seashore, dressed like a madman, following a plow to which was hitched a horse and a jackass. **Palamedes** (pal-a-**mē**-dēz), son of Nauplius, was not deceived. Famed, like Odysseus, for his cleverness, he had invented the alphabet, dice, numbers, and astronomy. Palamedes seized Telemachus from Penelopê's arms, raced to the beach, and cast the child into the sand before the blade of the plow: If Odysseus were mad, he would plow on, but if sane, he would spare his infant son. Odysseus stopped the plow and joined the expeditionary force.[9]

While they were still gathering at Aulis, **Calchas** (**kal**-kas), prophet of the expedition, declared that the Greeks would never take Troy without the help of Achilles, the son of Peleus and Thetis, who had been too young to be a suitor of Helen. When he was an infant, Thetis placed him on the hearth by night to burn away his mortal portions (as Demeter did to Demophon; see Chapter 9). When Peleus one night discovered them, Thetis angrily removed the child, cast him to the ground, and left the world of mortals to return to her father, Nereus, in the depths of the sea.[10]

Later, Achilles (like Jason) was entrusted to Chiron on Mount Pelion for his education (Fig. 19.4). There he was content to live the outdoor life, hunting every day with his companion, Patroclus. When he grew to maturity, however, Thetis took him to the island of Scyros, east of Euboea, and concealed him in the women's quarters, dressed like a girl. She hoped to prevent him from joining the upcoming war, where he surely would perish in the windy plain of Troy.

Calchas detected through his seercraft that Achilles was on Scyros, but he did not know just where. Odysseus devised a plan. He and Diomedes, pretending to be peddlers, appeared before the palace, hawking trinkets and gewgaws, dainty feminine things for the daughters of the king. The gifts were spread on a table, but a shield and a sword also were placed nearby. The girls were picking over the dainties when a trumpet blast sounded from the shore, as if to announce an attack by pirates. One "girl" seized the shield and sword and leapt to the top of the table, shouting "Let me at them!" "Surely you are Achilles," observed Odysseus, "and we need you for the war." Achilles agreed instantly. The plan to hide him among the women had been his mother's idea.

---

[9]Later, during the war, Odysseus took revenge on Palamedes. He planted a letter on a Trojan captive implying that Palamedes intended to betray the Greeks for gold. When the Greeks uncovered a sack of treasure in Palamedes' tent (which Odysseus placed there), they stoned him to death and left him to rot unburied, a traitor's death.

[10]A much later story, first attested in a Roman poet of the first century A.D., told how Thetis held Achilles by the heel and dipped him in the river Styx. He could never be wounded, except in the heel where her hand kept off the water, the origin of our phrase "Achilles' heel" to describe a point of vulnerability. Late in the war, Apollo guided an arrow, shot by Menelaüs, to hit Achilles in the heel, bringing about his death.

FIG. 19.4. Chiron with Achilles, Roman fresco painting from Herculaneum, c. A.D. 60. The wise Centaur instructs the young Achilles in the art of playing the lyre, hallmark of the Greek aristocrat.   (Museo Archeologico Nazionale, Naples; 1957)

The Journey to Troy

Finally all the warriors were gathered. Important figures, in addition to the suitors of Helen already named, were another Ajax, son of Oileus (unrelated to Ajax, son of Telamon); Nestor, king of Pylos and a son of Neleus (Pelias' brother; see Chart 18.1); Menestheus, king of Athens (he had expelled Theseus from the kingship); Idomeneus (ī-**dom**-e-nūs), king of Crete; Machaön and Podalirius, sons of Asclepius, surgeons and physicians to the army; and Diomedes, son of Tydeus of the Seven against Thebes.

They set out across the Aegean, but no one knew where Troy was (any more than the Argonauts knew how to find Colchis). Eventually they came ashore south of the Troad (the area around Troy), in a land called Mysia. The local king Telephus (**tel-**

e-fus), a son of Heracles, tried to drive them off, and Achilles wounded him in a skirmish. Realizing they were not at Troy and not knowing what to do, the Greeks got back in their ships and returned to Aulis.

The wound of Telephus refused to heal. Following an oracle that "only that which harmed you can cure you," Telephus crossed the sea, searching for his enemy Achilles. He found him at Aulis and agreed to lead them to Troy if Achilles would heal him. Achilles saw the true meaning of the oracle, scraped off some corrosion from his spear, and placed it in Telephus' wound. It healed at once.

Again the Greeks were ready to sail, but now the winds blew constantly in the wrong direction. They waited while the troops grew restless, food ran short, and disease threatened. At last Calchas revealed how Artemis was behind it all: Agamemnon once boasted, while hurling his spear at a deer, that "even Artemis could not do so well." To save the expedition, Agamemnon would have to sacrifice his own daughter **Iphigenia** (if-i-jen-ī-a).

Agamemnon sent a herald to bring Iphigenia to Aulis, pretending that he wanted to marry her to Achilles. Decked out in saffron wedding clothes, Iphigenia was led to a wood, where Agamemnon slashed her throat on an altar. The chorus in Aeschylus' play *Agamemnon,* the first in a trilogy called the *Oresteia* after Agamemnon's son, Orestes, performed in 458 B.C., tells of Agamemnon's initial hesitation, then commitment to the bloody deed (Fig. 19.5):

[218]   But once he bowed his neck to Necessity's yoke,
          a sigh gave proof of his terrible change of heart,
220   unholy, faithless, obscene.
          Grim and unyielding he stood, unmoved by scruple.
          Wicked intention arouses a sort of courage,
          stubborn, deranged, begetter of endless sorrow.
          He nerved himself to be his daughter's butcher,
225   to prosecute a war fought over a woman,
               to make this payment on his navy's budget.
          Her youth, her pleas, her anxious cries of "Father!"
          affected not at all the grim old men
               whose plans demanded war.
230   Her father finished reciting ritual prayers,
          and gave the acolytes their orders:
          to see her properly dressed (though collapsed and fainting);
          to bring her, quickly and smoothly, and lift her on the altar,
          just as they would a sacrificial goat; to gag her pretty mouth,
235   to silence her words with calm but wordless force,
          to keep unseemly cries from polluting her family.
               She let her wedding dress drop to the ground;
          she shot a piteous glance at each of her killers,
          eager to speak, like a picture from happier times,
240   when she used to sing at feasts in her father's halls,
          when the cheerful wine cup had passed three times.
          With clear maiden voice she would add to the grace
               of the luck-bringing hymn of Apollo.

FIG. 19.5. The sacrifice of Iphigenia, Roman fresco painting from Pompeii, c. A.D. 60. Two warriors, perhaps Odysseus and Diomedes, carry Iphigenia to the altar on the left, presided over by a statuette of Artemis accompanied by two hounds; Agamemnon stands waiting to perform the sacrifice, his head veiled in sorrow. To the right stands the prophet Calchas holding a prophetic wand(?) Above, Artemis watches as Iphigenia, riding on Artemis' deer, is carried away to the land of the Taurians. (Museo Archeologico Nazionale, Naples; University of Wisconsin, Madison Photo Archive)

> I saw no more; I have no more to tell,
> 245 but Calchas' prophecies always come true.
>
> AESCHYLUS, *Agamemnon* (218–251)

According to another tradition, similar to the story of Phrixus and Hellê (Chapter 18), at the last second Artemis sent down a doe as a substitute. The doe was killed, while the goddess carried Iphigenia to the land of the Taurians in the remote northern regions of the Black Sea, the modern Crimea. There she became priestess to a foreign and even more savage Artemis, who demanded the human sacrifice of all strangers.

As was predicted, the winds now blew fair. Again the fleet set sail, stopping at an island to take on water and to sacrifice to the gods. A snake crept from beneath the altar and bit **Philoctetes** on the foot. As the Greeks sailed on, Philoctetes' wound festered, ran with pus, and smelled so foul that his companions abandoned him in disgust on the island of Lemnos. There he eked out a wretched existence, lying at the mouth of a filthy cave, saved only by the bow he had received from Heracles as reward for lighting his pyre, with which he shot small game.

The Greeks approached the Troad, but an oracle had declared that the first to land would be first to die, and no one wanted to go ashore. Finally Protesilaüs (prō-te-si-**lā**-us) bravely leapt from the ship and ran up the beach. The Trojan warrior Hector came over a rise and cut him down, the first to die in the long war.[11]

Helen on the Wall

Odysseus and Menelaüs went to the city to ask for the return of Helen and the treasure and so settle the issue without further bloodshed.[12] For their efforts, they were nearly killed by treachery. Thus the fighting began. Our most complete source for the events of the Trojan War is Homer's *Iliad*. Although it focuses on a single incident in the ninth year of the war, the quarrel between Agamemnon and Achilles, it contains many descriptions of earlier episodes, including one that belongs to the first years of the war, often called "Helen on the Wall." The Trojan elders have climbed to the top of the city walls to overlook the host of warriors on the plain below. One elder complains at risking so much for the sake of a woman, when Helen herself comes to join them:

[150]   By now they were old and no longer able to enter the battle,
        but wise and skilled in counsel. As locusts perch in the foliage,
        endlessly chirping away in their thin and tremulous voices,
        so the old men of Troy conversed as they sat on the tower.
        Their words flew swift as arrows into the heart of the matter:
155   "No one can blame the Trojans or yet the well-greaved Achaeans,
        for enduring so much and so long for such a beautiful woman;
        to my eyes, indeed, she resembles the form of a goddess immortal.
        Yet beautiful as she is, let her sail away to her country,
        and not be left here in Troy, a scourge to us and our children."
160   So the old men chattered on, but Priam called out to Helen,
        "Hither, my daughter, come sit beside me here on the rampart,
        to watch your first husband, your brother-in-law, and your friends.
        You bear no blame in my eyes; the gods themselves were the authors
        of our war against the Achaeans and all the misery that followed.
165   Tell me, now, who is that man, a very giant in stature?
        What is his name, that Argive, that man so strong and so noble?

[11]Protesilaüs had just married Laodamia, who made a statue of him to comfort her while he was gone. When word of his death arrived, she prayed to Zeus to let him return, if only for a short time. Zeus agreed, and Protesilaüs' ghost came back to enter the statue for three hours. As he left to descend again to Hades, he asked Laodamia to follow him soon; she stabbed herself and joined him in the underworld.

[12]Possibly this mission took place before the expedition; the sources are not clear.

Others, I grant you, stand taller than he by as much as a head,
but these eyes of mine have never fallen upon one so handsome,
nor with such an appearance of power. He must be a king indeed!"

170 Helen, loveliest of women, replied to him with these words:
"Certainly, father. You know the respect and honor I owe you,
but—would I had met bitter death when I eloped with your son!
when I followed him here to Troy, abandoning husband and kindred,
even the daughter I loved, at the age when children are dearest.

175 Well, it was not to be thus, and I wither in self-reproach.
So let me answer the question and tell you what you inquire:
that man is the son of Atreus, Agamemnon, ruler of empire,
combining the wisdom of kings with a soldier's courage and skill.
Brother-in-law to a slut—but so distant it seems like a dream."

180 At that, old Priam gazed at the hero in wonder and murmured:
"Ah, lucky son of Atreus, favored by gods and by fortune,
how mighty a host are your subjects, the valiant youth of Achaea!
I once served, long ago, in Phrygia, country of vineyards,
and saw the Phrygian troops, their horses flashing with bronze,

185 the people of Otreus and Mygdon, kings very like the immortals,
advancing up the Sangarius to make their way into battle.
I was a young cadet, who had gone along for my training,
that day when the Amazons came, women, but equals of men.
But even that numberless host was less than these clear-eyed Achaeans."

190 Next, observing Odysseus, old Priam inquired of Helen,
"Now tell me, daughter, I pray, who that man is, over yonder,
the one who is short by a head of Atreus' son Agamemnon,
but broader, at least to my eye, of shoulder and deeper of chest.
He has laid his weapons aside, nearby on the life-giving earth.

195 Like a ram with a dirty coat he prowls the ranks of his soldiers,
a ram with a flock of ewes, bearers of fleeces of silver."
Helen, the daughter of Zeus, responded at once to his query:
"A different sort of man! for that is the crafty Odysseus,
son of Laërtes, brought up in rocky Ithaca's village,

200 skilled at all sorts of devices and clever deceitful maneuvers."
Then thoughtful Antenor° broke in and added this observation:
"My lady, what you remark is indeed nothing less than the truth.
Some time ago noble Odysseus, with Menelaüs the warrior,
came here to Troy to discuss the issues your presence had raised.

205 I entertained the two in my house as beloved companions,
and thus came to know their characteristics of body and spirit.
When they met the assembled Trojans and entered in the debating,
If they stood up, Menelaüs was taller and broader of shoulder,
but seated, Odysseus appeared to me of the two to be more impressive.

210 Again, when the time arrived for open (and secret) proposals,
Menelaüs, a man of few words, would bluntly offer suggestions,
brief ones, yes, but straightforward, the words of a younger man.
Then Odysseus would slowly arise. Hesitant, eyes on the floor,

201. *Antenor:* A Trojan nobleman. After the war he escaped to Italy, where he founded the city of Padua.

he stood with never a gesture, holding the scepter in silence.
215   People would say he was tongue-tied, or maybe exceedingly stupid;
you would think him dull and slow, or even a half-witted idiot.
But—when out of his throat a thunderous voice came resounding,
and words poured out like snow, blown by a blizzard in winter—
then no man on this earth dared argue against such a speaker;
220   no one who gazed on his face could refrain from admiring Odysseus."
    Thirdly, old Priam saw Ajax, and thus he inquired of Helen:
"And who is that other Achaean, so big, of such noble appearance,
taller than all the Argives by a head, and broader of shoulder?"
    Helen, the glory of women, she of the long-skirted gown,
225   replied: "That is Ajax the mighty, wall of defense to the Greeks.
Beyond him is Idomeneus, like a god in the midst of his Cretans,
whose marshals are gathered around him. Ah, many and many a time
the warlike king, Menelaüs, showed welcome to him in our palace,
whenever he came there from Crete. And many fierce-eyed Achaeans
230   stand there in my sight, men I know and whose names I could list.
But two men I cannot see, both of them rulers of peoples,
Polydeuces, mightiest of boxers, and Castor, tamer of horses.
One mother bore the pair, who indeed are full brothers of mine.
Perhaps they did not follow the army from fair Lacedaemon,
235   or they may be coming soon, in ships that traverse the ocean.
Again, they may not be willing to join in the battle of heroes,
fearing disgraceful reproach may follow the shame of their sister."
    So Helen answered Priam, but in fact the life-giving earth
of Lacedaemon, their own dear country, enshrouded the two.[13]

HOMER, Iliad (3.150–244)

The Anger of Achilles

The quarrel between Achilles and Agamemnon, which led to Achilles' unbridled anger and its fateful consequences, the main subject of Homer's *Iliad*, began in the ninth year of the war when Chryses (krī-sēz), a priest of Apollo, came to the Greek camp to ransom his daughter **Chryseïs** (krī-sē-is, "daughter of Chryses"), whom Achilles had captured in a raid. In the distribution of the booty, Chryseïs was given to Agamemnon. Although the assembled Greeks urged that the girl be given back to Chryses, Agamemnon bluntly announced that it would be unworthy for him as supreme commander to lack a girl as booty: According to the heroic code, booty, or war-prize (*geras*), is the outward and visible sign of a man's honor (*tīmê*, literally "value"), which a Homeric warrior covets above all else. Agamemnon brusquely dismissed Chryses: If ever again he appeared near the camp, Agamemnon would kill him.

Chryses walked away along the loud-resounding sea, then raised his arms to his special god, Apollo, lord of plague. Apollo heard his prayers for vengeance against the Greeks and loosed his plague-arrows on the camp. The funeral pyres burned day

---

[13]Homer does not seem to know the story about the Dioscuri sharing immortality between them.

The Beauty of Helen

The image of Helen stands for supreme feminine beauty, the pleasures and dangers that the female can offer to the male, and the eternal feminine. Her figure has inspired countless poets. English poet Christopher Marlowe (1564–1593), who may have written parts of several of Shakespeare's plays and who died at age thirty in a tavern brawl after a brilliant career in the theater, told in his *Dr. Faustus* the story of a man who sells his soul to the Devil in exchange for earthly pleasure and power. The hero announces to Mephistopheles (the Devil) that he wants to sleep with Helen, the most beautiful woman who ever lived. His famous words to her when she appears to him show how well known were the events of the Trojan saga to a popular audience in the late sixteenth century:

> Was this the face that launched a thousand ships
> And burnt the topless towers of Ilium?
> Sweet Helen, make me immortal with a kiss.

[She kisses him.]

> Her lips suck forth my soul. See where it flies!
> Come Helen, come, give me my soul again.
> Here will I dwell, for heaven is in these lips,
> And all is dross that is not Helena.
> I will be Paris, and for love of thee
> Instead of Troy shall Wittenberg° be sacked;
> And I will combat with weak Menelaus
> And wear thy colors on my plumèd crest.°
> Yea, I will wound Achilles in the heel
> And then return to Helen for a kiss.
> O, thou art fairer than the evening's air,
> Clad in the beauty of a thousand stars.
> Brighter art thou than flaming Jupiter
> When he appeared to hapless Semele,
> More lovely than the monarch of the sky
> In wanton Arethusa's° azured arms,
> And none but thou shalt be my paramour.

CHRISTOPHER MARLOWE, *Dr. Faustus* (99–118)

Wittenberg: Faustus's home.   . . . *crest:* The way a medieval knight would attach to his armor a piece of cloth given to him by his beloved.   *Arethusa:* Marlowe does a little myth-making of his own: Arethusa, a water nymph who governed a fountain on the island of Ortygia near Syracuse, was never loved by Zeus in recorded Greek myth.

American poet Edgar Allan Poe (1809–1849), master of Gothic tales of horror and inventor of the mystery story, also called on the image of Helen in a famous poem, *To Helen,* written for a woman he knew:

Helen, thy beauty is to me
Like those Nicaean° barks of yore,
That gently, o'er a perfumed sea,
    The weary wayworn wanderer bore
    To his own native shore.
On desperate seas long wont to roam,
    Thy hyacinth hair, thy classic face,
Thy Naiad° airs have brought me home
    To the glory that was Greece
And the grandeur that was Rome.°
Lo! in yon brilliant window-niche
    How statue-like I see thee stand!
The agate lamp within thy hand,
    Ah! Psyche,° from the regions which
    Are Holy Land!

Nicaean: Poe made up this adjective, which does, however, suggest the ancient port of Megara (named after Nisus, who had the single lock of purple hair).   Naiad: Female spirit of the water. *To the glory . . . Rome:* The source of this famous phrase.   Psyche: The Greek word for "soul."

and night. After nine years of exhausting war, the Greeks were no closer to victory than when they came, and now disease decimated their ranks.

Calchas announced that only by giving up Chryseïs could they be saved. Agamemnon is backed into a corner. He agrees in a public assembly to give her back, but declares that he will then take another woman, for honor's sake. Achilles reminds him that there are no unassigned girls stored away to give out, and that Agamemnon should wait until Troy is sacked, when he can have all the women he wants. If all the women are assigned, Agamemnon retorts, then he will take someone else's, even Achilles' own prize, **Briseïs** (brī-sē-is). After all, he is supreme commander and can do what he wants, words that fire Achilles' wrath:

[148]   Achilles, speedy of foot, glared at Agamemnon and answered:
           "See here, you arrogant scoundrel, greedy for ill-gotten profit,
150   why should an honest Achaean be ready to follow your orders,
           to take to the field, to battle even to death with the Trojans?
           I did not come here to fight their men in some personal quarrel;
           these men have done me no wrong, rustling my cattle or horses,
           or wasting the bountiful crops of the fertile meadows of Phthia.
155   Between us stretches a waste of thundering sea and dim mountains.
           No; it was you that we followed, scoundrel lacking in scruples,
           to win great glory for Menelaüs and you, you scavenging jackal.
           All this you ignore and pretend it is none of your business,
           and now you haughtily threaten to steal the prize of my valor,
160   for which I labored and fought, and which the Achaeans awarded.
           When we Achaeans have sacked a prosperous town of the Trojans,
           my share of loot is never the equal of what is awarded to you.
           Although my arms have always endured far more of the labor of battle,
           when the time to distribute has come, you get the bigger award,
165   and I reel back to the ships, worn out, consoled by a pittance.
               Very well; I shall return to Phthia. It is certainly better

to sail in the sharp-prowed vessels back again to my homeland,
than remain dishonored at Troy, amassing loot for your coffers."
     To this the lord Agamemnon, the leader of armies, retorted,
170 "Go ahead, if that's how you feel; I don't intend to implore you
to stay here just for my sake. I have plenty of other supporters,
who treat me with proper esteem, and among them Zeus the Adviser.
But you are the man I most hate of all these god-favored rulers,
for discord, quarrel and war are always your favorite pleasures.
175 You can fight, no credit to you; some god has given that talent.
So go on home with your ships, and take your Myrmidons with you
to serve as your subjects. I don't care at all what you do,
and I'm not afraid of your anger. But let me give you a warning:
Phoebus Apollo demands the return of Chryseïs; so be it;
180 I shall send her in my own ship, with an escort of my companions.
But you can be certain of this: I shall go myself to your shelter
and personally carry away your booty, the fair-cheeked Briseïs.
Then, perhaps, you will learn how much your better I am,
and others will hesitate to think of themselves as my equals."
185   The challenge enraged Achilles; his angry spirit debated:
should he draw his keen-edged sword, hanging down by his thigh,
thrust the others aside, and assassinate proud Agamemnon,
or should he swallow his anger, controlling his furious spirit?
He had barely started to draw his great sword out of its scabbard,
190 when down from the heavens Athena came flying, urged on by Hera,
who cared for both men in her heart and did her best to protect them.
Standing behind him, she caught at the yellow hair of Achilles,
appearing to him alone, unseen by the rest of the council.
Astounded, Achilles turned round, and at once knew Pallas Athena,
195 for her eyes flashed a terrible gleam. The hero addressed her
in words that flew to the target, "O daughter of Zeus of the aegis,
why have you come? to gaze at the folly of vain Agamemnon?
I tell you straight out what is sure: that Agamemnon will perish,
gasping out life for the folly he showed in his treatment of me."
200   At once to Achilles retorted the goddess, gray-eyed Athena:
"I have come to quiet your fury, so show some sense and obey me.
Hera, white-shouldered goddess, has sent me racing from heaven,
Hera, who cares for you both, and does her best to protect you.
So quit—at once!—your anger; stop fumbling about for your sword.
205 Stab him with words of scorn, show your irrevocable purpose.
For I can safely assert the consequence certain to follow:
he will be forced to concede gifts thrice the worth of Briseïs
to pay for this shameful behavior. Just listen to me and endure."
     Achilles, swiftest of runners, made this reply to Athena:
210 "A man must follow the orders of two such immortals as you,
however enraged he may be; such a course is always the wiser,
for whoever obeys the gods will find that they listen to him."
     With that, he checked his hand on the silver hilt of his weapon,
and thrust the mighty sword with a crash back into its scabbard,
215 obeying the words of Athena, who soared back up to Olympus,
to the house of Zeus of the aegis, amid the other immortals.

Once more the son of Peleus poured out his bitter invective
on Agamemnon, not checking the flow of his blistering fury:
"You sot, with the face of a mastiff to cover the heart of a doe,
220   your courage was never enough to drive you to put on your armor
and charge along with the rest of us into the heat of the battle,
or even to join with the bravest Achaeans in laying an ambush,
something you think is the equal of choosing to go to your death.
How much more pleasant to go through all the host of Achaeans,
225   stealing the prizes of any who dare to protest your embezzling!
A king who devours his people rules a nation of cowards;
otherwise, son of Atreus, your insolence now would be ended.
One more thing I shall say, and swear a great oath to confirm it:
look here, at this staff I hold. No more can branches and leaves
230   sprout from its stem, cut away so long ago in the mountains.
A bronze knife peeled bark and leaves: its life has forever departed.
Yet still the Achaeans take it in hand while making decisions;
they draw inspiration from Zeus, and make this scepter a token.
With it in my hand, I swear that soon desire for Achilles
235   will settle on all the Greeks. You too, Agamemnon, will share it,
but regret will do you no good when men fall dying by hundreds,
slain by the murderous hands of Hector. Your spirit will ache
and curse the way it dishonored the bravest of all the Achaeans."

HOMER, *Iliad* (1.148–244)

Achilles withdraws to his tent and sulks. Agamemnon's men come and take away Briseïs. Weeping, Achilles begs his mother, Thetis, for revenge on Agamemnon, who has wronged him, and on the Greeks who allowed him to do it. She asks Zeus, who owes her a favor, to destroy the Greeks, to make them realize their error when they dishonored Achilles by taking away his prize; Zeus agrees.

HECTOR AND ANDROMACHÊ

The fighting between Greeks and Trojans is in full fury when Hector returns briefly to the city, then, in one of the famous passages in ancient literature, leaves his wife, **Andromachê** (an-**drom**-a-kē), and his infant son, Astyanax (as-**tī**-a-naks, "king of the city"), and returns to battle. In this passage Homer sums up the roles of men, women, and children in a cruel, dangerous world:

[390]   Hector ran from the house, back again by the well-surfaced streets,
crossing the whole great city, and came to the Scaean gateway,
leading out of the town. There his wife came running to meet him,
Andromachê, rich in her dower, the daughter of noble Eëtion,
the king who once had dwelt by the wooded mountain of Placos,
395   above the city of Thebê, and had ruled the men of Cilicia.°
His daughter was married to Hector, hero with armor of bronze,

395. . . . *of Cilicia:* In southern Anatolia; Thebê is unconnected with Boeotian Thebes.

whom now she met by the gate. Beside her was walking a nursemaid,
bearing their good-humored baby, an infant still, on her bosom—
Hector's beloved small son, as bright as a star in his beauty.

400 "Scamandrius" Hector had named him; "Astyanax" everyone else,
for Hector, as everyone knew, was Troy's only hope of defense.
Hector stood there in silence, smiling down at the baby,
while Andromachê stood nearby, but could not hold back her tears.
She clasped his hand in her own and spoke her heartfelt entreaty:

405 "Hector," she pleaded, "your prowess is going to be your undoing.
Do you not pity at all this babe, or your poor troubled partner,
doomed to be called your widow, as soon as the gathered Achaeans,
making a charge, bring you low? Far better for me, if I lose you,
to pass at once to my grave. Thereafter no comfort, for sorrow

410 forever will follow my steps, once death has ended your days;
pain alone will be left. My father, my mother, have perished.
My father was slain by the hands of the glorious hero Achilles,
when he plundered the populous city, high-gated Cilician Thebê
and slew its defender, Eëtion. Yet he did not strip him of armor:

415 his chivalry paid due respect, leaving his well-fashioned weapons
to cover the corpse on the funeral pyre he heaped for my father.
Nymphs of the mountain, daughters of Zeus who carries the aegis,
surrounded the spot by planting a beautiful thicket of elm trees.
Those seven brothers I had, brought up with me in the palace—

420 where are they now? in a single day they descended to Hades:
Achilles, quick on his feet, dispatched them all in one battle,
in a raid for slow-gaited cattle and sheep with silvery fleeces.
My mother, one-time queen of the land under wood-covered Placos—
Achilles carried her hither as part of the loot of his foray,

425 but gladly released her again in exchange for a bountiful ransom;
Artemis, lady of archers, destroyed her,° at home in the palace.
    Thus, Hector, you have become to me both father and mother,
you have become my brother—but above all, the husband I cherish.
Now hear the prayer of my anguish: stay safely here on the tower,

430 lest your dear son be orphaned, and I be left as your widow.
    Check the advance of the army before it passes the fig tree,
where the city is hard to defend, and the wall is easy of access.
There three times the bravest Achaeans have probed our defenses,
led by the pair of Aiantes° and Idomeneus,° glorious hero,

435 by the two sons of Atreus, and by Tydeus' powerful son.°
Perhaps some seer has revealed a prophetic account of our ruin;
perhaps their own native courage is driving them on to attack."
    Hector, the shining-plumed hero, answered Andromachê thus:
"Dear wife, I constantly worry over all the matters you mention,

440 but even more for my fame in the mouths of the people of Ilium,

---

426. *Artemis . . . destroyed her:* Homer speaks of the sudden, nonviolent death of men as "dying by the arrows of Apollo," that of women as "dying by the arrows of Artemis."   434. *Aiantes:* Plural of Ajax (= Greek Aias): Ajax son of Telamon and Ajax son of Oileus. They are sometimes called the "greater" and the "lesser" Ajax.   434. *Idomeneus:* Leader of the Cretans.   435. *Tydeus' powerful son:* Diomedes.

both men and long-skirted women, if they discovered me skulking
like a coward here in the city, away from the tumult of battle.
Such feelings, indeed, have never kept me away from the fighting,
since the day I learned the lesson of how to summon my courage,
445   and always join the struggle amid the first ranks of the Trojans,
defending the fame of my father, and my own reputation as well.
But this too I know full well, down deep in my heart and my spirit:
the day will certainly come when holy Ilium shall perish,
and Priam of the stout ashwood spear, and all the people of Priam.
450   Yet not the misery coming hereafter to Troy and her people,
not even the woe of Lord Priam and of Hecabê, mother who bore me,
not yet the pains of my brothers, so many and so courageous,
destined to fall in the dust at the hands of implacable foemen,
affects me nearly as much as the thought of your terrible future,
455   when some bronze-armored Achaean shall ruthlessly drag you away,
mourning the loss of your freedom. As drudge for some other woman,
you will plod to and fro at the loom, perhaps in faraway Argos,
or labor beneath urns of water drawn from a faraway spring,
and bitter compulsion will force you to endure perpetual shame.
460   Perhaps somebody will notice your sorrow and tears and remark,
'That woman is widow of Hector, bravest of horse-taming Trojans,
he who protected the city, in the war they fought over Troy.'
So perhaps will he speak; fresh grief will rise in your spirit,
at the loss of the one man able to fend off slavery's approach.
465   Heaven grant that piled-up earth may long have covered my body,
before I hark to your screams and the brutal cries of abduction."
    So speaking, glorious Hector reached out for his little son,
but the baby whimpered and buried his head in his nurse's bosom,
scared at his father's array, the bronze and the horsehair crest,
470   as he saw it shaking and trembling above the peak of the helmet.
His father and lady mother together burst out into laughter,
but Hector at once took it off, set down the glittering helmet,
gave his small baby a kiss, and dandled the child in his arms,
offering up this entreaty to Zeus and the other immortals:
475   "O Zeus and the rest of you gods, grant that my son may develop
into a champion like me, a man of renown to the Trojans,
courageous and mighty in battle, a ruler of Troy by his might.
Some day people may say, as my son is returning from battle.
'Indeed, this man is much braver than even Hector, his father.'
480   May he bring blood-stained trophies, spoils of the enemy dead;
may his mother rejoice at heart, after all the woe she has suffered."
    He silently put the baby in the loving arms of his wife,
who hugged it close in her fragrant bosom, smiling through tears.
Hector watched her in pity, caressed her, and spoke to her thus:
485   "Don't be too troubled at heart; no one will send me to Hades,
until I am destined to fall. For no one, brave man or coward,
once he was born on the earth, has ever avoided that hour.
So go back to the palace, to all the tasks of the household,
back to the loom and shuttle, to keeping the maids at their work.
490   War is the task of all men born in Ilium—mine most of all."

Hector picked up his helmet, smoothing its horsehair crest,
while Andromachê slowly retreated, weeping, back to the palace.
She presently came to the well-built house of manslaying Hector;
within it, she found a group of her women all huddled together,
495   all of whom burst into tears to see her returning alone.
Those women lamented for Hector, not knowing he still was alive,
and did not imagine he ever would come unscathed from the battle,
or escape alive from the furious hands of the warlike Achaeans.

HOMER, Iliad (6.390–502)

The Embassy to Achilles

Zeus grants Thetis' request, and after much fighting the battle turns against the Greeks. Fearing they will be destroyed and regretting his own behavior, Agamemnon decides to offer Achilles an enormous reward to get him to come back and fight. Here Agamemnon speaks to his councilors, addressing Nestor, who has urged reconciliation with Achilles. The passage well exemplifies what was considered valuable in the eighth century B.C., and the extent of worldly power:

[115]   "O wise old man, how truly do you catalogue all my offenses!
How blind I have been! and I cannot deny your impeachment.
When Zeus delights in a man, that man is worth a whole army.
So he has honored Achilles and is ravaging all the Achaeans.
Since I am clearly to blame for my terrible blindness of spirit,
120   I will gladly make my amends with recompense knowing no limit,
and now in your ears will list the glorious gifts that I offer.
Seven tripods, not marked by the fire. Ten talents of gold.
Twenty well-burnished kettles. A dozen solid-hoofed horses,
winners of prizes, swift-footed victors in many a contest.
125   Nobody owning such horses could be considered a pauper,
nor could he ever be lacking in gold, that bringer of honor,
if the horses win such prizes as those they have won for me.
Seven women from Lesbos, all highly skilled with the needle,
whom I received as my share when the city was sacked by Achilles,
130   who in loveliness far outshine all other beautiful women.
These will I give, and with them will go Briseus' daughter,
she whom I dragged from Achilles. I shall also swear a great oath
I have never entered her bed, nor slept with her in the manner
which is common to all mankind, the joining of men and their women.
135   All this I promise at once. If the gods allow us to plunder
the mighty city of Priam, he may load a ship to the gunwales,
bronze and gold as he wishes, when we Greeks distribute the loot.
He may pick of the Trojan women whatever twenty he chooses,
of those who are next after Helen of Argos in womanly beauty.
140   If ever we make our way home to Argos, in fertile Achaea,
he may marry a daughter of mine and in honor equal Orestes,
my son, who is now being reared in a house of power and riches.
Three daughters I have in my palace, a house as firm as a rock:

Chrysothemis, Iphianassa,° Laodicê—his the decision,
145   which he shall take as his bride back to the household of Peleus,
paying no bride-price at all. I shall add by way of atonement
gifts like none ever offered to go with a daughter in marriage.
For he shall receive no less than seven populous cities:
Enopê; Cardamylê; Irê, surrounded by meadows:
150   Pherae, beloved by gods; the fertile fields of Anthia;
Aepia, fair to the eyes; and Pedasus, rich in its vineyards.
All these lie near to the sea, on the borders of Pylos the sandy.
Those who live in these towns are wealthy in sheep and in cattle,
and will reverence him as a god, paying him homage and tribute,
155   and obeying his righteous decrees beneath his benevolent scepter.
All this I will happily grant if he ceases his indignation;
let him not be like Hades, most hateful of gods to us mortals,
implacable, not to be swayed. May he yield to me and my pleading,
who am senior to him by as much as my kingly rank is the higher.

HOMER, *Iliad* (9.115–161)

144. *Iphianassa:* Evidently a variation of *Iphigenia;* Homer does not seem to know about the sacrifice at Aulis.

Odysseus, the great fighter Ajax, and Phoenix, Achilles' former tutor, who as an old man accompanied Achilles to Troy, walk along the sea to the tent of Achilles. They report Agamemnon's offer (Fig. 19.6). To their astonishment Achilles turns them down:

[308]   "Kingly son of Laërtes, thoughtful and clever Odysseus,
I must answer you frankly, declaring not only my feelings,
310   but my intention as well; I would not have you trying to talk me,
one of you after the other, into consent with your offer.
As much as I hate Hell's gate do I hate a man who says one thing,
secretly thinking another. I shall bluntly declare my decision.
It does not seem likely to me that Atreus' son Agamemnon
315   nor any other Danaän can persuade me to alter my purpose.
You see the thanks that I get for brutal and endless contention
with fierce and determined foes. As well to stay out of the battle
as enter and fight like a hero; the reward is exactly the same,
for equal honor is given to coward and soldier of courage.
320   Doers of mighty deeds die as surely as those who do nothing.
For year after worrisome year I risked survival in battle;
what does it profit me now? A bird brings food to her nestlings,
whatever morsel she catches, though she herself may go hungry.
Like her I have lain and tossed all through the sleepless nights
325   and battled the bloodstained days against men defending their women.
Twelve populous cities I sacked, attacking by sea in my ships;
eleven more did I capture by land, in the fertile-soiled Troad.
From all these cities I plundered rare and uncountable riches,
which I used to bring back and deliver to Atreus' son Agamemnon.
330   He for his part would stay behind by the swift-running vessels,
receiving the loot, and dealing it out in niggardly portions,

FIG. 19.6. The embassy to Achilles, Attic jug c. 480 B.C. Achilles, second from the right, sits gloomily on his stool, cloak pulled over his head, while Odysseus, seated before him and wearing the petasos, or traveler's cap, attempts to persuade Achilles to return to battle. Behind Odysseus stands Phoenix, Achilles' tutor, and behind Achilles his good friend Patroclus.   (Staatliche Antikensammlungen und Glyptothek, Munich; GL 8770)

keeping the bulk for himself. What he doles out to the nobles,
that he allows them to keep; from me alone of the army
by force he reclaims what he gives.
                                   He has a wife, freely chosen;
335 why can't he be contented to enjoy himself sleeping with her?
Why must the men of Argos embark to fight with the Trojans?
Why did the son of Atreus collect and bring the host hither?
Wasn't it all for the sake of a woman, the lovely-haired Helen?
He doubtless assumes that, of all the mortal race of mankind,
340 only the sons of Atreus have feelings of love toward their wives.
Someone should tell him that every decent intelligent husband
cherishes his—as I do, though she be but my captive and booty.
    Well, he has stolen my prize as well as cheating me roundly.
He'd best not try me again: I know him too well to believe him.
345 Perhaps he and you, Odysseus, and the other Achaean commanders
can work out a trick to save his ships from destruction by fire.
Just look at all the work he has done without my assistance.
Why, he has built him a wall, and a great wide moat to protect it,
and inside, a palisade of stakes bedded firm in the ground.
350 But even all this cannot hamper the fury of man-slaying Hector.
As long as I was in battle at the side of the other Achaeans,
Hector preferred not to sally forth from the walls of the city;
he would only advance as far as the Scaean gate and the oak tree,
where once he dared to engage me. He was lucky to get out alive.

355 But since I no longer desire to battle with glorious Hector,
tomorrow—first paying respect to Zeus and the other immortals—
I will drag my ships to the sea and load them up to the gunwales.
(come and watch if you like, if you really have any interest).
At break of day you will see, as they travel the fish-laden waters

360 of Hellespont, my ships and men, straining away at the oars.
Then, if the Shaker of Earth will grant me a quick happy voyage,
in three days I should arrive in the fertile region of Phthia.
There is the treasure I left—alas!—by voyaging hither;
there I shall pile up more, in gold and in ruddy bronze,

365 in women shapely of figure, in masses of tough gray iron—
all I acquired by lot. But the honor which he himself gave me,
imperious Agamemnon took back by force for himself.
    Give your report of my answer to Agamemnon in public
and give it in my own words, so that all the other Achaeans

370 will veto his next attempt to cheat some other Danaän.
For the man is devious and crooked, a shifty mongrel at heart,
and would never dare to confront me openly, face to face.
I certainly won't assist him, either by word or by deed;
he has lied to me and has cheated me shamelessly. Never again

375 will he swindle me with his tongue. Enough about Agamemnon;
he can go straight to hell. Zeus already has stolen his senses.
His gifts don't move me a bit; he himself is entirely worthless.
Suppose he gave me ten times, twenty times all that he owns,
as much as Orchomenus holds, or Thebes, that city of Egypt,

380 where treasure packs the houses, whose wall has a hundred gates,
each broad enough for two-hundred men with chariots and horses;
suppose he offered as many gifts as the sand of the seaside,
as specks of dust of the air—Agamemnon would make no impression
until he could make reparation for insults galling my spirit.

385 I shall not marry a daughter of Atreus' son Agamemnon,
though her beauty makes her a rival of Aphrodite the golden
and her skill is almost as great as that of gray-eyed Athena.
Very good; let him marry her off to one of the other Achaeans,
to someone more pliant than I, to a personage higher in station.

390 If the gods are willing to bring me in safety back to my homeland,
Peleus himself will find me a wife and arrange for my marriage.
In Hellas and Phthia are plenty of daughters of noble Achaeans,
rulers of towns; whichever I want I will take as my wife.
In days gone by, indeed, my strongest feelings would urge me

395 to woo and marry a wife, a good and suitable woman,
and settle down to enjoy the wealth that Peleus had gathered.
I value my life far more than all the treasure of Ilium,
which they say that populous city possessed in the days gone by,
long ago in the times of peace, before the Achaeans descended.

400 I value it more than all that the marble temple encloses,
the temple of Phoebus Apollo the archer, in rock-bounded Pytho.°
Cattle and sheep can be rustled, tripods and fine horses bought,

401. *rock-bounded Pytho:* Delphi.

but once his spirit departs and passes the gate of his teeth,
a man's life is gone beyond reach of any rustler or buyer.

405   Now silvery-footed Thetis, my goddess mother, informs me
that I must choose one or other manner of life and of death:
if I remain here, attacking the city and land of the Trojans,
all hope of returning is lost, but I win a glory undying.
If, however, I choose to return to the land of my fathers,

410 I must bid farewell to my glory, but survive to a quiet old age.
Death, the end of all men, will be slow and tardy to find me.
    If you others want my advice, I urge you to sail back home.
You will never succeed in the capture of Ilium's towering walls,
for the hand of far-sighted Zeus protects the city from danger,

415 and a confident people has gained new will and courage in battle.
So go you back and report to the very highest Achaeans,
and—privilege granted the aged—tell them to work out a program,
better than that which they tried, to save the Achaean armada,
and the men of Achaea too, who camp by their deep-holded vessels,

420 for the ruse their leaders concocted has foundered on my refusal.
    But Phoenix, I hope, will stay and sleep tonight in my quarters,
and tomorrow will follow me back again to my own dear homeland—
that is, if he so desires, for I would not dream of compulsion."

HOMER, *Iliad* (9.308–429)

The battle resumes, still without Achilles. Things go so badly for the Greeks that Patroclus, Achilles' best friend and tent-mate, comes to him in tears, begging that he relent in his wrath, which is killing so many of their former spear-mates. Or at least he should allow Patroclus to appear in battle wearing Achilles' armor, to give breathing space and save the ships, about to be set on fire under Hector's relentless assault. Achilles reluctantly agrees, but cautions Patroclus not to go near the walls of Troy, where Hector is strongest.[14]

Patroclus storms into battle and kills many, including Sarpedon, a son of Zeus. Then, carried away by bloodlust, he forgets Achilles' words, comes up under the walls, and three times jumps onto the escarpment. Hector corners him, kills him and strips off the armor—Achilles' own—and puts it on.

The Death of Hector

When Achilles hears that Patroclus is dead because of his own stubborn anger toward Agamemnon, he is maddened by grief. He thinks only of revenge. His mother, Thetis, brings him new armor made by Hephaestus to replace that taken by Hector. Like a demon he storms onto the plain, killing Trojans left and right. The river Scamander, which flows through the plain, is so choked with corpses that in self-defense it rears above the plain and attacks the hero, nearly drowning him. But Achilles escapes and continues to rout the Trojans, who pour into the city, except for Hector,

---

[14]An example of the folktale prohibition, whose violation always brings disaster.

FIG. 19.7. The duel of Achilles and Hector, from an Attic wine-drinking bowl, c. 490 B.C. Achilles has just dealt the fatal blow; blood gushes from Hector's wound as he staggers backward. The figures are labeled.   (British Museum, London; E 468)

who waits beside the Scaean Gate. His mother, Hecabê, and his father, Priam, climb to the walls and call down, begging him to come inside.

When Hector sees Achilles coming, he turns and runs three times around the walls, then makes his stand (Fig. 19.7). Achilles stabs his spear through Hector's throat, but misses the vocal cords. Hector begs Achilles for honorable burial. Achilles replies that he would rather eat Hector's flesh. Hector dies, prophesying that Achilles' death will follow soon.

Achilles ties Hector's body to his chariot and drags the corpse in the dust around the plain for days on end. A great funeral is held for Patroclus. Achilles cuts the throats of ten Trojan captives over the pyre and many animals besides. When the fire dies down, the Greeks gather Patroclus' bones and place them in an urn, to await Achilles' own.

In the middle of the night, the grief-stricken Priam loads a wagon and, helped by Hermes, penetrates the Greek lines. To Achilles' astonishment, Priam appears at the door of his tent and offers ransom for Hector's corpse (Fig. 19.8).[15] Achilles sees in the aged, broken king the image of his own father Peleus, soon to be childless too:

[15]Cf. the words of John Masefield, poet laureate of England, to British prime minister Neville Chamberlain on his return from meeting with Adolf Hitler at Munich in 1938:

"As Priam to Achilles for his son,
So you into the night, divinely led,
Went forth to end a war not yet begun,
Went begging young men's bodies, not yet dead."

Some consider these lines the first atrocity of World War II!

FIG. 19.8. The ransom of Hector, Attic cup, C. 480 B.C. The dead Hector lies under Achilles' couch, his body pierced by wounds. Old Priam stands to the left leaning on this staff, while Achilles, turning to a serving boy, asks that a meal be brought. Achilles' armor hangs from the walls of the tent.   (Kunsthistorisches Museum, Vienna; I 3039)

[472]   Inside his tent was Achilles.
In back sat his silent friends, respecting his sorrow; two only,
Automedon the hero and Alcimus, scion of Ares,

475   stood by to care for his needs. He had just now finished his supper;
the table, not yet cleared, lay cluttered with wine cups and dishes.
Nobody noticed great Priam, as he entered and knelt by Achilles,
embracing his knees, and kissing his terrible murderous hands—
the very hands that had slaughtered so many sons of old Priam.

480   As when, in folly and rage, back home in his own dear country,
someone murders a man and is forced to go into exile;
he enters some rich man's palace, to the pity of all who behold him.
Just so Achilles felt pity at the sight of godlike old Priam,
and all the attendants as well, exchanging glances of wonder.

485   But Priam knelt by Achilles and spoke with a suppliant's meekness.
"Achilles, peer of the gods, reflect on your own poor father,
an old man, just as I am, on the verge of death and extinction.
Like me, he may be surrounded by those who make life a misery,
with no one there to defend him against his looming destruction.

490   But as long as he hears the report that you are alive and uninjured,
his heart can rejoice in the hope that some day soon he will see you,
his own dear son, returning from the war and tumult of Troy.
But for me no hope can remain. I fathered glorious sons

here in broad-streeted Troy. Not a single one now is left me.
495 They numbered full fifty back then, before the Achaeans attacked us;
no less than nineteen of my boys were born by only one mother,
and all the rest were the sons of women here in my palace.
Most of the others fell to the onslaught of furious Ares;
the only one to survive, the city's only defender,
500 was he whom you have just slain as he fought defending his homeland,
Hector. To ransom his body I have ventured among the Achaeans,
into the heart of their ships. I set no bound to his ransom.
　　O Achilles, out of respect for the clemency loved by the gods,
take pity on me, and remember in pity your own aged father.
505 Yet my lot is surely the sadder, for—a thing no human before me
has ever been humbled to do—I held the hand of the slayer
of my own son to my lips, in token of deep supplication."
　　He stopped. Achilles' heart was shaken with grief for his father.
Taking the old man's hand, he quietly moved it away,
510 and both men remembered their sorrow. Priam, groveling in silence,
could not erase from his grief the picture of manslaying Hector.
Achilles sat openly mourning the helpless old age of his father,
but within him, the fate of Patroclus. Their misery filled all the camp.
　　But at last the noble Achilles, exhausted, lamented no further;
515 his sorrow ebbed from his mind, and with it the pain from his body.
Quickly he jumped from his chair to raise the prostrate old ruler,
pitying his old gray head, his chin and his scanty gray beard.
To Priam he spoke these words like arrows that fly to their target:
　　"Poor man, what a load of troubles have stricken you to the heart!
520 How could you summon the courage to make your lone way to our
　　　beachhead,
to me, who have stripped as a trophy the armor of your dead sons,
so many, and all so brave? Your heart must be made out of iron!
Come now, sit here beside me. Now let us allow our resentment
to slumber in quiet within us, though we cannot forget the pain.
525 We will find no profit in tears, no comfort in heart-freezing sorrow,
for the gods have decreed a life of permanent grief to poor mortals,
while they themselves enjoy an endless freedom from troubles.
　　Zeus has disposed two jars on either side of his doorway:
full of the lots that he gives, one of blessings, the other of curses.
530 If He who Delights in the Thunder mixes the two for a human,
at one time his life will be painful, but equally often a pleasure.
But if a human's allotment is unmixed shame and derision,
then torturing madness dogs his steps all the days of his life,
and he walks on the glorious earth despised by gods and by mortals.
535 Thus, from his birth the gods gave glorious honors to Peleus:
in wealth he surpassed all others; the Myrmidons were his subjects;
to him, though only a mortal, the gods gave a goddess in marriage.
But with this some god mixed evil: no child was born in his palace
to follow him on the throne, save one, soon fated to die.
540 What comfort am I to his gloomy old age, so far from my country,
lingering here in the Troad, a curse to you and your children?
You too, poor old man, so they tell me, were once as blessed as he,

holding the mainland of Phrygia from Lesbos, home of great Macar,
north to the Narrows of Hellê. Over all this land you were ruler,

545 and were blessed, moreover, with fortune and a mighty cohort of sons.
But since the gods on Olympus have brought this disaster upon you,
this endless war by your city, this endless bloodshed and slaughter,
all you can do is endure it; do not grieve for what cannot be altered.
You will not accomplish a thing by endlessly mourning for Hector;

550 you cannot bring him to life. And worse things are still to be suffered."

HOMER, *Iliad* (24.472–551)

In a magnanimous gesture, forgetting that Priam is father to the man who killed his friend, Achilles gives up the body without ransom. Priam returns to the city. "And so they buried horse-taming Hector," reads the last line of the *Iliad*.

OBSERVATIONS: HOMER, INVENTOR OF PLOT AND CHARACTER

Homer's great poems, the *Iliad* and the *Odyssey*, recorded in the earliest days of alphabetic literacy, have made stories about Troy some of the most widely known in the world. However, the *Iliad* is formally not the story of the whole Trojan War but of a single episode of several weeks' duration in the ninth year of the war, the "anger of Achilles." When the poem ends, Achilles is still alive and the city yet to be taken.

Homer realized the need for a plot—a story describing a struggle that has a beginning, middle, and end. As far as we know, the device of a plot was Homer's invention: Subsequent long poems, dramas, novels, and feature films are indebted to him. A good plot requires focus, and in the *Iliad* Homer focuses on the turbulent emotions of a single man who allows his anger to run away with him, destroying alike those he hates and those he loves and, finally, preparing his own destruction. There is nothing like it in pre-Hellenic literatures.

Homer is also the inventor of character ("imprint") in literature, although his methods of portraying character are different from a modern novelist's. He never describes to us the inner life of his characters but places them directly in the midst of events where they speak and act. He gives the sense that we are witnessing the lives of real men and women living in a real, although stylized, world. Helen is the lovely seductress, self-pitying but charming to every male. Odysseus is the clever man who can persuade anyone to do anything. Agamemnon is the blustering braggart, using political authority to swell his self-importance against the best interests of his people. Hector is the family man with much to protect but doomed to a frightful end, like his family, whom he cannot save. Achilles is the warrior–intellectual, questioning the very foundations of his traditional culture by rejecting Agamemnon's offer of the rich gifts that Athena promised him would come. His successors in Greek culture will create philosophy, a rejection of traditional (and "mythical") explanations in exchange for a reasoned investigation into the natural laws that govern the world. He is the man alone, pushing away the world around him and all it stands for, indulgent in self-destructive emotion but fearless to act on his conviction, regardless of consequence. In the final scene of the *Iliad*, when he sees his own father in his enemy Priam, he comes near to discovering "the brotherhood of man," a notion deeply alien to traditional Greek values.

Homer's figures are individuals yet ideal types, images and models for all human beings, as capable of touching the heart of modern humans as they excited the admiration and attention of the ancient Greeks.

KEY TERMS

Pelops, 510	Clytemnestra, 514
Oenomaüs, 511	Peleus, 516
Hippodamia, 511	Ajax, 516
Thyestes, 511	Hecabê, 519
Aegisthus, 511	Aulis, 520
Atreus, 511	Telemachus, 521
Menelaüs, 511	Palamedes, 521
Agamemnon, 511	Calchas, 521
Tyndareüs, 513	Iphigenia, 523
Leda, 513	Philoctetes, 525
Polydeuces, 514	Chryseïs, 527
Helen, 514	Briseïs, 529
Castor, 514	Andromachê, 531

FURTHER READING

Bloom, Harold, ed., *Homer's* The Iliad (New York, 1987). Collection of essays by leading scholars.

Edwards, Mark, *Homer, Poet of the* Iliad (Baltimore, 1987; reprinted Ithaca, 1990). Readable, sensible, up-to-date analysis of Homer's poem of war.

Griffin, Jasper, *Homer on Life and Death* (Oxford, U.K., 1980). Always interesting examination of major themes.

Kirk, G. S., *The Songs of Homer* (New York, 1962). A follower of the Parry–Lord school, Kirk brings many of his own original insights to the complex problems raised by the Homeric poems.

Luce, J. V., *Homer and the Heroic Age* (London, 1975). Astute comparison of the poems with archaeological data, with excellent illustrations.

Owen, E. T., *The Story of the* Iliad (New York, 1946; reprinted Waukonda, Ill., 1989). Admirably analyzes the plot of the *Iliad,* book by book.

Page, Denys, *History and the Homeric* Iliad (Berkeley, Calif., 1959; reprinted 1972). A major study of the relationship between historical records and the world of the poems.

Powell, B. B., and I. Morris, eds., *A New Companion to Homer* (Leiden, The Netherlands, 1997). Most up-to-date scholarly review of all aspects of Homeric studies.

Redfield, J. M., *Nature and Culture in the* Iliad: *The Tragedy of Hector* (Durham, N.C., 1993; expanded edition of first edition, Chicago, 1975). Studies the relationship between the *Iliad* and the society that produced it.

Schein, Seth, *The Mortal Hero: An Introduction to Homer's* Iliad (Berkeley, Calif., 1984). Synthesis of the vast scholarship, especially German, on the *Iliad*.

Weil, Simone, The Iliad: *The Poem of Force,* trans. by Mary McCarthy and often republished. Insightful essay written against the backdrop of World War II.

Whitman, C. H., *Homer and the Heroic Tradition* (Cambridge, Mass., 1958; reprinted New York, 1965). Close analysis of themes and plot.

Wolf, Christa, *Cassandra,* trans. from German by Jan Van Heurck (New York, 1984). A feminist rewriting of the *Iliad,* told by the scorned prophetess.

CHAPTER 20

THE TROJAN WAR

THE FALL OF TROY; THE RETURN OF AGAMEMNON

"Aagh! I am hit—a blow—deadly and deep!"

AESCHYLUS, *Agamemnon* 1343

THE MANY LATER EVENTS of the Trojan War—how the city fell and what happened when the Greeks returned home—were told in the lost Cyclic Epics, of which only summaries survive. In this chapter we review the most important of these events, to which Homer sometimes refers in passing.

THE GREEKS AT TROY

The Judgment of the Arms of Achilles

After Hector's death, allies from far afield came to assist the Trojans. **Penthesilea** (pen-thes-i-lē-a) led a contingent of Amazons but was cut down by Achilles. He did not know he was fighting a woman until her helmet rolled off, and then he took pity on her (Fig. 20.1). A Greek scoundrel, Thersites, called by Homer "the ugliest man who went to Troy," derided Achilles for killing a woman, so Achilles killed him too.

Paris, assisted by Apollo, shot down Achilles as he fought near the Scaean Gate. A great battle surrounded his body. At last Ajax got the corpse over his shoulder and fought his way back to the Greek lines through a rain of arrows. After a splendid funeral, the Greeks burned Achilles' body and mixed his ashes in the jar with those of Patroclus.

FIG. 20.1. The death of Penthesilea, interior of Attic wine-cup, c. 460 B.C. Achilles, accompanied by another warrior, plunges the sword into the throat of the Amazon queen; another Amazon lies dead at the right. The artist seems to follow the tradition that Achilles fell in love with Penthesilea as their eyes met, even as he struck the death blow—alas, too late.   (Staatliche Antikensammlungen und Glyptothek, Munich)

Achilles' armor was offered as prize to the next best warrior. Everybody knew this to be Ajax, son of Telamon, but for some reason (bribery?) the judges awarded the arms to Odysseus. Sophocles tells the story, in his earliest surviving play (the *Ajax*, written before 441 B.C.), how Ajax went mad with anger and grief and attacked the Greek captains, Menelaüs, Agamemnon, Odysseus, and the others, cutting them to pieces with his relentless bronze sword—so he thought. When he recovered his senses, he saw that he was standing in the midst of a flock of dead sheep, covered with blood from head to foot. The Greek commanders pointed and shook with laughter at his folly. Shamed, Ajax walked to a secluded cave near the shore and threw himself on his sword (Fig. 20.2). Agamemnon first ordered that the body be exposed, to be devoured by dogs and birds, but later relented and allowed a proper burial.

When Odysseus was in the underworld on his journey home, he saw the ghost of Ajax and tried to appease him:

FIG. 20.2. The suicide of Ajax, Attic jug, c. 530 B.C. The lonely hero, near a palm tree on the beach, plants the haft of his sword in the ground, preparing to fall upon it. He has set his armor to the side, reminding us of Achilles' armor, the reason for Ajax's suicide. His helmet seems to watch him, unconcerned. (Chateau-Musée, Boulogne-sur-Mer)

[541] The other sad ghosts stood about me, heroes now dead and gone,
       asking news of the comrades they had loved in the regions above.
       But all by himself stood the spirit of Ajax, Telamon's son,
       nursing a grudge because I had received the arms of Achilles,
545   offered by Thetis, his mother, as prize to the bravest Achaean—
       I wish I had never presented a claim to so splendid a trophy!
       The children of Troy adjudged them, along with Pallas Athena.
       Because of that armor the earth soon covered Ajax, the hero,
       handsomest of all Greeks but Achilles, and bravest in action.
550   Choosing my language with care, I spoke in words of appeasement:
           "Ajax, great Telamon's son, even in death can you never
       forget your quarrel with me, and the cursed arms of Achilles?
       The gods indeed laid sorrow and pain on the host of the Argives;
       we lost an impregnable tower when you died, and all the Achaeans
555   continue mourning your death, as deeply as that of Achilles.
       Yet blame should not be imputed to any bronze-clad Danaän;
       it was Zeus and his furious hatred that focused on you and your death.
       So stand no longer aloof, my lord, but approach me and listen
       to all that I have to tell, and calm your imperious spirit."
560   So I appealed, but he answered me never a word and departed,
       along with the other ghosts, to the gloomy place of the dead.

                                        HOMER, *Odyssey* (11.541–564)

The Trojan Horse

Although the greatest heroes on both sides were dead, the war still dragged on with no end in sight. Calchas explained that various conditions would have to be met if the city were ever to be taken: Achilles' son **Neoptolemus** (nē-op-**tol**-e-mus, "young fighter," also called Pyrrhus, "redhead"), conceived when Achilles lived in the women's quarters on Scyros, would have to join the army; a protective statue of Athena as city-protector, called the Palladium, which had fallen from heaven, would have to be taken from the city; and the bow of Heracles would have to be brought into the action.

Neoptolemus was summoned from Scyros; Odysseus and Diomedes, or Odysseus alone disguised as a beggar, sneaked into Troy and stole the statue; and Odysseus, in the company of Neoptolemus, sailed to Lemnos to recover the bow from Philoctetes, whom the Greeks had cruelly abandoned ten years before. Although consumed with hatred for the Greeks who had betrayed him, Philoctetes was eventually persuaded to give up the bow.[1] Podalirius, a son of Asclepius, healed his repulsive wound, and Philoctetes shot and killed Paris. But still the city did not fall.

Odysseus had an idea. He instructed Epeus (e-**pē**-us), an ingenious artisan, to construct an enormous wooden horse. Fifty warriors—among them Odysseus, Menelaüs, Diomedes, and Neoptolemus—concealed themselves in the horse's hollow belly (Fig. 20.3). The Greeks burned their tents and sailed away, pretending to go home, but actually they hid behind the nearby island of Tenedos. When the Trojans awoke the next day, they were astonished to see the plain empty of fighters, with only an enormous horse left behind. They went onto the plain, perplexed. A badly beaten Greek, Sinon (**sī**-non), emerged from the bush, and explained that the Greeks, without hope of taking Troy, had sailed home. The horse was an offering to Athena, to ensure their safe return. He himself had been designated as a human sacrifice to the idol but managed to escape, he said.

A humorous scene in the *Odyssey,* set in Sparta ten years after the war, describes the episode of the Trojan horse. Odysseus' son Telemachus has come to Sparta to seek news of his missing father and arrives in the midst of a wedding feast. To lighten their hearts, Helen offers Telemachus and Menelaüs a drugged wine and then praises the exploits of Telemachus' father, Odysseus, attempting to place her own role in a favorable light. Menelaüs offers a less flattering version of events:

[220] To the wine poured into the crater
from which they would drink she added a drug of mysterious power,
narcotic of pain and calmer of anger and all kinds of sorrow.
Whoever tasted the wine, once mixed with that drug in the crater,
for a day would remain apathetic, not shedding a single tear,
225 though his father and lady mother should perish before his eyes,
though he watched his son or brother die by a blow of the sword.
It was one of the most efficacious drugs in the keeping of Helen,
shown her by Polydamna, wife of Thon, the Pharaoh of Egypt,
a land whose nourishing earth is rich in herbs of great virtue;

---

[1]Sophocles tells the story in his play *Philoctetes.*

FIG. 20.3. The Trojan horse, Cycladic storage jar, c. 670 B.C. This relief from a large jar is one of the earliest surviving unequivocal references to myth in Greek art. The horse is on wheels and has openings through which we can see the heads of the heroes. From the portholes swords and shields are passed out. Some heroes have already come down and are striding off in full armor to the battle. Other scenes on the jar portray scenes of mayhem, the death of children, and the rape of women. (Archaeological Museum, Myconos; Mykonos 70)

230 compounds of some bring health, but others are venomous poison.
Each man is his own physician, skilled beyond all other mortals,
for all of them come of the race of Paeëon, greatest of healers.
So Helen mixed in her drug and, seeing the cups were replenished,
addressed the heroes again, urging them to go on with the story:
235   "Zeus-favored Menelaüs, and all you children of heroes,
we know that good and evil are assigned to us mortals by Zeus,

whose power extends to us all. Very well; recline at the banquet,
enjoying each other's adventures. My request is surely in reason,
for I myself could not list, even name, the trials of Odysseus.

240 But what an exploit was that, which he plotted and executed
in the very midst of the Trojans, at the lowest ebb of your hope!
He had himself lashed and beaten into bloody and shameful welts,
dressed in a dirty old cloak, and, disguised as a runaway slave,
got into the wide-streeted city. He changed his appearance again

245 to play the part of a beggar—how unlike the real Odysseus,
whom everyone knew as he was, encamped by the ships of Achaea!
Like a beggar he entered the town. No Trojan offered a challenge;
I was the only person to pierce his disguise and address him.
He cleverly tried to elude me, but when I was washing his body,

250 rubbing his skin with oil, and clothing his limbs in a garment,
I swore that until he was safe in camp by the swift-rowing ships,
no word would I utter revealing his entry into the city.
Then he told me in fullest detail the stratagem of the Achaeans.
On his way to the Argive camp to report what he had observed,

255 his sword had slain many Trojans, to the grief and despair of their women,
but my heart bounded in joy, for by now I was weary and homesick,
as I cursed the blindness and folly that Aphrodite injected,
bringing me into this land, so far from my dear native country,
carelessly leaving behind my daughter, my marriage, my husband,

260 a man who fell short in no virtue, either of mind or of body."
    Fair-haired Menelaüs replied, with a smile of approval:
"Every word you have uttered, dear wife, is truthfully spoken.
I have traveled in many lands; I know the mind and the counsel
of many a hero, but never have I found the like of Odysseus.

265 Think of his quickness of wit and courage in moments of peril,
like that in the wooden horse, when all we bravest Achaeans
crowded together to bring destruction and death to the Trojans.
Some spirit suggested a trick to shower the Trojans with glory,
waiting until you approached, with noble Deïphobus° following.

270 Thrice you walked by the horse and stroked the hollow deception,
and spoke to the noble Argives, calling on each by his name,
and simulating the voices of the wives of all the Achaeans.
Now I sat by Tydeus' son, in the middle, with noble Odysseus,
hearing your voice as you called by name on each of our comrades.

275 Diomedes and I started up in a frenzy of eager desire,
to burst from the horse, or at least to answer you from within.
But Odysseus grabbed us and checked our impulse to ruinous folly.
All the other Achaeans sat waiting in disciplined silence;
Only Anticlus tried to make some reply to your wheedling.

280 But Odysseus firmly squeezed on his mouth with powerful hands,
thus saving all the Achaeans, till Athena took you away."

HOMER, *Odyssey* (4.220–289)

---

269. *Deïphobus:* The man Helen took up with, after Paris had been killed.

FIG. 20.4. The death of Laocoön, second–first centuries B.C. One of the most famous works of sculpture to survive from the ancient world, this piece from the Hellenistic Period expresses unforgettably the anguish and terror of the Trojan priest and his sons.   (Vatican Museum, Rome; Author's photo)

A priest of Poseidon, **Laocoön** (lā-**ok**-o-on), also suspected that the horse held warriors. He came forward and declared Sinon, like all Greeks, to be a liar (hence the saying, "beware Greeks bearing gifts"). The horse was a trick, he said, and they should destroy it, and he hurled his spear into the horse's side. Two serpents suddenly arose from the sea, made straight for Laocoön and his two sons, and strangled them in their coils as the Trojans watched in horror (Fig. 20.4). Obviously the serpents were a sign of the divine anger against a man so impious as to strike the sacred image (in fact Laocoön's death had a different cause: He had intercourse with his wife within the temple precincts of Poseidon and now paid the price).

The Fall of Troy

To the sound of lutes, and in the midst of grand hilarity, the Trojans dragged the horse inside the citadel. That night a party of furious joy and abandon raged through the city. In the early hours of the morning, the Greeks descended to the ground from the horse's belly, opened the city's gates, and admitted their companions, who had returned from Tenedos. A blood-curdling cry pierced the night; children clung to their mothers' robes, and the slaughter began. The Trojan men were hunted down and killed, the women taken captive, their homes plundered and burned. In Euripides' antiwar play *The Trojan Women*, a chorus of Trojan captives sums up Troy's last agony. The play was produced in 415 B.C. just after the Athenians, in an especially nasty incident of the Peloponnesian War, slaughtered all the male inhabitants of the island of Melos and sold their women and children into slavery. The play may therefore be read as a commentary on Athenian behavior:[2]

[511]   *Chorus* Join with us, Muse, in our mournful dirge for Ilium;
         Sing through your tears her new song of sorrow.
         Mournfully sing the sorrows of Troy—
         how the four-legged wagon, loaded with Greeks,
515   ruined the city, made me a slave.
         The Greeks left the horse outside the gates of the city,
         horse with a frontlet gleaming with gold,
         horse that would raise the war cry to heaven.
         The people of Troy from the citadel's top
520   raised a great shout: "Now freed from your toil,
         come, bring in the image of well-polished wood
         for Athena of Ilium, daughter of Zeus."
         What maid, what old man but emerged from the house at the call?
            With songs in their hearts, they set hands to the ropes
525   to drag in betrayal and ruin.
         Phrygians° old, Phrygians young ran to the gates of the city,
         ready to offer, as gift to the goddess,
         pine from the mountain, sleek ambush of Argives,
         destruction of Dardanus' gullible race,
530   colt never broken, foal never to die.
         With ropes of spun linen, stout as a black ship's cables,
         they pulled the craft in, and up to its berth,
         the temple of marble, the floor soon to reek
         with worshipers' blood. They offered it there,
535   "to Pallas with thanks, on behalf of our country."
         On joy and rejoicing descended the night,
         amid music of flutes, amid Phrygian songs.
         The maidens' shrill song and quick-dancing feet spoke their joy,
           in every house the torch's dim beam
540   prevented the coming of slumber.
         I was there with the rest: in the jubilant hall

---

526. *Phrygians:* That is, the Trojans.

---

[2]Euripides' play is so effective a statement condemning war that it ran for more than ten years in New York City during the war in Vietnam; its message had as little effect then as did the original production 2,500 years earlier.

I had joined in the dance to honor the maiden,
the queen of the mountains, the daughter of Zeus.
When a blood-curdling cry rang out from the town and up the castle,
545 trembling children stretched little hands to their mother's lap.
  War sprang out of its ambush,
  the doing of maiden Athena.
Men were butchered beside the altar,
beheaded next to their brides,
550   who were dragged away as a trophy,
as breeders of sons for the Argives, of bitter sorrow for Troy.

EURIPIDES, The Trojan Women (511–567)

Perhaps the most horrific death was that of old King Priam, stabbed at the altar of Zeus by Achilles' son Neoptolemus. Vergil gives the graphic details in the second book of the *Aeneid:*

[506]   Perhaps you would like to ask me about the end of old Priam.
When he knew the town had fallen, the gates broken in by the foe,
the enemy storming each house in a frenzy of rapine and plunder,
he took down his rusty armor and fitted it over his shoulders,
510 trembling under the weight. His sword, too heavy to handle,
hung uselessly by his side as he stumbled out to destruction,
expecting to die in the thickest part of the enemy's phalanx.
  Now right in the central court of the palace, facing the sky,
stood a large and sacred altar, and beside it an ancient laurel,
515 shading the altar, where stood the household gods, the Penates.°
Like doves blown away as victims of a black and lowering tempest,
Hecuba° sat with her daughters, crowding closely around the altar,
clinging in desperate hope to the images of their protectors.
When Hecuba saw that Priam had donned his rusty old armor,
520 "Priam, my poor luckless partner, what desperate purpose is this?"
she screamed. "What frenzy spurs you to arm and hurry your fate?
Our condition no longer requires defense by armor like yours;
even my Hector himself could afford us no comfort whatever.
Admit, then, that we are beaten. If anything now can protect us,
525 it must be this altar; if not, we two will perish together."
She drew the old man to her arms, and with him sat by the altar.
  Polites, a son of Priam, escaping the murderous Pyrrhus,°
fled down the endless halls, now ringing with enemy weapons.
Reeling with wounds, he looked for safety in each empty chamber.
530 The rugged Pyrrhus, pursuing with spear poised ready to strike,
kept reaching out for the boy, who still eluded his captor.

---

515. . . . *the Penates:* Vergil's description fits a Roman household, but not a Homeric palace. The Penates were unique to Rome (see Chapter 22).   517. *Hecuba:* The Latin form of *Hecabê.*   527. *Pyrrhus:* Neoptolemus, Achilles' son.

At last he burst into sight, and under the gaze of his parents
he slipped and gasped out his life in a last outpouring of blood.
Priam, although now confronted by sure and immediate slaughter,
535   voiced his angry defiance in cries of embittered reproach:
     "If heaven can recognize justice, if any gods can be bothered
to avenge outrages like yours, may they make you recompense fully
your wickedness; may they impose due penalty for your offenses
on you, who forced me to watch as you butchered my son before me,
540   spattering a father's face with blood poured out by his child.
You lie, hypocritically claiming to be the son of Achilles;
he never acted like that toward Priam, his deadliest foeman,
but sent back the mangled body of Hector for proper interment
and me to my city again, observing his word and his promise."
545   With that the old man threw his spear, feebly, doing no damage.
The bronze shield rattled a bit as it parried the useless spear,
which dangled harmlessly down from the edge of the knob in the middle.
Sarcastically Pyrrhus replied, "Bring your report to my father,
Peleus' son, and tell in detail the deeds of shame I committed;
550   be sure he knows that his son is a weak and degenerate coward.
Now die!"
      Feeble old Priam collapsed in a puddle of blood from Polites.
Neoptolemus wound his left hand in his hair, and up to the altar
he dragged him, unresisting. His right drew his glittering sword,
and plunged it right to the hilt, deep into the bowels of Priam.
555   So ended the life of the king, a destiny long foretold.
This was the lot he had drawn: to live till the fall of the city,
till he saw Troy perish in flames, a city once monarch of Asia,
mistress of all her peoples. And now? a torso washed up on the seashore,
a head torn off from its body, a body without a name.

                        VERGIL, *Aeneid* (2.506–558)

Menelaüs found Helen in her bedroom with her new husband, Deïphobus, also a son of Priam, whom he killed and mutilated. Menelaüs was about to kill Helen too, but she bared her beautiful breasts to him and pleaded for her life. He hesitated, saying he would kill her later (in fact, they returned to Sparta and lived happily ever after). The other Ajax, son of Oïleus, raped Cassandra while she clung to an image of Athena; this crime excited Athena's wrath, who caused much of the trouble that befell the Greeks as they returned home. Of all the Trojan males, only a few escaped, the most important being Aeneas, who carried his lame father, Anchises, on his shoulders and led his young son Ascanius (also called Iulus) by the hand out of the burning city (see Chapter 22). The captive women were herded together outside the smoldering city, then distributed among the heroes. At the command of Odysseus, Astyanax, Hector's son, was ripped from Andromachê's bosom and thrown to his death from the walls; "only a fool kills the father and allows the son to live," Odysseus remarked. **Polyxena** (po-**lik**-se-na), youngest of Priam's daughters, was carried to the

The Trojan War in European Art

Stories from the Trojan War were important to Greek art from an early time; perhaps one fourth of the mythical subjects illustrated on Greek pots are related to the Trojan saga, and the tradition never stopped entirely. In *The Trojan Horse Disgorges Its Burden* (Fig. P 20.1a), from a late fifteenth-century French version of the Trojan story, three Greeks (perhaps Odysseus, Menelaüs, and Neoptolemus) emerge from the open hatch of the wooden horse to descend the ladder. The horse stands by a breach in the wall beside a gate labeled *la porte dardane,* the "Dardanian Gate." The story is told as a sequence of pictures. Beyond the horse are the Greeks, now emerged from the horse, then medieval city towers and a moat. In the courtyard beyond, the Greeks are in massed formation and dead Trojans litter the grounds. In the sky appears the label *la ville de troie,* the city of Troy.

The wedding of Peleus and Thetis, the Apple of Discord, and the subsequent determination which of the three goddesses—Hera, Aphrodite, or Athena—was the most beautiful are referred to casually in Book 24 of the *Iliad* (lines 28–70) but were treated fully in the lost epic poem the *Cypria* (perhaps = "myths about Aphrodite"),

FIG. P 20.1a. *The Trojan Horse Disgorges Its Burden,* late fifteenth-century manuscript of Raoul Lefèvre's *Recueil.* (Bibliothèque Nationale de France, Paris; MS. Fr. 22552, fol. 277v)

FIG. P 20.1b. Lucas Cranach the Elder (German, 1472–1553), *The Judgment of Paris,* c. 1528, tempra and oil on wood.   (Metropolitan Museum of Art, New York; Rogers Fund, 1928. Photo © 1986, Metropolitan Museum of Art, New York)

of which a summary has survived. A favorite motif of artists, it is seen here in the work of the German Lucas Cranach the Elder, who painted several versions of it with the same general composition but different details (Fig. P 20.1b). He took the opportunity to illustrate female anatomy by showing one woman from the side, one full front, and one from the back, a pose based on the ancient three Graces (see Perspective 6.2). However, it is hard to be sure which goddess is which. Cranach's Paris is a perfect German knight (like Cranach's patrons), slouched against the tree, the Apple of Discord in his left hand. Behind him is Hermes, with winged hat (peacocks!), holding a globe in his left hand (he travels the world) and a staff in his right (= caduceus). The landscape is a lively fantasy with a mountain citadel in the upper right, from which Paris came, and Troy in the center background. In the upper left is a cupid with drawn bow, ready to give success to Venus.

The Roman encyclopedist Pliny the Elder, who lived in the early Roman empire (A.D. 23–79), tells us that the emperor Vespasian (A.D. 69–79), builder of the Coliseum, had in his palace the most marvelous work ever made, a sculpture that portrayed the death of Laocoön and his sons carved from a single block of stone. In January 1506, some workers unearthed it (see Fig. 20.4) from a vineyard in the then-sparsely populated city of Rome. Pope Julius II, a warrior but patron of the arts, acquired it for the Vatican, where it is today one of the most famous works of art in the world. The *Laocoön*'s vivid portrayal of suffering and its understanding of the musculature of powerful masculine physique deeply influenced Michelangelo and many others. Hundreds of adaptations (and parodies) of the sculptural group exist, but the *Laocoön* of the visionary El Greco (1541–1614) is one of the best known (Fig. P 20.1c; El Greco, "the Greek," migrated to Toledo, Spain, from his home in Crete, hence the nickname). Here the Trojan priest, on the point of death, stares at the fangs of the serpent. The two naked figures on the right, long thought to be either Apollo and Artemis or Poseidon and Cassandra, are now thought to be Adam and Eve (Adam gazes at the fateful apple in his left hand). The carnal sin of Laocoön, who had intercourse with his wife in the temple of Poseidon, is thus compared with the sin of Adam and Eve, who disobeyed God's commandment and brought suffering, with the awareness of sexuality, into the world. In the background rises the medieval town of Toledo. Flamelike lines, distorted faces, elongated figures, and full, vibrant color combine to give the painting a curiously modern air. El Greco's paintings were, in fact, neglected until the twentieth century.

FIG. P 20.1c. El Greco (Domenikos Theotocopoulos; Spanish, born Greece, 1541– 1614), *Laocoön,* c. 1610–1614, oil on canvas.   (National Gallery of Art, Washington, D.C., Samuel H. Kress Collection)

FIG. P 20.1d. Frederic Leighton (English, 1830–1896), *Captive Andromache,* 1888, oil on canvas.   (City Art Galleries, Manchester)

In the nineteenth century, when the taste for suffering in literature was well developed, Frederic Leighton, president of the Royal Academy and leader of the Victorian art establishment, took up a pathetic theme from the *Iliad* (see Chapter 19): where Hector predicts to his wife Andromachê that one day, a slave, she will draw water from her master's well (Fig. P 20.1d). Here Leighton shows Andromachê forlorn among the Greek women, who draw water from the spring on the right. Perhaps the scene is set at the palace of Neoptolemus, whose captive she was. Most eyes turn to her, dressed in the black of mourning, her face covered and head bowed with sorrow, while the Greek women smile. The happy family at the bottom right imitates, and bitterly mocks, Homer's description of Hector, Andromachê, and the baby Astyanax at the Scaean Gate. But that was in a former time.

FIG. 20.5. The sacrifice of Polyxena, Etruscan jug, c. 570 B.C. Neoptolemus, son of Achilles, puts a sword into the throat of Polyxena, pouring the blood over his father's tomb. The three warriors holding the princess are named as Amphilochus, Antiphates, and Ajax, son of Oïleus. Behind Neoptolemus stand Diomedes and Nestor.   (British Museum, London: B 5507)

tomb of Achilles and her throat cut over it, the blood pouring into the grave to quench the dead warrior's thirst (Fig. 20.5).

AGAMEMNON'S RETURN

A genre of ancient epic told of the returns of the heroes from Troy and all that happened to them. These were called *Nostoi,* or "Homecomings."[3] Although the only epic account of a homecoming to survive is Homer's *Odyssey,* these stories often are referred to in other literary works. Agamemnon's return to Argos, his murder by Clytemnestra, and Orestes' revenge are known to us through Aeschylus' dramatic trilogy of 458 B.C., the *Oresteia* (or-es-tī-a, "story of Orestes"). It is made up of three plays, each complete in itself but also contributing to the larger group: *Agamemnon, Choëphoroe* (ko-**ef**-o-rē, "libation bearers"), and *Eumenides* (ū-**men**-i-dēz; "the kindly ones" = the Furies). Whereas Homer in his *Odyssey* concentrates on the tribulations Odysseus suffered while coming home and the difficulties he faced when he arrived, Aeschylus is concerned with bitter conflict within the family of Agamemnon and its resolution.

[3]Hence our word *nostalgia,* "homesickness."

Shakespeare's *Troilus and Cressida*

Shakespeare's play *Troilus and Cressida,* set during the eighth year of the Trojan War, revolves around many characters and incidents from ancient myth. But the central story of the play (Troilus' unhappy love for the fickle Cressida) proves, on close inspection, to have only a tenuous connection with the ancient sources. The play is a good example of the transformations undergone by ancient myth traveling through the Middle Ages and the Renaissance.

In the Middle Ages, all direct knowledge of Homer was gradually lost in Western, Latin-speaking Europe, and knowledge of the Greek language disappeared for about six hundred years. But the fame of the Trojan War lived on. It was known both from Vergil's account in the second book of the *Aeneid* and from the Latin translation of a Greek work by a "Dictys of Crete," the *Ephemeris belli Troiani,* "Diary of the Trojan War." Dictys claims actually to have been at Troy in the company of the Cretan commander, Idomeneus. Thus he was older than Homer and an eyewitness to the events of the war. We now know the work of so-called Dictys to be a fake of the second or third century A.D., but it was accepted as genuine by medieval scholars. So was the equally influential *De excidio Troiae historia,* "Concerning the Fall of Troy," by "Dares the Phrygian" (that is, a Trojan), a priest of Hephaestus, according to the *Iliad.* This Latin poem also is a fake, probably written in the fifth century A.D. In about 1160 a man named Benoît de Sainte-Maure, steeped in Dictys and Dares, wrote in French a *Roman de Troie,* "The Story of Troy," a classic of medieval romance. An Italian, Guido da Colonna, fashioned a prose version of Benoît's work, *Historia Troiana* (1272–1287), which was even more widely read because it was written in Latin, an international language. (The illustration of the Trojan Horse in Fig. P 20.1a comes from a translation back into French from Guido da Colonna's Latin version of Benoît's original French!) The story came to English readers through the *Troy Book* (1412–1420) of John Lydgate, based on Guido da Colonna, and William Caxton's *Recuyell of the Historyes of Troye* (1468–1471), which became the best-known version of the saga in English.

In Greek myth we learn only that Troilus was the youngest son of Priam and Hecabê and that Achilles killed him in an ambush. However, Dares portrays Troilus as a brave warrior fighting throughout the war. Benoît de Sainte-Maure and Guido da Colonna report the story of how the Trojan Troilus and the captive Briseida (= Briseïs) were lovers until the faithless Briseida forsook Troilus to take up with the Greek Diomedes. Then Boccaccio (1313–1375) changed the name of Briseida to Griseida (in his *De Casibus;* see Perspective 15.1), which eventually became the English Cressida, and made Pandarus, a bowman in the *Iliad,* into Troilus' dissolute companion. The English poet Chaucer depended on Boccaccio for his *Troylus and Cryseyde* (1372–1386), which delicately portrays the frailty of human love.

By Shakespeare's day (1564–1616) Cressida had become a byword for a depraved woman—for example, "Fetch forth the lazar [leprous] kite [a scavenging bird] of Cressid's kind, / Doll Tearsheet she by name" (Henry V, 2.1.73–74). Pandarus had become a byword for a procurer (hence our word *pander*), and Troilus was now the innocent young man brought to grief through love for a bad woman. Shakespeare develops these central themes in his play *Troilus and Cressida*, probably produced in 1602. Cressida is a giddy girl, a jilt, who first falls in love with Troilus, then thoughtlessly casts him aside for the sexier Diomedes. As background to the story, Shakespeare works in Agamemnon, Ajax, Ulysses (Odysseus), Nestor, and Achilles from the Greek side and Priam, Aeneas, Hector, Andromachê, Paris, and Helen from the Trojans.

Although audiences had lost direct connection with Greek literature, the story of the Trojan War continued to fascinate audiences in many countries throughout the European Middle Ages and later, when poets modified or built freely on inherited traditions to reflect contemporary literary styles and concerns.

The Murder of Agamemnon

The subject of the first play is Clytemnestra's murder of her husband on the day that he returns from Troy. In the opening scene a watchman perches on the roof of the palace, waiting for the beacon fire that will signal from across the sea, by a sort of primitive telegraph, that Troy has fallen. The watchman's opening words reflect the gloom enveloping the palace, where Clytemnestra has been having an affair with Agamemnon's cousin, Aegisthus, through the long years of the war. Suddenly the fire blazes up, signal that Troy has fallen. A war-weary herald arrives, reporting the imminent appearance of the great and triumphant king, Agamemnon.[4] The herald presents a gloomy picture of this famous conquest of wide-wayed Troy:

[555]   *Messenger*   Suppose I told you how all day long we rowed,
               how every night we tossed on cold hard decks,
               seldom allowed shore leave—even you who had no part
               would groan for our monotonous misery.
               But when we reached the coast, things were still worse:
560   crowded right underneath the walls of Troy,
               we tried to sleep, but rainfall from above
               and dampness from the ground soaked all our clothes,
               making both clothes and hair to swarm with lice.
               If I should tell you how the winter's cold
565   would freeze the very birds; how the drifting snow
               blew down, unbearable, from Ida's crags;
               or of the stifling heat of summer noons,
               when a windless sea slept in its waveless bed—
               but why rake up old torment? that has passed,
570   at least for those who died. No reveille
               will ever bother them for things to come.

                                AESCHYLUS, *Agamemnon* (555–569)

[4]Aeschylus has little interest in presenting the sequence of events in real time.

557

The herald describes the great storm that beset the fleet when it set out from Troy, a storm usually attributed to Athena's anger because of Ajax's rape of Cassandra:

[646] *Messenger* Arriving in a city blessed and wealthy,
        reporting glorious new of its deliverance,
        how dare I mix such news with tales of horror,
        or tell of the raging storm that struck the Achaeans,
650   sent by the angry gods? For fire and ocean,
        enemies immemorial, conspired with an oath,
        to annihilate the unhappy Argive fleet.
             In the black of night the sea began to rise.
        A gale swept down from Thrace to smash our ships
655   one on another; collision, screaming tempest,
        with blinding squalls of rain, forced us to run
        eyeless in darkness, helpless as driven sheep
        of a careless shepherd. When the pale dawn returned,
        we saw the Aegean dotted with Argive corpses,
660   floating like flowers among the shattered wrecks.
        We only and our ship escaped undamaged,
        saved by some god, who begged or stole our lives,
        ruling our helm with strong and practiced hand,
        a task too great for any mortal man.

AESCHYLUS, *Agamemnon* (646–664)

Where Menelaüs was driven, no one knew, but Agamemnon's ship, at least, has survived.

Agamemnon arrives in a chariot, accompanied by his mistress and "prize" (*geras*), Cassandra. He greets the city and is himself greeted by Clytemnestra, who comes out from the palace. She publicly complains of her suffering during her husband's absence, which nearly drove her to suicide, then invites her husband to enter the palace over a purple cloth, a central symbol in the play, a metaphor of the net by which Clytemnestra will trap and kill him: Deianira and Medea had used cloth to destroy their enemies too (Chapters 14, 18). At first Agamemnon refuses, saying this would be presumptuous, not befitting a mortal's place, but Clytemnestra urges him to put such thoughts from his mind. His triumphant return merits special display:

[958] *Clytemnestra* There is a sea which no one can drain dry.
        It endlessly renews its precious gift,
960   the crimson dye with which to stain our robes.°
        The gods be praised, my lord; of such robes we have plenty
        within the palace. Of those we fear no shortage.
        If an oracle had ordered, I could have made a boast
        of strewing endless garments in the way,
965   to show my thanks for your dear soul's return.

960. . . . *our robes:* The precious dye from a shellfish, a Phoenician manufacture.

> While the root survives, the tree can still bear leaves,
> to shade the house from the Dogstar's blazing heat.
> With your return to the heart of your own home,
> the heat of spring emerges from winter's cold.
> 970   But when in autumn the sour wine is stored
> Zeus makes it sweeten slowly through the winter,
> when, tasks completed, a man comes home once more.
> O Zeus above, who brings about all things,
> fulfill my prayer. May it fit in your design!

AESCHYLUS, Agamemnon (958–974)

Persuaded, Agamemnon removes his sandals, steps from the chariot, and enters the palace across the purple cloth.

Cassandra, who remains outside in her own chariot, foresees Agamemnon's doom and her own. Over the lintel of the palace she has a vision of Thyestes' curse hanging heavy on the house and a vision of his cannibal feast. Of course, no one understands her prophetic babble:

> [1214]   *Cassandra*   O horrible! O horrible! Most horrible!
> Again the crushing weight of truth foreseen
> staggers my mind with visions I scarce dare speak.
> Do you see those children floating above the house,
> the sort of shapes one only sees in nightmares?
> Dead, dead! at the will of those who ought to love them!
> 1220   Why are their hands full of their own roast flesh,
> their own entrails—they hold it out as food—
> O horror! their father takes it, tastes it, eats.
>   For this, I tell you, a certain mangy lion
> plots his revenge on my returning master
> 1225   (so I must name him; I bear the yoke of a slave),
> keeping his house and reveling in his bed.

AESCHYLUS, Agamemnon (1214–1225)

Cassandra herself turns and goes into the palace. From within a cry is heard as Clytemnestra strikes the death blow (Fig. 20.6). Clytemnestra comes forth, drenched in blood, looming over the murdered bodies of her husband and his mistress. Exulting, she declares how delicious was the murderous deed, which she prepared with her lover, Aegisthus:

> [1378]   *Clytemnestra*   My hatred was no sudden mindless growth;
> it rose from an old quarrel, which festered on.
> 1380   I stand here where I struck him. That work is finished.
> For it I offer no apology.
>   To keep the man from dodging and eluding death,
> I spread a sumptuous net, like one for fishes,
> rich robes but deadly; he could only struggle.
> 1385   Once, twice, I chopped. He gave two retching groans,
> his knees collapsed, he fell. With one more blow,

FIG. 20.6. The death of Agamemnon, Attic wine-mixing bowl, c. 470 B.C. Aegisthus has stabbed Agamemnon, who is wrapped in a weblike garment. Behind Aegisthus Clytemnestra runs up carrying a small ax (not visible). The woman behind Agamemnon is probably Cassandra, and the woman to the far right Electra. (Museum of Fine Arts, Boston; 63.1246)

a *coup de grâce*, I sent him down to Hades,
below the earth, comforter of the dead.
So he gasped out his life, and, as he fell,
1390   a rain of crimson drops, from his bitter death,
spattered upon me. My heart leaped up for joy,
exulting like a plot of budded wheat,
which Zeus is ripening with his hoped-for rain.
      Elders of Argos, you have heard my story;
1395   approve it or not. I glory in my deed.
If piety permitted such libation,
he would deserve it, more than any man.
For it was he who filled the accursed cup;
he has returned and drained its bitter dregs.

AESCHYLUS, *Agamemnon* (1378–1398)

Clytemnestra defends her treachery and murder, claiming as her motive Agamemnon's sacrifice of her daughter Iphigenia. Aegisthus joins her on the stage, and the play ends.

Orestes' Revenge

The second play of the trilogy takes place many years later. Agamemnon's son, **Orestes,** spirited from the house as a child and raised in Phocis (the territory around

Delphi), has come to manhood. Ordered by the Delphic Oracle, he returns to Argos in the company of his friend Pylades to avenge the murder of his father, even though this means killing his own mother. He goes to his father's grave and leaves a lock of hair upon it. The night before, Clytemnestra had a horrible dream: She gave birth to a viper that sucked at her breasts and bit them. Thinking that the dream was sent by the angry ghost of Agamemnon, she sends her daughter **Electra** to his grave to make drink-offerings, in company with a band of women: the "libation bearers" who make up the chorus in the play. Orestes reveals himself to his sister Electra, who is bitter and filled with hatred toward the mother who killed her father. Together they plot the murder of Clytemnestra.

Pretending that he is a messenger from Phocis to report his own death. Orestes gains admission to the palace. Aegisthus is summoned to hear the good news; Orestes slays him on the spot. Clytemnestra comes in to discover the corpse—and with it the truth. Orestes draws his sword to fulfill his mission; Clytemnestra, desperate for life, bares her breasts and pleads for mercy:

> No, no, my child! have pity on these breasts,
> from which, still half asleep, your baby gums
> so often sucked the milk that gave you strength.

> AESCHYLUS, *Choëphoroe* (896–898)

Orestes hesitates, but at the urging of Pylades kills her, then exults over the body and that of her lover, both lying at his feet:

[973] See, see the double tyrants of the land,
    who killed my father and who wrecked my home!
975   In arrogance they mounted to his throne,
    and even now they cling, these paramours,
    still bound by oath—or so their end suggests.
    Together they plotted Agamemnon's death;
    they swore to die together and kept that promise.
980 Now look again, all you that hear these horrors,
    upon the trap they set for my poor father,
    like fetters and manacles for feet and hands.
    Come, spread it out. Stand round it on all sides,
    and hold this winding-sheet in the plain sight
985 of the father—no, not mine, but Father Sun,
    who oversees all things—that he may know
    my mother's godless deeds, and stand by me
    as witness when at last I face my judges,
    to justify my compassing her death.
990 Killing Aegisthus bothers me not at all:
    he has paid the penalty the law decrees
    for such defilers. But as for her
    who schemed the shameful death of such a man
    as Agamemnon, who bore his children's weight
995 beneath her heart, a burden she once loved,
    but which by now she loathed—how do you judge?

A snake, I tell you, an adder, whose poisoned bite,
at first unnoticed, brings death and quick decay,
fruits of her passion and malicious heart.

AESCHYLUS, *Choëphoroe* (973–1004)

But already the **Furies** (Erinyes, e-**rin**-i-ēz), the persecuting spirits of murdered kin, surround Orestes. They work their vengeance by disturbing the mind of their victim, and Orestes slips into madness.

The Trial of Orestes

The last play of the trilogy, in which the Furies make up the chorus, opens in Delphi. Orestes has gone there for Apollo's protection from the Furies, for it was Apollo who advised him to kill his mother. Apollo orders Orestes to go to Athens to seek justice from the Athenian law court presided over by Athena. The scene shifts (something rare in Greek drama) to Athens, where Orestes falls down, a suppliant, at the statue of Athena. The Furies arrive and insist that the spilled blood of blood relatives must be atoned by more spilled blood, but Orestes claims that Apollo has purified him of pollution and appeals to Athena for help. The Furies claim that it is their divine prerogative to persecute those who murder their own blood kin, and that the upstart Olympians have no right to interfere with ancient privilege. Athena, seeing justice on either side, turns the case over to a jury of twelve Athenians, who hear the case on the Areopagus ("hill of Ares") below the Acropolis, the first trial scene in Western literature.

The Furies present their case: Without the ancient restraints there will be no check on crime. Orestes asks why they did not persecute Clytemnestra for killing Agamemnon—because, they reply, Clytemnestra and Agamemnon did not share the same blood. Apollo now takes up Orestes' case and claims the authority of Zeus, the protector of kings: Agamemnon's death is not to be compared with that of an adulterous woman. As for the primacy of blood-ties, the child's blood comes from the father who plants the seed, not from the mother who is but the soil in which the seed is sown. Athena herself is proof that the child is of the father—a modern twist to an old tale:

[657]   *Apollo*   Thus I declare: be sure I speak the truth.
           She who gives birth to what we call "her child"
           is not the parent of the new-sown growth;
660   rather, she is its nurse. Its parent is the man
           who gives his seed to her, a stranger woman,
           to keep for him, a stranger, as it swells,
           if so the gods decree. Here is the proof:
           a male can father children without a mother—
665   as witness she who stands among you here,
           Athena, daughter of Olympian Zeus.
           She was not fostered in a darkling womb;
           no goddess could give birth to such a child.

AESCHYLUS, *Eumenides* (657–666)

Therefore, Orestes' murder of Clytemnestra was, strictly speaking, not the shedding of kindred blood. Orestes was obliged to avenge the murder of his father, a scepter-bearing king. The jury's vote is evenly divided. Athena, who always sides with the male, casts the deciding vote:

[734]   *Athena* Mine is the last, mine the decisive vote:
735   this ballot, then, I cast—to acquit Orestes.
     No woman ever labored through my birth;
     my heartfelt fellow-feeling is for the man,
     save in one thing: he is obliged to marry.
     Thus siding with the father, I cannot place
740   an equal value on a woman's death,
     who killed her husband, guardian of the home.

AESCHYLUS, Eumenides (734–739)

Athena appeases the Furies, angry at the verdict, by assigning them a permanent place in Athens, but as beneficent spirits now, no longer malignant; hence their new name, **Eumenides,** "the kindly ones."

Apollo's argument, that the son is closer to the father than to the mother, strikes a modern as odd, but it is based on the ancient agricultural metaphor applied to human biology. The seed is planted in the earth, but is not of the earth; the rain from heaven, like semen, makes the seed grow, which otherwise would die. So the human female provides a soil in which the child may grow, but the child comes from the father. The reasoning is typical of arguments offered in real Athenian courts of the fifth century, when conclusions based on the plausibility of evidence were first being refined. A century and a quarter after the production of the *Oresteia*, Aristotle speculated on the roles of father and mother in producing children. Although he recognizes that both sexes contribute, he assigns the generative force (which includes the form the fetus is to assume) to the male contribution; the female contributes only its formless matter. In fact, the female's genetic contribution to human reproduction was not clarified until about two hundred years ago.

OBSERVATIONS: A PARABLE OF PROGRESS

Aeschylus, born in 525 B.C., grew up when the tyranny of Pisistratus and his sons was breaking down. He lived through the radical democratic reforms of Clisthenes and fought in the battles of Marathon, 490 B.C., and Salamis, 479 B.C. Alone of the major Athenian tragedians, he brought to his poetic vision the boundless optimism of the young democracy. In the *Oresteia* we see him refashion an old myth to proclaim this vision.

A leading theme in the trilogy is the question, "What is justice?" According to the ancient unwritten law of the clan, justice is revenge. Thyestes slept with Atreus' wife; Atreus gave Thyestes his own children to eat. Agamemnon killed Iphigenia; Clytemnestra killed Agamemnon; Orestes killed Clytemnestra. This is blood-vendetta, rooted in the ancient fear of ghosts who demand blood for blood, an eye for an eye, the old law that the Furies embody and execute.[5] But the constant killing for revenge has no logical limit. Somehow the vicious cycle must end.

Earlier, at Delphi, an advance over the primitive blood-vendetta had appeared. In a rite of purification performed there, a pig's blood was dripped over a murderer to release him and those who had contact with him from persecution by a ghost (see Fig 7.5). The progressive Athenian system of civic law to settle homicide, which Aeschylus proudly celebrates, was a momentous improvement over the Delphic system of magical purification (but note that Aeschylus gives Apollo credit for inspiring this advance). We use a similar system of civic law in the West today.

In Athenian civic law the juridical power of the family is curtailed and overridden by the authority of the state, whose will is communicated through laws recorded in alphabetic writing. Most upper-class Athenian males could read this script, and from 621 B.C. onward Athenian laws were engraved on wood or stone and displayed in the agora, where anyone could examine them and argue over their meaning. Some written law had existed before in Mesopotamia (never in Egypt), but such laws were presented as handed down by gods, immutable, divine, and inexorable; the Hebrews, too, viewed law as divinely willed. In Athens, by contrast, laws were drafted and approved by the people, constantly revised, and interpreted in open courts by a jury of one's fellow citizens. There was nothing divine about these laws, and there were no lawyers in Athens to present a definitive interpretation: A defendant had to represent himself in court.[6] The system of Athenian popular democratic laws recorded in alphabetic writing contributed greatly to the development of the arts of persuasion and led directly to the invention of logic and the elaborate philosophical speculations of Plato and Aristotle.

The Furies, on the other hand, stand for traditional, familial, and tribal ways. The avenging spirits of spilled blood take no interest in why familial blood was shed, but only that it was shed. These ancient powers of ghost-vengeance, the children of Night (Nyx), are by nature opposed to the younger Olympians, Athena and Apollo. Although they cannot be cast out completely or destroyed, they can be tamed and transformed into propitious powers that will support the new order: the Eumenides. Thus Athens, the ideal *polis,* replaces the violent, archaic, and heroic world with one that looks to a brighter future in which human intelligence can resolve primitive, self-destructive fear.

Aeschylus also incorporates numerous etiological details in the *Eumenides.* The institution of the Areopagus, a court with jurisdiction over homicide during Aeschylus' day, is traced back to the trial of Orestes; the rule that a tie vote stands for acquittal[7] begins with Athena's ruling; the cult of the Eumenides (which actually existed in caves beneath the rock of the Areopagus) is hereby explained; and the traditional political alliance between Argos and Athens in Classical times is traced to

---

[5]Cf. the biblical "If any harm follows, then you shall give life for life, eye for eye, tooth for tooth, hand for hand, foot for foot, burn for burn, wound for wound, stripe for stripe" (Exodus 21.23–25).

[6]Athenian females, who were never citizens, were excluded from this system of public governance and ordinarily were not allowed into court; when a woman was charged with a crime, a man would speak on her behalf.

[7]Still true today in parliamentary procedure, although of course not in criminal cases.

Orestes' gratitude for being freed of the Furies' persecution at Athens. Aeschylus' *Oresteia* is a good example of how the Greeks modified and transformed ancient, traditional tales to reflect contemporary issues and justify contemporary practice.[8]

KEY TERMS

Penthesilea, 545	Orestes, 560
Neoptolemus, 548	Electra, 561
Laocoön, 551	Furies, 562
Polyxena, 554	Eumenides, 563

FURTHER READING

Goldhill, Simon, *Reading Greek Tragedy* (Cambridge, U.K., 1986). Has two chapters on the *Oresteia*.

———, *Aeschylus:* The Oresteia (Cambridge, U.K. 1992). Excellent introduction to the social and political background of the trilogy, with a lucid interpretation.

Herington, J. *Aeschylus* (New Haven, Conn., 1986). A general study.

Huxley, G. L., *Greek Epic Poetry: From Eumelos to Panyasis* (Cambridge, Mass., 1969). Reconstruction of the lost Cyclic Poems on the basis of the fragments.

Lebeck, Ann, *The "Oresteia": A Study in Language and Structure* (Cambridge, Mass., 1971). A penetrating analysis of the sometimes desperate imagery and difficult themes in Aeschylus' tragedy, arguing that the central theme is a concern with causality.

Thomson, George, *Aeschylus and Athens* (London, 1941). A major study, but with a Marxist bias.

[8]For B. Malinowski's explanation of myth as justifying social custom, see Chapter 23.

CHAPTER 21

THE RETURN OF ODYSSEUS

But I imagine that the story of Odysseus is greater
than what he actually did, through the sweetness of Homer's verse;
for by his winged song he gives to lies a certain dignity,
and his poetic craft deceives us, leading us astray by myths.

PINDAR, *Nemean* 7.20–23

THE POETIC GENIUS Homer inherited a story about how Odysseus, one of the principal fighters at Troy, ran into a great deal of trouble trying to get home. After twenty years he arrived, only to find his son's life threatened, his father living like a pauper, and his wife besieged in her own house by lascivious, greedy, and politically ambitious men. Without allies, except experience and high intelligence, Odysseus appeared in disguise among his wife's suitors and, on a feast day of Apollo, killed them in cold blood. Of this gory story of revenge Homer made a parable of the human journey from life into death, and return again to life. In ancient times the *Iliad* was compared to tragedy because of its somber themes and deep personal conflict; the *Odyssey*, by contrast, was compared with comedy because (like the folktales whose patterns and symbols Homer borrows) it has a happy ending in which the family is reunited and the promise of the future is affirmed. The *Odyssey* is a towering artistic achievement, admired and still imitated by artists today, one of the most influential myths in the Western world.

ODYSSEUS' JOURNEY FROM TROY

The Cicones and the Lotus Eaters

In the *Odyssey*, Odysseus recounts his adventures at a banquet on the island of Phaeacia in the court of King Alcinoüs (al-**sin**-ō-us), where Odysseus is washed ashore. He has been away from home twenty years: ten at Troy, three lost at sea, and seven on the island of the mysterious nymph Calypso ("concealer"). Odysseus' first-person narrative of his travels occupies one sixth of Homer's *Odyssey*.

When Odysseus and his twenty ships leave Troy, they stop at Ismarus in Thrace, land of the Cicones (si-**kō**-nēz), and sack the city. Against the advice of their commander, they pause to devour the stolen sheep, cattle, and wine. On the next morning the neighboring Cicones attack, killing six men from every ship (each ship seems to have a crew of fifty).

The remaining Greeks escape by sea but are soon caught in a storm off the southern coast of the Peloponnesus. Violent winds blow them out of the everyday world into the land of the **Lotus Eaters.** The local inhabitants consume a drug that makes men forgetful of their home and their purpose:

[94] Once any of them had tasted the honey-sweet fruit of the lotus,
95   he lost his desire to return, to boast of his glorious exploits.
      All they wished was to stay in the land of the eaters of lotus,
      drowsily nibbling the fruit, and forgetting their hopes of return.
      Ignoring their tears, I frog-marched them back at once to the vessels,
      to lash them under the thwarts, in the bilge of the hollow ships.
100   Then I ordered the rest of my crew, shipmates sober and trusty,
      to embark in the ships right away, lest, after tasting the lotus
      some of them might be tempted to give up all hope of return.
      Quickly they hurried aboard and took their place on the benches;
      swinging together they caught at the foaming sea with their oars.

                    HOMER, *Odyssey* (9.94–104)

Polyphemus

At sea again, the Greeks come to the land of the **Cyclops** ("round-eye"), named **Polyphemus** (po-li-**fē**-mus, "much-renowned"). This story, one of the most famous in the world, surely had an independent existence before Homer adapted it to the story of Odysseus and seems to have been excerpted often from the longer poem for separate performance, once it was written down in the eighth century B.C.:

[105]   Forward we sailed, regretful of all we were leaving behind.
         In time we came to the land of the arrogant lawless Cyclopes,
         who sow no crops with their hands, nor harvest the ripened grain,
         but entrust all that to heaven; so all their needs are supplied—
         wheat and barley and vines which bear them wine in abundance,
110   fostered by Zeus's rain, without labor of seedtime or harvest,

They never unite in assembly for common decisions or laws,
but live in echoing caves on the highest peaks of the mountains,
alone, each ruling his wife and children, ignoring all others.
    A little outside a harbor along the Cyclopean coastline
115   stretches a wooded island, a breeding place for wild goats,
untroubled by wandering humans or hunters in search of game.
No danger ever concerns them as they wander over the hillsides,
no goat pens cumber the island, no plowland limits their range.
No humans inhabit the region, unplowed and fallow forever,
120   unharvested through the ages, a pasture for bleating goats.
For Cyclopes know nothing of ships with red-painted gunwales;
they have no shipwrights to build vessels of well-fitted benches,
to sail to the cities of men and return with whatever they lack—
crossing the sea in their vessels in search of something to trade.
125   Traders, indeed, might make of the island a prosperous city,
a source of all that is good, with nothing to threaten its safety.
By the coast of the foaming sea lie rich and well-watered meadows
which, planted with grapes, would yield almost perpetual vintage.
Plowmen could easily harvest abundant crops in their season
130   from the island's soil, so easy to harrow, so deep and so fertile.
The harbor, moreover, is perfect; a ship has no need of an anchor
or hawsers at either end, to hold her fast in her place:
just beach her and leave her alone, for as long a time as you fancy,
till the men are ready to sail and following breezes are rising.
135   Abundant fresh water runs from springs at the head of the harbor,
rising deep in a cave whose mouth is surrounded by poplars.
    Some god was surely the pilot who guided us into the harbor,
through the dark of night, for the dawn had not begun to appear.
Deep fog enveloped the ships, no moon was shining in heaven;
140   clouds had covered her face. No one saw the loom of the island,
nor did we see the long crests of the breakers rolling ashore,
till our vessels had already grounded and run on the sandy beach.
We jumped out into the water, removed the gear from the vessels,
then pulled our ships to safety and clambered up on the seashore,
145   where we sank into deepest slumber to wait for the breaking of dawn.
    Rose-fingered dawn at last revealed the coming of morning.
Gaping about in surprise, we wandered all over the island,
whose nymphs, the daughters of Zeus, the god adorned with the aegis,
roused up herds of wild goats, as breakfast for all my comrades.
150   From the ships we took curved bows and deeply socketed lances,
split ourselves into three groups, and then set off to the hunt.
The gods gave us wonderful luck: nine goats were allotted to each
of the dozen ships of my fleet, and ten to me as commander.
So we spent the whole day, till the sun was setting at evening,
155   feasting on endless fresh meat washed down with mellow old wine.
For the wine in our ships as yet was not completely exhausted,
wine that was part of our loot from the holy Ciconian city;
this we had poured in great jars and distributed plenty to each.
All that day we watched the land of the nearby Cyclopes,
160   seeing their smoke and hearing the sound of men and their flocks.

But after the sun had set and darkness come over the heavens,
we finally laid ourselves down to sleep by the edge of the water.
    Rose-fingered dawn at last revealed the coming of morning;
I rose to my feet, called the men, and issued them these as orders:
165   "My comrades, stay here a bit, while I and the crew of my vessel
go out to spy on the natives, what sort of people they are.
Uncivilized, maybe, and savage, having no vestige of honor,
or possibly kindly to strangers, with minds inspired by heaven."
    At this I climbed in my ship and ordered my comrades to follow,
170   to cast off the hawsers, board, and seat themselves at the oars.
Quickly they hurried aboard and took their place on the benches;
swinging together they caught at the foaming sea with their oars.
When we got to the nearby mainland we could see the mouth of a cavern,
down by the edge of the sea, high-vaulted, shaded by laurels,
175   where sheep and goats liked to sleep. Its front was a sort of corral,
fashioned of rough quarried stones piled up as high as the roof,
braced by long slender firs and trunks of high-foliaged oak trees.
Inside, there slept by himself a man of incredible stature,
a hermit, watching his sheep, avoiding the rest of his fellows,
180   in solitude making up fantasy, dreaming his god-accursed dreams.
His frame was enormous, atrocious, unlike that of bread-eating humans;
rather, he looked like a craggy spur of a desolate mountain,
standing alone and apart, its trees all gnarled and contorted.
    The rest of my loyal crew I told to remain with the vessel,
185   and to pull it up on the beach, while I myself with a dozen,
the best of the men, set out. With me I carried a goatskin
of wine, black, potent, and sweet, which Maron, son of Euanthes,
priest of Ismarean Apollo, gave me when we protected
himself with his wife and son, out of reverence for Apollo.
190   For Maron lived in a tree-studded meadow, the property of the god.
He had given magnificent gifts—seven talents of workable gold
and a bowl of the purest silver. As crown to this he included
fully a dozen double-eared jars, into which he decanted
a sweet and powerful wine, a drink to delight the immortals.
195   Nobody knew it existed, not even the slaves of the household;
Maron alone, his wife, and his stewardess knew of the secret.
Whenever he drank of the crimson wine with a heart sweet as honey,
he filled one cup and then added full twenty measures of water;°
at once the bowl breathed out a bouquet of heavenly fragrance,
200   a scent which I knew full well no man would dream of resisting.
With this I filled up a wineskin and hid it all in a knapsack,
for deep in my heart I suspected I soon would encounter a being
armed with invincible strength, but savage, barbaric, and lawless.
    We quickly got to the cave, but did not find its owner within it,
205   for he was herding fat sheep and moving from pasture to pasture.
Into the cave we wandered and looked around in amazement:
baskets loaded with cheeses, pens crowded with kids and with lambs,
milling about, group by group, the oldest, middling, and weanlings;

---

198. *water:* Ordinarily one mixed one part wine to two parts water; wine was never taken straight.

containers—pans, bowls, and buckets—carefully fashioned for milking.
210 Uneasily then my companions began to urge me, suggesting
that we borrow a few of the cheeses, and maybe a kid or a lamb,
driving them out from the sheepfolds. Then, hurrying back to the ship,
we should depart at once and set off on the briny dark waters.
But I refused their advice (later on, how I wished I had listened!),
215 for I wanted to see the owner, and see what gifts he might offer.°
(In fact, when he did appear, he was not at all nice to my comrades.)
    So we sat inside by a fire and nibbled bits of the cheeses,
offering some to the gods, while we waited for him to come back.
At last he returned from the pasture, with a heavy load of dry wood,
220 to give him light for his supper. He threw this down on the floor
inside the cave with a crash that frightened us off to a corner,
while he himself went out, to return with the ewes and the nannies,
leaving the rams and the billies corralled outside in the forecourt.
He then picked up a great rock and set it to serve as a barrier.
225 Twenty-two four-wheeled wagons could not shift it up from its threshold,
yet he easily moved this towering rock to block up the doorway.
Then down he sat to milk the ewes and the bleating nannies,
setting their young under each, with everything neat and in order.
Half the white milk he collected to curdle in wickerwork baskets;
230 the rest he poured into bowls, to take and drink for his supper.
He busied himself at his task, but when at last he was finished,
he blew up his fire, looked around, saw us, and thus he addressed us:
    "Gentlemen, who might you be? whence did you voyage the waters?
Are you come hither to trade, or are you wandering at random,
235 like pirates over the sea, cruising now this way, now that,
forever risking your lives and bringing destruction to others?"
    So he inquired, and we felt our poor hearts shatter within us,
hearing his thundering voice and seeing the mass of his body.
Yet I managed to answer his question in these diplomatical words:
240 "We are Achaeans, returning home from our warfare at Troy.
Winds of all sorts have scattered and driven us over the surges,
some in the way they would go, but us by a far different journey.
No doubt the inscrutable mind of Zeus has determined our fortune.
Know you that we are the people of Atreus' son, Agamemnon,
245 whose fame is the greatest of all men living under the heaven,
for the mighty city he sacked, the many peoples he conquered.
For our part, now we have met you, we beg you for only one thing:
grant us a kindly reception with a trifle to bid us good-bye,
the usual gift to a stranger, or show due respect to the gods.
250 Suppliants we kneel before you, whom Zeus, defender of strangers,
defends as fully as those to whom honor is owed as to guests."
    From deep in his evil heart the Cyclops gave me his answer,
"Stranger, you really are stupid, or else live a long way off,
if you warn me to dread the gods or fear that they may be offended.
255 We cyclopes pay no attention to Zeus or the other immortals,

---

215. *offer:* Odysseus hopes to receive the gifts appropriately given as an expression of *xenia,* "guest-friendship."

Ulysses

The figure of Odysseus, the Roman Ulysses, has always fascinated the imagination of the West. Although many meanings have been given to him, he is always cast in one of two categories: either glorified as the seeker of truth, the restless clever intelligence penetrating the secrets of the world, or damned as the treacherous deceiver, the exalter of intellect above the demands of the heart. Homer's Odysseus belongs to the first category, but the anti-Odysseus tradition appears as early as Sophocles' *Philoctetes* (409 B.C.) and is then refined by Euripides, Vergil, and others.

The Romans especially developed the tradition hostile to Odysseus because they claimed Aeneas, a Trojan, as their founder. In his *Divine Comedy,* Dante Alighieri (1265–1321) follows this tradition, for he saw legitimate political power in his own world as descending from the Roman state. Dante's is the first important portrayal of Odysseus in a nonclassical language. In the twenty-sixth canto of the *Inferno,* Dante stands with his guide, Vergil, and looks down in the pit reserved for deceitful counselors. Dante and Vergil are near Hell's deepest caverns and beneath them see flames that look like fireflies in the darkness. Vergil explains that one flame, split at the top, is Ulysses, crafty inventor of the Trojan horse, who through guile sneaked into Troy (with Diomedes) and stole the protecting statue of Athena, the Palladium. Ulysses is condemned to Hell because of his successful stratagems against the Roman's Trojan forebears, but Dante also condemns him for the restlessness of his intellect and his search for truth, a sinful exploration that can lead only to destruction. The flame speaks and tells a tale never told in the ancient world: how Odysseus never reached home, but was lost, still searching, in the high seas beyond the Pillars of Heracles. The voice is prophetic, foretelling the age of discovery when the restless Europeans, cultural descendants of Greece and Rome, crossed the Atlantic Ocean and sailed around Africa to discover new worlds. Although dependent on the Roman Vergil's portrayal of Ulysses, Dante has rediscovered the side of the Greek character that scorns comfort in order to pursue fame and explore the unknown.

The pro-Odysseus tradition reappears in "Ulysses" of Alfred, Lord Tennyson (1809–1902), the most famous English poet of the Victorian age, who glorifies the very qualities Dante condemns. The poem is set on Ithaca. Ulysses has grown old, but is determined to leave home again in pursuit of fresh adventure:

> It little profits that an idle king,
> By this still hearth, among these barren crags,
> Matched with an aged wife, I mete and dole
> Unequal laws unto a savage race,
> That hoard, and sleep, and feed, and know not me.
> I cannot rest from travel; I will drink
> Life to the lees. . . .
> Old age hath yet his honour and his toil.
> Death closes all; but something ere the end,

Some work of noble note, may yet be done,
Not unbecoming men that strove with gods.
The lights begin to twinkle from the rocks;
The long day wanes; the slow moon climbs; the deep
Moans round with many voices. Come, my friends,
'Tis not too late to seek a newer world.
Push off, and sitting well in order smite
The sounding furrows; for my purpose holds
To sail beyond the sunset, and the baths
Of all the western stars, until I die. . . .
We are not now that strength which in old days
Moved earth and heaven; that which we are, we are;
One equal temper of heroic hearts,
Made weak by time and fate, but strong in will
To strive, to seek, to find, and not to yield.

FROM ALFRED, LORD TENNYSON, "Ulysses"

A sympathetic perception also underlies the most celebrated recasting of Odysseus in the twentieth century in James Joyce's (1882–1941) novel *Ulysses* (1922). In this long and difficult work (768 pages), really a satire, Ulysses appears as Leopold Bloom, an Irish Jew, forever the outsider, who makes a modest living selling advertising for a newspaper. The book describes his wanderings on a single day through the streets of Dublin, whose humdrum everyday life replaces the exotic lands of Homer's story. Telemachus is replaced by Stephen Dedalus, whose name combines those of Stephen, the first Christian martyr, and Daedalus, the master artist of Athens. He is a world-weary dropout whose mind is preoccupied with the relationship between Hamlet and his father (as Telemachus is seeking his father). The princess Nausicaä, whom Homer's Odysseus compared to Artemis in beauty, is a crippled shop-girl who inspires Leopold Bloom to masturbate in his pants as he watches her on the beach. Penelopê, Leopold's wife, Molly, is conducting a torrid affair with Blazes Boylan (= the suitors, who in this case have succeeded in seducing the lady of the house); although Leopold knows about her tryst on that afternoon, he can think of no way to prevent it. Yet Molly in her own way, in her heart, is truly like Penelopê, faithful to her beloved "Poldy."

because we are stronger by far. And if a whim should possess me,
my fear of the anger of Zeus would not save you or your friends.
But tell me, where did you moor your stout and well-founded ship,
close by, or off at a distance? I really would like to know."
260   His clumsy attempt to trap me did not deceive my astuteness:
I innocently gave him an answer in lying treacherous words:
"Poseidon, Shaker of Earth, has smashed my ship on a reef
as a rising wind drove her close to a point we wanted to weather.
Only these men and I survived her utter destruction."
265   Even this tale did not soften the flinty heart of the Cyclops.
Springing erect, he grabbed with his hands, caught two of my sailors,
and smashed them down on the rock, as you kill a superfluous puppy.
Their brains burst out from their skulls and ran all over the floor.

He twisted one limb from another (his way of preparing his supper),
270 and, crunching them down like a wildcat, left never a morsel uneaten,
not entrails or muscle, not even the bones and their succulent marrow.
What could we do but rage as we lifted our hands to the heavens,
while watching this horrible crime? Despair crushed all other emotion.
When the Cyclops finally ended stuffing his monstrous great belly
275 with swallows of human flesh, washed down with milk by the bucket,
he stretched himself out in his cave, in the very midst of the sheep.
For a moment I planned to approach, to draw the sword by my side,
to feel for the lethal spot where the diaphragm covers the liver,
and stab him under the chest. But second thought gave me pause:
280 we too would die in the cave and suffer a horrible ending,
for I saw no way human hands could budge his rock from the doorway.
So all night long we lay groaning and waiting for dawn to appear.
Rose-fingered dawn at last revealed the coming of morning.
The Cyclops rekindled the fire and milked his magnificent sheep,
285 in smooth and efficient fashion, then set each lamb to its mother.
Next, this duty completed, he grabbed two more of my comrades
to gobble them up for his breakfast. Then he easily lifted the stone,
drove his fat sheep outdoors, and put back the boulder behind them,
just as one does when replacing the lid on a quiver of arrows,
290 and with many a merry whistle drove off his flock to the mountains.
There I was, left to brood and to fashion a terrible vengeance,
hoping Athena would grant my prayers and an opportune moment.
This plan suggested itself to my heart as by far most effective:
the Cyclops had cut a bludgeon of olive, still pliant and green,
295 and left it to dry by the pens. To us it looked fully as heavy
as the mast of a twenty-oared ship, black-sided, broad in the beam,
plodding its way through the surge, heavily loaded with cargo;
such was its length to our eyes, such was its cumbersome thickness.
From this I chopped off a piece, a length of fully a fathom,
300 and handed it on to my comrades to smooth it and taper it down.
They made the shaft of the weapon all smooth and easy to handle,
while I first pointed the tip, then hardened it well in the fire.
This done, I carefully hid it by burying it under a dungheap,
plenty of which, of course, was everywhere piled in the cavern.
305 Lastly, I told the men to draw lots to decide who should join me
in the perilous job of lifting and twisting the ponderous timber
around in the Cyclops' eyeball, when he drifted off to sweet dreams.
Four volunteers they chose, and I added myself to the number.
At evening he reappeared, his wooly sheep going before him.
310 He drove the fat creatures onward, into the depths of the cavern,
this time not leaving a one outside in the spacious forecourt;
perhaps some deity moved him, or perhaps he suspected the truth.
Once more he lifted the boulder and set it over the doorway,
then sat him down to his milking of bleating nannies and ewes
315 in smooth and efficient fashion, then set each lamb to its mother.
Next, this duty completed, he seized two more of my comrades
and devoured them for his supper. At last I spoke to the Cyclops,
standing beside him and holding a punchbowl of strong black wine.

"Cyclops, drink up," said I, "now your cannibal orgy is over,
320 so you may learn what sort of drink we carried as cargo.
See, I have brought you a drop; I hope you will show me your mercy
and send me back to my home, giving up your boorish behavior,
which I really can stand no more. How can you dream for a minute
that anyone ever will come, from any nation of mortals,
325 if they hear the way you have acted, and the nasty way you behave?"
At that he reached for the bowl and drained it all at a gulp.
The sweet wine delighted his heart, and thus he addressed me again:
"Give me another big drink. But tell me, what is your name?
I shall certainly give you a present, one you will surely enjoy.
330 Oh yes, our land, rich in grapes, yields us Cyclopes a vintage
good in its way, and fostered by showers sent us by Zeus.
But that with which you have plied me is truly a fountain of nectar!"
So he exclaimed, and I poured him a sparkling bumper of wine.
Three times I offered him more; three times he drank in his folly.
335 At last, when the fumes had addled the brain and wits of the Cyclops,
I spoke to him once again with words deceitful of purpose:
"Cyclops, a moment ago you asked me to tell you my name.
I shall tell you, if you in return give me the present you promised.
'Nobody' is my name, for my dear mother and father
340 gave me this name at my birth, and since then all my companions."
These were my words, and this the reply of his arrogant heart:
"'Nobody,' then, will be last, after all his friends, to be eaten;
before him, the rest will go down. That will be my farewell gift!"°
Collapsing, he sprawled on his back, his head drooping off to one side,
345 and slumber, who conquers all mortals, received him into its charge.
The wine and the half-chewed flesh of humans spewed from his gullet,
vomited up by the drunkard. Then I thrust the stake in the embers,
and, while it heated, inspired the hearts of all my companions,
hoping that no one would fail me or flinch in a spasm of terror.
350 Green though it was, the olive-wood stake was about to catch fire
and shone with a red-hot glare. Approaching, I lifted it out;
the others stood by me to help, and some god fired their courage.
They picked up the olive-wood log, red-hot and sharp at the tip,
and swung it into his eye. Against it I threw my whole weight,
355 and spun it around, like a shipwright drilling a hole in a timber:
he guides the drill, while his helpers, standing on either side,
saw the thong back and forth as the drill° sinks deeper and deeper.
So I and my men rotated the stake in the eye of the Cyclops:
hissing, his blood spurted out, and the heat singed eyelid and brow;
360 the eyeball, scorched to its roots, crackled and boiled in the fire.

343. *farewell gift:* The gift of Cyclops parodies, by inversion, the custom of *xenia*—Odysseus will be eaten last!   357. *drill:* The auger described here is like a bow drill, whose forward thrust comes from the weight of the user as he leans against it. The twist of the drill came from a long thong wrapped in a single turn around it; men at each end pushed and pulled so it turned, now clockwise, now counterclockwise, like the drill of someone starting a fire by friction. But the simile is somewhat mixed: How could Odysseus both guide the stake and twist it, especially if its weight was carried by four other men?

FIG. 21.1. The blinding of Polyphemus, on a large Attic jug from Eleusis, c. 670 B.C. (the jar was used to
bury a child). Odysseus and two
companions, lifting the fire-hard-
ened stake on their shoulders, blind
Polyphemus. In this early mythic
representation, the artist has exper-
imented by painting Odysseus
white, to distinguish him from the
other figures; white usually was reserved for female figures. Note the
cup in Polyphemus' hand, referring
to the detail that Odysseus first got
him drunk.   (Archaeological Museum,
Eleusis; 546)

As when a blacksmith is quenching a big bronze° adze or an ax-head,
he plunges it into cold water, which makes it sizzle and scream,
but gives the temper required, the strength and toughness of iron;
just so his eyeball squealed as the stake of olive-wood entered (Fig. 21.1).

365 He let out a horrible cry, which the rocky cavern reechoed,
scaring us back in terror. He plucked at the blood-smeared stake,
wrenched it out from his eye, and in torment hurled it away.
He shouted to other Cyclopes, who lived in the nearby caves
dotted about the wind-blown hillsides, to come to his rescue.

370 Hearing his call, they came at a run from every direction,
and standing before his cave, they asked him what was the matter:
"What troubles you so, Polyphemus, making you call us to help,
and rousing us from our slumber, so late in the god-given night.
Perhaps some rascally mortal is trying to rustle your sheep,

375 or is somebody bent on your murder by treachery or brute force?"
The mighty Polyphemus replied from the mouth of his cave:
"Nobody wants to kill me, by treachery, not by brute force."
To this the others replied in words aimed right at the mark:
"If nobody's using force on a man alone and defenseless,

361. *bronze:* The Homeric poems took form at the time when iron was slowly replacing bronze; the
smith is said to quench a bronze ax, which gives "the strength and toughness of iron." For centuries
the effectiveness of tempering iron (immersion does nothing for bronze) was thought to come from
substances dissolved in the water into which the hot metal was plunged, not from the sudden cooling of the metal.

380 you must have an inescapable sickness, sent by great Zeus.
The best thing for you to do is to pray to your father Poseidon."
     With this retort they departed. I laughed in my inmost heart,
gloating over my shrewdness, and seeing them tricked by my name.
The Cyclops groaned in his pain and suffered spasms of torture.
385 Groping about with his hands, he lifted the rock from the doorway,
meanwhile feeling around, as he sat him there at the entrance,
expecting to catch whoever might try to get out with the sheep,
and even hoping that I might be foolish enough to attempt it.
But I was pondering deeply, to make things turn out for the best,
390 and to find some way to avoid disaster for me and my comrades.
In this matter of life and death, in the face of imminent peril,
this was the method that seemed the best of all possible courses:
the cave held plenty of well-fed rams with thick shaggy fleeces
(big ones, handsome, all covered with heavy dark-colored wool),
395 which I quietly tied in threes with pliant shoots of the willow
where the monster Cyclops slept, planning his criminal horrors.
The rams in the middle each carried a man; the two on the outside
trotted along beside them, and thus protected my comrades.
So three rams carried each man, but I myself was left over,
400 as also the noblest ram of the flock enclosed in the sheepfold.
Approaching the beast from behind and stretching under its belly,
I lay there, my hands holding tight to the animal's glorious wool.
So we lay in discomfort and awaited the light of the dawning.
     Rose-fingered dawn at least revealed the coming of morning.
405 The Cyclops drove all the males of the flock away to the pasture,
but the unmilked females remained, with udders swollen to bursting,
bleating in pain, in the cave. Tormented by horrible anguish,
their owner felt the back of each ram as it went out to pasture—
stupid! he never suspected my men were lashed under their bellies.
410 Last of all the bellwether approached and was nearing the doorway,
slowed by the weight of his wool and of me, a man of resources.
Gently caressing its back, Polyphemus the might addressed it:
     "My good old ram, how is it that you are last of my flock
to hurry out of the cavern? The others have never outstripped you,
415 as you proudly galloped along, the first to taste of the grasses,
to get to the stream, and to hurry home to the fold in the evening.
But today you are last of all. Is it grief for your master's eye,
which Nobody blinded, the scoundrel, he and his evil companions,
after getting me drunk? But I tell you, he hasn't yet gotten away
420 from the death he deserves. How I wish that you could stand here beside me
and tell me in human speech how he managed to duck from my power!
I'd smash him down on the floor, his brains would spatter all over
in every part of the cave! and that would lighten the burden
of all the sorrow I feel, which that no-good Nobody caused me."
425   With this he dismissed the ram to go free from the door and away.
As soon as the ram and I were far enough from the doorway,
I freed my hands from the wool, and undid the bonds of my comrades.
Turning the fat and shambling sheep away from their pasture,
we drove them back to the ship, and were greeted with great relief—

430 those of us who survived. For the rest they began to lament,
but sorrow I could not allow, and shook my head at each mourner.
Instead, I told them to hurry and load the heavy-wooled sheep
down in the bilge of the ships, and set sail on the billowy ocean.
At once they hurried aboard and took their place on the benches;
435 swinging together they caught at the foaming sea with their oars.
When we had gone as far as the sound of a man's voice will carry,
I shouted back at the Cyclops in words of taunt and abuse:
     "Cyclops, your luck was bad. No coward was he, whose companions
you seized with violent hands in the hollow cave and devoured.
440 Your sin has found you out, your insolent treatment of strangers;
unscrupulously you killed and ate them, right in your dwelling!
Revenge has fallen upon you from Zeus and the other immortals."
     So I jeered at the Cyclops, who raged even more in his heart.
He broke off the topmost peak of a mighty mountain nearby
445 and flung it out at the ship. Flying over, it landed beyond us.
The cresting sea swelled up where the rock fell into its waters,
in a surge which hurtled our vessel headlong back to the shore,
a huge wave out of the deep, driving us in to destruction.
Hastily grabbing a spar, I reached it down to the bottom,
450 fended her off, and in silence signaled the oarsmen to heave,
to strain at the oars, if they hoped to break away from the peril.
They fell to their oars and rowed, until, by churning the sea,
we had opened a gap twice as wide as that we had earlier trusted.
Again I taunted the Cyclops, while my sailors tried to restrain me,
455 assailing me from all sides with clever attempts at persuasion:
     "Why do you have to keep on infuriating this savage?
Just now he hurled that great rock beyond us out into the ocean,
washing us back to the shore, where we fully expected destruction.
If you had made the least sound, or if he had heard what you uttered,
460 he would have smashed our bodies and ships into one bloody mess
with the toss of one jagged rock at that incredible distance."
     So they attempted in vain to persuade my imperious spirit.
Once more I called in an angry voice and showed my defiance:
"Cyclops, if ever a human asks how you came by your blindness,
465 or who it was that disfigured your eye, just give him the answer:
'Odysseus put out my eye, Odysseus, sacker of cities,
the son of Laërtes, who dwells in Ithaca, lord of its palace.'"
     Hearing, he gave a great moan and sadly made this reply:
"Alas, the words of a prophet have now returned to my mind.
470 There once was a seer among us, a prophet wise and sagacious,
Telemus, son of Eurymus, a man who excelled at divining,
grown old among the Cyclopes, for whom he practiced his science.
Long ago he assured me I was doomed to loss of my eyesight
at the hands of a certain Odysseus. This man, I assumed, would appear
475 big and impressive to look at, wearing the trappings of power.
But the man who put out my eye is little, feeble, and sluggish,
who could only do what he wanted by getting me drunk on his wine.
Come back to me then, Odysseus, so I can give you a present
fitting for your departure, by persuading the Shaker of Earth

480 to escort you off on your way and grant you a prosperous voyage.
For I am his son, and Poseidon is proud that he is my father;
he himself, if he pleases, will escort you off on the journey,
not leaving the task to another, be it human or blessed immortal."
He tried to wheedle me so, but I quickly gave him my answer:
485 "I wish I were able to rob you of life and send you to Hades!
Still, even the Shaker of Earth can never restore you your vision."
So I replied. The Cyclops then prayed to lordly Poseidon,
lifting his suppliant hands to the star-studded heaven above:
"Hear my prayer, Poseidon, thou dark-haired Shaker of Earth:
490 if I am truly your son, if you boast of being my fathers,
grant that the sacker of cities, Odysseus, son of Laërtes,
whose house is in Ithaca, never again may return to his home.
But if Fate ordains that he must revisit the land of his father,
that he look on his friends again and enter his well-built palace,
495 grant this: may he come as a beggar, a vagrant for long weary years,
bereft of his comrades' lives, with no one left to support him;
may he come in a ship not his own, and find his household a chaos."
Such was his prayer, and the dark-haired god approved his petition.
But the Cyclops seized on a rock, far bigger in size than before,
500 which he whirled up over his head, and exerting incredible force,
he threw it a little behind the stern of the dark-sided vessel,
barely failing to carry to the blade of the oar of the helmsman.
The cresting sea surged up where the rock fell into its waters,
making our dark ship yaw and plunge headlong right to the island.
505 We made our way to the shore, where our other well-fitted ships
lay drawn up all in a group, with their worried crews sitting alongside,
always keeping a lookout and waiting till we should appear.
Arriving, we beached the vessel, and pulled her up on the sand.
We ourselves disembarked there by the side of the water,
510 brought the sheep of the Cyclops from out of the smooth-gliding vessel,
and divided them up so no one should leave without a fair share.
But to me as a special portion my well-armed comrades awarded
the noble ram who had brought me out of the cave of the Cyclops.
Of him I made an offering there on the shore of the ocean.
515 to dark-clouded Zeus, son of Cronus, ruler of all that has being,
the animal's succulent thighs.° But Zeus ignored my offering,
and schemed to destroy my well-fitted ships and trusty companions.
So we sat at the feast, all day to the coming of sunset,
eating unlimited meat and washing it down with sweet wine.
520 At last the sun went down and darkness fell from the heavens;
then we lay down to sleep along the edge of the seashore.
But when the rose-fingered dawn announced the coming of daylight,
I roused my sleeping companions and bade them climb to the benches,
and to cast off the cables that moored us fast to the nearby shore.
525 At once they hurried aboard and took their place on the benches;
swinging together they caught at the foaming sea with their oars.

516. *thighs:* He burned the thigh bones in the fire, as was customary in Greek sacrifice.

From there we sailed on forward, saddened and sick at heart,
grieving the loss of our comrades, but happy that we had survived.

HOMER, *Odyssey* (9.105–566)

Aeolus, the Laestrygonians, and Circê

Odysseus next tells how he came to the island of **Aeolus** (ē-o-lus), the wind king,[1] who spends his days dining with his six sons and six daughters, all married to one another. Aeolus feasts Odysseus and his men and gives him a special gift in accordance with the customs of *xenia*: a sealed cow-hide bag that contained the dangerous winds, which he warns him not to untie under any conditions.[2]

Favored by the good winds not enclosed in the bag, Odysseus and his men come so close to Ithaca that they can see men tending fires on the shore. In his exhaustion Odysseus falls asleep, and his men begin to murmur among themselves. Their commander probably has gold in the bag, they say, which he doubtless wants to keep for himself. Greedily they untie the bag, the dangerous winds escape, and the fleet is caught in a storm. The Greeks find themselves back at the island of Aeolus. Observing that they must be bitterly hated by the gods to have suffered such a fate, Aeolus gruffly orders them away.

Next the Greeks come to the land of the **Laestrygonians** (lest-tri-**gōn**-i-ans, perhaps "gnashers"). They park their ships in a long, narrow bay bordered by high cliffs, a sort of fjord, and send out men to reconnoiter. The king's daughter meets them and leads the advance party to her father, but the king promptly gobbles one down; the Laestrygonians, like the Cylops, are cannibals! Other Laestrygonians run in from far and wide, take up position on either side of the fjord, and smash the ships below with giant boulders. They harpoon the men wiggling in the water like eels, pull them out, and eat them alive. Everyone is killed and every ship destroyed—all except Odysseus and his lucky crew, who cleverly moored their vessel outside the entrance to the harbor.

On they sail and come to Aeaea, land of **Circê** (**sir**-sē), daughter of Helius the sun and sister of Aeëtes, Medea's father. The island is heavily forested, surrounded by a mist so dense that one cannot see where the sun rises or sets. A wisp of smoke rises from the center of the island. Half the grew go inland to investigate, while Odysseus remains by the ship. Soon a member of the crew, Eurylochus, returns in a panic. They came to the house of a beautiful woman, he says, who sang a beautiful song while she wove. For some reason he hung back and watched as the others sat down to drink a potion the woman prepared. She touched them with her wand and instantly they turned into pigs (Fig. 21.2).

Odysseus says he will take care of the matter and sets forth alone along the path. In the middle of the forest Hermes appears and gives Odysseus a magic herb called *moly,* with black root and brilliant white flower (perhaps a mandrake root). When Odysseus reaches the hut, he is greeted by animals—enchanted men, evidently—

---

[1]Apparently unconnected with Aeolus, the ancestor of Jason.
[2]Another instance of the motif of the folktale prohibition.

FIG. 21.2. Circê enchants the companions of Odysseus, Attic wine-cup, c. 550 B.C. Seductive Circê stands naked in the center, stirring a magic drink and offering it to Odysseus' companions, already turning into animals—the one in front of Circê into a pig, the next to the right into a ram, and the third into a wolf. The figure behind Circê has the head of a boar; on the far left is a lion, beside whom Odysseus comes with sword drawn. On the far right, one of the companions (Eurylochus) escapes.
(Museum of Fine Arts, Boston; 99.518)

who fawn upon him. He hears Circê singing from within. He enters her house and sits down at table. She offers him a drink, but nothing happens when she touches him with her wand; the *moly* protects him. You must be Odysseus, she observes: A prophecy foretold that a man would one day defy her magic.[3]

She then invites him to her bed, but Odysseus, remembering advice given by Hermes, draws his sword and forces her to swear a great oath: to do him no harm. If he did not extort this promise, she would castrate him, Hermes had warned. Circê swears the oath, and then they go to bed.

Afterward, Circê releases Odysseus' men from their enchantment; they remain on the island for a year, feasting and taking their pleasure. At last Odysseus' men remind the commander of their purpose: to return home. Circê agrees that they may go, but first they must cross the river Ocean to gather information from the ghost of Tiresias; they will need to survive the Sirens and Scylla (**sil**-la) and Charybdis (ka-**rib**-dis) too, and under no circumstances should they eat the Cattle of Helius.

Sirens, Scylla and Charybdis, the Cattle of Helius, and Calypso

And so they cross the river Ocean. Odysseus speaks with the ghosts of many, including Tiresias (Chapter 11). Again they embark and approach the island of the **Sirens,**

[3]Similarly, Polyphemus was warned by a prophecy of Odysseus' coming.

FIG. 21.3. Odysseus and the Sirens, Attic jug, c. 450 B.C. Odysseus, bound to the mast, hears the Sirens' song while his men, their ears plugged with wax, row past the island. Two stand on the cliffs, while the third falls to her death, evidently because Odysseus escaped their alluring song. Note the apotropaic eye on the prow of the ship.   (British Museum, London; PS 113104)

whose song no man can resist. Odysseus, on Circê's advice, stops up the ears of his men—but not his own—with wax and orders himself bound to the mast. If he cries out when he hears the Sirens' song, they are only to bind him tighter.

In art, the Sirens have the heads and breasts of a woman but the wings and bodies of birds (like the Harpies; Fig. 21.3).[4] At their feet lie the rotting corpses of the many sailors who have heeded their sweet song, which draws all who hear it to their death. Odysseus, ravished by their song, begs his men to release him, but they only bind him more tightly until they pass in safety.

Next they come to a double evil. On one side of a narrow strait is **Charybdis,** an enormous whirlpool that sucks down and spits up a torrent of water three times a day, and on the other, beneath a cliff as sheer as glass, lives **Scylla,** a monster with twelve feet, all misshapen, and six long necks, each with its own head; in each head lie three rows of teeth. Up to her middle she is hidden in a cave, but she holds her head out to snatch passersby.[5] Because Charybdis promises certain death, Odysseus orders that they hug the cliff while he stands at the prow, sword drawn against the monster. Scylla, unimpressed, reaches down, seizes six men, and devours them gruesomely as the others row with all their might.

[4]This image is taken from the Egyptian ba-bird, a picture of the soul.
[5]Hence the proverbial saying for an impossible situation, to be "between Scylla and Charybdis." Scylla seems to have no connection with the Megarian princess, daughter of Nisus, who fell in love with Minos.

They come to Thrinacia, the island of Helius, where his cattle graze, which Circê had forbidden them to devour. Held on the island by contrary winds, the men soon begin to starve and are reduced to eating fish (real heroes eat red meat). While Odysseus reconnoiters inland, Eurylochus agitates against their commander, saying that he would rather die with a full belly than live like this. When Odysseus comes down from the hills, where he had fallen asleep, he smells the rich scent of beef roasting on spits and hears the mooing of the spitted cows (for they are magic cows). It is too late; the damage is done.

When the winds blow fair, they set out again, but Zeus, acting on a complaint from the angry Helius, smashes the ship with a thunderbolt. Everyone drowns except Odysseus, who clings to a mast. He drifts back toward the straits of Scylla and Charybdis and feels himself sucked down, but at the last second seizes a fig tree growing on a cliff above the whirlpool. The mast is ripped away as he hangs suspended, while Charybdis whips round and round, exposing the sandy bottom of the deep sea. At last Charybdis spits up again, Odysseus drops back onto the mast, and again he is swept away. Days later he washes up on Ogygia, "the navel of the sea," Calypso's island.

Odysseus lives on Ogygia for seven years. **Calypso** is a beautiful nymph who loves him and even offers him eternal life, if he will only marry her. Odysseus longs to go home and every day goes down to the shore. Looking across the trackless deep, he weeps with desire for his beloved wife, Penelopê, and his home. Athena, his protectress, asks Zeus to release Odysseus at last from his suffering and the persecutions of Poseidon. Zeus consents, and Hermes descends to inform Calypso. Bitterly she agrees.

Observations: Historical and Mythical Travel

About 800 B.C. Greeks from the island of Euboea traveled in small open boats across perilous seas all the way to Italy, where they founded the earliest Greek colonies. Homer's *Odyssey,* by far the best known of the returns from Troy, seems to have been composed and written down on the island of Euboea at about this same time, between 800 and 750 B.C.[6] Its natural audience was one of men listening to seamen who had actually traveled to the far West, and Odysseus' adventures were from an early time identified with specific geographic features in and around Italy: Calypso's island with Malta, Polyphemus' island with Sicily, Scylla and Charybdis with the Straits of Messina between Italy and Sicily, the island of Aeolus with the Lipari Islands north of Sicily, the Sirens' land with the promontory of Sorrento, and Circê's island with Ischia in the Bay of Naples.

Homer must have heard many sailors' tales about adventure in Italy, and he may have gone there himself. It is a mistake, however, to see in the *Odyssey* a sailor's log or to reconstruct a close identity between mythical and real locations. Homer fashions his narrative to appeal to an audience of wanderers yet creates a symbolic voyage, a vision of moral purpose and national identity. Sometimes Odysseus nearly for-

[6]According to the author's research; many scholars prefer a somewhat later date.

gets his purpose, as when he lies in Circê's arms; at other times he is the lonely Greek set in defiance against the alien outside world and its barbarous, sometimes disgusting customs. Cyclops and the Laestrygonians are portrayed as cannibals, repulsive to the civilized Greek; the shepherd Cyclopes do not cultivate grains, have assemblies, respect the gods, or understand the responsibilities of *xenia*. They lack the arts of civilization, very like the actual peoples with whom the Greeks struggled in Italy, Sicily, and further west. Such peoples are perceived as dangerous but stupid, and in the end no match for the wily Greek. A beautiful island, ripe for development, lies just off Cyclops' island, perfect place for a colony, but Cyclopes have no ships to explore the world, preferring to live alone amid piles of dung in the brain-splattered darkness of their caves.

RETURN TO ITHACA

Phaeacia and Nausicaä

On Ogygia, the hero builds a raft and sets out to sea. After drifting many days, he comes near the shore of Scheria, island of the **Phaeacians** (fē-ā-shunz).[7] As Odysseus is about to land, Poseidon, returning from the land of the blameless Ethiopians where he has richly dined, sees him on his raft. Still angry because Odysseus blinded his son, Polyphemus, Poseidon sends a great storm. Caught in the violent waves and wind, the raft breaks up and throws Odysseus into the sea.

He swims for three days and nights and would have drowned had it not been for the sea goddess Leucothea (lū-ko-**thē**-a, "white goddess," who once was Ino, nurse of Dionysus and wife of Athamas). She rises from the waves and gives him her veil to tie around his chest, which has magical powers of protection. He comes ashore where a stream pours into the sea. Exhausted and scaly with brine, he climbs into the bushes, makes a dark nest, and falls asleep.

That night **Nausicaä** (naw-**sik**-a-a), adolescent daughter of the Phaeacian king Alcinoüs, has a dream. Athena appears to her in disguise and advises that she wash her clothes to attract a husband; surely no man likes a woman who neglects her laundry! Next morning, Nausicaä receives her father's permission to go to the sea with her attendants, leading a wagon stuffed with dirty clothes.

Nausicaä and her friends, *parthenoi* all, spread the clothes on the shore to dry, then for relaxation throw a beach ball back and forth. The ball goes astray and falls into the stream, and the girls' excited shrieks wake up Odysseus. He staggers stark naked out of the bushes, but modestly holds a branch before his private parts, so as not to be too frightening (Fig. 21.4). The maidens, except for Nausicaä, flee down the beach. The tattered and weary but courtly wanderer praises her beauty:

[148] "I drop to my knees, my lady. Are you goddess, or are you human?
       If in fact you are one of the gods who dwell above in the heavens,
150   to judge by your outward form you are Artemis, daughter of Zeus,

[7]Identified by Thucydides (fifth century B.C.) with Corcyra, on the coastal route to Italy.

FIG. 21.4. Odysseus and Nausicaä, Attic vase, c. 440 B.C. A naked Odysseus, holding a bough in front of his genitals, with twigs in his hair, Athena at his side, speaks to Nausicaä, half-turned to run away. The princess's clothes hang from the tree behind the hero.   (Staatliche Antikensammlungen und Glyptothek, Munich; 2322 vas)

whom in stature, bearing, and form I think you most closely resemble.
But if indeed you are human, one of us who dwells on the earth,
thrice blest in you are your father and the honored lady your mother,
thrice blest also your brothers, whose hearts are warmed with delight,

155   watching your willowy movement as you come and go in the dance.
But most blest of all is the lucky suitor who carries you homeward,
offering the richest presents in the contest to make you his bride.
I tell you, these eyes have never beheld your like among mortals,
neither woman nor man, and I gaze at your every action in wonder.

160   Once, on the island of Delos, by the altar of Phoebus Apollo
(I and my men had stopped on the way that would lead to such sorrow),
I noticed a fair young sapling arising out of a palm tree,
a shoot like no tree had ever made spring up out of the earth.
As I looked on that, the same emotions arose in my spirit—

165   wonder, astonishment, fear—as strike me, kneeling before you.
        Yesterday I was cast ashore from the wine-colored ocean,
on the twentieth day since first I was driven by wind and by wave
from the isle of Ogygia. Doubtless some god directed me hither,

170   to suffer, perhaps, even here; my troubles are surely not over.
Before my day of releasing, the gods will yet bring me more sorrow.
But, lady, I pray you, have pity. To you I direct my appeal,
for of others I know not a one who rules in this land and its city.
Show me the way to the palace, and give me a rag like a beggar's,
some cover, perhaps, from the linen you brought to wash on the seashore.
175   Lastly I pray that the gods may grant you a husband and home,
a household of peace and love, for nothing is dearer or finer
than concord of husband and wife who share their hopes for the family,
the envy of all their foes and the glory of those who respect them.

HOMER, Odyssey (6.148–185)

Nausicaä, flattered and unafraid, calls back her maids. They give Odysseus a bath, from which he emerges shining like a young man, handsome and comely. Wearing some of the laundry, Odysseus follows Nausicaä to the city, hidden in a mist and keeping a certain distance (or the neighbors would gossip!). In the court of King Alcinoüs, Odysseus tells his famous adventures.

Ithaca, Argus, and Euryclea

The Phaeacians are marvelous seafarers and give Odysseus many gifts, then transport him to Ithaca and, while he is asleep, put him ashore in a fog. He awakes and cannot at first believe he has touched his native soil, but Athena appears and reassures him. He makes his way to the hut of his own swineherd, **Eumaeus** (ū-mē-us), who of course does not recognize his master after so many years. Still, Eumaeus, who understands correct behavior, offers what hospitality he can.

    Telemachus (tel-**em**-a-kus), Odysseus' only son and therefore in danger from the suitors, had gone abroad to Pylos and Sparta in hopes of finding some news about his father. The suitors have laid an ambush, which he avoids by landing on the backside of the island and also coming to the swineherd's hut. Odysseus reveals his true identity to his son, who tells him the situation in his house. For many years the suitors have pressed their demand that Penelopê marry one of them; in the meanwhile, they devour Odysseus' wealth, sleep with the maids, and scorn the youthful Telemachus.

    Disguised as a beggar, Odysseus makes his way inland to the palace. Just outside the gate his faithful dog Argus is asleep on a dung heap, old now and near death. As a pup he was Odysseus' favorite hound, before the hero went to Troy. Argus peers up, recognizes his master, cocks his ears, and drops over dead from excitement.

    Inside the palace, Odysseus stands in the shadows of the great hall. The suitors, led by Antinoüs (an-**tin**-o-us), revile the beggar: One throws a stool at his head, another a piece of bone. They complain how Penelopê had promised to marry as soon as she finished weaving a burial robe for Laërtes, Odysseus' father, now sleeping on a bed of leaves in the countryside, but each night she sneaked into the hall and undid as much of the weaving as she had done that day (Fig. 21.5, compare Fig. P 21.3a). The suitors had discovered the trick long ago, yet still she will not choose a husband.

FIG. 21.5. Penelope before the web, from an Attic cup, c. 440 B.C. Penelopê sits in a melancholy pose before her loom, the shroud partly done, while her son Telemachus stands before her with two spears, viewing her with skepticism. A griffin, a horse, and a man, all winged, are embroidered into the bottom band.   (Museo Civico, Chiusi; University of Wisconsin, Madison Photo Archive.)

The beggar requests an audience with the queen, his own wife. He informs Penelopê that her husband is still alive. He has himself seen him, he says, and Odysseus will soon be home. Penelopê does not believe a word, but in thanks for the pleasant thought she asks the old nurse **Euryclea** (ū-ri-**klē**-a), who suckled Odysseus when he was an infant, to wash the beggar's stinking feet.

Euryclea hauls out an enormous bronze cauldron and fills it with hot water. As she scrubs away, suddenly she feels a scar on his thigh. When Odysseus was young, a boar had sliced him there. Odysseus sees that she has recognized him and seizes her scrawny throat with his powerful hand. One sound out of her, he warns, and she dies.

Penelopê, Telemachus, and the Suitors

Penelopê, with a little help from Athena, suddenly decides that she will marry after all, on the very next day. She arranges a contest to help her decide: She will marry whoever can string her husband's bow, stored all these years in a closet, and with the bow shoot an arrow through the haft holes of twelve axheads aligned and fixed on stakes in the floor of the dining hall. The bow was a gift of Iphitus (son of the great bowman Eurytus), whom Heracles threw from the walls of Tiryns.

The suitors try to string the bow but are too weak from years of carousing. A sneering Telemachus suggests that they let the beggar try his hand, and he gives the bow to Odysseus. Ignoring the indignant noblemen, the beggar takes the wonderful weapon, warms it by the fire, and easily strings it, like a poet who puts a string to his lyre. The beggar nocks an arrow and in a moment of high drama fires it through the axheads. Then:

[1] Stripping himself of his rags, the shrewd foresighted Odysseus
     sprang up to straddle the threshold, holding his bow and a quiver

Cavafy's "Ithaca"

With the possible exception of Chinese, the Greek language has been recorded longer than any other language still spoken on Earth, in Linear B script and a related script from Cyprus from about 1400 to 1100 B.C. and in alphabetic writing from about 800 B.C. up to the present. (The oldest parts of the Hebrew Bible, once thought to be the oldest writing, date in their present form to about 600 B.C.). Although today the language is restricted mainly to the borders of modern Greece, fine poets continue to appear who reinterpret for modern Greek speakers the traditions of ancient times. Such a poet was Constantine Cavafy (1863–1933).

Born in the Greek community in Constantinople, now almost extinct, he belonged to a prominent commercial family who moved soon after his birth to Alexandria in Egypt, founded by Alexander the Great. There he worked for most of his life as a clerk, but he knew and influenced the British writers E. M. Forster, T. S. Eliot, Arnold Toynbee, D. H. Lawrence, and Lawrence Durrell. Cavafy often celebrated erotic love between men, but in "Ithaca" (1894) he recreates Odysseus' homeland as a symbol for the journey that is itself the goal, the Odyssey of everyone's life:

Ithaca*

As you set out on your journey to Ithaca,
pray that your journey be a long one,
filled with adventure, filled with discovery.
Laestrygonians and Cyclopes,
the angry Poseidon—do not fear them:
you'll never find such things on your way
unless your sight is set high, unless a rare
excitement stirs your spirit and your body.
The Laestrygonians and Cyclopes,
the savage Poseidon—you won't meet them
so long as you do not admit them to your soul,
as long as your soul does not set them before you.
Pray that your road is a long one.
May there be many summer mornings
when with what pleasure, with what joy,
you enter harbors never seen before;
may you stop at Phoenician trading stations
to buy fine things,
mother of pearl and coral, amber and ebony,
and voluptuous perfumes of every kind
—buy as many voluptuous perfumes as you can;
and may you go to many Egyptian cities

*Translated by Barry B. Powell from the Greek text printed in *C. Cavafy, Poiêmata: 1897–1933* (Ikaros, 1989).

to learn and learn from those who know.
Always keep Ithaca in your mind.
You are destined to arrive there.
But don't hurry your journey at all.
Far better if it takes many years,
and if you are old when you anchor at the island,
rich with all you have gained on the way,
not expecting that Ithaca will give you wealth.
Ithaca has given you a beautiful journey.
Without her you would never have set out.
She has no more left to give you.
And if you find her poor, Ithaca has not mocked you.
As wise as you have become, so filled with experience,
you will have understood what these Ithacas signify.

      loaded with swift-flying arrows, which he poured out, ready for use,
      onto the ground at his feet. Then he turned and spoke to the suitors:
5   "So ends the meaningless contest, the silly purposeless pastime.
      Now I shall shoot at a mark which no man has ever transfixed;
      I shall know at once if I hit it. Apollo, grant me that glory!"
       Straight at the suitor he shot his arrow, bitter and deadly,
      where Antinoüs sat, reaching out to receive a beautiful goblet,
10   twin-handled, golden, into his hands, to drink of its wine [Fig. 21.6],
      with no thought of death in his heart. Who indeed would ever imagine
      that one single man, in the midst of banqueters crowded around him
      (however strong he might be), could bring him death and destruction?
      Odysseus' arrow, well-aimed, struck its victim square in the gullet,
15   and its head sped on through the tenderest part of Antinoüs' neck.
      His body slumped to one side; the cup in the hand of the dead man
      clanged to the floor; from his nostrils spurted a jet of his blood.
      In a dying spasm his legs jerked out and kicked back the table,
      spilling the food in a dirty puddle of bread and hot meat.
20   From all the house the suitors ran with a shout to the body
      of him who was murdered. Some jumped in alarm from their places,
      peering around all through the well-built rooms of the palace.

HOMER, *Odyssey* (22.1–24)

The suitors think it is some terrible mistake, but Odysseus tells them the truth:

[34]   Wily Odysseus, glaring, addressed the men in this fashion:
35   "You curs, you thought that I would never return to my homeland,
      from Troy, and seized on the chance to ravage my prosperous household.
      Your violence forced the women, my slaves, to give way to your lust,
      and while I was still alive you hoped you might marry my wife.
      You showed no fear of the gods, the mighty dwellers in heaven,
40   nor did you worry that human vengeance might strike you hereafter.
      But now—the crisis of death is waiting for you and your fellows."

HOMER, *Odyssey* (22.34–41)

FIG. 21.6. Odysseus slays the suitors, Attic cup, c. 440 B.C. Odysseus draws his bow as two serving-girls look on. The suitors uselessly struggle to defend themselves. Two are on a couch, while a third crouches behind a table. Note the dapper mustache of the suitor on the far right. (Antikenmuseum, Staatliche Museen, Berlin; I 2588; I 2589)

Helped by Telemachus, Eumaeus, and another retainer, Odysseus massacres the 108 unarmed men (Fig. 21.6). The hall reeks of blood and gore when Penelopê, wakened by Euryclea, descends from the upper chambers. She has just enjoyed the best nap, she says, since the day that Odysseus went to Troy. She sees the man drenched in their blood but refuses to believe that he is her husband. Nonetheless, she is grateful and, so that the man might rest, asks Euryclea to bring out her Master's bed. Odysseus is amazed at her coldness:

[166] "You're a strange woman all right. To you beyond all women
have the Olympians given a hard heart.
No other woman would harden her heart as you,
and stand away from her husband who after desperate suffering
170 had come to her in the twentieth year, to his native land.
All right nurse, make up a couch so I may lay down alone,
for her heart is iron." Then wise Penelope answered him:
"Odd fellow, I am not proud, nor do I scorn you,
nor yet am I so amazed, for well I knew you,
175 when you went forth from Ithaca on your long-oared ship.
Yet come, Euryclea, strew for him the stout bedstead
outside the well-built bridal chamber which he himself made.
Bring for him the stout bedstead from there, and cast bedding on it,
fleeces and cloaks and shining coverlets."
180 So she spoke, testing her husband.
     But Odysseus, in a burst of anger, spoke to his true-hearted wife,
and said: "Woman, truly you have spoken a bitter word.
Who has set my bed elsewhere? Hard would it be for one to do,
although highly skilled, unless a god should come
185 and easily by his will move it to another place.
But of men there is no mortal alive, no matter
how young and strong, who could easily pry it from its place,
for a great token is set in the well-built bed,
and it was I who built it and no one else.
190 A long-leafed olive tree was growing in the court, strong, vigorous,
thick and round like a pillar. Around this I built my bedchamber,
working on it until it was done, all of close-set stones,
and I roofed it too, and added joined doors that fit close.
Then I cut away the leafy branches of the long-leafed olive,
195 and, trimming the trunk up from the root,
I smoothed it around with the adze,
well and cunningly, and made it straight to the line.
In this way I made the bed-post. Then I bored it all
with the augur. Beginning in this way
200 I made my bed, working on it till I was done,
inlaying it with gold and silver and ivory,
and I stretched on it a thong of ox-hide,
bright with purple. There is my token.
I do not know, woman, whether my bedstead is still fast in its place,
205 or whether by now some man has cut from beneath
the olive stump, and set the bedstead elsewhere."
So he spoke, and her knees went slack where she sat,
and her heart melted, as she knew the sure tokens
which Odysseus told her. Then with a burst of tears she ran straight toward
     him, and flung
210 her arms about the neck of Odysseus, and kissed his head.

HOMER, *Odyssey* (23.166–208)

Penelopê was only testing him, after all (as Odysseus had tested so many others).
They go upstairs to make love and chat about all that has happened. Odysseus tells

her everything, although he skims rapidly past the beautiful Circê and Calypso. So ends Homer's *Odyssey*.

Curious tales from other sources report the end of Odysseus' career: how his restless nature carried him away again to the mainland, where he took another wife even while Penelopê was alive. He returned to Ithaca, there to meet his death. While living with Circê, he had fathered a child, Telegonus (tel-**eg**-o-nus, "begotten afar"), who grew up and came in search of his father. He arrived on Ithaca with some companions, but not knowing where he was, drove off some cattle. Telemachus and the aged Odysseus attacked the invaders and in the fight Telegonus stabbed Odysseus with his spear tipped with a stingray's poisonous tail. Thus a prophecy given by Tiresias in the underworld was fulfilled: that Odysseus would "die a gentle death from the sea." According to a still odder tale, Telegonus then married Penelopê and carried her and Telemachus back to Circê's island, where Telemachus married the ageless witch. But such bizarre intricacies, unfriendly to our expectations about a hero's career, are foreign to the spirit of Homer's timeless tale.

Observations: Symbols of Rebirth in the Folktale of the Man Who Came Home, Tested by Woman and the World

Homer's *Odyssey*, viewed as a whole, is the story of a hero who came home after a long absence, found his household in the hands of usurpers, and killed them to reestablish his ascendancy. The older generation—tough, smart, and wise in the need for just behavior—is triumphant over the younger—brash, indolent, and self-indulgent, taking what it wants.[8] Because the youthful usurpers threaten traditional property rights, the poem appears to be a simple tale of revenge, of human justice triumphant over wrong. Not the gods' enmity, but their own thoughtless behavior, brings about the suitors' destruction. This powerful theme is set in the beginning of the poem when Zeus complains that humans blame gods for their troubles, but it is their own recklessness that brings them to grief. Zeus cites the example of Aegisthus: Warned not to sleep with Clytemnestra, he did so anyway. No wonder he paid the price! Similarly, Odysseus' foolish men dawdle in the land of the Cicones, eat the dangerous Lotus, open the bag of the winds, and devour the Cattle of the Sun. Justice is based on restraint, on the ability to hold back and not give in to one's animal appetite. Food is good, but when it is forbidden by gods, on Helius' island, or when it belongs to someone else, on Ithaca, you should not eat it. Sex is pleasurable, but when your husband is absent you must do without. Sometimes, however, these simple morals, typical of folktales, are contradicted by the story itself. Although Zeus explains that humans are responsible for their own troubles, Poseidon, a god, harasses Odysseus in revenge for the blinding of Polyphemus, and Poseidon's enmity also seems to explain the destruction of Odysseus' men.

[8]Modern feature films, by contrast, ordinarily show the younger generation, respectful of the environment and in love, triumphant over the older, which is politically corrupt and sexually predacious: Entertainers know their audience, then as now.

But the underlying structure of the story is much older than the moral posture Homer gives it; we noticed in Chapter 12 how the epic of Gilgamesh and Homer's *Odyssey* begin with nearly the same words. This is the story of a journey where deadly dangers threaten, but of eventual return. The hero must slay his dragon, and in fact Odysseus overcomes many deadly enemies. Even the 108 suitors who besiege Odysseus' home are, in a realistic mode, the same old dragon, described repeatedly as voracious ("devouring his substance") and sexually threatening ("whoring with the maidservants") while seeking to marry his wife; in the same way, the mythical dragon devours everything in sight and sexually threatens a woman. In the myth of the dragon-combat, the monster is often overcome by a trick, sometimes at a banquet, and slain with a special weapon; even so Odysseus tricks the beast with 108 mouths by entering the palace in disguise, surprising the suitors in the dining hall, then killing them with a special bow that no one else can string. As the dragon-slayer receives a princess as reward, Odysseus too "marries" the woman.

In Mesopotamian cosmogonic myth and in Hesiod (see Chapter 4) such stories describe the triumph of the ordered world over the disordered, of life and progress over death and stagnation, even as a prominent theme in Homer's poem is the hero's victory over death—so closely interwoven are myths of creation, the epic hero, and the folktale hero. The enemies of Odysseus are death's allies: sleep (Odysseus falls asleep at crucial junctions in the stories of Aeolus and the cattle of Helius), narcosis (the Lotus Eaters), darkness (the cave of Polyphemus, the shadowy land of the Cimmerians), or forgetfulness of purpose (Circê). Declared by all to be dead, Odysseus travels across water, the element separating this world from the next, to the land of the Cimmerians, where he interrogates the actual spirits of the dead and sees the torments of the damned (Chapter 11). The eternal life offered him by Calypso, whose name means "concealer" and whose island is the "navel of the sea," is eternal death for the inquisitive man ever thirsting for experience: Death hovers in the still-central point of the boundless water, "concealing" the dead from the living (*Hades* means "unseen"). Water is death and its god, Poseidon, is Odysseus' relentless enemy. Like Polyphemus and the Laestrygonians, death is a cannibal, devouring the living in the tomb's dark and hungry maw. Within the dark cave of the Cyclops, Odysseus is "Nobody"—nameless, without identity, nonexistent. As dragons of death are stupid, so Polyphemus is made drunk by the wine, fooled by the trick of the name, then wounded by the special weapon of the pointed stake; the same pattern underlies the slaying of the suitors. When Odysseus escapes from the cave, passing from darkness into light, from death into life, he gets his name back and shouts to Polyphemus, "I am Odysseus!"; after he kills the suitors, Penelopê sees who he is and they retire to the wedding bed.

Triumph over death leads to rebirth. Odysseus, like a baby leaving the "navel of the sea," passes through waters to emerge naked on the shore of Phaeacia. He takes refuge in a womblike hole in the dark bushes, then is welcomed by Nausicaä, a *parthenos* who has dreamed of imminent marriage, like the marriage that unites Odysseus and Penelopê at the end of the poem. Nausicaä's role as deliverer, as new mother, is explicit as Odysseus is about to depart for Ithaca and she says to him, "Never forget me, for I gave you life."

The Legends of Odysseus

The story of Penelopê's efforts to trick the suitors by promising to marry after finishing a shroud for Odysseus' father, then unraveling it at night, is represented in this early eighteenth-century painting by French artist François Lemoyne (Fig. P 21.3a), known for his luminous sensuousness. Penelopê is seated before her loom. Her trick discovered at last, she points to the finished shroud, which handmaids spread out for inspection. On the left, suitors bear gifts, tempting her to marriage, but Odysseus' ship even now draws into port, visible in the distance beyond the porch (to the right of the tree).

Lemoyne was commissioned to paint this subject for the wife's room in an elegant private Paris house; thus he pays tribute to fidelity and the strength of the marriage vows to inspire the room's occupant.

FIG. P 21.3a. Francois Lemoyne (French, 1688–1737), *The Work of Penelope*, c. 1729–37, oil on canvas. (Musée Rodin, Paris)

FIG. P 21.3b. J.M.W. Turner (English, 1775–1851), *Ulysses Deriding Polyphemus*, 1829, oil on canvas.   (National Gallery, London)

The paintings of J.M.W. Turner are among the outstanding achievements of the nineteenth century. Known for his seascapes and misty landscapes, he is the first to isolate color apart from form, prefiguring the abstract painters of the twentieth century. Here (Fig. P 21.3b) Odysseus, dressed in a scarlet cloak, stands beside the left mast to shout his defiance at the shadowy figure of the Cyclops above the cliff on the upper left (hard to make out!). The writhing Polyphemus, just blinded, invokes the vengeance of his father Poseidon. Some companions on the crowded ship try to restrain Odysseus; others are urged by a figure with upraised arms to row faster. Still others unfurl the sails to speed the boat away from danger. The ship shows two flags, the red pennant at the top with Odysseus' name in Greek, and the white one below with a painting of the dragging of the Trojan horse into the city. The prow of the ship is a sea-monster, with the anchor hanging from it like a great hook. Mermaids play in the water. The horses of the Sun rise above the horizon in the lower right. For Turner the interest in this painting is the landscape/seascape, the misty colors of a never-never land satisfying to the Romantic taste for the picturesque and sublime. The painter John Constable described Turner's style as "airy visions, painted with tinted steam."

FIG. P 21.3c. Dosso Dossi (1479–1542), *Circe and Her Lovers in a Landscape*, mid 16th century, oil on canvas   (National Gallery, Washington).

Dossi was a painter at the court of Duke Alfonso d'Este at Ferrara and familiar with the duke's favorite poet, Ariosto Lodovico (1474–1533), whose *Orlando Furioso* combined elements of classical tales with medieval romance. Ariosto's enchantress Alcina appears to be a blend of Homer's Circe and Morgan le Fay of the Arthurian legend. Dosso Dossi may have been thinking of Alcina when he painted this Circe and her lovers (Fig. P 21.3c).

In this sensuous representation of the queen and enchantress who changed men into animals, Circe recites her spell from a tablet with cryptic signs, having consulted the book of magic still open at her feet. The deer, the fishing spoonbill, and possibly the dogs at her feet may once have been men.

Claude was a classicizing painter who studied in Rome with a specialist in harbor scenes (Fig. P 21.3d). In this anachronistic setting of Odysseus' mission to take Agamemnon's concubine/war booty Chryseis to her father, the priest of Apollo, Chryseis herself is a diminutive figure seated on a hatbox just left of center in the foreground. Her luggage is piled beside her as if she had just taken a long sea journey instead of being seized as wartime plunder.

FIG. P 21.3d. Claude Lorrain (Claude Gelle) (1600–1682), Ulysses Returning Chryseis to Her Father, oil on canvas   (Musee de Louvre, Paris; Scala/Art Resource, NY)

Achilles had taken Chryseis prisoner, and in the division of the plunder she was allotted to Agamemnon. Her father caused a pestilence to fall on the Greeks because of Agamemnon's refusal to return his daughter. When Agamemnon was finally forced to return Chryseis, he seized Achilles' concubine Briseis to replace her, thus beginning the fateful wrath of Achilles, the subject of Homer's *Illiad*.

In cosmogonic myth, the primordial being is female, like Tiamat or Gaea, who begets monstrous creatures that oppose the establishment of the ordered world; or she is herself the enemy. But the female is ambiguous and may also conspire with the hero to overthrow the monsters of chaos, as Gaea conspired with Cronus to defeat Uranus, or as Rhea conspired with Zeus to overthrow Cronus. The ambiguity of the female in such stories is paralleled in the extraordinary array of female types in the *Odyssey*, good and evil, who oppose or help Odysseus' efforts to return home and reestablish order. At one end of the spectrum are the dangerous seductive women Calypso and Circê, so like the seductive but deadly Inanna/Ishtar. Calypso, although beautiful, is the "concealer." Circê, although beautiful, wants to castrate Odysseus, a symbolic death; she turns men into pigs by the irresistible female power that reduces the male to pure animal lust, snorting and groveling in the dirt. The female Scylla eats them whole; the female Sirens, like perverted Muses, lead men to their deaths through the alluring promise of secret knowledge, dressed in beautiful song.

On the positive end of the scale stand Athena, Odysseus' protector; Nausicaä, the uncorrupted *parthenos,* cast as both potential mate for Odysseus and symbolic mother; and Penelopê, who resists sexual temptation for twenty years. In Zeus's speech about human folly, Clytemnestra is cited as an example of humans who act recklessly and pay the price. Throughout the poem Clytemnestra is the implied opposite to Penelopê. Clytemnestra is the wicked woman who gave in to sexual desire, betrayed the strict rules of wifely fidelity, and murdered her husband. Penelopê, by contrast, is the ideal woman, long-suffering, ever-faithful, and ingenious in preserving the honor of her home. Beset by a dangerous crisis, she courageously decides to take a second husband, thus setting up (unknowingly) the slaughter of the suitors. Clever like her husband, she cooly tests Odysseus with the token of the bed, in its immovability the symbol for their own marriage, as the olive tree from which it is made stands for the life of the family uncorrupted by adultery. In the contrasting but parallel stories of the royal houses of Mycenae and Ithaca, Odysseus is like Agamemnon, each returning from Troy to find his house in the hands of enemies; Telemachus is like Orestes, fighting to restore family right and honor. The difference between the parallel legends lies in the character of the woman: Odysseus survives because Penelopê is woman as she should be, while Agamemnon is cut down like a dog. That too, is a moral of the tale.

KEY TERMS

FURTHER READING

Bloom, Harold, ed., *Homer's* The Odyssey (New York, 1988). Collection of modern essays.

Clarke, Howard, *The Art of the "Odyssey"* (Englewood Cliffs, N.J., 1967). A good introduction to the poem.

Clay, Jenny Strauss, *The Wrath of Athena* (Princeton, N.J., 1983). Brilliant study of the goddess' role in the *Odyssey*.

Cohen, B., ed., *The Distaff Side: Representing the Female in Homer's* Odyssey (Oxford, U.K., 1995). Essays with a contemporary theoretical, often feminist, perspective.

Finley, Moses I., *The World of Odysseus*, 2nd ed. (New York, 1978). Good on social background to the poem.

Kazantzakis, Nikos, The Odyssey: *A Modern Sequel* (New York, 1985). Notable adaptation by the modern Greek writer.

Malkin, Irad, *The Returns of Odysseus* (Berkeley, Calif., 1998). Stimulating study from myth and history of early Greek western colonization.

Page, Denys, *Folktales in Homer's "Odyssey"* (Cambridge, Mass., 1973). A penetrating look at this aspect of the poem, although one must beware of Page's desire to attribute the poem to many authors.

Stanford, W. B., *The Ulysses Theme* (Ann Arbor, Mich., 1968). Odysseus from Homer through the tragedians, Vergil, Dante, Tennyson, up to James Joyce and Nikos Kazantzakis's The Odyssey: *A Modern Sequel*.

———, and J. V. Luce, *The Quest for Ulysses* (New York, 1974). Essays, lavishly illustrated, exploring the relationship of Homer's descriptions in the *Odyssey* to actual locations on Ithaca and elsewhere.

Tracy, Steve, *The Story of the* Odyssey (Princeton, N.J., 1991). Highly readable retelling of Homer's story—a good guide to the poem.

Walcott, Derek, *Omeros* (New York, 1990). Recreation of the *Odyssey*, set in the Caribbean.

CHAPTER 22

ROMAN MYTH

When the age has come as the centuries glide their unhurrying path,
the royal line of the Trojans will enslave the home of Achilles,
with famous Mycenae as well, and will rule by conquest in Argos.
Caesar° will then be born, a Trojan of glorious lineage,
Julius, a name handed down from your son, the mighty Iulus,
whose rule will end at the ocean, whose fame will end at the stars.

VERGIL, Aeneid 1.283–288

Caesar: Probably Augustus. Very little is made of his adoptive father, Julius Caesar, in the *Aeneid*. In fact, the name of the Julian *gens* ("clan") is not derived from the three-syllable name of I-ū-lus, as Vergil suggests.

W E HAVE NOW LOOKED at a large number of Greek myths in a systematic way and some from the Near East as well. We have found in these rich and diverse stories a complex blend of religious symbol, national legend, and folktale. What of later developments in Rome, when the stories of the Greeks were adopted and modified by a people of different language, culture, and geography? Roman religious and social patterns of thought were quite different from those of the Greeks, as were their economic and political institutions.

In the native Roman tradition, there is no creation story and almost no divine myth, as we have defined it in Chapter 1. Roman myth is Roman *legend*, intimately bound up with Roman history and equated with it by the Romans themselves. Nonetheless, there is little that is truly historical in these legends. Mostly they are myths in our modern sense, propaganda, designed to elicit support for social patterns, and they did in fact prove remarkably effective in maintaining Roman power.

The Romans knew that their legends worked as propaganda but accepted their validity, just as we still teach children that George Washington cut down a cherry tree and, because he could not tell a lie, confessed to his father. Even if Washington never really did this, he might have done so; the moral of the story is more important than its historical truth.[1] Roman "myth," then, looks like traditional story and is modeled after Greek myth, but ethical and political purposes (as in Athenian myth) have become preeminent. The stories of early Rome have exercised a profound influence on Western civilization and continue to do so today. Whenever one is asked to suppress one's personal interests for the common good, the wonderful deeds of early Rome come to mind and take on fresh meaning. Such has always been an important function of myth: to define a culture to itself, to inform a people what is real in their world and important in their personal and social lives, and to offer bases for the difficult decisions everyone must face.

In this chapter we first say something about the religious and political background of Roman myth, then describe the myths themselves.

ROMAN RELIGION

The direct ancestors of the Romans were the *Latini,* who may have entered the Italian peninsula as early as 1500 B.C. and occupied the site of Rome by 1200 B.C. They gave their name to Latium (lā-shum), the territory west of the central Apennine range and south of the Tiber as far as the fertile plain of Campania, behind the Bay of Naples (see Map IV). Dominating Latium on the south and east rose the Alban Hills, with many important Latin towns in the sixth and fifth centuries B.C. Among these were Alba Longa, at the western edge of the hills, and Lavinium toward the coast, which figure in stories about the early Roman state. These early peoples had religious practices and attitudes rather different from those found in Greece.

Numina and *Sacrificium*

We noted earlier (Chapter 1) that myths are stories, whereas religion is belief and the course of action that follows from belief. Religion is a system of assumptions about how external powers affect our behavior, and the things we do to maintain good relations with these external powers. Greek myth was inextricably mixed with religion. Roman myth was too, but the profoundly different nature of the Roman divinities created special conditions for the development of Roman myth. Greek religion regarded its deities as endowed with superhuman powers and, in general, with immortality, but the Greek anthropomorphic gods also possess a human psychology: They lust, lie, cheat, fight, love, forgive, hate, and avenge, and many help the humans they favor. Native Roman deities, by contrast, seem to have been mostly personifications of various qualities and were strictly limited in their function, having

---

[1]Many of the imaginary stories (including this one) about the first American president go back to the *Life and Memorable Actions of George Washington* (c. 1800) by an Episcopal minister, Mason Weems.

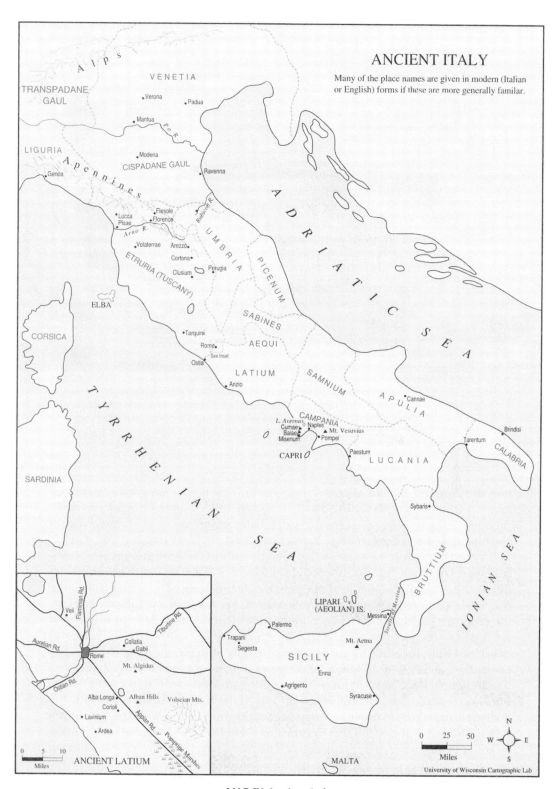

ANCIENT ITALY

Many of the place names are given in modern (Italian or English) forms if these are more generally familar.

TRANSPADANE GAUL

A L P S

VENETIA

Verona

Padua

Mantua

LIGURIA

Modena

CISPADANE GAUL

Ravenna

Genoa

A p e n n i n e s

Lucca

Pisae

Fiesole

Florence

Arno R.

Rubicon R.

UMBRIA

Volaterrae

Arezzo

Cortona

Clusium

Perugia

PICENUM

ELBA

ETRURIA (TUSCANY)

SABINES

CORSICA

Tarquinii

AEQUI

Rome

See Inset

Ostia

LATIUM

Anzio

SAMNIUM

A D R I A T I C S E A

APULIA

Cannae

T Y R R H E N I A N   S E A

CAMPANIA

L. Avernus

Cumae

Naples

Balae

Mt. Vesuvius

Misenum

Pompei

CAPRI

Paestum

LUCANIA

Brindisi

Tarentum

CALABRIA

SARDINIA

Sybaris

BRUTTIUM

I O N I A N   S E A

Strait of Messina

LIPARI
(AEOLIAN) IS.

Messina

Trapani

Palermo

Segesta

Mt. Aetna

SICILY

Enna

Agrigento

Syracuse

MALTA

0   25   50

Miles

N
W   E
S

University of Wisconsin Cartographic Lab

ANCIENT LATIUM

Veii

Flaminian Rd.

Aurelian Rd.

Tiburtine Rd.

Collatia

Gabii

Rome

Mt. Algidus

Ostian Rd.

Alba Longa

Corioli

Alban Hills

Volscian Mts.

Lavinium

Appian Rd.

Pomptine Marshes

Ardea

0   5   10

Miles

MAP IV. Ancient Italy

597

FIG. 22.1. A river *numen*, marble sculpture, c. second century A.D. Almost everything had its indwelling spirit. This one is labeled "Marforio," evidently sometime in the medieval period. Most medieval and Renaissance paintings of the baptism of Christ have a figure representing the *numen* of the River Jordan.   (Musei Capitolini, Rome; Author's photo)

only the right to refuse or assent to requests. The Latin verb *nuo* means "nod" and hence "assent," and from this word such deities are called **numina** (singular **numen**), "nodders." The *numina* are spirits that can inhabit almost any object or serve almost any function, petty or grand (Fig. 22.1).

A good example is the *numen* called by some authors Robigus, grammatically masculine, and by others Robigo, grammatically feminine—that is, a spirit whose gender was unimportant. Robigus/o had one power, either to bring or hold back fungus disease in the grain crop. At a sacrifice called the Robigalia, held annually on April 25, the priest of Quirinus (kwi-**rī**-nus), a *numen* representing the Roman people, would ask Robigus/o to hold back the blight. In return, the priest offered him/her a sort of bribe of wine, incense, the gut of a sheep, and the entrails of a filthy red dog. The ceremony was called *sacrificium*, a "making sacred," the origin of our word *sacrifice*.

Sacrificium was a legal transfer of something into the ownership of the *numen*, who was then expected to fulfill his or her side of the bargain. Both parties to a contract gave something in order to receive something in return—*do ut des*, "I grant you this, so that you will give me that in exchange." Such a notion, applied to the gods, removed them from moral responsibility. The priest acted as a lawyer for the Roman people in fulfilling their side of the contract, and the *numen* was expected to fulfill his or her obligations as well.

FIG. 22.2. Two-faced Janus, on a Roman coin, third century B.C. A spirit of the doorway, he gave his name to the month of January, which looks forward to the new, backward to the old. Starting in 153 B.C. the Roman year began in January; February was devoted to purifications (*februa*); farming and war began in March.
(Museum of Fine Arts, Boston; 22.729)

The functions of *numina* sometimes were subdivided by anxious souls eager to do everything exactly right. We have several lists of such subdeities, who had no temples or cult but were invoked separately on appropriate occasions. For example, at the Cerealia, a ceremony on April 19 in honor of Ceres (sē-rēz), *numen* of the grain harvest, and *Tellus Mater* ("Mother Earth"), a priest invoked the favor of First-Plower, Second-Plower, Maker-of-Ridges-between-Furrows, Implanter, Over-Plower, Harrower, Hoer, Weeder, Harvester, Bringer-In, Storer, and Bringer-Out. Such beings later excited the scornful mirth of the fathers of the Christian Church.

Although the Roman *numina* were remote and colorless, some of them took on roles of service to the state and the family and enjoyed a central place in Roman civic and home life—roles that grew as Greek influence helped them assume more personality. One of the best-known Roman *numina* was **Janus** (jā-nus), "gate," in origin a *numen* of bridges, hence of going forth and returning. He was represented as a man with two faces, one looking forward, the other back (Fig. 22.2). He came to be viewed as presiding over beginnings of all kinds, and the first month of our year was named after him. In the Forum stood a gate without a building: Janus himself. His doors were opened when Rome went to war and closed when it was at peace. Until the final victory of Augustus in 31 B.C., they had stood open for more than two hundred years; the emperor proudly proclaimed, "I closed Janus." From this *numen* seems to come the Roman triumphal arch.

Roman Deities Equated with Greek

When the Roman poets fell under the influence of the Greeks living in southern Italy, they began to think of these bloodless abstractions, the *numina*, as being like

FIG. 22.3. The Roman gods, marble relief from the Arch of Trajan at Beneventum, 114–117 A.D. In the center forefront are Jupiter with his staff and a bundle, perhaps the *fasces;* on one side Minerva, with her helmet; on the other Juno, dressed as a priestess with cloak over her head. Jupiter, Minerva, and Juno are often called the Capitoline Triad. Behind them, left to right: Hercules (with his club), Bacchus (with vines in his hair), Ceres (with the torch), and Mercury (with winged helmet). The sculptural style goes back to Greek models on the Athenian Parthenon.   (University of Wisconsin, Madison Photo Archive)

the anthropomorphic gods of the Greeks. The Roman equivalents to Greek gods as named in Vergil, Ovid, and other poets were largely a poetic invention with little basis in native Roman religion, although there were also important political motivations, especially during the reign of the first emperor Augustus (27 B.C.–A.D. 14), for establishing such identifications (Fig. 22.3).

The first syllable of the name of **Jupiter**[2] (also called Jove), originally *numen* of the sky, is etymologically identical to Zeus (see Chapter 6); he must descend from the common cultural, linguistic, and racial heritage shared by all speakers of Indo-European languages. Jupiter was worshiped in many manifestations (for example, as *Juppiter pluvius,* "Jupiter as the rain"). As *Juppiter lapis,* a sacred stone supposed to be a thunderbolt, he received pigs sacrificed with a stone knife, a rite descended from neolithic times. Jupiter became the incarnation of the striking power of the Roman state, and his emblem, the eagle, appeared on the standards of the Roman legions. His temple sat on top of the Capitoline Hill, hence our word *capitol.*

Juno was the *numen* who presided over women as members of the family, hence her equation with Hera; she had close ties with the moon. **Ceres,** *numen* of wheat, was from an early time equated with Demeter. **Diana,** the Roman Artemis, shares the same Indo-European root *di-,* "shining," with Zeus, Jupiter, the Indian sky god Dyaus, and the Norse war god Tiu. Perhaps in origin a spirit of the wood, Diana, like Juno, was associated with women and childbirth.

Mercury has no ancient Italian heritage but is Hermes introduced to the Latins under a title suggestive of his commercial activities (*merx* is Latin for "merchandise").

---

[2]His name is spelled with two *p*s in Latin, one in English.

Vulcan's name is not Latin. Identified with Hephaestus, he may have come from the eastern Mediterranean through Etruria; he was a god of volcanic and other forms of destructive fire. **Neptune** was the *numen* of water, although not specifically the sea until identified with Poseidon. Apollo was never successfully identified with a Latin *numen,* but came early to Latium through Etruria and the Greek colonies of southern Italy.

The origins of **Mars,** assimilated to the Greek Ares, are obscure. Closely associated with the wolf, he may once have protected flocks or been a primordial god of war (a spear kept in the forum had the name *Mars*). He gave his name to the month of March, a good time for beginning military operations. **Minerva,** an Etruscan import, was *numen* of handicrafts, hence associated with the Greek Athena. Liber (**lē**-ber, "free"), *numen* of wine, was equated with Dionysus; according to the etymologizing of the Romans, always suspect, his name was taken to be a translation of the Greek epithet for Dionysus, *luaios,* "looser" from care. Liber had a female counterpart, Libera. **Faunus** (**faw**-nus; "kindly one") is named euphemistically: He was *numen* of the unreasoning terror of the lonely forest and was identified with Pan.

Venus seems once to have been a *numen* of fresh water, especially springs; an early inscription from the volcanic country in southern Italy is a dedication "to the Stinking Venus," presumably the *numen* of a sulphurous spring. Water is, of course, essential for the cultivation of plants, especially in gardens, and the name of the *numen* may derive from the Latin word for "pleasant," *venustus.* From being a *numen* of vegetable fertility, Venus, under Greek influence, also took animal and human fertility under her protection.

A literary passage reflecting the transformation of Venus appears in the opening of the *De rerum natura,* "On the Nature of Things," a philosophical poem by one of Rome's finest poets, Lucretius, written about 60 B.C. Venus, Lucretius writes, is a being "who stings every heart on land and sea and air, the leaf-laden trees and the birds, the green and flourishing land, with insistent desire that lures them on to propagate their kind." In these lines she functions still as *numen,* a natural force with a name. A few lines further, however, she becomes the Greek Aphrodite, in whose arms "reclines fierce Mars,[3] stabbed with love's undying wound. His head droops back; he feeds desire with gazing in your [Venus'] eyes, and his breath is locked to your responsive lips." The humanization of Venus presented by Lucretius in 60 B.C. has much advanced forty years later in Vergil's *Aeneid,* where she functions as any Greek god, protecting her son Aeneas in his trials.

To **Hercules** belongs the earliest foreign cult received at Rome. The form of his name reflects Western Greek pronunciation, as does *Aesculapius,* the Latin form of *Asclepius,* and *Proserpina* (pro-**ser**-pi-na), the Latin form of *Persephonê* (as *Ulysses* is the Latin form of *Odysseus*). *Dis* (dis), the Roman Hades, is an abbreviation of Latin *dives,* "riches," a translation of the Greek *Pluto* (which in Greek means "enricher"), a euphemism for Hades.

[3]That is, Ares.

FIG. 22.4. The master of the household with his Lares, painting on plaster from Pompeii, c. 70 A.D. The Lares hold horns of plenty and baskets. The serpent, about to eat a honey cake, also protects the house, like the serpent in the House of Erechtheus on the Acropolis in Athens. (House of the Vetti, Pompeii; Author's photo)

Gods of the Family and the State

The divinities associated with the Roman family always retained their own identities, despite Greek influence. This may have been because the Greeks had no deities to correspond to these particular gods or because they were so embedded in Roman life that nothing could replace them. One such deity was the Lar (plural Lares, **lar-ēz**), protector of the people in a household; the name apparently is derived from the Etruscan word for a spirit of the dead. The **Lares** were worshiped in small shrines at crossroads where the boundaries of four farms came together; there every year a doll was suspended for each member of the family and a ball of wool for each slave, perhaps a substitute for human sacrifice (Fig. 22.4). The **Penates** (pe-**nā**-tēz), often confused with the Lares, protected a household's things and especially its food. In origin the *numina* of the storehouse (*penus* means "cupboard"), they became identified with the welfare of the state. The Trojan gods whom Hector's ghost entrusted to Aeneas as he fled the burning city of Troy were identified with the state Penates.

The religious activity of the family revolved around the *gens* (roughly, "clan"; plural *gentes*) and the *familia* ("household," including slaves). Citizenship meant membership in a *gens* and was confined to males. The head of the *familia*, at least in theory, had absolute power over all members of the *familia*, including the right to kill even his own sons (some instances are recorded). The *patria potestas*, "power of the father,"[4] invested in the *paterfamilias*, "father of the family," rarely was exercised to the full but was always a real threat, especially for slaves. One term from Roman familial religion has passed into our own speech, although its meaning has changed.

[4]Augustus (and later emperors) used the title *pater patriae* ("Father of the Fatherland"). After death the emperor sometimes became *divus* ("a divinity by act of the Senate"). Not until late in the empire did live emperors become *dei*—"full gods."

FIG. 22.5. The temple of Vesta, first century A.D. The building stands in the Roman Forum, where burned the eternal flame of the Roman state. Its round shape is perhaps inspired by the primitive huts that once stood on the hills around the Forum. (Author's photo)

A man's *genius,* "begetter," was a sort of double, the part of him he had inherited from his father and would pass on to his sons. The *genius* of Augustus, and later emperors, was worshiped throughout the Roman world.

The Romans felt that the state was a family writ large. This notion becomes clear in the cult of the *numen* **Vesta,** whose name corresponds etymologically to the Greek *Hestia.* Like her, Vesta is protectress of hearth and home. In Rome she was served by six Vestal Virgins, each chosen at the age of seven from the great families. The Vestals served for thirty years, after which they could marry, although few did. In their round temple in the Forum near the ancient house of the Roman kings (fig. 22.5), they performed services for the state analogous to the work of unmarried girls in a private home: ritual baking, spring cleaning, and tending the sacred flame on the hearth, said to have been brought from Troy by Aeneas and never allowed to go out. If a Vestal was caught having sexual relations, she was buried alive in a tomb containing a loaf of bread, a jug of water, and a lighted lamp (some did meet their end in this way). Although Vesta was among the most sacred and revered deities of Roman religion, she has few myths (like the Greek Hestia) but remained a *numen* throughout Roman history.

Perhaps the Romans' vision of the state as an enlarged family is most clear from the exaltation in myth and other propaganda of a set of duties called **pietas** (pē-e-tas). The term has little in common with its derivatives *piety* and *pity* but refers to the extraordinary devotion that one shows first to the *paterfamilias,* then, by extension, to the abstraction of the state itself and its gods. The Roman exaltation of *pietas* as the highest virtue was prominent from an early time and was claimed in titles used by Roman emperors and the poets who wrote for them, especially Vergil, who constantly calls his hero *pius Aeneas.* The virtue of *pietas* could legitimize the suppression of political opposition because the ruler embodies the country, and opposition to him shows a lack of *pietas.* No doubt it was the native Roman predisposition to regard abstractions as divine that enabled them to transfer pious devotion from the head of a family to an invisible entity, the state. Greek religious anthropomorphism, by contrast, stood in the way of granting obedience to a divine abstraction. Although the Greeks (in Athens especially) made tentative efforts to replace family moral authority with that of the city, their political divisions continued, and they never—until the Roman conquest—united as a single nation.

THE FOUNDING OF ROME

Roman Politics and History

In its earliest days, Rome was ruled by kings. About 500 B.C. the monarchy, then Etruscan, was destroyed by an alliance of wealthy land-owning families, the *patricians,* who met together in the Senate, "body of old men," to pass laws and decide on peace and war. Those excluded from this privileged class, the majority, were the *plebeians,* who especially in the fourth century B.C. struggled to gain their own representation, with limited success. Under the *Republic,* as modern historians call the period of Rome rule after the expulsion of the kings (from the Latin *res publica,* "business of the people"), elections, usually rigged, were held among the members of the ruling patrician oligarchy; there were never more than thirty or so ruling families at any time. Under the Republic the legislative branch, we might say, normally held the power, while the normally weak executive consisted of two *consuls* elected annually. The power of the consuls was checked by their short term of office and the power of veto each held over the other. A consul possessed *imperium,* the power to command the army and enforce the law, including imposition of the death penalty, a vestige of royal power inherited by the new ruling oligarchy. The symbol of *imperium* was the *fasces,* an axhead surrounded by a bundle of rods carried by bearers called lictors, who preceded the consul wherever he went: The rods were for whipping and the ax for beheading.[5]

---

[5]From this word comes the modern term *fascism,* because the twentieth-century Italian political leader Benito Mussolini claimed to be reconstructing the ancient Roman state. The *fasces* appeared

Having set up a government by means of a small clique from their own number, the patrician families fabricated a legendary tradition of their own ancestors to bolster their monopoly of power. But the rule—and the wealth—of Rome expanded enormously as in the third to first centuries B.C. the Roman state took over virtually the entire Mediterranean world. By 31 B.C., the Republic gave way to a new monarchy under Augustus. Modern historians call this new monarchy the Roman Empire, when *imperium* resided permanently in the hands of a single man.

Julius Caesar (100–44 B.C.), a key figure in the disintegration of the Republic, was in his enemies' eyes a man who violated *pietas* and placed personal ambition before the interests of the state. He destroyed the senatorial armies that opposed him and became sole ruler, but he was murdered by conspirators. As he fell—as Shakespeare tells the story in Julius Caesar—Caesar cried out to his good friend Marcus Brutus, *Et tu, Brute,* "You too, Brutus?"[6] Not so coincidentally, this same Marcus Brutus claimed descent from an earlier tyrant-slayer also named Brutus, alleged founder of the Republic five hundred years before.

Caesar's enemies thought that his death would restore the power of the senatorial oligarchy, but Caesar's party rallied under Mark Antony, Caesar's general, and Octavian (after 27 B.C. called Augustus, "greater than human"), Caesar's grandnephew and heir. They conquered the senatorial armies and divided the world between them, Octavian taking the West and Antony the East. Antony's infamous affair with Queen Cleopatra of Egypt[7] and other quarrels led in 31 B.C. to a new war and Octavian's final victory. The monarchy instituted by Octavian/Augustus was to last (in the east) until the fall of Constantinople to the Turks in A.D. 1453.

Augustus calmed the remains of the old senatorial party by retaining the outward trappings of the old Republican government. The religious, artistic, and literary program he sponsored, from which come most of our surviving accounts of Roman myth, was heavily propagandistic, with the aim of making the new regime appear to be a continuation of the old Republic. Two writers whose work we examine are particularly important in this movement: Vergil[8] (70–19 B.C.), author of the *Aeneid,* and the historian Livy (59 B.C.–A.D. 17). But many other writers prominent under Augustus, especially Ovid, alluded often to the tales of early Rome, with the intent of linking the present political situation with the past.

The Origins of Rome: Vergil and the *Aeneid*

Vergil, in his immensely complicated and influential poem the *Aeneid,* used the legend of Aeneas, the founder of Rome, to create a document to rival those of the

---

on the reverse side of the United States Mercury dime, standard issue during the 1940s, apparently in reverence to the forms of government pioneered by Rome. The symbol remained, even when the United States was at war with Italy.

[6]According to ancient sources, he cried out in Greek, "And you, my son?" which Brutus was rumored to be; the Latin version appears in an early English translation of Plutarch, who wrote in Greek.

[7]Not an Egyptian, but descended from Ptolemy, the Macedonian general of Alexander the Great.

[8]Sometimes erroneously spelled *Virgil.*

Greeks, even Homer. Vergil was born in 70 B.C. near Mantua, in the north of Italy. In 41 B.C., if we can believe suggestions in his own verses, he lost his farm. Helped by Maecenas, a friend and minister of Augustus, he became a trusted member of Augustus' art council. He wrote the *Eclogues,* graceful pastoral poetry celebrating the uncorrupted emotions and clever wit of imaginary shepherds, and the *Georgics,* a long poem ostensibly on farming in four books that praise the physical beauty of Italy and the old-fashioned virtues of its people. The last ten years of his life Vergil spent on the *Aeneid,* which he left not quite finished when he died in 19 B.C. Although the poet had ordered his literary executors to burn the incomplete poem, Augustus intervened. We now examine his story.

In Homer's *Iliad,* Aeneas was the son of Anchises and a cousin of Hector; he hoped to succeed Priam as king, although they were on bad terms. His mother was the goddess Aphrodite (see Chapter 8). It is unusual for a hero to have a mortal father and a divine mother, although the same was true of Achilles. Aeneas was destined to survive the Trojan War, as Poseidon explains to Artemis and Hera:

[300] "Come, let us bring Aeneas away from the clutches of death,
       averting the fury of Cronus' son, if he learns that Achilles
       has slain the man whom destiny calls to escape from this fate—
       all this, that Dardanus' line may not perish in utter oblivion,
       Dardanus, dearer to Zeus than all the rest of the children
305   born as the fruit of his loving embrace with the daughters of men.°
       You know how the son of Cronus now hates the household of Priam;
       know too that mighty Aeneas is to hold the rule of the Trojans,
       he and his children's children, for generations to come."

HOMER, *Iliad* (20.300–308)

305. . . . *daughters of men:* Dardanus was the son of Zeus and Electra, a daughter of Atlas.

As we noted earlier, the Romans had no ancient explanation for their origins. This passage from the *Iliad* suggested a possible illustrious ancestor for them, complete with a divine parent. By the time of Augustus, the story had been elaborated: Aeneas had fought valiantly for Troy, but when the city burned, he escaped to the far West and founded Lavinium in Latium. His son **Iulus** (ī-ū-lus), who allegedly gave his name to the Julian clan to which Julius Caesar and Augustus belonged, then founded Alba Longa. Eventually his descendants, Romulus (**rom**-u-lus) and Remus (**rē**-mus), born in Alba Longa, founded Rome. But Aeneas was *pater* of the whole race of victorious Romans and the direct ancestor of Augustus.

The *Aeneid* opens with an explanation, in mythical terms, of the bitter rivalry that was to exist between Carthage,[9] a Phoenician colony close to modern Tunis, and Rome. Juno is the protector of Carthage, as Venus, mother of Aeneas and sponsor of the Julian clan, favors Rome:

[9]From Semitic *Qeret Hadshah* = "Newtown"; similarly, Naples is from the Greek *Neapolis* = "Newtown." Vergil places the founding of Carthage at the same time as the burning of Troy; in fact it was founded about 800 B.C., the same time as the western expansion of the Greeks reflected in the *Odyssey.*

[1]   I sing of ancient wars and an exile, by Destiny's order,
        who sailed from the seashore of Troy, pursued over land and sea
        by the might of the gods who heeded great Juno's implacable anger.
        To Italy's mainland he came, to the coast of the land of Lavinia;
5   once more he fought to the death, as he tried to establish a city,
        and settle his gods in Latium, whence rose the race of the Latins,
        the noble rulers of Alba, and the towering ramparts of Rome.
            O Muse, recall to my mind the insulted godhead of Juno:
        what did the queen so resent that she forced so pious° a hero
10   to suffer such trials and labor? Can divinity harbor such passion?
            There once was an ancient city, founded by Tyrian settlers,
        far to Italy's south, but facing the mouths of the Tiber,
        Carthage, dowered with wealth, skilled and resourceful in warfare.
        Juno is said to have cherished this city, more than all others,
15   Samos alone excepted; here she kept her weapons and chariot.
        Even as early as this the goddess was planning and helping
        to make—if fate should permit—of her city the ruler of nations.
        She heard that a race was arising from the conquered rulers of Troy,
        which some day would dash to the ground the new-built Tyrian city.
20   From this race was destined to come a warlike imperial people,
        Libya's° bane and destruction. And the fated time was approaching.
        Saturnian° Juno trembled at this, but remembered the struggle
        which once she had waged at Troy at the head of the Argives she loved.
        The cause of that war and the bitter resentment it roused in her spirit
25   had never vanished away: deep down in her heart she remembered
        the judgment of Paris, the wounding shame that her beauty was slighted,
        her rival's° hated descendants, and abducted Ganymede's honors.
        Already embittered by this, she had blocked the way for the Trojans
        (survivors of war with the Greeks and the wrath of savage Achilles),
30   and driven them over the seas, far from the promise of Latium.
        Truly a mighty task was the founding of Rome and its people!

                            VERGIL, *Aeneid* (1.1–33)

9. *pious:* The first reference to the *pietas* of Aeneas—his respect for family, country, and gods.
21. *Libya's:* = North Africa = Carthage, utterly destroyed by Rome in 146 B.C. after a hundred years
of war.   22. *Saturnian:* Saturn = Cronus, father of Juno/Hera. He appears in Latin authors as
the ruler of Italy in the Golden Age but also as a cynical old man, the equivalent of "crooked-coun-
seling Cronus," which gives us the English word *saturnine* = gloomy.   27. *rival's:* Electra, on
whom Zeus fathered Dardanus, ancestor of the Trojans.

    Aeneas and twelve shiploads of refugees have for seven years been wandering
across the Mediterranean, drifting ever westward.[10] They have just left Sicily when
Juno persuades Aeolus, king of the winds, to raise a killer storm. Some of Aeneas'
ships are lost, but others reach the coast of North Africa. Aeneas' mother, Venus,
sends Cupid to breathe passion into **Dido** (dī-dō), queen of nearby Carthage and

[10]Literary critics call this technique of beginning a poem *in medias res,* jumping "into the middle of
things," after a phrase from the Roman poet Horace (65–8 B.C.). Vergil derives it from the *Iliad*
and the *Odyssey,* both of which begin in the same manner.

FIG. 22.6. Aeneas escaping with his father and son from the flames of Troy, painting on plaster from Pompeii, c. A.D. 70. On his shoulder Aeneas carries his father, who holds a special box, perhaps containing the Lares. He holds his son, Ascanius, by the hand. (Museo Archeologico Nazionale, Naples)

herself a refugee. She had left Phoenician Tyre after her husband, Sychaeus (si-**kē**-us), was treacherously murdered and had sworn to his ghost a vow of perpetual chastity.

At a banquet in honor of the newcomers, Aeneas tells Dido and her court about the fall of Troy: the wooden horse, Sinon, Laocoön, the death of Priam, his own escape through darkened streets, and the disappearance of his wife, Creüsa. Carrying on his shoulders his lame father, Anchises, and his household gods, he led his son Ascanius (as-**kā**-ni-us, another name for Iulus) through the fire and carnage (a striking image of the Roman patriarchal family; see Fig. 22.6). He and other refugees managed to build ships and sail away. In a voyage deliberately reminiscent of Odysseus' travels, Aeneas describes how he and his companions stopped in Thrace but were warned away by the ghost of Aeneas' murdered cousin Polydorus, Priam's youngest son. From Thrace they sailed to the sacred island of Delos, where Apollo's oracle told them to seek the land of the founder of their race, Dardanus. They supposed this land to be Crete, but once there they were beset by plague. Dardanus, Aeneas now learned, was in fact born in Italy. Heading further west, the Trojans put in at the island of the Harpies, who predicted they would travel until "hunger made them eat their tables."

Disheartened, they made their way up the coast of the modern Albania. Putting to land, they met the prophet Helenus, himself a refugee and the last surviving son of Priam. Helenus described the route to Italy and warned Aeneas to land on its western coast. He told him that he must found his city in a secluded valley by a stream, where he had found a white sow with thirty piglets.

They crossed the Adriatic, edged along the southern coast of Italy, and put in to Sicily. Escaping the enraged and blinded Polyphemus—for Odysseus had been there before—they continued west. Anchises died and was buried in Sicily. Then they were caught in the storm that brought them to Dido's palace.

Dido, inspired with hopeless love for Aeneas (thanks to Cupid's arrows), listens to the story with fascination. A few days later, Aeneas and Dido are out hunting. A thunderstorm bursts above them, and the royal couple take refuge in a cave, where they fall into one another's arms. Soon the rumor of their affair reaches the ears of a neighboring king, to whom Dido had refused marriage because of her vow to Sychaeus. In anger he prays to Jupiter, who sends Mercury to order Aeneas to leave Africa: His destiny is to found the Roman race, not to idle away his life in the arms of a foreign princess.

Dido hears of Aeneas' preparations to leave and throws his treachery in his face:

[305] "Traitor, did you expect to conceal the crime you were planning,
and quietly sneak away from my land? Was our love unable to hold you,
or the mutual vows that we gave, or the thought of Dido abandoned,
doomed to a piteous death? Pray, why pick the middle of winter
for hurriedly readying ships to sail into a furious tempest?
310 Have you no heart?" . . .
    So Dido poured out her pain, but Aeneas, by Jupiter's order,
displayed no trace of emotion and repressed his anguish of heart.
At last he muttered an answer: "If the choice were entirely mine,
not a single word of the many which you so justly can utter,
315 O queen who deserved so much better of me, would I try to deny.
As long as self-consciousness lasts, or body hearkens to spirit,
never will I be ashamed to acknowledge my debt to Elissa.°
Still, the plain truth demands a few words of exculpation:
I never tried to conceal my hurried departure—no, never!
320 I never held the bridegroom's torch, nor acknowledged a marriage.
If destiny so had allowed, I would live my life as I pleased,
easing the cares that attack, in whatever way seemed to me best.
I would cherish the city of Troy and whatever remained of my people;
Priam's great hall would survive, and the Pergama° shake off its ashes,
325 raised up by my own hand, restored to a once beaten people.
But now such a prospect is gone. The voice of Grynean° Apollo
and the Lycian tablets of fate° have expounded Destiny's order:
to Italy now must I voyage, to great Italy turn my endeavors.
That is the land that I love, and that is the land of my fathers.
330   Mighty Carthage detains you, and the sight of your Libyan city,
Phoenician though you were born. By what right, then, do you murmur
if the Trojans at last find their promised home in Ausonia's° land?
Surely we too are entitled to a kingdom in lands not our own.

317. *Elissa:* Dido's real name. *Dido* is an epithet of the Phoenician goddess Astartê as moon goddess.   324. *Pergama:* "Citadel," "stronghold," a word Homer uses to describe the walls of Troy. 326. *Grynean:* The epithet derives from Apollo's shrine in Mysia, south of Troy.   327. *fate:* That is, Apollo's oracles on Delos: *Lycian* is a common epithet of Apollo.   332. *Ausonia:* The borderland between Latium and Campania; here simply Italy.

Night never covers the earth with misty shadows and darkness,
335   the stars never rise in the east to march on their fiery courses,
but the troubled ghost of my father brings panic into my slumber,
urging me on to my task. My son, too, appears in my dreams,
reproaching me for my damage to the hopes of one so beloved,
in cheating him of a kingdom, his destined Hesperian° acres.
340   And last, great Jove himself—I swear by your head and my own—
has sent his herald to bring my orders down through the tempest.
By the clearest light of the day I saw him enter the city,
and when he addressed me I listened with all my closest attention.
So please, give over inflaming both yourself and me with your protests;
345   though not by my own free will, to Italy I make my venture!"

VERGIL, Aeneid (4.305–361)

339. *Hesperian:* That is, western.

Dido loses control and threatens suicide. Aeneas sails anyway, just before sunrise; as he goes, he turns to see distant smoke rising from her funeral pyre, spiraling into the sky. She has died by her own hand, and with her last breath curses Aeneas and those begotten of him.

The fleet stops in Sicily to hold funeral games for Anchises. There the Trojan women rebel against their long wandering and attempt to burn the ships. Aeneas leaves them behind, with some cowardly men as well, to found their own colony. The Trojans travel north toward what is today the Bay of Naples, where the helmsman Palinurus falls overboard and is drowned, for Neptune had demanded the death of one of the crew before he would allow a safe landing.

At Cumae, Aeneas consults the Sibyl, a local prophetess. From a magical tree he plucks a golden bough, sign of the elect, and he and the Sibyl penetrate the underworld (Chapter 11). On the banks of the River Styx Aeneas sees the ghost of Palinurus, still unburied (as Odysseus encountered the unburied Elpenor). Charon allows them to enter his boat and ferries them over the gloomy water. On the other bank, the Sibyl drugs the ferocious Cerberus with a honey cake. Nearby, on the "mourning fields," populated by those who died for love, Aeneas espies the ghost of Dido:

[450]   Among them Phoenician Dido was wandering deep in the forest,
still showing her wound. As Aeneas came, he peered through the shadow,
like a man who sees or imagines the rise of the dim new moon,
gleaming faint through the clouds. Unable to hold back from weeping,
and touched by still tender affection, Aeneas spoke through his tears:
455   "So the word, poor Dido, was true, that reported that your life had ended,
and that you had met your fate from a weapon in your own hands!
Was I the cause of your death? I swear by the stars in the heaven,
by the gods above, by whatever has force in the depths of earth,
that I sailed away from your country, O queen, against my desire.
460   The orders of heaven forced me, and the gods' irresistible power,
which forces me now to explore this region of darkness and mildew.
How could I have foreseen what anguish my leaving would bring you?
No, no! Wait for a while; turn not away from my presence.

465

This is the last time ever that fate will allow me to plead."
    With words like this, with a flood of tears, Aeneas attempted
to mollify angry Dido's scowling implacable specter.
She fixed her eyes on the ground, and, silently turning her back,
seemed no more moved by his pleading than would be a block of flint
or a statue of Parian marble. At last she regained self-control,

470

and, still unforgiving, ran off to the shadowy depths of the forest,
where at once her husband Sychaeus consoled her with mutual affection.
Aeneas still watched as she went, deeply shaken by Dido's misfortune,
shedding his tears of pity as long as she still could be seen.

VERGIL, *Aeneid* (6.450–476)

They pass Tartarus, where the worst sinners suffer, but the Sibyl will not allow Aeneas to enter. Next they come to the Fields of Elysium, abode of the blessed dead. Aeneas vainly attempts to embrace the spirit of his father, Anchises. Nearby, ghosts drink from the River Lethê, "forgetfulness," and Anchises explains that these spirits will soon be reincarnated, having purified their souls of crimes committed in earlier lives. Anchises points out to Aeneas the souls of Romulus, the other early kings of Rome, the great generals of Rome, and the spirit of Augustus himself. Anchises' words about Rome's destiny are central to the poem:

[847]

Others will chisel the bronze so subtly it seems to be breathing;
others, no doubt, will extract a lifelike face from the marble.
Tongues more fluent than ours will plead the rights of their clients;

850

sages will measure the heavens and tell of the rise of the stars.
But you, Roman, never forget your duty to govern the nations.
Your god-given skill will be this: to impose good conduct on peace,
to thrust the proud from the throne, to forgive the beaten and humble.

VERGIL, *Aeneid* (6.847–853)

After returning to the upper world, Aeneas and his followers again board their ships and land at the mouth of the Tiber in Latium. The Harpy's prophecy is fulfilled when they eat breadcakes that, for want of dishes, they had to use as platters.

At Latium, they encounter the local king, Latinus. His daughter, Lavinia, had been betrothed to **Turnus,** the king of the nearby Rutulians, but a prophecy directed Latinus to give Lavinia to a foreigner. When Aeneas accepts her, war erupts between the indigenous Italians and the Trojan interlopers. The angry, jilted Turnus organizes a coalition of local warriors, including Camilla, a warrior-maiden from the neighboring tribe of the Volsci.

The river god Tiber persuades Aeneas to form an alliance with King Evander, a Greek who had settled on the Palatine Hill. On the way up river, Aeneas sees a white sow with a litter of thirty piglets: Here he will found Lavinium, according to the prophecy of Helenus. Evander shows Aeneas sites later to be famous in Rome and agrees to support Aeneas in the war. He suggests that they also strike an alliance with the Etruscans.

Meanwhile, Turnus has surrounded the Trojan camp. In a skirmish Ascanius kills his first man. In a glorious scene of battle, Turnus, trapped alone inside the walls of the camp, single-handedly kills many Trojans, then dives into the river to escape. In the company of Pallas, the son of Evander, Aeneas returns to the Trojan camp. Turnus lies in wait and kills Pallas. In the heat of war, the brave Camilla, dedicated to the warrior goddess Diana as an infant, kills many Trojans:

[648] Right at the heart of the fray, like an Amazon, baring one breast,
the better to join in the battle, Camilla, with quiver of arrows,
650   raged now this way, now that; one moment, with battle-hard muscle
she filled the air with her shafts; the next, unwearied, she pounded
the foe with a two-bitted ax she had seized in her powerful hand.
Her golden bow, like Diana's, sang loud, drawn back to her shoulder;
even when forced to retreat in the face of superior foemen,
655   backward she turned her bow and, running, let fly with her arrows.

VERGIL, *Aeneid* (11.648–654)

Aruns, an Etruscan, takes careful aim at Camilla and strikes her down. At last Aeneas and Turnus agree to settle the quarrel by single combat. The winner will marry Lavinia and rule over Latium. Aeneas wounds Turnus, who falls to the ground and begs for his life. Aeneas nearly shows him mercy, but when he sees Pallas' sword-belt tied to Turnus' chest as a trophy, he angrily plunges his sword into the breast of the Italian warrior. So ends the *Aeneid*.

Observations: An Epic of National Rebirth

At first glance, the *Aeneid* and the *Iliad* or *Odyssey* look much the same: Both authors use an apparatus of gods to manipulate the action, set their poems in the days of the Trojan War, treat issues of honor and destiny, and present gory descriptions of death and physical violence.

The first half of the *Aeneid* is a sort of *Odyssey*, a tale of a hero's wandering as he tries to reach a new home. The second part resembles the *Iliad*, a chronicle of warfare. The meter is the same dactylic hexameter of Homer, introduced to Latin about two hundred years before Vergil and by his time fairly well naturalized (although Vergil was the first Roman to use it with true facility). All three poems use many of the same technical devices, such as the use of such fixed descriptive epithets as "swift-footed Achilles" and "pious Aeneas."

But the differences are profound. Homer was an oral entertainer in a boisterous, unlettered age that lacked political unity or great wealth; Vergil was highly literate, steeped in written Greek poetry and philosophy and in personal contact with the most powerful men who had ever lived. Homer composed on the fly to entertain; our versions of the *Iliad* and *Odyssey* were (apparently) taken down by dictation. Vergil's poem was painstakingly learned, self-conscious, and created in writing with deliberate compression and elegant expression. Greek oral epic, usually complete in a single sitting, differed with every performance—our Homeric poems are snapshots of a single artificially extended performance; the *Aeneid*, composed in writing, was not finished even after ten years.

In Homer's stories people act: They become angry, do clever things, kill cruelly, or die nobly. The meaning of the story is in the action, and the characters are who they pretend to be. But Vergil's myths, like the Athenian myths of Theseus, are purposeful propaganda, to prove that Augustus deserved his place in the world and that Rome's destiny in history was willed by divine intelligence. Characters and events in Vergil's myths have various levels of meaning; they stand for more than meets the eye. All events and characters are subordinated to his patriotic purpose of satisfying Rome's need for a tradition of national origin, a tale telling in the language of legend how this great empire was made. Its story of far away and long ago, when cows munched grass on the Palatine hill, satisfied contemporary literary taste for an escapist setting yet made it possible for Vergil to proclaim, in symbolic form, the divine necessity of Rome's conquest of the world and Augustus' ascendancy in it.

In order to provide justification for the new regime, Vergil needed a philosophy that could explain the whole sweep of Roman history, culminating in the purposes and achievement of Augustus. The old Roman *numina* lacked the authority to satisfy this requirement. Vergil needed a theory of destiny, an unchanging and inescapable plan laid down by immortal power, operating through all the ages. He found this theory in the philosophy of Stoicism, which taught that the world is ruled by the divine *logos,* an untranslatable word that means something like "purpose," "structure," and "order" (the origin of our word *logic*).[11] The force of the logos permeates all history and predetermined Rome's ascendancy over all other nations. Rome's triumph is simply the working out among mortals of divine will.

To Vergil, his hero must be shown as obedient to his country, above all other obligations. Vergil may have had political motives for this attitude, but Stoic philosophy again provided a convenient framework because the Stoics taught that one must always do one's duty. Aeneas is *pius,* placing duty above all, and he is not an independent agent; he is *fato profugus,* "driven by Fate." Fate is much the same as the *logos;* Latin *fatum* means "something spoken" or "decreed," and the Greek *logos* is derived from *legô,* "to say." The world of the *Aeneid,* and hence by implication the world of Rome under Augustus, is not controlled by a self-indulgent sky god who squabbles with his wife and lusts after young maidens. As Anchises reveals in the underworld, even Jupiter serves the impersonal *logos/fatum,* the divine order. Aeneas may appear to be heartless for placing his duty to found Rome above his love for Dido, but the *pius* man must do his duty to the divine command, regardless of consequences to his personal life. He does what he must do, the only behavior that admits the possibility of human happiness, according to Stoic philosophical teaching. For the founding of empire, one must place personal interests behind those of the state. The Trojan women who tired of wandering and were left in Sicily are not worthy of

---

[11]The Stoic *logos,* although it lacked personality, was close enough to the Judeo-Christian God to appear in the opening of the gospel of John (1.1): "In the beginning was the *logos,* and the *logos* was with God, and the *logos* was God, and without the *logos* was nothing made that was made." The usual translation, *word,* is inadequate. Stoicism was founded by Zeno from Citium in Cyprus, about 300 B.C.; it is named after a colonnade (= stoa) in Athens where Zeno taught. A central moral theme of this complicated philosophy was that one should live in harmony with nature, whose transformations reflect the underlying *logos.*

empire: The weak must be purged before the great task can begin. Palinurus, the helmsman who fell from the ship off the Bay of Naples, is not just a member of the crew but stands for every noble Roman who gave his life, at divine behest, that Rome might be great: The individual will perish, but empire grows.

Vergil's complex myth therefore places empire in the context of a divine plan for human history while glorifying the moral qualities necessary for the foundation of empire. The quality of *pietas,* devotion to duty, is the most important positive quality in a ruler. Vergil also shows what features rulers should not have. Aeneas during his seven years of wandering has purged himself of material and sexual excess, which the exotic eastern city of Troy symbolized in ancient literature, where gold-drenched Priam produced fifty sons, each with his own chamber. He spurns the glorious new city that Dido is building and rejects his passion for her, so like that between Paris and Helen, who in placing personal desire above communal good gave rise to the catastrophic Trojan War.

In Dido, Vergil embodies many mythical and historical associations: Dido is not only like Helen of Troy, who gave in to her passion, but also like Circê and Calypso, enchantresses who would sway the hero from his purpose, and like Euripides' savage Medea, who represents all that is barbaric. In her the contemporary Roman reader would also recognize Cleopatra, who seduced Mark Antony and turned him against Augustus and Rome. In short, Dido represents the moral failings of broken faith and Eastern passion. Although she had sworn to Sychaeus that she would have no other, she slept with Aeneas. Instead of transcending her heartbreak and pain (as a true Roman woman would), she took her life in an act of vindictive self-destruction. Dido also is an incarnation of Carthage, Rome's greatest enemy, who under the extraordinary general Hannibal (247–183 B.C.) nearly destroyed the Roman state. Such was the working out of Dido's curse on Aeneas and his descendants.

The Romans were an amalgam of many clans and tribes whose primitive tribal identity was submerged in the greater being of the state. In Vergil's poem, Latinus the Latin, Tarchon the Etruscan, and Evander the Greek stand for the peoples fused into Rome. All work together toward the common enterprise. Brazen and hotheaded, Turnus is too like Achilles or Mark Antony to survive. Morally, he is not wrong; he may be right. After all, he was engaged to Lavinia before Aeneas appeared and carried off his promised bride. Still, he must lose because he opposes the pattern of destiny. The personal and local pride that Turnus represents must succumb if empire will bestow its many benefits on humankind.

LEGENDS OF THE ROMAN MONARCHY

Romulus and Remus

As we have seen, such Roman mythographers, "writers of myth," as Vergil and Livy had to fill in the embarrassing gap of 450 years between the burning of Troy, traditionally placed at about 1200 B.C., and the "founding" of Rome in 753 B.C., according to conventional belief. The most common stories told that Aeneas founded

Lavinium, named after his wife, Lavinia, then died. Ascanius/Iulus founded Alba Longa and was succeeded by a sequence of kings. In the twelfth generation after Aeneas—that is, about 450 years later—**Romulus** and **Remus** were born, who founded Rome on seven low hills on the banks of the Tiber. In this way the legends of Aeneas and Romulus and Remus were brought together.

Livy wrote an enormous history of the Roman people in 142 papyrus rolls, of which 35 survive, in which he celebrated the political settlement of Augustus, who personally encouraged him. His history is called *Ab urbe condita* ("From the Founding of the City"), after its first three words. His prose version of the story of Romulus and Remus is a good specimen of the Roman's understanding of his early past:

> The next king [of Alba Longa] was Proca. He had two sons, Numitor and Amulius; to Numitor, the elder, he bequeathed the ancient throne of the Silvian dynasty.° But neither a father's intention nor respect for the claims of an elder son proved to be any match for violence when Amulius drove his brother out into exile. Then, piling crime on crime, he killed all Numitor's sons, and stripped away all hope of male issue from his brother's daughter Rhea Silvia by giving her the empty honor of being a Vestal, and thus condemned to lifelong virginity.
>
> But surely the origin of so great a city, and an empire second only to the domain of the gods, must be ascribed to Destiny itself. The Vestal presently gave birth to twins, the result, she claimed, of violent rape. She named Mars as their father, either because she really believed it, or because she felt that putting the responsibility on a god would lessen her own dishonor. Be that as it may, neither gods nor man defended the Vestal or her sons from the savagery of the king. She was chained and flung into a dungeon, and an order was given for the boys to be thrown into a running stream. By some piece of divine providence it happened that the Tiber had overflowed its banks and spread out into sluggish ponds, so that its normal bed could nowhere be approached. This led the men who were carrying out the babies to hope that they could toss them into any water that was moving, however slowly, and could thus feel that they were carrying out the royal command. So they abandoned the boys on the nearest mud bank, by the site of the present *Ficus Ruminalis* ["fig tree of the sucklings"], which, it is said, was then called the Romular ["of Romulus"]. Now in those days there were wild areas all through the region. The story goes on that when the slow-moving water ebbed away, it left the basket that carried the boys stranded on the dry bank. Presently a thirsty she-wolf from the nearby hills came down to drink. Hearing a childish wail, she turned aside to the boys, and offered them her teats so gently that, when a shepherd of the king's block found her a little later, she was licking them with her tongue. The shepherd's name is said to have been Faustulus ["lucky"]. He brought the boys back to his hut and gave them to his wife Larentia to bring up. True, some people maintain that Larentia was the local whore to whom the shepherds gave the nickname of Lupa ["she-wolf"], and that this was the source of the story—be it legend or miracle.

Livy, Ab urbe condita (1.3.10–1.4.7)

Silvian dynasty: So called from Aeneas Silvius, grandson of Aeneas.

The origin of the story of Romulus and Remus, perhaps the best-known foundation story from classical myth, is not clear. Some think it a genuine Roman tradition, but other scholars find in it a compendium of elements drawn consciously from Greek models. Native elements would include Romulus' name, an eponym of *Roma*, itself of Etruscan origin. Remus' name, however, has never been adequately explained. The detail about the Ruminal Fig seems to be an etiological tag to explain a real tree venerated as the site of a *numen* called Rumina, "breast-nourisher" (because the milk of the fig looks like milk from the human breast). Faustulus is perhaps related to the Roman woodland spirit Faunus,[12] identified with the Greek Pan. A *numen* with underworld associations, said to be mother to the Lares, was also called Larentia.

But the narrative details of the story recall Greek examples. The exposure of the children reminds us of Oedipus and other figures like Paris, who was exposed and suckled by a bear, and Zeus, who was suckled by a goat[13] (Fig. 22.7). Royal brothers appear in Greek myth, notably in the story of the city founders Amphion and Zethus. Danaë, a virgin like **Rhea Silvia,** was imprisoned in an underground cavern, but Zeus seduced her anyway and she and her child were set afloat on the sea. The rivalry between the colorless Numitor and Amulius may be consciously modeled on that between Eteocles and Polynices.[14] We cannot determine whether such elements were borrowed deliberately from Greek stories to concoct a Roman foundation story or whether the story arose from a native oral tradition parallel to but independent of the Greek.

When Romulus and Remus grew up, they became great hunters (like all traditional heroes), first of animals, then of bandits, whose loot they honorably divided with other shepherds. But one day the bandits captured Remus and handed him over to King Amulius, who for some reason gave him to Numitor to be punished. Numitor recognized his son, Romulus was brought into the conspiracy, and the brothers killed the wicked Amulius. Livy continues:

> Thus the throne of Alba was restored to Numitor. But Romulus and Remus were eager to build a city in the place where they had been exposed and brought up. There were already too many people in Alba, both Albans and Latins, and beside them there were the shepherds—so many, all told, that it was quite reasonable to believe that Alba and Lavinium would look like little hamlets compared to the town now being founded. But into these rosy dreams intruded the ancestral blight of ambition to be king, and a shameful quarrel arose from a trifling argument. Since Romulus and Remus were twins, respect for seniority could not determine whose name should be given to the new city and which of them should rule once it was founded. Romulus therefore occu-

---

[12]As in Claude Debussy's famous *Afternoon of a Faun;* cf. Perspective 7.2.

[13]Sargon of Akkad c. 2500 B.C., greatest ruler of Mesopotamia in the third millennium; the Hebrew Moses, c. 1200 B.C.; and Cyrus the Great, founder of the Persian empire in the sixth century B.C., were all, like Romulus and Remus, abandoned in baskets on a river: So difficult is it to disentangle history from myth!

[14]But the motif occurs earlier in the biblical stories of Cain and Abel and Jacob and Esau and in the Egyptian story of Osiris and Seth.

FIG. 22.7 The Capitoline wolf, Etruscan bronze from the fifth century B.C. The twins are not original but were added by a Florentine artist of the fifteenth century, probably Pollaiuolo. According to Livy the Ruminal fig tree grew up where the wolf suckled the twins. Rumina was a *numen* of nursing, connected with ruma, "a breast."
(Musei Capitolini, Rome; University of Wisconsin Photo Archive, Madison)

pied the Palatine and Remus the Aventine° to observe the signs by which the local gods might show them the answers. Remus, so goes the story, was the first to receive a portent, six vultures. But this sign had just been announced when twice that number appeared to Romulus. Both men were promptly hailed as king by their own henchmen, Remus on grounds of priority, Romulus on grounds of number.

They began to argue, but their quarrel soon turned to violence, and in the fighting Remus was killed. There is a better known story that Remus contemptuously jumped over his brother's half-built wall. Romulus, furious at the slight, killed him, adding the bitter jest: "This is what will happen to anyone else who tries the same!" Thus Romulus became sole ruler, and his name was given to the city he had founded.

LIVY, *Ab urbe condita* (1.6.3–1.7.3)

Palatine . . . Aventine: The Palatine and Aventine were hills of Rome.

The founding of Rome in fratricide was sometimes interpreted as foretelling the civil wars of the first century B.C., but in origin the story of the two brothers may have advocated the sanctity of the consuls' dual rule in the state as the best refuge against kingship and tyranny, or it may reflect tensions in the fourth century B.C. between patricians and plebeians. That Rome claimed the murder of Remus by Romulus as the story of its founding is a tantalizing puzzle.

The Rape of the Sabine Women

Rome was founded and named, but there was no one to live in it except runaway slaves, bandits, and murderers who assembled from the hills. If they were to grow in number, the Romans needed wives. Romulus approached local communities and requested their women, but no one wanted to marry his daughter to a Roman bandit. Romulus conceived a plan. During a festival large crowds flocked to Rome from neighboring Latin townships, including the **Sabines** (sā-bīnz). As soon as the festival began, the Romans rushed through the crowd and seized the young Sabine women. The festival broke up in a panic, and the girls' parents, shouting curses, were forced to abandon their daughters.

The abducted women were angry and fearful for the future, but Romulus assured them that everything would turn out well and that they would enjoy the privileges of married women. Their children, when they came, would bind them closely to their new husbands, whom they would learn to love. The men, too, spoke honeyed words and swore that passionate love had prompted their offense, a tactic, as Livy observes, that "touches a woman's heart." Indeed, the women soon forgot their resentment.

No doubt Sabines did contribute significantly to the early Roman bloodline, but behind the story must also lie an early custom of the communal exchange of women, forced or voluntary; such practices occur in many societies. Even in classical Roman marriage the maid was pulled away from her mother in a mock show of force and her hair parted with a spear.

Titus Tatius, Tarpeia, and the Death of Romulus

The king of the Sabines, Titus Tatius (tī-tus tā-shus), promptly made war on the Romans. The struggle went on for years. At one point the Sabines gained entry to the Capitoline Hill by bribing **Tarpeia** (tar-pē-a),[15] daughter of the Roman commander, who demanded in return "what the Sabines wear on their left arms," meaning their big gold bracelets. But once inside, they crushed her under the weight of their shields, which they also wore on their left arms. A cliff on the Capitoline Hill, where Tarpeia was supposed to have allowed the Sabines to enter the fortifications, was allegedly named after her: It was a place of execution, down which traitors were thrown.

The day of the decisive battle arrived. The two armies drew up facing each other, ready to fight, when between the lines ran the women with their young children, beg-

---

[15]Another tradition holds that she fell in love with Titus Tatius. Scylla, Medea, and Ariadnê also fell in love with their fathers' enemies.

ging fathers and brothers on one side, husbands on the other, not to shed kindred blood. Both armies laid down their arms and united as one people.

Romulus died mysteriously. He went into the forest with a group of senators and never came out. One tradition reports that he was murdered by senators jealous of his royal power, his body dismembered and hidden under their togas; another holds that he was raised into heaven. In any event, he became a god and was ever after worshiped as the ancient *numen* Quirinus.

The Horatii and the Curiatii

Rome was ruled by a sequence of seven kings, the first four Romano-Sabine, the last three Etruscan. The odd-numbered kings were valiant and warlike, the even-numbered devoted to the arts of peace. During the Roman monarchy occurred one of the most celebrated examples of Roman valor. The Romans, fighting against Alba Longa, agreed to decide the dispute by a duel between three Roman and three Alban brothers, the **Horatii and the Curiatii** (ho-**rā**-shi-ī, kūr-i-**ā**-shi-ī).[16] The fighting began, and almost immediately two of the Horatii, after wounding their opponents, were cut down. The remaining Horatius, seeing himself outnumbered three to one, turned and ran. As the Curiatii pursued, they strung themselves out. Suddenly the surviving Horatius spun round and cut down his pursuer, then ran back to cut down the next. Only one wounded Curiatius remained, and the single Horatius killed him easily.

This inspiring lesson in Roman steadfastness was marred when the surviving Horatius, returning from the field, saw his sister weeping: She had been engaged to one of the Curiatii. In a rage Horatius drew his sword and plunged it into her breast, crying, "Go to your lover, since you have forgotten your brothers, dead and living, and your country too! May every Roman woman die who laments an enemy!"

Horatius was tried, but acquitted, compelled only to walk beneath a yoke with his head covered as a sign that he submitted to Roman law.

The Etruscan Dynasty and Tullia

Tarquin the Elder, the fifth king of Rome, who had come to Rome from Etruria to establish his ascendancy, was killed by the jealous sons of the fourth king, who resented Tarquin's usurpation of power. However, they did not succeed in regaining the throne, which fell next to Servius Tullius. His mother had been a slave in the royal house (Servius Tullius = "Tullius the slave") who was impregnated by the household Lar, which took the form of a phallus of ash on the hearth and leapt out upon the girl. When Servius Tullius was a child, flames danced around his head, convincing Tarquin's wife, Tanaquil, a prophetess, that he was a man of destiny. After her husband's murder, Tanaquil conspired to place Servius Tullius on the throne.

---

[16]*Horatii/Curiatii* are plurals, *Horatius/Curiatius* singular.

David's *Oath of the Horatii*

Little was known of ancient art and architecture until the mid-eighteenth century, when several publications by seasoned travelers who had visited the ruins of ancient cities in the Near East and Greece inspired an enthusiasm for all things ancient and classical. Between 1776 and 1788 appeared Edward Gibbon's long and learned *The Decline and Fall of the Roman Empire,* which has never been out of print. Sensational archaeological discoveries at Pompeii and Herculaneum, beginning in 1748, fed the admiration for classical antiquity, and in 1755 the founder of ancient art history, Johann Winckelmann, published (in German) his *Thoughts on the Imitation of Greek Art in Painting and Sculpture.* Such developments inspired an artistic movement called Neoclassicism, which lasted well into the nineteenth century. Its central idea was of an unchanging eternal truth underlying appearance (in this

FIG. P 22.1. Jacques Louis David (1748–1825), *Oath of the Horatii,* 1784–1785, oil on canvas.   (Musée du Louvre, Paris; 3692)

respect, Neoclassicism shared intellectual foundations with Renaissance neoplatonism).

In France, Jacques Louis David (da-**vēd**, 1748–1825) was a leading exponent of the movement, and his *Oath of the Horatii* of 1784 illustrates his political didacticism and admiration for classical geometric form (Fig. P 22.1). The story was familiar to Parisian audiences not only through Livy, but through a play by Pierre Corneille (1606–1684; see Perspective 18.2). The picture shows the three brothers as they swear on their swords to return with their shields or upon them, oblivious to the anguish of their sisters, one of whom is engaged to a Curiatius. The figures, enclosed by a rigorous architectural frame, are sculpted in the near foreground like ancient reliefs and posed almost like statues. The stiff, manly forms of the warriors contrast with the soft, grieving women: The men embody the superior and virile qualities of patriotism, duty, and dedication to the state, while the women give in to love and sorrow.

David's hard-edged, glazed paintings reveal the painter–ideologist of the French Revolution. He was a friend of Robespierre and a member of the National Convention that voted for the execution of King Louis XVI. As Roman myth served as propaganda for the Roman empire, so did David's paintings for the Napoleonic era. He believed that the "marks of heroism and civic virtue offered to the eyes of the people will electrify its soul, and plant the seeds of glory and devotion to the fatherland." The picture aroused a great commotion when placed on public view in 1785. Henceforth European art became increasingly political in its aims.

Servius Tullius ruled long and well, and his daughters, both named Tullia,[17] married sons of Tarquin the Elder, the murdered fifth king of Rome. But when Servius Tullius grew old, one of the Tullias, a woman as wicked as Clytemnestra, began a passionate love affair with her brother-in-law, soon to be the seventh and last king of Rome, called **Tarquin the Proud.** She urged him to murder his wife (her sister) and his brother (her husband) and to get rid of her father (Servius Tullius) so that together they could rule Rome. Soon they were married to one another, and one day Tarquin the Proud sat down in Tullius' seat in the Senate house. When the old king came to see what was happening, Tarquin hurled him down the steps into the street. At that moment the wicked Tullia herself arrived in the Forum. Livy tells the story:

> Everybody agrees that Tullia, driving her carriage into the Forum, paid no attention to the assembled crowd of men, but shouted to her husband to come out from the Senate House, and was the first to hail him as king. He told her to go away, because the crowd might become dangerous. But on her way home she had just reached the top of Cyprian Street (where the Temple of Diana stood until a little while ago) and was turning right onto the Urban Hill to get to the Esquiline, when her coachman halted in terror, reined in the

---

[17]Roman women had no first names: they bore the name of their *gens* with a feminine ending (Julia, Cornelia) and, if necessary, a number (Claudia Quinta = Claudia the fifth, Antonia Minor = Antonia the younger).

horses, and showed her the mutilated body of Servius Tullius as it lay in the road. The savage and brutal act Tullia then committed is commemorated by the place it occurred, which they now call Crime Alley (*vicus sceleratus*). For it was there that Tullia, crazed by the vengeful spirits of her sister and husband, is said to have driven her carriage right over her father's corpse. She herself was spattered with his blood, and on the gory vehicle she brought back bits of his flesh to the household of herself and her husband. The gods of the home were so enraged by this terrible start of Tarquin's reign that an equally terrible end presently caught up with the pair.

LIVY, Ab urbe condita (1.48.5–7)

In the days of Tarquin the Proud, the patrician fear of excessive power in one man's hands was fully realized. The king laid terrible burdens on his people and was feared by all.

Lucretia and the End of Monarchy

Several young army officers, including Tarquin's son Sextus Tarquin (= Tarquin the Sixth) and his cousin Tarquin Collatinus, were on military service near Rome. They were comparing the beauty and virtue of their wives, each boasting that his wife was most virtuous. To settle the argument they visited Rome unannounced to see what the women were doing. They found most of the women drinking and gossiping, but **Lucretia** (lu-**krē**-sha), wife of Tarquin Collatinus, was virtuously spinning wool with her women servants. Sextus Tarquin, astonished by her beauty no less than by her modesty, formed a vile plan.

Returning alone a few nights later, he was politely received, but as soon as the house was quiet he drew his sword and demanded that she yield to him. When she indignantly refused, he threatened to kill her and one of her slaves, then tell her husband that he had found the pair together in bed, thus joining shame to her death. Lucretia sadly gave in, but the next day summoned her family and a few friends, including a certain Lucius Brutus, associate of her husband and a cousin of the Tarquins. His real name was Lucius Junius, but to ensure his safety he had carefully cultivated the appearance of a fool, and so received the nickname Brutus, "stupid":

> Shattered by such a horror, Lucretia sent the same message to her father in Rome and her husband in Ardea, to come to her, each with one trustworthy friend; both speed and action were imperative; something dreadful had happened. Spurius Lucretius came with Publius Valerius, the son of Volesus, and Tarquin Collatinus with Lucius Junius Brutus, with whom he happened to be returning to Rome when he met the messenger. They found Lucretia sitting dejectedly in her bedroom; tears sprang to her eyes when her husband asked her, "Are you all right?" "Certainly not," she answered, "How can a woman be all right when her shame and modesty have been torn away? In your bed, Collatinus, are the marks of another man. But only my body has been violated; my soul is still guiltless—and this I shall prove by my death. But this you must promise: the adulterer shall not go untouched. He is Sextus Tarquin, who

PERSPECTIVE 22.2

The *Lucretia* of Rembrandt and Shakespeare

Rembrandt van Rijn (1606–1669) was a prolific painter and printmaker who produced some three thousand works of art. In 1664 he painted the first of two versions of the rape of Lucretia (Fig. P 22.2). He selects the moment just before Lucretia plunges the knife into her breast. Lucretia wears a red gown with white drapery at bust, a style contemporary with the artist. Her body faces the viewer squarely, but her head turns away in shame. Immediately noticeable is the deathly pallor of her face. She has just told her tale of rape and demanded revenge, then drawn the hidden dagger. With her other hand she keeps her family at a distance. Rembrandt may depend partly on Livy's account, but his more likely inspiration is a famous poem of Shakespeare, *The Rape of Lucrece* (1,855 lines), published in 1594 and influential throughout Europe. In the following selection, Sextus Tarquin has stolen into Lucrece's bedchamber:

> Lucrece, quoth he, this night I must enjoy thee.
> If thou deny, then force must work my way,
> For in thy bed I purpose to destroy thee.
> That done, some worthless slave of thine I'll slay,
> To kill thine honour with thy life's decay;
>   And in thy dead arms do I mean to place him,

FIG. P 22.2. Rembrandt van Rijn (Dutch, 1606–1669), *Lucretia,* 1664, oil on canvas. (National Gallery of Art, Washington; Andrew Mellon Collection)

Swearing I slew him, seeing thee embrace him.
So thy surviving husband shall remain
The scornful mark of every open eye;
Thy kinsmen hang their heads at this disdain,
Thy issue blurr'd with nameless bastardy;
And thou the author of their obloquy,
    Shalt have thy trespass cited up in rhymes.
    And sung by children in succeeding times.
But if thou yield, I rest thy secret friend.
The fault unknown is as a thought unacted.

(512–528)

Lucretia yields but the next morning, dressed in mourning, calls her father and husband:

Here with a sigh as if her heart would break,
She throws forth Tarquin's name. He, he, she says,
But more than "he" her poor tongue could not speak,
Till after many accents and delays,
Untimely breathings, sick and short assays,
    She utters this "He, he, fair lords, 'tis he
    That guides this hand to give this wound to me."
Even here she sheathed in her harmless breast
A harmful knife, that thence her soul unsheathed.

(1716–1724)

After much lamenting, the soldiers carry Lucrece's bleeding body through Rome, denouncing Tarquin for his dastardly deed. Seeing her thus, "The Romans plausibly did give consent / To Tarquin's everlasting banishment" (1854–1855).

came last night in the guise of a friend, but in fact a bitter enemy, and made a plunder of this delight, a plunder deadly to me—and, if you are men, to himself." One after the other the men promised what she asked, meanwhile trying to console her sorrow by shifting the blame from the victim to the guilty man: crime, they assured her, was a matter of the mind, not the body, and where there was no intent there could be no offense. But Lucretia only answered, "You must determine his punishment. As for me, even though I acquit myself of guilt, I must still pay the penalty; from now on no adulteress can live with Lucretia as her model." She had hidden a dagger in her clothing; at this she plunged it into her heart and fell dying upon her wound.

Livy, *Ab urbe condita* (1.58.5–12)

Brutus drew the gory dagger from her breast, and on its hilt swore to drive out the Tarquins. He summoned the people, repeated the tale, and led them in the expulsion of the tyrant and his brood. A new order was established. Henceforth the state would be ruled by the Senate, presided over by two consuls, and there would be no more kings. The state was to be a *res publica,* a "public affair," not a plaything of kings. The first two consuls were Brutus himself and Tarquin Collatinus, the husband of Lucretia.

HEROES OF THE EARLY REPUBLIC

Many patriotic tales, designed to inculcate traditional values, were told of early figures in the newly organized state.

Brutus and His Sons

Brutus, "founder of the Roman Republic," allegedly the ancestor of Marcus Brutus, a leader in the conspiracy to murder Julius Caesar, had his own story. One day, before the revolution, a serpent appeared in the royal palace. Alarmed, Tarquin the Proud sent his two sons to ask the Delphic Oracle what he should do. For laughs the envoys took "stupid" Brutus along. The oracle ignored their direct inquiry but reported, "He who first kisses his mother will succeed to the highest place in Rome." Returning to Rome, the sons ran to kiss their mother, but the clever Brutus, who saw the oracle's true meaning, pretended to stumble, fell to the ground, and kissed the earth—the mother of all. Of course he became one of the first consuls.

For some reason Brutus' own sons were unhappy with the Tarquins' expulsion and plotted with the enemy to overthrow the newly founded Republic. When caught, they made no defense; the evidence was incontrovertible. Brutus handed them over to the lictors, who threw the boys to the ground, whipped them with their rods, then beheaded them with the ax. Although others turned away, Brutus, as his office required, kept his eyes fixed on the execution: Criminals against Rome must pay the price, and sentiment had no place in obedience to the state. Brutus fell in battle fighting the Etruscans, serving his country to the last.

Horatius at the Bridge

Tarquin the Proud fled from Rome into Etruria, his homeland, and appealed to Lars Porsenna, an Etruscan king, to restore him. Porsenna raised a great army, marched on Rome, and ravaged the countryside, but could not reach the city until he captured the only bridge across the Tiber. **Horatius** Cocles (ho-**rā**-shus **kō**-klēz) and two others occupied the northern end of the bridge to hold off the foe, until the rest of the Romans could chop down the bridge behind them. Horatius' companions retreated just before it fell, but Horatius, wounded, was forced to swim back in full armor—a model of bravery for every good Roman.

Mucius Scaevola

While the Etruscans lay encamped across the river, one of Rome's bravest men, Gaius Mucius (**mū**-shus), sneaked through the enemy lines, determined to kill Porsenna.

He approached where the king sat with his nobles, but, not knowing the king's appearance, he killed the king's secretary by mistake. Brought before the Etruscan king, he announced that he was but the first of three hundred Romans who had sworn to kill the invader. To prove his determination, Mucius held his right hand in the fire on an altar until it was burned off. Porsenna was so impressed that he gave up his attack and sent Mucius in honor back to Rome, where he received the nickname **Scaevola** (sē-vo-la, "Lefty").

Thus the Etruscans were expelled from Rome forever, and the Republic was firmly established.

Other Patriotic Heroes

Many other patriotic tales were told of the early days of the Republic. Gnaeus Marcius had earned the name **Coriolanus** (ko-ri-ō-lā-nus) by conquering the town of Corioli. Despite his glorious service to the state, he was expelled from the city because of his intolerable arrogance and opposition to men of common birth, the plebeians. In anger, he went over to the hostile city of Volsci and led them against Rome. Rome was in mortal peril. Although the senators begged Coriolanus not to destroy his own people, he was deaf to their plea. Only when his wife, carrying their young sons, and his mother ran between the armies into the battlefield and begged him to relent did Coriolanus at last withdraw.[18] To preserve the memory of his mother and wife as fine examples of Roman womanhood, the Romans built a temple to the Destiny of Women but exiled Coriolanus; on his return to the Volscians, he was assassinated by its disappointed rulers.

Cincinnatus (sin-sin-ā-tus), an exconsul, was living and working with his own hands on his farm in 458 B.C. when word was brought that, to repel an enemy attack, he had been chosen dictator, a legal office of one-man rule used in extreme emergencies. He left his plow, saved the Roman army, defeated the enemy, and returned to his farm—all within sixteen days.[19]

OBSERVATIONS: AN IMAGINARY PAST PRESERVES THE PRESENT

There was very little change in Rome's system of government for five hundred years between the sixth and first centuries B.C. The external world, by contrast, changed enormously, swiftly, and radically between the founding of the Republic, when Rome controlled perhaps 100 square miles, and the murder of Caesar, when Rome controlled most of Europe and the Mediterranean world. Rarely in human history has a small power grown so large so fast, and never has a political power lasted so long.

---

[18]Shakespeare wrote a play on the topic, *Coriolanus.*
[19]This inspiring tale of dedication to the simple life, constant readiness, and selfless devotion to the state gave the name to the Society of the Cincinnati, a fraternal and patriotic organization founded in 1783 by officers of the Continental Army, including George Washington, after the American Revolution. The society still exists and has given its name to the city of Cincinnati.

The Roman political achievement is unparalleled in history and is likely never to be equaled.

Rome was not a tyrant state, gobbling up everything in its path, taking what it wanted and offering nothing in return. Control by Rome was in most cases preferable to the dangers of freedom, for Rome offered military protection in a cut-throat world, communication, free trade across the wonderful Roman roads, equal treatment (in theory) under written law, and freedom from religious and social persecution. Military superiority may grant any state an initial advantage over its neighbors, but only moral advantage can bestow permanence to conquest and rule.

This moral advantage, as the Romans themselves understood it, was responsible for Roman victory where others failed. Changes in the size of the empire, and in the way of life that followed the accumulation of enormous wealth in the hands of the Roman ruling class, were viewed as superficial and incidental. The Romans wanted to know where they came from and how they got to where they were, but surviving traditions about the early days were unreliable. The Trojan ancestry of the Romans was first suggested by Greek historians of Sicily, a suggestion the Romans discovered, and approved, after entering into relations with the Greeks living in the West. Perhaps building on a local story, they claimed that the Trojan Aeneas' descendants, Romulus and Remus, founded the city of Rome four hundred years after Aeneas. But the monarchy that Romulus founded had concentrated power in the hands of one man, anathema to the ideals of the expanding Roman state; the Republic, by contrast, spread power among a small class, the very class that directed Rome's expansion and benefited from it. Thus did Roman stories also support ideals of the Roman Republic through examples of men—such as Coriolanus—who at first helped the city, then came to a bad end for "aiming at the kingship." During the one-man rule of Augustus, and his successors, the trick was to pretend that nothing had changed; for this reason Augustus always called himself *princeps,* "first citizen," never *rex,* "king." Only some were fooled. Roman legend was an important force in stabilizing and conserving the Roman state, but in the end Time, the great devourer, swallowed that too.

KEY TERMS

numen, numina, 598
Janus, 599
Jupiter, 600
Juno, 600
Ceres, 600
Diana, 600
Mercury, 600
Vulcan, 601
Neptune, 601
Mars, 601
Minerva, 601
Faunus, 601

Venus, 601
Hercules, 601
Lares, 602
Penates, 602
Vesta, 603
pietas, 604
Iulus, 606
Dido, 607
Turnus, 611
Romulus, 615
Remus, 615

Rhea Silvia, 616
Sabines, 618
Tarpeia, 618
Horatii and the Curiatii, 619
Tarquin the Proud, 621
Lucretia, 622
Brutus, 625
Horatius, 625
Scaevola, 626
Coriolanus, 626
Cincinnatus, 626

FURTHER READING

Bloom, Harold, *Virgil: Modern Critical Views* (New York, 1986). Collection of essays by leading scholars.

Bremmer, J. N., and N. M. Horsfall, *Roman Myth and Mythography* (London, University of London, Institute of Classical Studies, No. 52, 1987). A scholarly but readable and original study of several Roman myths, including Aeneas and Romulus and Remus.

Cairns, Francis, *Virgil's Augustan Epic* (Cambridge, U.K., 1989). The interrelation between poetry and politics in Vergil's Rome.

Donaldson, Ian, *The Rapes of Lucretia: A Myth and Its Transformations* (New York, 1982). Reviews the legend throughout European literature.

Dumézil, Georges, *Archaic Roman Religion*, 2 vols., trans. Philip Krapp (Chicago, 1970). A long, learned, and often compelling study that attempts to justify Dumézil's theory about the tripartite structure of early Indo-European society (see Chapter 23).

Galinsky, G. Karl, *Aeneas, Sicily, and Rome* (Princeton, N. J., 1969). The origins of the legend of Aeneas, with much interesting evidence from art and archaeological finds.

Gardner, Jane F., *Roman Myths* (Austin, Tex., 1993). Succinct review with good illustrations.

Grant, Michael, *Roman Myths* (New York, 1971). A complete review, accessible to the amateur and attractive to the specialist.

Livy, *The Early History of Rome,* trans. Aubrey de Sélincourt (Baltimore, 1960). A principal source for Roman myth. Contains Books 1–5 of Livy's great *The History of Rome from Its Foundations.*

Rose, H. J., *Religion in Greece and Rome* (New York, 1959). Contains succinct, scholarly, although somewhat old-fashioned synopses.

Wiseman, T. P., *Remus, A Roman Myth* (Cambridge, U.K., 1996). Ingenious and learned attempt to explain why Romulus murdered Remus.

CHAPTER 23

THEORIES OF MYTH INTERPRETATION

There are no facts; only interpretations.

FRIEDRICH NIETZSCHE (1844–1900)

W̲HERE DO MYTHS COME FROM? What do these stories handed down from the unknown past, often bizarre or mysterious, signify? Disturbed by the irrational and often immoral content of their traditional tales, Greek intellectuals had already posed these questions in ancient times, initiating a long tradition of theoretical inquiry into the nature and meaning of myth. Some ancient Greeks rejected the traditional stories completely, but others developed elaborate theories to show that the myths contained profound truths, despite their initial implausibility. This tradition was developed further in the medieval period and the Renaissance. In the modern era, with the development of new fields of inquiry, the factual or philosophic truth of myth has ceased to be the only question considered. Anthropologists, for example, are concerned with the social function of myth, and psychologists develop theories about the emotional needs that myth reflects and satisfies. In the following pages we trace some of the major phases in the history of the interpretation of myth from ancient to modern times.

GREEK THEORIES

Through their **rationalism** the Greeks were the first people to become fully self-conscious and critical of their own traditions. The inquiry was closely bound up with

Greek philosophy, which began partly in speculation about the nature of myth, then developed into a system of reasoning about causes and effects and about the nature of things that was independent of traditional—that is, mythical—explanations. The Greek philosophers wanted to reduce dependence on explanations that used the anthropomorphic categories of Greek religion so prominent in Greek traditional tales. They criticized the traditional stories for their implausible and irrational details or immoral content. Already in the sixth century B.C. **Xenophanes** (ksen-o-fan-ēz) of Colophon (in Asia Minor) complained of the ethical weakness of the Olympians, insisting that popular notions about the gods must be wrong:

> In my opinion mortals have created their gods with the dress and voice and appearance of mortals. If cattle and horses had hands and wanted to draw or carve as men do, the cattle would show their gods in the form of cattle and horses would show them as horses, with the same form and appearance as their own. The Ethiopians say that their gods have snub noses and black skins, while the Thracians say that theirs have blue eyes and red hair.

XENOPHANES, fragment 21 B 14–16 (Diels–Krans)

And

> One god is greatest among gods and men, but his appearance and thought are nothing like ours.

XENOPHANES, fragment 21 B 23 (Diels–Krans)

Xenophanes, who lived about two hundred years after Homer, questions the very existence of the gods that populate Greek myth and, by implication, attacks the truth of the traditional tales cherished by the Greeks as their cultural heritage. Plato, a friend of Socrates and founder of the immensely influential Academy during the fourth century B.C. in Athens, criticized such tales even more severely. He thought that the irrational stories of Homer and other poets had a corrupting influence because they presented to the untutored mind a false image of reality. In his ideal state, described in *The Republic*, Plato banned the poets and their lying tales. On the other hand, Plato was aware that some important truths lie beyond the grasp of human reason. Indeed, the burden of his philosophy was to demonstrate the existence of timeless eternal realities that lay behind the transient and changing surface of the everyday world, realities Plato called "Ideas" or "Forms" (Greek *eidos* = "shape").[1] Although opposing traditional myth, Plato considered mythlike stories to be an appropriate vehicle for giving expression to these truths. So he wrote his own "myths," dealing especially with the soul's fate after death as in the "myth of Er" ("eschatological myth," see Chapter 11) but also with the nature of being and of the perfect political order. The "myth of Atlantis," a wealthy powerful city on an island that later disappeared beneath the sea, was Plato's invention.

Other Greek thinkers went beyond Plato, asserting that even the traditional myths Plato had criticized so vigorously could be seen to contain a kernel of philo-

---

[1] Hence our word *idealism,* belief in values not apparent in the material world.

sophical or historical truth. The task, they thought, was to interpret the myths so that this kernel would come to light. Despite their bizarre or immoral content, the traditional stories meant something other than what they appeared at first glance to mean. Therefore, there was no need to dismiss the myths as mere errors, containing nothing that need be taken seriously. They must be allegories, the Greeks argued, stories that look like one thing on the surface but are really something else inside.

Allegory is a Greek word that means "saying something in a different way" or "saying something different from what appears to be said." In allegorizing myth, the story is translated from its initial frame of reference into another that is more acceptable. For example, Daphnê's transformation into a laurel tree to escape the clutches of Apollo can be explained as an allegory about chastity. The story does not mean that a girl, pursued by Apollo, literally was changed into a tree, but promulgates the view that abstinence from sexual intercourse can, at least for a woman, be desirable. Allegory is closely related to **symbolism,** "something put together with something else," because in both allegory and symbolism one thing points to and brings another thing to mind. Thus Daphnê can be interpreted as a symbol of virginity.

The allegorical or symbolic meaning found in any given story depended entirely on the frame of reference that the ancient interpreter believed to be true. Because Greek philosophers were concerned primarily with "the truth" in such fields as cosmology, history, and—as in the case of Daphnê—morality, the meanings they found in myth generally originated in these spheres.

Physical Allegory

Theagenes (thē-**a**-jen-ēz), who lived in southern Italy during the later sixth century B.C., is said to have been the first to use the allegorical method. None of his writing survives, but later commentators say that he explained mythical accounts of battle among the gods as representing conflicts among natural forces. In Theagenes' cosmology, dry is opposite to wet, hot to cold; water extinguishes fire, fire evaporates water. Such natural oppositions, Theagenes thought, must be embodied in Homer's story in the *Iliad* (20.54ff.) of Apollo who, armed with his arrows, faces Poseidon: Apollo stands for fire, Poseidon for water. The mythical conflict of the two gods is the allegorical expression of a basic cosmological principle concerning the opposition of fire and water. Other allegorists did not hesitate to apply allegory in psychological interpretations as well, making Athena personify rational thought; Ares, irrational violence; Aphrodite, desire; and Hermes, reason.

During the Hellenistic Period, the Stoic philosophers refined physical allegory into a powerful tool that could be applied to any myth. For example, they argued that the Greek creation myths contained profound truths about the origin of the universe. The story of Uranus' castration was explained as meaning that the original creative element of the universe, "fiery air" (= Uranus), begot its offspring spontaneously without the assistance of sexual union. Likewise, the Stoics identified Cronus with *chronos* = "time," and his role in creation was interpreted to mean that all things were begotten by time. The children of Cronus are the ages, and the story that

Cronus devoured them means that "time consumes the ages." The story that Zeus overthrew Cronus and bound him in the underworld means that time, although great in extent, is nonetheless limited (compare Perspective 4.1).

The interpretation of Cronus as *chronos* illustrates how the Stoics used **etymology,** speculation about "the true meaning of a word" to reinforce allegory; they believed that the meaning of a word or name can reveal the meaning of a myth. The famous biographer Plutarch (c. A.D. 50–125) offers another example. He interprets the story of Demeter and Persephonê as an allegory conveying an important insight about life after death. According to Plutarch, Demeter is the earth, Hades the shadow cast by the earth, and Persephonê the moon, which reflects the light of the sun. He proves this by reminding us that Persephonê's other name, Korê, means in Greek not only "girl," but also "pupil of the eye." As the eye (Korê = "pupil") acts like a mirror reflecting little images of objects, so does the moon reflect the light of the sun. Korê, or pupil/Persephonê, is the moon, and the story of Persephonê's descent into the underworld and subsequent return refers to the waxing and waning of the moon, when the moon slips in and out of the shadow of the earth, Hades' realm. By extension, the story of Persephonê's descent and return means that after losing their bodies at death, human beings exist as souls and minds in Hades. If they are blameless, however, they may subsequently escape to the sun as pure minds. By adding a philosophical meaning, Plutarch's physical allegory turns the myth into a vehicle for deeper truth.

The etymologies offered by the Stoics, which depended on similarity in sound, must have seemed reasonable in a society where myth was still part of the living, aural language. In reality, their etymologies were often quite fantastic because the science of linguistics was unknown in the ancient world. We now know that the name Cronus is etymologically unrelated to the word *chronos*. But through this false etymology arose the common picture of Father Time as the Grim Reaper, an old man carrying a sickle, because C(h)ronus/Time castrated his father with a sickle.

Roman writers who followed the Stoic philosophy also used Latin etymologies to interpret myths. For example, they argued that Juno (corresponding to Hera in Greek myth) was really air because the Greek (and Latin) word for air (*aêr, aura*) sounded like *Hera*. This etymology was supported by the belief that air lay just beneath the aether, or upper atmosphere, symbolized in myth by Jupiter. The position of air (= Juno) just beneath aether (= Jupiter, Juno's mate) was the true meaning of the story that Jupiter united with Juno in sexual embrace.

These physical allegorical interpretations attempted to explain a cultural inheritance from a distant, preliterate past in light of sophisticated philosophical thought about forces in nature. The allegorists had no notion that myths arose at different times and in different cultural conditions and for different reasons (a mistake easy to make). Through their explanations, the allegorists were able to maintain the respectability of the traditional tales, which were otherwise liable to rejection because of their patent factual errors or offensive moral content. In addition to protecting the respectability and social utility of traditional stories, physical allegory was a philosophically respectable way of bringing to light hidden, even mysterious truths about the world.

Historical Allegory: Euhemerism

Allegorical interpretation of myth goes back to the sixth century B.C., but about 300 B.C. the Greek mythographer Euhemerus (ū-**hē**-mer-us) offered a new approach, according to which myth was thought to reveal historical rather than cosmological truth. Euhemerus wrote a book describing a journey to three fabulously wealthy islands in the Indian Ocean. On the main island, Panchaea (modeled after Plato's Atlantis), Euhemerus said that he had found a golden column on which was inscribed the history of the reigns of early human kings. This alleged history suggested a very different interpretation of Greek myth.

First to rule, according to Euhemerus' story, was Uranus, so called because he was learned in the study of the heavens. From union with his human wife, Hestia, Uranus begot the Titans and Cronus. The column gave further information about Uranus' successors, Cronus, Zeus, and their families. The war in heaven and Cronus' swallowing his children were explained as recollections of palace intrigues. During his reign, according to the column, Zeus was said to have traveled the earth teaching the arts of civilized life, banning such reprehensible religious practices as cannibalism and founding temples. According to the story, he actually lived for a while on Mount Olympus, then, at the end of a long life, Zeus retired to Crete, died, and was buried near Cnossus. That is why the Cretans spoke of "the tomb of Zeus."

Although Euhemerus' story of the inscribed column is a fiction, his underlying theory is quite plausible and enters many modern interpretations of myth. By asserting that gods were in origin great men, so respected that they were worshiped after death, he attempted to explain myth as a form of early history. From his book comes the modern term *euhemerism,* the thesis that gods once were human. Many features of the Greek mythical tradition lent themselves to explanation along these lines. After all, the gods were organized in a family on Olympus, and they looked and acted like Greek aristocrats. The god Asclepius shows many signs of having once been a real man, a famous doctor.[2] As for such deified heroes as Heracles, everyone always thought them to be real men anyway, who had actually lived, founded cities, and done great deeds. Euhemerus' thesis derived convenient support from the politics of Hellenistic monarchs, especially in Egypt, who presented themselves to their peoples as gods incarnate and who included the native gods in their dynastic genealogies. The deification of dead Hellenistic rulers made more plausible the notion that great humans of the past had, with the passage of time, become more than human. Behind myth lay history.

An approach closely related to that of Euhemerus is found in a handbook on myth called *On Incredible Things,* of which an excerpt survives, written by Palaephatus (pal-**ē**-fat-us), a contemporary of Euhemerus. Palaephatus' special contribution was to explain myths as originating from a misunderstanding of language. According to Palaephatus, Actaeon, for example, was not really transformed into a stag and torn apart by his dogs; rather, he was ruined by spending too much money on his hunting dogs. The myth arose when neighborhood gossip began to tell of how "poor

---

[2]Recent research suggests that in fact he was a healing god from the northern Levant.

Actaeon is being devoured by his dogs." Similarly, the Lernaean Hydra against which Heracles fought was not really a many-headed monster, although Palaephatus' interpretation of this myth is more complex. Lernus, he claimed, was a king in the Peloponnesus who went to war with the Mycenaeans. Near Lernus' border was a town called Hydra, garrisoned by fifty archers in a tower. According to Palaephatus, Heracles was sent with some troops to attack the town, but when he used fire against the archers, two new ones would take the place of every one who fell. Lernus called in additional help from a mercenary army led by a certain Carcinus (= "crab"). Carcinus was so effective that Iphicles, Heracles' nephew, had to come to his uncle's aid with another contingent from Thebes. At last they succeeded in burning Hydra. In origin, then, the myth told of a "General Heracles who destroyed Watertown ('Hydra'), defended by General Crabb, by using fire as an assault weapon against persistent defenders." The interpretation of myth as a "disease of language" was to undergo a surprisingly successful renaissance in the theories of Max Müller in the nineteenth century A.D. (see later in this chapter).

Moral Allegory

The interpretation of myth as a system of advice on good and bad behavior, or moral allegory, was more highly developed than physical or historical allegory. We have already seen a crude example of it in the explanation of the story of Apollo and Daphnê as exhorting young women to remain chaste. So the Harpies who rob Phineus of his food are really prostitutes who ruin young men through their high fees. The goddesses in the Judgment of Paris represent three kinds of life: the active (Hera), the contemplative (Athena), and the amorous (Aphrodite), among which every man (Paris) must choose. The coupling of Leda and the Swan is an allegory for the joining of Power (Zeus) and Injustice (Leda, who is raped), whose fruit is inevitably scandal and discord (Helen).

   Such interpretations, like those of the physical and historical allegorists, fail to preserve myth, whatever the intentions of their practitioners, for they remove the charm of the original story and replace it with a trite truism or historical or physical incident. An intellectual movement linked loosely to Platonism dealt with myth more positively and gently. Although Plato himself rejected traditional myths, later writers influenced by Plato were able to find in these same myths allegorical expressions of profound metaphysical truths. In the final centuries of the pagan era (A.D. 200–500), a school known as **neoplatonism** revived and developed many of Plato's theories and became the major philosophic movement of the day. Neoplatonists, like their founder, Plato, believed in a higher dimension of reality beyond the limits of time and space, where perfection and absolute truth—that which is always and everywhere the same—could be found. This higher world is accessible to us through our minds, if they are freed from our bodies and senses. The material universe, by contrast, yields only an inferior knowledge based on sense perception, at best imperfect and ultimately false because everything in the material world is always changing. The material world in which we live, reported to us by our senses, is nonetheless to some extent modeled after the perfect rational world. By virtue of that

Apuleius' Allegory of Cupid and Psychê

Sometimes allegory is an interpretation that the interpreter teases out of the story, suggesting, for example, that the marriage of Zeus/Jupiter and Hera/Juno really refers to the Upper Air, which lies upon the Lower. At other times, the allegory appears to have been consciously in the mind of the storyteller. The philosopher Apuleius of Madaura in North Africa (mid–second century A.D.) included one such story, much beloved in Europe after the Middle Ages, in a long Latin prose novel titled, like Ovid's work, the *Metamorphoses,* but usually called *The Golden Ass.* The story, told by an old woman to comfort a girl kidnapped by robbers, tells of the love between Cupid (= Greek Eros), "sexual desire," and Psychê (sī-kē), "soul," a Greek word almost as vague as the English.

Psychê was the youngest and most beautiful of three sisters, so beautiful that she aroused the jealousy of Venus. No one dared court her for fear of the goddess, and her father consulted an oracle, which ordered him to dress her as if for a marriage, but then to expose her on a cliff to a winged monster of whom even Zeus was afraid. Psychê, left alone, was picked up by a wind that bore her to a garden of a beautiful palace; a delicious meal was set for her and heavenly music played, although no one was in sight. She went to bed and in the black of night awoke to realize that someone was in bed with her, who warned her that she must never see him or she would lose him forever. Her new husband visited her night after blissful night, but she never saw him by day. Reluctantly, he allowed her to have her sisters visit her. Fiercely jealous, they persuaded her to kill her husband, who, they insisted, was the monster of whom the oracle had spoken. Psychê therefore armed herself with a knife, lit a lamp, and entered her bedroom; so surprised was she to see the handsome, sleeping young man with wings that she let a drop of hot oil fall on him. Cupid—for it was he—leaped up, flew to the top of a tree, and bade poor Psychê farewell. The girl rushed off in despair to one of her sisters, told her the whole story, and added that her husband had announced that he much preferred the sister. The vain woman ran to a cliff and jumped off, expecting to be borne up by the wind, but was dashed to bits on the rocks. The same thing was repeated with the second sister.

Cupid, tormented by the hot oil, could not protect Psychê from the anger of his mother, Venus, who, aided by her servants Convention, Worry, and Gloom, beat and tormented the girl. She was forced to sort a heap of mixed seeds in one night; she succeeded when a swarm of ants came to her aid. She had to bring golden wool from a flock of man-eating sheep by a river; friendly reeds plucked it for her. She had to bring Venus water from a stream guarded by a dragon; the eagle of Zeus himself fetched it for her. Finally, she had to go down to Hades to bring back the Water of Youth—a journey beset with traps laid by Venus. The girl evaded all these, but finally, although forbidden, drank some of the water, and at once fell into a profound sleep.

Cupid had by now recovered. He found Psychê, awakened her with a prick of his arrows, and appealed to Zeus to let him have his beloved. Zeus consented, Venus was appeased, they had a grand marriage feast, and Psychê became immortal.

The story contains many motifs familiar from folktale: the jealous sisters, like those of Cinderella; and miraculous assistance at an impossible task, like that of the dwarf who spun Rapunzel's gold. Like many of the stories of the Grimm brothers, this too is told by an old serving woman. On the other hand, the frame is that of an intentional allegory—a story with a further meaning obvious from the names of the characters: the longing of Soul (Psychê) for union with Desire (Cupid), who must overcome hindrances set up by Convention, Worry, and Gloom.

connection, the changing, imperfect material world has many features that point to, or symbolize, the unchanging perfect blueprint that lies behind the corrupt world of the senses. Thus transient physical beauty, such as a sunset, symbolizes eternal beauty. In the same way, say the neoplatonists, myths give us hints about the moral world beyond. Neoplatonism lends itself to allegory, although of a kind that does not reduce myth to literal fact but expands it into a vehicle for discovering profound truths, usually moral, about a higher domain hidden behind appearance (compare Perspective 8.1).

Plotinus, the founder of neoplatonism in the third century A.D., held that myth describes timeless realities in the form of temporal events. He saw a correspondence between the sequence

- Uranus

- Cronus

- Zeus

and the three great principles of reality:

- Unity (unchanging, the same in all parts = Uranus)

- Intellect (unchanging, but plural = Cronus)

- Soul (plural and subject to change and motion = Zeus)

Plotinus' student Porphyry produced an extremely complex interpretation of Homer's description of the cave of the nymphs on Ithaca, where Odysseus hides his treasure after returning from his wanderings (*Odyssey* 13.102–112). The cave, he argues, represents the universe because it is generated from matter and its natural; the nymphs, as spirits of water, represent the ceaseless flow of events within time; the looms of stone on which they weave represent souls descending to incarnation, as the flesh is woven on the bones (the stones of the body). The moral truths are obvious: The material world, including our bodies, is an illusion and unworthy of our aspiration. The increasing interest of neoplatonists in such allegories reflects an effort to rehabilitate myth and to establish its value for revealing higher truths in face of the growing threat from Christianity. In the end Christianity swallowed neoplatonism: St. Augustine (A.D. 354–430) began as a dualist (believer in two opposed principles), became a neoplatonist, and ended as one of the greatest of Christian theologians.

MEDIEVAL AND RENAISSANCE THEORIES

Platonic modes of thinking exerted powerful influence on early Christian theology. Both myth itself and the various methods devised for interpreting it were part and parcel of the cultural heritage taken over by the church. Although some church fathers rejected allegory on the ground that it was a way of holding onto pagan myth, most found allegorical interpretations a legitimate way to interpret pagan myth, especially when a moral encouragement of righteous conduct could be found lurking within the tale. The allegorical method whereby moral meanings were drawn from old stories was also applied extensively to the Bible. For example, the frankly erotic content of the *Song of Solomon,* which tells of sexual love between a man and a woman, was explained as an allegory of God's love for the church (in fact the poem descends from secular Egyptian love poetry). Euhemerism was a useful method of analysis for the Christians because it served to justify the authority of the church by proving that pagan religion was idolatry, just as Christians and Jews had always maintained.

The ancient methods of interpretation lived on, but direct acquaintance with classical culture and its literature declined drastically, especially in the Latin-speaking West. The myths were now known principally through handbooks, which became increasingly important and elaborate. One of the most influential was the *Mythologies* of Fulgentius (ful-**jen**-shus), a North African Christian of the sixth century A.D. On reading his account of some god, the reader would find a succinct entry that included both the facts of the story and a moral based on an allegorical interpretation.[3] For example, the story of Liber (the Latin equivalent of the Greek Dionysus) was understood to be an allegory in which Semelê and her three sisters represent four stages of intoxication: (1) too much wine, (2) the forgetfulness it causes, (3) lust, and (4) sheer madness. The interpretation is supported with typical etymological explanations: the first sister (and first stage of drunkenness) is *Ino,* linked to *vinum* and *oinos,* the Latin and Greek words for "wine"; *Autonoë* is fancifully said to mean in Greek "ignorant of herself"; *Semelê* is explained as a combination of *soma* = "body" and *luein* = "release"—a "release from bodily inhibitions, hence lust"; *Agavê* is insanity because she cut off her son's head, which only an insane person could do. Drunkenness, obviously, is to be avoided at all costs.

Such material reappeared in other handbooks over the next centuries and for a long time made up the basic source of myths available in the West. Interpretation had become more complex and important than the myths themselves, whose telling might consist of little more than a few key details. Allegory continued to focus on acceptable moral meanings. *Ovide moralizé* ("Ovid Moralized"), a text originally in French that went through many versions from 1300 on, listed interpretations of the often racy myths retold in Ovid's poetry. The story of Daphnê transformed into a laurel tree to escape the lustful Apollo is explained as an allegory for the moral that chastity, like the laurel, remains as cool as a river and always blooms, but never bears fruit. The story may also be understood as a botanical allegory (the warmth of the sun, Apollo, when combined with water, Daphnê, makes the laurel flourish) or even a medical allegory (chased by a rapist, she dies from exhaustion under a laurel tree).

---

[3]Fulgentius gives the allegorical interpretation of the Judgment of Paris mentioned earlier.

FIG. 23.1. Odysseus at the mast, relief from a fourth-century A.D. Roman sarcophagus. The story of Odysseus' journey was easily adapted to Christian allegory. Here the Greek hero is another Christ on the cross, at the same time representing all believers who escape the Sirens' temptation to sin during the voyage through life. The Sirens are shown as women with the feet of birds; a cupid strides off to the right, perhaps the redeemed soul of the dead Christian.   (Museo Nazionale delle Terme, Rome; 201G14L)

Such interpretations reached a wider public through Christian sermons, which could use Odysseus' encounter with the Sirens, for example, as an object lesson of the temptations posed by pleasure during a Christian's voyage through life (Fig. 23.1).

Part of the renewed emphasis given to classical culture at the time of the Renaissance came from interest in Platonism. The Platonic conviction that myth contains profound symbolic truth concerning higher spiritual realms was highly attractive to Christian culture and led to a vogue for even more elaborate allegory that combined pagan and Christian elements. Repeating arguments made earlier by the neoplatonists, whom they deeply admired, students of classical myth during the Renaissance maintained that bizarre, shocking features were actually the surest sign of truth in a myth. Only those who earnestly sought the truth would not be put off by repulsive surface appearances, but would penetrate to the deeper riches hidden beneath.

For example, Hesiod's description of the birth of Aphrodite is a raw, even brutal account, beginning with a son's mutilation of his father's genitals. The foam that gathers around the penis is a pun on the Greek *aphros*, "foam," but the image is taken from actual intercourse. From these gory events and viscous fluids emerged a figure that is in appearance the opposite: lovely and lithesome, the object of desire. Yet within remains the blood and the foam, a woman's deceptive nature, occluded by giggles and the irresistible sweetness of always destructive passion. From the same story Botticelli, a master artist of the fifteenth century, drew an entirely different lesson (see Figure P 8.1).

Botticelli was a member of the circle of the rich and powerful Lorenzo de' Medici's Platonic Academy of Philosophy, whose guiding genius was Marsilio Ficino, a Greek scholar of high achievement. Ficino, following the neoplatonists of the third to sixth centuries A.D., taught that the universe was a hierarchy of descending spheres reaching from the oneness of God through angelic spheres to our own world of base matter. Before birth, the human soul (= Botticelli's *Venus*) was perfect and lived in the angelic spheres, then was caught at birth in the dark material world (= the shell, the cloak in Botticelli's painting). Only through God's love, as expressed in the beauty of creation, was it possible for the soul to regain its original perfection and be saved from vile matter. Through the contemplation of beauty (Botticelli's very picture of the birth of Venus), the soul could perceive the abstract beauty behind the material expression, which would then restore the soul to its spiritual nature.

The medieval and Renaissance alchemists, who believed that a knowledge of nature's secrets would allow them to transform common metals into gold or silver, found a different kind of truth in classical myth, reviving in new form Greek physical allegory. Accepting neoplatonic ideas about the relationship between matter and spirit, they put allegorical interpretation of myth to use in their description of secret physical processes. The figure of Hermes (= Mercury), for example, was taken to be a ready-made allegory of chemical facts about the element Mercury. The alchemical work *Atalanta Fugiens* ("Atalanta Running Away"), published in 1617 by Michael Maier, is an excellent case in point. Building on a long tradition, he provided his text with pictures and a musical score, "so that your eyes and ears may take in the emblems, but your reason searches out the hidden signs." Both text and pictures treat the mythical tradition as a treasure trove of alchemical allegory (Fig. 23.2). Atalanta was identified with "volatile" mercury, which "flees," and Hippomenes, her suitor, is the sulfur that overcomes her, that is, effects a chemical reaction. The golden apples are another ingredient retarding the process.

Along with such specialized esoteric texts, handbooks continued to provide basic information for artists or writers along with interpretations. Myth had virtually become a language for talking about timeless truths, and in the seventeenth century the theory that pagan myth was a distorted version of biblical history reemerged with vigor. Scholars gathered evidence intended to show that many details in Homer were muddled versions of events in the Old Testament. The siege of Troy was explained as a recasting of Joshua's attack on Jericho. Odysseus' wanderings reflected those of the patriarchs. Nysa, the mountain where Dionysus was raised, becomes an anagram for *Syna* (= Sinai).

THEORIES OF THE ENLIGHTENMENT

Such interpretations fell under serious attack in the eighteenth century as part of the profound cultural revolution called the **Enlightenment.** As the institutional power of the church waned in response to political and social changes in Europe, everything traditional was subject to reexamination, usually with a notable lack of sympathy. Because few things were so traditional as myth, the authority of mythical accounts (including the Bible) and the value of allegory for preserving their worth were increasingly questioned.

EMBLEMA XXXIX. *De fecretis Naturæ.* 165
Oedypus Sphynge fuperata & trucidato Lajo patre
matrem ducit in uxorem.

EPIGRAMMA XXXIX.

*S Phyngem ænigmatico Thebis fermone timendam
  Oedypus ad propriam torferat arte necem:
Quæfitum eft cui mane pedes fint bis duo, luce
  Sed mediâ bini, tres ubi vefper adeft.
Victor abhinc Lajum nolentem cedere cædit,
  Ducit & uxorem quæ fibi mater erat.*   X 3   BA-

FIG. 23.2. Oedipus in *Atalanta Fugiens* by Michael Maier (1617). The story of Oedipus was interpreted as an alchemical allegory. In clockwise order beginning at the top, the snaky-tailed sphinx besieges Thebes, Oedipus meets Jocasta, and Oedipus kills Laius. In the foreground is the riddle of the three ages, really about the laws of nature: the triangle on the old man's (= Old Age) forehead is body/soul/spirit, the hemisphere on the mature man (= Maturity) is the moon, and the square on the baby (= Childhood) is the four elements. At the left the sphinx is about to leap from a cliff in despair at her defeat. The Latin poetic text means

> While Thebes lies quaking in dread of the riddling monster's enigma,
>   Oedipus cleverly twists the Sphinx's word to its doom.
> The creature had asked, "Who, pray, has twice two legs in the morning,
>   at noonday only a pair; eventide sets him on three?"
> Oedipus, puffed up in triumph, bids Laius, "Get out of my way!,"
>   kills him—then takes as his wife she who had given him birth.

Bernard Fontenelle's book *De l'origine des fables,* "Concerning the Origin of Fables" (1724), is a monument of the radical change in attitude taking place, initially in France, and paved the way for many of the central ideas of the Enlightenment. Fontenelle took a detached, wholly disenchanted stance and laid down a whole range of new principles for dealing with myth. Instead of seeking deep, esoteric truths, he saw in myth the product of error, beyond saving by allegory. Myth was rooted in the ignorance of humans living at earlier stages of cultural development. Fontenelle shifted the emphasis of theory from interpreting myth to explaining the origin of myth, which, he asserts, originates and develops in savagery and ignorance. Some scholars date the modern meaning of "myth" as a fanciful tale, or the notion that it exists as a discrete category at all, to Fontenelle's writings.

Information about the cultures of the American Indians and other preliterate peoples coming in from missionaries or colonial administrators was a source for Fontenelle's ideas. Such information justified his distinguishing the "primitive" mind from the enlightened and his finding of parallels between the "primitive" cultures of his day and that of the early Greeks. Greek myth, too, he assumed, was the product of a "primitive" mode of thought. This radical, new, and dramatic approach, taking as its premise the notion of progressive evolutionary development away from an earlier condition of savagery to present conditions of civilization, was destined to shape Western thought for the coming centuries and continues to do so today.

The Italian **Giambattista Vico** (jom-ba-tēs-ta vē-kō), sometimes regarded as the first modern historian (*Scienza Nuova,* "New Science," 1725), accepted this evolutionary approach to the understanding of the past. History, he thought, was the study of the origin and unfolding of human society and institutions. This view was unlike that of his contemporaries, who regarded history as the biographies of great men or the record of the unfolding of God's will. Vico argued that history moves in great cycles, each of which has three phases, the same in every cycle but modified by new circumstances and developments.

The first phase in each cycle is the Age of Gods. In our own cycle, this was the period immediately after the flood. In the Age of Gods human activity is limited to a struggle for physical survival. People live close to nature, whose power they understand only as a display of anger by a mighty god. From this phase comes the image of God and of gods as terrible and wrathful beings and what we have called divine myth. In the next phase, the Age of Heroes, nature becomes separated from humankind. Emerging social institutions are connected with personified gods and heroes about whom stories are told; from the Age of Heroes descend "legends." The third and last stage (we live in one now) is the Age of Man, in which reason replaces instinctive imagination and passion. Philosophy arises in this phase.

Vico's theory is one of the earliest of many efforts to understand myth as part of an all-embracing history of ideas. Allegory, in his view, deals only with particular myths. What was really needed, Vico thought, was to discover a principle of myth itself in human consciousness. Myth originated in the earlier phases of culture, when humankind's thinking was highly concrete. At that time language, originally monosyllabic and versified, expressed a poetry and ritual more powerful than any we know today, a direct representation of reality. This is why myth is so personal and dramatic, so disconcerting to those who live in the "rational" Age of Man. By recognizing that ways of thinking change fundamentally, Vico avoided two common pitfalls associated with evolutionary schemes: He did not simply idealize preliterate culture, and he recognized that earlier forms of understanding, which cannot be fully grasped by the standards of rational thought, are valid in their own terms.

THEORIES OF THE NINETEENTH AND TWENTIETH CENTURIES

Romantic Theories

Although there have been many disagreements in emphasis, approaches to myth since the Enlightenment have either used an evolutionary perspective, which assumes that myths are the relics of savagery, or have studied myth with the methods of the social sciences, which assume that myth reflects ways of thinking different from our own. Both approaches are closely related, and in either case the effect is to reduce myth to a cultural relic. However, the counterview of myth as valid and understandable in its own terms did not entirely disappear at the time of the Enlightenment, and it surfaced again in the Romantic movement during the late eighteenth and early nineteenth centuries.

Romanticism was a reaction against what many saw as the arrogance, superficiality, and outright blindness of the Enlightenment. Opposing the Enlightenment's confident rationalism, the Romantics saw the emotional side of experience as most distinctively human: intense feeling, awareness of powerful but obscure forces, abnormal states, and a direct intuitive relationship to nature. Whereas thinkers of the Enlightenment attacked myth as a product of primitive mental and emotional states, the Romantics returned to myth as a vehicle for regaining lost truths. Such ideals were expressed mostly in poetry, painting (Fig. 23.3), and music, but ambitious philosophical theories, especially in Germany, argued for the timeless truth of myth and for its continuing vital role in the modern world.

An explanation of how this could be, that myth embodies timeless truths, was given by **Friedrich Creuzer** in his long book *Symbolism and Mythology of the Ancient Peoples, Especially the Greeks* (1810). Creuzer made much of recently discovered material on the myths of ancient India and interpreted all myth, in neoplatonic fashion, as a set of symbols for universal truths. Indian religious texts, he argued, contained an extremely ancient revelation of absolute truth. As the Aryans—that is, the Indo-Europeans—spread from their homeland, the once pristine truth became obscure, preserved only in symbolic forms by a priestly elite, refracted like pure light broken into various colors by a lens. The different mythologies of the Indo-European peoples are those colors, each expressing in its own idiom a truth that was originally, Creuzer thought, symbolized visually by means of hieroglyphs like those of Egypt.

According to Creuzer, myth is a way of dealing with absolute, infinite truth in finite narrative form. But whereas truth is ultimately rational and abstract, myth is dramatic and concrete. For example, the golden rope by which Zeus could suspend sea and earth if he chose (*Iliad* 8.18–19) symbolizes the divine energy that supports the world. This is the same cosmic energy described as a thread of pearls in the Sanskrit classic *Bhagavad Gita*, "Song of the Blessed One." Each mythic image—the golden rope and the string of pearls—descends ultimately from a single primordial revelation to humankind of truth about the nature of reality.

Another imaginative, partly Romantic theory was advanced by **Johann Bachofen** (*Das Mutterrecht*, "Mother Right," 1861), a student of Roman law who noticed that women enjoyed considerable status in some ancient legal and social systems. All modern theories of a matriarchal phase in early human social development go back to Bachofen, who concluded that the patriarchal authority, which has dominated all present-day societies, was preceded by a stage during which women exercised great influence in their capacity as mothers. Much of his evidence for this claim came from classical myth, which he considered to contain hidden truths about early human social structure. According to Bachofen's explanation, the earliest nomadic hunting phase, represented in myth by Aphrodite, was lawless, when women were victims of violence. In a later phase, represented by Demeter, the institutions of agriculture and marriage were introduced, and values clustering around the mother encouraged peace and feelings of communal affection. On the other hand, the aggressive potential in woman's nature was reflected in myths about the Amazons.

Although Bachofen described favorably the early "mother right," he recognized a third, and higher, Apollonian phase, represented by Rome. Here the older, more primitive communal mother right was overthrown, and authority was invested in law that embodied the higher values of patriarchy, individuality, and rationality. His scheme, which influenced later Marxist theory, combined speculation about a happier, maternal past with a typically evolutionary pattern that moved through earthly and lunar phases to the present solar triumph of the patriarchal principle.

Friedrich Engels, one of the founding fathers of modern communism, took Bachofen's position in his book *The Origin of the Family, Private Property, and the State* (1883). Before the evolution of the state and the family, women ruled society and were free to have intercourse with whomever they pleased, so that no son ever knew his father. The eminent Russian folklorist Vladimir Propp (1895–1970), writing under the Soviet regime, pointed out that such was the situation of Oedipus: The myth must therefore be a historical reminiscence of the shift from a matriarchal to a patriarchal organization of society. According to Propp, the shepherds in the Greek legend, who transported Oedipus to the wild and then to Corinth, stand for the foster parents who in a primitive matriarchy cared for the children. Oedipus' age-mates reflect some early collective, before the evolution of the family.[4]

Anthropological Theories

The flood of information about newly discovered cultures pouring into Europe from colonial outposts and journeys of exploration did seem to support the view that myth is a symptom of intellectual backwardness, and students of myth formulated many variations on the concept of "primitive" societies and "primitive" ways of thinking by

[4]In the communist People's Republic of China such teaching is still official doctrine.

which classical myth could be understood. During the second half of the nineteenth century, the process of integrating diverse data into general theories of development was further encouraged by Charles Darwin's theory of biological evolution advanced in *The Origin of Species* (1859). From such studies emerged what is now called anthropology.

One of the most influential of these formulations was advanced by British anthropologist **Edward Tylor,** who presented his theory of universal cultural evolution proceeding through several stages in *Primitive Culture* (1871). Tylor explained the "quaint fancies and wild legends of the lower tribes" in terms of an original stage that he called "animistic." Animism is the belief that everything has a soul. Myth and religion, which are natural consequences of such a belief, do not ultimately come from inherently poetic language, as Vico thought. Instead, myth is a mistaken science or philosophy, rooted in fear or ignorance but designed to explain natural phenomena.

A number of other theories were advanced about the primitive state through which all human societies must pass. The model for the evolution of human societies was drawn from the biological evolution of a species. Thus societies that represent earlier stages can exist, although only in isolated backwaters, at the same time as more evolved societies. Technologically primitive communities still intact in Australia, or practices and beliefs of European peasants, were sources of information.

This general approach was especially popularized by British author Andrew Lang (*Myth, Literature, and Religion,* 1887). Trained as a classicist, he was a prolific essayist, historian, poet, sports writer, and critic, one of the leading intellectuals of his day.[5] Deeply affected by the interest in evolution, he at first accepted Tylor's laws of cultural development, but as he examined the evidence more critically, he came to believe that there must have been more than a single pattern of development. Myth was indeed, as Tylor maintained, a protoscientific effort at explanation, but the primitive stage of culture was not always a time of confused ideas about natural forces. Faced with examples of what seemed to be ethical monotheism among "savages," Lang argued that monotheism must in some cases have actually preceded animism and polytheistic myth, into which it subsequently degenerated.

To most scholars, then, myth was explicable essentially as reflecting an early, clumsy effort to do what science later did better: explain why things are the way they are. **Sir James Frazer,** a classical scholar and one of the founders of modern anthropology, accepted the validity of social evolution as an explanation with universal application. With immense industry Frazer gathered evidence from all over the world, from American Indians, from Africans, from Melanesians, as scientific evidence from which decisive conclusions about the meaning of myth could be drawn.

Frazer's celebrated book, *The Golden Bough,* is often ranked as one of the most influential works of modern times. It began as two volumes published in 1890 and reached twelve volumes in the 1911–1915 edition. Frazer started by inquiring into the ancient tradition that a "King of the Wood" ruled at Aricia, a village near Rome.

---

[5]His retelling of traditional stories in the *Blue Fairy Book* and others, which he published with his wife, are still popular among children.

The King of the Wood, so the story went, was never secure in his power because at any time another man might challenge him to hand-to-hand combat, kill him, and take over the realm. Before the duel could take place, however, the challenger had to break off a golden bough from a sacred tree in the grove, hence the title of Frazer's book.[6]

Frazer searched the world over for evidence of his thesis that the story of the golden bough is a late survival of a primordial human social and religious institution in which the King of the Wood embodied and ensured the fertility of the realm. When his waning power threatened the well-being of the people, the king had to be killed and a young, vital successor placed on the throne. The king must die that the people might live. As embodiment of a fertility or "corn"[7] god, his life and death represent the fundamental vitality of nature. The stories of Attis, Adonis, Osiris, and Dionysus are mythical projections of this pattern.

On the basis of this hypothetical primordial rite, Frazer attempted to account for much that we find in myths and religions worldwide. The king's life was hemmed in by an elaborate system of taboos. If he broke a taboo, his ability to help his people would be lessened, much as a grounded battery loses its charge. Here, Frazer argued, is the origin of the do's and don'ts in every religion and of the many violated taboos in myth. Because the old king must die, many myths tell of the death of kings and gods. These stories, he thought, arose as explanations for real rituals in which a king actually was killed. The origin of myth is thus closely tied to religious ritual. This is the **ritual theory of myth.**

Frazer's understanding of myth as a secondary elaboration of ritual exerted considerable influence. Like others influenced by evolutionary thought, Frazer wanted to formulate a comprehensive theory of cultural development. To that end he replaced Tylor's "animism" with "magic," understood as a mechanical operation used by primitive peoples as part of a ritual to coerce impersonal natural or supernatural forces to obey human wishes. When humans realized that magic was often ineffective, religion was born. The propitiation of quasihuman gods replaced coercion through magic. Science, in turn, was destined to replace religion. Myth is associated especially with the religious phase of development because myth is characterized by a belief in personal forces that act in stories, whereas science and magic are concerned with impersonal forces.

Europeans of the late nineteenth century were preoccupied by the concept of progress. Especially in England, progress was thought of as change for the better and, in fact, implicit in the principle of evolution. Like writers on myth during the Enlightenment, Frazer ignored the possibility that change may not always bring improvement. Frazer himself did no field work. He integrated into his master scheme a vast body of data, often carelessly gathered, and manipulated it to fit his theory.

In the twentieth century, anthropological method was much improved by Bronislaw Malinowski (*Magic, Science, and Religion,* 1948), who was born in Poland but pursued his career chiefly in England. Influenced by French sociological thought,

[6]No connection, apparently, with the golden bough in Vergil's story of Aeneas' descent into the underworld (see Chapters 11, 22).

[7]*Corn,* in British usage, means any sort of grain; in American usage *corn* usually is limited to maize.

his own theory was based directly on field work carried out between 1914 and 1918 among the Trobrianders, the people of a remote island complex southeast of New Guinea. Objecting to the evolutionary understanding of myth as protoscience, Malinowski held that its purpose was to serve as a "charter," a justification for the way things are. This is the **charter theory of myth.**

For example, a story might be told to justify so-and-so's ownership of a certain part of the island—because that is where so-and-so's ancestors sprang from the ground. According to Malinowski, myths justify and validate economic, political, social, and religious realities. Myth is not to be explained according to hypothetical patterns of cultural evolution at all, but from its social function, from how myth helps to deal with the practical problems of living.[8]

Linguistic Theories

The science of Indo-European linguistics, which made great advances in the nineteenth century, was the basis for another allegorical approach to myth in theories advanced by Max Müller (1823–1900), the leading Sanskrit scholar of his day, a vigorous rival of Andrew Lang. Müller, a German-born Oxford don, saw in nearly every myth, whether about heroes or gods, an allegory of the struggle between sunlight and darkness. Hence this method of interpretation is called **solar mythology.** Müller's theory, like others inspired by evolutionary thought and the rapid growth of science, sought to understand myth as the effort of early peoples to explain prominent natural phenomena, such as storms or celestial bodies, but Müller's theory was unusually influential because of the linguistic support he provided for the central role assigned to the sun.

Take, for example, the fairly obscure story of Endymion and Selenê. Endymion was a handsome youth whom Selenê ("moon") saw as he lay sleeping in a cave. She fell deeply in love with him and bore him many children. The two were separated when Zeus allowed Endymion to choose anything he wanted: He chose to sleep forever, never growing old. Because the Greek *endyein* originally meant "to dive," the name *Endymion* at first simply described the sun's setting ("diving") in the sea. The original meaning of *endyein* faded and was misunderstood to refer to a person, Endymion ("Diver"). The mythical story of the love of Selenê and Endymion, then, began with the words "Selenê embraces Endymion," that is, "Moon embraces Diver," which in the metaphorical "primitive" expression of early peoples was a way of saying "the sun is setting and the moon is rising."

In effect, Max Müller combined ancient physical allegory with the theories of Palaephatus about the distortion of language. Myth, he thought, begins through a "disease of language" whereby the original meaning of language, especially in observations about solar phenomena, was gradually misunderstood and reinterpreted. Müller and his followers were able in this way to argue that bloody death in myth was

[8]Malinowski usually is considered the founder of *functionalism,* the notion that the function of a practice determines the form it takes.

really the red-streaked sunset, that Odysseus' imprisonment in a cave was the waxing and waning year, and that Achilles' destruction of his enemies was really the splendid sun breaking through the clouds. Midas was the sun gilding everything it touches, and the story of Phaëthon describes how excessive heat (Phaëthon's ride) causes drought that is finally broken by a thunderstorm (the bolt hurled by Zeus to kill Phaëthon).

It is easy to ridicule Müller's theories, but he did attempt to furnish a theoretical explanation for shifts in the meaning of the names of mythical figures. In this he differed from his many predecessors in the long history of allegory, who simply proclaimed, without justification, the truth of whatever came to their minds. Still, it was all too easy for Müller and his followers to find the sun everywhere. Like many ambitious theories of myth, this one began to refute itself. The theory was wittily parodied in a learned article by Andrew Lang that proved, by Müller's methods, that Müller had never existed, but was himself a solar myth!

Solar mythology arose under the influence of one of the great intellectual discoveries of modern times, that most European languages (except Basque, Finnish, Hungarian, and Estonian) and many others spoken as far east as central India (including Armenian, Iranian, and Sanskrit, but not the Semitic languages) are descended from the hypothetical parent language called proto–Indo-European.[9] If it is possible to elucidate the origin and inner structure of modern European languages by comparing them with Greek, Latin, and Sanskrit, it should also be possible, according to the supporters of **Indo-European comparative mythology,** to elucidate European mythology in the same way and to discover essential patterns and original meanings of myth. For example, the Romans told a story about Mucius Scaevola ("Lefty"), who deliberately burned off his right hand to demonstrate Roman bravery to an enemy king. The Norsemen, Indo-European speakers like the Romans, told a story about the war god Tiu (hence "Tuesday"), whose right hand was bitten off by the wolf Fenris, an enemy of the present order of creation: While biting off Tiu's hand, the distracted wolf was bound by an unbreakable chain. We could thus infer the existence of an original Indo-European story about a man who sacrificed his hand for the good of all. This story becomes a patriotic tale among the Romans, who emphasized civic duty, but among the Norsemen, who were concerned with the opposition between the cosmic forces of order and chaos, it became a tale of temporary world redemption (one day the Fenris wolf will escape its bonds and the world will end).

Indo-European comparative mythologists maintain that myths accompany language as it is passed on. They seek a common "grammar" or inner structure in the stories. Such a grammar ought also to reveal something characteristic of Indo-European social traditions. This sort of interpretation was refined in the mid–twentieth century by French scholar Georges Dumézil (1898–1986), who correlated three hypothetical original classes in Indo-European society with the roles played by cer-

---

[9]The discovery usually is credited to Sir William Jones, chief justice of India, founder of the Royal Asiatic Society, presented in a lecture in 1796.

tain deities in Indo-European myth. These classes are rulers and priests, warriors, and food producers. Consider, for example, the story of the Judgment of Paris. Why does Hera attempt to bribe Paris with an offer of royal power, while Athena offers him military glory and Aphrodite offers him Helen? Because the three choices represent the three fundamental activities in Indo-European society: Hera stands for royal authority, the ruling class; Athena stands for the warrior class; and Aphrodite, who sponsors reproduction and sustenance, represents the food producers.[10] The division of the first function into rulers and priests is also reflected in myths about early Roman history. The first four kings, in order, are the political founder Romulus, a religious leader (Numa), a warrior (Tullus Hostilius), and a provider (Ancus Marcius). Dumézil thus combines features of Malinowski's functional approach (myth justifies social patterns) with features of the structural approaches, which we consider shortly.

Psychological Theories

New fields of study of the past century inspired corresponding new theories of myth. Sociology and anthropology led to functionalism, linguistics led to Indo-European comparative mythology. Psychology, too, has brought with it both a key myth—the story of Oedipus—and a variety of new psychological theories.

At the time when anthropological approaches were developing, **Sigmund Freud** (1856–1939) advanced a view of myth based in the individual rather than in society. Myth, he thought, was a byproduct of personal psychological forces. Freud's theories of myth began with his thinking about the dreams of individuals. The mind of a sleeper works by different rules from the mind of the wakeful, although dream symbols can be correlated with things in the waking world. Freud formulated rules by which translation from symbolism in dreams to everyday reality takes place. For example, condensation occurs when several things from the waking world are fused together in a dream, perhaps with disturbing effect. Displacement occurs when something in a dream stands for something quite different in the waking world, even its opposite, as when an enemy represents a lover whom the sleeper does not entirely trust. Condensation and displacement are necessary to the dreamer because the true thought is morally or emotionally repugnant to the waking consciousness. Because the thought is still there, however, it must be dealt with, and the mind releases tension by dealing with the problem indirectly. Dreams are symptoms of psychological tensions that can affect the waking world of those suffering from mental disease, from neuroses.

How do the dreams of individuals result in myths, which belong to a whole people? They do, Freud thought, because myths are the collective and recurrent dreams of the race. An example in myth of dream condensation would be the mythical Centaurs or Sirens, made up of two separate beings fused together; an example in myth

---

[10]We would expect Demeter, because Aphrodite's concerns are preeminently with human sexuality; furthermore, Aphrodite is a goddess of Semitic origin. However, Dumézil must accept the story as it is given. In fact, the theory works poorly with Greek material.

of dream "displacement" would be the upward anatomical shift of a woman's pubic region to create the face of Medusa.

Freud also held that neuroses and their symbolic expression in dreams go back to the infant's experience of his or her personal sexuality. He emphasized the **Oedipus complex,** first set forth in *The Interpretation of Dreams* (1900). From this story Sigmund Freud developed his notion that adult male psychology arises from the infant boy's sexual attraction to his mother and his hostility and jealousy toward his father. Freud did not seek the origins of the legend in social history, as had the Soviet folklorist Vladimir Propp, but in the incest dreams of his patients, which he took to represent suppressed desires of childhood. The son wishes sexual contact with his mother, from whose breasts he feeds and in whose warm body he is daily encompassed. He resents the father's sexual demands on the mother, which displace him from her embrace. He wants to kill the father, that he might have the mother to himself. Only by overcoming such hidden, taboo, and obviously unspoken desires might one become an adult, Freud thought.

The myth of Oedipus, then, emerges from primeval dreams. To make his point Freud ignored inconvenient parts of the legend, above all the story that at the end of his life Oedipus may even have been taken up by the gods. Freud also ignores Oedipus' exposure as an infant and his great intelligence. Critics of Freud starkly complain that Freud's true intentions in his fantasies about human psychology were to denigrate human nature, to reduce it to raw and amoral animal impulse, a vision much in favor at the end of the nineteenth century. Like Oedipus, Freud says, we live in ignorance of our inner wishes that are so repugnant to morality, which Nature has forced upon us, but when we see them clearly, we seek to close our eyes. Critics have also asked whether Oedipus himself had an Oedipus complex; he does not seem to, but Freud was little interested in explaining the story itself.

In Freudian interpretation, stories that describe heroes slaying dragons and marrying maidens are really forms of the Oedipus complex because they echo the son's repressed desire to kill his father (= the dragon) and have sexual intercourse with his mother (= the maid). Cronus castrated Uranus because sons want to deprive their fathers of sexual power, and they fear the same treatment from their own sons in turn. Mythical kings and queens represent parents, sharp weapons are the male sexual organ, and caves, rooms, and houses symbolize the mother's containing womb. The imagery of myths can therefore be translated into that of sex, often in specifically anatomical ways.

Freud saw myths as arising among a race in the way that dreams arise in the individual, but he also argued that individual psychological development repeats the psychological history of the whole race.[11] This is an adaptation of evolutionary thinking. The individual's dreams reflect the same primitive mode of consciousness that we find in myth, which are collective dreams preserved from the primitive childhood of the race. His theory is yet another that connects the mythical with the primitive and the irrational, an approach common since the Enlightenment. A Freudian read-

---

[11]The notion that "ontogeny recapitulates phylogeny" (the development of the individual goes through the same stages as that of the race) was developed by embryologist August Weissman (1834–1914) some time before Freud.

ing of myth is allegory in yet another guise, translating mythical patterns and events into psychological patterns and events. But like Max Müller, and unlike earlier interpreters, Freud explained not merely how but also why shifts occur from one meaning to another.

Freud's associate **Carl Jung** (yung, 1875–1961) continued to explore the notion of an unconscious part of human nature. Like Freud, Jung discerned a complex symbolism that both conceals the unconscious and, to the psychiatrist, furnishes access to it. Jung did not believe, however, that the symbolism of the unconscious mind was predominantly sexual in nature, nor even that dream symbolism ultimately belonged to the individual.

Jung's theory resembles Eastern religious teachings in some respects. For him the consciousness of the individual is like a bay or an inlet on a great ocean of psychic activity, which he called the **collective unconscious** (Freud had implied as much, with his notion of racial dreaming). Into the bay swim, from time to time, great beings that inhabit the deep. These are the *archetypes* (a Greek term also used by neoplatonists), timeless recurrent images on which our emotional world and our myths are built. Certain groups of archetypes may dominate the consciousness of entire cultures for periods of time. Jung spoke of such different archetypes as the Wise Old Man, the Earth Mother, and the Divine Child. The *mandala,* a perfectly symmetrical, geometric visual figure used for focusing the consciousness in Buddhist meditation, was considered by Jung to be an emblem of the total psychological integration that each person seeks and that myth reflects. In this sense myth can never be discarded from human life. Whether we know it or not, we live out myths in our own lives.[12]

A follower of Jung, Erich Neumann (1905–1960), used Jung's method to explain the common myth of the dragon-combat. The myth, he argued, symbolizes the breaking away of an individual's consciousness from the great collective unconscious of the world. The dragon represents the collective unconscious, always trying to swallow the hero, who symbolizes individual consciousness. The collective unconscious is also represented by the Great Mother goddess, the mother of all things, a recurrent type of myth and in the history of religion. Although the source of individual consciousness and of life itself, she threatens to swallow her own progeny. For this reason, the male hero, who typically undergoes great dangers, is often threatened by evil female forces—witches like Circê or monsters like Tiamat. At some point the monster may actually swallow the hero (as the whale swallowed Jonah), but defeat is always temporary. The psychological truth represented by the hero's ultimate victory over the dragon is the emergence of personal identity, the victory of the individual consciousness over the threatening collective unconscious. The hero's reward—

---

[12]Deeply influenced by Jung is Joseph Campbell, whose many books and even a TV series have popularized the notion of *Myths to Live By* (the title of one of Campbell's books: New York, 1981). Although his works are interesting to read, they have limited value to scholars because of Campbell's failure to distinguish between myth and religion and because of his eagerness to find a central hidden meaning (like so many before him) in all myths from all cultures. Most widely read is *The Hero with a Thousand Faces,* 2nd ed. (New York, 1968); see also *The Masks of God,* 4 vols. (New York, 1959–1968) and *The Power of Myth,* with Bill Moyers (New York, 1988).

princess or treasure—represents the devouring collective unconscious in a tamed-down form, defeated, and now made fecund. The combat myth is really a description of an individual's psychological destiny.

Structuralist Theories

A highly influential theory of myth interpretation is **structuralism,** especially as propounded by French anthropologist **Claude Lévi-Strauss** (1908–1994). Meaning in a traditional story is not conveyed by the content, he maintains, but by the structural relations one can discover behind the content. In this most rationalistic and abstract of theories, the meaning of myth is its pure form. Structural relations often are so subtle that they can be made clear only by means of diagrams, charts, and formulas, which resemble mathematical formulas. The meaning of a story, then, is independent of any particular telling of it, residing ultimately in all possible variants of the story taken together. Far from confining himself to "traditional tales," Lévi-Strauss declared that even the interpretation of a myth is to be considered part of the myth, including Lévi-Strauss's own analyses, which are simply additional variants!

Lévi-Strauss finds the origin of myth in the principle that "mythical thought always works from the awareness of opposition toward their progressive mediation." Humans perceive the world in terms of sharp, intolerable dualities: hot and cold, bitter and sweet, raw and cooked, life and death. Because by nature we cannot tolerate opposition for which intermediaries do not exist, we bridge perceived contradictions by telling stories. For example, the story of Cronus fathering his children but refusing to allow them to be born, and of Uranus' son Cronus swallowing his children after they were born, could be said to mediate between the opposites of birth and death. The irreconcilable opposites are brought together by telling a story in which the same creature both generates and consumes his progeny. Homer's *Odyssey,* the story of a man who went to the land of the dead and returned, brings together the irreconcilable opposites of life and death: Although life and death are opposites, in myth we can tell how a man journeyed to the land of the dead and returned. Our binary perception of the world derives, Lévi-Strauss thought, from the binary physical structure of our brains, which is supposed to make consciousness possible. Because of this binary structure, perceived oppositions can never be fully and finally reconciled—hence the dynamic quality of myth.

In 1955 Lévi-Strauss offered a celebrated new interpretation of the myth of Oedipus. Despite its obscurity, his reading of the myth has attracted widespread comment. According to Lévi-Strauss, the myth has no message but is the expression of the perception of irreconcilable claims about human origins. The Thebans claimed to be autochthonous, "sprung from the earth" (the teeth of the dragon). Thus Oedipus, "swollen-footed," is so called because creatures who spring from the earth, such as the snaky-footed Giants, have something wrong with their feet. On the other hand, the Thebans obviously sprang from their mothers' wombs, and Oedipus is certainly born from Jocasta. Therefore the myth of Oedipus is alleged to bridge, through story, what cannot be bridged through logic.

Lévi-Strauss's interpretations are difficult to assess, in part because of the obscurity of his style. He summarizes his argument about the myth of Oedipus in this way: The "Overvaluation of blood relations is to their undervaluation as the attempt to escape autochthony is to the impossibility of succeeding in it"! It is also hard to know when a true structure has been found because different possibilities for analysis so often exist. As an anthropologist, Lévi-Strauss worked principally among South American Indians, through whose myths he wanted not only to discover the deep concerns, fears, and ambitions of these peoples, but to lay open the inner workings of the whole human mind. In this he follows the ancient tradition of commentators wanting to prove that secrets about human nature and human destiny are hidden in traditional tales. More specifically, Lévi-Strauss echoes the neoplatonists' program of discovering behind the stuff of myth an abstract pattern or code that explains the very nature of things.

In spite of its limitations, Lévi-Strauss's structural method of interpretation has had considerable exploratory power because it brings out hitherto unnoticed facets of myth by bringing together whole systems of myth and, beyond that, by relating myth to broader aspects of culture. The method has been followed up for Greek myth by a group of Lévi-Strauss's followers, especially J.-P. Vernant, P. Vidal-Naquet, and M. Detienne. These authors, together with Claude Lévi-Strauss himself, are often called the **Paris school of myth criticism.**

We can take as an example of their method their treatment of the Greek pantheon. The usual way (the method adopted in this book) of studying the pantheon is to examine each god in isolation, speculating on his or her origin and saying something about associated myths and rituals. According to Vernant, however, no one god can ever be understood in isolation, any more than can a single word; one must seek the "syntax," the complicated interrelations that bind together all the gods in myth. Only then can one understand the conceptual universe of the Greeks.

For example, the traveler Pausanias noted that on the base of Phidias' statue of Zeus in Olympia were linked the names of Hestia and Hermes. Why? Because, according to Vernant, Hestia and Hermes embody the contrary but complementary aspects of the Greeks' apprehension of space. Hestia is the fixed point, the hearth at the center of the household and of the city; Hermes represents transition, movement, change, the connecting link between oppositions. The same polarity is echoed in Greek social life. As Hestia is to Hermes, so is woman to man: The woman stays at home, while the man travels abroad, conducts business, and wages war. Neither Hestia nor Hermes, then, can be understood in isolation because they constitute opposite poles of a single concept. To us this single concept is represented by the word *space,* but the Greeks, who are supposed to have lacked this abstract expression, represented the same notion by the different but complementary activities of Hestia and Hermes.[13]

By selecting and linking apparently disparate items taken from all aspects of culture, structuralist interpretations attempt to detect the rules shaping myth. The

---

[13]In fact, several words in Greek do roughly correspond to our *space.*

complexity of the enterprise points to both its possibilities and its hazards. Interplay between details and larger patterns yields fascinating insights, but the objectivity and significance of what emerges are a persistent difficulty. The universal claims of structuralist theory, professing as it does to be based on the very laws of human thought, permit it to be applied practically everywhere but open it to criticism on the familiar ground of attempting too much.

Contextual Approaches

Such weaknesses are well described by the German scholar Walter Burkert in his book *Structure and History in Greek Mythology and Ritual* (1979), which has exercised strong influence on classical scholars. Burkert accepts the importance of structure in the study of myth, agreeing that the very identity of a tale is maintained by a structure of sense within it. The existence of this constant, partly invisible, internal structure makes it possible for us to say that Homer's story of Oedipus and Sophocles' story are both, despite their differences, "the myth of Oedipus." However, Burkert opposes Lévi-Strauss's indifference to changing cultural and historical conditions, which constantly impart different collective meanings to a myth. Cultural and historical context must always be taken into account, Burkert insists.

Reviving in part the ritual theory of myth, Burkert argues that the structures that inform myth reflect biological or cultural **programs of action.** An example of a cultural program of action can be found in the hunting practices of Paleolithic man. Forced to kill his prey in order to survive but feeling a close relationship with and affection for animals, the hunter assuages his feelings of guilt through various ceremonies. After killing an animal, he makes a mock restoration by setting up its bones. This program of action can explain details in the myth of the hunter Actaeon, who was turned into a stag by Artemis, a goddess of hunting, and torn to pieces by his own dogs. The story reflects a prehistoric ritual in which real animals were hunted by men in animal disguise—thus the dogs are personified in the mythical tradition to the extent of being given individual names. In one version of this myth, the dogs' grief-stricken howling at Actaeon's death is brought to an end when the Centaur Chiron makes an image of Actaeon, which the dogs mistake for their slain master. This making of the image of the slain man/animal, in Burkert's view, reflects the very old ritual reconstruction of the dead animal by the guilt-ridden hunter, actually practiced by tribal peoples.

Surely many ritual elements are reflected in Greek myth, including, no doubt, some drawn from Paleolithic hunting practice, and Burkert's remarks on religion and myth are always enlightening. However, his thesis that Greek sacrificial ritual, and the myths that reflect it, derive from ancient hunting practice leaves unexplained why Greek sacrificial ritual always used domestic animals, never wild animals captured for the purpose. His conviction that ancient hunters felt "guilty" about killing their prey is also open to criticism. Although hunters undoubtedly respect their prey, we usually think of guilt as an emotion arising from violating the social mores; killing animals did not violate the mores of Paleolithic hunters. No doubt one reason that ancient hunters reconstructed their slain prey was to ensure, through magic, that there might be still more animals to kill.

Feminist critics may also apply a contextual approach, using myth to cast light on underlying social realities related to gender or show how myths may actually construct reality; so the myth of Demeter explained to Greek women expected roles in marriage, childbearing, and religious cult, making such roles seem intrinsic and natural. Always, of course, such criticism must work with literary material generated by and for males.

The contextual approach to myth is complex, making use of insights from structural, historical, and comparative methods and appealing broadly to what we know about human biology, the history of religion, language, and anthropology.

CONCLUSION

What are we to make of this long development, the history of the interpretation of Greek myths, of which we have here given only brief highlights? One cannot help but be impressed by the abiding fascination that the Greek mythical tradition has exercised over the human mind. But what validity do these systems of interpreting myth have for our understanding of myth, if by "understanding" we mean placing something in a larger and more familiar context?

The ancient Greek theorists, puzzled by the strangeness of traditions taken from a preliterate and prephilosophic past, attempted to explain their own myths by assimilating them to "correct" models of reality as created by philosophy. They saw in myths allegories for philosophic descriptions of the physical world or, in Euhemerism, as a source for historical reconstruction of the human past, or as a set of examples for how one should behave. Later methods have worked much the same way, adapting myths to new models of reality as they emerged from Christian to modern times. We need to be aware that the scientific model of reality, which has increasingly dominated thought since the Enlightenment and especially since the nineteenth century, is only the latest in a long line of such models. Although the nineteenth-century theory of myth as a "disease of language" centering on natural phenomena was encouraged by scientific linguistics, it is remarkably similar to the interpretation proposed by Palaephatus in 300 B.C. Modern psychological theories, especially those of Jung and Lévi-Strauss, offer explanations that in important ways repeat and refine an approach used by much earlier interpreters who sought in myth allegories of spiritual and psychological truths.

The strength of science lies in defining ideas precisely and treating them within strictly controlled guidelines. The power of humanistic studies, on the other hand, lies in their concern with the capacity of humans, as symbol-making beings, to create alternative worlds. Myth is one such alternative world, and the interpretation of myth is another; each is an expression of the same human capacity. Historically, the interpretation of myth is fully as important as myth itself and in fact occurs on a far grander scale. The interchangeable use of the words *myth* (the story itself) and *mythology* (reflection on myth) in English usage unintentionally points to this critical confusion, a fact recognized by structuralists when they suggest that interpretations of myths are only the addition of new myths to old. If myth embodies the tensions, values, and intellectual currents of the society that produces it, myth interpretation embodies those currents no less faithfully. A sketch of the history of myth interpretation turns out to be a sketch of the history of ideas. In the history of myth interpretation we can watch and study ever-changing intellectual fashions in relation to an unchanging body of material.

The grand theorizers about myth like to pick out this or that story, this or that figure, make impressive observations, and then speak as if their conclusions were applicable to all myths from all times and all places. But myths are so different from one another that any universal definition is bound to be arbitrary and to serve the theoretical interests of the definer; the history of the interpretation of myth richly demonstrates this fact. The scope of Greek myth both invites and refutes the fatal tendency to comprehensive claims because Greek myth affords so rich a choice of test cases. With careful selection any theory will work well in particular instances, elucidating even minor points with astonishing clarity. Applied to the next myth, the theory may be unable to deal plausibly with even obvious features.

Classical myth taken together is too complex, too many-faceted, to be explained by a single theory, as is fully recognized by the contextual approach, which we have favored throughout this book. The complexity of myth is bound up with the complexity of human consciousness itself and with the special role that the Greeks, the inventors of the alphabet, played in the transition from an oral traditional culture to one that was alphabetic and self-critical. Greek myth therefore is a special case in the history of the human spirit. To understand it, we must make use of insights offered by different schools of interpretation. No one method of analysis will dissolve the endless mysteries of classical myth.

KEY TERMS

rationalism, 629
Xenophanes, 630
allegory, 631
symbolism, 631
etymology, 632
euhemerism, 633
neoplatonism, 634
Enlightenment, 639
Bernard Fontenelle, 641
Giambattista Vico, 641
Romanticism, 642
Friedrich Creuzer, 642
Johann Bachofen, 643
Edward Tylor, 644

Sir James Frazer, 644
ritual theory of myth, 645
charter theory of myth, 646
solar mythology, 646
Indo-European comparative mythology, 647
Sigmund Freud, 648
Oedipus complex, 649
Carl Jung, 650
collective unconscious, 650
structuralism, 651
Claude Lévi-Strauss, 651
Paris school of myth criticism, 652
program of action, 653

FURTHER READING

GENERAL

Bremmer, Jan, and Fritz Graf, eds., *Interpretations of Greek Mythology* (London, 1987). A collection of essays on various topics, by leading critics.

Cohen, Percy, "Theories of Myth," *Man,* new series 4 (1969): 337–353. Concise review of theories on the interpretation of myth.

Dundes, Alan, ed., *Sacred Narrative: Readings in the Theory of Myth* (Berkeley, Calif., 1984). Gathers important essays by major scholars on myth interpretation, edited by a leading folklorist.

Edmunds, Lowell, ed., *Approaches to Greek Myth* (Baltimore, 1990). Essays on modern schools of myth interpretation, including myth and ritual, myth and history, Greek and Near Eastern mythology, Indo-European mythology, folklore, structuralism, psychoanalytic interpretation, and myth and Greek art.

Kirk, G. S., *Myth: Its Meaning and Functions in Ancient and Other Cultures* (Berkeley, Calif., 1970). Good general study that attempts to apply Straussian methods of interpretation to Mesopotamian myth.

————, *The Nature of Greek Myths* (New York, 1974). Discusses "five monolithic theories"—nature myths, etiological myths, charter myths, myths that evoke a creative era, and myths that derive from rituals—and adds five additional theories that view myths as products of the psyche.

Peradotto, John, *Classical Mythology. An Annotated Bibliographical Survey* (Ann Arbor, Mich., 1973; reprinted Boulder, Colo., 1977). Review of bibliography to 1973.

Sebeok, T. A., ed., *Myth: A Symposium* (Bloomington, Ind., 1955; reprinted 1971). Good general collection of essays on myth interpretation.

Segal, Robert A., ed., *Literary Criticism and Myth* (New York, 1996), 6 vols. Essays by exponents of different critical schools.

GREEK THEORIES

Guthrie, W.K.C., *The Greek Philosophers, from Thales to Aristotle* (New York, 1960). Lucid condensation of how philosophy emerged in the Archaic and Classical periods, with bibliography for further exploration.

Hersman, Anne Bates, *Studies in Greek Allegorical Interpretation* (Chicago, 1906). Sketch of allegorical interpretation before Plutarch.

Kirk, G. S., and J. E. Raven, *The Presocratic Philosophers: A Critical History with a Selection of Texts* (Cambridge, U.K., 1962). The earliest critics of traditional explanations of the world, including Xenophanes.

MEDIEVAL AND RENAISSANCE THEORIES

Allen, Don Cameron, *Mysteriously Meant: The Rediscovery of Pagan Symbolism and Allegorical Interpretation in the Renaissance* (Ann Arbor, Mich., 1970). Surveys the use of allegory in the Renaissance.

Allen, Susan Heuck, ed., et al., *Survival of the Gods: Classical Mythology in Medieval Art* (Providence, R.I., 1987). Based on an exhibition, contains excellent essay on facets of the survival of classical myth, with excellent illustrations.

Bolgar, R. R., *The Classical Heritage and Its Beneficiaries: From the Carolingian Age to the End of the Renaissance* (New York, 1964).

Bush, Douglas, *Mythology and the Renaissance Tradition in English Poetry* (Minneapolis, 1932; New York, 1963). Good on the postclassical uses of mythology, with a list, chronologically arranged, of poems on mythological subjects.

Seznec, Jean, *The Survival of the Pagan Gods: The Mythological Tradition and Its Place in Renaissance Humanism* (New York, 1953; reprinted Princeton, N.J., 1994). Scholarly description of how the Greek gods were recast and reinterpreted in European literature and art after the triumph of Christianity—the most useful book on this topic.

THEORIES OF THE ENLIGHTENMENT

Marsak, L. M., trans. and ed., *The Achievement of Bernard le Bovier de Fontenelle* (New York, 1970). Introduction to Fontenelle, with selections from his works.

ROMANTIC THEORIES

Georgoudi, Stella, "Creating a Myth of the Matriarchy," in P. S. Pantel, ed., *A History of Women* (Cambridge, Mass., 1992).

Kamenetsky, Christa, *The Brothers Grimm and Their Critics, Folktales and the Quest for Meaning* (Athens, Ohio, 1992). The place of the Grimm's collection in the Romantic movement; extensive review of theories of folktale interpretation.

ANTHROPOLOGICAL THEORIES

Fontenrose, Joseph, *The Ritual Theory of Myth* (Berkeley, Calif., 1966; reprinted 1971). Argument against the theory that myth derives from ritual, by a leading scholar.

Frazer, J. G., *The New Golden Bough,* ed. T. Gaster (New York, 1959). A modern condensation of this seminal work.

Malinowski, Bronislaw, *Magic, Science, and Religion, and Other Essays* (New York, 1948; reprinted Prospect Heights, Ill., 1992). The anthropologist sets forth his charter theory of myth.

Vickery, John B., *The Literary Impact of* The Golden Bough (Princeton, N.J., 1973). Résumé of Frazer's arguments and their influence.

LINGUISTIC THEORIES

Dorson, R. M., "The Eclipse of Solar Mythology," in T. A. Sebeok, ed., *Myth: A Symposium* (Bloomington, Ind., 1971), pp. 25–63. A witty account of the rise and fall of Max Müller's theory of nature mythology.

Müller, F. Max, *Comparative Mythology: An Essay,* ed. A. Smythe Palmer (London, 1909; reprinted Salem, N.H., 1977, ed. R. M. Dorson). Müller's major statement on the principles of solar mythology.

Puhvel, Jaan, *Comparative Mythology* (Baltimore, 1987; reprinted 1989). An up-to-date review of Indo-European elements in Greek myth, including the theories of Georges Dumézil (most of whose many publications are in French).

PSYCHOLOGICAL THEORIES

Fordham, Frieda, *An Introduction to Jung's Psychology,* with a foreword by Jung, 3rd ed. (Baltimore, 1966).

Jung, Carl G., et al., *Man and His Symbols* (New York, 1968). Jung and his followers expound the theory of unconscious archetypes.

Mullahy, Patrick, *Oedipus, Myth and Complex, A Review of Psychoanalytic Theory* (New York, 1948; reprinted 1955).

Neumann, Erich, *The Origins and History of Consciousness,* trans. R.F.C. Hull (Princeton, N.J., 1954; reprinted 1970). A student of Carl Jung, Neumann analyzes the story of the dragon-combat in terms of unconscious archetypes.

Wollheim, Richard, *Freud* (London, 1971). An introduction to Freud's thought for the beginner.

STRUCTURALISM

Detienne, Marcel, *The Creation of Mythology,* trans. Margaret Cook (Chicago, 1986). An important contribution to the "Paris school."

Gordon, R. L., ed., *Myth, Religion and Society. Structuralist Essays by M. Detienne, L. Gernet, J.-P. Vernant and P. Vidal-Naquet* (Cambridge, U.K., 1981). Writings from the "Paris school."

Leach, Edmund, *Claude Lévi-Strauss,* revised edition (New York, 1974; reprinted Chicago, 1989). Excellent presentation of the Straussian analysis of myth.

Lévi-Strauss, Claude, "The Structural Study of Myth," reprinted in T. A. Sebeok, ed., *Myth: A Symposium* (Bloomington, Ind., 1971), pp. 81–106. A classic, much-criticized essay analyzing the myth of Oedipus.

———, *The Raw and the Cooked,* trans. J. and D. Weightman (Chicago, 1980). This is volume 1 of his four-volume *Mythologiques* and a good introduction to his method and theories.

Vernant, J.-P., *Myth and Society in Ancient Greece,* trans. J. Lloyd (New York, 1990). Major statement by a leading member of the "Paris school."

CONTEXTUAL APPROACHES

Burkert, Walter, *Structure and History in Greek Mythology and Ritual* (Berkeley, Calif., 1979). An influential modern contribution to theoretical approaches to Greek mythology. Contains a lucid explication and criticism of the school of Lévi-Strauss.

Buxton, R., *Imaginary Greece: The Contexts of Mythology* (Cambridge, U.K., 1994). Locates the stories within their originally peasant communities; analyzes narrative and social contexts.

APPENDIX

Roman and Greek Forms of Classical Names:
Spelling and Pronunciation

THE PROPER NAMES OF CLASSICAL MYTH are mostly Greek in origin and were later transliterated into the Latin alphabet. In this process a few changes had to be made, and the Latin forms, therefore, are somewhat different from the Greek. Latin presently broke up into the Romance languages (Italian, French, Spanish, Portuguese), each of which had its own peculiarities of spelling and pronunciation. English is not a Romance language, but its speakers were members of the western Christian Church, which—in its Roman Catholic branch—used Latin for its liturgy and for almost all its business down to the mid–twentieth century. In consequence, through all western Europe Latin was a universal second language for educated classes for about fifteen hundred years. For this reason the most familiar spellings of the proper names of classical myth are Latinized forms of Greek names, sometimes further altered in standard English. Because of their familiarity, these are the forms used (mostly) in this book. About a hundred years ago, however, some scholars and translators urged a reform of this system and the use of the Greek forms of classical names rendered in the Roman alphabet, so that one may find tales about "Klytaimnestra," "Akhilleus," and others. To aid reference, because such forms often appear in English translations, the following index gives the Greek forms one is likely to encounter in parentheses after the Latinized forms. The principal differences between the Latinized and Greek forms are as follows:

Latin *j* = Greek *i:* Jason = Iason

Latin *c* = Greek *k:* Calypso = Kalypso

Latin *ae* or *e* = Greek *ai:* Gaea = Gaia; Clytemnestra = Klytaimnestra

Latin *e* or *i* = Greek *ei:* Rhea = Rheia; Chiron = Kheiron

Latin *i* = Greek *oi:* Delphi = Delphoi

Latin *oe* = Greek *oi:* Oedipus = Oidipous

Latin *u* = Greek *ou:* Creusa = Kreousa

Latin *y* = Greek *u* (sometimes): Clytemnestra = Klutaimnestra

Latin final *a* = Greek *e:* Athena = Athene

Latin final *um* = Greek *on:* Palladium = Palladion

Latin final *us* = Greek *os:* Linus = Linos

Finally, the Greek letter *chi* (χ) is rendered *ch* in Latin but either *ch* or *kh* in the Greek forms.

The value of the sounds of names in classical myth as pronounced in English, especially those of vowels, is another matter, one on which people agree to disagree; certainly an ancient Greek would be astonished at the ordinary English pronunciation of his or her name. So one often hears the name of the Athenian playwright pronounced as *E*-schylus or *Ē*-schylus or sometimes *Ī*-schylus. Is the famous king of Thebes called *E*-dipus or *Ē*-dipus? Professional classicists may use any of these versions. Consonants, which arouse less dispute, tend to follow these rules in the anglicized forms of words Latinized from the original Greek:

- The letters *c* and *g* are "soft" before *e* and *i* sounds (not necessarily letters) and "hard" before *a, o,* and *u* sounds in words of Greek or Latin origin: for example, *c*enter, *C*aesar, *c*ivic, *c*ycle; *g*entle, Eu*g*ene, a*g*ile, but *c*ategory, *c*ooperate, *c*uneiform; *g*arrulous, *g*onad, *g*usto. Notice the requirement "in words of Greek or Latin origin": "*g*et" and "*g*ive" are of Germanic origin and do not follow the rule.

- The Greek letter *chi* (χ), written *ch*, represented a sound like *k* but pronounced back in the throat; in English it is pronounced like the "hard" *c* in *c*ard," not like the *ch* of "*ch*icken."

- Final *e* must be pronounced as a separate syllable: Daph-n*ē*, Cir-c*ē*. To remind the reader of this rule, I place a circumflex over the *e* in such syllables (except for the common Aphrodite): Daphnê, Circê. Final *es* is also pronounced, as Achill*ēs*.

Another problem is accent—where to stress the word. Latin and Greek relied chiefly on pitch and quantity, whereas English depends on stress. Quantity is the length of time it takes to pronounce a syllable; pitch is the register of the voice. Because of the influence of Latin on Western culture, the English accent on proper names follows the rule that governs the pronunciation of Latin: If the next to last syllable is "long," it is accented; if it is not "long," the syllable before it is accented.

How does one know whether a syllable is "long" or "short"? If the next-to-last sylla-ble ends with two consonants, or if it contains a diphthong (-*ae*-, -*oe*-, -*au*-, -*ei*-), or if it contains a vowel "long" by nature, it must be accented. Otherwise, the accent goes on the third syllable from the end. But how does one know whether a vowel is long by nature? Unfortunately, only by knowing Latin well can you know whether a vowel is long by nature. A further complication arises from the fact that the combinations of vowels -*ae*-, -*oe*-, -*au*-, and -*ei*- are not always diphthongs (two vowels pronounced as one) but are sometimes pronounced separately. In these cases I place a dieresis (two superimposed dots) over the second vowel: The mother of Perseus was Danaë, pro-nounced **dan**-a-ē.

These rules are useful but complex. For many it will be easiest simply to consult the pronunciation given after each name in the text and in the following Index, where the syllable to be accented is printed in **bold** characters. Vowels should be pro-nounced according to this key:

ā = p*ay*

ē = b*e*

ī - w*i*fe

ō = n*o*

ū = c*u*te

INDEX

Heliades (hel-i-**a**-dēz), "children of the sun," turned into poplars mourning for Phaëthon, their tears into amber, 78, 197

Helicon (**hel**-i-kon), a mountain in Boeotia, 60, 321

Helius (**he**-li-us), sun god, son of Hyperion, father of Phaëthon, 5, 61, 77, 104, 139, 173, 174, 179, 185, 230, 361, 363, 367, 384, 421, 428, 475, 496, 499, 579, 580, 582, 591, 592

Hellê (**hel**-lē), daughter of Athamas and Nephelê, sister of Phrixus, fell from the golden ram into the Hellespont, 341, 474, 475, 507, 524, 542

Hellen (**hel**-len), son of Pyrrha and Deucalion, eponymous ancestor of the Hellenes, 26, 129, 133, 474

Hellenes (**hel**-ēnz), the Greeks, inhabitants of Hellas, 26, 129, 329, 473, 519

Hellenistic, referring to Greek culture between Alexander's death in 323 B.C. and the ascendancy of Rome, 19, 42, 138, 141, 142, 155, 195, 215, 229, 276, 306, 311, 329, 340, 369, 430, 508, 551, 631, 633

Hellespont, straits between the Aegean Sea and the Sea of Marmora (= the Dardanelles), 254, 272, 475, 478, 507, 509, 537

Hemera (**hē**-mer-a), "day," one of the first beings, daughter of Erebus and Nyx, 73, 74

Hephaestus (he-**fēs**-tus), Greek god of smiths, son of Zeus and Hera or Hera alone, husband of faithless Aphrodite (= Roman Vulcan), 53, 91, 92, 112, 114, 118, 129, 133, 135, 146, 148, 149, 151, 170–176, 179, 254, 384, 386, 387, 398, 401, 404, 442, 449, 510, 518, 538, 556, 601

Hera (**hē**-ra), daughter of Cronus and Rhea, wife and sister of Zeus (= Roman Juno), 50, 85, 134–141, 144–150, 157–159, 170–172, 177, 190, 199, 217, 220, 250, 251, 258, 272, 276, 287, 301, 303, 324–328, 348, 349, 351–354, 360, 363, 366, 369, 378–382, 413, 466, 473, 476, 482, 490, 504, 517–520, 530, 600, 606, 607, 632, 634, 635, 648

Heracles (**her**-a-klez), son of Zeus and Alcmena, greatest of Greek heroes, 21, 38, 41, 83, 92, 98, 112, 138, 145, 147, 151, 161, 211, 299, 318, 323, 326, 340, 341, 342, 345–382, 391, 397, 398, 401, 403, 404, 414–416, 426, 444, 458, 477–479, 487, 500, 502, 503, 505, 507, 510, 511, 514, 517, 519, 523, 525, 548, 586, 633, 634

Heraclids (**her**-a-klids), descendants of Heracles, 346, 379, 381, 511

Hercules, Roman form of Heracles, 68, 341, 345, 360, 362, 370, 372, 373, 600, 601, 627

Hermaphroditus (her-ma-fro-**dī**-tus), son of Hermes and Aphrodite, became bisexual when united with the nymph Salmacis, 195, 215

Hermes, son of Zeus and Maia, Greek god of travel, tricks, commerce and thievery, who stole Apollo's cattle (= Roman Mercury), 50, 90, 94, 114, 116, 135, 151, 155, 159, 168, 169, 174–195, 200–203, 213, 223, 236, 237, 240, 250, 251, 286, 288, 289, 294, 299, 324, 325, 332, 361, 365, 371, 379, 384, 388, 419, 420, 451, 510, 519, 539, 579, 580, 582, 600, 631, 639, 652

Hermionê (her-**mī**-o-nē), only daughter of Helen and Menelaüs, 510, 516, 520

Herodotus (her-**o**-do-tus), Greek historian, 5th century B.C., 25, 76, 164, 222, 403

Hersê (**her**-sē), "dew," daughter of Cecrops, 384, 385, 386, 387, 388

Hesiod, Greek poet, 8th century B.C., composer of *Works and Days* and *Theogony*, 22, 51, 73, 80, 81, 83–94, 99, 101–123, 129, 132–135, 141, 144, 146, 179, 186, 193–196, 285, 297, 301, 313, 320, 347, 367–369, 396, 409, 458, 487, 488, 516, 592, 638

Hesperides (hes-**per**-i-dēz), "daughters of the West" who protected the tree with golden apples, 110, 147, 360,

366–370, 381, 487, 505

Hestia (**hes**-ti-a), daughter of Cronus and Rhea, Greek goddess of the hearth (= Roman Vesta), 85, 134, 135, 170, 192, 193, 198, 199, 215, 248, 603, 604, 633, 652

hetaira (he-**tī**-ra) "companioness," Greek courtesan, 31, 249

hierophant (hī-**er**-o-fant), "revealer of the sacred things," priestly office at Eleusis, 244, 245, 246

hieros gamos, "holy marriage," ritual sexual union to enhance fertility, 220, 247, 440

Hipparchus (hi-**par**-kus. Hipparkhos), Athenian leader, son of Pisistratus, 6th century B.C., brother of Hippias, 415

Hippias (**hi**-pi-as), brother of Hipparchus, 415

Hippodamia (hip-po-da-**mī**-a), daughter of Oenomaüs, wife of Pelops, 413; bride of Pirithoüs, 511, 512

Hippolyta (hip-**pol**-i-ta. Hippolyte), queen of the Amazons, killed by Heracles, 363, 370, 381, 402

Hippolytus (hip-**pol**-i-tus. Hippolytos), son of Theseus and Antiopê, betrayed by Phaedra and killed, 168, 362, 405–411, 417, 440, 506–508

Hippomedon (hip-**po**-me-don), one of the seven against Thebes, 460

Hippomenes (hi-**po**-me-nēz), defeated Atalanta in a footrace (or it was Milanion), 505, 639

Hittites (**hi**-tīts), Indo-European warrior people in central Anatolia, 58, 99, 104, 105

Homer, composer of the *Iliad* and the *Odyssey,* 3, 20, 41, 76, 130, 134–141, 144–156, 170, 172, 175, 204, 205, 207, 211–213, 250, 254, 255, 272, 280, 283–295, 300, 301, 303, 304, 308, 313, 314, 326, 329, 349, 379, 380, 396, 412, 418, 442, 444, 453–455, 458, 463, 473, 474, 476, 487, 488, 489, 509, 519, 525, 527, 531, 532, 534, 535, 538, 542–547, 550, 555, 556, 566, 567, 571, 572, 579, 582, 585, 588–594, 606, 609, 612, 613, 630, 631, 636, 639, 651, 653

Homeric Hymns, 62, 105, 157, 217, 229, 247, 250, 396

Homeric poems, 543, 575, 613

hoplites (**ho**-plīts), heavy-armed Greek warriors of classical period, 31, 404

Horae (**hō**-rē),"hours," the Seasons, offspring of Zeus and Themis, 83, 140, 141, 159

Horatii (ho-**rā**-shi-ī), three Roman brothers who defeated the three Curiatii from Alba Longa, 619, 621, 627

Horatius Cocles (ho-**rā**-shus **kō**-klēz), defended bridge over Tiber single-handed, 625

Horus, the child of Isis and Osiris, 222, 223, 350

human sacrifice, 39, 125, 209, 210, 225, 276, 384, 418, 436, 440, 470, 524, 548, 602

Humbaba (hum-**ba**-ba), monster killed by Gilgamesh and Enkidu, 315, 316, 320, 368, 507

Hyacinth (**hī**-a-sinth. Hyakinthos), beloved of Apollo, turned into a hyacinth plant, 166

Hydra (**hi**-dra), "water-snake," many-headed serpent killed by Heracles at Lerna, 82, 83, 297, 342, 358, 368, 369, 376, 378, 381, 634

Hygieia (hī-**jē**-a), "health," daughter of Asclepius, 168

Hylas (**hī**-las), beloved of Heracles, snatched by water nymphs on voyage of the Argo, 478

Hyllus (**hī**-lus. Hyllos), son of Heracles and Deianira, 346, 354, 377–379

Hymen (**hī**-men), god of marriage, 391

Hymettus (hī-**met**-tus. Hymettos), mountain near Athens, 197, 389

Hyperboreans (hi-per-bor-**ē**-anz), "beyond the north wind," a mythical people who lived there, 155

Hyperion (hi-**per**-ion), a Titan, father of Helius, Selenê, and Eos, 75, 161, 179, 230, 231, 391

Hypsipylê (hip-**sip**-i-lē), queen of Lemnos, consort of Jason, 478

I

Iacchus (i-**ak**-kus' Iakkhos), personification of a ritual cry, another name for Dionysus, 265

Iambê (i-**am**-bē), servant of Celeus and Metanira at Eleusis who amused Demeter, 234

Iapetus (ī-**ap**-e-tus. Iapetos), a Titan, father of Prometheus, Epimetheus , Atlas, 61, 75, 88, 108, 109, 112

Icarus (**ik**-a-rus. Ikaros), drowned when he disobeyed his father Daedalus' instructions not to fly close to the sun, 384, 432–435

ichor (**ī**-kor), the fluid in the veins of the gods, 149, 487

Ida (**ī**-da), Mount, on Crete. another mountain near Troy, 136, 138, 144, 199, 220, 226, 422, 428, 503, 519, 520, 557

Idas (**ī**-das), brother of Lynceus, an Argonaut who competed with Apollo for Marpessa, 477

Idmon, seer on the Argo, 213, 477

Idomeneus (ī-**dom**-i-nūs), king of Crete, fought at Troy, 522, 527, 532, 556

Ilium (Ilion), another name for Troy, 203, 304, 509, 528, 532, 533, 537, 538, 552

Illyria, the northeast coast of the Ionian Sea (coast of former Yugoslavia), 449, 471

Ilus (**ī**-lus. Ilos), early king of Troy, 304, 519

Imbros, island in the northeast Aegean, 152

imperium, supreme authority in Rome, power to conduct war and to kill, 604, 605

Inachus (**īn**-a-kus. Inakhos), river near Argos, 323, 324, 326, 338

Inanna (in-**an**-na), Sumerian fertility goddess, 53, 99, 193, 194, 216–220, 223, 225, 229, 243, 247, 316, 317, 412, 593

Indians, 641, 644, 652

Inferno, of Dante, 296, 302, 303, 571

Ino (**ī**-nō), daughter of Cadmus and Harmonia, sister of Semelê, nurse of Dionysus, wife of Athamas, 250, 251, 255, 257, 261, 264, 267, 269, 273, 274–276, 281, 353, 449, 474, 475, 583, 637

Io (**ī**-ō), Argive princess, beloved of Zeus, turned into cow, 177, 323–327, 338, 344, 366, 396, 419, 423, 446

Iolaüs (ī-ō-**lā**-us. Iolaos), Heracles' nephew, 345, 346, 357, 358, 369

Iolcus (ī-**ol**-kus. Iolkos), city in Thessaly, home of Jason, 473, 474, 476, 489, 490, 492, 494, 500, 502, 507

Iolê (ī-**ō**-lē), daughter of Eurytus, won by Heracles in an archery contest, 371, 375, 378, 381

Ion (**ī**-on), son of Apollo, eponymous ancestor of the Ionians, 129

Ionians, division of the Greek people, 21, 129, 400, 416

Iphicles (**if**-i-klēz), son of Amphitryon and Alcmena, father of Iolaüs, 346–351, 502, 634

Iphigenia (if-i-jen-**ī**-a), daughter of Agamemnon and Clytemnestra, sacrificed by her father at Aulis (or transported to Tauris), 42, 517, 518, 523, 524, 535, 536, 543, 560, 563

Iphigenia in Aulis, by Euripides, 517, 518

Iphitus (**if**-i-tus. Iphitos), son of Eurytus, brother of Iolê, thrown from a tower by Heracles, 371, 380, 586

Iris (**ī**-ris), "rainbow," messenger of the gods, 159, 236

Ishtar, Akkadian fertility goddess (= Sumerian Inanna), 55, 193, 194, 216, 223, 316, 317, 320, 321, 372, 412, 429, 441, 593

Isis (**ī**-sis), Egyptian goddess, wife of Osiris, 216, 221–224, 229, 247, 326, 327

Isles of the Blessed, 121, 122

Ismarus (**is**-ma-rus. Ismaros), city in Thrace, sacked by Odysseus, 567

Ismenê (is-**mē**-nē), daughter of Oedipus, sister of Antigonê, 449, 454, 460, 465, 467, 469, 471

Ismenus River, near Thebes, 258

Italy, 17, 18, 42, 78, 81, 83, 91, 122, 142, 166, 189, 245, 291, 298, 302, 310, 333, 336, 364, 370, 376, 404, 436, 486, 498, 499, 526, 582, 583, 599, 601, 605–610, 631

Ithaca (Ithaka), off the northwest coast of Greece, home of Odysseus, 247, 281, 286, 287, 291, 312, 417, 516, 521, 526, 543, 571, 577–579, 585–594, 636

Itys (**it**-is), son of Tereus and Procnê, served in a stew to his father, 386, 391, 394, 395, 417

Iulus (**ī**-**ū**-lus), son of Aeneas, also called Ascanius, ancestor of the Julian clan, 304, 519, 554, 595, 606, 608, 615, 627

Ixion (ik-**sī**-on), father of Centaurus, tried to rape Hera, bound to a wheel in Tartarus, 138, 301, 303, 306, 413, 502

J

Janus (**jā**-nus), *numen* of gates, bridges, and archways, 599, 627

Jason, son of Aeson, husband of Medea, leader of the Argonauts, 67, 210, 211, 397, 406, 421, 445, 473–502, 507, 508, 521, 579, 660

Jesus, 110, 189, 222, 277, 458

Jocasta (jō-**kas**-ta), mother/wife of Oedipus, 449, 452, 456–458, 471, 640, 651

Joppa, port city on the coast of Palestine (= modern Tel Aviv), 335

Joshua, biblical leader, 639

Jove, another name for Jupiter, 600, 610

Joyce, James, 572, 594

Julius Caesar, see Caesar, Julius, 43, 302, 342, 595, 605, 606, 625

Jung (yung), Carl, 472, 650, 654, 655, 657, 658

Juno, Roman counterpart of Greek Hera, 144, 391, 600, 607, 608, 627, 632, 635

Jupiter, Roman counterpart of Greek Zeus, 49, 113, 126, 127, 136, 214, 297, 300, 340, 419, 528, 600, 609, 613, 627, 632, 635

K

Keats, John, 189

Ki (**kē**), Sumerian god of, 55, 57, 95, 103, 107, 108, 133

Kingu, Tiamat's marshal, killed by Marduk, from whose blood humans were made, 96, 97, 99, 107

Korê (**kō**-rē), "girl," another name for Persephonê, 229, 241, 243, 246, 247, 632

Kumarbi (ku-**mar**-bē), Hittite enemy of the storm god Teshub, 100, 101, 103, 225

L

Labdacus (**lab**-da-kus), father of Laius, grandfather of Oedipus, 449, 452, 455

labrys, "double-ax," Minoan symbol, 19, 440

Labyrinth (**lab**-e-rinth), Cretan maze, home of the Minotaur, 399, 414, 415, 425, 430, 432, 434, 440, 442

Lacedaemon (las-e-**dē**-mon. Lakedaimon), another name for Sparta, or the territory around it, 16, 527

Lachesis (**lak**-e-sis), "apportioner," the Fate who measures out the thread of life, 141, 295

Laconia (la-**kōn**-i-a), territory in the southern Peloponnesus surrounding Sparta, 16, 20

Ladon (**lā**-don), serpent that guarded the tree with the golden apples in the garden of the Hesperides, 110, 147, 366, 487

Laelaps (**le**-laps), dog that always caught its prey, gift from Minos to Procris, 388, 391, 395, 417, 421

M

T

The Greek and Roman Pantheon

Greek Name (Roman Name)	Parentage	Origin	Concern	Attributes
Zeus (Jupiter, Jove)	Cronus + Rhea	Indo-European sky-god	Kingship, law; weather	Thunderbolt, scepter
Hera (Juno)	Cronus + Rhea	Mother-goddess	Marriage, family	Middle-aged, round hat
Demeter (Ceres)	Cronus + Rhea	Mother-goddess	Harvest	Grain; with Persephonê
Poseidon (Neptune)	Cronus + Rhea	Consort of earth?	Water, sea; earthquakes	Trident, team of dolphins
Hestia (Vesta)	Cronus + Rhea	The hearth	Household	Rarely shown
Artemis (Diana)	Zeus + Leto	Mother-goddess	Hunting, wild things	Bow, short dress, often with animals
Aphrodite (Venus)	Zeus + Dionê (or born from the foam)	Asian fertility-goddess	Human sexuality	Nude, doves, with Eros
Hermes (Mercury)	Zeus + Maia	Personified road marker	Travel, trade, lies, thieves	Winged shoes, caduceus
Hephaestus (Vulcan)	Hera (alone)	Fire spirit	Crafts	Lame, bald, hammer
Apollo	Zeus + Leto	Lycia, Thrace; shaman	Music, healing, plague, prophecy	Beardless; lyre, bow
Ares (Mars)	Zeus + Hera	Thrace	War, violence	Spear, shield
Athena (Minerva)	Zeus + Metis	City-goddess	Civilization; crafts	Helmet, aegis
[Dionysus][a] (Liber)	Zeus + Semelê	Thrace, Phrygia	Ecstasy; the vine, wine	Ivy, panthers, Maenads
[Pan] (Faunus)	Hermes + nymph	Arcadia	Cattle; terror	Horns, hoofs, pipes
[Heracles] (Hercules)	Zeus + Alcmenê	Deified hero	—	Club, lion-skin, bow
[Asclepius] (Aesculapius)	Apollo + Coronis	Deified hero	Medicine	Staff with snake entwined
[Hades] (Dis)	Cronus + Rhea	Underworld	The dead	Rarely shown
[Persephonê] (Proserpina)	Zeus + Demeter	New crop; doublet of Demeter	The dead	Young woman, with Demeter

[a]Deities in brackets are not Olympians.

10,000 B.C.	**Neolithic** ("New Stone") **Period** begins in the Near East with the development of agriculture and sedentary communities
4000 B.C.	
	Sumerian cuneiform writing is developed, c. 3400
	Egyptian hieroglyphic writing, Pharaonic civilization emerge, c. 3100
3000 B.C.	**EARLY BRONZE AGE** begins in Greece with introduction of bronze metallurgy, c. 3000–2000
	Sumerian cities flourish in Mesopotamia, c. 2800–2340
	Minoan civilization flourishes in Crete, c. 2500–1200
	Akkadian empire in Mesopotamia, c. 2334–2220
	Sumerian revival, c. 2200–2000
	MIDDLE BRONZE AGE begins with arrival of Indo-European Greeks in Balkan Peninsula, c. 2000–1600
2000 B.C.	Old Babylonian Empire in Mesopotamia c. 2000–1550
	LATE BRONZE AGE (or **MYCENAEAN AGE**) begins, c. 1600
	Hittite empire rules in Anatolia, c. 1600–1200
1500 B.C.	Phoenician syllabic writing appears, c. 1500
	Trojan War occurs, c. 1250
	DARK (or **IRON**) **AGE** begins with destruction of Mycenaean cities in Greece, c. 1200–1100
1000 B.C.	Greek colonies are settled in Asia Minor, c. 1000
	Greek colonies in Southern Italy and Sicily, c. 800–600
	ARCHAIC PERIOD begins with invention of Greek alphabet, c. 800
	Iliad and the *Odyssey*, attributed to **Homer**, are written down, c. 800–750
	Olympic games begin, 776
	Rome, allegedly, is founded, 753
	Hesiod's *Theogony* is written down, c. 750–700
	Homeric Hymns, c. 700–500
	Cyclic poets, c. 650–500
	Age of Tyrants, c. 650–500
	Cyrus the Great of Persia, c. 600–529
	Xenophanes, c. 570–460
	Pindar, 518–438
	Simonides, sixth–fifth century
	Alleged date of the expulsion of the Etruscan dynasty at Rome and the foundation of the "Roman Republic," 510
500 B.C.	**Bacchylides,** fifth century
	Persians invade Greece; battle of Marathon, 490
	Persians invade Greece again; destruction of Athens; Greek victories at Salamis and Plataea, 480–479
	CLASSICAL PERIOD begins with end of Persian Wars, 480
	Aeschylus, 525–456
	Sophocles, 496–406
	Herodotus, c. 484–420

Euripides, 480–406
Roman *Twelve Tables* are committed to writing, 451
Socrates, 469–399
Peloponnesian War, 431–404
Thucydides, c. 470–400
Biblical book of *Genesis* reaches present form, c. 400

400 B.C.

Plato, 427–437
Hippocrates, c. 400
Aristotle, 384–322
The Gauls sack the city of Rome, 390
Philip II of Macedon, Alexander's father, conquers Greece,
putting an end to local rule, 338–337
Alexander the Great conquers the Persian empire
and makes Greek culture world culture, 336–323
HELLENISTIC PERIOD begins with death of Alexander
in 323

300 B.C.   Callimachus, c. 305–240
Apollonius of Rhodes, third century

200 B.C.   Punic Wars are waged between Rome and Carthage, 264–146
Plautus, Roman playwright, dies, c. 180
ROMAN PERIOD begins when Greece becomes Roman province,
146
Roman civil wars, Marius-Sulla, Caesar-Pompey,
Augustus-Antony, are waged, 88–31
Catullus, 84–54
Vergil, 70–19
Livy, 57 B.C.–17 A.D.
Julius Caesar rules as dictator, 46–44
Ovid, c. 43 B.C.–17 A.D.
Augustus defeats Antony and Cleopatra at battle of Actium and
annexes Egypt, 31
Augustus Caesar reigns, 27 B.C.–14 A.D.
Apollodorus' *Library,* first century A.D. (?)
Plutarch c. 46–120 A.D.

100 A.D.   Pausanias, second century
Apuleius, second century

200 A.D.
300 A.D.

Constantine, 280?–337; Edict of Milan freeing Christian
church from persecution, 313

400 A.D.

MEDIEVAL PERIOD begins with fall of Western Roman Empire, 476

500 A.D.